THE LOEB CLASSICAL LIBRARY

FOUNDED BY JAMES LOEB 1911

EDITED BY

JEFFREY HENDERSON

ARISTOTLE

VII

LCL 397

ARISTOTLE

METEOROLOGICA

WITH AN ENGLISH TRANSLATION BY

H. D. P. LEE

HARVARD UNIVERSITY PRESS
CAMBRIDGE, MASSACHUSETTS
LONDON, ENGLAND

First published 1952
Reprinted 1962, 1978, 1987, 2004

LOEB CLASSICAL LIBRARY® is a registered trademark
of the President and Fellows of Harvard College

ISBN 0-674-99436-1

Printed and bound by Edwards Brothers, Ann Arbor, Michigan
on acid-free paper made by Glatfelter, Spring Grove, Pennsylvania

CONTENTS

PREFACE TO SECOND EDITION

THE present edition is reprinted without change from that of 1952. There is however one publication, which has appeared since that date, to which reference should be made, Dr. Gottschalk's paper in *C.Q.* N.S. xi (May 1961) on the authorship of Book IV. G. agrees that the view that the book is the work of Strato is untenable, and that the " broad outlook of this book is not so very different from Aristotle's." But he thinks that it contains un-Aristotelian elements, notably the doctrine of πόροι, of which he would not accept the interpretation suggested on p. xviii of my Introduction. This and other features of the book are, he argues, more characteristic of Theophrastus, and his conclusion is that it is " a thorough revision of an Aristotelian work by a pupil of Theophrastus." Chapters 8-9 in particular he thinks are by " Theophrastus entirely," pointing out, quite rightly, that they break awkwardly into the sequence of thought in the book. It should also be noted that all the references to πόροι (apart from one at 381 b 1, where a non-technical meaning gives perfectly good sense) are in these chapters ; and G. may well be right to regard them as un-Aristotelian. The case for so regarding the rest of the book is perhaps less strong ; G. himself considers it basically Aristotelian, and the question at issue is to how much revision, if any, it has been subjected and by whom.

WINCHESTER COLLEGE
   September 1961

H. D. P. L.

PREFACE TO FIRST EDITION

THIS translation was begun shortly before the war, laid aside in 1940, and finally completed in August 1948. I have added, in proof stage, some references to publications since that date, but have not been able to use them in detail. I have acknowledged in the appropriate places help that has generously been given to me, but I should like to record here in particular my gratitude to Professor Fobes for permission to use his text and index, and my sense of indebtedness to E. W. Webster's version in the Oxford Translation.

H. D. P. L.

CLIFTON COLLEGE
September 1951

viii

INTRODUCTION [a]

THE *Meteorologica* falls into two well-defined parts, Books I-III and Book IV. The first three books form a complete work by themselves. The programme set out in Book I. ch. 1 contains nothing that can plausibly be said to look forward to Book IV and appears to have been completed by the end of Book III,[b] and the last chapter of Book III looks forward to a treatment of metals and minerals, which Book IV does not contain. Book IV is in fact a separate treatise, as had already been noticed by the Greek commentators.[c] The two parts of the work may therefore be treated separately in this Introduction.

A. BOOKS I-III

1. *Authenticity and place.* The authenticity of these books has not been seriously questioned, and there seems no reason to doubt that they are by Aristotle.[d]

[a] I am grateful to Prof. Hackforth for reading this Introduction in manuscript and for his comments.
[b] See introductory note to Book I. ch. 1 : *cf.* W. Capelle, " Das Proömium der Meteorologie," *Hermes* xlvii (1912), pp. 514-535.
[c] Alex. 179. 3, Olymp. 273. 21.
[d] W. Capelle, *loc. cit.*, argues cogently for the authenticity of Book I. ch. 1, and, by implication, of Books I-III. *Cf.* also Ideler i. pp. vi ff., St.-Hilaire pp. lxv ff.

Their place in the series of his physical works is defined in the opening chapter of Book I. There Aristotle gives, in effect, the following arrangement : (1) *The Physics*, dealing with first causes and natural movement in general ; (2) the *De Caelo* i and ii, dealing with astronomy ; (3) *De Caelo* iii and iv and *De Generatione et Corruptione*, dealing with the four elements, their mutual transformations and the general principles of the consequent processes of generation and destruction ; (4) the *Meteorologica* ; (5) the works on biology.

2. *Contents.* The subjects dealt with in Books I-III appear to us very miscellaneous. They are summarized by Aristotle in Book I. ch. 1, but can perhaps best be seen at a glance in chapter headings.

Book I. Ch. 1. Introduction : the place of Meteorology in the Natural Sciences and summary of matters to be dealt with.

Chs. 2-3. Preliminaries. Ch. 2. Recapitulation of the conclusions reached on the four elements in *De Caelo* iii, iv and *De Gen. et Corr.*

Ch. 3. The relative dispositions of air and fire in the terrestrial sphere.

Ch. 4. Shooting stars.

Ch. 5. The Aurora Borealis.

Chs. 6-7. Comets.

Ch. 8. The Milky Way.

Ch. 9. Rain, cloud and mist.

Ch. 10. Dew and hoar-frost.

Ch. 11. Snow.

It will be seen at once that we have here subjects dealt with to-day by several sciences, by astronomy, geography, geology and seismology, as well as meteorology in its modern connotation. But this is typical of a stage in the development of the natural sciences in which they had not yet fully differentiated out from an all-embracing Natural Philosophy. The process of differentiation was largely started by Aristotle, and Book I. ch. 1 shows us how far he had taken it. He places the *Meteorologica*, whose subject he himself seems to feel to be somewhat ill-defined, after the *De Caelo* iii and iv and *De Gen. et Corr.* In the *De Caelo* Books I-II he deals with astronomy and cosmology. He believes the universe to be spherical in form, and accepts the system of Eudoxus which accounts for the movements of the stars and planets by a system of concentric spheres, fitting inside each other, whose combined motions produce the apparent movements of the heavenly bodies. This system of

INTRODUCTION

spheres is not described in detail in the *De Caelo*, though it is apparently assumed (Book II. ch. 12, 293 a 5 ff.) ; the only description of it which we have is that in *Met.* Λ. ch. 8. The spheres are made of a fifth element (*cf. Meteor.* i. 2) and the innermost set of spheres is that of the moon. The region below the moon, the " terrestrial " or " sublunar " sphere, is filled by the four elements, earth, air, fire and water. They form four further concentric spheres, each element having its own natural place, but there is a constant process of intermixture between them which produces all the phenomena of the terrestrial world as we know it (*cf.* note at end of Book I. ch. 3). *De Caelo* Books III-IV outline the general doctrine of the four elements, and of their four natural places ; the *De Gen. et Corr.* deals with the general principles which govern their intermixture and the consequent processes of generation and destruction which constitute the natural world. In the *Meteorologica* Aristotle comes to deal with these processes in detail. The first, and in a sense the most obvious group of them, is the meteorological group (including those astronomical phenomena which Aristotle regarded as meteorological) : shooting-stars, meteors, comets and the milky way, rain, hail, snow, frost, thunder and lightning, winds of all sorts, haloes and rainbows. But though the opening words of the description in Book I. ch. 1 of the scope of the work [a] indicate that these phenomena will be its main concern, Aristotle cannot confine it within these bounds. So in Book I we have an account of rivers and springs and of coast

---

[a] 338 b 21 περὶ τὸν γειτνιῶντα μάλιστα τόπον τῇ φορᾷ τῇ τῶν ἄστρων : it is concerned with phenomena " in the region which borders most nearly on the movements of the stars."

erosion and silting, and in Book II of the sea and of earthquakes, topics which can hardly be classed as μετέωρα, though they are not unrelated to the remaining topics in these books and their inclusion is therefore not altogether surprising. But whereas Book I. ch. 1 [a] indicates that the *Meteorologica* will be followed immediately by the biological works, Book III, 378 a 15 ff., promises a treatise on metals and minerals, on the grounds that these also are products of the two exhalations studied earlier in the work.

The fact is that in the *Meteorologica* Aristotle embarks on an account of the processes of change in the four elements whose general principles have been laid down in *De Gen. et Corr.* He starts with meteorological processes and includes with them certain allied topics. But these two groups between them clearly do not exhaust the processes and products of the transformation and mixture of elements: there is a vast field of physical and chemical changes and substances left unaccounted for, and even Aristotle with his strong bias towards biology cannot have been unaware of them. Hence the promise (never fulfilled in the extant works) at the end of Book III, and hence also the inclusion of Book IV in its present position, for it is just those processes of chemical change, interpreted in terms of Aristotle's doctrine of the four elements, and certain physical properties of materials that are its subject.

B. BOOK IV

1. *Authenticity.* The authenticity [b] of Book IV has

---

[a] 339 a 5.
[b] See Preface to the second edition of this volume, p. vii.

been doubted, and Ross [a] says that it is " pretty certainly not genuine," while Jaeger [b] refers to it as " spurious." On the other hand, Joachim [c] treats it as genuine. The only attempt to argue the case against its authenticity is that by I. Hammer-Jensen,[d] who has in turn been criticized by Dr. V. C. B. Coutant.[e]

As Dr. Coutant remarks, H.-J.'s argument turns mainly on " an analysis of the natural philosophy behind the book "; or, more precisely, on an attempt to show that certain ideas in the book are un-Aristotelian, for, " asserting the character of the book to be very mechanical and atomistic in its explanation of certain phenomena, she ventures to ascribe the work to Strato of Lampsacus, on the ground that Strato was the most atomistic of the Peripatetics." [f] Such arguments from the ideas expressed in a particular book and their consistency or inconsistency with the main tenets of a philosopher expressed in the main body of his work are bound to be, to some extent, subjective : but I agree with Dr. Coutant that H.-J. has failed to make a convincing case, and

[a] *Aristotle* (3rd ed.), p. 11.
[b] *Aristotle* (Eng. trans.), p. 386.
[c] *Aristotle on Coming-to-be and Passing-away* and article on " Aristotle's Conception of Chemical Combination," *J.Ph.* xxix (1903).
[d] " Das sogennante IV. Buch der Meteorologie des Aristoteles," *Hermes*, l (1915), pp. 113-136.
[e] In a dissertation for the degree of D.Ph. at Columbia University entitled *Alexander of Aphrodisias : Commentary on Book IV of Aristotle's Meteorologica*, privately printed, 1936. I am grateful to Mr. D. J. Allan of Balliol College for lending me his copy of this work (reviewed by him in *C.R.* li (Nov. 1937)), of which copies are deposited at Columbia University but which is not generally available.
[f] *Op. cit.* p. 8.

it is surprising that her arguments have remained unanswered so long.[a]

H.-J.'s two main arguments are (1) that the explanations of natural processes given in the book are of a very "mechanistic" kind, the characteristic Aristotelian insistence on the final cause being absent ; (2) that the use made of the ideas of πόροι and ὄγκοι in chs. 3, 8 and 9 is un-Aristotelian and indicates a connexion with Atomism.

(1) The answer to the first of these objections is supplied by Aristotle himself in ch. 12 and overlooked by H.-J. Briefly, it is to be found in the words τὸ γὰρ οὗ ἕνεκα ἥκιστα ἐνταῦθα δῆλον, ὅπου δὴ πλεῖστον τῆς ὕλης " (390 a 3). "The final cause is least obvious where matter predominates." Throughout the book Aristotle is dealing with changes that arise from the mutual relations of the four "prime contraries" and the four elements through which they operate, which are the *material* basis of the universe. The formal and final causes are not entirely overlooked [b] : but, as Aristotle is careful to point out in the final chapter, they are in the nature of things less obvious when one is dealing with matter and material processes in the more elementary stages ; they become obvious only when we get higher in the scale of creation, in particular when we reach plants and animals. It is true [c] that in ch. 12 Aristotle speaks of the homoeomerous substances as being formed " by hot and cold and the motions set up by them " (*i.e.* by material and efficient causes only), while in *De Gen. An.* ii. 1, 734 b 29 ff. he speaks as if a final-formal cause were also

[a] W. Capelle in *Pauly-Wissowa*, Supp. Bd. vi (1935), pp. 339-342, is unconvinced by them but does not give his reasons.
[b] *Cf.* 379 b 25, 381 a 1, 388 a 20.
[c] H.-J. p. 127.

necessary for their formation. But, as Dr. Coutant points out, he is not consistent elsewhere on this point in *De Gen. An.* itself [a]; and what he says in ch. 12 is not that a final cause is ever entirely absent, but that in material processes of the kind dealt with in Book IV it is difficult to perceive, and can therefore, it is implied, be ignored. The homoeomerous bodies are, clearly, a borderline case and can be spoken of in either way.

There is therefore nothing inconsistent with Aristotle's philosophy of nature in the comparative absence of the final-formal cause from Book IV. The subject matter is, on Aristotle's own showing, such as to make that absence likely; and it is perhaps worth adding that the same is true of the first three books, which are undoubtedly genuine, and which could with equal plausibility be argued to be "mechanical." [b] Nor is H.-J.'s contention [c] that Aristotle was hardly aware of the problems of mechanical causation and the antithesis οὖ ἔνεκα—ἐξ ἀνάγκης till they were brought to his attention by Strato as author of *Meteor.* IV in the least plausible. Aristotle was acutely aware of these problems, both in *Physics* B and in *De Part. An.* (cf. Book I. ch. 1 in particular) and *De Gen. An.*; and *Physics* B and the main groundwork of his biological work were certainly completed before the end of his residence in the Troad and Lesbos.[d]

---

[a] 743 a 7 states the same view as *Meteor.* iv. 12 and clearly refers to it.

[b] *Cf.* Coutant, *op. cit.* p. 10.

[c] P. 126.

[d] For the *Physics cf.* the Introduction to Ross's edition. H.-J. makes no reference to the *Physics* and erroneously assumes (p. 129), with Jaeger, that the biological works are late: *cf.* my paper in *C.Q.* (July-Oct. 1948). There is no

INTRODUCTION

(2) H.-J. finds traces of atomistic doctrine in the references to ὄγκοι and πόροι in chs. 3, 8 and 9.[a] But there is no evidence that a belief in πόροι was characteristic of the Atomists. For if Democritus used the word in connexion with sense perception, so also did a number of other early philosophers[b]; and the use of the idea of πόροι as part of the theory of the constitution of matter is characteristic not of the atomists but of Empedocles. It is true that in *De Gen. et Corr.* i. 8 Aristotle associates the theory of " pores " with the doctrine of the Atomists on the grounds that the empty spaces between the atoms are analogous to the " pores " of Empedocles,[c] but it is clear that the two doctrines are different, that the association is made by Aristotle himself for purposes of criticism, and that the theory of pores is not part of atomist doctrine.[d] The case is little better with ὄγκοι. The word is used by the Atomists and may mean " atoms," but the use is very occasional[e] and the meaning uncertain, and in Epicurus at any rate it seems to mean little more than " particle " without any specific reference to atoms.[f]

---

evidence that Strato attended the Lyceum during the lifetime of Aristotle. He is said to have been a pupil of Theophrastus, whom he succeeded as head of the Lyceum, dying *circa* 270–268 B.C. He cannot have been more than a child in the decade 350–340 B.C. and can therefore hardly be responsible for having drawn Aristotle's attention to difficulties of which he was at that time well aware. *Cf.* Zeller, *Aristotle and the Earlier Peripatetics*, ii. p. 451, note 1.

[a] P. 122.   [b] *Cf.* Diels, *Vors.* Index, *s.v.*
[c] *Cf.* 325 b 5-11.
[d] *Cf.* Joachim's notes on this chapter (*Aristotle on Coming-to-be and Passing-away*, pp. 156 ff.); and Bailey, *Greek Atomists*, chs. 2 and 3.
[e] Diels, *Vors.* Index, *s.v.*; Bailey, *op. cit.* p. 156, note 1.
[f] Bailey, *op. cit.* pp. 577-579.

INTRODUCTION

The general meaning " particle," in fact, suits the two [a] contexts in which the word occurs in Book IV very well. In both Aristotle is speaking of water penetrating and melting or softening other bodies, and it is natural enough to talk of particles of water penetrating into other materials. Similarly it is not unnatural in these contexts to speak, without using the words in any technical sense, of " pores " into which the particles of water penetrate. The obvious example which presents itself is that of a sponge : and this is, in fact, used by Aristotle when speaking of pores in 386 b 5, 7 and 17. It is easy to extend the idea to penetration by fire (387 a 19, 21) and, with the analogy of the sponge in mind (386 b 5), to compressibility (386 b 2 ff.). In all these cases the body concerned can be called " porous " without stretching the ordinary meaning of the word far. Nor need it be stretched much farther to make it cover the breaking or splitting of materials (386 a 15, 387 a 2) : the grain of wood (387 a 2), for example, is a kind of *path* (another meaning of πόρος) along which it splits.[b]

The references to πόροι and ὄγκοι are thus best explained by taking the words in their non-technical ordinary meaning : and Olympiodorus' explanation [c] that by πόροι Aristotle means τὰ εὐπαθέστερα μόρια is not far wrong. There is no reason whatever to see any reference to atomism.[d] But even if the refer-

[a] 385 a 30, b 20.
[b] The passages in which πόροι are mentioned may be grouped as follows : penetration by moisture 381 b 1, 3, 385 a 29, b 20, 24, 25 ; penetration by fire 387 a 19, 21 ; compressibility 386 b 2, 4, 5, 6, 9 ; breakability 386 a 15 ; fissibility 387 a 2. [c] 313. 18.
[d] H.-J.'s case is not improved by an attempt (p. 122) to read atomism into 387 a 12 ff., where there is no conceivable reference to it.

ences to atomism were proved, this would not necessarily indicate Strato as author. For though Strato is said to have abandoned the Aristotelian teleology, to have regarded heat and cold as ultimate causes, and to have adopted the atomists' conception of the void, he is also said to have refused to accept the atomic theory itself on the grounds that the possibility of infinite division made the existence of a minimum physical body impossible.[a]

H.-J.'s two main arguments thus seem to be ill founded. Without them the others can hardly carry much weight and in themselves are lacking in cogency. Most of them turn on discrepancies between statements in Book IV and statements made elsewhere by Aristotle. But as Dr. Coutant points out (p. 10, note 18), Aristotle is frequently inconsistent on minor matters ; and the search for minor inconsistencies in his works really throws little light on their authenticity. Thus if Aristotle in this book (ch. 4, 381 b 24, and 382 a 4) says that all bodies are compounded of earth and water, while in *De Gen. et Corr.* 334 b 31 ff. he says that all bodies are composed of all four elements, the difference is one of point of view rather than of fundamental doctrine. For in this book all four elements are still involved in the composition of bodies ; but two are regarded as active, and therefore as efficient cause, two as passive, and therefore as material cause. In ch. 4, 382 a 3, water is called the element most characterized by moisture, in *De*

---

[a] Zeller, *Phil. der Griechen* ii³. 2, pp. 901 ff. : Eng. trans. *Aristotle and the Earlier Peripatetics*, pp. 456-460. H.-J.'s statement (p. 125), " Von Straton wissen wir, dass er Peripatitiker war, und doch der atomischen Lehre, die er ausbaute, seine Zustimmung gab," seems to contradict what Zeller, to whom she refers, in fact says.

Gen. et Corr. 331 a 4 it is said to be characterized by cold rather than moisture : but Aristotle is not consistent on this point in *De Gen. et Corr.* itself and at 334 b 34 implies that water is characteristically moist, which agrees with what is said here in ch. 4.[a] Again, there is no radical inconsistency between what Aristotle says about olive oil in ch. 7, 383 b 20 ff., and what he says in *De Gen. An.* 735 b 12 ff., and I agree with Dr. Coutant that there is no conflict between what Aristotle says at 379 a 26 about ἡ οἰκεία θερμότης and what he says in Book II, 355 b 9, about the ἔμφυτος θερμότης.[b] But further detailed argument may be omitted here.

Finally, there are certain positive indications that the book is by Aristotle. There are three fairly clear references to it in the biological works (with which ch. 12 deliberately links it) : *De Part. An.* ii. 2, 649 a 33 ff. refers to chs. 6-8 and 10, *De Gen. An.* ii. 6, 743 a 3-7 refers to chs. 4-7, and v. 4, 784 b 8 refers to ch. 1, 379 a 16. The doctrine of ch. 12 is, as has been indicated above, thoroughly Aristotelian, and indeed an important passage for Aristotle's views on teleology in organic and inorganic nature. The use of the parallel between τέχνη and φύσις (*cf.* ch. 2, note *a* on p. 298 and ch. 3, note *b* on p. 308) is typically Aristotelian, and can be found, for example, running through *Physics* B and *De Part. An.* i. 1. The treatment of hard and soft as the primary qualities in chs. 4 ff. is, as H.-J. herself points out (p. 120), consistent with what Aristotle says elsewhere on the subject (*De Gen. et Corr.* ii. 2, 329 b 32 ff., *De Anima* ii. 11, 423 b 27 ff., iii. 13, 435 a 21 ff.), and what is said about

---

[a] *Cf.* ch. 4, note *c* on p. 312.
[b] *Cf.* chap. 1, note *a* on p. 294.

INTRODUCTION

the four prime contraries and the four elements in
general is in complete accord with *De Caelo* iii and iv
and *De Gen. et Corr.* (which is perhaps why Alexander
grouped the book with the *De Gen. et Corr.*). Lastly,
in the latter part of the book the homoeomerous substances are given a place in the constitution of the
physical world similar to that given to them in *De
Part. An.* ii. 1, 646 a 12 ff.

I conclude that the case against the authenticity
of Book IV has not been made out, that what indications there are point to it being genuine, and that
it should be accepted as such until a far stronger case
is made out against it than hitherto.

2. *Contents.* Book IV, as has been remarked,[a] is
concerned with chemical change and various properties of matter.[b] In it Aristotle deals in detail
with processes of what we should to-day call chemical
change, whose general principles he has laid down in
the *De Gen. et Corr.* : he deals also with various
secondary properties of matter, secondary, that is, to
the four "prime contraries," which have also been
dealt with in *De Gen. et Corr.* The sequence of
thought in the book is by no means easy to follow,
and can best be seen in a brief analysis of its contents.

A. Chs. 1-3. The effects of heat and cold.
  Ch. 1. Summary of the doctrine
    of four prime contraries (hot,
    cold, moist, dry) and four
    elements (fire, air, water,
    earth). Heat and cold as
    active factors are responsible
    for generation and destruc-
    tion.

[a] P. xiii above. [b] *Cf.* Joachim, *loc. cit., J.Ph.* xxix (1903).

C. Date

The evidence for the date of the composition of the *Meteorologica* is inconclusive. Positive indications in the work are as follows :

I. 7, 345 a 1, mentions a comet which appeared in the archonship of Nicomachus 341/0 B.C.

At III. 1, 371 a 31, the burning of the temple at Ephesus (356 B.C.) is referred to as having taken place νῦν, which would seem to mark it as a recent event.

At III. 2, 372 a 28, Aristotle, speaking of the appearance of a rainbow at night, says " we have only met with two instances of it over a period of more than fifty years "; and it may be argued that this indicates, though not conclusively, that Aristotle was not a young man at the time he wrote it.[a]

These indications are not conclusive, and are mutually inconsistent. For the first and third indicate a date after 340 : the second a date not far from 356.

Two further arguments are used by Ideler (i. p. ix) :

(1) That Aristotle's references to the Caspian and Aral Seas (Book I. ch. 13, 351 a 8, Book II. ch. 1, 354 a 3) argue a date prior to Alexander's expedition, on the grounds that after Alexander the two seas were supposed to be one and to be a gulf of the Ocean (cf. Ideler's notes ad i. 13, l. 29, and ii. 1, l. 10). But this argument is invalidated by Tarn's discussion.[b]

(2) That the observations on the position of the constellation of the Crown in Book II. ch. 5, 362 b 9, appear to be made as from the latitude of Athens. But the passage is of doubtful authenticity (cf. O.T. note ad loc.) and in any case would only indicate a date after 335 or before 347.

It cannot therefore be said that internal evidence gives any conclusive evidence of date. On other general grounds Ross [c] and Jaeger,[d] followed by Dr. Coutant,[e] favour a later date. But they base themselves on Jaeger's conclusion that the biological works, with their attention to detail, are the products of Aristotle's later years, and that other works, showing a similar attention to detail, must be referred to the same period. Jaeger's view of the date of the biological works is ill founded, and all indications

[a] Cf. Jaeger, *Aristotle* (Eng. trans.), p. 307, note 1.
[b] *Alexander the Great*, ii. pp. 6 ff. Cf. Note on Aristotle's Geography, Bk. I. ch. 13.
[c] *Aristotle*, p. 19.   [d] *Loc. cit.*
[e] *Op. cit.* p. 18.

point to an early origin for them [a]; and this argument for a later date for the *Meteorologica* therefore fails. But there is undoubtedly some connexion between it and the biological works. The introduction (Book I. ch. 1) looks forward to them in a way which suggests that Aristotle may have started work on them; and the conclusion of Book IV. ch. 12 again deliberately links itself with them. In addition, the only clear references to the *Meteorologica* elsewhere are in the biological works.[b]

The evidence, therefore, if inconclusive, would seem to indicate that the *Meteorologica* was started not later than Aristotle's period of residence in the Troad and Lesbos, when so much of his biological work was done. The connexion with the biological works and the reference to the temple of Ephesus both point to this. At the same time Aristotle without doubt continued to revise and bring up to date his work on the subject, and this accounts, for instance, for the reference to the archonship of Nicomachus, which must certainly be later than 340 B.C. We know that Aristotle's extant works are either lecture-notes or connected closely with his teaching work; and the one thing any lecturer is constantly doing is to revise and bring his notes up to date.

D. CONCLUSION

That the *Meteorologica* is a little-read work is no doubt due to the intrinsic lack of interest of its contents. Aristotle is so far wrong in nearly all his conclusions that they can, it may with justice be said,

[a] *Cf.* above, p. xvi, note *d*.
[b] *Cf.* above, p. xx, and Bonitz, *Index*, p. 102 b 49.

have little more than a passing antiquarian interest. Certain passages there are which have an interest of their own, and which are less well known than they otherwise might be because of their context. Such are Book I. ch. 1, with its review of the physical sciences, perhaps the best-known passage in the work and the basis for the accepted arrangement of Aristotle's works ; Book I. ch. 13, 350 a 14 ff. and Book II. ch. 5, 362 b 12 ff., from which we learn Aristotle's view of the nature and extent of the habitable world and the extent of his geographical knowledge ; passages in Book I of considerable interest for the history of Greek astronomy, for instance, those which give the views of Aristotle and of his predecessors on comets and the Milky Way (chs. 6-7, and 8 ; Aristotle's view of the former was to hold the field until Newton[a]) ; Book IV. ch. 12, which adds considerably to our understanding of Aristotle's views on the place of the final-formal cause in nature.

But, apart from these passages of special interest, the main interest of the work is to be found not so much in any particular conclusions which Aristotle reaches, as in the fact that all his conclusions are so far wrong and in his lack of a method which could lead him to right ones. In this he is typical of Greek science. The comparative failure of the Greeks to develop experimental science was due to many causes, which cannot be considered here. They lacked instruments of precision—there were, for instance, no accurate clocks until Galileo discovered the pendulum. They did not produce until a comparatively late date any glass suitable for chemical experiment or lens-making. Their iron-making technique was elemen-

[a] Heath, *Aristarchus of Samos*, p. 217.

tary, which precluded the development of the machine. Their mathematical notation was clumsy and unsuited to scientific calculation. All these things would have severely limited the development of an experimental science had the Greeks fully grasped its method. But the experimental method eluded them. They observed but they did not experiment, and between observation and experiment there is a fundamental difference, which it is essential to recognize if the history of Greek thought is to be understood.[a] This difference can be clearly seen in the *Meteorologica*. There is plenty of observation : Books I-III are full of it, and Book IV shows a keen observation of the processes of the kitchen and garden in terms of which Aristotle tries to explain chemical change in general. But there is practically no experiment, and in those experiments which Aristotle does quote the results given are wrong (*cf.* Book II. ch. 3, note *b* on p. 156 and note *a* on p. 158). A good example of his attitude and method is the theory of exhalations, which plays so prominent a part in Books I and II.[b] It has a basis in observation : Aristotle had obviously observed the phenomena of evaporation. Yet not only has it no basis in experiment but it is not designed to be verified experimentally, nor is it easy to conceive any experiment which could either confirm or invalidate it. It is this absence of the awareness for the necessity of an experimental test that is the mark of thought that is rational but not yet scientific, of the natural philosopher rather than the natural scientist. And of Aristotle's natural philosophy and of Greek natural philosophy in general it is true that it re-

---

[a] Burnet, *E.G.P.*[4], p. 27, for instance, fails to recognize it.
[b] *Cf.* note at the end of Book I. ch. 3.

mained rational without being scientific, that it never passed from natural philosophy to natural science. There are, of course, exceptions both in Aristotle and elsewhere in Greek thought. Greek medicine comes very near to being scientific,[a] so also do Aristotle's biological works; and the Greeks made further progress in astronomy than in any of the other physical sciences, though this was just because their astronomy involved no experiment, but only observation and mathematical calculation. But these are exceptions. Of the more general tendency the *Meteorologica* is typical; it is a product of the natural philosopher, not the natural scientist, and it is in this that its main interest lies.

TEXT

The text printed in this edition is that of Professor Fobes, to whom I wish to express my thanks and gratitude for his permission to use it. I have occasionally and with great diffidence adopted a different reading from that given in his text, in an attempt to produce a version that would give better sense. I have noted these variations, and also in some places where the text is obscure some of the alternative readings given in his apparatus.

BIBLIOGRAPHY

The following are the works to which most frequent reference is made and the abbreviations used in referring to them.

[a] *Cf.* W. H. S. Jones, *The Medical Writings of Anonymus Londiniensis*, Excursus I, pp. 148 ff., and *Philosophy and Medicine in Ancient Greece*, p. 32.

INTRODUCTION

I. L. Ideler, *Aristotelis Meteorologi-*   Ideler.
corum Libri IV, Lipsiae, 1836.

F. H. Fobes, *Aristotelis Meteorologi-*   Fobes.
corum Libri Quattuor, Harvard,
1918.

J. Barthélemy-Saint-Hilaire, *Météoro-*   St.-Hilaire.
logie d'Aristote, Paris, 1863.

The Works of Aristotle, translated into   O.T.
English, vol. iii containing *Me-*
teorologica, by E. W. Webster,
Oxford, 1931 (the " Oxford translation ").

F. C. E. Thurot, " Observations cri-   Thurot.
tiques sur les Meteorologica
d'Aristote," *Revue Archéologique*
xx (1869), pp. 415-420, xxi
(1870), pp. 87-93, 249-255, 339-
346, 396-407.

Alexandri in Aristotelis Meteorologi-   Alex. or A.
corum libros Commentaria, ed. M.
Hayduck, Berlin, 1899.

Olympiodori in Aristotelis Meteora Com- Olymp. or O.
mentaria, ed. Guil. Stüve, Berlin,
1900.

Ioannis Philoponi in Aristotelis Meteoro- Philop. or P.
logicorum librum primum Commen-
tarium, ed. M. Hayduck, Berlin,
1901.

In the notes on the text I have added, following
Fobes, to the initial letter of the commentator the
letters c, l, or p to indicate whatever the reading
referred to is to be found in a citation, in a lemma, or
in the paraphrase and commentary.

INTRODUCTION

A fuller bibliography, concerned primarily with more recent publications, will be found in Fobes pp. xlii-xliii. To it may be added :

D'Arcy Thompson, " The Greek Winds," *Classical Review*, xxxii (1918), pp. 49-56.

D. E. Eichholz, " Aristotle's Theory of the Formation of Metals and Minerals," *Classical Quarterly*, xliii (July-October, 1949), p. 141.

V. C. B. Coutant, *Alexander of Aphrodisias : Commentary on Book IV of Aristotle's Meteorologica* : dissertation submitted to Columbia University, privately printed, 1936.

Sir T. L. Heath, *Aristarchus of Samos : a History of Greek Astronomy to Aristarchus*, Oxford, 1913.

Sir W. Napier Shaw, *Manual of Meteorology*, vol. i : *Meteorology in History*, Cambridge, 1932.

Of the older commentators, who fall outside the scope of Fobes' bibliography, the most noteworthy (apart from Ideler) is :

F. Vicomercatus, *In quatuor libros Aristotelis meteorologicorum Commentarii*, Paris, 1556, and Venice, 1565.

To these should be added :

Ingemar Düring, *Aristotles's Chemical Treatise Meteorologica Book IV*, Göteborg, 1944,

which did not come into my hands until this book was in proof. Düring's chief object is to prove *Meteorologica IV* to be " a genuine work from the hand of Aristotle by a thorough-going comparison of the contents and the language of this treatise with the treatises of undisputed Aristotelian origin " (p. 20). His arguments supplement those given in my Introduction.

THE TRADITIONAL ORDER of the works of
Aristotle as they appear since the edition of
Immanuel Bekker (Berlin, 1831), and their
division into volumes in this edition.

THE TRADITIONAL ORDER

THE TRADITIONAL ORDER

THE TRADITIONAL ORDER

ARISTOTLE
METEOROLOGICA

ΑΡΙΣΤΟΤΕΛΟΥΣ
ΜΕΤΕΩΡΟΛΟΓΙΚΩΝ

A

CHAPTER I

ARGUMENT

The scope and subject-matter of Meteorology and its place in the system of Natural Philosophy. Natural Philosophy comprises (1) *Physics, which deals with first principles and the various kinds of natural motion (the* Physics*) ;* (2) *Astronomy (the* De Caelo*) ;* (3) *the general theory of the elements and their transformation (*De Caelo *iii, iv,* De Generatione et Corruptione*) ;* (4) *Meteorology, the subject of the present work ;* (5) *Zoology and Botany.*

Note.—In section (4), 338 a 26—339 a 5, *Aristotle gives a summary of the subjects to be treated in the first three books. It is a preliminary survey, not a table of contents, and we must not look for too precise a correspondence between it and the contents of the work and the order of treatment : thus the milky way, comets and meteors are mentioned here in the reverse order to that in which they are in fact treated, and no specific mention is made of the contents of Book I. ch. 5. But broadly speaking the contents of the first three books do correspond to the summary here given. There are only three passages which cause difficulty.*

(1) 338 b 24 ὅσα τε θείημεν ἂν ἀέρος εἶναι κοινὰ πάθη καὶ

2

ARISTOTLE
METEOROLOGICA
BOOK I
CHAPTER I

ARGUMENT (*continued*)

ὕδατος. *These words most naturally refer to Book I. chs. 9-12 (which are summed up as a unit at the end of ch. 12) : but they may refer to Book III. chs. 2-6 as the commentators suppose.*

(2) 338 b 25 ἔτι δὲ γῆς ὅσα μέρη καὶ εἴδη καὶ πάθη τῶν μερῶν. *These words describe not very exactly the contents of Book I. ch. 13-Book II. ch. 3, and it seems best to suppose with the O.T. that it is to them that reference is intended, and to take ἐξ ὧν 338 b 25 as marking sequence only and not causal connexion.*

(3) 339 a 4 καὶ τῶν ἄλλων τῶν ἐγκυκλίων, ὅσα διὰ πῆξιν συμβαίνει πάθη τῶν αὐτῶν σωμάτων τούτων. τῶν αὐτῶν . . . τούτων can hardly refer to thunderbolts, etc., and must therefore presumably be taken to refer to air and water, the two elements most recently mentioned (338 b 24, cf. Alex. 3. 25). ἐγκύκλιος is used of any recurrent phenomenon, and though it might more easily be used to describe rain, hail, etc., i.e. Book I. chs. 9-12, it is not impossible to interpret it to refer to haloes, rainbows, etc., described in Book III. chs. 2-6. These are all due to condensation, which is what πῆξις seems to mean here. Cf. W. Capelle, " Das Proömium der Meteorologie," Hermes xlvii, pp. 514-535.*

338 a 20 Περὶ μὲν οὖν τῶν πρώτων αἰτίων τῆς φύσεως καὶ περὶ πάσης κινήσεως φυσικῆς, ἔτι δὲ περὶ τῶν κατὰ τὴν ἄνω φορὰν διακεκοσμημένων ἄστρων καὶ περὶ τῶν στοιχείων τῶν σωματικῶν, πόσα τε καὶ ποῖα, καὶ τῆς εἰς ἄλληλα μεταβολῆς, καὶ περὶ
25 γενέσεως καὶ φθορᾶς τῆς κοινῆς εἴρηται πρότερον. λοιπὸν δ' ἐστὶ μέρος τῆς μεθόδου ταύτης ἔτι θεωρητέον, ὃ πάντες οἱ πρότεροι μετεωρολογίαν ἐκά-
338 b λουν· ταῦτα δ' ἐστὶν ὅσα συμβαίνει κατὰ φύσιν μέν, ἀτακτοτέραν μέντοι τῆς τοῦ πρώτου στοιχείου τῶν σωμάτων, περὶ τὸν γειτνιῶντα μάλιστα τόπον τῇ φορᾷ τῇ τῶν ἄστρων, οἷον περί τε γάλακτος καὶ κομητῶν καὶ τῶν ἐκπυρουμένων καὶ κινουμένων φασμάτων, ὅσα τε θείημεν ἂν ἀέρος εἶναι κοινὰ
25 πάθη καὶ ὕδατος, ἔτι δὲ γῆς ὅσα μέρη καὶ εἴδη καὶ πάθη τῶν μερῶν, ἐξ ὧν περί τε πνευμάτων καὶ
339 a σεισμῶν θεωρήσαιμεν ἂν τὰς αἰτίας καὶ περὶ πάντων τῶν γιγνομένων κατὰ τὰς κινήσεις τὰς τούτων· ἐν οἷς τὰ μὲν ἀπορούμεν, τῶν δὲ ἐφαπτόμεθά τινα τρόπον· ἔτι δὲ περὶ κεραυνῶν πτώσεως καὶ τυφώνων καὶ πρηστήρων καὶ τῶν ἄλλων τῶν
5 ἐγκυκλίων, ὅσα διὰ πῆξιν συμβαίνει πάθη τῶν αὐτῶν σωμάτων τούτων.

Διελθόντες δὲ περὶ τούτων, θεωρήσωμεν εἴ τι δυνάμεθα κατὰ τὸν ὑφηγημένον τρόπον ἀποδοῦναι

---

a Physics.
b Physics, esp. Books V-VIII.
c De Caelo i and ii.
d De Caelo iii and iv, De Gen. et Corr.
e The fifth element of which the heavenly bodies and their spheres are made.

(1) WE have already dealt with the first causes of nature [a] and with all natural motion [b] ; (2) we have dealt also with the ordered movements of the stars in the heavens,[c] (3) and with the number, kinds and mutual transformations of the four elements, and growth and decay in general.[d] (4) It remains to consider a subdivision of the present inquiry which all our predecessors have called Meteorology. Its province is everything which happens naturally, but with a regularity less than that of the primary element [e] of material things, and which takes place in the region which borders most nearly on the movements of the stars. For instance the milky way,[f] comets,[g] shooting stars and meteors,[h] all phenomena that may be regarded as common to air and water,[i] and the various kinds and parts of the earth and their characteristics.[j] There follows the investigation of the causes of winds [k] and earthquakes [l] and all occurrences associated with their motions. Of all these phenomena, some we find inexplicable, others we can to some extent understand. We shall also be concerned with the fall of thunderbolts,[m] with whirlwinds,[n] with firewinds,[n] and with all other recurrent conditions which affect these same bodies owing to condensation.[o]

(5) After we have dealt with all these subjects let us then see if we can give some account, on the lines

---

[f] i. 8.   [g] i. 6-7.   [h] i. 4.
[i] i. 9-12, and perhaps iii. 2-6, 378 a 14.
[j] i. 13-ii. 3, though it is difficult to find a precise reference for this phrase. It can hardly, however, refer to Book IV.
[k] ii. 4-6.   [l] ii. 7-8.
[m] ii. 9, iii. 1.   [n] iii. 1.
[o] " Same bodies " : not thunderbolts, etc., but presumably air and water. iii. 2-6, 378 a 14, or i. 9-12.

339 a

περὶ ζῴων καὶ φυτῶν, καθόλου τε καὶ χωρὶς··
σχεδὸν γὰρ τούτων ῥηθέντων τέλος ἂν εἴη γεγονὸς
τῆς ἐξ ἀρχῆς ἡμῖν προαιρέσεως πάσης.
10 Ὧδ' οὖν ἀρξάμενοι λέγωμεν περὶ αὐτῶν πρῶτον.

ᵃ The zoological works, with which should be included the
De Anima.
ᵇ A reference to the lost work On Plants : cf. Bonitz,
Index 104 b 38.

CHAPTER II

ARGUMENT

*There is one element in the celestial region, in the terrestrial
there are four, earth, air, fire and water. These four are the*

339 a 11 Ἐπειδὴ γὰρ διώρισται πρότερον ἡμῖν μία μὲν
ἀρχὴ τῶν σωμάτων, ἐξ ἧς¹ συνέστηκεν ἡ τῶν ἐγκυκλίως φερομένων σωμάτων φύσις, ἄλλα δὲ τέτταρα σώματα διὰ τὰς τέτταρας ἀρχάς, ὧν διπλῆν
15 εἶναί φαμεν τὴν κίνησιν, τὴν μὲν ἀπὸ τοῦ μέσου
τὴν δ' ἐπὶ τὸ μέσον· τεττάρων δ' ὄντων τούτων,
πυρὸς καὶ ἀέρος καὶ ὕδατος καὶ γῆς, τὸ μὲν τούτοις
πᾶσιν ἐπιπολάζον εἶναι πῦρ, τὸ δ' ὑφιστάμενον γῆν·
δύο δὲ ἃ πρὸς αὐτὰ τούτοις ἀνάλογον ἔχει (ἀὴρ μὲν
γὰρ πυρὸς ἐγγυτάτω τῶν ἄλλων, ὕδωρ δὲ γῆς)· ὁ
20 δὴ περὶ τὴν γῆν ὅλος κόσμος ἐκ τούτων συνέστηκε
τῶν σωμάτων· περὶ οὗ τὰ συμβαίνοντα πάθη φαμὲν

---

¹ ἐξ ἧς Vicomercatus O.T.   ἐξ ὧν codd.

ᵃ Hot, cold, dry, moist which combine to form the four
elements, here called " bodies." Earth is a combination of

6

we have laid down, of animals [a] and plants,[b] both in general and in particular ; for when we have done this we may perhaps claim that the whole investigation which we set before ourselves at the outset has been completed.

With this introduction let us begin our discussion of the subject in hand.

CHAPTER II

ARGUMENT (continued)

material cause, the eternal motion of the celestial region the efficient cause of all that happens in the terrestrial region.

WE have previously laid down that there is one element from which the natural bodies in circular motion are made up, and four other physical bodies produced by the primary qualities,[a] the motion of these bodies being twofold, either away from or towards the centre. These four bodies are fire, air, water and earth : of them fire always rises to the top, earth always sinks to the bottom, while the other two bear to each other a mutual relation similar to that of fire and earth—for air is the nearest of all to fire, water to earth. The whole terrestrial [b] region, then, is composed of these four bodies, and it is the conditions which affect them which, we have said,

cold and dry ; air of hot and wet ; fire of hot and dry ; water of wet and cold. *De Gen. et Corr.* ii. 3. *Cf.* Book IV. ch. 1, note *a* on p. 290.

  [b] *i.e.* below the sphere of the moon ; *cf.* 339 b 5.

εἶναι ληπτέον. ἔστιν δ' ἐξ ἀνάγκης συνεχὴς οὗτος
ταῖς ἄνω φοραῖς, ὥστε πᾶσαν αὐτοῦ τὴν δύναμιν
κυβερνᾶσθαι ἐκεῖθεν· ὅθεν γὰρ ἡ τῆς κινήσεως
ἀρχὴ πᾶσιν, ἐκείνην αἰτίαν νομιστέον πρώτην.
25 πρὸς δὲ τούτοις ἡ μὲν ἀίδιος καὶ τέλος οὐκ ἔχουσα
τῷ τόπῳ τῆς κινήσεως, ἀλλ' ἀεὶ ἐν τέλει· ταῦτα
δὲ τὰ σώματα πάντα πεπερασμένους διέστηκε
τόπους ἀλλήλων. ὥστε τῶν συμβαινόντων περὶ
αὐτὸν πῦρ μὲν καὶ γῆν καὶ τὰ συγγενῆ τούτοις
ὡς ἐν ὕλης εἴδει τῶν γιγνομένων αἴτια χρὴ νομίζειν
30 (τὸ γὰρ ὑποκείμενον καὶ πάσχον τοῦτον προσαγο-
ρεύομεν τὸν τρόπον), τὸ δ' οὕτως αἴτιον ὡς[1] ὅθεν
ἡ τῆς κινήσεως ἀρχή, τὴν τῶν ἀεὶ κινουμένων
αἰτιατέον δύναμιν.

[1] ὡς om. Fobes : habent E𝔚F_corr. Ap.

---

[a] I have translated δύναμις " capacity for movement "
because it is the capacity of the elements for movement, and
so for change and combination, which Aristotle seems to have
in mind.

[b] The characteristics of circular motion.

[c] Each of the four elements has its " natural place " to
which it has a natural tendency to move in a straight line
(*cf.* a 16-19 above). I have taken πρὸς δὲ τούτοις a 24 . . .
ἀλλήλων a 27 as a parenthesis in which the circular motion

CHAPTER III

ARGUMENT

*The argument of this chapter is somewhat involved because
Aristotle approaches the solution of its main problem—the
disposition of earth and fire in the terrestrial region—in-*

are the subject of our inquiry. This region must be continuous with the motions of the heavens, which therefore regulate its whole capacity for movement [a] : for the celestial element as source of all motion must be regarded as first cause. (Besides, the celestial element is eternal and moves in a path that is spatially endless but always complete,[b] while the terrestrial bodies have each their distinct and limited regions).[c] Fire, earth and the kindred elements must therefore be regarded as the material cause of all sublunar events (for we call the passive subject of change the material cause) ; while the driving power of the eternally moving bodies must be their cause in the sense of the ultimate source of their motion.

of the celestial region is contrasted with the linear motion of the terrestrial, linear motion lacking, according to Aristotle, the perfection of circular. The parenthesis may perhaps have a further implication. Left to themselves the four elements would each move to its natural place and come to rest ; they have not done so because the celestial motion keeps them stirred up, as it were, to form the world that we know. Thus the celestial motion is ἀρχὴ κινήσεως of the processes in the terrestrial region. The reference to natural places in the parenthesis may be intended to recall this and so to enforce the previous statement of the dependence of the terrestrial on the celestial region.

CHAPTER III

ARGUMENT (continued)

directly, by discussing certain other, though closely related, problems. It may be analysed as follows :

1. There are four elements. Earth is comparatively small in bulk and lies, with water (seas, rivers, etc.), at the centre of the universe. What is the position of air ? And, more generally, what is the nature of the substance or substances that occupy the space between the earth and the farthest stars (339 a 33–b 16) ?

2. The celestial region is composed of a divine fifth element which we may identify with the traditional " aether " (339 b 16-30). So (a) the stars are not made of fire nor set in fire (339 b 30—340 a 3) ; (b) nor are the intervals between them full of air (340 a 3-17).

3. We are left with two problems : (a) the disposition of air and fire below this fifth element ; (b) how heat reaches us from the stars (340 a 17-22). (A discussion of (b) is necessary now the stars have been shown not to be made of fire and so not to be hot.)

3 (a). Let us first deal with air, and approach the solution of our main problem by means of a discussion of the question, why do not clouds form in the upper air as one might on the face of it expect (340 a 22-32) ?

339 a 33 Ἀναλαβόντες οὖν τὰς ἐξ ἀρχῆς θέσεις καὶ τοὺς εἰρημένους πρότερον διορισμούς, λέγωμεν περί τε 35 τῆς τοῦ γάλακτος φαντασίας καὶ περὶ κομητῶν καὶ τῶν ἄλλων ὅσα τυγχάνει τούτοις ὄντα συγγενῆ.

Φαμὲν δὴ πῦρ καὶ ἀέρα καὶ ὕδωρ καὶ γῆν γίγνε-
339 b σθαι ἐξ ἀλλήλων, καὶ ἕκαστον ἐν ἑκάστῳ ὑπάρχειν τούτων δυνάμει, ὥσπερ καὶ τῶν ἄλλων οἷς ἕν τι καὶ ταὐτὸν ὑπόκειται, εἰς ὃ δὴ ἀναλύονται ἔσχατον.

Πρῶτον μὲν οὖν ἀπορήσειεν ἄν τις περὶ τὸν καλούμενον ἀέρα, τίνα τε χρὴ λαβεῖν αὐτοῦ τὴν φύσιν
5 ἐν τῷ περιέχοντι κόσμῳ τὴν γῆν, καὶ πῶς ἔχει
τῇ τάξει πρὸς τἆλλα τὰ λεγόμενα στοιχεῖα τῶν
σωμάτων. ὁ μὲν γὰρ δὴ τῆς γῆς ὄγκος πηλίκος ἄν
τις εἴη πρὸς τὰ περιέχοντα μεγέθη, οὐκ ἄδηλον·
ἤδη γὰρ ὦπται διὰ τῶν ἀστρολογικῶν θεωρημάτων

---

*a i.e. in the De Caelo and De Gen. et Corr., to which re-
ference has been made above.*

(i) *Introduction : any solution which implied that the whole region was full of air, or air-cum-vapour, would upset the balance of the elements unduly (340 a 32–b 3).*

(ii) *Aristotle's own solution :*

a. *The motion of the celestial sphere generates heat (which prevents clouds) in the part of the terrestrial nearest to it (340 b 4-14). β. There are in fact two strata in this region, an upper one of fire, a lower one of air. So clouds will not form in it because it contains fire as well as air (340 b 14-32). γ. The whole mass, fire and air, must move round with the motion of the celstial sphere ; and this would prevent cloud formation (340 b 32—341 a 12).*

3 (b). *a. The sun generates heat by its motion, like a projectile. This alone is enough to account for all the heat in the terrestrial region (341 a 12-30).*

β. The fire that surrounds the terrestrial sphere is sometimes driven inwards by the motion of the heavens (341 a 30-31).

LET us then recall our initial assumptions and the definitions given earlier,[a] and then proceed to discuss the milky way, comets, and other similar phenomena.

1. The problem—what occupies the space between the earth and the farthest stars ?

We maintain that fire, air, water and earth are transformable one into another, and that each is potentially latent in the others, as is true of all other things that have a single common substratum underlying them into which they can in the last resort be resolved.[b]

Our first difficulty concerns what we call the air. What are we to suppose its nature to be in the terrestrial region ? And what is its position in relation to the other so called elements of physical things ? (For there is no doubt about the relative size of the earth and of the masses which surround it, as astronomical researches have now made it clear that

[b] *De Gen. et Corr.* ii. 1, 4 ; *De Caelo* iii. 6, 7.

339 b

ἡμῖν ὅτι πολὺ καὶ τῶν ἄστρων ἐνίων ἐλάττων ἐστίν.
10 ὕδατος δὲ φύσιν συνεστηκυῖαν καὶ ἀφωρισμένην
οὔθ' ὁρῶμεν οὔτ' ἐνδέχεται κεχωρισμένην εἶναι τοῦ
περὶ τὴν γῆν ἱδρυμένου σώματος, οἷον τῶν τε
φανερῶν, θαλάττης καὶ ποταμῶν, κἂν εἴ τι κατὰ
βάθους ἄδηλον ἡμῖν ἐστιν. τὸ δὲ δὴ μεταξὺ τῆς
γῆς τε καὶ τῶν ἐσχάτων ἄστρων πότερον ἕν τι
15 νομιστέον εἶναι σῶμα τὴν φύσιν ἢ πλείω, κἂν εἰ
πλείω, πόσα, καὶ μέχρι ποῦ διώρισται τοῖς τόποις;

Ἡμῖν μὲν οὖν εἴρηται πρότερον περὶ τοῦ πρώτου
στοιχείου, ποῖόν τι τὴν δύναμίν ἐστιν, καὶ διότι
πᾶς ὁ περὶ τὰς ἄνω φορὰς κόσμος ἐκείνου τοῦ
σώματος πλήρης ἐστί. καὶ ταύτην τὴν δόξαν οὐ
20 μόνον ἡμεῖς τυγχάνομεν ἔχοντες, φαίνεται δὲ ἀρ-
χαία τις ὑπόληψις αὕτη καὶ τῶν πρότερον ἀνθρώ-
πων· ὁ γὰρ λεγόμενος αἰθὴρ παλαιὰν εἴληφε τὴν
προσηγορίαν, ἣν Ἀναξαγόρας μὲν τῷ πυρὶ ταὐτὸν
ἡγήσασθαί μοι δοκεῖ σημαίνειν· τά τε γὰρ ἄνω
πλήρη πυρὸς εἶναι, κἀκείνους[1] τὴν ἐκεῖ δύναμιν
25 αἰθέρα καλεῖν ἐνόμισε, τοῦτο μὲν ὀρθῶς νομίσας·
τὸ γὰρ ἀεὶ σῶμα θέον ἅμα καὶ θεῖόν τι τὴν φύσιν
ἐοίκασιν ὑπολαβεῖν, καὶ διώρισαν ὀνομάζειν αἰθέρα
τὸ τοιοῦτον ὡς ὂν οὐδενὶ τῶν παρ' ἡμῖν τὸ αὐτό·
οὐ γὰρ δὴ φήσομεν ἅπαξ οὐδὲ δὶς οὐδ' ὀλιγάκις
τὰς αὐτὰς δόξας ἀνακυκλεῖν γιγνομένας ἐν τοῖς
30 ἀνθρώποις, ἀλλ' ἀπειράκις. ὅσοι δὲ πῦρ καθαρὸν

---

[1] κἀκείνους ci. Thurot : κἀκεῖνος codd.

[a] Cf. De Caelo ii. 14, 297 b 30 ff., Heath, *Aristarchus*, p. 236.　　[b] De Caelo i. 2, 3.

[c] Cf. below ii. 9, 369 b 14 and v. Diels 56 A 43, 73, 84.

[d] As if αἰθήρ were derived from ἀεί and θεῖν, with a play on θεῖος as well. For this etymology cf. Plato, *Cratylus* 410 B, [Aristotle], *De Mundo* 2, 392 a 5.

12

the earth is far smaller even than some of the stars [a] :
while water we never see existing as a separate and
distinct physical substance, nor can it so exist apart
from the mass of it situated round the earth, by which
I mean both that which we can see, for instance sea
and rivers, and any that may be hidden from us
underground.) But to return—are we to consider
that one physical substance occupies the space between the earth and the farthest stars, or more than
one ? And if more than one, then how many are
there and what are the limits of the various regions
which they occupy ?

Now we have already discussed the primary
element and its properties, and explained why the
whole region of the celestial motions is filled by that
body.[b] This opinion moreover is one that we are not
alone in holding, for it appears to be an ancient belief
and one held by men in former times ; for what is
called the aether was given this name in antiquity.
Anaxagoras seems to think that the name means the
same as fire,[c] since he considered that the upper
regions are full of fire and that the ancients meant
by " aether " the substance which fills them. In the
latter belief he was right. For men seem to have
supposed that the body that was in eternal motion was
also in some way divine in nature, and decided to call
a body of this kind aether,[d] as it is different from all
terrestrial things. For we maintain that the same
opinions recur in rotation among men, not once or
twice or occasionally, but infinitely often.[e] (a) On the

2. The celestial region composed of the fifth element.

Two other views refuted.

[e] For the doctrine of a recurrent cycle of knowledge cf.
De Caelo i. 3, 270 b 16, *Met.* Λ 8, 1074 b 1-14, *Politics* vii. 9,
1329 b 25 : see also Jaeger, *Aristotle*, pp. 128 ff., and cf.
ch. 14 below, note a on p. 115.

339 b

εἶναί φασι τὸ περιέχον καὶ μὴ μόνον τὰ φερόμενα
σώματα, τὸ δὲ μεταξὺ γῆς καὶ τῶν ἄστρων ἀέρα,
θεωρήσαντες ἂν τὰ νῦν δεικνύμενα διὰ τῶν μαθη-
μάτων ἱκανῶς ἴσως ἂν ἐπαύσαντο ταύτης τῆς
παιδικῆς δόξης· λίαν γὰρ ἁπλοῦν τὸ νομίζειν μικρὸν
35 τοῖς μεγέθεσιν εἶναι τῶν φερομένων ἕκαστον, ὅτι
φαίνεται θεωροῦσιν ἐντεῦθεν ἡμῖν οὕτως. εἴρηται
μὲν οὖν καὶ πρότερον ἐν τοῖς περὶ τὸν ἄνω τόπον
θεωρήμασι· λέγωμεν δὲ τὸν αὐτὸν λόγον καὶ νῦν.
340 a εἰ γὰρ τά τε διαστήματα πλήρη πυρὸς καὶ τὰ σώματα συνέστηκεν ἐκ πυρός, πάλαι φροῦδον ἂν ἦν
ἕκαστον τῶν ἄλλων στοιχείων. ἀλλὰ μὴν οὐδ' ἀέρος γε μόνου πλῆρι· πολὺ γὰρ ἂν ὑπερβάλλοι τὴν
5 ἰσότητα τῆς κοινῆς ἀναλογίας πρὸς τὰ σύστοιχα
σώματα, κἂν εἰ δύο στοιχείων πλήρης ὁ μεταξὺ
γῆς τε καὶ οὐρανοῦ τόπος ἐστίν· οὐδὲν γὰρ ὡς
εἰπεῖν μόριον ὁ τῆς γῆς ἐστιν ὄγκος, ἐν ᾧ συνεί-
ληπται πᾶν καὶ τὸ τοῦ ὕδατος πλῆθος, πρὸς τὸ
περιέχον μέγεθος. ὁρῶμεν δ' οὐκ ἐν τοσούτῳ
10 μεγέθει γιγνομένην τὴν ὑπεροχὴν τῶν ὄγκων, ὅταν
ἐξ ὕδατος ἀὴρ γένηται διακριθέντος ἢ πῦρ ἐξ ἀέρος·
ἀνάγκη δὲ τὸν αὐτὸν ἔχειν λόγον ὃν ἔχει τὸ τοσονδὶ
καὶ μικρὸν ὕδωρ πρὸς τὸν ἐξ αὐτοῦ γιγνόμενον
ἀέρα, καὶ τὸν πάντα πρὸς τὸ πᾶν ὕδωρ. διαφέρει
δ' οὐδὲν οὐδ' εἴ τις φήσει μὲν μὴ γίγνεσθαι ταῦτα
15 ἐξ ἀλλήλων, ἴσα μέντοι τὴν δύναμιν εἶναι· κατὰ
τοῦτον γὰρ τὸν τρόπον ἀνάγκη τὴν ἰσότητα τῆς
δυνάμεως ὑπάρχειν τοῖς μεγέθεσιν αὐτῶν, ὥσπερ

---

[a] Perhaps Heracleitus, as he is definitely referred to at
b 34 (see note b).

[b] Heracleitus believed the sun was the size it looks to us,
" about a foot across " ; Diels 22 A 1 (141, 12), 22 B 3.

14

other hand those [a] who maintain that not only the bodies in motion but also the element surrounding them are composed of pure fire, and that the space between the earth and the stars is filled by air, would perhaps have ceased to hold this childish opinion if they had studied what mathematics has now sufficiently demonstrated. For it is too simple to believe that each of the moving bodies is really small in size because it so appears to us when we look at it from the earth.[b] The matter is one we have already discussed in our consideration of the celestial region,[c] but let us repeat the argument again here. If the intervals between the bodies were full of fire and the bodies also composed of fire each of the other elements would long ago have disappeared. (b) But neither can the intervals be full of air alone : for air would then far exceed its due proportion in relation to its fellow elements, even if the space between earth and sky were filled with two elements, as the bulk of the earth, including the whole mass of water, is, we may say, a mere nothing when compared in size with the surrounding universe. But in fact we see no such excessive disproportion of masses when air is formed by separation from water or fire from air : yet any small quantity of water of given volume must necessarily bear the same proportion to the air which is formed from it, as the total aggregate of air bears to the total aggregate of water. And this still holds even if you deny that the elements can be transformed one into another, but say that they have equal powers of action ; for on this argument certain quantities of them must be equal in powers of action just

[c] *De Caelo* ii. 7 (stars and surrounding element not fire), *ibid.* ii. 14, 297 b 30 ff. (the smallness of the earth).

15

340 a

κἂν εἰ γιγνόμενα ἐξ ἀλλήλων ὑπῆρχεν. ὅτι μὲν οὖν οὔτ᾽ ἀὴρ οὔτε πῦρ συμπεπλήρωκε μόνον τὸν μεταξὺ τόπον, φανερόν ἐστι.

Λοιπὸν δὲ διαπορήσαντας εἰπεῖν πῶς τέτακται
20 τὰ δύο πρὸς τὴν τοῦ πρώτου σώματος θέσιν, λέγω δὲ ἀέρα τε καὶ πῦρ, καὶ διὰ τίν᾽ αἰτίαν ἡ θερμότης ἀπὸ τῶν ἄνωθεν ἄστρων γίγνεται τοῖς περὶ τὴν γῆν τόποις. περὶ ἀέρος οὖν εἰπόντες πρῶτον, ὥσπερ ὑπεθέμεθα, λέγωμεν οὕτω καὶ περὶ τούτων πάλιν.

Εἰ δὴ γίγνεται ὕδωρ ἐξ ἀέρος καὶ ἀὴρ ἐξ ὕδατος,
25 διὰ τίνα ποτ᾽ αἰτίαν οὐ συνίσταται νέφη κατὰ τὸν ἄνω τόπον; προσῆκε γὰρ μᾶλλον ὅσῳ πορρώτερον ὁ τόπος τῆς γῆς καὶ ψυχρότερος, διὰ τὸ μήθ᾽ οὕτω πλησίον εἶναι τῶν ἄστρων θερμῶν ὄντων μήτε τῶν ἀπὸ τῆς γῆς ἀνακλωμένων ἀκτίνων, αἳ κωλύουσι
30 πλησίον τῆς γῆς συνίστασθαι, διακρίνουσαι τῇ θερμότητι τὰς συστάσεις· γίγνονται γὰρ αἱ τῶν νεφῶν ἀθροίσεις, οὗ λήγουσιν ἤδη διὰ τὸ σχίζεσθαι εἰς ἀχανὲς αἱ ἀκτῖνες.

Ἢ οὖν οὐκ ἐξ ἅπαντος τοῦ ἀέρος πέφυκεν ὕδωρ γίγνεσθαι, ἢ εἰ ὁμοίως ἐξ ἅπαντος, ὁ περὶ τὴν γῆν οὐ μόνον ἀήρ ἐστιν ἀλλ᾽ οἷον ἀτμίς, διὸ πάλιν
35 συνίσταται εἰς ὕδωρ. ἀλλὰ μὴν εἰ τοσοῦτος ὢν ὁ ἀὴρ ἅπας ἀτμίς ἐστι, δόξειεν ἂν πολὺ ὑπερβάλλειν

---

[a] Cf. *De Gen. et Corr.* ii. 6, esp. 333 a 16-27, where Aristotle argues that if the elements are mutually comparable (*e.g.* by any form of measurement) they must be mutually transformable. For the reference to Empedocles see Diels 31 B 17, l. 27.

[b] This is a problem because Aristotle believes the stars

16

as they would be if transformation were possible.[a]
It is clear therefore that neither air nor fire fills the
space between earth and the outermost heaven.

It now remains for us to discuss and give our solution of two problems—what positions these two,
that is air and fire, occupy in relation to that of the
first element, and what is the cause of the heat that
reaches the places in the neighbourhood of the earth
from the stars in the upper region.[b] Let us therefore
deal with air first, as we proposed, and then proceed
to deal with these problems.

3. Two problems : (a) disposition of air and fire ; (b) heat from stars.

If water is produced from air and air from water,
why are no clouds formed in the celestial region ?
The farther the region from the earth and the lower
its temperature the more readily should clouds form
there : and its temperature should be low because
it is not so very near to the heat of the stars nor to
the rays reflected from the earth, which by their heat
break up cloud-formations and so prevent clouds
gathering near the earth—for clouds gather where
the rays begin to lose their force by dispersion in
the void.

(a) approached by discussing the question why do not clouds form in the upper air, as one might expect ?

Either then water is not naturally produced from
all air, or, if it is, what immediately surrounds the
earth is not air simply but a sort of vapour which can
condense into water again.[c] But if the whole expanse
of the air is all vapour, then the amount of the sub-

(i) Introduction.

(with which of course he includes the sun and planets) are
not made of fire and so not hot : cf. note c on p. 15 above.
[c] Two alternatives : either there are two strata of air, one
(the lower) of which will condense and form clouds and one
of which will not, or all air will condense but the stratum of
air immediately round the earth contains an admixture of
vapour so that clouds form more readily in it. Cf. Alex. 11.
31 f., Phil. ad 340 a 32.

340 a

ἡ τοῦ ἀέρος φύσις καὶ ἡ τοῦ ὕδατος, εἴπερ τά τε
340 b διαστήματα τῶν ἄνω πλήρη ἐστὶ σώματός τινος,
καὶ πυρὸς μὲν ἀδύνατον διὰ τὸ κατεξηράνθαι ἂν
τἆλλα πάντα, λείπεται δ' ἀέρος καὶ τοῦ περὶ τὴν
γῆν πᾶσαν ὕδατος· ἡ γὰρ ἀτμὶς ὕδατος διάκρισίς
ἐστιν.

Περὶ μὲν οὖν τούτων ἠπορήσθω τοῦτον τὸν
5 τρόπον· ἡμεῖς δὲ λέγωμεν ἅμα πρός τε τὰ λεχθη-
σόμενα διορίζοντες καὶ πρὸς τὰ νῦν εἰρημένα. τὸ
μὲν γὰρ ἄνω καὶ μέχρι σελήνης ἕτερον εἶναι σῶμά
φαμεν πυρός τε καὶ ἀέρος, οὐ μὴν ἀλλ' ἐν αὐτῷ
γε τὸ μὲν καθαρώτερον εἶναι τὸ δ' ἧττον εἰλικρινές,
10 καὶ διαφορὰς ἔχειν, καὶ μάλιστα ᾗ καταλήγει πρὸς
τὸν ἀέρα καὶ πρὸς τὸν περὶ τὴν γῆν κόσμον.
φερομένου δὲ τοῦ πρώτου στοιχείου κύκλῳ καὶ
τῶν ἐν αὐτῷ σωμάτων, τὸ προσεχὲς ἀεὶ τοῦ κάτω
κόσμου καὶ σώματος τῇ κινήσει διακρινόμενον
ἐκπυροῦται καὶ ποιεῖ τὴν θερμότητα. δεῖ δὲ νοεῖν
15 οὕτως καὶ ἐντεῦθεν ἀρξαμένους. τὸ γὰρ ὑπὸ τὴν
ἄνω περιφορὰν σῶμα οἷον ὕλη τις οὖσα καὶ δυνάμει θερμὴ καὶ ψυχρὰ καὶ ξηρὰ καὶ ὑγρά, καὶ ὅσα
ἄλλα τούτοις ἀκολουθεῖ πάθη, γίγνεται τοιαύτη
καὶ ἔστιν ὑπὸ κινήσεως καὶ ἀκινησίας, ἧς τὴν
αἰτίαν καὶ τὴν ἀρχὴν εἰρήκαμεν πρότερον. ἐπὶ
20 μὲν οὖν τοῦ μέσου καὶ περὶ τὸ μέσον τὸ βαρύτατόν
ἐστιν καὶ ψυχρότατον ἀποκεκριμένον, γῆ καὶ ὕδωρ·
περὶ δὲ ταῦτα καὶ ἐχόμενα τούτων, ἀήρ τε καὶ ὁ

---

[a] O.T. takes this to refer to " the region between air
properly so called and the moon " : so also Ideler (i. p. 346).
This seems very unnatural. Alex., Phil. and Ol. all take it
to refer to the celestial region and the fifth element, as does
also Heath, *Aristarchus*, p. 228 : and I have followed their

18

stances air and water will be unduly large : for the spaces between the heavenly bodies must be filled by some substance, and if this cannot be fire because everything else would have been burnt up if it were, then it must be air and the water that surrounds the earth—for vapour is evaporated water.

So much then for the difficulties involved—let us now give our own statement of the matter with reference both to what we have already said and to our future discussions. We maintain that the celestial region as far down as the moon is occupied by a body which is different from air and from fire, but which varies in purity and freedom from admixture, and is not uniform in quality, especially when it borders on the air and the terrestrial region.[a] Now this primary substance and the bodies set in it as they move in a circle set on fire and dissolve by their motion that part of the lower region which is closest to them and generates heat therein. We are also led to the same view if we reason as follows : The substance beneath the motion of the heavens is a kind of matter, having potentially the qualities hot, cold, wet and dry and any others consequent upon these [b] : but it only actually acquires and has any of these in virtue of motion or rest, about whose originating cause we have already spoken elsewhere.[c] So what is heaviest and coldest, that is, earth and water, separates off at the centre or round the centre : immediately round them are air and what we are accustomed

(marginal notes) (ii) Solution : α. Celestial sphere generates heat.

β. Two strata, one fire, one air.

interpretation, taking μέχρι to mean " down as far as " and the σῶμα to be the fifth element.

[b] De Gen. et Corr. ii. 2-3.

[c] Ibid. ii. 10, where the sun's annual movement in the ecliptic is stated to be the efficient cause of terrestrial change. Cf. 341 a 19 below, and ch. 2, note c on p. 8.

340 b

διὰ συνήθειαν καλοῦμεν πῦρ, οὐκ ἔστι δὲ πῦρ·
ὑπερβολὴ γὰρ θερμοῦ καὶ οἷον ζέσις ἐστὶ τὸ πῦρ.
ἀλλὰ δεῖ νοῆσαι τοῦ λεγομένου ὑφ᾿ ἡμῶν ἀέρος τὸ
25 μὲν περὶ τὴν γῆν οἷον ὑγρὸν καὶ θερμὸν εἶναι διὰ τὸ
ἀτμίζειν τε καὶ ἀναθυμίασιν ἔχειν γῆς, τὸ δὲ ὑπὲρ
τοῦτο θερμὸν ἤδη καὶ ξηρόν. ἔστιν γὰρ ἀτμίδος μὲν
φύσις ὑγρὸν καὶ ψυχρόν,[1] ἀναθυμιάσεως δὲ θερμὸν
καὶ ξηρόν· καὶ ἔστιν ἀτμὶς μὲν δυνάμει οἷον ὕδωρ,
30 ἀναθυμίασις δὲ δυνάμει οἷον πῦρ. τοῦ μὲν οὖν ἐν
τῷ ἄνω τόπῳ μὴ συνίστασθαι νέφη ταύτην ὑποληπτέον αἰτίαν εἶναι, ὅτι οὐκ ἔνεστιν ἀὴρ μόνον ἀλλὰ
μᾶλλον οἷον πῦρ. οὐδὲν δὲ κωλύει καὶ διὰ τὴν
κύκλῳ φορὰν κωλύεσθαι συνίστασθαι νέφη ἐν τῷ
ἀνωτέρω τόπῳ· ῥεῖν γὰρ ἀναγκαῖον ἅπαντα τὸν
35 κύκλῳ ἀέρα, ὅσος μὴ ἐντὸς τῆς περιφερείας λαμβάνεται τῆς ἀπαρτιζούσης ὥστε τὴν γῆν σφαι-
ροειδῆ εἶναι πᾶσαν· φαίνεται γὰρ καὶ νῦν ἡ τῶν
ἀνέμων γένεσις ἐν τοῖς λιμνάζουσι τόποις τῆς γῆς,
341 a καὶ οὐχ ὑπερβάλλειν τὰ πνεύματα τῶν ὑψηλῶν
ὀρῶν. ῥεῖ δὲ κύκλῳ διὰ τὸ συνεφέλκεσθαι τῇ τοῦ
ὅλου περιφορᾷ. τὸ μὲν γὰρ πῦρ τῷ ἄνω στοιχείῳ,
τῷ δὲ πυρὶ ὁ ἀὴρ συνεχής ἐστιν· ὥστε καὶ διὰ τὴν
5 κίνησιν κωλύεται συγκρίνεσθαι εἰς ὕδωρ, ἀλλ᾿ ἀεὶ

---

[1] ψυχρόν E₁ 𝔚 Ross, *Aristotle*, p. 109, n. 4, O.T., cf.
Thurot : θερμόν Fobes cett.

---

[a] I agree with Ross that the logic of the passage requires
ψυχρόν here. The " part of what we call air " immediately
surrounding the earth is moist and hot because it is ἀτμίς
(moist and cold) plus ἀναθυμίασις (hot and dry). 360 a 23
speaks of ἀτμίς as wet and cold and 367 a 34 implies the same.
De Gen. et Corr. 330 b 4 speaks of air as hot and moist,
adding οἷον ἀτμὶς γὰρ ὁ ἀήρ. But I do not think this necessarily implies that ἀτμίς is hot and moist : air is οἷον ἀτμίς,
not the same thing as ἀτμίς, and the present passage seems

20

to call fire, though it is not really fire : for fire is an excess of heat and a sort of boiling. But we must understand that of what we call air the part which immediately surrounds the earth is moist and hot because it is vaporous and contains exhalations from the earth, but that the part above this is hot and dry. For vapour is naturally moist and cold [a] and exhalation hot and dry : and vapour is potentially like water, exhalation like fire. We must suppose therefore that the reason why clouds do not form in the upper region is that it contains not air only but rather a sort of fire. At the same time there is no reason why the formation of clouds in the upper region should not also be prevented by the circular motion. For the whole encircling mass of air must necessarily be in motion, except that part of it which is contained within the circumference that makes the earth a perfect sphere.[b] (Thus in fact we find that winds rise in low marshy districts of the earth, and do not blow above the highest mountains.) It moves in a circle because it is carried round by the motion of the heavens. For fire [c] is contiguous with the element in the celestial regions, and air contiguous with fire, and their movement prevents any condensation ;

γ. Motion of air and fire.

to imply that air combines the characteristics of ἀτμίς and ἀναθυμίασις, while the " fire " that surrounds it has those of ἀναθυμίασις only : cf. Ross, *Aristotle*, pp. 109-110, and the note on the arrangement of the elements at the end of this chapter.

[b] The earth is not a perfect sphere because of the mountains and valleys on its surface. The " circumference that makes the earth a perfect sphere " will have as its radius the distance from the centre of the earth to the top of the highest mountains.

[c] *i.e.* " what we are accustomed to call fire " : 340 b 22 above.

21

ὅ τι ἂν βαρύνηται μόριον αὐτοῦ ἐκθλιβομένου εἰς
τὸν ἄνω τόπον τοῦ θερμοῦ κάτω φέρεται, ἄλλα δ'
ἐν μέρει συναναφέρεται τῷ ἀναθυμιωμένῳ πυρί,
καὶ οὕτω συνεχῶς τὸ μὲν ἀέρος διατελεῖ πλῆρες ὂν
τὸ δὲ πυρός, καὶ ἀεὶ ἄλλο καὶ ἄλλο γίγνεται ἕκαστον
αὐτῶν.

10 Περὶ μὲν οὖν τοῦ μὴ γίγνεσθαι νέφη μηδ' εἰς
ὕδωρ σύγκρισιν, καὶ πῶς δεῖ λαβεῖν περὶ τοῦ
μεταξὺ τόπου τῶν ἄστρων καὶ τῆς γῆς, καὶ τίνος
ἐστὶν σώματος πλήρης, τοσαῦτα εἰρήσθω.

Περὶ δὲ τῆς γιγνομένης θερμότητος, ἣν παρέχεται
ὁ ἥλιος, μᾶλλον μὲν καθ' ἑαυτὸ καὶ ἀκριβῶς ἐν τοῖς
15 περὶ αἰσθήσεως προσήκει λέγειν (πάθος γάρ τι τὸ
θερμὸν αἰσθήσεώς ἐστιν), διὰ τίνα δ' αἰτίαν γίγνεται
μὴ τοιούτων ὄντων ἐκείνων τὴν φύσιν, λεκτέον καὶ
νῦν. ὁρῶμεν δὴ τὴν κίνησιν ὅτι δύναται διακρίνειν
τὸν ἀέρα καὶ ἐκπυροῦν, ὥστε καὶ τὰ φερόμενα
τηκόμενα φαίνεσθαι πολλάκις. τὸ μὲν οὖν γίγνε-
20 σθαι τὴν ἀλέαν καὶ τὴν θερμότητα ἱκανή ἐστιν
παρασκευάζειν καὶ ἡ τοῦ ἡλίου φορὰ μόνον· ταχεῖάν
τε γὰρ δεῖ καὶ μὴ πόρρω εἶναι. ἡ μὲν οὖν τῶν
ἄστρων ταχεῖα μὲν πόρρω δέ, ἡ δὲ τῆς σελήνης
κάτω μὲν βραδεῖα δέ· ἡ δὲ τοῦ ἡλίου ἄμφω ταῦτα

ᵃ i.e. of fire surely, not " air " (O.T.). The point of the
passage (a 5-9) is that the terrestrial region (outside the
highest mountains) has an upper layer of " fire " and a lower
of " air " and that air and fire are in a constant process of
change one into other. ἄλλα (l. 6) . . . πυρί (l. 7) refers
to the change into fire : so ἀλλ' ἀεὶ (l. 5) . . . φέρεται (l. 6)
must refer to the change back to air or ἀτμίς (cf. O.T. note on
βαρύνηται, " i.e. becomes ἀτμίς "). Aristotle uses μόριον without further qualification because he is apparently thinking

22

for any particle [a] that becomes heavy sinks down, the heat in it being expelled and rising into the upper region, and other particles in turn are carried up with the fiery exhalation : thus the one layer is always and continually full of air, the other of fire, and each one of them is in constant process of transformation into the other.

These then are the reasons why clouds do not form and why the air is not condensed into water, and this is the correct description of the space between the stars and the earth and the substance with which it is filled.

[a]. A separate and exact account of the heat gener-ated by the sun's action would be more in place in a treatise on sensation [b] (for heat is a sensible quality) : but we may explain now the reason why it is gener-ated although the heavenly bodies themselves are not naturally hot. We see that motion can rarefy and in-flame air, so that, for example, objects in motion are often found to melt. The sun's motion is therefore in itself sufficient to produce warmth and heat : for to produce heat a motion must be rapid and not far off. The motion of the stars is rapid but far off: that of the moon close but slow : but the sun's motion has both required characteristics to a sufficient degree. That

3 (b) Heat that reaches the earth due to two causes.

of the substance, which fills the region, as a whole, and saying that any part of it that becomes heavy sinks, while other parts " rise with the exhalation " ; so the region con-sists of two strata each constantly changing into the other. Thus air and fire are (a) in constant circular motion, (b) in constant process of mutual transformation. (b) is presumably due to (a) (this I take to be the force of the ἀλλά 341 a 5), and the non-formation of clouds due to (a) and (b) and to (a) through (b).

[b] No such account is to be found either in the De Anima or in the De Sensu.

23

ἔχει ἱκανῶς. τὸ δὲ μᾶλλον γίγνεσθαι ἅμα τῷ ἡλίῳ
25 αὐτῷ τὴν θερμότητα εὔλογον, λαμβάνοντας τὸ
ὅμοιον ἐκ τῶν παρ' ἡμῖν γιγνομένων· καὶ γὰρ
ἐνταῦθα τῶν βίᾳ φερομένων ὁ πλησιάζων ἀὴρ
μάλιστα γίγνεται θερμός.. καὶ τοῦτ' εὐλόγως συμ-
βαίνει· μάλιστα γὰρ ἡ τοῦ στερεοῦ διακρίνει κίνησις
αὐτόν. διά τε ταύτην οὖν τὴν αἰτίαν ἀφικνεῖται
30 πρὸς τόνδε τὸν τόπον ἡ θερμότης, καὶ διὰ τὸ τὸ
περιέχον πῦρ τὸν ἀέρα διαρραίνεσθαι τῇ κινήσει
πολλάκις καὶ φέρεσθαι βίᾳ κάτω.

Σημεῖον δ' ἱκανὸν ὅτι ὁ ἄνω τόπος οὐκ ἔστι
θερμὸς οὐδ' ἐκπεπυρωμένος καὶ αἱ διαδρομαὶ τῶν
ἀστέρων. ἐκεῖ μὲν γὰρ οὐ γίγνονται, κάτω δέ·
35 καίτοι τὰ μᾶλλον κινούμενα καὶ θᾶττον, ἐκπυροῦται
θᾶττον. πρὸς δὲ τούτοις ὁ ἥλιος, ὅσπερ μάλιστα
εἶναι δοκεῖ θερμός, φαίνεται λευκὸς ἀλλ' οὐ πυρώδης ὤν.

---

[a] *Cf.* with this account *De Caelo* ii. 7, 289 a 29 ff. The
" air " which is ignited by the motions of the sun and stars
is the fiery layer of air referred to above, 340 b 22 ff. It is
described as ὑπέκκαυμα and as " fire " in ch. 4 below, 341
b 14 ff. The chief difficulty in Aristotle's account seems to
be that this " air " is strictly speaking only in contact with
the innermost of the spheres of the celestial region. Mr.
Guthrie (Aristotle, *On the Heavens*, L.C.L. p. 179) suggests

NOTE ON THE STRATA IN ARISTOTLE'S
UNIVERSE

The following note on the arrangement of the elements and
the stratification of the atmosphere in Aristotle's natural
philosophy may be useful at this point.

1. *The Elements.* There are five elements. The fifth
element is the material from which stars and planets and
the spheres which carry them are made. These constitute the

the heat is increased by the presence of the sun is easily enough explained by considering analogies from our own experience : for here too the air in the neighbourhood of a projectile becomes hottest. That this should be so is easily explicable, for the movement of a solid object disintegrates it most. This then is one reason why heat is transmitted to the terrestrial region.[a] β. Another reason is that the fire which surrounds it is frequently scattered by the motion of the heavens and forcibly carried downwards.

(A sufficient proof that the celestial region is not hot or fiery is provided by shooting stars. For they do not originate there but in the terrestrial region : and yet the longer and more rapid its movement the more rapidly does an object catch fire.[b] A further proof is that the sun which appears to be the hottest of the heavenly bodies is bright rather than fiery in appearance.)

that Aristotle perhaps " saw a way of escape in the thesis that the fifth element exists in purity only at the outer extreme of the universe, and gets more and more contaminated at its lower levels " (cf. above, 340 b 6). See also Heath, *Aristarchus*, p. 242.

[b] And so if the celestial sphere could catch fire it would, as its motion is fastest of all. This last paragraph is an afterthought or footnote to the last section of the argument and has been omitted from the analysis at the head of the chapter.

Celestial or Heavenly Sphere, the outermost layer of the Universe: Fig. 1, a (p. 26). Beneath the Celestial Sphere is the Terrestrial or Sub-Lunar Sphere (the moon being the innermost of the planets). Celestial and Terrestrial spheres are contiguous and the Celestial is the source of motion in the Terrestrial : cf. ch. 2 above, 339 a 21 ff.

In the terrestrial sphere the four terrestrial elements are arranged in concentric spherical strata, with earth at the centre (e) and water, air and fire above in that order (d, c, b).

But this stratification is not rigid. Dry land rises above water, and fire burns on the earth ; and in addition all four

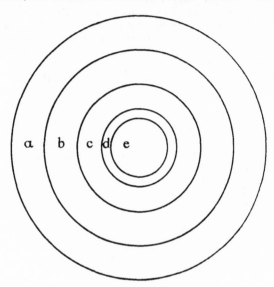

Fig. 1

elements are in constant process of change one into the other (*cf. De Gen. et Corr.* ii. 4 and 341 a 5, with ch. 3, note *a* on p. 22, for the constant interchange of " air " and " fire "). The four concentric spheres represent, rather, the " natural places " to which each of the four elements naturally move and in which the main bulk of each is found.

But " air " and " fire " are still further analysed in terms of Aristotle's theory of " exhalations." This theory is mentioned in this chapter, 340 b 23, and recurs constantly throughout the work : *e.g.* ch. 4 and Book II. ch. 4. The earth when heated by the sun gives off two kinds of exhala-

NOTE ON THE STRATA

tion, one hot and dry, from the earth itself (the πνευματώδης or καπνώδης ἀναθυμίασις of ch. 4 : often called ἀναθυμίασις simply), the other cool and moist, from the water on the earth (ἀτμίς). The outermost terrestrial stratum (b) to which Aristotle often refers as " fire," is, strictly speaking, composed of the hot-dry exhalation, which rises above the cool-moist : it is a highly inflammable material (ὑπέκκαυμα), which is the material of which shooting stars, etc. are composed (ch. 4 below) and which is ignited to produce the sun's heat (341 b 10 and note a on p. 24). The inner stratum, " air," is composed of a mixture of the two exhalations, and is therefore hot and moist : cf. 340 b 23 and ch. 3, note a on p. 20. It is the material from which cloud, rain, etc. are formed.

2. *Stratification of the Atmosphere.* There are thus two main strata of what we may call the atmosphere, " air " and " fire." But within the sphere of air there are certain further differentiations. (a) Clouds cannot form beyond the tops of the highest mountains : for the air beyond them is carried round with the celestial motion and clouds cannot therefore form in it (340 b 32) : cf. 361 a 22 for the celestial motion being imparted to air. (b) Clouds also cannot form close to the earth, because the heat reflected from the earth prevents it (340 a 31).

We thus reach an arrangement illustrated in Fig. 2, where m-m-m are the mountain tops and the stratum a-a is the stratum in which clouds can form.

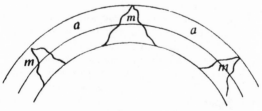

Fig. 2

But Aristotle is not always consistent and it is difficult to see where the calm region " near the earth " in which haloes are formed (373 a 23) is situated.

ARISTOTLE

CHAPTER IV

ARGUMENT

The subject of the chapter is " burning flames, shooting stars, torches and goats," different kinds of meteoric phenomena, with which Aristotle rightly classes so-called shooting stars (341 b 1-5). These are due to two causes. (1) There are two kinds of exhalation that rise from the earth, one vaporous, one dry and hot. The dry and hot exhalation is lighter and rises to the top, forming a sheath of " fire " round the terrestrial sphere, the more vaporous exhalation or " air " lying below it. Though we must call it fire for lack of a better word it is not fire in the ordinary sense, but rather a kind of inflammable material (ὑπέκκαυμα) (341 b 5-22). This inflammable material is liable, when set in motion by the celestial

341 b 1 Τούτων δὲ διωρισμένων, λέγωμεν διὰ τίν' αἰτίαν
αἵ τε φλόγες αἱ καιόμεναι φαίνονται περὶ τὸν οὐρανὸν καὶ οἱ διαθέοντες ἀστέρες καὶ οἱ καλούμενοι
ὑπό τινων δαλοὶ καὶ αἶγες· ταῦτα γὰρ πάντ' ἐστὶν
5 τὸ αὐτὸ καὶ διὰ τὴν αὐτὴν αἰτίαν, διαφέρει δὲ τῷ
μᾶλλον καὶ ἧττον.

Ἀρχὴ δέ ἐστιν καὶ τούτων καὶ πολλῶν ἄλλων
ἥδε. θερμαινομένης γὰρ τῆς γῆς ὑπὸ τοῦ ἡλίου
τὴν ἀναθυμίασιν ἀναγκαῖον γίγνεσθαι μὴ ἁπλῆν, ὥς
τινες οἴονται, ἀλλὰ διπλῆν, τὴν μὲν ἀτμιδωδεστέραν
τὴν δὲ πνευματωδεστέραν, τὴν μὲν τοῦ ἐν τῇ γῇ
10 καὶ ἐπὶ τῇ γῇ ὑγροῦ ἀτμίδα, τὴν δ' αὐτῆς τῆς γῆς
οὔσης ξηρᾶς καπνώδη· καὶ τούτων τὴν μὲν πνευ-
ματώδη ἐπιπολάζειν διὰ τὸ θερμόν, τὴν δὲ ὑγροτέραν ὑφίστασθαι διὰ τὸ βάρος. καὶ διὰ ταῦτα
τοῦτον τὸν τρόπον κεκόσμηται τὸ πέριξ· πρῶτον
μὲν γὰρ ὑπὸ τὴν ἐγκύκλιον φορὰν ἐστι τὸ θερμὸν

CHAPTER IV

ARGUMENT (continued)

sphere immediately above it, to burst into flames. The par-
ticular kind of meteoric phenomenon produced depends on
the position, amount and consistency of the inflammable
material available (341 b 22-35). (2) These phenomena are
also caused by heat being ejected forcibly downwards by pres-
sure, when air condenses owing to cold (341 b 35—342 a 16).
Cause (1) operates in the upper atmosphere, cause (2) in the
lower. The direction taken depends on the position, etc. of
the exhalation, which is the material cause in both cases, the
efficient in (1) being the heavenly motion, in (2) condensation
(342 a 16-30). All these phenomena take place below the moon,
as their motion shows (342 a 30-33).

HAVING laid down these principles let us now explain
what is the cause of the appearance of burning flames
in the sky, of shooting stars and of what some people
call " torches " and " goats." All these phenomena
are the same thing and due to the same cause, and
only differ in degree.

Subject— meteoric phenomena.

Their origin, as the origin of many other phenomena, is as follows. The exhalations that arise from
the earth when it is heated by the sun must be not,
as some think, of a single kind, but of two kinds ; one
is more vaporous in character, the other more windy,
the vapour arising from the water within and upon
the earth, while the exhalations from the earth itself,
which is dry, are more like smoke. The windy exhalation being hot rises to the top, the more watery
exhalation being heavy sinks below it. And therefore the region round the earth is arranged as follows :
first, immediately beneath the circular celestial

Caused (1) by firing of ὑπέκκαυμα,

341 b

15 καὶ ξηρόν, ὃ λέγομεν πῦρ (ἀνώνυμον γὰρ τὸ κοινὸν
ἐπὶ πάσης τῆς καπνώδους διακρίσεως· ὅμως δὲ
διὰ τὸ μάλιστα πεφυκέναι τὸ τοιοῦτον ἐκκαίεσθαι
τῶν σωμάτων οὕτως ἀναγκαῖον χρῆσθαι τοῖς ὀνό-
μασιν), ὑπὸ δὲ ταύτην τὴν φύσιν ἀήρ. δεῖ δὴ
νοῆσαι οἷον ὑπέκκαυμα τοῦτο ὃ νῦν εἴπομεν πῦρ
20 περιτετάσθαι τῆς περὶ τὴν γῆν σφαίρας ἔσχατον,
ὥστε μικρᾶς κινήσεως τυχὸν ἐκκαίεσθαι πολλάκις
ὥσπερ τὸν καπνόν· ἔστι γὰρ ἡ φλὸξ πνεύματος
ξηροῦ ζέσις. ᾗ ἂν οὖν μάλιστα εὐκαίρως ἔχῃ ἡ
τοιαύτη σύστασις, ὅταν ὑπὸ τῆς περιφορᾶς κινηθῇ
πως, ἐκκάεται.

Διαφέρει δ' ἤδη κατὰ τὴν τοῦ ὑπεκκαύματος θέσιν
25 ἢ τὸ πλῆθος· ἂν μὲν γὰρ πλάτος ἔχῃ καὶ μῆκος τὸ
ὑπέκκαυμα, πολλάκις ὁρᾶται καιομένη φλὸξ ὥσπερ
ἐν ἀρούρᾳ καιομένης καλάμης, ἐὰν δὲ κατὰ μῆκος
μόνον, οἱ καλούμενοι δαλοὶ καὶ αἶγες καὶ ἀστέρες.
[ἐὰν μὲν πλέον τὸ ὑπέκκαυμα ᾖ κατὰ τὸ μῆκος ἢ
30 τὸ πλάτος,][1] ὅταν μὲν οὖν[2] ἀποσπινθηρίζῃ ἅμα
καιόμενον (τοῦτο δὲ γίγνεται διὰ τὸ παρεκπυ-
ροῦσθαι, κατὰ μικρὰ μέν, ἐπ' ἀρχὴν δέ), αἲξ καλεῖ-

---

[1] ἐὰν . . . πλάτος seclusi.   [2] οὖν N : οἷον Fobes.

---

[a] Cf. 340 b 25-27 above.   [b] Cf. 340 b 23 above.

[c] I have bracketed ἐὰν μὲν (28) . . . τὸ πλάτος (27) as a
gloss on κατὰ μῆκος (27). The words appear in all the mss.
and in Phil. and Alex. with some variations (v. Fobes'
apparatus) : but they are not required by the logic of the
passage and only serve to give it a rather confused appearance (cf. Ideler i. pp. 368-370). They do in fact explain the
meaning of κατὰ μῆκος, which is a somewhat odd phrase,
but which must mean, I take it, " with greater length than

30

motion comes a warm and dry substance which we call fire [a] (for we have no common name to cover every subspecies of the smoky exhalation : but because it is the most inflammable of all substances, we must adopt this nomenclature) ; below this substance comes air. Now we must think of the substance we have just called fire as extending round the outside of the terrestrial sphere like a kind of inflammable material, which often needs only a little motion to make it burst into flames, like smoke : for flame is the boiling up of a dry current of air.[b] Wherever then conditions are most favourable this composition bursts into flame when the celestial revolution sets it in motion.

The result differs according to the position and quantity of the inflammable material. If it extends both lengthwise and breadthwise we often see a burning flame of the kind one sees when stubble is being burnt on ploughland : if it extends lengthwise only, then we see the so-called torches and goats and shooting stars. When [c] it throws off sparks as it burns (which happens when small portions of matter catch fire at the side but in connexion with the main

whose different disposition causes different phenomena;

breadth "—as we talk of a " long " object : so Alex. 21. 1 b (cf. Phil. 59. 20, 23) interprets it. The bracketed words might have been a gloss to explain an odd phrase and have found their way into the text later. If we omit them, and read οὖν in l. 29 with N, we have a passage whose logic is fairly clear, and which may be analysed as follows : (1) ἂν μὲν γὰρ πλάτος ἔχῃ καὶ μῆκος, (25) . . . φλόξ (2) ἐὰν δὲ κατὰ μῆκος μόνον (27) . . . δαλοὶ καὶ αἶγες καὶ ἀστέρες, (a) ὅταν μὲν οὖν (29) . . . αἴξ, (b) ὅταν δ' ἄνευ τούτου (32) . . . δαλός, (c) ἐὰν δὲ (33) . . . ἀστέρες. The omitted clause is thus quite unnecessary to the logic of the passage, which it merely serves to confuse by repeating what has already been stated in κατὰ μῆκος.

341 b

ται, ὅταν δ᾽ ἄνευ τούτου τοῦ πάθους, δαλός. ἐὰν
δὲ τὰ μέρη[1] τῆς ἀναθυμιάσεως κατὰ μικρά τε καὶ
πολλαχῇ διεσπαρμένα ᾖ καὶ ὁμοίως κατὰ πλάτος
35 καὶ βάθος, οἱ δοκοῦντες ἀστέρες διάττειν γίγνονται.
Ὁτὲ μὲν οὖν ὑπὸ τῆς κινήσεως ἡ ἀναθυμίασις
ἐκκαιομένη γεννᾷ αὐτά· ὁτὲ δὲ ὑπὸ τοῦ διὰ τὴν
342 a ψύξιν συνισταμένου ἀέρος ἐκθλίβεται καὶ ἐκκρίνεται τὸ θερμόν, διὸ καὶ ἔοικεν ἡ φορὰ ῥίψει μᾶλλον
αὐτῶν, ἀλλ᾽ οὐκ ἐκκαύσει. ἀπορήσειε γὰρ ἄν τις
πότερον ὥσπερ ἡ ὑπὸ τοὺς λύχνους τιθεμένη ἀνα-
5 θυμίασις ἀπὸ τῆς ἄνωθεν φλογὸς ἅπτει τὸν κάτωθεν
λύχνον (θαυμαστὴ γὰρ καὶ τούτου ἡ ταχυτής ἐστιν
καὶ ὁμοία ῥίψει, ἀλλ᾽ οὐχ ὡς ἄλλου καὶ ἄλλου
γιγνομένου πυρός), ἢ ῥίψεις τοῦ αὐτοῦ τινος σώματός εἰσιν αἱ διαδρομαί. ἔοικε δὴ δι᾽ ἄμφω· καὶ
γὰρ οὕτως ὡς ἡ ἀπὸ τοῦ λύχνου γίγνεται, καὶ ἔνια
10 διὰ τὸ ἐκθλίβεσθαι ῥιπτεῖται, ὥσπερ οἱ ἐκ τῶν
δακτύλων πυρῆνες, ὥστε καὶ εἰς τὴν γῆν καὶ εἰς
τὴν θάλατταν φαίνεσθαι πίπτοντα, καὶ νύκτωρ καὶ
μεθ᾽ ἡμέραν καὶ αἰθρίας οὔσης. κάτω δὲ ῥιπτεῖται
διὰ τὸ τὴν πύκνωσιν εἰς τὸ κάτω ῥέπειν τὴν ἀπ-
ωθοῦσαν. διὸ καὶ οἱ κεραυνοὶ κάτω πίπτουσιν[2].
15 πάντων γὰρ τούτων ἡ γένεσις οὐκ ἔκκαυσις ἀλλ᾽
ἔκκρισις ὑπὸ τῆς ἐκθλίψεώς ἐστιν, ἐπεὶ κατὰ φύσιν
γε τὸ θερμὸν ἄνω πέφυκε φέρεσθαι πᾶν.

[1] μέρη E$_{corr. m. 1}$ 𝔚 N Ideler : μήκη Plp Fobes.
[2] τοῦ πυρὸς ἄνω φερομένου κατὰ φύσιν post πίπτουσιν
habent Pl Fobes : om. codd.

[a] So the O.T., following Alex. 21. 20, Phil. 59. 37 ff.
Ideler and Saint-Hilaire take the words to mean " when
consumed bit by bit, but entirely."
[b] I have omitted the words τοῦ πυρὸς . . . φύσιν (v. crit.
note) because they do not seem to add anything to the passage.

body ⁱ) it is called a goat : when this characteristic
is absent it is called a torch : and if the parts of the
exhalation are broken up small and scattered in many
directions both vertically and horizontally, then what
are commonly thought to be shooting stars are produced.

Sometimes then the exhalation produces these (2) By condensation
phenomena when ignited by the heavenly motion. of air.
But sometimes heat is ejected by pressure when the
air contracts owing to cold ; and then they take a
course more like that of a projectile than of a fire.
For one might be uncertain whether shooting stars
are the result of a process like that in which, when
one lamp is placed beneath another, the exhalations
from the lower one cause it to be lit from the flame
of the upper (the speed with which this takes place
is extraordinary and resembles the action of a projectile rather than of a train of fire), or whether again
they are caused by the projection of a single body.
Probably both causes operate, and some of these phenomena are produced in the same way as the flame
from the lamp, others are shot out under pressure,
as fruit stones from the fingers. And we see them
falling onto the earth and into the sea, both at night
and by day, from a clear sky. They are shot downwards because the condensation which propels them
has a downward inclination. For this reason thunderbolts too fall downwards : for all these phenomena
are produced ᵵot by combustion but by projection
under pressure, since naturally all heat tends to rise
upwards.ᵇ

Aristotle says the same thing in ll. 15-16, which surely makes
the words superfluous here : and Pl seems the only authority
for them.

342 a

Ὅσα μὲν οὖν [μᾶλλον]¹ ἐν τῷ ἄνω² τόπῳ συνίσταται, ἐκκαιομένης γίγνεται τῆς ἀναθυμιάσεως, ὅσα δὲ κατώτερον, ἐκκρινομένης διὰ τὸ συνιέναι
20 καὶ ψύχεσθαι τὴν ὑγροτέραν ἀναθυμίασιν· αὕτη γὰρ συνιοῦσα καὶ κάτω ῥέπουσα ἀπωθεῖ πυκνουμένη καὶ κάτω ποιεῖ τοῦ θερμοῦ τὴν ῥῖψιν· διὰ δὲ τὴν θέσιν τῆς ἀναθυμιάσεως, ὅπως ἂν τύχῃ κειμένη τοῦ πλάτους καὶ τοῦ βάθους, οὕτω φέρεται ἢ ἄνω ἢ κάτω ἢ εἰς τὸ πλάγιον. τὰ πλεῖστα δ' εἰς τὸ
25 πλάγιον διὰ τὸ δύο φέρεσθαι φοράς, βίᾳ μὲν κάτω, φύσει δ' ἄνω· πάντα γὰρ κατὰ τὴν διάμετρον φέρεται τὰ τοιαῦτα. διὸ καὶ τῶν διαθεόντων ἀστέρων ἡ πλείστη λοξὴ γίγνεται φορά.

Πάντων δὴ τούτων αἴτιον ὡς μὲν ὕλη ἡ ἀναθυμίασις, ὡς δὲ τὸ κινοῦν ὁτὲ μὲν ἡ ἄνω φορά, ὁτὲ
30 δ' ἡ τοῦ ἀέρος συγκρινομένου πῆξις. πάντα δὲ κάτω ταῦτα σελήνης γίγνεται. σημεῖον δ' ἡ φαινομένη αὐτῶν ταχυτὴς ὁμοία οὖσα τοῖς ὑφ' ἡμῶν ῥιπτουμένοις, ἃ διὰ τὸ πλησίον εἶναι ἡμῶν πολὺ δοκεῖ τῷ τάχει παραλλάττειν ἄστρα τε καὶ ἥλιον καὶ σελήνην.

¹ μᾶλλον om. E Ap Ol : habet Fobes.
² ἄνω E 𝔚 Ol : ἀνωτάτω Pl Fobes : ἀνωτέρω Ap.

ᵃ On the readings in l. 17 the O.T. has the following note :
" Omit μᾶλλον and read ἄνω with E and the lemma in

CHAPTER V

ARGUMENT

The aurora borealis is due to the condensation of air. This may produce the phenomena mentioned in the last chapter ;
34

When therefore formation takes place in the upper Summary.
part of this region, the phenomenon is produced by
combustion of the exhalation [a] : when in the lower,
by ejection consequent upon the condensation and
cooling of the more humid exhalation, which inclines
downwards when it condenses and as it contracts
propels the heat and causes it to be shot downwards.
The motion is upwards, downwards or sideways according to the position of the exhalation and whether
it happens to lie vertically or horizontally. The
motion is most often sideways because it is a combination of two motions, an impressed motion downwards and a natural motion upwards, and bodies under
these conditions move obliquely.[b] Therefore the
movement of shooting stars is commonly transverse.

The material cause then of all these phenomena
is the exhalation, the moving cause in some cases the
celestial motion, in others the condensation of the air
as it contracts. And all of them take place below the
moon : a proof of which is the fact that the speed of
their movement is comparable to that of objects thrown
by us, which seem to move much faster than the
stars and sun and moon because they are close to us.

Olympiodorus. μᾶλλον and the superlative ἀνωτάτω are explanations of ἄνω." So also is Alex.'s ἀνωτέρω.

[b] As Thurot (p. 89) points out, Aristotle's mechanics here
are at fault.

CHAPTER V

ARGUMENT (*continued*)

*but may also, when it takes place to a lesser degree and when
the air is also lit up by reflection, produce the various phenomena of the aurora.*

ARISTOTLE

(The O.T. supposes that the chapter deals with " phenomena of cloud coloration." Ideler says it deals with the aurora and produces evidence that this can be seen as far south as

342 a 34   Φαίνεται δέ ποτε συνιστάμενα νύκτωρ αἰθρίας
  35 οὔσης πολλὰ φάσματα ἐν τῷ οὐρανῷ, οἷον χάσματά
τε καὶ βόθυνοι καὶ αἱματώδη χρώματα. αἴτιον δὲ
342 b ἐπὶ τούτων τὸ αὐτό· ἐπεὶ γὰρ φανερός ἐστι συνιστάμενος ὁ ἄνω ἀὴρ ὥστ' ἐκπυροῦσθαι, καὶ τὴν
ἐκπύρωσιν ὁτὲ μὲν τοιαύτην γίγνεσθαι ὥστε φλόγα
δοκεῖν καίεσθαι, ὁτὲ δὲ οἷον δαλοὺς φέρεσθαι καὶ
ἀστέρας, οὐδὲν ἄτοπον εἰ χρωματίζεται ὁ αὐτὸς
  5 οὗτος ἀὴρ συνιστάμενος παντοδαπὰς χρόας· διά
τε γὰρ πυκνοτέρου διαφαινόμενον ἔλαττον φῶς καὶ
ἀνάκλασιν δεχόμενος ὁ ἀὴρ παντοδαπὰ χρώματα
ποιήσει, μάλιστα δὲ φοινικοῦν ἢ πορφυροῦν, διὰ
τὸ ταῦτα μάλιστα ἐκ τοῦ πυρώδους καὶ λευκοῦ
φαίνεσθαι μειγνυμένων κατὰ τὰς ἐπιπροσθήσεις,
  10 οἷον ἀνίσχοντα τὰ ἄστρα καὶ δυόμενα, ἐὰν ᾖ καῦμα,
καὶ διὰ καπνοῦ φοινικᾶ φαίνεται. καὶ τῇ ἀνακλάσει
δὲ ποιήσει, ὅταν τὸ ἔνοπτρον ᾖ τοιοῦτον ὥστε μὴ
τὸ σχῆμα ἀλλὰ τὸ χρῶμα δέχεσθαι. τοῦ δὲ μὴ
πολὺν χρόνον μένειν ταῦτα ἡ σύστασις αἰτία ταχεῖα
οὖσα.
  15 Τὰ δὲ χάσματα ἀναρρηγνυμένου τοῦ φωτὸς ἐκ
κυανοῦ καὶ μέλανος ποιεῖ τι βάθος ἔχειν δοκεῖν.
πολλάκις δ' ἐκ τῶν τοιούτων καὶ δαλοὶ ἐκπίπτουσιν,
ὅταν συγκριθῇ μᾶλλον· συνιὸν δ' ἔτι χάσμα δοκεῖ.

ᵃ I have translated συνίστασθαι etc. " condense," " condensation " (with O.T.) because it seemed to make the best

Greece and so might be known to Aristotle (i. p. 374) : *Heath*, Aristarchus (p. 243), *also supposes Aristotle is referring here to the aurora.*)

SOMETIMES on a clear night a number of appearances can be seen taking shape in the sky, such as " chasms," " trenches " and blood-red colours. These again have the same cause. For we have shown that the upper air condenses [a] and takes fire and that its combustion sometimes produces the appearance of a burning fire, sometimes of " torches " or stars in motion ; it is therefore to be expected that this same air in process of condensation should assume all sorts of colours. For light penetrating more feebly through a thicker medium, and the air when it permits reflection, will produce all sorts of colours, and particularly red and purple : for these colours are usually observed when fire-colour and white are superimposed and combined, as happens for instance in hot weather when the stars at their rising or setting appear red when seen through a smoky medium. The air will also produce the same effects by reflection, when the reflecting medium is such as to reproduce colour only and not shape. The cause of the brief duration of these phenomena is that the condensation lasts for a short time only.

Chasms have an appearance of depth because the light breaks out from a dark blue or black background. Similar conditions often cause the fall of " torches " when there is a greater degree of condensation : but while the process of contraction is

sense. The word can bear this meaning (*cf.* 342 a 1), and πυκνοτέρου l. 5 and συγκριθῇ l. 17 seem to indicate that it bears it here.

The αἴτιον . . . τὸ αὐτό of the previous sentence must then refer to cause (2) of the last chapter.

342 b

ὅλως δ' ἐν τῷ μέλανι τὸ λευκὸν πολλὰς ποιεῖ ποι-
κιλίας, οἷον ἡ φλὸξ ἐν τῷ καπνῷ. ἡμέρας μὲν οὖν
20 ὁ ἥλιος κωλύει, νυκτὸς δ' ἔξω τοῦ φοινικοῦ τὰ
ἄλλα δι' ὁμόχροιαν οὐ φαίνεται.

Περὶ μὲν οὖν τῶν διαθεόντων ἀστέρων καὶ τῶν
ἐκπυρουμένων, ἔτι δὲ τῶν ἄλλων τῶν τοιούτων
φασμάτων ὅσα ταχείας ποιεῖται τὰς φαντασίας,
ταύτας ὑπολαβεῖν δεῖ τὰς αἰτίας.

---

^a Thurot (p. 90) finds these words (συνιόν . . . δοκεῖ ll. 17-
18) " unintelligible," and suggests reading συνιὸν δέ τι ⟨βόθυνος
εἶναι τὸ⟩ χάσμα δοκεῖ, a suggestion which the O.T. adopts and
translates " When the ' chasm ' contracts it presents the
appearance of a ' trench.' " This has the advantage that it
provides us with a definition of the βόθυνοι in 342 a 36, which

CHAPTER VI

ARGUMENT

Comets. A. Previous views stated and criticized. (1) *Anaxagoras and Democritus—Comets are due to a conjunction of
planets* (342 b 27-29). (2) (a) *The Pythagoreans believe that
comets are a planet which only appears at long intervals* (342 b
29-35). 2 (b) *Hippocrates and Aeschylus agree, but suppose
that the tail is due to reflection of the sun in moisture attracted*

342 b 25 Περὶ δὲ τῶν κομητῶν καὶ τοῦ καλουμένου γάλακτος λέγωμεν, διαπορήσαντες πρὸς τὰ παρὰ τῶν
ἄλλων εἰρημένα πρῶτον.

Ἀναξαγόρας μὲν οὖν καὶ Δημόκριτός φασιν εἶναι
τοὺς κομήτας σύμφασιν τῶν πλανήτων ἀστέρων, ὅταν
διὰ τὸ πλησίον ἐλθεῖν δόξωσι θιγγάνειν ἀλλήλων.
30 Τῶν δ' Ἰταλικῶν τινες καλουμένων Πυθαγορείων

38

going on a chasm appears.[a] In general, white thrown on black produces a variety of colours, as does flame on smoke. In the day time the sun prevents their appearance, at night all other colours except red are lost because they provide no contrast with the background of darkness.

These then must be assumed to be the causes of shooting stars and fires and of other such phenomena whose appearance is of brief duration.[b]

otherwise remain unmentioned. But it is not unlike Aristotle to leave them unmentioned, particularly as they are so evidently similar to χάσματα ; and I have accordingly left the text as it stands in Fobes, and taken συνιόν to mean the same as συνιστάμενος. This when read in conjunction with the first part of the sentence makes good sense.

[b] These last words sum up the contents of chs. 4 and 5.

CHAPTER VI

ARGUMENT (continued)

by the comet : and add further explanations of its infrequent appearance (342 b 35—343 a 20). All these views are incorrect : criticisms, (I) of 2 (a) and (b) (343 a 20–b 6), (II) of 1 and 2 jointly (343 b 7-25), (III) of 1 (343 b 25—344 a 2). With this chapter cf. Heath, Aristarchus, pp. 243 ff.

OUR next subjects are comets and the so-called milky way. First let us examine the views of others on these subjects.

1. Anaxagoras [a] and Democritus [b] say that comets are a conjunction of planets, when they appear to touch each other because of their nearness.

2 (a). Of the Italian schools some of the so-called

Previous Views.
1. Anaxagoras and Democritus.

2 (a). The Pythagoreans.

[a] Diels 59 A 81 : A 1 (ii. 6. 3).   [b] *Ibid.* 68 A 92.

342 b

ἕνα λέγουσιν αὐτὸν εἶναι τῶν πλανήτων ἀστέρων,
ἀλλὰ διὰ πολλοῦ τε χρόνου τὴν φαντασίαν αὐτοῦ
εἶναι καὶ τὴν ὑπερβολὴν ἐπὶ μικρόν, ὅπερ συμβαίνει καὶ περὶ τὸν τοῦ Ἑρμοῦ ἀστέρα· διὰ γὰρ τὸ
μικρὸν ἐπαναβαίνειν πολλὰς ἐκλείπει φάσεις, ὥστε
35 διὰ χρόνου φαίνεσθαι πολλοῦ.

Παραπλησίως δὲ τούτοις καὶ οἱ περὶ Ἱππο-
343 a κράτην τὸν Χῖον καὶ τὸν μαθητὴν αὐτοῦ Αἰσχύλον
ἀπεφήναντο, πλὴν τήν γε κόμην οὐκ ἐξ αὐτοῦ
φασιν ἔχειν, ἀλλὰ πλανώμενον διὰ τὸν τόπον
ἐνίοτε λαμβάνειν ἀνακλωμένης τῆς ἡμετέρας ὄψεως
5 ἀπὸ τῆς ἑλκομένης ὑγρότητος ὑπ᾽ αὐτοῦ πρὸς τὸν
ἥλιον. διὰ δὲ τὸ ὑπολείπεσθαι βραδύτατα τῷ
χρόνῳ διὰ πλείστου χρόνου φαίνεσθαι τῶν ἄλλων
ἄστρων, ὡς ὅταν ἐκ ταὐτοῦ φανῇ ὑπολελειμμένον

---

^a Diels 42. 5.

^b The mathematician. Heath, *Greek Maths.* i. pp. 182 ff.;
Diels 42. 5.   ^c *Ibid.*

^d We normally speak only of the object being reflected by
the mirror to the eye: Aristotle here speaks of the sight
(ὄψις) being reflected by the mirror to the object. Fig. 1
illustrates this theory of Hippocrates and Aeschylus (I have
followed Alex. 27 and Phil. 77).

^e Two reasons are given for the infrequent appearance of
comets. (1) The planet " is slowest of all in falling behind "
(*v.* note *f*). (2) It does not acquire a tail, and so appear as a
comet, in every region of the sky, but only when its course
lies towards the north.

^f ὑπολείπεσθαι is the ordinary word for the apparent retro-
grade motion of the planets, which seem " to fall behind "
the motion of the fixed stars. And early cosmologies supposed that this was in fact what happened, the stars moving
more quickly than the planets, which were consequently left
behind and so appeared to have a " backward " motion of
their own (Heath, *Aristarchus*, pp. 108-109; Cornford,
Plato's Cosmology, p. 112; Alex. 27. 13). Alex. (27. 15 ff.)

Pythagoreans [a] say that a comet is one of the planets, but that it appears only at long intervals and does not rise far above the horizon. This is true of Mercury too; for because it does not rise far above the horizon, many of its appearances are invisible to us, and so it is only seen at long intervals of time.

2 (b). Hippocrates [b] of Chios and his disciple Aeschylus [c] held views similar to this. But they maintain that the tail does not belong to the comet itself, but that it acquires it when in its passage through space it draws up moisture which reflects [d]

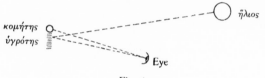

Fig. 1

Sun's image reflected in moisture produces appearance of comet's tail.

our vision towards the sun. It appears at longer intervals than any of the other stars [e] because it is the slowest of all in falling behind the sun,[f] and when it reappears again at the same point it has completed

takes this to be the meaning of the word here. But it is difficult to see how this could account for the comet-planet appearing more seldom; indeed, as Philoponus (79. 27) remarks, it would have the opposite effect. He accordingly supposes (78) that ὑπολείπεσθαι here means not " fall behind the stars " but " fall behind the sun "; and that this accounts for its rare appearance, because it remains for a long time too close to the sun to be visible. The analogy with Mercury, one of the slowest planets on this view, thus gains point (Phil. 79. 35). Ideler (i. p. 385, quoting Vicomercatus) and Heath (p. 243) follow Philoponus.

41

ὅλον τὸν ἑαυτοῦ κύκλον· ὑπολείπεσθαι δ' αὐτὸν καὶ
πρὸς ἄρκτον καὶ πρὸς νότον. ἐν μὲν οὖν τῷ μεταξὺ
τόπῳ τῶν τροπικῶν οὐχ ἕλκειν τὸ ὕδωρ πρὸς
10 ἑαυτὸν διὰ τὸ κεκαῦσθαι ὑπὸ τῆς τοῦ ἡλίου φορᾶς·
πρὸς δὲ νότον ὅταν φέρηται, δαψίλειαν μὲν ἔχειν
τῆς τοιαύτης νοτίδος, ἀλλὰ διὰ τὸ μικρὸν εἶναι τὸ
ὑπὲρ τῆς γῆς τμῆμα τοῦ κύκλου, τὸ δὲ κάτω πολ-
λαπλάσιον, οὐ δύνασθαι τὴν ὄψιν τῶν ἀνθρώπων
φέρεσθαι κλωμένην πρὸς τὸν ἥλιον οὔτε τῷ τρο-
15 πικῷ τόπῳ[1] πλησιάζοντος οὔτ' ἐπὶ θεριναῖς τροπαῖς
ὄντος τοῦ ἡλίου· διόπερ ἐν τούτοις μὲν τοῖς τόποις
οὐ γίγνεσθαι κομήτην αὐτόν· ὅταν δὲ πρὸς βορέαν
ὑπολειφθεὶς τύχῃ, λαμβάνειν κόμην διὰ τὸ μεγάλην
εἶναι τὴν περιφέρειαν τὴν ἄνωθεν τοῦ ὁρίζοντος,
τὸ δὲ κάτω μέρος τοῦ κύκλου μικρόν· ῥᾳδίως γὰρ
20 τὴν ὄψιν τῶν ἀνθρώπων ἀφικνεῖσθαι τότε πρὸς τὸν
ἥλιον.

Πᾶσιν δὲ τούτοις τὰ μὲν κοινῇ συμπίπτει λέγειν
ἀδύνατα, τὰ δὲ χωρίς.

Πρῶτον μὲν οὖν τοῖς λέγουσιν ὅτι τῶν πλανω-
μένων ἐστὶν εἷς ἀστέρων ὁ κομήτης· οἱ γὰρ πλα-
νώμενοι πάντες ἐν τῷ κύκλῳ ὑπολείπονται τῷ τῶν
25 ζῳδίων, κομῆται δὲ πολλοὶ ἑωραμένοι εἰσὶν ἔξω

---

[1] νότῳ E_1 $H_{corr.}$: τροπικῷ οὔτε τ νότῳ $E_{rec.}$: τροπικῷ οὔτε
τῷ νότῳ (overline: νοτίῳ) $\mathfrak{W}$: τροπικῷ F : νοτίῳ τόπῳ (overline: τόπῳ) Pl : (νοτίου μέρους Ap).

---

[a] It is visible only for a short period and must complete
its " backward " orbit and come back to the same relative
position before it is visible again.
[b] Though the text is uncertain it seems clear what the
meaning must be. When the planet's course falls south of
the tropics, then, though there is plenty of moisture, reflection

its backward orbit.[a] It falls behind both to the north
and to the south. In the zone between the tropics
it cannot draw up water to itself because the sun in
its course dries up that whole region. In its south-
ward course it finds plenty of the requisite moisture,
but as only a small segment of its course is visible
above our horizon, the greater part of it being below,
human vision is incapable of being reflected as far as
the sun either when it approaches its southern limit
or at the summer solstice.[b] In these regions therefore
it does not become a comet. But when it falls behind
towards the north, then it gets its tail because the
segment of its course that is above the horizon is a
large one, and the arc of its circle below the horizon
small, and when this is so, human vision can easily
reach the sun by reflection.

There are impossibilities in all these views, some
of which apply to all, others to some only.

(I) Let us first deal with those who say the comet
is one of the planets. (i) The planets all fall into
retrogradation within the zodiac circle, but many
comets have been seen outside that circle. (ii) Again,

Criticisms:
(I) of the
Pytha-
goreans,
Hippocrates
and
Aeschylus.

is impossible, either when the sun approaches the southern
or the northern limit of its course. We have the northern
in the summer solstice (θεριναῖς τροπαῖς l. 15); and the words
τροπικῷ τόπῳ should define the southern, but as they stand
hardly do. νότῳ or νοτίῳ appears in some MSS., and some
phrase with one or the other would give the necessary sense.
But it is difficult to see exactly what the reading should be.
(Thurot's note here (p. 90) seems to rest on a misunderstand-
ing. Ll. b 4-7, to which he refers, can have no relation to this
passage, which states the conditions under which comets *do
not* appear: b 4-7 deals with conditions under which they
do and should be related to a 17-20. The view that comets
cannot appear in the south at the summer solstice is not inconsistent with the view that they *can* appear then in the
north.)

43

343 a

τοῦ κύκλου. εἶτα καὶ πλείους ἑνὸς ἅμα γεγένηνται
πολλάκις. πρὸς δὲ τούτοις, εἰ διὰ τὴν ἀνάκλασιν
τὴν κόμην ἴσχουσι, καθάπερ φησὶν Αἰσχύλος καὶ
Ἱπποκράτης, ἔδει ποτὲ φαίνεσθαι καὶ ἄνευ κόμης
τὸν ἀστέρα τοῦτον, ἐπειδήπερ ὑπολείπεται μὲν καὶ
30 εἰς ἄλλους τόπους, τὴν δὲ κόμην ἴσχει οὐ πανταχοῦ·
νῦν δ' οὐδεὶς ὦπται παρὰ τοὺς πέντε ἀστέρας·
οὗτοι δὲ πολλάκις ἅμα πάντες μετέωροι φαίνονται
ὑπὲρ τοῦ ὁρίζοντος. καὶ φανερῶν δὲ ὄντων αὐτῶν
ἁπάντων καὶ μὴ φαινομένων πάντων, ἀλλ' ἐνίων
ὄντων πρὸς τῷ ἡλίῳ, οὐδὲν ἧττον κομῆται φαίνον-
35 ται γιγνόμενοι πολλάκις. ἀλλὰ μὴν οὐδὲ τοῦτο
ἀληθές, ὡς ἐν τῷ πρὸς ἄρκτον τόπῳ γίγνεται
343 b κομήτης μόνον, ἅμα καὶ τοῦ ἡλίου ὄντος περὶ
θερινὰς τροπάς· ὅ τε γὰρ μέγας κομήτης ὁ γενόμενος περὶ τὸν ἐν Ἀχαΐᾳ σεισμὸν καὶ τὴν τοῦ
κύματος ἔφοδον ἀπὸ δυσμῶν τῶν ἰσημερινῶν ἀν-
έσχεν, καὶ πρὸς νότον ἤδη πολλοὶ γεγόνασιν. ἐπὶ
5 δ' ἄρχοντος Ἀθήνησιν Εὐκλέους τοῦ Μόλωνος
ἐγένετο κομήτης ἀστὴρ πρὸς ἄρκτον μηνὸς Γαμη-
λιῶνος περὶ τροπὰς ὄντος τοῦ ἡλίου χειμερινάς·
καίτοι τοσοῦτον ἀνακλασθῆναι καὶ αὐτοὶ τῶν
ἀδυνάτων εἶναί φασι.

Κοινὸν δὲ καὶ τούτοις καὶ τοῖς τὴν σύναψιν λέγουσιν πρῶτον μὲν ὅτι καὶ τῶν ἀπλανῶν λαμβά-
10 νουσι κόμην τινές. καὶ τοῦτ' οὐ μόνον Αἰγυπτίοις
πιστεῦσαι δεῖ, καίτοι κἀκεῖνοί φασιν, ἀλλὰ καὶ
ἡμεῖς ἐφεωράκαμεν· τῶν γὰρ ἐν τῷ ἰσχίῳ τοῦ

---

a As said above, 2 (*b*), 343 a 6 ff.
b In a 17-20 it was only stated that comets appear in the

more than one comet has frequently appeared at the same time. (iii) Besides, if they owe their tails to reflection, as Aeschylus and Hippocrates say, the star in question should sometimes appear without its tail, since it falls into retrogradation in several regions but does not have a tail in all of them [a] ; but in fact no planet has been seen other than the five, and all of these are often visible in the sky together above the horizon, and comets have appeared with equal frequency both when all the planets are visible and when some are not, being too close to the sun. (iv) Nor is it true that comets only appear in the northern part of the sky when the sun is at the summer solstice.[b] For the great comet, which appeared about the time of the earthquake in Achaea [c] and the tidal wave, rose in the west.[d] And there have been many in the south. And when Euclees, son of Molon, was archon [e] at Athens, there was a comet towards the north in the month Gamelion [f] about the time of the winter solstice : and even the upholders of this theory are prepared to admit that reflection at such a distance is impossible.

(II) Objections which apply both to those who hold this theory and also to those who suppose comets are due to conjunction of two planets are (i) that some of the fixed stars have tails. And for this we need not rely only on the evidence of the Egyptians who say they have observed it ; we have observed it also ourselves. For one of the stars in the thigh of the

(II) Applying to all alike.

northern part of the sky ; the further condition " and at the summer solstice " was omitted.

[c] 373–372 B.C. Also referred to at b 18, 344 b 34, 368 b 6.

[d] Lit. " towards the equinoctial sunset," cf. ch. 13 below and Heidel, *Frame of Greek Maps.*

[e] 427/6 B.C. [f] Jan.–Feb.

κυνὸς ἀστήρ τις ἔσχε κόμην, ἀμαυρὰν μέντοι·
ἀτενίζουσιν μὲν γὰρ εἰς αὐτὸν ἀμυδρὸν ἐγίγνετο
τὸ φέγγος, παραβλέπουσι δ' ἠρέμα τὴν ὄψιν πλέον.
15 πρὸς δὲ τούτοις ἅπαντες οἱ καθ' ἡμᾶς ὠμμένοι ἄνευ
δύσεως ἠφανίσθησαν ἐν τῷ ὑπὲρ τοῦ ὁρίζοντος
τόπῳ ἀπομαρανθέντες κατὰ μικρὸν οὕτως, ὥστε
μήτε ἑνὸς ἀστέρος ὑπολειφθῆναι σῶμα μήτε πλειόνων, ἐπεὶ καὶ ὁ μέγας ἀστὴρ περὶ οὗ πρότερον
ἐμνήσθημεν ἐφάνη μὲν χειμῶνος ἐν πάγοις καὶ
20 αἰθρίαις ἀφ' ἑσπέρας, ἐπὶ Ἀστείου ἄρχοντος, καὶ
τῇ μὲν πρώτῃ οὐκ ὤφθη ὡς προδεδυκὼς τοῦ ἡλίου,
τῇ δ' ὑστεραίᾳ ὤφθη· ὅσον ἐνδέχεται γὰρ ἐλάχιστον
ὑπελείφθη, καὶ εὐθὺς ἔδυ· τὸ δὲ φέγγος ἀπέτεινε
μέχρι τοῦ τρίτου μέρους τοῦ οὐρανοῦ οἷον ἅλμα[1]·
διὸ καὶ ἐκλήθη ὁδός. ἐπανῆλθε δὲ μέχρι τῆς ζώνης
25 τοῦ Ὠρίωνος, καὶ ἐνταυθοῖ διελύθη.

Καίτοι Δημόκριτός γε προσπεφιλονείκηκεν τῇ
δόξῃ τῇ αὑτοῦ· φησὶ γὰρ ὦφθαι διαλυομένων τῶν
κομητῶν ἀστέρας τινάς. τοῦτο δὲ οὐχ ὁτὲ μὲν
ἔδει γίγνεσθαι ὁτὲ δὲ οὔ, ἀλλ' ἀεί. πρὸς δὲ τούτοις καὶ οἱ Αἰγύπτιοί φασι καὶ τῶν πλανήτων καὶ
πρὸς αὐτοὺς καὶ πρὸς τοὺς ἀπλανεῖς γίγνεσθαι
30 συνόδους, καὶ αὐτοὶ ἑωράκαμεν τὸν ἀστέρα τὸν τοῦ
Διὸς τῶν ἐν τοῖς διδύμοις συνελθόντα τινὶ ἤδη καὶ
ἀφανίσαντα, ἀλλ' οὐ κομήτην γενόμενον. ἔτι δὲ
καὶ ἐκ τοῦ λόγου φανερόν· οἱ γὰρ ἀστέρες κἂν εἰ
μείζους καὶ ἐλάττους φαίνονται, ἀλλ' ὅμως ἀδι-
35 αίρετοί γε καθ' ἑαυτοὺς εἶναι δοκοῦσιν. ὥσπερ οὖν
καὶ εἰ ἦσαν ἀδιαίρετοι, ἁψάμενοι οὐδὲν ἂν ἐποίησαν

---

[1] ἅμμα E₁ F₁ : ἅμα J.

Dog had a tail, though a dim one : if you looked hard at it the light used to become dim, but to a less intent glance it was brighter. (ii) Further, all the comets seen in our time disappeared without setting, gradually fading away in the sky above the horizon and leaving behind neither one star nor more than one. For instance, the great comet which we mentioned before [a] appeared during the winter in clear frosty weather in the west, in the archonship of Asteius : on the first night it was not visible as it set before the sun did, but it was visible on the second, being the least distance behind the sun that would allow it to be seen, and setting immediately. Its light stretched across a third of the sky in a great *jump*,[b] as it were, and so was also called a *path*. It rose as high as Orion's belt, and there dispersed.

(III) Democritus, however, has defended his view vigorously, maintaining that stars have been seen to appear at the dissolution of some comets. (i) But this ought, on his view, to happen not sometimes but always. (ii) And further, the Egyptians say that there are conjunctions both of planet with planet and of planets and fixed stars, and we ourselves have observed the planet Jupiter in conjunction with one of the stars in the Twins and hiding it completely, but no comet resulted. (iii) Besides, the theory can be shown to be wrong on purely logical grounds. For though some of the stars seem to be bigger, some smaller than others, yet individually they seem to be indivisible points. As therefore, if they were indivisible points, the addition of one to another

(III) Of Democritus.

---

[b] οἷον ἅλμα, " like a jump," is an odd phrase : the alternative reading ἅμμα, " like a cord (or band)," is perhaps better.

343 b

μέγεθος μεῖζον, οὕτως καὶ ἐπειδὴ οὐκ εἰσὶν μὲν
344 a φαίνονται δὲ ἀδιαίρετοι, καὶ συνελθόντες οὐδὲν φα-
νοῦνται μείζους τὸ μέγεθος ὄντες.

Ὅτι μὲν οὖν αἱ λεγόμεναι περὶ αὐτῶν αἰτίαι
ψευδεῖς οὖσαι τυγχάνουσιν, εἰ μὴ διὰ πλειόνων,
ἀλλὰ καὶ διὰ τούτων ἱκανῶς δῆλόν ἐστιν.

---

^a Aristotle regarded the geometrical point as indivisible
(ἀδιαίρετον) ; the line cannot be composed of points, the
point is not part of the line. Thus the point has no magnitude,
and cannot increase or decrease a magnitude (*cf. Phys.* vi.

CHAPTER VII

ARGUMENT

Comets (continued). B. *Aristotle's own theory.* Comets
have two causes. (1) *As has been said, the outermost part of
the terrestrial sphere consists of a hot dry exhalation, which is
carried round by the motion of the heavenly sphere with which
it is contiguous. When this motion sets up a fiery principle
of moderate strength and this meets a suitably constituted
exhalation, a comet is produced. (It will be a* " comet " κομήτης *or* " bearded-star " πωγωνίας *according to the shape of the
exhalation.) A comet of this kind is in fact a self-contained
shooting star* (344 a 8-33). (2) *When the exhalation is formed
by one of the stars this star becomes a comet, and is followed
by a tail just as the sun and moon are sometimes followed by*

344 a 5 Ἐπεὶ δὲ περὶ τῶν ἀφανῶν τῇ αἰσθήσει νομίζομεν
ἱκανῶς ἀποδεδεῖχθαι κατὰ τὸν λόγον, ἐὰν εἰς τὸ
δυνατὸν ἀναγάγωμεν, ἔκ τε τῶν νῦν φαινομένων
ὑπολάβοι τις ἂν ὧδε περὶ τούτων μάλιστα συμβαίνειν.

could not give an increase in magnitude, so now, since they appear to be indivisible points even though they really are not, their conjunction will bring no appearance of an increase in magnitude.[a]

Though more could be said, this is enough to demonstrate the falsity of current theories of the causes of comets.

chs. 1, 2). So here he argues that as the stars *look* like points, their conjunction (addition) can bring no *appearance* of increase in magnitude.

CHAPTER VII

ARGUMENT (*continued*)

haloes [a] (344 a 33–b 8). *Comets of type* (2) *have the same motion as the star in question : type* (1) *move with the terrestrial sphere and so fall behind the stars* (344 b 8-12). *Confirmation of this view that comets are fiery is that they are generally the sign of winds and drought : the more of them there are the more likely are these to occur* (344 b 12-31). *Examples* (344 b 31—345 a 5). *The reason why comets are rare is that the motion of the sun and stars not only causes the hot principle to form but also dissolves it* (345 a 5-10).

We consider that we have given a sufficiently rational explanation of things inaccessible to observation by our senses if we have produced a theory that is possible : and the following seems, on the evidence available, to be the explanation of the phenomena now under consideration.

[a] " Comets are thus bodies of vapour in a state of slow combustion either moving freely or in the wake of a star," Heath, *Aristarchus*, p. 246.

Ὑπόκειται γὰρ ἡμῖν τοῦ κόσμου τοῦ περὶ τὴν
10 γῆν, ὅσον ὑπὸ τὴν ἐγκύκλιόν ἐστιν φοράν, εἶναι τὸ
πρῶτον μέρος ἀναθυμίασιν ξηρὰν καὶ θερμήν· αὕτη
δὲ αὐτή τε καὶ τοῦ συνεχοῦς ὑπ᾽ αὐτὴν ἀέρος ἐπὶ
πολὺ συμπεριάγεται περὶ τὴν γῆν ὑπὸ τῆς φορᾶς
καὶ τῆς κινήσεως τῆς κύκλῳ· φερομένη δὲ καὶ
κινουμένη τοῦτον τὸν τρόπον, ᾗ ἂν τύχῃ εὔκρατος
15 οὖσα, πολλάκις ἐκπυροῦται· διὸ φαμὲν γίγνεσθαι
καὶ τὰς τῶν σποράδων ἀστέρων διαδρομάς. ὅταν
οὖν εἰς τὴν τοιαύτην πύκνωσιν ἐμπέσῃ διὰ τὴν
ἄνωθεν κίνησιν ἀρχὴ πυρώδης, μήτε οὕτω πολλὴ
λίαν ὥστε ταχὺ καὶ ἐπὶ πολὺ ἐκκαίειν, μήθ᾽ οὕτως
ἀσθενὴς ὥστε ἀποσβεσθῆναι ταχύ, ἀλλὰ πλείων καὶ
20 ἐπὶ πολύ,[1] ἅμα δὲ κάτωθεν συμπίπτῃ ἀναβαίνειν
εὔκρατον ἀναθυμίασιν, ἀστὴρ τοῦτο γίγνεται κομήτης, ὅπως ἂν τὸ ἀναθυμιώμενον τύχῃ ἐσχηματι-
σμένον· ἐὰν μὲν γὰρ πάντῃ ὁμοίως, κομήτης, ἐὰν
δ᾽ ἐπὶ μῆκος, καλεῖται πωγωνίας. ὥσπερ δὲ ἡ
τοιαύτη φορὰ ἀστέρος φορὰ δοκεῖ εἶναι, οὕτως καὶ
25 ἡ μονὴ ἡ ὁμοία ἀστέρος μονὴ δοκεῖ εἶναι· παραπλήσιον γὰρ τὸ γιγνόμενον οἷον εἴ τις εἰς ἀχύρων
θημῶνα καὶ πλῆθος ὤσειε δαλὸν ἢ πυρὸς ἀρχὴν
ἐμβάλοι μικράν· φαίνεται γὰρ ὁμοία καὶ ἡ τῶν
ἀστέρων διαδρομὴ τούτῳ· ταχὺ γὰρ διὰ τὴν εὐφυΐαν
τοῦ ὑπεκκαύματος διαδίδωσιν ἐπὶ μῆκος. εἰ δὴ
30 τοῦτο μείνειε καὶ μὴ καταμαρανθείη διελθόν, ᾗ
μάλιστα ἐπύκνωσε τὸ ὑπέκκαυμα, γένοιτ᾽ ἂν ἀρχὴ

We have laid down that the outer part of the
terrestrial world, that is, of all that lies beneath the
celestial revolutions, is composed of a hot dry exhalation. This and the greater part of the air which is
continuous with and below it are carried round the
earth by the movement of the circular revolution :
as it is carried round its movement frequently causes
it to catch fire, wherever it is suitably constituted,
which we maintain is the cause of scattered shooting
stars.[a] Now when as a result of the upper motion
there impinges upon a suitable condensation a fiery
principle which is neither so very strong as to cause
a rapid and widespread conflagration, nor so feeble
as to be quickly extinguished, but which is yet strong
enough and widespread enough ; and when besides
there coincides with it an exhalation from below of
suitable consistency ; then a comet is produced, its
exact form depending on the form taken by the exhalation—if it extends equally in all directions it is
called a comet or long-haired star, if it extends
lengthwise only it is called a bearded star. And
just as a phenomenon of this sort when it moves
seems to be a shooting star, so when it remains
stationary it seems to be a stationary star. An
analogy may be found in what happens when one
thrusts a burning torch into a large quantity of chaff
or drops a spark onto it ; for the course of a shooting
star is similar in that because the fuel is suitable it
runs quickly along it. But if the fire were not to run
through the fuel and burn itself out, but were to stand
still at a point where the fuel-supply was densest,

Two types of comet : (1) formed by a fiery principle in the hot exhalation ;

[a] Ch. 3, 340 b 14 ff. and ch. 4, 341 b 5 ff.

---

[1] καὶ ἐπὶ πολύ del. Thurot.

344 a

τῆς φορᾶς ἡ τελευτὴ τῆς διαδρομῆς. τοιοῦτον ὁ
κομήτης ἐστὶν ἀστήρ, ὥσπερ διαδρομὴ ἀστέρος,
ἔχων ἐν ἑαυτῷ πέρας καὶ ἀρχήν.

   "Οταν μὲν οὖν ἐν αὐτῷ τῷ κάτω τόπῳ ἡ ἀρχὴ
35 τῆς συστάσεως ᾖ, καθ' ἑαυτὸν φαίνεται κομήτης·
ὅταν δ' ὑπὸ τῶν ἄστρων τινός, ἢ τῶν ἀπλανῶν
ἢ τῶν πλανήτων, ὑπὸ τῆς κινήσεως συνιστῆται ἡ
344 b ἀναθυμίασις, τότε κομήτης γίγνεται τούτων τις·
οὐ γὰρ πρὸς αὐτοῖς ἡ κόμη γίγνεται τοῖς ἄστροις,
ἀλλ' ὥσπερ αἱ ἅλῳ περὶ τὸν ἥλιον φαίνονται καὶ
τὴν σελήνην παρακολουθοῦσαι, καίπερ μεθιστα-
5 μένων, ὅταν οὕτως ᾖ πεπυκνωμένος ὁ ἀὴρ ὥστε
τοῦτο γίγνεσθαι τὸ πάθος ὑπὸ τὴν τοῦ ἡλίου πο-
ρείαν, οὕτω καὶ ἡ κόμη τοῖς ἄστροις οἷον ἅλως
ἐστίν· πλὴν ἡ μὲν γίγνεται δι' ἀνάκλασιν τοιαύτη
τὴν χρόαν, ἐκεῖ δ' ἐπ' αὐτῶν τὸ χρῶμα φαινόμενόν
ἐστιν.

   "Οταν μὲν οὖν κατ' ἀστέρα γένηται ἡ τοιαύτη
10 σύγκρισις, τὴν αὐτὴν ἀνάγκη φαίνεσθαι φορὰν
κινούμενον τὸν κομήτην ἥνπερ φέρεται ὁ ἀστήρ·
ὅταν δὲ συστῇ καθ' αὑτόν, τότε ὑπολειπόμενοι
φαίνονται. τοιαύτη γὰρ ἡ φορὰ τοῦ κόσμου τοῦ
περὶ τὴν γῆν.

   (Τοῦτο γὰρ μάλιστα μηνύει μὴ εἶναι ἀνάκλασίν
τινα τὸν κομήτην, ὡς ἅλω ἐν ὑπεκκαύματι καθαρῷ,[1]
15 πρὸς αὐτὸν τὸν ἀστέρα γιγνομένην, καὶ μὴ ὡς
λέγουσιν οἱ περὶ Ἱπποκράτην, πρὸς τὸν ἥλιον, ὅτι

---

[1] interpunxit O.T.

---

[a] The point of this comparison appears to be as follows.

52

then this point at which the fire stops would be the beginning of the orbit of a comet.[a] So we may define a comet as a shooting star that contains its beginning and end in itself.[b]

When therefore the material gathers in the lower region, the comet is an independent phenomenon. But when the exhalation is formed by the movement of one of the stars—either of the planets or of the fixed stars—then one of them becomes a comet. The tail is not attached to the stars themselves, but is a kind of stellar halo, like the haloes which appear to accompany the sun and moon as they move, when the air has condensed in such a way as to produce such formations beneath the sun's course. The difference between them is that whereas the colour of the sun's halo is due to reflection, the colour of the comet's tail is what it actually appears to be.

(2) formed by a star.

When therefore the formation of matter occurs in connexion with a star, the comet must necessarily appear to follow the same course as that on which the star is moving : when it is an independent formation it seems to fall behind the stars, as it follows the movement of the terrestrial sphere.

Motion of these two types of comet.

(A conclusive disproof that the comet is a reflection, not to the sun, as the school of Hippocrates maintain, but to the star itself—thus being a kind of halo in the clear inflammable material—is that a comet often

---

[a] If you ignite a large quantity of inflammable material (*e.g.* chaff), if it is scattered over an area, the fire will run quickly across it. This is analogous to a shooting star. If the material is gathered together in a heap, then the fire will burn at the place where the heap is. This is analogous to a comet (*cf.* Alex. 34. 24 ff. and Phil. 93. 28).

[b] *i.e.* burns in a single place, like the heap of chaff, and does not " shoot " like a shooting star proper.

344 b

καὶ καθ' αὑτὸν γίγνεται κομήτης πολλάκις καὶ
πλεονάκις ἢ περὶ τῶν ὡρισμένων τινὰς ἀστέρων.
περὶ μὲν οὖν τῆς ἅλω τὴν αἰτίαν ὕστερον ἐροῦμεν.)

Περὶ δὲ τοῦ πυρώδη τὴν σύστασιν αὐτῶν εἶναι
20 τεκμήριον χρὴ νομίζειν ὅτι σημαίνουσι γιγνόμενοι
πλείους πνεύματα καὶ αὐχμούς· δῆλον γὰρ ὅτι
γίγνονται διὰ τὸ πολλὴν εἶναι τὴν τοιαύτην ἔκκρισιν,
ὥστε ξηρότερον ἀναγκαῖον εἶναι τὸν ἀέρα, καὶ
διακρίνεσθαι καὶ διαλύεσθαι τὸ διατμίζον ὑγρὸν ὑπὸ
τοῦ πλήθους τῆς θερμῆς ἀναθυμιάσεως, ὥστε μὴ
25 συνίστασθαι ῥᾳδίως εἰς ὕδωρ. σαφέστερον δ' ἐροῦμεν καὶ περὶ τούτου τοῦ πάθους, ὅταν καὶ περὶ
πνευμάτων λέγειν ᾖ καιρός.

Ὅταν μὲν οὖν πυκνοὶ καὶ πλείους φαίνωνται,
καθάπερ λέγομεν, ξηροὶ καὶ πνευματώδεις γίγνονται
οἱ ἐνιαυτοὶ ἐπιδήλως· ὅταν δὲ σπανιώτεροι καὶ
ἀμαυρότεροι τὸ μέγεθος, ὁμοίως μὲν οὐ γίγνεται
30 τὸ τοιοῦτον, οὐ μὴν ἀλλ' ὡς ἐπὶ τὸ πολὺ γίγνεταί
τις ὑπερβολὴ πνεύματος ἢ κατὰ χρόνον ἢ κατὰ
μέγεθος, ἐπεὶ καὶ ὅτε ὁ ἐν Αἰγὸς ποταμοῖς ἔπεσε
λίθος ἐκ τοῦ ἀέρος, ὑπὸ πνεύματος ἀρθεὶς ἐξέπεσε
μεθ' ἡμέραν· ἔτυχε δὲ καὶ τότε κομήτης ἀστὴρ
γενόμενος ἀφ' ἑσπέρας. καὶ περὶ τὸν μέγαν ἀστέρα
35 τὸν κομήτην ξηρὸς ἦν ὁ χειμὼν καὶ βόρειος, καὶ τὸ
κῦμα δι' ἐναντίωσιν ἐγένετο πνευμάτων· ἐν μὲν γὰρ
345 a τῷ κόλπῳ βορέας κατεῖχεν, ἔξω δὲ νότος ἔπνευσε

---

[a] I take it that Aristotle is meeting a possible modification
of Hippocrates' theory. This seems to be how Phil. (98. 19)
took the passage : it is not clear from Alex. (35. 23 f.) that
he had the same text, as he seems to find only a simple reference to the opinion of Hippocrates above, ch. 6, 342 b 36. I
have bracketed the passage in my translation because it

54

appears independently, indeed more often than
round one of the stars.[a] The cause of the halo we
will explain later.[b])

We may regard as a proof that their constitution
is fiery the fact that their appearance in any number
is a sign of coming wind and drought. For it is evident
that they owe their origin to this kind of exhalation
being plentiful, which necessarily makes the air drier,
while, at the same time, the moist evaporation is
disintegrated and dissolved by the quantity of the
hot exhalation so that it will not readily condense
into water. But we will give a clearer explanation
of this when the time comes to deal with winds.[c]

So when comets appear frequently and in considerable numbers, the years are, as we say, notoriously
dry and windy. When they are less frequent and
dimmer and smaller in size, these effects are not so
considerable, though as a rule the wind is excessive
either in duration or in strength. For instance when
the stone fell from the air at Aegospotami [d] it had
been lifted by the wind and fell during the day time :
and its fall coincided with the appearance of a comet
in the west. Again at the time of the great comet [e]
the winter was dry and the wind strong and northerly,
and the tidal wave was due to a conflict of winds, for
the north wind was blowing inside the gulf, while
outside it there was a southerly gale. Again in the

Proof that comets are fiery.

seems to be rather a parenthesis or footnote than part of the
main argument : and I have therefore also omitted it from
the chapter analysis.

[b] Book III. ch. 2. [c] Book II. chs. 4 ff.

[d] The fall of this meteor attracted the attention of Anaxagoras (Diels 59 A 11, 12 : cf. 71). He was even said to have
foretold it (Diels 59 A 1, ii. 6. 9).

[e] Cf. 343 b 1, ch. 6, note c on p. 45.

345 a

μέγας. ἔτι δ' ἐπ' ἄρχοντος Νικομάχου ἐγένετο
ὀλίγας ἡμέρας κομήτης περὶ τὸν ἰσημερινὸν κύκλον,
οὐκ ἀφ' ἑσπέρας ποιησάμενος τὴν ἀνατολήν, ἐφ' ᾧ
5 τὸ περὶ Κόρινθον πνεῦμα γενέσθαι συνέπεσεν.

Τοῦ δὲ μὴ γίγνεσθαι πολλοὺς μηδὲ πολλάκις
κομήτας, καὶ μᾶλλον ἐκτὸς τῶν τροπικῶν ἢ ἐντός,
αἴτιος ἡ τοῦ ἡλίου καὶ ἡ τῶν ἀστέρων κίνησις, οὐ
μόνον ἐκκρίνουσα τὸ θερμόν, ἀλλὰ καὶ διακρίνουσα
τὸ συνιστάμενον. μάλιστα δ' αἴτιον ὅτι τὸ πλεῖστον
10 εἰς τὴν τοῦ γάλακτος ἀθροίζεται χώραν.

CHAPTER VIII

ARGUMENT

*The Milky Way. A. Previous views stated and criticized.
(1) The Pythagoreans say it is the path of a star that fell in
Phaethon's time or else the path the sun once described (345 a
13-17). Criticisms (345 a 17-25). (2) Anaxagoras and
Democritus say that it is the light of the stars that fall within
the shadow cast by the earth when the sun passes beneath it :
for the light of these stars is not overpowered by that of the
sun (345 a 25-31). Criticisms (345 a 31-b 9). (3) A third
view which supposes that it is due to reflection of our sight to
the sun (like the view of comets above, ch. 6 (2) (b) (345 b
9-12). Criticisms (345 b 12-31).*

*B. Aristotle's own view. The Milky Way is formed in the
same way as the type of comet formed by a star ; only the
formation affects a whole circle of the heavens (345 b 31—*

345 a 11 "Οπως δὲ καὶ διὰ τίν' αἰτίαν γίγνεται καὶ τί ἐστι
τὸ γάλα, λέγωμεν ἤδη. προδιέλθωμεν δὲ καὶ περὶ
τούτου τὰ παρὰ τῶν ἄλλων εἰρημένα πρῶτον.

archonship of Nicomachus [a] a comet appeared in the equinoctial circle for a few days (this one had not risen in the west), and this coincided with the storm at Corinth.

The reason why comets are few in number and infrequent, and why they appear more outside the tropics than within them, is that the movement of the sun and stars not only separates off the hot substance but also disintegrates it as it is forming. But the chief reason is that most of it collects in the area of the Milky Way.[b] Why comets are few.

[a] 341/0 B.C.   [b] Cf. 346 b 7 below.

CHAPTER VIII

ARGUMENT (continued)

346 a 11). *In the zodiac circle the formation of the necessary exhalation is prevented by the movement of the sun and planets : and similarly sun and moon do not have tails (346 a 11-16). The Milky Way extends beyond the tropic circles, and contains very many bright stars which cause the exhalation to gather there : that this is the cause is indicated by the fact that it is brighter where it is double and that it is there that the stars are thickest (346 a 16-30). So, assuming our account of comets to be reasonable, we may define the Milky Way as the tail of the greatest circle, due to exhalation (346 a 30–b 6). (So comets are rare because the material for them collects in the Milky Way (346 b 7-10).) So much for the upper atmosphere (346 b 10-15).*

LET us now explain how the Milky Way is formed, and what is its cause and nature : and let us again first review what others have said on the subject.

345 a

Τῶν μὲν οὖν καλουμένων Πυθαγορείων φασί
15 τινες ὁδὸν εἶναι ταύτην οἱ μὲν τῶν ἐκπεσόντων
τινὸς ἀστέρων, κατὰ τὴν λεγομένην ἐπὶ Φαέθοντος
φθοράν, οἱ δὲ τὸν ἥλιον τοῦτον τὸν κύκλον φέρεσθαί
ποτέ φασιν· οἷον οὖν διακεκαῦσθαι τὸν τόπον τοῦτον ἤ τι τοιοῦτον ἄλλο πεπονθέναι πάθος ὑπὸ τῆς
φορᾶς αὐτῶν.

Ἄτοπον δὲ τὸ μὴ συννοεῖν ὅτι εἴπερ τοῦτ᾽ ἦν
20 τὸ αἴτιον, ἔδει καὶ τὸν τῶν ζῳδίων κύκλον οὕτως
ἔχειν, καὶ μᾶλλον ἢ τὸν τοῦ γάλακτος· ἅπαντα
γὰρ ἐν αὐτῷ φέρεται τὰ πλανώμενα καὶ οὐχ ὁ
ἥλιος μόνος. δῆλος δ᾽ ἡμῖν ἅπας ὁ κύκλος· αἰεὶ
γὰρ αὐτοῦ φανερὸν ἡμικύκλιον τῆς νυκτός. ἀλλὰ
πεπονθὼς οὐδὲν φαίνεται τοιοῦτον, πλὴν εἴ τι
25 συνάπτει μόριον αὐτοῦ πρὸς τὸν τοῦ γάλακτος
κύκλον.

Οἱ δὲ περὶ Ἀναξαγόραν καὶ Δημόκριτον φῶς
εἶναι τὸ γάλα λέγουσιν ἄστρων τινῶν· τὸν γὰρ
ἥλιον ὑπὸ τὴν γῆν φερόμενον οὐχ ὁρᾶν ἔνια τῶν
ἄστρων. ὅσα μὲν οὖν περιορᾶται ὑπ᾽ αὐτοῦ, τούτων μὲν οὐ φαίνεσθαι τὸ φῶς (κωλύεσθαι γὰρ ὑπὸ
30 τῶν τοῦ ἡλίου ἀκτίνων)· ὅσοις δ᾽ ἀντιφράττει ἡ
γῆ ὥστε μὴ ὁρᾶσθαι ὑπὸ τοῦ ἡλίου, τὸ τούτων
οἰκεῖον φῶς εἶναί φασι τὸ γάλα. φανερὸν δ᾽ ὅτι

---

[a] Diels 58 B 37 c. The second view is attributed also to
Oenopides ; Diels 41. 10 (Heath, *Aristarchus*, p. 133).
[b] Diels 59 A 1 (ii. 6. 2) ; 42 (ii. 16. 31) ; 80.
[c] *Ibid.* 68 A 91.
[d] " As we have seen, he (Anaxagoras) thought the sun to
be smaller than the earth. Consequently, when the sun in
its revolution passes below the earth, the shadow cast by the
earth extends without limit. The trace of this shadow on
the heavens is the Milky Way. The stars within this shadow

The so-called Pythagoreans give two explanations. Some say that the Milky Way is the path taken by one of the stars at the time of the legendary fall of Phaethon : others say that it is the circle in which the sun once moved.[a] And the region is supposed to have been scorched or affected in some other such way as a result of the passage of these bodies.

But it is absurd not to see that if this is the cause, the circle of the zodiac should also be so affected, indeed more so than the Milky Way : for all the planets, as well as the sun, move in it. But though the whole zodiac circle is visible to us (for we can see half of it at any time during the night) it shows no sign of being so affected, except when a part of it overlaps the Milky Way.

The schools of Anaxagoras [b] and Democritus [c] maintain that the Milky Way is the light of certain stars. The sun, they say, in its course beneath the earth, does not shine upon some of the stars ; the light of those upon which the sun does shine is not visible to us, being obscured by its rays, while the Milky Way is the light peculiar to those stars which are screened from the sun's light by the earth.[d] This

are not interfered with by the light of the sun, and we there- fore see them shining ; those stars, on the other hand, which are outside the shadow are overpowered by the light of the sun, which shines on them even during the night, so that we cannot see them." So Heath (*Aristarchus*, p. 83) summarizes this passage. What is not easy to understand is why, on Anaxagoras' theory, we see any stars outside the Milky Way, if the light of stars outside it is " overpowered by the light of the sun." Alex. 37. 24-27 implies that such stars owe their light to reflection from the sun. Anaxagoras was the first to discover that the moon owes its light to the sun (Heath, *op. cit.* p. 78) ; he may have held that the stars outside the Milky Way did too.

345 a

καὶ τοῦτ' ἀδύνατον· τὸ μὲν γὰρ γάλα ἀεὶ τὸ αὐτὸ
ἐν τοῖς αὐτοῖς ἐστιν ἄστροις (φαίνεται γὰρ μέγιστος
ὢν[1] κύκλος), ὑπὸ δὲ τοῦ ἡλίου ἀεὶ ἕτερα τὰ οὐχ
35 ὁρώμενα διὰ τὸ μὴ ἐν ταὐτῷ μένειν τόπῳ. ἔδει
οὖν μεθισταμένου τοῦ ἡλίου μεθίστασθαι καὶ τὸ
γάλα· νῦν δὲ οὐ φαίνεται τοῦτο γιγνόμενον. πρὸς
345 b δὲ τούτοις, εἰ καθάπερ δείκνυται νῦν ἐν τοῖς περὶ
ἀστρολογίαν θεωρήμασιν, τὸ τοῦ ἡλίου μέγεθος
μεῖζόν ἐστιν ἢ τὸ τῆς γῆς καὶ τὸ διάστημα πολ-
λαπλασίως μεῖζον τὸ τῶν ἄστρων πρὸς τὴν γῆν ἢ
5 τὸ τοῦ ἡλίου, καθάπερ τὸ τοῦ ἡλίου πρὸς τὴν γῆν
ἢ τὸ τῆς σελήνης, οὐκ ἂν πόρρω που τῆς γῆς ὁ
κῶνος ὁ ἀπὸ τοῦ ἡλίου συμβάλλοι τὰς ἀκτῖνας,
οὐδ' ἂν ἡ σκιὰ πρὸς τοῖς ἄστροις εἴη τῆς γῆς, ἡ
καλουμένη νύξ· ἀλλ' ἀνάγκη πάντα τὸν ἥλιον τὰ
ἄστρα περιορᾶν, καὶ μηδενὶ τὴν γῆν ἀντιφράττειν
αὐτῶν.

10 Ἔτι δ' ἐστὶν τρίτη τις ὑπόληψις περὶ αὐτοῦ·
λέγουσιν γάρ τινες ἀνάκλασιν εἶναι τὸ γάλα τῆς
ἡμετέρας ὄψεως πρὸς τὸν ἥλιον, ὥσπερ καὶ τὸν
ἀστέρα τὸν κομήτην.

Ἀδύνατον δὲ καὶ τοῦτο· εἰ μὲν γὰρ τό τε ὁρῶν
ἠρεμοίη καὶ τὸ ἔνοπτρον καὶ τὸ ὁρώμενον ἅπαν,
ἐν τῷ αὐτῷ σημείῳ τοῦ ἐνόπτρου τὸ αὐτὸ φαίνοιτ'
15 ἂν μέρος τῆς ἐμφάσεως· εἰ δὲ κινοῖτο τὸ ἔνοπτρον
καὶ τὸ ὁρώμενον ἐν τῷ αὐτῷ μὲν ἀποστήματι πρὸς
τὸ ὁρῶν καὶ ἠρεμοῦν, πρὸς ἄλληλα δὲ μήτε ἰσοταχῶς μηδ' ἐν τῷ αὐτῷ ἀεὶ διαστήματι, ἀδύνατον

---

[1] μέγιστος ὢν Pl : μέγας E₁ 𝔚 : μέγιστος E_var. : μέγιστος
ὢν ὁ Oc : μέσον ὢν ὁ Ol : μέγιστος εἶναι Ald.

---

[a] The text is uncertain and the meaning of μέγιστος κύκλος,
" greatest circle," doubtful. But by referring to the Milky

theory is also manifestly impossible. For the Milky Way always remains stationary among the same constellations, and is clearly a greatest circle *a* : whereas the stars on which the sun does not shine change constantly as the sun changes its position. The Milky Way should therefore change with the sun's change of position : but in fact no such change is observed. Besides, astronomical researches have now shown that the size of the sun is greater than that of the earth and that the stars are far farther away than the sun from the earth, just as the sun is farther than the moon from the earth : therefore the vertex of the cone formed by the rays of the sun will not fall very far from the earth, nor will the earth's shadow (which we call night) reach the stars. The sun must therefore shine on all the stars, nor can the earth screen any of them from it.

There is still a third theory about the Milky Way. (3) a third For some say that it is a reflection of our vision to view. the sun, just as a comet was supposed to be.*b*

But this too is an impossibility. For if the eye and the mirror and the whole of the object seen were at rest, the same part of the image would always appear at the same point in the mirror. But if mirror and object are in motion, keeping the same distance from the eye, which is at rest, but moving with different speeds and so not keeping the same distance from

Way as " a (or " the ") greatest circle, " Aristotle appears to mean that it lies on the outermost celestial sphere. The phrase occurs again at 346 a 17 and 346 b 6.
b Diels 42. 6. He attributes the theory to Hippocrates and Aeschylus. There seems no explicit independent evidence that it is theirs, but the words ὥσπερ . . . κομήτην b 11-12 refer to their theory of comets (ch. 6, 2 (*b*)) and perhaps suggest that this theory of the Milky Way was theirs too.

345 b

τὴν αὐτὴν ἔμφασιν ἐπὶ τοῦ αὐτοῦ εἶναι μέρους τοῦ
ἐνόπτρου. τὰ δ' ἐν τῷ τοῦ γάλακτος κύκλῳ φερό-
20 μενα ἄστρα κινεῖται καὶ ὁ ἥλιος πρὸς ὃν ἡ ἀνάκλασις, μενόντων ἡμῶν, καὶ ὁμοίως καὶ ἴσον πρὸς
ἡμᾶς ἀπέχοντα, αὐτῶν δ' οὐκ ἴσον· ὁτὲ μὲν γὰρ
μέσων νυκτῶν ὁ δελφὶς ἐπιτέλλει, ὁτὲ δὲ ἕωθεν,
τὰ δὲ μόρια τοῦ γάλακτος τὰ αὐτὰ μένει ἐν ἑκάστῳ.
25 καίτοι οὐκ ἔδει, εἰ ἦν ἔμφασις, ἀλλὰ μὴ ἐν αὐτοῖς
τι ἦν τοῦτο τὸ πάθος τοῖς τόποις.

Ἔτι δὲ νύκτωρ ἐν ὕδατι καὶ τοῖς τοιούτοις ἐνόπτροις τὸ μὲν γάλα ἐμφαίνεται θεωροῦσι, τὸ δὲ τὴν
ὄψιν ἀνακλᾶσθαι πρὸς τὸν ἥλιον πῶς δυνατόν;

Ὅτι μὲν οὖν οὔτε ὁδὸς τῶν πλανήτων οὐδενὸς
οὔτε φῶς ἐστι τῶν μὴ ὁρωμένων ἄστρων οὔτ'
30 ἀνάκλασις, ἐκ τούτων φανερόν. σχεδὸν δὲ ταῦτ'
ἐστὶν μόνον τὰ μέχρι τοῦ νῦν παραδεδομένα παρὰ
τῶν ἄλλων.

Ἡμεῖς δὲ λέγωμεν ἀναλαβόντες τὴν ὑποκειμένην
ἀρχὴν ἡμῖν. εἴρηται γὰρ πρότερον ὅτι τὸ ἔσχατον
τοῦ λεγομένου ἀέρος δύναμιν ἔχει πυρός, ὥστε τῇ
κινήσει διακρινομένου τοῦ ἀέρος ἀποκρίνεσθαι τοι-
35 αύτην σύστασιν οἵαν καὶ τοὺς κομήτας ἀστέρας εἶναί
φαμεν. τοιοῦτον δὴ δεῖ νοῆσαι γιγνόμενον ὅπερ ἐπ'

346 a

ἐκείνων, ὅταν μὴ αὐτὴ καθ' αὑτὴν γένηται ἡ τοιαύτη ἔκκρισις, ἀλλ' ὑπό τινος τῶν ἄστρων ἢ τῶν
ἐνδεδεμένων ἢ τῶν πλανωμένων· τότε γὰρ οὗτοι
φαίνονται κομῆται διὰ τὸ παρακολουθεῖν αὐτῶν τῇ

---

[a] Which is close to the Milky Way.

[b] Alex. 40. 16 and Phil. 108 *ad loc.* explain this to mean
that the double reflection that would be necessary is impossible at such a distance.

[c] 340 b 4 f., 341 b 6 f.

each other, it is impossible for the same image to remain in the same part of the mirror. But the stars whose course lies through the circle of the Milky Way are in motion, and so also is the sun from which the reflection comes. And while their distances from us, who are at rest, remain constant and equal, their distances from each other vary : for the Dolphin *a* sometimes rises at midnight, sometimes at dawn. But the constitution of the Milky Way remains the same in each case. But this should not be so if it were a reflection and not a characteristic of the region.

Besides, we can see the Milky Way reflected at night in water and similar reflecting surfaces : but how can our sight in these circumstances be reflected to the sun ? *b*

This shows clearly enough that the Milky Way is not the path of one of the planets, nor the light of stars unlit by the sun, nor a reflection : and these are more or less the only views on the subject previously put forward.

Let us now recall the first principle we have laid down and then proceed to give our own explanation of the matter. We have previously said *c* that the outer part of what is commonly called air has the properties of fire, and that when the air is disintegrated by motion there is separated off a kind of mixture out of which, we maintain, comets are formed.*d* We must then suppose that the same thing happens here as when a comet is formed not by an independent formation of the requisite material but by one of the stars—either one of the fixed stars or one of the planets. For the stars then appear as comets because there accompanies their motion a

Aristotle's own view.

d 344 a 7 f.

346 a

φορᾷ ὥσπερ τῷ ἡλίῳ τὴν τοιαύτην σύγκρισιν, ἀφ'
5 ἧς διὰ τὴν ἀνάκλασιν τὴν ἅλω φαίνεσθαί φαμεν,
ὅταν οὕτω τύχῃ κεκραμένος ὁ ἀήρ. ὃ δὴ καθ' ἕνα
συμβαίνει τῶν ἀστέρων, τοῦτο δεῖ λαβεῖν γιγνόμενον περὶ ὅλον τὸν οὐρανὸν καὶ τὴν ἄνω φορὰν
ἅπασαν· εὔλογον γάρ, εἴπερ ἡ ἑνὸς ἄστρου κίνησις,
καὶ τὴν τῶν πάντων ποιεῖν τι τοιοῦτον καὶ ἐκριπίζειν ἀέρα τε καὶ διακρίνειν διὰ τὸ τοῦ κύκλου
10 μέγεθος.[1] καὶ πρὸς τούτοις ἔτι καθ' ὃν τόπον
πυκνότατα καὶ πλεῖστα καὶ μέγιστα τυγχάνουσιν
ὄντα τῶν ἄστρων. ὁ μὲν οὖν τῶν ζῳδίων διὰ τὴν
τοῦ ἡλίου φορὰν καὶ τὴν τῶν πλανητῶν διαλύει τὴν
τοιαύτην σύστασιν· διόπερ οἱ πολλοὶ τῶν κομητῶν
ἐκτὸς γίγνονται τῶν τροπικῶν. ἔτι δ' οὔτε περὶ
15 τὸν ἥλιον οὔτε περὶ σελήνην γίγνεται κόμη· θᾶττον
γὰρ διακρίνουσιν ἢ ὥστε συστῆναι τοιαύτην σύγκρισιν. οὗτος δ' ὁ κύκλος ἐν ᾧ τὸ γάλα φαίνεται
τοῖς ὁρῶσιν, ὅ τε μέγιστος ὢν τυγχάνει καὶ τῇ
θέσει κείμενος οὕτως ὥστε πολὺ τοὺς τροπικοὺς
ὑπερβάλλειν. πρὸς δὲ τούτοις ἄστρων ὁ τόπος
20 πλήρης ἐστὶν τῶν μεγίστων καὶ λαμπροτάτων, καὶ
ἔτι τῶν σποράδων καλουμένων (τοῦτο δ' ἐστὶν καὶ
τοῖς ὄμμασιν ἰδεῖν φανερόν), ὥστε διὰ ταῦτα συνεχῶς καὶ ἀεὶ ταύτην πᾶσαν ἀθροίζεσθαι τὴν σύγκρισιν. σημεῖον δέ· καὶ γὰρ αὐτοῦ τοῦ κύκλου
πλέον τὸ φῶς ἐστιν ἐν θατέρῳ ἡμικυκλίῳ τῷ τὸ

---

[1] ἀέρα . . . μέγεθος om. J E 𝔚 : (in voc. ἐκριπίζειν cadit
Pl) : post μέγεθος ⟨ἀνάγκη τοίνυν τῶν αὐτῶν μεγίστων κύκλων
μάλιστα τὴν μέλλουσαν τοῦτο ποιήσειν φοράν . . . χρὴ γὰρ τοῦτο,
ἵνα πολλὴ κίνησις ᾖ διὰ τὸ μέγεθος γιγνομένη καὶ πλείονα τὴν
ἔξαψιν ποιήσῃ.⟩ Fobes, praebet Ol : om. codd.

64

formation similar to that which follows the sun and causes, so we maintain, the appearance of a halo when the constitution of the air is suitable. We must assume then that what happens to one of the stars happens to the whole heaven and the whole upper motion. For it is reasonable to suppose that, if the motion of a single star can produce this effect and set the air on fire or disintegrate it because of the size of the circle,[a] the movement of all the stars can do so too [b]; and especially in a region in which the stars are thickest, most numerous and largest in size. In the zodiac circle any such mixture is dissolved because of the movement of the sun and the planets —and consequently the majority of comets fall outside the tropics. Besides, no tail appears around the sun or moon because they dissolve any such mixture before it can form. But this circle in which the Milky Way appears to our eyes is the greatest circle and is so placed that it extends far beyond the tropics. And in addition the region is full of stars of greatest size and brilliance, and also of what are called scattered stars (you can see this clearly enough if you look). So for these reasons all this mixture always continues to gather there. A proof of this is the following : the light of the circle itself is stronger in that half of it in which the Milky Way is double,

---

[a] Cf. 345 a 7.

[b] As they stand the words inserted by Fobes do not construe easily, if at all: as he indicates, there is a lacuna after φοράν. It seems that the words might be a gloss on διὰ τὸ τοῦ κύκλου μέγεθος, meaning roughly " The circle must be one of the greatest; for thus its motion will be great because of its size, and the conflagration caused greater "—a fairly intelligible comment. I have accordingly omitted them, but retained ἀέρα ... μέγεθος with Fobes.

346 a

25 δίπλωμα ἔχοντι· ἐν τούτῳ γὰρ πλείω καὶ πυκνότερά
ἐστιν ἄστρα ἢ ἐν θατέρῳ, ὡς οὐ δι' ἑτέραν τιν'
αἰτίαν γιγνομένου τοῦ φέγγους ἢ διὰ τὴν τῶν
ἄστρων φοράν· εἰ γὰρ ἔν τε τῷ κύκλῳ τούτῳ γίγνεται ἐν ᾧ τὰ πλεῖστα κεῖται τῶν ἄστρων, καὶ
αὐτοῦ τοῦ κύκλου[1] ἐν ᾧ μᾶλλον φαίνεται κατα-
30 πεπυκνῶσθαι καὶ μεγέθει καὶ πλήθει ἀστέρων,
ταύτην εἰκὸς ὑπολαβεῖν οἰκειοτάτην αἰτίαν εἶναι
τοῦ πάθους.

Θεωρείσθω δ' ὅ τε κύκλος καὶ τὰ ἐν αὐτῷ ἄστρα
ἐκ τῆς ὑπογραφῆς. τοὺς δὲ σποράδας καλουμένους
οὕτω μὲν εἰς τὴν σφαῖραν οὐκ ἔσται τάξαι διὰ τὸ
μηδεμίαν διὰ τέλους ἔχειν φανερὰν ἕκαστον θέσιν,
35 εἰς δὲ τὸν οὐρανὸν ἀναβλέπουσίν ἐστι δῆλον· ἐν
μόνῳ γὰρ τούτῳ τῶν κύκλων τὰ μεταξὺ πλήρη
τοιούτων ἀστέρων ἐστίν, ἐν δὲ τοῖς ἄλλοις διαλείπει

346 b

φανερῶς. ὥστ' εἴπερ καὶ περὶ τοῦ φαίνεσθαι
κομήτας ἀποδεχόμεθα τὴν αἰτίαν ὡς εἰρημένην
μετρίως, καὶ περὶ τοῦ γάλακτος τὸν αὐτὸν ὑποληπτέον τρόπον ἔχειν· ὃ γὰρ ἐκεῖ περὶ ἕνα ἐστὶν
5 πάθος ἡ κόμη, τοῦτο περὶ κύκλον τινὰ συμβαίνει
γίγνεσθαι τὸ αὐτό, καὶ ἔστιν τὸ γάλα, ὡς εἰπεῖν
οἷον ὁριζόμενον, ἡ τοῦ μεγίστου διὰ τὴν ἔκκρισιν
κύκλου κόμη.

(Διὸ καθάπερ πρότερον εἴπομεν, οὐ πολλοὶ οὐδὲ
πολλάκις γίγνονται κομῆται, διὰ τὸ συνεχῶς ἀπο-

---

[1] post κύκλου fortasse πάλιν πλεῖον γίνεται scribenda :
praebet Ap (43. 4. 5).

---

[a] If the words from Alex. are inserted the translation
would read " and *if again it is stronger* in that segment."
The sense remains substantially the same in either case.

and in this half the stars are greater in number and density than in the other, which indicates that the cause of the light is none other than the movement of the stars : for if the Milky Way lies on the circle in which are the greatest number of stars, and [a] in that segment of the circle in which the stars appear to be of a greater density and size, it is reasonable to assume that this is the most likely cause of the phenomenon.

The circle and the stars in it can be seen on the diagram.[b] It is not possible to mark the so-called scattered stars on the sphere in the same way because none of them has a clear permanent position : but they are clear enough to anyone who looks up at the sky. For in this one alone of the circles the intervening spaces are full of stars of this sort, in the others they are clearly absent. So that if the cause of the appearance of comets given above is accepted as reasonable, it is to be assumed that something similar holds good for the Milky Way : for that which produces the tail in a single star affects a whole circle in the same way, so that the Milky Way might perhaps be defined as the tail of the greatest circle produced by the material formation we have described.

(For this reason, as we have said before,[c] comets occur neither often nor in large numbers, because the requisite formation of material has been and (So comets are infrequent.)

[b] Aristotle's extant works are lecture-notes, or were written to be used in close conjunction with the teaching work in the Lyceum. References like the present are to diagrams displayed on the walls of the lecture-room ; l. 33 suggests that it also contained a celestial globe. *Cf.* Jackson, *J. Ph.* xxxv. pp. 191 ff.

[c] 345 a 8 above.

κεκρίσθαι καὶ ἀποκρίνεσθαι καθ᾽ ἑκάστην περίοδον
10 εἰς τοῦτον τὸν τόπον αἰεὶ τὴν τοιαύτην σύστασιν.)

Περὶ μὲν οὖν τῶν γιγνομένων ἐν τῷ περὶ τὴν
γῆν κόσμῳ τῷ συνεχεῖ ταῖς φοραῖς εἴρηται, περί
τε τῆς διαδρομῆς τῶν ἄστρων καὶ τῆς ἐκπιμπρα-
μένης φλογός, ἔτι δὲ περί τε κομητῶν καὶ τοῦ
καλουμένου γάλακτος· σχεδὸν γάρ εἰσιν τοσαῦτα
15 τὰ πάθη τὰ φαινόμενα περὶ τὸν τόπον τοῦτον.

CHAPTER IX

ARGUMENT

*The lower atmosphere, the sphere of water and air below
the sphere of fire (346 b 16-20). The moisture on the earth's
surface is evaporated by the sun : when it rises into the atmosphere it is cooled again, condenses and falls as rain (346 b
20-31). Cloud is condensed vapour, mist the residue of cloud*

346 b 16 Περὶ δὲ τοῦ τῇ θέσει μὲν δευτέρου τόπου μετὰ
τοῦτον, πρώτου δὲ περὶ τὴν γῆν, λέγωμεν· οὗτος
γὰρ κοινὸς ὕδατός τε τόπος καὶ ἀέρος καὶ τῶν
συμβαινόντων περὶ τὴν ἄνω γένεσιν αὐτοῦ. λη-
20 πτέον δὲ καὶ τούτων τὰς ἀρχὰς καὶ τὰς αἰτίας
πάντων ὁμοίως.

Ἡ μὲν οὖν ὡς κινοῦσα καὶ κυρία καὶ πρώτη τῶν
ἀρχῶν ὁ κύκλος ἐστίν, ἐν ᾧ φανερῶς ἡ τοῦ ἡλίου
φορὰ διακρίνουσα καὶ συγκρίνουσα τῷ γίγνεσθαι
πλησίον ἢ πορρώτερον αἰτία τῆς γενέσεως καὶ
τῆς φθορᾶς ἐστι. μενούσης δὲ τῆς γῆς, τὸ περὶ
25 αὐτὴν ὑγρὸν ὑπὸ τῶν ἀκτίνων καὶ ὑπὸ τῆς ἄλλης
τῆς ἄνωθεν θερμότητος ἀτμιδούμενον φέρεται ἄνω·

continues to be separated off and collected at each revolution of the heavens into this region.)

This completes our account of the phenomena in the region of the terrestrial world which is continuous with the heavenly motions; that is, shooting stars and burning flames, comets and the so-called Milky Way—for these are practically all the phenomena which characterize that region.

CHAPTER IX

ARGUMENT (continued)

(346 b 32-35). *The process varies with the sun's course in the ecliptic, evaporation being greater in summer, rainfall in winter (346 b 35—347 a 8). (Difference of drizzle and rain (347 a 8-12).)*

LET us next deal with the region which lies second beneath the celestial and first above the earth. This region is the joint province of water and air, and of the various phenomena which accompany the formation of water [a] above the earth. And we must deal with their principles and causes also.

The efficient, controlling and first cause is the circle Rain. of the sun's revolution.[b] For it is evident that as it approaches or recedes the sun produces dissolution and composition and is thus the cause of generation and destruction. The earth is at rest, and the moisture about it is evaporated by the sun's rays and the other heat from above and rises upwards: but when the

---

[a] αὐτοῦ l. 19 must refer to water: so O.T. and Ideler i. p. 423.   [b] Cf. ch. 2 above; De Gen. et Corr. ii. 10.

346 b

τῆς δὲ θερμότητος ἀπολιπούσης τῆς ἀναγούσης
αὐτό, καὶ τῆς μὲν διασκεδαννυμένης πρὸς τὸν ἄνω
τόπον, τῆς δὲ καὶ σβεννυμένης διὰ τὸ μετεωρίζεσθαι
πορρώτερον εἰς τὸν ὑπὲρ τῆς γῆς ἀέρα, συνίσταται
30 πάλιν ἡ ἀτμὶς ψυχομένη διά τε τὴν ἀπόλειψιν τοῦ
θερμοῦ καὶ τὸν τόπον, καὶ γίγνεται ὕδωρ ἐξ ἀέρος·
γενόμενον δὲ πάλιν φέρεται πρὸς τὴν γῆν. ἔστι
δ' ἡ μὲν ἐξ ὕδατος ἀναθυμίασις ἀτμίς, ἡ δ' ἐξ ἀέρος
εἰς ὕδωρ νέφος· ὁμίχλη δὲ νεφέλης περίττωμα τῆς
εἰς ὕδωρ συγκρίσεως. διὸ σημεῖον μᾶλλόν ἐστι
35 εὐδίας ἢ ὑδάτων· οἷον γάρ ἐστιν ἡ ὁμίχλη νεφέλη
ἄγονος.

Γίγνεται δὲ κύκλος οὗτος μιμούμενος τὸν τοῦ ἡλίου
347 a κύκλον· ἅμα γὰρ ἐκεῖνος εἰς τὰ πλάγια μεταβάλλει
καὶ οὗτος ἄνω καὶ κάτω. δεῖ δὲ νοῆσαι τοῦτον
ὥσπερ ποταμὸν ῥέοντα κύκλῳ ἄνω καὶ κάτω,
κοινὸν ἀέρος καὶ ὕδατος· πλησίον μὲν γὰρ ὄντος
τοῦ ἡλίου ὁ τῆς ἀτμίδος ἄνω ῥεῖ ποταμός, ἀφιστα-
5 μένου δὲ ὁ τοῦ ὕδατος κάτω. καὶ τοῦτ' ἐνδελεχὲς
ἐθέλει γίγνεσθαι κατά γε τὴν τάξιν· ὥστ' εἴπερ
ἠνίττοντο τὸν ὠκεανὸν οἱ πρότερον, τάχ' ἂν τοῦτον
τὸν ποταμὸν λέγοιεν τὸν κύκλῳ ῥέοντα περὶ τὴν
γῆν.

Ἀναγομένου δὲ τοῦ ὑγροῦ αἰεὶ διὰ τὴν τοῦ θερμοῦ
δύναμιν καὶ πάλιν φερομένου κάτω διὰ τὴν ψύξιν
10 πρὸς τὴν γῆν, οἰκείως¹ τὰ ὀνόματα τοῖς πάθεσιν
κεῖται καί τισιν διαφοραῖς αὐτῶν· ὅταν μὲν γὰρ
κατὰ μικρὰ φέρηται, ψακάδες, ὅταν δὲ κατὰ μείζω
μόρια, ὑετὸς καλεῖται.

70

heat which caused it to rise leaves it, some being dispersed into the upper region, some being quenched by rising so high into the air above the earth, the vapour cools and condenses again as a result of the loss of heat and the height and turns from air into water : and having become water falls again onto the earth.[a] The exhalation from water is vapour ; the formation of water from air produces cloud. Mist is the residue of the condensation of air into water, and is therefore a sign of fine weather rather than of rain ; for mist is as it were unproductive cloud.[b]

Cloud and Mist.

This cycle of changes reflects the sun's annual movement : for the moisture rises and falls as the sun moves in the ecliptic. One should think of it as a river with a circular course, which rises and falls and is composed of a mixture of water and air. For when the sun is near the stream of vapour rises, when it recedes it falls again. And in this order the cycle continues indefinitely. And if there is any hidden meaning in the " river of Ocean " of the ancients, they may well have meant this river which flows in a circle round the earth.

Winter and Summer.

Moisture then is always made to rise by heat and to fall again to the earth by cold ; and there are appropriate names for these processes and for some of their sub-species—for instance when water falls in small drops it is called drizzle, when in larger drops, rain.

Drizzle and Rain.

[a] Cf. 359 b 34 ff.
[b] Vapour condenses into cloud, which subsequently falls as rain. Mist is what is left over in the process of condensation ; it is therefore " unproductive " in the sense that it will not produce rain, and is thus a sign of fine weather.

___

[1] δὲ post οἰκείως coll. Thurot, qui ἀναγομένου . . . γῆν cum antecedentibus coniungit.

CHAPTER X

ARGUMENT

Dew and hoar frost are due to moisture which has evaporated during the day, but has not risen far and falls again when cooled at night. When the vapour freezes before condensing the result is hoar frost, when it condenses the result

347 a 13 Ἐκ δὲ τοῦ καθ' ἡμέραν ἀτμίζοντος ὅσον ἂν μὴ μετεωρισθῇ δι' ὀλιγότητα τοῦ ἀνάγοντος αὐτὸ
15 πυρὸς πρὸς τὸ ἀναγόμενον ὕδωρ, πάλιν καταφερόμενον ὅταν ψυχθῇ νύκτωρ, καλεῖται δρόσος καὶ πάχνη, πάχνη μὲν ὅταν ἡ ἀτμὶς παγῇ πρὶν εἰς ὕδωρ συγκριθῆναι πάλιν (γίγνεται δὲ χειμῶνος, καὶ μᾶλλον ἐν τοῖς χειμερινοῖς τόποις), δρόσος δ' ὅταν συγκριθῇ εἰς ὕδωρ ἡ ἀτμίς, καὶ μήθ' οὕτως ἔχῃ ἡ
20 ἀλέα ὥστε ξηρᾶναι τὸ ἀναχθέν, μήθ' οὕτω ψῦχος ὥστε παγῆναι τὴν ἀτμίδα αὐτὴν διὰ τὸ ἢ τὸν τόπον ἀλεεινότερον ἢ τὴν ὥραν εἶναι· γίγνεται γὰρ μᾶλλον ἡ δρόσος ἐν εὐδίᾳ καὶ ἐν τοῖς εὐδιεινοτέροις τόποις, ἡ δὲ πάχνη, καθάπερ εἴρηται, τοὐναντίον· δῆλον
25 γὰρ ὡς ἡ ἀτμὶς θερμότερον ὕδατος (ἔχει γὰρ τὸ ἀνάγον ἔτι πῦρ), ὥστε πλείονος ψυχρότητος αὐτὴν πῆξαι. γίγνεται δ' ἄμφω αἰθρίας τε καὶ νηνεμίας· οὔτε γὰρ ἀναχθήσεται μὴ οὔσης αἰθρίας, οὔτε συστῆναι δύναιτ' ἂν ἀνέμου πνέοντος.

Σημεῖον δ' ὅτι γίγνεται ταῦτα διὰ τὸ μὴ πόρρω μετεωρίζεσθαι τὴν ἀτμίδα· ἐν γὰρ τοῖς ὄρεσιν οὐ
30 γίγνεται πάχνη. αἰτία δὲ μία μὲν αὕτη, ὅτι ἀνάγεται ἐκ τῶν κοίλων καὶ ἐφύδρων τόπων, ὥστε καθάπερ φορτίον φέρουσα πλέον ἢ ἀνάγουσα θερμό-

CHAPTER X

ARGUMENT (*continued*)

is dew. Dew forms in warm and fine weather, frost in cold and clear (347 a 13-28). A proof that they are so caused is that hoar frost does not form on mountains : reasons for this (347 a 29-35). Conditions in which dew forms (347 a 35-b 11).

ANY moisture evaporated during the day that does not rise far because the amount of the fire raising it compared to the amount of water that is being raised is small, falls again when it is chilled during the night and is called dew or hoar frost. It is hoar frost when the evaporation is frozen before it has condensed into water again ; this happens in winter, and more readily in wintry places than elsewhere. It is dew when the vapour has condensed into water and the heat is not so great as to dry up the moisture that has risen nor the cold so intense as to freeze the vapour, either because the district or the season is too warm. Dew tends to form rather in fair weather and mild districts ; hoar frost, as said, under opposite conditions. For it is obvious that vapour is warmer than water, as it still contains the fire that caused it to rise, and so needs more cold to freeze it. Both dew and hoar frost form in clear calm weather : no moisture will rise except in clear weather, and no condensation is possible in a wind.

A proof that they are due to the vapour not rising very far is that no hoar frost is formed on mountains. There are two reasons for this : firstly, that vapour rises from hollow, damp places, so that the heat which is causing it to rise is unable, as if it were carrying

Cause of dew and frost.

A proof that this is the cause.

73

347 a

της ἢ καθ' ἑαυτὴν οὐ δύναται μετεωρίζειν ἐπὶ
πολὺν τόπον αὐτὸ τοῦ ὕψους, ἀλλ' ἐγγὺς ἀφίησι
πάλιν· ἑτέρα δ' ὅτι καὶ ῥεῖ μάλιστα ὁ ἀὴρ ῥέων
35 ἐν τοῖς ὑψηλοῖς, ὃς διαλύει τὴν σύστασιν τὴν τοιαύτην.

Γίγνεται δ' ἡ δρόσος πανταχοῦ νοτίοις, οὐ βορείοις, πλὴν ἐν τῷ Πόντῳ. ἐκεῖ δὲ τοὐναντίον·
347 b βορείοις μὲν γὰρ γίγνεται, νοτίοις δ' οὐ γίγνεται.
αἴτιον δ' ὁμοίως ὥσπερ ὅτι εὐδίας μὲν γίγνεται,
χειμῶνος δ' οὔ· ὁ μὲν γὰρ νότος εὐδίαν ποιεῖ, ὁ δὲ
βορέας χειμῶνα· ψυχρὸς γάρ, ὥστ' ἐκ τοῦ χειμῶνος
τῆς ἀναθυμιάσεως σβέννυσι τὴν θερμότητα. ἐν
5 δὲ τῷ Πόντῳ ὁ μὲν νότος οὐχ οὕτως ποιεῖ εὐδίαν
ὥστε γίγνεσθαι ἀτμίδα, ὁ δὲ βορέας διὰ τὴν ψυχρότητα ἀντιπεριστὰς τὸ θερμὸν ἀθροίζει, ὥστε
πλέον ἀτμίζει μᾶλλον. πολλάκις δὲ τοῦτο καὶ ἐν
τοῖς ἔξω τόποις ἰδεῖν γιγνόμενον ἔστιν· ἀτμίζει γὰρ
τὰ φρέατα βορείοις μᾶλλον ἢ νοτίοις· ἀλλὰ τὰ μὲν
10 βόρεια σβέννυσιν πρὶν συστῆναί τι πλῆθος, ἐν δὲ
τοῖς νοτίοις ἐᾶται ἀθροίζεσθαι ἡ ἀναθυμίασις.

Αὐτὸ δὲ τὸ ὕδωρ οὐ πήγνυται, καθάπερ ἐν τῷ
περὶ τὰ νέφη τόπῳ.

---

[a] *Cf.* above, ch. 3, 340 b 33 ff. and note *ad loc.*
[b] On ἀντιπεριστάναι *cf.* ch. 12, note *b* on p. 82 below.
Here it means to " surround and compress," the " compress "
being repeated in ἀθροίζει.

a burden too heavy for it, to lift it to a great height, but lets it fall again while still close to the earth. Secondly, that the flow of air is especially strong at great heights and this dissolves a formation of this kind.[a]

Dew is formed by south winds, and not by north, everywhere except in Pontus. There the opposite is true, for it is produced there by north winds and not by south. The cause is the same as that which makes it form in mild weather and not in wintry ; for the south wind brings mild weather, while the north wind, being cold, brings wintry weather, by which the heat of the exhalation is quenched. But in Pontus the south wind does not make the weather mild enough to produce vapour : while the north wind, because it is cold, surrounds [b] and compresses the heat and so causes more evaporation. This is a thing which it is often possible to observe happening in places outside Pontus. For instance, wells give off vapour in north winds rather than in south ; but the north winds quench the heat before any quantity of it has collected, while the south winds allow the exhalation to accumulate.[c]

The water formed from vapour does not freeze on the earth as it does in the region of the clouds.[d]

Conditions of formation of dew.

---

[c] And so, except in Pontus, dew forms in south winds and not in north.

[d] The point of this sentence, which the next chapter elaborates, is that while to dew and frost on the earth there correspond rain and snow in the clouds, there is nothing on the earth to correspond to hail. As Ideler i. p. 432 notes, the sentence comes rather awkwardly at the end of this chapter and might be better placed at the beginning of the next ; but I have kept the conventional chapter division to avoid confusion.

ARISTOTLE

CHAPTER XI

ARGUMENT

*From the clouds there fall as a result of refrigeration rain,
snow and hail. Rain and snow correspond to dew and frost
respectively, are due to similar causes and differ only in
degree : rain is due to the condensation of a large quantity*

347 b 12 Ἐκεῖθεν γὰρ τρία φοιτᾷ σώματα συνιστάμενα διὰ
τὴν ψῦξιν, ὕδωρ καὶ χιὼν καὶ χάλαζα. τούτων δὲ
15 τὰ μὲν δύο ἀνάλογον καὶ διὰ τὰς αὐτὰς αἰτίας
γίγνεται τοῖς κάτω, διαφέροντα τῷ μᾶλλον καὶ
ἧττον καὶ πλήθει καὶ ὀλιγότητι· χιὼν γὰρ καὶ
πάχνη ταὐτόν, καὶ ὑετὸς καὶ δρόσος, ἀλλὰ τὸ μὲν
πολὺ τὸ δ' ὀλίγον. ὁ μὲν γὰρ ὑετὸς ἐκ πολλῆς
ἀτμίδος γίγνεται ψυχομένης· τούτου δ' αἴτιον ὅ τε
20 τόπος πολὺς καὶ ὁ χρόνος ὤν, ἐν ᾧ συλλέγεται καὶ
ἐξ οὗ. τὸ δ' ὀλίγον ἡ δρόσος· ἐφήμερος γὰρ ἡ
σύστασις καὶ ὁ τόπος μικρός· δηλοῖ τε ἥ τε γένεσις
οὖσα ταχεῖα καὶ βραχὺ τὸ πλῆθος. ὁμοίως δὲ καὶ
πάχνη καὶ χιών· ὅταν γὰρ παγῇ τὸ νέφος, χιών
ἐστιν, ὅταν δ' ἡ ἀτμίς, πάχνη. διὸ ἢ ὥρας ἢ χώρας
25 ἐστὶν σημεῖον ψυχρᾶς· οὐ γὰρ ἂν ἐπήγνυτο ἔτι
πολλῆς ἐνούσης θερμότητος, εἰ μὴ ἐπεκράτει τὸ
ψῦχος· ἐν γὰρ τῷ νέφει ἔτι ἔνεστιν πολὺ θερμὸν τὸ
ὑπόλοιπον τοῦ ἐξατμίσαντος ἐκ τῆς γῆς τὸ ὑγρόν.[1]

Χάλαζα δ' ἐκεῖ μὲν γίγνεται, ἐν δὲ τῷ πλησίον
τῆς γῆς ἀτμίζοντι τοῦτ' ἐκλείπει· καθάπερ γὰρ εἴ-
30 πομεν, ὡς μὲν ἐκεῖ χιών, ἐνταῦθα γίγνεται πάχνη,
ὡς δ' ἐκεῖ ὑετός, ἐνταῦθα δρόσος· ὡς δ' ἐκεῖ χάλαζα,

CHAPTER XI

ARGUMENT (*continued*)

of vapour, dew of a small quantity, snow is frozen cloud, as frost is frozen vapour (347 b 12-28). But there is no analogy on the earth itself to hail (347 b 28-33).

For from the clouds there fall three bodies formed by refrigeration, water, snow and hail. Two of these correspond to and are due to the same causes as dew and frost on the earth, differing from them only in degree and amount. For snow is the same as frost, rain the same as dew, there being a merely quantitative difference between them. For rain is the result of the cooling of a large body of vapour, which owes its quantity to the length of time during which and the size of space in which it collects. Dew, on the other hand, is produced by small quantities of vapour, which collect for a day only and over a small area, as is shown by the rapidity with which it forms and its scanty quantity. The same is true of hoar frost and snow : when cloud freezes snow is produced, when vapour, hoar frost. So snow is a sign of a cold season or a cold country. For the cloud would not have frozen, since it still contains much heat, unless the cold predominated : for a good deal of the heat which caused the moisture to evaporate from the earth is still left in the cloud.

Hail forms at higher levels, but there is nothing to correspond to it in the evaporation close to the earth : for as we have said, snow above corresponds to frost below, rain above to dew below : but there

---

[1] ὑγρὸν πυρός E_rec. Fobes : πυρός om. E_1 F Ap O.T.

347 b

ἐνταῦθα οὐκ ἀνταποδίδωσι τὸ ὅμοιον. τὸ δ' αἴτιον
εἰποῦσι περὶ χαλάζης ἔσται δῆλον.

CHAPTER XII

ARGUMENT

Hail. A. Difficulties. (1) *Hail is ice : yet hailstorms are
commonest in spring and summer, i.e. in warm weather.*
(2) *How does the necessary water remain in the air long enough
to be frozen* (347 b 34—348 a 14) ? *B. Anaxagoras's view.
Hail is due to cloud being forced into the upper atmosphere
and there frozen* (348 a 14-20). *Criticisms* (348 a 20-b 2).
*C. Aristotle's own view. Heat and cold react on one another.
When cold is compressed by heat surrounding it, it may* (a)
cause heavy rain or (b), *when the compression is greater and
the consequent refrigeration quicker, cause hail. The nearer*

347 b 34   Δεῖ δὲ λαβεῖν ἅμα καὶ τὰ συμβαίνοντα περὶ τὴν
35 γένεσιν αὐτῆς, τά τε μὴ πλανῶντα καὶ τὰ δοκοῦντ'
εἶναι παράλογα.

Ἔστι μὲν γὰρ ἡ χάλαζα κρύσταλλος, πήγνυται δὲ
τὸ ὕδωρ τοῦ χειμῶνος· αἱ δὲ χάλαζαι γίγνονται
348 a ἔαρος μὲν καὶ μετοπώρου μάλιστα, εἶτα δὲ καὶ
τῆς ὀπώρας, χειμῶνος δ' ὀλιγάκις, καὶ ὅταν ἧττον
ᾖ ψῦχος. καὶ ὅλως δὲ γίγνονται χάλαζαι μὲν ἐν
τοῖς εὐδιεινοτέροις τόποις, αἱ δὲ χιόνες ἐν τοῖς
ψυχροτέροις.

5 Ἄτοπον δὲ καὶ τὸ πήγνυσθαι ὕδωρ ἐν τῷ ἄνω
τόπῳ· οὔτε γὰρ παγῆναι δυνατὸν πρὶν γενέσθαι
ὕδωρ, οὔτε τὸ ὕδωρ οὐδένα χρόνον οἷόν τε μένειν
μετέωρον ὄν. ἀλλὰ μὴν οὐδ' ὥσπερ αἱ ψακάδες
ἄνω μὲν ὀχοῦνται διὰ μικρότητα, ἐνδιατρίψασαι δ'

is no analogous phenomenon below to correspond to hail above. The reason for this will become clear when we have dealt with hail.

CHAPTER XII

ARGUMENT (continued)

the earth and the more intense the refrigeration, the heavier the rain and the larger the hailstones. Hail is more frequent in spring and autumn because there is more moisture in the air at these seasons (348 b 2-30). Refrigeration takes place more quickly if the water is warmed first (so hail will form more easily in warm weather) (348 b 30—349 a 4). This is also the reason for the violent summer rainfalls in Arabia and Aethiopia (349 a 4-9). So much for rain, dew, snow, frost and hail (349 a 9-11).

In considering the process by which hail is produced, we must take into account both facts whose interpretation is straightforward and those which appear to be inexplicable.

(1) Hail is ice, and water freezes in the winter : A. Difficulties. yet hailstorms are commonest in spring and autumn, rather less common at the end of the summer, and rare in winter when they only occur when it is not very cold. And, in general, hailstorms occur in milder districts, snowstorms in colder.

(2) It is also odd that water should freeze in the upper region ; for it cannot freeze before it becomes water, and yet having become water it cannot remain suspended in the air for any length of time. Nor can we maintain that just as drops of water ride aloft because of their minuteness and rest on the

348 a

ἐπὶ τοῦ ἀέρος, ὥσπερ καὶ ἐπὶ τοῦ ὕδατος γῆ καὶ
10 χρυσὸς διὰ μικρομέρειαν πολλάκις ἐπιπλέουσιν, οὕτως ἐπὶ τοῦ ἀέρος τὸ ὕδωρ, συνελθόντων δὲ πολλῶν
μικρῶν μεγάλαι καταφέρονται ψακάδες· τοῦτο
γὰρ οὐκ ἐνδέχεται γενέσθαι ἐπὶ τῆς χαλάζης· οὐ
γὰρ συμφύεται τὰ πεπηγότα ὥσπερ τὰ ὑγρά. δῆλον
οὖν ὅτι ἄνω τοσοῦτον ὕδωρ ἔμεινεν· οὐ γὰρ ἂν
ἐπάγη τοσοῦτον.

15 Τοῖς μὲν οὖν δοκεῖ τοῦ πάθους αἴτιον εἶναι τούτου
καὶ τῆς γενέσεως, ὅταν ἀπωσθῇ τὸ νέφος εἰς τὸν
ἄνω τόπον μᾶλλον ὄντα ψυχρὸν διὰ τὸ λήγειν ἐκεῖ
τὰς ἀπὸ τῆς γῆς τῶν ἀκτίνων ἀνακλάσεις, ἐλθὸν
δ' ἐκεῖ πήγνυσθαι τὸ ὕδωρ· διὸ καὶ θέρους μᾶλλον
καὶ ἐν ταῖς ἀλεειναῖς χώραις γίγνεσθαι τὰς χαλάζας,
20 ὅτι ἐπὶ πλέον τὸ θερμὸν ἀνωθεῖ ἀπὸ τῆς γῆς τὰς
νεφέλας. συμβαίνει δ' ἐν τοῖς σφόδρα ὑψηλοῖς
ἥκιστα γίγνεσθαι χάλαζαν· καίτοι ἔδει, ὥσπερ καὶ
τὴν χιόνα ὁρῶμεν ἐπὶ τοῖς ὑψηλοῖς μάλιστα γιγνομένην. ἔτι δὲ πολλάκις ὦπται νέφη φερόμενα σὺν
25 ψόφῳ πολλῷ παρ' αὐτὴν τὴν γῆν, ὥστε φοβερὸν
εἶναι τοῖς ἀκούουσιν καὶ ὁρῶσιν ὡς ἐσομένου τινὸς
μείζονος. ὁτὲ δὲ καὶ ἄνευ ψόφου τοιούτων ὀφθέν-
των νεφῶν χάλαζα γίγνεται πολλὴ καὶ τὸ μέγεθος
ἄπιστος, καὶ τοῖς σχήμασιν οὐ στρογγύλη, διὰ τὸ
μὴ πολὺν χρόνον γίγνεσθαι τὴν φορὰν αὐτῆς ὡς
30 πλησίον τῆς πήξεως γενομένης τῆς γῆς, ἀλλ' οὐχ
ὥσπερ ἐκεῖνοί φασιν. ἀλλὰ μὴν ἀναγκαῖον ὑπὸ
τοῦ μάλιστ' αἰτίου τῆς πήξεως μεγάλας γίγνεσθαι
χαλάζας· κρύσταλλος γὰρ ἡ χάλαζα, καὶ τοῦτο
παντὶ δῆλον. μεγάλαι δ' εἰσὶν αἱ τοῖς σχήμασιν

80

air, like minute particles of earth or gold that often float on water, so here the water floats on the air till a number of the small drops coalesce to form the large drops that fall. This cannot take place in the case of hail, because frozen drops cannot coalesce like liquid ones. Clearly then drops of water of the requisite size must have been suspended in the air : otherwise their size when frozen could not have been so large.

Some [a] then think that the cause of the origin of hail is as follows : when a cloud is forced up into the upper region where the temperature is lower because reflection of the sun's rays from the earth does not reach it,[b] the water when it gets there is frozen : and so hailstorms occur more often in summer and in warm districts because the heat forces the clouds up farther from the earth. But (1) in the very high places hail falls very infrequently ; but on their theory this should not be so, for we can see that snow falls mostly in high places. (2) Clouds have often been seen swept along with a great noise close to the earth, and have struck fear into those that heard and saw them as portents of some greater catastrophe. But sometimes, when such clouds have been seen without any accompanying noise, hail falls in great quantities and the stones are of an incredible size, and irregular in shape ; the reason being that they have not had long to fall because they were frozen close to the earth, and not, as the theory we are criticizing maintains, far above it. (3) Moreover, large hailstones must be formed by an intense cause of freezing : for it is obvious to everyone that hail is ice. But hail-

B. Anax-agoras's view.

---

[a] Anaxagoras, as Aristotle tells us at b 12 below : Diels 59 A 85.   [b] Cf. 340 a 27 ff.

348 a

μὴ στρογγύλαι. τοῦτο δ' ἐστὶ σημεῖον τοῦ παγῆναι
35 πλησίον τῆς γῆς· αἱ γὰρ φερόμεναι πόρρωθεν διὰ
τὸ φέρεσθαι μακρὰν περιθραυόμεναι γίγνονται τό
τε σχῆμα περιφερεῖς καὶ τὸ μέγεθος ἐλάττους.

348 b Ὅτι μὲν οὖν οὐ τῷ ἀπωθεῖσθαι εἰς τὸν ἄνω
τόπον τὸν ψυχρὸν ἡ πῆξις συμβαίνει, δῆλον.

Ἀλλ' ἐπειδὴ ὁρῶμεν ὅτι γίγνεται ἀντιπερίστασις
τῷ θερμῷ καὶ ψυχρῷ ἀλλήλοις (διὸ ἔν τε ταῖς
ἀλέαις ψυχρὰ τὰ κάτω τῆς γῆς καὶ ἀλεεινὰ ἐν τοῖς
5 πάγοις), τοῦτο δεῖ νομίζειν καὶ ἐν τῷ ἄνω γίγνεσθαι
τόπῳ, ὥστ' ἐν ταῖς ἀλεεινοτέραις ὥραις ἀντιπερι-
ιστάμενον εἴσω τὸ ψυχρὸν διὰ τὴν κύκλῳ θερμό-

ᵃ The largest hailstones need the intensest cold to form
them : therefore on this theory they should be formed high
up, where it is coldest : but their shape shows that they are
not formed high up but close to the ground : therefore the
theory must be wrong. This argument is an extension of (2)
showing, like it, that hail forms low down and not high up.

ᵇ ἀντιπεριίστημι(and ἀντιπερίστασις correspondingly)has two
meanings given, by L & Sⁿ, as (1) to oppose by surrounding, to
compress : *pass.* to be compressed, (2) *pass.* to be replaced by
another substance. It occurs in meaning (2) at 360 b 25 and at
382 a 12, 14, where it is used of water which yields place to
any body immersed in it. It is used in the same sense in
De Resp. 472 b 16 ; and the words ἀντιμεθίστημι, -μετάστασις
are used at *Phys.* 208 b 2, 209 b 25, 211 b 27 with the same
meaning of replacement of one substance by another. At
Phys. 215 a 15, 267 a 16, 18 ἀντιπερίστασις is used to describe
the Platonic theory of the motion of a projectile by περίωσις :
Timaeus 79 A ff., *cf.* Cornford, *Plato's Cosmology*, pp. 315 f.
For a full definition of the word in this sense *cf.* Simplicius
ad Phys. viii. 267 a 16 : quoted Bonitz, *Index* 65 b 14. Sense
(1) of the verb is found at 347 b 6, 361 a 1, 382 b 10 and
in the present chapter 348 b 6, 16 ; of the noun at 349 a 8.

stones that are not rounded in shape are large in size, which is a proof that they have frozen close to the earth : for stones which fall farther are worn down in the course of their fall and so become round in shape and smaller in size.[a]

It is clear then that the freezing does not take place because the cloud is forced up into the cold upper region.

Now we know that hot and cold have a mutual reaction [b] on one another (which is the reason why subterranean places are cold in hot weather and warm in frosty weather). This reaction we must suppose takes place in the upper region, so that in warmer seasons the cold is concentrated within by the surrounding heat. This sometimes causes a rapid forma-

C. Aristotle's own view. Mutual reaction of heat and cold the cause.

Examples from elsewhere are, verb *Problems* 909 a 23, 936 b 16, 943 a 11 ; noun *Problems* 867 b 32, *De Somn.* 457 b 2, 458 a 27 (sleep due to a concentration (*cf.* συνεωσμένη 458 a 10) of vital warmth by cold). There remains the use of the noun in the present passage 348 b 2, which L&S list under sense (2). At first sight this meaning seems to suit it better : yet twice in the next dozen lines the verb is used clearly in sense (1), and it is therefore more likely that the noun bears this sense too. The apparent ambiguity perhaps throws some light on the relation of the two senses. Substance *a* gives place to substance *b* (sense (2)) : from this it is not a long step to think of *a* and *b* exercising a mutual reaction or repulsion (*cf.* the O.T.'s " recoil " here). This explains the example which Aristotle gives, that caves are warm in winter, cold in summer. For in winter the surrounding cold drives the heat underground, in summer vice versa : *cf.* Alex. 50. 23, where the meaning hovers instructively between mutual replacement (*cf.* ἀντιμεθιστάμενον l. 26) and mutual repulsion. Finally we get compression when a larger quantity of *a* (or *b*) drives together, as it were, and so compresses a smaller quantity of *b* (or *a*). This is the way hail is formed : compare the account of sleep in the *De Somn.* (sleep due to the vital warmth being driven together by cold).

348 b

τητα ότὲ μὲν ταχὺ ὕδωρ ἐκ νέφους ποιεῖ[1]· διὸ καὶ
αἱ ψακάδες πολὺ μείζους ἐν ταῖς ἀλεειναῖς γίγνονται
10 ἡμέραις ἢ ἐν τῷ χειμῶνι, καὶ ὕδατα λαβρότερα·
λαβρότερα μὲν γὰρ λέγεται ὅταν ἀθρούτερα, ἀθρούτερα δὲ διὰ τὸ τάχος τῆς πυκνώσεως. (τοῦτο δὲ
γίγνεται αὐτὸ τοὐναντίον ἢ ὡς Ἀναξαγόρας λέγει·
ὁ μὲν γὰρ ὅταν εἰς τὸν ψυχρὸν ἀέρα ἐπανέλθῃ φησὶ
15 τοῦτο πάσχειν, ἡμεῖς δ᾽ ὅταν εἰς τὸν θερμὸν κατ-
έλθῃ, καὶ μάλιστα ὅταν μάλιστα.) ὅταν δ᾽ ἔτι
μᾶλλον ἀντιπεριστῇ ἐντὸς τὸ ψυχρὸν ὑπὸ τοῦ ἔξω
θερμοῦ, ὕδωρ ποιῆσαν ἔπηξεν καὶ γίγνεται χάλαζα.
συμβαίνει δὲ τοῦτο ὅταν θᾶττον ᾖ ἡ πῆξις ἢ ἡ τοῦ
ὕδατος φορὰ ἡ κάτω· εἰ γὰρ φέρεται μὲν ἐν τοσῷδε
20 χρόνῳ, ἡ δὲ ψυχρότης σφοδρὰ οὖσα ἐν ἐλάττονι
ἔπηξεν, οὐδὲν κωλύει μετέωρον παγῆναι, ἐὰν ἡ
πῆξις ἐν ἐλάττονι γίγνηται χρόνῳ τῆς κάτω φορᾶς.
καὶ ὅσῳ δ᾽ ἂν ἐγγύτερον καὶ ἀθρωτέρα γένηται
ἡ πῆξις, τά τε ὕδατα λαβρότερα γίγνεται καὶ αἱ
ψακάδες καὶ αἱ χάλαζαι μείζους διὰ τὸ βραχὺν
25 φέρεσθαι τόπον. καὶ οὐ πυκναὶ αἱ ψακάδες αἱ
μεγάλαι πίπτουσιν διὰ τὴν αὐτὴν αἰτίαν. ἧττον
δὲ τοῦ θέρους γίγνεται ἢ ἔαρος καὶ μετοπώρου,
μᾶλλον μέντοι ἢ χειμῶνος, ὅτι ξηρότερος ὁ ἀὴρ
τοῦ θέρους· ἐν δὲ τῷ ἔαρι ἔτι ὑγρός, ἐν δὲ τῷ μετ-
οπώρῳ ἤδη ὑγραίνεται. γίγνονται δέ ποτε, καθ-
30 άπερ εἴρηται, καὶ τῆς ὀπώρας χάλαζαι διὰ τὴν
αὐτὴν αἰτίαν.

[1] post ποιεῖ add. ὁτὲ δὲ χάλαζα N_rec., ὁτὲ δὲ χάλαζαν Pc PlM.

---

[a] " Omit ὅτε δὲ χάλαζαν in l. 8, with all the mss. except
N_corr. ὁτὲ μὲν is answered by ὅταν δ᾽ b 15 below and the inter-
84

tion of water from cloud.[a] And for this reason you get larger raindrops on warm days than in winter and more violent rainfall—rainfall is said to be more violent when it is heavier, and a heavier rainfall is caused by rapidity of condensation. (The process is just the opposite of what Anaxagoras says it is. He says it takes place when cloud rises into the cold air : we say it takes place when cloud descends into the warm air and is most violent when the cloud descends farthest). Sometimes, on the other hand, the cold is even more concentrated within by the heat outside it, and freezes the water which it has produced, so forming hail. This happens when the water freezes before it has time to fall. For if it takes a given time (t^1) to fall, but the cold being intense freezes it in a lesser time (t^2), there is nothing to prevent it freezing in the air, if the time (t^2) taken to freeze it is shorter than the time (t^1) of its fall. The nearer the earth and the more intense the freezing, the more violent the rainfall and the larger the drops or the hailstones because of the shortness of their fall. For the same reason [b] large raindrops do not fall thickly. Hail is rarer in the summer than in spring or autumn, though commoner than in winter, because in summer the air is drier : but in spring it is still moist, in autumn it is beginning to become so. For the same reason hailstones do sometimes occur in late summer, as we have said.[c]

vening lines διὸ καὶ . . . ὅταν μάλιστα are parenthetical . . ." (O.T.).

[b] It is not at all clear why this is so, cf. Alex. 51. 32 and Phil. 130. 4. Perhaps Aristotle thinks of large *and few* as an alternative to small *and many* : if a given amount of vapour is condensed into large drops, as here, there will be fewer of them than if it was condensed into small.   [c] 348 a 1.

Συμβάλλεται δ' ἔτι πρὸς τὴν ταχυτῆτα τῆς
πήξεως καὶ τὸ προτεθερμάνθαι τὸ ὕδωρ· θᾶττον
γὰρ ψύχεται. διὸ πολλοὶ ὅταν τὸ ὕδωρ[1] ψῦξαι
ταχὺ βουληθῶσιν, εἰς τὸν ἥλιον τιθέασι πρῶτον,
35 καὶ οἱ περὶ τὸν Πόντον ὅταν ἐπὶ τοῦ κρυστάλλου
σκηνοποιῶνται πρὸς τὰς τῶν ἰχθύων θήρας (θηρεύ-
ουσι γὰρ διακόπτοντες τὸν κρύσταλλον), ὕδωρ
349 a θερμὸν περιχέουσι τοῖς καλάμοις διὰ τὸ θᾶττον
πήγνυσθαι· χρῶνται γὰρ τῷ κρυστάλλῳ ὥσπερ τῷ
μολύβδῳ, ἵν' ἠρεμῶσιν οἱ κάλαμοι. θερμὸν δὲ
γίγνεται ταχὺ τὸ συνιστάμενον ὕδωρ ἔν τε ταῖς
χώραις καὶ ταῖς ὥραις ταῖς ἀλεειναῖς.
5 Γίγνεται δὲ καὶ περὶ τὴν Ἀραβίαν καὶ τὴν Αἰθιο-
πίαν τοῦ θέρους τὰ ὕδατα καὶ οὐ τοῦ χειμῶνος, καὶ
ταῦτα ῥαγδαῖα, καὶ τῆς αὐτῆς ἡμέρας πολλάκις,
διὰ τὴν αὐτὴν αἰτίαν· ταχὺ γὰρ ψύχεται τῇ ἀντι-
περιστάσει, ἢ γίγνεται διὰ τὸ ἀλεεινὴν εἶναι τὴν
χώραν ἰσχυρῶς.
10 Περὶ μὲν οὖν ὑετοῦ καὶ δρόσου καὶ νιφετοῦ καὶ
πάχνης καὶ χαλάζης, διὰ τίν' αἰτίαν γίγνεται καὶ
τίς ἡ φύσις αὐτῶν ἐστιν, εἰρήσθω τοσαῦτα.

---

[1] τὸ ὕδωρ corr. F Ap : τὸ θερμὸν F₁ cet. PlV : om. PlM.

---

[a] τὸ θερμόν, the reading adopted by the O.T. " with all the

CHAPTER XIII

ARGUMENT

Our next subjects are wind, rivers and the sea.
(I) Wind.—Some people say wind is a current of air :

If the water has been previously heated, this con- Warm water cools more quickly.
tributes to the rapidity with which it freezes : for it
cools more quickly. (Thus so many people when they
want to cool water [a] quickly first stand it in the sun :
and the inhabitants of Pontus when they encamp on
the ice to fish—they catch fish through a hole which
they make in the ice—pour hot water on their rods
because it freezes quicker, using the ice like solder
to fix their rods.) And water that condenses in the
air in warm districts and seasons gets hot quickly.[b]

For the same reason in Arabia and Aethiopia rain Arabia and Aethiopia.
falls in the summer and not in the winter, and falls
with violence and many times on the same day : for
the clouds are cooled quickly by the reaction due to
the great heat of the country.

So much then for our account of the causes and
nature of rain, dew, snow, hoar frost and hail.

mss.," must be wrong in spite of the mss. authority. The only
point in putting the water in the sun is to warm it so that it
may cool more quickly. If it is already warm when put in
the sun the whole point of the process is lost.

[b] Aristotle is returning to the argument of ll. 30-32, which
he interrupted at διό l. 32 in order to give examples (Thurot :
cf. Ol. 93. 34) ; διό . . . κάλαμοι 349 a 3 is really parenthetical and is printed as a parenthesis in the translation.
The point of the paragraph is to give another reason for the
formation of hail (ice) in summer, τὸ συνιστάμενον ὕδωρ being
the water which freezes into hail.

CHAPTER XIII

ARGUMENT (continued)

some produce the ludicrous view that all winds are the same
wind blowing in different directions. We must investigate

the nature and origin of wind (349 a 12–b 1). (Aristotle here drops the subject of wind, and does not resume it until Book II. ch. 4.)

(II) *Rivers.—There are some who believe that rivers flow from subterranean reservoirs fed by rainfall* (349 b 1-15). *Criticisms (in the course of which Aristotle's own view emerges).* (1) *Such reservoirs would have to be impossibly large* (349 b 15-19). (2) *Condensation produces water below the earth as well as above it* (349 b 19-27). (3) *Rainfall does not collect into reservoirs. Most of it is absorbed by mountains*

349 a 12   Περὶ δὲ ἀνέμων καὶ πάντων πνευμάτων, ἔτι δὲ ποταμῶν καὶ θαλάττης λέγωμεν, πρῶτον καὶ περὶ τούτων διαπορήσαντες πρὸς ἡμᾶς αὐτούς· ὥσπερ
15 γὰρ καὶ περὶ ἄλλων, οὕτως καὶ περὶ τούτων οὐδὲν παρειλήφαμεν λεγόμενον τοιοῦτον ὃ μὴ κἂν ὁ τυχὼν εἴπειεν.

Εἰσὶ δέ τινες οἵ φασι τὸν καλούμενον ἀέρα κινούμενον μὲν καὶ ῥέοντα ἄνεμον εἶναι, συνιστάμενον δὲ τὸν αὐτὸν τοῦτον πάλιν νέφος καὶ ὕδωρ, ὡς τῆς αὐτῆς φύσεως οὔσης ὕδατος καὶ πνεύματος, καὶ
20 τὸν ἄνεμον εἶναι κίνησιν ἀέρος. διὸ καὶ τῶν σοφῶς βουλομένων λέγειν τινὲς ἕνα φασὶν ἄνεμον εἶναι πάντας τοὺς ἀνέμους, ὅτι συμπέπτωκε καὶ τὸν ἀέρα τὸν κινούμενον ἕνα καὶ τὸν αὐτὸν εἶναι πάντα, δοκεῖν δὲ διαφέρειν οὐδὲν διαφέροντα διὰ τοὺς
25 τόπους ὅθεν ἂν τυγχάνῃ ῥέων ἑκάστοτε, παραπλησίως λέγοντες ὥσπερ ἂν εἴ τις οἴοιτο καὶ τοὺς ποταμοὺς πάντας ἕνα ποταμὸν εἶναι. διὸ βέλτιον οἱ πολλοὶ λέγουσιν ἄνευ ζητήσεως τῶν μετὰ ζητήσεως οὕτω λεγόντων· εἰ μὲν γὰρ ἐκ μιᾶς ἀρχῆς ἅπαντες ῥέουσι, κἀκεῖ τὰ πνεύματα τὸν αὐτὸν

and high ground, which act as a kind of sponge and, in addition, being cold, cause condensation ; it then gradually trickles together to form springs (349 b 27—350 a 13). This is confirmed by the fact that all the largest rivers flow from mountains : a brief geographical review to demonstrate this (350 a 14–b 22). Summary (350 b 22-30). There are of course bodies of water underground, as is proved by rivers that are swallowed up by the earth : this happens when no other outlet can be found to the sea. Examples (350 b 30— 351 a 18).

LET us go on to deal with winds and all kinds of disturbances in the air, and also with rivers and the sea. And here again let us first discuss the difficulties involved : for on this subject as on many others we know of no previous theory that could not have been thought of by the man in the street.

There are some [a] who say that wind is simply a (I) Wind. moving current of what we call air, while cloud and water are the same air condensed ; they thus assume that water and wind are of the same nature, and define wind as air in motion. And for this reason some people, wishing to be clever, say that all the winds are one, on the ground that the air which moves is in fact one and the same whole, and only seems to differ, without differing in reality, because of the various places from which the current comes on different occasions : which is like supposing that all rivers are but one river. The unscientific views of ordinary people are preferable to scientific theories of this sort. If all rivers flowed from a single source, and something analogous were true of winds, there

[a] Alex. and Ol. both refer to Hippocrates, περὶ φυσῶν : the passage is given by Diels 64 C 2 (under Diogenes). *Cf.* also Diels 12 A 24 (Anaximander).

349 a

30 τρόπον, τάχα λέγοιεν ἄν τι οἱ λέγοντες οὕτως· εἰ
δ' ὁμοίως ἐνταῦθα κἀκεῖ, δῆλον ὅτι τὸ κόμψευμα
ἂν εἴη τοῦτο ψεῦδος, ἐπεὶ τοῦτό γε προσήκουσαν
ἔχει σκέψιν, τί τ' ἐστὶν ὁ ἄνεμος, καὶ γίγνεται πῶς,
καὶ τί τὸ κινοῦν, καὶ ἡ ἀρχὴ πόθεν αὐτῶν, καὶ
πότερον ἄρ' ὥσπερ ἐξ ἀγγείου δεῖ λαβεῖν ῥέοντα
35 τὸν ἄνεμον, καὶ μέχρι τούτου ῥεῖν ἕως ἂν κενωθῇ
349 b τὸ ἀγγεῖον, οἷον ἐξ ἀσκῶν ἀφιέμενον, ἢ καθάπερ
καὶ οἱ γραφεῖς γράφουσιν, ἐξ αὑτῶν τὴν ἀρχὴν
ἀφιέντας.

Ὁμοίως δὲ καὶ περὶ τῆς τῶν ποταμῶν γενέσεως
δοκεῖ τισιν ἔχειν· τὸ γὰρ ἀναχθὲν ὑπὸ τοῦ ἡλίου
ὕδωρ πάλιν ὑόμενον ἀθροισθὲν ὑπὸ γῆν ῥεῖν ἐκ
5 κοιλίας μεγάλης, ἢ πάντας μιᾶς ἢ ἄλλον ἄλλης·
καὶ οὐ γίγνεσθαι ὕδωρ οὐδέν, ἀλλὰ τὸ συλλεχθὲν
ἐκ τοῦ χειμῶνος εἰς τὰς τοιαύτας ὑποδοχάς, τοῦτο
γίγνεσθαι τὸ πλῆθος τὸ τῶν ποταμῶν. διὸ καὶ
μείζους ἀεὶ τοῦ χειμῶνος ῥεῖν ἢ τοῦ θέρους, καὶ
τοὺς μὲν ἀενάους εἶναι τοὺς δ' οὐκ ἀενάους· ὅσων
10 μὲν γὰρ διὰ τὸ μέγεθος τῆς κοιλίας πολὺ τὸ συλλε-
γόμενον ὕδωρ ἐστίν, ὥστε διαρκεῖν καὶ μὴ προανα-
λίσκεσθαι πρὶν ἐπελθεῖν τὸ ὄμβριον ἐν τῷ χειμῶνι
πάλιν, τούτους μὲν ἀενάους εἶναι διὰ τέλους, ὅσοις
δὲ ἐλάττους αἱ ὑποδοχαί, τούτους δὲ δι' ὀλιγότητα
τοῦ ὕδατος φθάνειν ξηραινομένους πρὶν ἐπελθεῖν τὸ
15 ἐκ τοῦ οὐρανοῦ, κενουμένου τοῦ ἀγγείου.

Καίτοι φανερόν, εἴ τις βούλεται ποιήσας οἷον
ὑποδοχὴν πρὸ ὀμμάτων τῷ καθ' ἡμέραν ὕδατι
ῥέοντι συνεχῶς νοῆσαι τὸ πλῆθος· ὑπερβάλλοι γὰρ

---

[a] Cf. *Odyssey* x. 19.
[b] Cf. *De Mot. An.* 2, 698 b 25.
[c] Anaxagoras : Diels 59 A 42 (ii. 16. 13).

might be something in such a theory : but if nothing of the sort is true in either case, it is clear that the theory, though ingenious, is false.   In fact, the following questions are worth investigation : What is the wind and how does it arise ?   What is the motive cause of winds, and what their origin ?   Are we to suppose that the wind flows like a stream from some vessel, and continues to flow until the vessel is empty, like wine poured from wineskins ? [a]   Or are the winds rather self-originating as the painters depict them ? [b]

Some people [c] hold similar views about the origin (II) Rivers. of rivers.   They suppose that the water drawn up The Reservoir theory. by the sun when it falls again as rain is collected beneath the earth into a great hollow from which the rivers flow, either all from the same one or each from a different one : no additional water is formed in the process,[d] and the rivers are supplied by the water collected during the winter in these reservoirs. This explains why rivers always run higher in winter than in summer, and why some are perennial, some are not.   When the hollow is large and the amount of water collected therefore great enough to last out and not be exhausted before the return of the winter rains, then rivers are perennial and flow continuously : when the reservoirs are smaller, then, because the supply of water is small, rivers dry up before the rainy weather returns to replenish the empty container.

(1) But it is evident that if anyone tries to compute Criticisms. the volume of water constantly flowing each day and then to visualize a reservoir for it, he will see that to

----

[d] *e.g.* by condensation, as Aristotle himself maintains, 349 b 23 below.

ἂν τῷ μεγέθει τὸν τῆς γῆς ὄγκον ἢ οὐ πολὺ ἂν
ἐλλείποι τὸ δεχόμενον πᾶν τὸ ῥέον ὕδωρ εἰς τὸν
ἐνιαυτόν.

20 Ἀλλὰ δῆλον ὅτι συμβαίνει μὲν καὶ πολλὰ τοιαῦτα πολλαχοῦ τῆς γῆς, οὐ μὴν ἀλλ' ἄτοπον εἴ
τις μὴ νομίζει διὰ τὴν αὐτὴν αἰτίαν ὕδωρ ἐξ ἀέρος
γίγνεσθαι δι' ἥνπερ ὑπὲρ γῆς καὶ ἐν τῇ γῇ. ὥστ'
εἴπερ κἀκεῖ διὰ ψυχρότητα συνίσταται ὁ ἀτμίζων
ἀὴρ εἰς ὕδωρ, καὶ ὑπὸ τῆς ἐν τῇ γῇ ψυχρότητος τὸ
25 αὐτὸ τοῦτο δεῖ νομίζειν συμβαίνειν, καὶ γίγνεσθαι
μὴ μόνον τὸ ἀποκεκριμένον ὕδωρ ἐν αὐτῇ, καὶ
τοῦτο ῥεῖν, ἀλλὰ καὶ γίγνεσθαι συνεχῶς.

Ἔτι δὲ τοῦ μὴ γιγνομένου ἀλλ' ὑπάρχοντος ὕδατος
καθ' ἡμέραν μὴ τοιαύτην εἶναι τὴν ἀρχὴν τῶν ποτα-
30 μῶν, οἷον ὑπὸ γῆν λίμνας τινὰς ἀποκεκριμένας, καθάπερ ἔνιοι λέγουσιν, ἀλλ' ὁμοίως ὥσπερ καὶ ἐν τῷ
ὑπὲρ γῆς τόπῳ μικραὶ συνιστάμεναι ῥανίδες, καὶ
πάλιν αὗται ἑτέραις, τέλος μετὰ πλήθους καταβαίνει
τὸ ὑόμενον ὕδωρ, οὕτω καὶ ἐν τῇ γῇ ἐκ μικρῶν συλ-
λείβεσθαι τὸ πρῶτον καὶ εἶναι οἷον πιδώσης εἰς ἓν
35 τῆς γῆς τὰς ἀρχὰς τῶν ποταμῶν. δηλοῖ δ' αὐτὸ
350 a τὸ ἔργον· οἱ γὰρ τὰς ὑδραγωγίας ποιοῦντες ὑπο-
νόμοις καὶ διώρυξι συνάγουσιν, ὥσπερ ἂν ἰδιούσης
τῆς γῆς ἀπὸ τῶν ὑψηλῶν. διὸ καὶ τὰ ῥεύματα τῶν
ποταμῶν ἐκ τῶν ὀρῶν φαίνεται ῥέοντα, καὶ πλεῖστοι
καὶ μέγιστοι ποταμοὶ ῥέουσιν ἐκ τῶν μεγίστων
5 ὀρῶν. ὁμοίως δὲ καὶ αἱ κρῆναι αἱ πλεῖσται ὄρεσιν

---

[a] Rainfall is not the only source of supply : there is also
subterranean condensation.

[b] *i.e.* by condensation.

[c] Construe τοῦ . . . ὕδατος with λίμνας (Thurot) : a literal
translation would run " the source of rivers is not as it were

contain the whole yearly flow of water it will have to be as large as the earth in size or at any rate not much smaller.

(2) And though it is true that there are many such reservoirs in different parts of the earth, yet it is absurd for anyone not to suppose that the same cause operates to turn air into water below the earth as above it. If then cold condenses vaporous air into water above the earth, the cold beneath the earth must be presumed to produce the same effect. So not only does water form separately within the earth and flow from it, but the process is continuous.[a]

(3) Besides, even if one leaves out of account water so produced [b] and considers only the daily supply of water already existing,[c] this does not act as a source of rivers by segregating into subterranean lakes, as it were, in the way some people maintain : the process is rather like that in which small drops form in the region above the earth, and these again join others, until rain water falls in some quantity ; similarly inside the earth quantities of water, quite small at first, collect together and gush out of the earth, as it were, at a single point and form the sources of rivers. A practical proof of this is that when men make irrigation works they collect the water in pipes and channels, as though the higher parts of the earth were sweating it out. So we find that the sources of rivers flow from mountains, and that the largest and most numerous rivers flow from the highest mountains. Similarly the majority of springs are in the

Aristotle's own view.

lakes of ready-made as opposed to produced water." Thurot would read ὑπάρχειν for γίγνεσθαι in l. 25—" car Aristote oppose l'eau qui se forme (γίγνεσθαι) à cette qui est toute formée (ὑπάρχειν) "—and transpose καθ᾽ ἡμέραν l. 29 to l. 28 after γιγνομένου.

ARISTOTLE

καὶ τόποις ὑψηλοῖς γειτνιῶσιν· ἐν δὲ τοῖς πεδίοις
ἄνευ ποταμῶν ὀλίγαι γίγνονται πάμπαν. οἱ γὰρ
ὀρεινοὶ καὶ ὑψηλοὶ τόποι, οἷον σπόγγος πυκνὸς
ἐπικρεμάμενοι, κατὰ μικρὰ μὲν πολλαχῇ δὲ δια-
πιδῶσι καὶ συλλείβουσι τὸ ὕδωρ· δέχονταί τε γὰρ
10 τοῦ κατιόντος ὕδατος πολὺ πλῆθος (τί γὰρ διαφέρει
κοίλην καὶ ὑπτίαν ἢ πρηνῆ τὴν περιφέρειαν εἶναι
καὶ κυρτήν; ἀμφοτέρως γὰρ τὸν ἴσον ὄγκον περι-
λήψεται σώματος) καὶ τὴν ἀνιοῦσαν ἀτμίδα ψύχουσι
καὶ συγκρίνουσι πάλιν εἰς ὕδωρ.

Διό, καθάπερ εἴπομεν, οἱ μέγιστοι τῶν ποτα-
15 μῶν ἐκ τῶν μεγίστων φαίνονται ῥέοντες ὀρῶν.
δῆλον δ' ἐστὶ τοῦτο θεωμένοις τὰς τῆς γῆς
περιόδους· ταύτας γὰρ ἐκ τοῦ πυνθάνεσθαι παρ'
ἑκάστων οὕτως ἀνέγραψαν, ὅσων μὴ συμβέβηκεν
αὐτόπτας γενέσθαι τοὺς λέγοντας. ἐν μὲν οὖν τῇ
20 Ἀσίᾳ πλεῖστοι μὲν ἐκ τοῦ Παρνασσοῦ καλουμένου
φαίνονται ῥέοντες ὄρους καὶ μέγιστοι ποταμοί,
τοῦτο δ' ὁμολογεῖται πάντων εἶναι μέγιστον τὸ
ὄρος τῶν πρὸς τὴν ἕω τὴν χειμερινήν· ὑπερβάντι
γὰρ ἤδη τοῦτο φαίνεται ἡ ἔξω θάλαττα, ἧς τὸ
πέρας οὐ δῆλον τοῖς ἐντεῦθεν. ἐκ μὲν οὖν τούτου
ῥέουσιν ἄλλοι τε ποταμοὶ καὶ ὁ Βάκτρος καὶ ὁ
Χοάσπης καὶ ὁ Ἀράξης· τούτου δ' ὁ Τάναϊς ἀπο-
25 σχίζεται μέρος ὢν εἰς τὴν Μαιῶτιν λίμνην. ῥεῖ
δὲ καὶ ὁ Ἰνδὸς ἐξ αὐτοῦ, πάντων τῶν ποταμῶν
ῥεῦμα πλεῖστον. ἐκ δὲ τοῦ Καυκάσου ἄλλοι τε

---

[a] So condensation, as well as rainfall, contributes to the
supply : cf. 349 b 23 and note a on p. 92 above, Alex. 56. 31.
[b] More correctly Paropamisus : the Hindu Kush. For
the geography of this passage and Book II. ch. 5 see the note
at the end of this chapter.

neighbourhood of mountains and high places, and there are few sources of water in the plains except rivers. For mountains and high places act like a thick sponge overhanging the earth and make the water drip through and run together in small quantities in many places. For they receive the great volume of rain water that falls (it makes no difference whether a receptacle of this sort is concave and turned up or convex and turned down : it will contain the same volume whichever it is) : and they cool the vapour as it rises and condense it again to water.[a]

Hence the largest rivers flow, as we said, from the highest mountains. You can see this if you look at the maps of the earth, which have been drawn up by their authors from their own first-hand knowledge or, when this failed, from inquiries made from others. We find that most of the rivers in Asia and the largest of them flow from the mountain range called Parnassus,[b] which is commonly regarded as the highest mountain towards the winter dawn.[c] For when you have crossed it the outer ocean, whose farther limit is unknown to the inhabitants of our part of the world, is already in sight. There flow from this mountain among other rivers the Bactrus,[d] the Choaspes,[e] and the Araxes,[f] from the last of which the Tanaïs [g] branches off and flows into Lake Maeotis.[h] From it also flows the Indus, the greatest of all rivers. From the Caucasus there flow many rivers, extraordinary

Geographical review.

Asia.

---

[c] South-east ; the direction in which the sun rises at the winter solstice.　　　　　　[d] Oxus.

[e] Karun : or possibly Kabul River.

[f] Or Iaxartes : Syr Darya.

[g] Don.　　　　　　[h] Sea of Azov.

350 a

ρέουσι πολλοὶ καὶ κατὰ πλῆθος καὶ κατὰ μέγεθος
ὑπερβάλλοντες, καὶ ὁ Φᾶσις· ὁ δὲ Καύκασος μέγιστον ὄρος τῶν πρὸς τὴν ἔω τὴν θερινήν ἐστιν καὶ
30 πλήθει καὶ ὕψει. σημεῖα δὲ τοῦ μὲν ὕψους ὅτι
ὁρᾶται καὶ ἀπὸ τῶν καλουμένων βαθέων καὶ εἰς
τὴν λίμνην εἰσπλεόντων, ἔτι δ' ἡλιοῦται τῆς νυκτὸς
αὐτοῦ τὰ ἄκρα μέχρι τοῦ τρίτου μέρους ἀπό τε τῆς
ἔω καὶ πάλιν ἀπὸ τῆς ἑσπέρας· τοῦ δὲ πλήθους ὅτι
πολλὰς ἔχον ἕδρας, ἐν αἷς ἔθνη τε κατοικεῖ πολλὰ
35 καὶ λίμνας εἶναί φασι μεγάλας, †ἀλλ' ὅμως πάσας
τὰς ἕδρας εἶναί φασι φανερὰς μέχρι τῆς ἐσχάτης
κορυφῆς.†

350 b 'Εκ δὲ τῆς Πυρήνης (τοῦτο δ' ἐστὶν ὄρος πρὸς
δυσμὴν ἰσημερινήν[1] ἐν τῇ Κελτικῇ) ῥέουσιν ὅ τε
"Ιστρος καὶ ὁ Ταρτησσός. οὗτος μὲν οὖν ἔξω
στηλῶν, ὁ δ' "Ιστρος δι' ὅλης τῆς Εὐρώπης εἰς τὸν
Εὔξεινον πόντον. τῶν δ' ἄλλων ποταμῶν οἱ πλεῖ-
5 στοι πρὸς ἄρκτον ἐκ τῶν ὀρῶν τῶν 'Αρκυνίων·
ταῦτα δὲ καὶ ὕψει καὶ πλήθει μέγιστα περὶ τὸν
τόπον τοῦτόν ἐστιν. ὑπ' αὐτὴν δὲ τὴν ἄρκτον ὑπὲρ
τῆς ἐσχάτης Σκυθίας αἱ καλούμεναι 'Ρῖπαι, περὶ
ὧν τοῦ μεγέθους λίαν εἰσὶν οἱ λεγόμενοι λόγοι
μυθώδεις· ῥέουσι δ' οὖν οἱ πλεῖστοι καὶ μέγιστοι
10 μετὰ τὸν "Ιστρον τῶν ἄλλων ποταμῶν ἐντεῦθεν,
ὥς φασιν.

'Ομοίως δὲ καὶ περὶ τὴν Λιβύην οἱ μὲν ἐκ τῶν

---

[1] πρὸς δυσμὴν ἰσημερινὴν fortasse post στηλῶν l. 3 collo-
canda censet Heidel.

[a] Rion.   [b] North-east.   [c] Cf. 351 a 11 below.
[d] " This is unintelligible: our text, though it goes back to
Alexander (Alex. 57. 32 f.), must be corrupt " (O.T.). I agree,
and have accordingly obelized the words.
[e] The Pyrenees.

both in number and in size, among them the Phasis.[a]
The Caucasus is the largest mountain range, both in
extent and height, towards the summer sunrise.[b]
A proof of its height is the fact that it is visible both
from the so-called Deeps [c] and also as you sail into
Lake Maeotis ; and also that its peaks are sunlit for
a third part of the night, both before sunrise and
again after sunset. A proof of its extent is that it
contains many habitable regions in which there live
many tribes and in which there are said to be many
great lakes. †And yet they say that all these regions
are visible up to the last peak.† [d]

From Pyrenê [e] (this is a mountain range towards Europe.
the equinoctial sunset in Celtice [f]) there flow the
Istrus [g] and the Tartessus.[h] The latter flows into
the sea outside the pillars of Heracles, the Istrus flows
right across Europe into the Euxine. Most of the
remaining European [i] rivers flow northward from the
Arkynian [j] mountains which are the largest both in
height and extent in that region. Beneath the Bear
itself [k] beyond the farthest part of Scythia is a range
of mountains called the Rhipae [l] : the stories told of
their size are too fanciful for credence, but they say
that from them the greatest number and, after the
Istrus, the largest of other European rivers flow.

Similarly in Libya from the Aethiopian moun- Africa.

[f] A general name for France and Spain.
[g] Danube.
[h] Or Baetis : Guadalquivir.
[i] I have inserted " European " here and at b 9 below,
though it is not in the Greek : Aristotle must be thinking
of Europe here and not of the world as a whole.
[j] The mountains of Central Europe, the Alps to the Car-
pathians.
[k] i.e. in the extreme North : cf. 362 b 9.
[l] These seem to be purely mythical, as Aristotle indicates.

Αἰθιοπικῶν ὀρῶν, ὅ τε Αἰγὼν καὶ ὁ Νύσης, οἱ δὲ
μέγιστοι τῶν διωνομασμένων, ὅ τε Χρεμέτης
καλούμενος, ὃς εἰς τὴν ἔξω ῥεῖ θάλατταν, καὶ τοῦ
Νείλου τὸ ῥεῦμα τὸ πρῶτον, ἐκ τοῦ Ἀργυροῦ καλουμένου ὄρους.

15 Τῶν δὲ περὶ τὸν Ἑλληνικὸν τόπον ὁ μὲν Ἀχελῷος
ἐκ Πίνδου, καὶ ὁ Ἴναχος ἐντεῦθεν, ὁ δὲ Στρυμὼν
καὶ Νέσσος καὶ ὁ Ἕβρος ἅπαντες τρεῖς ὄντες ἐκ
τοῦ Σκόμβρου· πολλὰ δὲ ῥεύματα καὶ ἐκ τῆς
Ῥοδόπης ἐστίν.

Ὁμοίως δὲ καὶ τοὺς ἄλλους ποταμοὺς εὕροι τις
20 ἂν ῥέοντας· ἀλλὰ μαρτυρίου χάριν τούτους εἴπομεν·
ἐπεὶ καὶ ὅσοι αὐτῶν ῥέουσιν ἐξ ἑλῶν, τὰ ἕλη ὑπὸ
ὄρη κεῖσθαι συμβαίνει πάντα σχεδὸν ἢ τόπους
ὑψηλοὺς ἐκ προσαγωγῆς.

Ὅτι μὲν οὖν οὐ δεῖ νομίζειν οὕτω γίγνεσθαι τὰς
ἀρχὰς τῶν ποταμῶν ὡς ἐξ ἀφωρισμένων κοιλιῶν,
φανερόν· οὔτε γὰρ ἂν ὁ τόπος ἱκανὸς ἦν ὁ τῆς γῆς
25 ὡς εἰπεῖν, ὥσπερ οὐδ᾽ ὁ τῶν νεφῶν, εἰ τὸ ὂν ἔδει
ῥεῖν μόνον, ἀλλὰ μὴ τὸ μὲν ἀπῄει τὸ δ᾽ ἐγίγνετο,
ἀλλ᾽ αἰεὶ ἀπὸ ὄντος ἐταμιεύετο· τό τε ὑπὸ τοῖς
ὄρεσιν ἔχειν τὰς πηγὰς μαρτυρεῖ διότι τῷ συρρεῖν
εἰς ὀλίγον καὶ κατὰ μικρὸν ἐκ πολλῶν νοτίδων
30 διαδίδωσιν ὁ τόπος καὶ γίγνονται οὕτως αἱ πηγαὶ
τῶν ποταμῶν.

Οὐ μὴν ἀλλὰ καὶ τοιούτους εἶναι τόπους ἔχοντας
πλῆθος ὕδατος, οἷον λίμνας, οὐδὲν ἄτοπον, πλὴν
οὔτι τηλικαύτας ὥστε τοῦτο συμβαίνειν, οὐδὲν μᾶλ-

---

^a Unidentifiable.
^b Unidentifiable.
^c Later called the Mountains of the Moon : perhaps
Mts. Kilimanjaro and Kenya or the Ruwenzori range.

tains there flow the Aegon[a] and the Nyses[b]; from the so-called Silver Mountains[c] the two largest of rivers distinguished by names, the river called the Chremetes,[d] which flows into the outer ocean, and the most important of the sources of the Nile.[e]

Of the rivers in Greek lands, the Acheloüs flows from Mount Pindus, as does also the Inachus, and the trio Strymon, Nessos and Hebrus from Mount Scombrus : and there are also many rivers that flow from Mount Rhodopê.

Further investigation would show that all other rivers flow similarly from mountains : these have simply been given as examples. For even when rivers flow from marshes it will almost always be found that these marshes lie beneath either mountains or gradually rising ground.

We can now see that the supposition that rivers Summary. spring from definite hollows in the earth is a false one. For, firstly, the whole earth, we might say, would hardly be room enough, nor the region of the clouds, if the flow were fed only by water already existing, and if some waters were not in fact vanishing in evaporation, some re-forming all the time, but all were produced from a ready-made supply. Secondly, the fact that rivers have their sources at the foot of mountains proves that the place accumulates water little by little by a gradual collection of many drops, and that the sources of rivers are formed in this way.

It is not, of course, at all impossible that there do Subterexist such places containing large volumes of water, ranean like lakes : but they cannot be so large as to act in rivers. the way this theory maintains, any more than one waters and

[d] Probably the Senegal River.   [e] The White Nile.

λον ἢ εἴ τις οἴοιτο τὰς φανερὰς εἶναι πηγὰς τῶν
ποταμῶν· σχεδὸν γὰρ ἐκ κρηνῶν οἱ πλεῖστοι
35 ῥέουσιν. ὅμοιον οὖν τὸ ἐκείνας καὶ τὸ ταύτας
νομίζειν εἶναι τὸ σῶμα τὸ τοῦ ὕδατος πᾶν.

Ὅτι δ' εἰσὶν τοιαῦται φάραγγες καὶ διαστάσεις
351 a τῆς γῆς, δηλοῦσιν οἱ καταπινόμενοι τῶν ποταμῶν.
συμβαίνει δὲ τοῦτο πολλαχοῦ τῆς γῆς, οἷον τῆς μὲν
Πελοποννήσου πλεῖστα τοιαῦτα περὶ τὴν Ἀρκαδίαν
ἐστίν. αἴτιον δὲ διὰ τὸ ὀρεινὴν οὖσαν μὴ ἔχειν
5 ἐκροὰς ἐκ τῶν κοίλων εἰς θάλατταν· πληρούμενοι
γὰρ οἱ τόποι καὶ οὐκ ἔχοντες ἔκρυσιν αὐτοῖς εὑρί-
σκονται τὴν δίοδον εἰς βάθος, ἀποβιαζομένου τοῦ
ἄνωθεν ἐπιόντος ὕδατος. περὶ μὲν οὖν τὴν Ἑλλάδα
μικρὰ τοιαῦτα παντελῶς ἐστιν γιγνόμενα· ἀλλ' ἥ
10 γε ὑπὸ τὸν Καύκασον λίμνη, ἣν καλοῦσιν οἱ ἐκεῖ
θάλατταν[1]· αὕτη γὰρ ποταμῶν πολλῶν καὶ μεγάλων
εἰσβαλλόντων οὐκ ἔχουσα ἔκρουν φανερὸν ἐκδίδωσιν
ὑπὸ γῆν κατὰ Κοραξούς, περὶ τὰ καλούμενα βαθέα
τοῦ Πόντου· ταῦτα δ' ἐστὶν ἄπειρόν τι τῆς θαλάττης
βάθος· οὐδεὶς γοῦν πώποτε καθεὶς ἐδυνήθη πέρας
εὑρεῖν. ταύτῃ δὲ πόρρω τῆς γῆς σχεδὸν περὶ τρια-
15 κόσια στάδια πότιμον ἀναδιδωσιν ὕδωρ ἐπὶ πολὺν
τόπον, οὐ συνεχῆ δέ, ἀλλὰ τρισσαχῆ. καὶ περὶ τὴν
Λιγυστικὴν οὐκ ἐλάττων τοῦ Ῥοδανοῦ καταπίνεταί
τις ποταμός, καὶ πάλιν ἀναδίδωσιν κατ' ἄλλον
τόπον· ὁ δὲ Ῥοδανὸς ποταμὸς ναυσιπέρατός ἐστιν.

---

[1] θάλατταν φανερά S$_{rec.}$ Cam. : θάλατταν μεγάλη ci. Thurot.

---

[a] And it cannot be merely the spring which we see at the
source that supplies the river with water : it must rather be
the whole process of accumulation described at b 27 and
350 a 7 above. *Cf.* Alex. 58. 20 ff.

could reasonably suppose that their visible sources supply all the water for the rivers, most of which flow from springs.[a] It is thus equally unreasonable to believe either that lakes or that the visible sources are the sole water supply.

But the rivers that are swallowed up by the earth prove that there are chasms and cavities in the earth. This happens in many places : in the Peloponnese, for example, one finds it most often in Arcadia. The reason is that because the country is mountainous there are no outlets from the valleys to the sea : so when these valleys get filled with water and there is no outlet, the water flowing in from above forces its way out and finds a way through into the depths of the earth. In Greece this only happens in quite a small way. But there is the lake [b] beneath the Caucasus, which the inhabitants call a sea [c] : for this is fed by many great rivers, and having no obvious outlet runs out beneath the earth in the district of the Coraxi [d] and comes up somewhere about the so-called deeps of Pontus. (This is a part of the sea whose depth is unfathomable : at any rate no sounding has yet succeeded in finding the bottom.) Here at about three hundred stades' distance from shore fresh water comes up over a large area, an area not continuous but falling into three divisions. And in Liguria a river [e] as large as the Rhone (and the Rhone is large enough to be navigable) is swallowed up, and comes up again in another place.

[b] The Caspian Sea.

[c] Thurot inserts μεγάλη after θάλατταν to answer to μικρά in l. 7.

[d] On the east coast of the Black Sea.

[e] Perhaps the Po. " Pliny alleges (falsely) that it flows underground (Pliny iii. 6) " (O.T.).

ARISTOTLE

NOTE ON ARISTOTLE'S GEOGRAPHY

From the geographical review in this chapter, and from the passage in Book II. ch. 5, 362 a 32 ff. on the zones of the earth, we learn Aristotle's views about the dimensions and geography of the habitable world.

Aristotle believed the earth to be a sphere, of no great relative size, situated at the centre of the universe (Book I. ch. 3, 339 b 6-8, 340 a 6-8: *cf. De Caelo* ii. 14, 298 a 10 ff., where he quotes an estimate of 400,000 stades = about 46,000 miles for its circumference). There are two habitable zones of the earth, " one, in which we live, towards the upper pole, the other towards the other, that is the south pole." The zone in which we live is bounded by the tropic of Cancer on the south and the Arctic circle on the north, the other sector zone by the tropic of Capricorn and the Antarctic circle. They are the only habitable regions, the zone between the tropics being uninhabitable owing to the heat, the zones beyond the Arctic and Antarctic circles owing to the cold. The habitable zones thus extend right round the globe in two broad strips : and the length of the portion of our strip which we know, that is, from " the pillars of Heracles to India," exceeds its breadth in the proportion of 5 to 3. " Beyond the Pillars of Heracles and India lies the ocean which severs the habitable zone and prevents it forming a continuous belt," though if it were not for the ocean the complete circuit could be made.

Such is the account of the zones of the earth in Book II. ch. 5, and it gives us the general dimensions (length 5 : breadth 3) of the maps (περιόδους 350 a 16) which Aristotle has in mind in Book I. ch. 13. In this chapter he is not, of course, setting out to give an account of the geography of the known world ; he is using geography to illustrate the theme that the largest rivers flow from the highest mountains. But it seems clear that he had a map or maps in mind, if not before him, and it should therefore be possible to draw a map that will illustrate what he says.

Such a map is given here (Map 1) together with a map of the same area as we know it to-day (Map 2). In making this map, and in identifying the rivers and mountains to which Aristotle refers, I have been guided largely by the following works (in addition to Ideler and the O.T.) : Bunbury, *History of Ancient Geography*, vol. i ; Tozer, *History of*

MAP 1

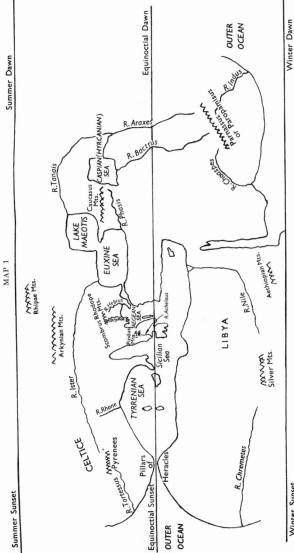

Summer Dawn

Equinoctial Dawn

Winter Dawn

Summer Sunset

Equinoctial Sunset

Winter Sunset

Rhipae Mts.

Arkynian Mts.

R. Ister

R. Rhone

CELTICE

Pyrenees

R. Tartessus

Pillars of Heracles

TYRRENIAN SEA

OUTER OCEAN

Sicilian Sea

Silver Mts.

R. Chremetes

LIBYA

R. Nile

Aethiopian Mts.

Scombrus Rhodope Mts.

R. Hebrus

Strymon

Pindus Mts.

AEGEAN SEA

R. Achelous

EUXINE SEA

LAKE MAEOTIS

R. Tanais

Caucasus Mts.

R. Phasis

CASPIAN (HYRCANIAN) SEA

R. Araxes

R. Bactrus

R. Choaspes

Parapamisus or Parnassus

R. Indus

OUTER OCEAN

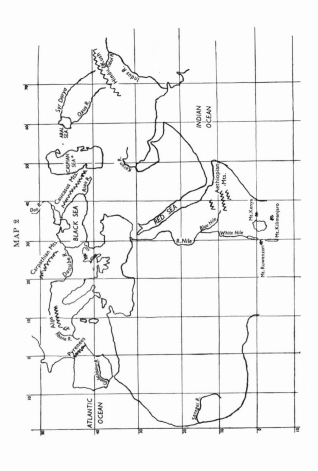

MAP 2

NOTE ON ARISTOTLE'S GEOGRAPHY

Ancient Geography (Ed. 2, with additional notes by M. Cary);
E. H. Warmington, *Greek Geography*; Heidel, *The Frame of the Ancient Greek Maps*; J. L. Myres, article on Herodotus's maps in the *Geographical Journal*, 8, 1896; P. Bolchert, *Aristoteles Erdkunde von Asien und Libyen*. Prof. Heidel's book I have found particularly useful, as it explains very clearly how the three co-ordinates, summer-equinoctial-winter-sunrise and sunset, were used as the frame within which Greek maps were drawn (see Map 1). To these authors the reader is referred for further information, but the following notes on particular identifications may be useful.

1. Mountains.

Parnassus 350 a 19. By this Aristotle must mean the range which later writers called Paropanisus or Paropamisus : *i.e.* the Hindu-Kush (Tozer, p. 133, Bunbury, p. 400, Heidel, p. 42, note 107). Aristotle locates it " towards the *winter* dawn," which Heidel thinks too far south. But there is no authority for a change of the text to read " equinoctial " or " summer dawn " as Heidel suggests ; and it looks as if in Aristotle's map *Parnassus* balances *Caucasus* (350 a 26) which is towards the *summer* dawn (the Greeks liked their maps to be symmetrical : *cf.* Myres, *loc. cit.* p. 608) ; though it is true that with the present reading the course of the Araxes-Tanaïs is very long. Heidel (*loc. cit.*) also thinks Aristotle puts the *Pyrenees* too far south, and has suggested that the text should be amended (*v.* 350 b 1 and note *ad loc.*). But Herodotus, who thought the Ister (Danube) rose " from the city of Pyrenê " (ii. 33), seems to locate it very far south (*cf.* maps in How and Wells's Commentary, p. 303, Tozer, p. 75, Bunbury, p. 172), and it is still possible to draw a map without altering the text. But the map could of course quite easily be re-drawn if these two amendments of Heidel were adopted.

The *Silver Mountains* (350 b 14), the source of the Chremetes and the Nile, are more difficult to place. But Olymp. 105. 30 identifies them with the mountains called later the Mountains of the Moon, which Tozer (p. 352) supposes to be Mounts Kilimanjaro and Kenya. Warmington (p. 144) suggests the Ruwenzori range " which, though equatorial, has miles of snow and glacier." I have placed them in Central Africa where they balance the mountain masses in Central Europe. For Herodotus thought that the Nile followed an easterly course in its upper reaches, and it was

ARISTOTLE

not until the Ptolemies that a fuller knowledge of it was gained.

2. RIVERS.

Choaspes, called by Herodotus v. 52 " the river on which Susa stands," and so presumably the Karun River. But Aristotle may have a different Choaspes in mind : Bunbury, p. 434 (*cf.* Bolchert, p. 39), suggests the Cabul River.

Bactrus " is probably the ' river of Bactria '—that is, the Oxus " (Bunbury, *loc. cit.*).

Araxes : it seems generally agreed that by this Aristotle means the Iaxartes or Syr Darya : *cf.* Bunbury, pp. 400 and 434, Tozer, pp. 82, 135 and additional notes, p. xviii, and for Herodotus's confusions about the Araxes, How and Wells, i. pp. 152 and 202.

The *Chremetes* is otherwise unknown, unless it is to be identified with the Chretes of the Periplus of Hanno, which was probably the Senegal River or a branch of it. It is possible that Aristotle may have had some knowledge of the voyage of Hanno, just as the persistent Greek tradition about the shallowness of the sea beyond the pillars of Heracles (Book II. ch. 1, 354 a 22 : *cf.* Plato, *Timaeus* 25 D) may reflect the experience of Himilco in the Sargasso Sea : see Bunbury, pp. 324-325, 335 and 401 (Hanno), and 402-403 (Himilco), Tozer, pp. 111-112 (Himilco).

The lack of any reference to the *Tigris* or *Euphrates* is surprising, for they were known to Herodotus and could have been used to illustrate Aristotle's thesis.

CHAPTER XIV

ARGUMENT

The same districts of the earth are not always wet and dry, nor the same places always sea and land. The reason for this is that different parts of the earth grow old and dry up at different times, while others correspondingly revive and grow wet (351 a 19–b 8). But the whole process takes a long time to complete, and peoples perish by war, pestilence or famine before it is complete, so that no record of it is preserved (351 b 8-22). So also a people forgets its own first settlement in

104

The traditional consensus of opinion (*cf.* Tozer, pp. 134, 136, Bunbury, p. 401) is that Aristotle did not distinguish the Caspian and Aral : and I have drawn the map accordingly. But Aristotle speaks at Book II. ch. 1, 354 a 3 of the Hyrcanian and Caspian as distinct (*cf.* Book II. ch. 1, note *a* on p. 126), and Tarn (*Alexander the Great*, vol. ii. pp. 5 ff.) has argued that he believed the two seas to be separate, his name for our Caspian being Hyrcanian, for our Aral Caspian. Tarn's argument is persuasive ; but the reference in Book II. ch. 1 is the only reference in Aristotle's genuine works to either sea, it is a passing reference, not made in the course of his geographical review, and it is not easy to draw any firm conclusions from it. If Tarn's view is accepted it must be on the strength of his contention that the truth was known to Alexander before his expedition ; for if this is so, it is reasonable to suppose, in view of this reference, that it was known to Aristotle and that Alexander learned it from him. If Aristotle believed the two seas to be separate, then the map should be redrawn to show the Araxes and Bactrus falling into the Caspian-Aral, though this makes the course of the Araxes-Tanaïs even more awkward and perhaps strengthens the case for Heidel's emendment of 350 a 21.

J. O. Thomson, *History of Ancient Geography*, to which reference may also be made, appeared when this note had already gone to the press, as did also L. Pearson's article in *C.Q.* xliv (N.S. i) (1951), pp. 80 ff., in which he criticizes Tarn.

CHAPTER XIV

ARGUMENT (*continued*)

a district and the character of the district at the time of settlement, as has happened in Egypt. We can, however, infer from the evidence we have that this is a district that is drying up. It has been formed by the silt deposited by the Nile : the deposit is at first marshy but improves as it dries and is then inhabited, while other districts deteriorate and become too dry for habitation. A similar improvement and deterioration has taken place in Argos and Mycenae. The same process

takes place on a larger scale and affects larger areas (351
b 22—352 a 17).

The cause of these changes is not, as some say, a change in
the universe as a whole—this is to lose sight of the relatively
small size of the earth—but periodical seasons of rain, as it
were winters in a great year, which affect different parts of
the earth at different times : e.g. Deucalion's flood (352 a

351 a 19 Οὐκ αἰεὶ δ' οἱ αὐτοὶ τόποι τῆς γῆς οὔτ' ἔνυγροί
20 εἰσιν οὔτε ξηροί, ἀλλὰ μεταβάλλουσιν κατὰ τὰς τῶν
ποταμῶν γενέσεις καὶ τὰς ἀπολείψεις· διὸ καὶ τὰ
περὶ τὴν ἤπειρον μεταβάλλει καὶ τὴν θάλατταν, καὶ
οὐκ αἰεὶ τὰ μὲν γῆ τὰ δὲ θάλαττα διατελεῖ πάντα
τὸν χρόνον, ἀλλὰ γίγνεται θάλαττα μὲν ὅπου χέρσος,
25 ἔνθα δὲ νῦν θάλαττα, πάλιν ἐνταῦθα γῆ. κατὰ μέντοι
τινὰ τάξιν νομίζειν χρὴ ταῦτα γίγνεσθαι καὶ περίοδον. ἀρχὴ δὲ τούτων καὶ αἴτιον ὅτι καὶ τῆς γῆς
τὰ ἐντός, ὥσπερ τὰ σώματα τῶν φυτῶν καὶ ζῴων,
ἀκμὴν ἔχει καὶ γῆρας. πλὴν ἐκείνοις μὲν οὐ κατὰ
μέρος ταῦτα συμβαίνει πάσχειν, ἀλλ' ἅμα πᾶν
30 ἀκμάζειν καὶ φθίνειν ἀναγκαῖον· τῇ δὲ γῇ τοῦτο
γίγνεται κατὰ μέρος διὰ ψύξιν καὶ θερμότητα.
ταῦτα μὲν οὖν αὔξεται καὶ φθίνει διὰ τὸν ἥλιον καὶ
τὴν περιφοράν, διὰ δὲ ταῦτα καὶ τὴν δύναμιν τὰ
μέρη τῆς γῆς λαμβάνει διαφέρουσαν, ὥστε μέχρι
τινὸς ἔνυδρα δύναται διαμένειν, εἶτα ξηραίνεται καὶ
35 γηράσκει πάλιν· ἕτεροι δὲ τόποι βιώσκονται καὶ
ἔνυδροι γίγνονται κατὰ μέρος. ἀνάγκη δὲ τῶν μὲν
351 b τόπων γιγνομένων ξηροτέρων τὰς πηγὰς ἀφανίζεσθαι, τούτων δὲ συμβαινόντων τοὺς ποταμοὺς
πρῶτον μὲν ἐκ μεγάλων μικρούς, εἶτα τέλος γίγνεσθαι ξηρούς, τῶν δὲ ποταμῶν μεθισταμένων καὶ
ἔνθεν μὲν ἀφανιζομένων ἐν ἄλλοις δ' ἀνάλογον

17–b 2). *The effects of such a deluge last a long time, and longer in districts with suitable mountain ranges to retain the moisture (352 b 2-16). These changes must take place : and the facts show that they have. Evidence :—Egypt has been formed by Nile deposits, and lies lower than the Red Sea : clearly it was once all continuous sea. Lake Maeotis is similarly silting up (352 b 16—353 a 14). Conclusion (353 a 14-28).*

THE same parts of the earth are not always moist or dry, but change their character according to the appearance or failure of rivers. So also mainland and sea change places and one area does not remain earth, another sea, for all time, but sea replaces what was once dry land, and where there is now sea there is at another time land. This process must, however, be supposed to take place in an orderly cycle. Its originating cause is that the interior parts of the earth, like the bodies of plants and animals, have their maturity and age. Only whereas the parts of plants and animals are not affected separately but the whole creature must grow to maturity and decay at the same time, the parts of the earth are affected separately, the cause of the process being cold and heat. Cold and heat increase and decrease owing to the sun's course, and because of them the different parts of the earth acquire different potentialities ; some are able to remain moist up to a certain point and then dry up and become old again, while others come to life and become moist in their turn. As places become drier the springs necessarily disappear, and when this happens the rivers at first dwindle from their former size and finally dry up ; and when the rivers are removed and disappear in one place, but come into existence correspondingly in another, the

Changes in humidity and in relative positions of sea and land.

107

351 b

5 γιγνομένων μεταβάλλειν τὴν θάλατταν· ὅπου μὲν
γὰρ ἐξωθουμένη ὑπὸ τῶν ποταμῶν ἐπλεόναζεν,
ἀπιοῦσαν ξηρὰν ποιεῖν ἀναγκαῖον, ὅπου δὲ τοῖς
ῥεύμασιν πληθύουσα¹ ἐξηραίνετο προσχουμένη,² πάλιν ἐνταῦθα λιμνάζειν.

Ἀλλὰ διὰ τὸ γίγνεσθαι πᾶσαν τὴν φυσικὴν περὶ
τὴν γῆν γένεσιν ἐκ προσαγωγῆς καὶ ἐν χρόνοις
10 παμμήκεσι πρὸς τὴν ἡμετέραν ζωήν, λανθάνει ταῦτα
γιγνόμενα, καὶ πρότερον ὅλων τῶν ἐθνῶν ἀπώλειαι
γίγνονται καὶ φθοραὶ πρὶν μνημονευθῆναι τὴν τούτων μεταβολὴν ἐξ ἀρχῆς εἰς τέλος. μέγισται μὲν
οὖν φθοραὶ γίγνονται καὶ τάχισται ἐν τοῖς πολέμοις,
15 ἄλλαι δὲ νόσοις, αἱ δὲ ἀφορίαις, καὶ ταύταις αἱ μὲν
μεγάλαι αἱ δὲ κατὰ μικρόν, ὥστε λανθάνουσι τῶν
γε τοιούτων ἐθνῶν καὶ αἱ μεταναστάσεις διὰ τὸ
τοὺς μὲν λείπειν τὰς χώρας, τοὺς δὲ ὑπομένειν
μέχρι τούτου μέχριπερ ἂν μηκέτι δύνηται τρέφειν
ἡ χώρα πλῆθος μηδέν. ἀπὸ τῆς πρώτης οὖν ἀπο-
20 λείψεως εἰς τὴν ὑστέραν εἰκὸς γίγνεσθαι μακροὺς

---

¹ πληθύουσι ci. O.T.
² πληθύουσα ηὐξάνετο προσχουμένη 𝔐 𝔄 : πληθύουσα ἐξηραίνετο προσχουμένη N₁ : πληθύουσα ἐξηραίνετο προσχουμένη
N_rec. : ἐξηραίνετο (in ras.) πληθύουσα (in ras.) προσχουμένη
(-σ- fortasse postea add.) E₁ : ηὐξάνετο ὀχουμένη 𝔚 : πλήθουσα
ἐξηραίνετο προσχουμένη Ald.

ᵃ Rivers fall into the sea at A, push it back by silting and
cause it to flood the land at B ; when the rivers dry up the
sea will recede from B (first ὅπου clause 5-6), and at the same
time flood the land made by the river silt at A (second ὅπου
clause 6-8). The two ὅπου clauses are concerned with the
same process but the first considers the flooding and subsequent drying of B, the second the formation and subsequent
flooding of land at A. An example of the process as it affects

sea too must change. For wherever it has encroached
on the land because the rivers have pushed it out, it
must when it recedes leave behind it dry land : while
wherever it has been filled and silted up by rivers and
formed dry land, this must again be flooded.[a]

But these changes escape our observation because
the whole natural process of the earth's growth takes
place by slow degrees and over periods of time which
are vast compared to the length of our life, and whole
peoples are destroyed and perish before they can
record the process from beginning to end. Of such
destructions the most extensive and most rapid are
caused by war, others by disease and famine. Famines
may be either immediately destructive or else so
gradual that the disappearance of the people affected
goes unnoticed ; for when the inhabitants emigrate
in relays, some leaving, some remaining until at last
the land is unable to support any population at all,
the time that elapses between the first and last

These changes take too long for records of them to survive.

A can be found at 352 b 20 below. The whole of Egypt
has been formed by the Nile silt. It lies lower than the
Red Sea, which shows that the whole area was once sea
(352 b 20-30). So presumably when the Nile dries up the
land will again flood. As the O.T. points out, Aristotle is
more familiar with one side of the process, the encroaching
of land on sea.

(My explanation in the first paragraph follows the O.T.
closely. Alex. gives the same explanation of the first ὅπου
clause : but takes λιμνάζειν in the second to refer to a stage
in the process of silting up. So he supposes that each clause
describes a way in which land is formed (by retirement of the
sea or by silting), rather than that each describes from a
different point of view the same process of reciprocal land
formation and flooding. The O.T. explanation seems the
better. Its variant reading πληθύουσι does not materially
affect the sense. The text of the passage is doubtful, as the
note on the text indicates.)

351 b

χρόνους, ὥστε μηδένα μνημονεύειν, ἀλλὰ σῳζο-
μένων ἔτι τῶν ὑπομενόντων ἐπιλελῆσθαι διὰ χρόνου
πλῆθος. τὸν αὐτὸν δὲ τρόπον χρὴ νομίζειν καὶ
τοὺς κατοικισμοὺς λανθάνειν πότε πρῶτον ἐγένοντο
τοῖς ἔθνεσιν ἑκάστοις εἰς τὰ μεταβάλλοντα καὶ
25 γιγνόμενα ξηρὰ ἐξ ἑλωδῶν καὶ ἐνύδρων· καὶ γὰρ
ἐνταῦθα κατὰ μικρὸν ἐν πολλῷ γίγνεται χρόνῳ ἡ
ἐπίδοσις, ὥστε μὴ μνημονεύειν τίνες πρῶτοι καὶ
πότε καὶ πῶς ἐχόντων ἦλθον τῶν τόπων.

Οἷον συμβέβηκεν καὶ τὰ περὶ Αἴγυπτον· καὶ γὰρ
οὗτος ἀεὶ ξηρότερος ὁ τόπος φαίνεται γιγνόμενος
30 καὶ πᾶσα ἡ χώρα τοῦ ποταμοῦ πρόσχωσις οὖσα
τοῦ Νείλου, διὰ δὲ τὸ κατὰ μικρὸν ξηραινομένων
τῶν ἑλῶν τοὺς πλησίον εἰσοικίζεσθαι τὸ τοῦ χρόνου
μῆκος ἀφήρηται τὴν ἀρχήν. φαίνεται οὖν καὶ τὰ
στόματα πάντα, πλὴν ἑνὸς τοῦ Κανωβικοῦ, χειρο-
ποίητα καὶ οὐ τοῦ ποταμοῦ ὄντα, καὶ τὸ ἀρχαῖον
35 ἡ Αἴγυπτος Θῆβαι καλούμεναι. δηλοῖ δὲ καὶ
Ὅμηρος, οὕτως πρόσφατος ὢν ὡς εἰπεῖν πρὸς τὰς
352 a τοιαύτας μεταβολάς· ἐκείνου γὰρ τοῦ τόπου ποιεῖται
μνείαν ὡς οὔπω Μέμφιος οὔσης ἢ ὅλως ἢ οὐ τηλι-
καύτης. τοῦτο δ᾽ εἰκὸς οὕτω συμβαίνειν· οἱ γὰρ
κάτωθεν τόποι τῶν ἄνωθεν ὕστερον ᾠκίσθησαν·
ἑλώδεις γὰρ ἐπὶ πλείω χρόνον ἀναγκαῖον εἶναι τοὺς
5 ἐγγύτερον τῆς προσχώσεως διὰ τὸ λιμνάζειν ἐν
τοῖς ἐσχάτοις ἀεὶ μᾶλλον. μεταβάλλει δὲ τοῦτο

---

[a] *i.e.* before starvation or emigration has removed the last
of the original inhabitants.

[b] In spite of the lack of records we can prove that the pro-

emigration is likely to be too long for memory to cover, and indeed so long that memory fails before the last survivors have died out.[a] In the same way we must suppose that the time of the first settlement of the various peoples in places that were in process of change from wet and marshy to dry has been forgotten. For here, too, the advance is gradual and takes a long time, so that there is no record of who the first settlers were or when they came or in what state they found the land.

This has happened in Egypt. This is a land which is obviously in the process of getting drier, and the whole country is clearly a deposit of the Nile : but because the adjacent peoples have only encroached on the marshes gradually as they dried up, the beginning of the process has been lost in the lapse of time. We can see, however,[b] that all the mouths of the Nile, except the one at Canopus, are artificial and not formed by the action of the river itself ; and the old name of Egypt was Thebes. Homer's evidence [c] proves this last point, though in relation to such changes he is comparatively modern : for he mentions the country as though Memphis either did not exist as yet at all or at any rate were not a place of its present importance. And it is quite likely that this was in fact so. For the higher lands were inhabited before the lower-lying, because the nearer a place is to the point where silt is being deposited the longer it must remain marshy, as the land last formed is always more water-logged. But this land changes

Examples : Egypt.

cess has taken place by adducing the following facts as evidence.
[c] Homer, *Il.* ix.- 381 ; *cf. Od.* iv. iv. 83-85, 229 ff., xiv. 245 ff., 295.

111

352 a

καὶ πάλιν εὐθενεῖ· ξηραινόμενοι γὰρ οἱ τόποι ἔρ-
χονται εἰς τὸ καλῶς ἔχειν, οἱ δὲ πρότερον εὐκραεῖς
ὑπερξηραινόμενοί ποτε γίγνονται χείρους.

    Ὅπερ συμβέβηκε τῆς Ἑλλάδος καὶ περὶ τὴν
10 Ἀργείων καὶ Μυκηναίων χώραν· ἐπὶ μὲν γὰρ τῶν
Τρωικῶν ἡ μὲν Ἀργεία διὰ τὸ ἑλώδης εἶναι ὀλίγους
ἐδύνατο τρέφειν, ἡ δὲ Μυκηναία καλῶς εἶχεν (διὸ
ἐντιμοτέρα ἦν), νῦν δὲ τοὐναντίον διὰ τὴν προειρη-
μένην αἰτίαν· ἡ μὲν γὰρ ἀργὴ γέγονεν καὶ ξηρὰ
πάμπαν, τῆς δὲ τὰ τότε διὰ τὸ λιμνάζειν ἀργὰ νῦν
15 χρήσιμα γέγονεν. ὥσπερ οὖν ἐπὶ τούτου τοῦ τόπου
συμβέβηκεν ὄντος μικροῦ, ταὐτὸ δεῖ νομίζειν τοῦτο
συμβαίνειν καὶ περὶ μεγάλους τόπους καὶ χώρας
ὅλας.

    Οἱ μὲν οὖν βλέποντες ἐπὶ μικρὸν αἰτίαν οἴονται
τῶν τοιούτων εἶναι παθημάτων τὴν τοῦ ὅλου μεταβολὴν ὡς γιγνομένου τοῦ οὐρανοῦ· διὸ καὶ τὴν
20 θάλατταν ἐλάττω γίγνεσθαί φασιν ὡς ξηραινομένην,
ὅτι πλείους φαίνονται τόποι τοῦτο πεπονθότες νῦν
ἢ πρότερον. ἔστιν δὲ τούτων τὸ μὲν ἀληθὲς τὸ δ'
οὐκ ἀληθές· πλείους μὲν γάρ εἰσιν οἱ πρότερον
ἔνυδροι νῦν δὲ χερσεύοντες, οὐ μὴν ἀλλὰ καὶ τοὐναν-
τίον· πολλαχῇ γὰρ σκοποῦντες εὑρήσουσιν ἐπελη-
25 λυθυῖαν τὴν θάλατταν. ἀλλὰ τούτου τὴν αἰτίαν οὐ
τὴν τοῦ κόσμου γένεσιν οἴεσθαι χρή· γελοῖον γὰρ
διὰ μικρὰς καὶ ἀκαριαίας μεταβολὰς κινεῖν τὸ πᾶν,
ὁ δὲ τῆς γῆς ὄγκος καὶ τὸ μέγεθος οὐδέν ἐστι δή
που πρὸς τὸν ὅλον οὐρανόν· ἀλλὰ πάντων τούτων

---

in its turn and in time becomes thriving. For as places dry they improve, and places that formerly enjoyed a good climate deteriorate and grow too dry.

This has happened in Greece to the land about Greece. Argos and Mycenae. In the time of the Trojan War Argos was marshy and able to support few inhabitants only, while Mycenae was good land and therefore the more famous. Now the opposite is the case for the reason given above : for Mycenae has become unproductive and completely dry, while the Argive land that was once marshy and unproductive is now under cultivation. What has happened in this small district may therefore be supposed to happen to large districts and whole countries.

Those whose vision is limited think that the cause The cause of these effects is a universal process of change, the of these whole universe being in process of growth. So they periodical say the sea is becoming less because it is drying up,[a] deluges. their reason being that we find more places so affected now than in former times. There is some truth in this, but some falsehood also. For it is true that there is an increase in the number of places that have become dry land and were formerly submerged ; but the opposite is also true, for if they will look they will find many places where the sea has encroached. But we must not suppose that the cause of this is the growth of the universe : for it is absurd to argue that the whole is in process of change because of small changes of brief duration like these ; for the mass and size of the earth are of course nothing compared to that of the universe.[b] Rather we should

belief that the sea is drying up is attributed in ii. 3, 356 b 10, a passage Diels quotes as 68 A 100.
    [b] Cf. ch. 3, note a on p. 12.

352 a

αἴτιον ὑποληπτέον ὅτι γίγνεται διὰ χρόνων εἱμαρ-
30 μένων, οἷον ἐν ταῖς κατ' ἐνιαυτὸν ὥραις χειμών,
οὕτως περιόδου τινὸς μεγάλης μέγας χειμὼν καὶ
ὑπερβολὴ ὄμβρων. αὕτη δὲ οὐκ ἀεὶ κατὰ τοὺς
αὐτοὺς τόπους, ἀλλ' ὥσπερ ὁ καλούμενος ἐπὶ Δευ-
καλίωνος κατακλυσμός· καὶ γὰρ οὗτος περὶ τὸν
Ἑλληνικὸν ἐγένετο τόπον μάλιστα, καὶ τούτου περὶ
35 τὴν Ἑλλάδα τὴν ἀρχαίαν. αὕτη δ' ἐστὶν ἡ περὶ
352 b Δωδώνην καὶ τὸν Ἀχελῷον· οὗτος γὰρ πολλαχοῦ
τὸ ῥεῦμα μεταβέβληκεν· ᾤκουν γὰρ οἱ Σελλοὶ
ἐνταῦθα καὶ οἱ καλούμενοι τότε μὲν Γραικοὶ νῦν δ'
Ἕλληνες. ὅταν οὖν γένηται τοιαύτη ὑπερβολὴ
ὄμβρων, νομίζειν χρὴ ἐπὶ πολὺν χρόνον διαρκεῖν,
5 καὶ ὥσπερ νῦν τοῦ ἀενάους εἶναί τινας τῶν ποταμῶν
τοὺς δὲ μὴ οἱ μέν φασιν αἴτιον εἶναι τὸ μέγεθος
τῶν ὑπὸ γῆς χασμάτων, ἡμεῖς δὲ τὸ μέγεθος τῶν
ὑψηλῶν τόπων καὶ τὴν πυκνότητα καὶ ψυχρότητα
αὐτῶν (οὗτοι γὰρ πλεῖστον καὶ δέχονται ὕδωρ καὶ
στέγουσιν καὶ ποιοῦσιν· ὅσοις δὲ μικραὶ αἱ ἐπικρε-
10 μάμεναι τῶν ὀρῶν συστάσεις ἢ σομφαὶ καὶ λιθώδεις
καὶ ἀργιλώδεις, τούτους δὲ προαπολείπειν), οὕτως
οἴεσθαι δεῖν[1] τότε, ἐν οἷς ἂν γένηται ἡ τοιαύτη τοῦ
ὑγροῦ φορά, οἷον ἀενάους ποιεῖν τὰς ὑγρότητας τῶν
τόπων μᾶλλον.[2] τῷ χρόνῳ δὲ ταῦτα ξηραίνεται
15 [γιγνόμενα][3] μᾶλλον, θάτερα δ' ἔλαττον[4] τὰ ἔφυδρα,[5]

---

[1] δεῖ 𝔚 O.T.
[2] om. O.T. : ποταμῶν pro τόπων μᾶλλον habent Par. 2032 Ol.
[3] secl. Ideler O.T., cf. Ap 62. 33-34.
[4] ἔλαττον O.T., cf. Ap 62. 34 ; ἐλάττω Fobes.
[5] τὰ ἔφυδρα secl. Ideler.

suppose that the cause of all these changes is that, just as there is a winter among the yearly seasons, so at fixed intervals in some great period of time [a] there is a great winter and excess of rains. This does not always happen in the same region of the earth : for instance, the so-called flood of Deucalion took place largely in the Hellenic lands and particularly in old Hellas, that is, the country round Dodona and the Acheloüs, a river which has frequently changed its course. Here dwelt the Selloi and the people then called Greeks and now called Hellenes. Whenever such an excess of rains occurs it must be supposed to suffice for a long time. To give an analogy—We have just said that the cause of some rivers flowing perennially, some not, is considered by some to be the size of the chasms beneath the earth, but that we consider it to be the size and frequency and low temperature of mountainous districts, for such districts catch, contain and produce most water ; while if the mountain systems overhanging a district are either small or porous and composed of stones and clay, the supply of water runs out earlier : so then we must suppose that where the fall of water is so large, it tends to make the moisture of the districts almost inexhaustible. But in course of time districts of the second kind dry up more, the others, that is those of the

[a] Perhaps a great year, the period which it takes the heavenly bodies to return to the same relative positions. This is an old idea : cf. Heath, *Aristarchus*, and Taylor, *Commentary on Plato's Timaeus*, p. 215, *ad* 39 D. There is no association of the great year in this passage with periodic cataclysms : but the idea that there are such cataclysms occurs several times in Plato, *Tim.* 22 B-C, 23 A-B, *Laws* 677 A, *Critias* 109 D, *cf. Politicus* myth 268 E ff., esp. 273 A. Compare the doctrine of a recurrent cycle of knowledge, ch. 3, note *e* on p. 13.

ἕως ἂν ἔλθῃ πάλιν ἡ καταβολὴ τῆς περιόδου τῆς
αὐτῆς.

Ἐπεὶ δ' ἀνάγκη τοῦ ὅλου γίγνεσθαι μέν τινα
μεταβολήν, μὴ μέντοι γένεσιν καὶ φθοράν, εἴπερ
μένει τὸ πᾶν, ἀνάγκη, καθάπερ ἡμεῖς λέγομεν, μὴ
τοὺς αὐτοὺς ἀεὶ τόπους ὑγρούς τ' εἶναι θαλάττῃ καὶ
20 ποταμοῖς καὶ ξηρούς. δηλοῖ δὲ τὸ γιγνόμενον· οὓς
γὰρ φαμὲν ἀρχαιοτάτους εἶναι τῶν ἀνθρώπων
Αἰγυπτίους, τούτων ἡ χώρα πᾶσα γεγονυῖα φαίνεται
καὶ οὖσα τοῦ ποταμοῦ ἔργον. καὶ τοῦτο κατά τε
τὴν χώραν αὐτὴν ὁρῶντι δῆλόν ἐστιν, καὶ τὰ περὶ
τὴν ἐρυθρὰν θάλατταν τεκμήριον ἱκανόν· ταύτην
25 γὰρ τῶν βασιλέων τις ἐπειράθη διορύττειν (οὐ γὰρ
μικρὰς εἶχεν ἂν αὐτοῖς ὠφελείας πλωτὸς πᾶς ὁ
τόπος γενόμενος· λέγεται δὲ πρῶτος Σέσωστρις
ἐγχειρῆσαι τῶν παλαιῶν), ἀλλ' εὗρεν ὑψηλοτέραν
οὖσαν τὴν θάλατταν τῆς γῆς· διὸ ἐκεῖνός τε πρότερον καὶ Δαρεῖος ὕστερον ἐπαύσατο διορύττων,
30 ὅπως μὴ διαφθαρῇ τὸ ῥεῦμα τοῦ ποταμοῦ συμμι-
γείσης τῆς θαλάττης. φανερὸν οὖν ὅτι θάλαττα
πάντα μία ταύτῃ συνεχὴς ἦν. διὸ καὶ τὰ περὶ τὴν

ᵃ The text and interpretation of ll. 8-15 are doubtful. My
interpretation follows the O.T. and makes ταῦτα (13) refer
to the latter of the two types of district described in the
parenthesis, *i.e.* to ὅσοις δέ . . . προαπολείπειν (9-11) : θάτερα
then refers to οὗτοι γάρ . . . ποιοῦσι 8-9, words which describe a type of district that may fairly be described as ἔφυδρος
(14-15). On this interpretation Aristotle is contrasting two
types (οὗτοι γάρ and ὅσοις δέ) of districts and saying that after
a deluge one retains its moisture longer than the other.
    Thurot makes ταῦτα refer to the wet districts described in
ll. 12-13, and alters ll. 13-15 to read as follows—τῷ χρόνῳ δὲ

moist kind, less,[a] until the beginning of the same cycle returns again.

Since some change must necessarily take place in the whole, but this change cannot be growth and decay as the universe is permanent, it must be as we say that the same districts are not always moistened by sea and rivers nor always dry. The facts prove this. For the land of the Egyptians, who are supposed to be the most ancient of the human race, appears to be all made ground, the work of the river. This is clear to anyone who looks at the country itself, and further proof is afforded by the facts about the Red Sea. One of the kings tried to dig a canal to it. (For it would be of no little advantage to them if this whole region was accessible to navigation : Sesostris is said to be the first of the ancient kings to have attempted the work.) It was, however, found that the sea was higher than the land : and so Sesostris first and Dareius after him gave up digging the canal for fear the water of the river should be ruined by an admixture of sea-water.[b] This makes it clear that there was once a continuous sea here, which again is

Evidence of such changes in Egypt and the Red Sea.

ταῦτα ξηραινόμενα γίγνεται ἐλάττω τὰ ἔφυδρα, θάτερα δὲ πλείω, ἕως . . . Thus the contrast is between districts subject to the deluge and in consequence wet, which shrink while other districts not subject to it and so dry correspondingly expand.

γιγνόμενα (14) is condemned by Ideler (i. p. 487) as well as by O.T. and Thurot, and does not seem to have been read by Alex. I have therefore bracketed it. ἐλάττον seems necessary in l. 14 on the interpretation I have adopted.

[b] Cf. Herod. ii. 108, 158, Strabo xvii. 25, Diodorus i. 33, Pliny, Nat. Hist. vi. 33; and How and Wells's Commentary on Herodotus, vol. i. pp. 245-246. The canal ran from the Nile at Bubastis to the Bitter Lakes and thence southwards to the Red Sea. Strabo, Diodorus and Pliny all mention the difficulty caused by the difference in levels, which Diodorus says was overcome by means of a lock.

117

352 b

Λιβύην τὴν Ἀμμωνίαν χώραν ταπεινότερα φαίνεται καὶ κοιλότερα παρὰ λόγον τῆς κάτωθεν χώρας· δῆλον γὰρ ὡς ἐγχώσεως μὲν γενομένης ἐγένοντο
35 λίμναι καὶ χέρσος, χρόνου δὲ γενομένου τὸ ἐναπο-
353 a λειφθὲν καὶ λιμνάσαν ὕδωρ ξηρανθέν ἐστιν ἤδη φροῦδον. ἀλλὰ μὴν καὶ τὰ περὶ τὴν Μαιῶτιν λίμνην ἐπιδέδωκε τῇ προσχώσει τῶν ποταμῶν τοσοῦτον, ὥστε πολλῷ ἐλάττω μεγέθει πλοῖα νῦν εἰσπλεῖν πρὸς τὴν ἐργασίαν ἢ ἔτος ἑξηκοστόν· ὥστε
5 ἐκ τούτου ῥᾴδιον ἀναλογίσασθαι ὅτι καὶ τὸ πρῶτον, ὥσπερ αἱ πολλαὶ τῶν λιμνῶν, καὶ αὕτη ἔργον ἐστὶ τῶν ποταμῶν, καὶ τὸ τελευταῖον πᾶσαν ἀνάγκη γενέσθαι ξηράν. ἔτι δὲ ὁ Βόσπορος ἀεὶ μὲν ῥεῖ διὰ τὸ προσχοῦσθαι, καὶ ἔστιν ἔτι ταῦτα καὶ τοῖς ὄμμασιν ἰδεῖν ὅν τινα συμβαίνει τρόπον· ὅτε γὰρ
10 ἀπὸ τῆς Ἀσίας ἠόνα ποιήσειεν ὁ ῥοῦς, τὸ ὄπισθεν λίμνη ἐγίγνετο μικρὰ τὸ πρῶτον, εἶτ᾽ ἐξηράνθη ἄν, μετὰ δὲ τοῦτο ἄλλη ἡ ἀπὸ ταύτης ἠών, καὶ λίμνη ἀπὸ ταύτης· καὶ τοῦτο ἀεὶ οὕτως συνέβαινεν ὁμοίως· τούτου δὲ γιγνομένου πολλάκις ἀνάγκη χρόνου προϊόντος ὥσπερ ποταμὸν γενέσθαι, τέλος δὲ καὶ τοῦτον ξηρόν.
15 Φανερὸν τοίνυν, ἐπεὶ ὅ τε χρόνος οὐχ ὑπολείψει καὶ τὸ ὅλον ἀΐδιον, ὅτι οὔτε ὁ Τάναϊς οὔτε ὁ Νεῖλος ἀεὶ ἔρρει, ἀλλ᾽ ἦν ποτε ξηρὸς ὁ τόπος ὅθεν ῥέουσιν· τὸ γὰρ ἔργον ἔχει αὐτῶν πέρας, ὁ δὲ χρόνος οὐκ ἔχει. ὁμοίως δὲ τοῦτο καὶ ἐπὶ τῶν ἄλλων ἁρμόσει ποταμῶν λέγειν. ἀλλὰ μὴν εἴπερ καὶ οἱ ποταμοὶ
20 γίγνονται καὶ φθείρονται καὶ μὴ ἀεὶ οἱ αὐτοὶ τόποι τῆς γῆς ἔνυδροι, καὶ τὴν θάλατταν ἀνάγκη μεταβάλλειν ὁμοίως. τῆς δὲ θαλάττης τὰ μὲν ἀπολειπούσης τὰ δ᾽ ἐπιούσης ἀεὶ φανερὸν ὅτι τῆς πάσης

why the district of Ammon [a] in Libya is unexpectedly found to be lower and hollower than the land to seaward of it : for clearly what happened was that the river deposited silt which formed dry land and lakes, but that in course of time the water left in the lakes dried up and has now disappeared. Furthermore, Lake there has been such a great increase of river silt on the Maeotis. shores of Lake Maeotis that the ships that ply there now for trade are far smaller in size than they used to be sixty years ago. And from this fact it is easy to deduce that, like most other lakes, this too was originally produced by rivers and that eventually it must all become dry. Besides, there is always a current through the Bosphorus as a result of the silting, and one can even see with one's own eyes how the process works. For whenever the current made a sandbank off the shore of Asia, there formed behind it at first a small lake, which subsequently dried up : then a further sandbank formed in front of this one and another lake, and so the process went on. When this has happened often enough the channel must in course of time be narrowed till it is like a river, and even this in the end must dry up.

It is therefore clear that as time is infinite and the Conclusion. universe eternal that neither Tanaïs nor Nile always flowed but the place whence they flow was once dry : for their action has an end whereas time has none. And the same may be said with truth about other rivers. But if rivers come into being and perish and if the same parts of the earth are not always moist, the sea also must necessarily change correspondingly. And if in places the sea recedes while in others it encroaches, then evidently the same parts of the earth

[a] Qattara Depression.

119

353 a

γῆς οὐκ ἀεὶ τὰ αὐτὰ τὰ μέν ἐστιν θάλαττα τὰ δ᾽
ἤπειρος, ἀλλὰ μεταβάλλει τῷ χρόνῳ πάντα.

25 Διότι μὲν οὖν οὐκ ἀεὶ ταὐτὰ οὔτε χερσεύει τῆς
γῆς οὔτε πλωτά ἐστιν, καὶ διὰ τίν᾽ αἰτίαν ταῦτα
συμβαίνει, εἴρηται· ὁμοίως δὲ καὶ διὰ τί οἱ μὲν
ἀέναοι οἱ δ᾽ οὒ τῶν ποταμῶν εἰσιν.

as a whole are not always sea, nor always mainland, but in process of time all change.

We have now explained why the same parts of the earth are not always either dry land or navigable water and what the reason for this is : and we have explained similarly why some rivers are perennial, some not.

B

CHAPTER I

ARGUMENT

The sea and its nature. (I) Previous views. The theologians believed that the sea has sources (like a river) ; the secular philosophers believed that it had a beginning in time and give various accounts of its saltness (353 a 32-b 16). (II) The sea cannot have sources. A (1) Water that has a

353 a 32 Περὶ δὲ θαλάττης, καὶ τίς ἡ φύσις αὐτῆς, καὶ διὰ τίν' αἰτίαν ἁλμυρὸν τοσοῦτόν ἐστιν ὕδατος πλῆθος, ἔτι δὲ περὶ τῆς ἐξ ἀρχῆς γενέσεως λέγωμεν.

35 Οἱ μὲν οὖν ἀρχαῖοι καὶ διατρίβοντες περὶ τὰς **353 b** θεολογίας ποιοῦσιν αὐτῆς πηγάς, ἵν' αὐτοῖς ὦσιν ἀρχαὶ καὶ ῥίζαι γῆς καὶ θαλάττης· τραγικώτερον γὰρ οὕτω καὶ σεμνότερον ὑπέλαβον ἴσως εἶναι τὸ λεγόμενον, ὡς μέγα τι τοῦ παντὸς τοῦτο μόριον ὄν· καὶ τὸν λοιπὸν οὐρανὸν ὅλον περὶ τοῦτον συνεστάναι 5 τὸν τόπον καὶ τούτου χάριν ὡς ὄντα τιμιώτατον καὶ ἀρχήν.

Οἱ δὲ σοφώτεροι τὴν ἀνθρωπίνην σοφίαν ποιοῦσιν αὐτῆς γένεσιν· εἶναι γὰρ τὸ πρῶτον ὑγρὸν ἅπαντα

BOOK II

CHAPTER I

ARGUMENT (continued)

*source is either running or artificial, the sea is neither ; (2)
some seas are land locked and their sources would have been
discerned (353 b 17—354 a 5). B (1) Though the sea does
flow in places this is due (1) to confinement in narrow straits,
(2) to differences of depth (354 a 5-34).*

OUR next subject is the sea and its nature, the problem of why so great a volume of water is salt and of
its original formation.

(I) The ancients who concerned themselves with The Theo-
theology [a] make it have sources, their purpose being logians.
to provide both land and sea with origins and roots.
They perhaps supposed that this would give a more
dramatic and grander air to their theories, according
to which the earth was an important part of the
universe, the whole of the rest of which had formed
around it and for its sake, as if the earth were the
most important and primary part of it.

Those who were more versed in secular philosophy The Philo-
suppose it to have had a beginning. They say that sophers.

[a] *Cf.* Hesiod, *Theogony* 282, 785-792.

353 b

τὸν περὶ τὴν γῆν τόπον, ὑπὸ δὲ τοῦ ἡλίου ξηραινό-
μενον τὸ μὲν διατμίσαν πνεύματα καὶ τροπὰς ἡλίου
καὶ σελήνης φασὶ ποιεῖν, τὸ δὲ λειφθὲν θάλατταν
10 εἶναι· διὸ καὶ ἐλάττω γίγνεσθαι ξηραινομένην
οἴονται, καὶ τέλος ἔσεσθαί ποτε πᾶσαν ξηράν.
ἔνιοι δ' αὐτῶν θερμαινομένης φασὶν ὑπὸ τοῦ ἡλίου
τῆς γῆς οἷον ἱδρῶτα γίγνεσθαι· διὸ καὶ ἁλμυρὰν
εἶναι· καὶ γὰρ ὁ ἱδρὼς ἁλμυρός. οἱ δὲ τῆς ἁλμυρό-
15 τητος αἰτίαν τὴν γῆν εἶναί φασιν· καθάπερ γὰρ τὸ
διὰ τῆς τέφρας ἠθούμενον ἁλμυρὸν γίγνεται, τὸν
αὐτὸν τρόπον καὶ ταύτην ἁλμυρὰν εἶναι μειχθείσης
αὐτῇ τοιαύτης γῆς.

Ὅτι μὲν οὖν πηγὰς τῆς θαλάττης ἀδύνατον εἶναι,
διὰ τῶν ὑπαρχόντων ἤδη θεωρεῖν δεῖ.

Τῶν γὰρ περὶ τὴν γῆν ὑδάτων τὰ μὲν ῥυτὰ τυγ-
20 χάνει ὄντα τὰ δὲ στάσιμα. τὰ μὲν οὖν ῥυτὰ πάντα
πηγαῖα· περὶ δὲ τῶν πηγῶν εἰρήκαμεν πρότερον ὅτι
δεῖ νοεῖν οὐχ ὥσπερ ἐξ ἀγγείου ταμιευομένων[1] τὴν

---

[1] ταμιευομένων E$_{corr.}$ 𝔚 Thurot O.T.: ταμιευσομένων (ut
videtur) E$_1$: ταμιευόμενον Fobes.

---

[a] Alex., on the authority of Theophrastus, attributes this
view to Anaximander and Diogenes of Apollonia (cf. Diels
12 A 27 and 64 A 9, 17): though there is also perhaps some
reminiscence of Thales and of Anaximenes (Diels 13 A 7 (5)).
There are, however, two views of the cause of the solstices
to be found in this and the following chapter: (1) that the sun
is fed by moisture and the solstices are due to the lack of it,
354 b 34—355 a 5; (2) that they are due to the resistance of
the air 353 b 7, 355 a 22-25. The second view was held by
Anaximenes (Diels 13 A 15); and also, according to Theophrastus, by Anaximander and Diogenes. Ideler (i. p. 509)
seems right in attributing the first view to Heracleitus: cf.
Burnet, *E.G.P.*[4], pp. 155-156, and especially the passage

at first the whole region about the earth was wet,[a] and that as it dried up the water that evaporated became the cause of winds and the turnings of sun and moon,[b] while what was left is the sea : consequently they believe that the sea is still drying up and becoming less, and that in the end a time will come when it is all dried up. Some [c] again believe that the sea is, as it were, the sweat of the earth which it sweats out when the sun heats it : which is the reason why it is salt because sweat is salt. Others [d] suppose that the earth is the cause of its saltness : just as water strained through ashes becomes salt, so the sea is salt because earth with this property is mixed with it.

(II) We must therefore now show by an examination of the facts that the sea cannot have sources.

The sea cannot have sources.

A (1) The water on the earth's surface is either running or standing. Running water flows from sources. (We have spoken about sources above and said that a source must not be supposed to be the point at which a supply of water flows out of a kind

quoted from the Περὶ Διαίτης. But Burnet, Diels and Heath all ignore the passage 354 b 34—355 a 5 in which this first view is given.

[b] Heath, *Aristarchus*, p. 33 (following Zeller, *Phil. der Griechen*[6], i. p. 298, note 1), doubts if τροπαί can mean solstice here. But his doubts are partly based on his interpretation of 355 a 25 (on which see ch. 2, note *b* on p. 135), and of the reference to the moon here he says " τροπαί could be used of the moon in a sense sufficiently parallel to its use for solstices." It seems better, therefore, to take τροπαί in what is its natural sense as referring to the limits of the variations in the course of the sun (solstices) and of the moon. *Cf.* Burnet, *E.G.P.*[4], p. 63, note 2.

[c] Empedocles : *cf.* 357 a 24 and Diels 31 A 66. Also Democritus (Diels 68 A 99 A) and Antiphon (87 B 32).

[d] Xenophanes : Diels 21 A 33 (4) ; Metrodorus : Diels 70 A 19 ; Anaxagoras : Diels 59 A 90.

353 b

ἀρχὴν εἶναι πηγήν, ἀλλ' εἰς ἣν[1] ἀεὶ γιγνόμενον καὶ
συρρέον ἀπαντᾷ[2] πρώτην. τῶν δὲ στασίμων τὰ
μὲν συλλογιμαῖα καὶ ὑποστάσεις, οἷον τὰ τελμα-
25 τιαῖα καὶ ὅσα λιμνώδη, πλήθει καὶ ὀλιγότητι διαφέροντα, τὰ δὲ πηγαῖα. ταῦτα δὲ πάντα χειρόκμητα,
λέγω δ' οἷον τὰ φρεατιαῖα καλούμενα· πάντων γὰρ
ἀνωτέρω δεῖ τὴν πηγὴν εἶναι τῆς ῥύσεως. διὸ τὰ
μὲν αὐτόματα ῥεῖ τὰ κρηναῖα καὶ ποτάμια, ταῦτα
δὲ τέχνης προσδεῖται τῆς ἐργασομένης. αἱ μὲν οὖν
30 διαφοραὶ τοσαῦται καὶ τοιαῦται τῶν ὑδάτων εἰσίν·
τούτων δ' οὕτω διωρισμένων ἀδύνατον πηγὰς εἶναι
τῆς θαλάττης. ἐν οὐδετέρῳ γὰρ τούτων οἷόν τ'
εἶναι τῶν γενῶν αὐτήν· οὔτε γὰρ ἀπόρρυτός ἐστιν
οὔτε χειροποίητος, τὰ δὲ πηγαῖα πάντα τούτων
θάτερον πέπονθεν· αὐτόματον δὲ στάσιμον τοσοῦτον
35 πλῆθος οὐδὲν ὁρῶμεν πηγαῖον γιγνόμενον.

354 a

Ἔτι δ' ἐπεὶ πλείους εἰσὶ θάλατται πρὸς ἀλλήλας
οὐ συμμειγνύουσαι κατ' οὐδένα τόπον, ὧν ἡ μὲν
ἐρυθρὰ φαίνεται κατὰ μικρὸν κοινωνοῦσα πρὸς τὴν
ἔξω στηλῶν θάλατταν, ἡ δ' Ὑρκανία καὶ Κασπία
κεχωρισμέναι τε ταύτης καὶ περιοικούμεναι κύκλῳ,
5 ὥστ' οὐκ ἂν ἐλάνθανον αἱ πηγαί, εἰ κατά τινα
τόπον αὐτῶν ἦσαν.

Ῥέουσα δ' ἡ θάλαττα φαίνεται κατά τε τὰς
στενότητας, εἴ που διὰ τὴν περιέχουσαν γῆν εἰς
μικρὸν ἐκ μεγάλου συνάγεται πελάγους, διὰ τὸ

---

[1] ἣν E_1 𝔐 𝔄 H $N_{corr. m. 1}$ Thurot O.T. : ἐν Fobes.
[2] ἀπαντᾷ E_1 𝔚 𝔐 𝔄 H N Ap Thurot O.T. : ἀπαντᾶν Fobes.

---

[a] Aristotle's language here, with the plural participles,
implies, as Tarn remarks (*Alexander the Great*, ii. p. 6, note 3),
that the Hyrcanian and Caspian are separate seas. If this

of vessel, but the point at which water which is continually forming and trickling together first gathers.)
Of standing water some collects and remains static,
for instance swamps and lakes, which differ only in
size ; some springs from sources, but is always made
to do so artificially, as for instance the water in wells.
For the source must always be higher than the stream
it feeds : and hence water in springs and rivers runs
of its own accord, but well-water always needs an
artificial construction. This is a complete enumeration of the various species of water : and from this
classification one can see that it is impossible for the
sea to have sources. For water that has a source is
either running or artificial : but the sea has neither
of these characteristics, and therefore cannot fall
into either class. And we know of no volume of water
of comparable size that has sources and yet stands
of its own accord.

(2) Besides, there are many seas that have no connexion with each other at any point ; for instance the
Red Sea communicates with the ocean outside the
straits by only a narrow channel, and the Hyrcanian [a]
and Caspian have no connexion with the outer ocean
and are inhabited all round, and so their sources
would have been observed if they had any any-
where.

B (1) The sea, however, obviously flows in narrow
places where a large expanse of water is contracted
by the surrounding land into a small space : but this

is Aristotle's real view, and he is not merely confused by a
single sea having *two* names (*cf.* Bunbury, *Ancient Geography*,
i. p. 401, and P. Bolchert, *Aristoteles Erdkunde von Asien
und Libyen*, p. 10), then the seas in question must be the
Caspian (Ὑρκανία) and Aral (Κασπία). See also Note on
Aristotle's Geography at end of Book I. ch. 13.

354 a

ταλαντεύεσθαι δεῦρο κἀκεῖσε πολλάκις. τοῦτο δ᾽
ἐν μὲν πολλῷ πλήθει θαλάττης ἄδηλον· ᾗ δὲ διὰ
10 τὴν στενότητα τῆς γῆς ὀλίγον ἐπέχει τόπον, ἀναγκαῖον τὴν ἐν τῷ πελάγει μικρὰν ταλάντωσιν ἐκεῖ
φαίνεσθαι μεγάλης.

Ἡ δ᾽ ἐντὸς Ἡρακλείων στηλῶν ἅπασα κατὰ
τὴν τῆς γῆς κοιλότητα ῥεῖ, καὶ τῶν ποταμῶν τὸ
πλῆθος· ἡ μὲν γὰρ Μαιῶτις εἰς τὸν Πόντον ῥεῖ,
15 οὗτος δ᾽ εἰς τὸν Αἰγαῖον. τὰ δ᾽ ἤδη τούτων ἔξω
πελάγη ἧττον ποιεῖ τοῦτ᾽ ἐπιδήλως. ἐκείνοις δὲ
διά τε τὸ τῶν ποταμῶν πλῆθος συμβαίνει τοῦτο
(πλείους γὰρ εἰς τὸν Εὔξεινον ῥέουσιν ποταμοὶ καὶ
τὴν Μαιῶτιν ἢ τὴν πολλαπλασίαν χώραν αὐτῆς)
20 καὶ διὰ τὴν βραχύτητα τοῦ βάθους· ἀεὶ γὰρ ἔτι
βαθυτέρα φαίνεται οὖσα ἡ θάλαττα, καὶ τῆς μὲν
Μαιώτιδος ὁ Πόντος, τούτου δ᾽ ὁ Αἰγαῖος, τοῦ δ᾽
Αἰγαίου ὁ Σικελικός· ὁ δὲ Σαρδονικὸς καὶ Τυρρη-
νικὸς βαθύτατοι πάντων. τὰ δ᾽ ἔξω στηλῶν βραχέα
μὲν διὰ τὸν πηλόν, ἄπνοα δ᾽ ἐστὶν ὡς ἐν κοίλῳ τῆς
θαλάττης οὔσης. ὥσπερ οὖν καὶ κατὰ μέρος ἐκ
τῶν ὑψηλῶν οἱ ποταμοὶ φαίνονται ῥέοντες, οὕτω
25 καὶ τῆς ὅλης γῆς ἐκ τῶν ὑψηλοτέρων τῶν πρὸς
ἄρκτον τὸ ῥεῦμα γίγνεται τὸ πλεῖστον· ὥστε τὰ
μὲν διὰ τὴν ἔκχυσιν οὐ βαθέα, τὰ δ᾽ ἔξω πελάγη
βαθέα μᾶλλον. περὶ δὲ τοῦ τὰ πρὸς ἄρκτον εἶναι
τῆς γῆς ὑψηλὰ σημεῖόν τι καὶ τὸ πολλοὺς πεισθῆναι
30 τῶν ἀρχαίων μετεωρολόγων τὸν ἥλιον μὴ φέρεσθαι

---

is because the sea ebbs and flows frequently. In a large expanse this motion is unnoticeable; but where the expanse is small because the shores constrict it the ebb and flow which in the open sea seemed small now seems strong.[a]

(2) The whole Mediterranean flows according to the depth of the sea-bed and the volume of the rivers. For Lake Maeotis flows into the Pontus and this into the Aegean. In the remaining seas the process is not so obvious. In the seas mentioned it takes place because of the rivers—for more rivers flow into the Euxine and Lake Maeotis than into other areas many times their size—and because of their shallowness. For the sea seems to get deeper and deeper, the Pontus being deeper than Lake Maeotis, the Aegean deeper than the Pontus, and the Sicilian sea deeper than the Aegean, while the Sardinian and Tyrrhenian are the deepest of all. The water outside the pillars of Heracles is shallow because of the mud but calm because the sea lies in a hollow.[b] As, therefore, rivers in particular are found to flow down from high places, so in general the flow is greatest from the higher parts of the earth which lie towards the north. So some seas are shallow because they are always being emptied, while the outer seas are deeper. An indication that the northerly parts of the earth are high is the opinion of many of the ancient meteorologists [c] that

and flow (lit. swinging to and fro) of the sea, for he had no real knowledge of the tides.

[b] " *i.e.* it is shallow, yet the water does not flow back (as you might expect on the analogy of Maeotis, etc.) because the sea lies in a hollow as is proved by the calm (Alexander) " (O.T.). For the shallowness of the sea beyond the Pillars of Heracles *cf.* Plato, *Timaeus* 25 D.

[c] Anaximenes : Diels 13 A 7 (b) 14.

ARISTOTLE

ὑπὸ γῆν ἀλλὰ περὶ τὴν γῆν καὶ τὸν τόπον τοῦτον,
ἀφανίζεσθαι δὲ καὶ ποιεῖν νύκτα διὰ τὸ ὑψηλὴν
εἶναι πρὸς ἄρκτον τὴν γῆν.

Ὅτι μὲν οὖν οὔτε πηγὰς οἷόν τ' εἶναι τῆς θαλάττης, καὶ διὰ τίν' αἰτίαν οὕτως φαίνεται ῥέουσα,
τοιαῦτα καὶ τοσαῦθ' ἡμῖν εἰρήσθω.

CHAPTER II

ARGUMENT

*The sea (continued). (III) Its origin and saltness. Our
predecessors regarded the sea as the main body of water ; and
some thought that rivers flow out of it as well as into it (354
b 1-18). But why then is it salt ? Water surrounds the earth
just as air surrounds water : and the sun evaporates fresh
water, which subsequently falls as rain (354 b 18-33). (The
sun cannot be fed by moisture as some have maintained, for
(1) the analogy with flame which they use is not valid ; (2) fire*

Περὶ δὲ τῆς γενέσεως αὐτῆς, εἰ γέγονε, καὶ τοῦ
χυμοῦ, τίς ἡ αἰτία τῆς ἁλμυρότητος καὶ πικρότητος,
λεκτέον.

Ἡ μὲν οὖν αἰτία ἡ ποιήσασα τοὺς πρότερον
οἴεσθαι τὴν θάλατταν ἀρχὴν εἶναι καὶ σῶμα τοῦ
5 παντὸς ὕδατος ἥδ' ἐστίν· δόξειε γὰρ ἂν εὔλογον
εἶναι, καθάπερ καὶ τῶν ἄλλων στοιχείων ἐστὶν
ἠθροισμένος ὄγκος καὶ ἀρχὴ διὰ τὸ πλῆθος, ὅθεν
μεταβάλλει τε μεριζόμενον καὶ μείγνυται τοῖς
ἄλλοις—οἷον πυρὸς μὲν ἐν τοῖς ἄνω τόποις, ἀέρος
δὲ πλῆθος τὸ μετὰ τὸν τοῦ πυρὸς τόπον, γῆς δὲ
10 σῶμα περὶ ὃ ταῦτα πάντα κεῖται φανερῶς· ὥστε

the sun does not pass under the earth but round its northerly part, and that it disappears and causes night because the earth is high towards the north.

So much then for our proofs that the sea cannot have sources, and for the reason why it seems to flow as it does.

CHAPTER II

ARGUMENT (*continued*)

is not fed by the water which it heats ; (3) when water is evaporated an equivalent amount always condenses and falls again (354 b 33—355 a 32).) The fresh water, then, is evaporated, the salt water is left. The process is analogous to the digestion of liquid food. The place occupied by the sea is the natural place of water : and fresh water evaporates more quickly and easily when it reaches and is dispersed in the sea (355 a 32–b 32). Criticism of the account of rivers and the sea given in the Phaedo (355 b 32—356 b 2).

(III) We must now deal with the origin of the sea, if it had one, and the reason for its salt and bitter taste.

The reason that made our predecessors think that the sea is the primary and main body of water is that they thought it reasonable to suppose that what was true of the other elements must be true of water. For of each of them there is one mass which is primary because of its volume, and from which come those parts of it which change and are mixed with the other elements : thus there is a mass of fire in the upper regions, of air in the region beneath that of fire, and a main body of earth round which it is obvious that

Predecessors' views.

131

354 b

δῆλον ὅτι κατὰ τὸν αὐτὸν λόγον καὶ περὶ ὕδατος
ἀνάγκη ζητεῖν. τοιοῦτον δ' οὐδὲν ἄλλο φαίνεται
σῶμα κείμενον ἀθρόον, ὥσπερ καὶ τῶν ἄλλων στοιχείων, πλὴν τὸ τῆς θαλάττης μέγεθος· τὸ γὰρ τῶν
ποταμῶν οὔτ' ἀθρόον οὔτε στάσιμον, ἀλλ' ὡς γι-
15 γνόμενον ἀεὶ φαίνεται καθ' ἡμέραν. ἐκ ταύτης δὴ
τῆς ἀπορίας καὶ ἀρχὴ τῶν ὑγρῶν ἔδοξεν εἶναι καὶ
τοῦ παντὸς ὕδατος ἡ θάλαττα. διὸ καὶ τοὺς ποταμοὺς οὐ μόνον εἰς ταύτην ἀλλὰ καὶ ἐκ ταύτης
φασί τινες ῥεῖν· διηθούμενον γὰρ γίγνεσθαι τὸ
ἁλμυρὸν πότιμον. ἀντίκειται δὲ ἑτέρα πρὸς ταύτην
20 τὴν δόξαν ἀπορία, τί δή ποτ' οὐκ ἔστιν τὸ συνεστὸς
ὕδωρ τοῦτο πότιμον, εἴπερ ἀρχὴ τοῦ παντὸς ὕδατος,
ἀλλ' ἁλμυρόν. τὸ δ' αἴτιον ἅμα ταύτης τε τῆς
ἀπορίας λύσις ἔσται, καὶ περὶ θαλάττης τὴν πρώτην
λαβεῖν ὑπόληψιν ἀναγκαῖον ὀρθῶς.

Τοῦ γὰρ ὕδατος περὶ τὴν γῆν περιτεταμένου,
25 καθάπερ περὶ τοῦτο ἡ τοῦ ἀέρος σφαῖρα καὶ περὶ
ταύτην ἡ λεγομένη πυρός (τοῦτο γάρ ἐστι πάντων
ἔσχατον, εἴθ' ὡς οἱ πλεῖστοι λέγουσιν εἴθ' ὡς
ἡμεῖς), φερομένου δὲ τοῦ ἡλίου τοῦτον τὸν τρόπον,
καὶ διὰ ταῦτα τῆς μεταβολῆς καὶ γενέσεώς τε καὶ
φθορᾶς οὔσης, τὸ μὲν λεπτότατον καὶ γλυκύτατον
30 ἀνάγεται καθ' ἑκάστην ἡμέραν καὶ φέρεται διακρινόμενον καὶ ἀτμίζον εἰς τὸν ἄνω τόπον, ἐκεῖ δὲ
πάλιν συστὰν διὰ τὴν ψύξιν καταφέρεται πάλιν
πρὸς τὴν γῆν. καὶ τοῦτ' ἀεὶ βούλεται ποιεῖν ἡ
φύσις οὕτως, καθάπερ εἴρηται πρότερον.

Διὸ καὶ γελοῖοι πάντες ὅσοι τῶν πρότερον ὑπέλαβον τὸν ἥλιον τρέφεσθαι τῷ ὑγρῷ· καὶ διὰ τοῦτ'
355 a ἔνιοί γέ φασιν καὶ ποιεῖσθαι τὰς τροπὰς αὐτόν· οὐ

the other two lie. Clearly, therefore, we must look for something analogous for water. But there is no obvious single mass of water, as there is of the other elements, except the sea. For the water of the rivers is neither a single mass nor standing, but appears to change continuously from day to day. It was this difficulty which led people to suppose that the sea was the primary source of moisture and of all water. So some say that rivers not only flow into it but out of it,[a] and that the salt water becomes drinkable by being filtered. But there is a further difficulty in the way of this view—Why is not this body of water fresh and not salt, if it is the origin of all water? A knowledge of the reason for this will provide us with an answer to the difficulty and also ensure that our basic ideas about the sea are correct.

Water surrounds the earth just as the sphere of air surrounds water and the so-called sphere of fire surrounds that of air—fire being the outermost both on the commonly accepted view and on ours. As the sun moves in its course—and by its movement causes change, generation and destruction—it draws up the finest and sweetest water each day and makes it dissolve into vapour and rise into the upper region, where it is then condensed by the cold and falls again to the earth. This is the natural and normal course of events as we have said above.[b]

(So it is absurd to believe as some of our predecessors have that the sun is fed by moisture. Indeed some say that this is the cause of the solstice,[c] as the

Water surrounds earth.

The sun not fed by moisture.

---

[a] Xenophanes : Diels 21 B 30.

[b] Book I. ch. 9.

[c] Heracleitus : ch. 1, note a on p. 124. It is not clear to whom, besides Heracleitus, Aristotle is referring in ὅσοι, 354 b 33 ; possibly to Heracleitus's followers.

355 a

γὰρ αἰεὶ τοὺς αὐτοὺς δύνασθαι τόπους παρασκευάζειν αὐτῷ τὴν τροφήν· ἀναγκαῖον δ᾿ εἶναι τοῦτο
συμβαίνειν περὶ αὐτὸν ἢ φθείρεσθαι· καὶ γὰρ τὸ
φανερὸν πῦρ, ἕως ἂν ἔχῃ τροφήν, μέχρι τούτου ζῆν,
5 τὸ δ᾿ ὑγρὸν τῷ πυρὶ τροφὴν εἶναι μόνον,—ὥσπερ
ἀφικνούμενον μέχρι πρὸς τὸν ἥλιον τὸ ἀναγόμενον
τοῦ ὑγροῦ, ἢ τὴν ἄνοδον τοιαύτην οὖσαν οἷανπερ
τῇ γιγνομένῃ φλογί, δι᾿ ἧς τὸ εἰκὸς λαβόντες οὕτω
καὶ περὶ τοῦ ἡλίου ὑπέλαβον. τὸ δ᾿ οὐκ ἔστιν
10 ὅμοιον· ἡ μὲν γὰρ φλὸξ διὰ συνεχοῦς ὑγροῦ καὶ
ξηροῦ μεταβαλλόντων γίγνεται καὶ οὐ τρέφεται (οὐ
γὰρ ἡ αὐτὴ οὖσα διαμένει οὐδένα χρόνον ὡς εἰπεῖν),
περὶ δὲ τὸν ἥλιον ἀδύνατον τοῦτο συμβαίνειν, ἐπεὶ
τρεφομένου γε τὸν αὐτὸν τρόπον, ὥσπερ ἐκεῖνοί
φασιν, δῆλον ὅτι καὶ ὁ ἥλιος οὐ μόνον καθάπερ
Ἡράκλειτός φησιν, νέος ἐφ᾿ ἡμέρῃ ἐστίν, ἀλλ᾿ ἀεὶ
15 νέος συνεχῶς. ἔτι δ᾿ ἡ ὑπὸ τοῦ ἡλίου ἀναγωγὴ
τοῦ ὑγροῦ ὁμοία τοῖς θερμαινομένοις ἐστὶν ὕδασιν
ὑπὸ πυρός· εἰ οὖν μηδὲ τὸ ὑποκαόμενον τρέφεται
πῦρ, οὐδὲ τὸν ἥλιον εἰκὸς ἦν ὑπολαβεῖν, οὐδ᾿ εἰ πᾶν
θερμαίνων ἐξατμίσειεν τὸ ὕδωρ. ἄτοπον δὲ καὶ τὸ
μόνον φροντίσαι τοῦ ἡλίου, τῶν δ᾿ ἄλλων ἄστρων
20 αὐτοὺς παριδεῖν τὴν σωτηρίαν, τοσούτων καὶ τὸ
πλῆθος καὶ τὸ μέγεθος ὄντων. τὸ δ᾿ αὐτὸ συμβαίνει καὶ τούτοις ἄλογον καὶ τοῖς φάσκουσι τὸ
πρῶτον ὑγρᾶς οὔσης καὶ τῆς γῆς, καὶ τοῦ κόσμου
τοῦ περὶ τὴν γῆν ὑπὸ τοῦ ἡλίου θερμαινομένου,
ἀέρα γενέσθαι καὶ τὸν ὅλον οὐρανὸν αὐξηθῆναι, καὶ
25 τοῦτον πνεύματά τε παρέχεσθαι καὶ τὰς τροπὰς
αὐτοῦ ποιεῖν· φανερῶς γὰρ ἀεὶ τὸ ἀναχθὲν ὁρῶμεν

ᵃ Diels 22 B 6.

same regions cannot always provide it with nourishment yet nourishment it must have or of necessity perish, just as the fire we can see burns as long as it has fuel to feed it, and moisture is the only fuel that will feed fire. This supposes that the moisture which is drawn up reaches as far as the sun and that it rises in the same way as flame does ; for this theory of the sun is based on the analogy of fire. But (1) in fact there is no such analogy. Flame is the result of a constant metabolism of wet and dry : it is not a *thing* that can be fed, for it can hardly be said to remain one and the same for any length of time. But this cannot be true of the sun : for if it were fed in the same way as a flame, as they say, clearly there would not only be, as Heracleitus [a] says, a new sun every day, but a new sun every second. (2) Besides, the drawing up of moisture by the sun is similar to the heating of water by fire : so that if the fire beneath is not fed by the water above it, there is no reason to suppose that the sun is fed by water either, even if its heat were to evaporate all the water there is. And it is absurd to think of the sun only and say nothing about the maintenance of the other stars, when they are so many and so large. (3) And they are open to the same objection as those who maintain that at first the earth also was moist, and that subsequently the universe about the earth was heated by the sun ; that this produced air and led to the growth of the whole heaven, and that the air caused winds and the solstices.[b] For we can see clearly that the

[b] See ch. 1, note a on p. 124. It seems unnecessary to take αὐτοῦ to refer to οὐρανόν as Heath suggests (*op. cit.* p. 33). Neither τοῦτον (l. 24) nor αὐτοῦ is unambiguous ; and it seems to give the best sense if τοῦτον is taken as referring to ἀέρα and αὐτοῦ to ἡλίου : *cf.* Burnet, *E.G.P.*⁴, p. 64, note 1.

καταβαῖνον πάλιν ὕδωρ· κἂν μὴ κατ' ἐνιαυτὸν ἀπο-
διδῷ καὶ καθ' ἑκάστην ὁμοίως χώραν, ἀλλ' ἔν γέ
τισιν τεταγμένοις χρόνοις ἀποδίδωσι πᾶν τὸ ληφθέν,
ὡς οὔτε τρεφομένων τῶν ἄνωθεν, οὔτε τοῦ μὲν μέ-
30 νοντος ἀέρος ἤδη μετὰ τὴν γένεσιν, τοῦ δὲ γιγνομένου καὶ φθειρομένου πάλιν εἰς ὕδωρ, ἀλλ' ὁμοίως
ἅπαντος διαλυομένου καὶ συνισταμένου πάλιν εἰς
ὕδωρ.

Τὸ μὲν οὖν πότιμον καὶ γλυκὺ διὰ κουφότητα πᾶν
ἀνάγεται, τὸ δ' ἁλμυρὸν ὑπομένει διὰ βάρος οὐκ ἐν
35 τῷ αὑτοῦ οἰκείῳ τόπῳ· τοῦτο γὰρ οἰητέον ἀπορη-
355 b θῆναί τε προσηκόντως (ἄλογον γὰρ εἰ μή τίς ἐστιν
τόπος ὕδατος ὥσπερ καὶ τῶν ἄλλων στοιχείων) καὶ
ταύτην εἶναι λύσιν· ὃν γὰρ ὁρῶμεν κατέχουσαν
τόπον τὴν θάλατταν, οὗτος οὐκ ἔστιν θαλάττης
ἀλλὰ μᾶλλον ὕδατος. φαίνεται δὲ θαλάττης, ὅτι
5 τὸ μὲν ἁλμυρὸν ὑπομένει διὰ τὸ βάρος, τὸ δὲ
γλυκὺ καὶ πότιμον ἀνάγεται διὰ τὴν κουφότητα,
καθάπερ ἐν τοῖς τῶν ζῴων σώμασιν. καὶ γὰρ ἐν
τούτοις τῆς τροφῆς εἰσελθούσης γλυκείας ἡ τῆς
ὑγρᾶς τροφῆς ὑπόστασις καὶ τὸ περίττωμα φαίνεται πικρὸν ὂν καὶ ἁλμυρόν· τὸ γὰρ γλυκὺ καὶ
10 πότιμον ὑπὸ τῆς ἐμφύτου θερμότητος ἑλκυσθὲν εἰς
τὰς σάρκας καὶ τὴν ἄλλην σύνταξιν ἦλθεν τῶν
μερῶν, ὡς ἕκαστον πέφυκεν. ὥσπερ οὖν κἀκεῖ
ἄτοπον εἴ τις τῆς ποτίμου τροφῆς μὴ νομίζοι τόπον
εἶναι τὴν κοιλίαν, ὅτι ταχέως ἀφανίζεται, ἀλλὰ τοῦ
περιττώματος, ὅτι τοῦθ' ὁρᾷ ὑπομένον, οὐκ ἂν
15 ὑπολαμβάνοι καλῶς. ὁμοίως δὲ καὶ ἐν τούτοις·
ἔστιν γάρ, ὥσπερ λέγομεν, οὗτος ὁ τόπος ὕδατος·
διὸ καὶ οἱ ποταμοὶ ῥέουσιν εἰς αὐτὸν ἅπαντες καὶ
πᾶν τὸ γιγνόμενον ὕδωρ· εἴς τε γὰρ τὸ κοιλότατον

water drawn up always falls again. Even if the correspondence is not exact in any one year or any one
place, yet in a certain fixed period what was taken
is returned. So it cannot feed the heavenly bodies,
nor can some of it become and remain air while some
after becoming air turns into water again ; all alike
is resolved into air and all condenses again into water.)

The fresh and sweet water, then, as we said, is all
drawn up because it is light, while the salt water
because it is heavy remains, but not in its own natural
place. For this is a difficulty which may be properly
raised (for it would be unreasonable that water should
not have its natural place like the other elements)
and its solution is as follows : The place which we see
the sea occupying is not really its natural place [a] but
rather that of water. But it seems to be the sea's
because the salt water gets left behind because it is
heavy, and the sweet and fresh drawn up because
it is light. Something similar happens in the bodies
of living things. For here the food when it goes in
is sweet, but the sediment and residue from liquid
food is bitter and salty—for the sweet and fresh part
of it is drawn off by the natural heat of the body and
passes into flesh and the other constituent parts of
the body as appropriate.[b] But it would be absurd
not to regard the belly as the proper place of fresh
liquid food because it vanishes so quickly, but of
residue because this is observed to remain. Similar
remarks apply in our present subject. The place
occupied by the sea is, as we say, the proper place of
water, which is why all rivers and all the water there
is run into it : for water flows to the deepest place,

Fresh water evaporates salt water remains.

---

[a] *Cf.* above, 354 b 23 ff., and note at end of Book I. ch. 3.
[b] *Cf.* Book IV. ch. 1, note a on p. 294.

355 b

ἡ ῥύσις, καὶ ἡ θάλαττα τὸν τοιοῦτον ἐπέχει τῆς
γῆς τόπον· ἀλλὰ τὸ μὲν ἀναφέρεται ταχὺ διὰ τὸν
20 ἥλιον ἅπαν, τὸ δ' ὑπολείπεται διὰ τὴν εἰρημένην
αἰτίαν. τὸ δὲ ζητεῖν τὴν ἀρχαίαν ἀπορίαν, διὰ τί
τοσοῦτον πλῆθος ὕδατος οὐδαμοῦ φαίνεται (καθ'
ἑκάστην γὰρ ἡμέραν ποταμῶν ῥεόντων ἀναρίθμων
καὶ τὸ μέγεθος ἀπλέτων οὐδὲν ἡ θάλαττα γίγνεται
πλείων), τοῦτο οὐδὲν μὲν ἄτοπον ἀπορῆσαί τινας,
25 οὐ μὴν ἐπιβλέψαντά γε χαλεπὸν ἰδεῖν. τὸ γὰρ
αὐτὸ πλῆθος ὕδατος εἰς πλάτος τε διαταθὲν καὶ
ἀθρόον οὐκ ἐν ἴσῳ χρόνῳ ἀναξηραίνεται, ἀλλὰ
διαφέρει τοσοῦτον ὥστε τὸ μὲν διαμεῖναι ἂν ὅλην
τὴν ἡμέραν, τὸ δ' ὥσπερ εἴ τις ἐπὶ τράπεζαν μεγάλην περιτείνειεν ὕδατος κύαθον, ἅμα διανοου-
30 μένοις ἂν ἀφανισθείη πᾶν. ὃ δὴ καὶ περὶ τοὺς
ποταμοὺς συμβαίνει· συνεχῶς γὰρ ῥεόντων ἀθρόων
ἀεὶ τὸ ἀφικνούμενον εἰς ἀχανῆ καὶ πλατὺν τόπον
ἀναξηραίνεται ταχὺ καὶ ἀδήλως.

Τὸ δ' ἐν τῷ Φαίδωνι γεγραμμένον περί τε τῶν
ποταμῶν καὶ τῆς θαλάττης ἀδύνατόν ἐστιν. λέ-
35 γεται γὰρ ὡς ἅπαντα μὲν εἰς ἄλληλα συντέτρηται
356 a ὑπὸ γῆν, ἀρχὴ δὲ πάντων εἴη καὶ πηγὴ τῶν ὑδάτων
ὁ καλούμενος Τάρταρος, περὶ τὸ μέσον ὕδατός τι
πλῆθος, ἐξ οὗ καὶ τὰ ῥέοντα καὶ τὰ μὴ ῥέοντα ἀναδίδωσιν πάντα· τὴν δ' ἐπίρρυσιν ποιεῖν ἐφ' ἕκαστα
τῶν ῥευμάτων διὰ τὸ σαλεύειν ἀεὶ τὸ πρῶτον καὶ
5 τὴν ἀρχήν· οὐκ ἔχειν γὰρ ἕδραν, ἀλλ' ἀεὶ περὶ τὸ
μέσον εἰλεῖσθαι· κινούμενον δ' ἄνω καὶ κάτω ποιεῖν
τὴν ἐπίχυσιν τοῖς ῥεύμασιν. τὰ δὲ πολλαχοῦ μὲν
λιμνάζειν, οἷον καὶ τὴν παρ' ἡμῖν εἶναι θάλατταν,
πάντα δὲ πάλιν κύκλῳ περιάγειν εἰς τὴν ἀρχήν,

and the sea occupies the deepest place on the earth. But one part of it [a] is all quickly drawn up by the sun, while the other for the reasons given is left behind. The old question why so great an amount of water disappears (for the sea becomes no larger even though innumerable rivers of immense size are flowing into it every day) is quite a natural one to ask, but not difficult to answer with a little thought. For the same amount of water does not take the same time to dry up if it is spread out as if it is concentrated in a small space : the difference is so great that in the one case it may remain for a whole day, in the other, if for instance one spills a cup of water over a large table, it will vanish as quick as thought. This is what happens with rivers : they go on flowing in a constricted space until they reach a place of vast area when they spread out and evaporate rapidly and imperceptibly.

Plato's description of rivers and the sea in the *Phaedo* [b] is impossible. He says they all flow into each other beneath the earth through channels pierced through it, and that their original source is a body of water at the centre of the earth called Tartarus, from which all waters running and standing are drawn. This primary and original mass causes the flow of the various rivers by surging perpetually to and fro ; for it has no fixed position but is always oscillating [c] about the centre, and its motion up and down fills the rivers. Many of them form lakes, one example of which is the sea by which we live, but all of them pass round again in a circle to the original source from which they

The *Phaedo*.

---

[a] *i.e.* the fresh water.   [b] *Phaedo* 111 c ff.
[c] On the meaning of εἰλεῖσθαι *cf.* Cornford, *Plato's Cosmology*, p. 122.

ὅθεν ἤρξαντο ῥεῖν, πολλὰ μὲν κατὰ τὸν αὐτὸν
10 τόπον, τὰ δὲ καὶ καταντικρὺ τῇ θέσει τῆς ἐκροῆς,
οἷον εἰ ῥεῖν ἤρξαντο κάτωθεν, ἄνωθεν εἰσβάλλειν.
εἶναι δὲ μέχρι τοῦ μέσου τὴν κάθεσιν· τὸ γὰρ λοιπὸν
πρὸς ἄναντες ἤδη πᾶσιν εἶναι τὴν φοράν. τοὺς δὲ
χυμοὺς καὶ τὰς χρόας ἴσχειν τὸ ὕδωρ δι᾽ οἵας ἂν
τύχωσι ῥέοντα γῆς.
15 Συμβαίνει δὲ τοὺς ποταμοὺς ῥεῖν οὐκ ἐπὶ ταὐτὸν
ἀεὶ κατὰ τὸν λόγον τοῦτον· ἐπεὶ γὰρ εἰς τὸ μέσον
εἰσρέουσιν ἀφ᾽ οὗπερ ἐκρέουσιν, οὐδὲν μᾶλλον
ῥευσοῦνται κάτωθεν ἢ ἄνωθεν, ἀλλ᾽ ἐφ᾽ ὁπότερ᾽
ἂν ῥέψῃ κυμαίνων ὁ Τάρταρος. καίτοι τούτου συμβαίνοντος γένοιτ᾽ ἂν τὸ λεγόμενον ἄνω ποταμῶν·
ὅπερ ἀδύνατον.
20 Ἔτι τὸ γιγνόμενον ὕδωρ καὶ τὸ πάλιν ἀναγόμενον
πόθεν ἔσται; τοῦτο γὰρ ἐξαίρειν ὅλον ἀναγκαῖον,
εἴπερ ἀεὶ σώζεται τὸ ἴσον· ὅσον γὰρ ἔξω ῥεῖ, πάλιν
ῥεῖ πρὸς τὴν ἀρχήν.
Καίτοι πάντες οἱ ποταμοὶ φαίνονται τελευτῶντες
εἰς τὴν θάλατταν, ὅσοι μὴ εἰς ἀλλήλους· εἰς δὲ γῆν
25 οὐδείς, ἀλλὰ κἂν ἀφανισθῇ, πάλιν ἀναδύουσιν.
μεγάλοι δὲ γίγνονται τῶν ποταμῶν οἱ μακρὰν
ῥέοντες διὰ κοίλης· πολλῶν γὰρ δέχονται ῥεύματα
ποταμῶν, ὑποτεμνόμενοι τῷ τόπῳ καὶ τῷ μήκει
τὰς ὁδούς· διόπερ ὅ τ᾽ Ἴστρος καὶ ὁ Νεῖλος μέγιστοι τῶν ποταμῶν εἰσιν τῶν εἰς τήνδε τὴν
30 θάλατταν ἐξιόντων. καὶ περὶ τῶν πηγῶν ἄλλοι
λέγουσιν ἑκάστου τῶν ποταμῶν ἄλλας αἰτίας διὰ
τὸ πολλοὺς εἰς τὸν αὐτὸν ἐμβάλλειν. ταῦτα δὴ
πάντα φανερὸν ὡς ἀδύνατόν ἐστι συμβαίνειν ἄλλως
τε καὶ τῆς θαλάττης ἐκεῖθεν τὴν ἀρχὴν ἐχούσης.
Ὅτι μὲν οὖν ὕδατός τε ὁ τόπος ἐστὶν οὗτος καὶ

flowed ; many return to it again at the same place, others at a point opposite to that of their outflow, for instance if they flowed out from below they return from above. They fall only as far as the centre, when once that is passed all motion is uphill. And water gets its tastes and colours from the different kinds of earth through which it happens to flow.

But (1) on this account rivers do not always flow Objections. in the same sense. For if they flow towards the centre and also away from it, they will flow uphill as much as down, according to the direction in which the surge of Tartarus inclines. And if this is so we have the proverbial impossibility of rivers flowing uphill.

(2) Besides, where is the water that forms as rain and is again drawn up to come from ? It must be entirely left out of account if equality is to be preserved, for the same amount flows back to the source as flowed from it.

(3) And again all rivers that do not flow into each other manifestly flow into the sea : none of them flow into the earth, and even if they do disappear underground they come up again. The great rivers are those which flow for great distances through valleys, but they are joined by many tributaries whose courses they intercept because of the length and position of their course. That is why the Istros and the Nile are the largest of the rivers flowing into our sea ; and because so many rivers flow into them different accounts are given of the sources from which they rise. But clearly none of these things could possibly happen on this theory, especially as it maintains that Tartarus is-the source of the sea.

This completes our proof that the place the sea Conclusion.

356 a
35 οὐ θαλάττης, καὶ διὰ τίν᾿ αἰτίαν τὸ μὲν πότιμον
ἄδηλον πλὴν ῥέον, τὸ δ᾿ ὑπομένον, καὶ διότι τελευτὴ
356 b μᾶλλον ὕδατος ἢ ἀρχή ἐστιν ἡ θάλαττα, καθάπερ
τὸ ἐν τοῖς σώμασιν περίττωμα τῆς τροφῆς πάσης,
καὶ μάλιστα τὸ τῆς ὑγρᾶς, εἰρήσθω τοσαῦθ᾿ ἡμῖν.

CHAPTER III

ARGUMENT

*The sea (continued). If the universe as a whole had a be-
ginning, then the sea had. But Democritus's theory that it
will dry up is no better than a fable of Aesop. Evaporation
and rainfall balance each other (356 b 4—357 a 3). The
sea is not salt either (1) because it is a residue left by evaporation or (2) because of an admixture of earth : nor (3) is it
any explanation to call it the sweat of the earth (357 a 3–b 21).
The sea is constant in volume though the water composing it
changes. Its saltness is due to the dry exhalation, of which*

356 b 4 Περὶ δὲ τῆς ἁλμυρότητος αὐτῆς λεκτέον, καὶ
5 πότερον αἰεί ἐστιν ἡ αὐτή, ἢ οὔτ᾿ ἦν οὔτ᾿ ἔσται
ἀλλ᾿ ὑπολείψει· καὶ γὰρ οὕτως οἴονταί τινες.
Τοῦτο μὲν οὖν ἐοίκασι πάντες ὁμολογεῖν, ὅτι
γέγονεν, εἴπερ καὶ πᾶς ὁ κόσμος· ἅμα γὰρ αὐτῆς
ποιοῦσι τὴν γένεσιν. ὥστε δῆλον ὡς εἴπερ ἀίδιον
τὸ πᾶν, καὶ περὶ τῆς θαλάττης οὕτως ὑποληπτέον.
10 τὸ δὲ νομίζειν ἐλάττω τε γίγνεσθαι τὸ πλῆθος,
ὥσπερ φησὶ Δημόκριτος, καὶ τέλος ὑπολείψειν,
τῶν Αἰσώπου μύθων οὐδὲν διαφέρειν ἔοικεν ὁ πε-
πεισμένος οὕτως· καὶ γὰρ ἐκεῖνος ἐμυθολόγησεν

---

occupies is the natural place of water and not of the sea, and our explanation of why fresh water is always running water, salt water standing ; and of why the sea is the terminus rather than the source of water, being analogous to the residue of all food, and particularly of liquid food in living creatures.

CHAPTER III

ARGUMENT (*continued*)

we have already spoken, which is analogous to the residues left in combustion and digestion, and like them salty. This dry exhalation is mixed with the moist exhalation, is carried down with it in rain, and so makes the sea salt (357 b 21—358 a 27). Hence south winds and autumn winds are brackish (358 a 27–b 12). So the sea increases in saltness, for little or no salt is lost in the process of evaporation (358 b 12-34). Examples to show that saltness is due to an admixture of an appropriate substance (358 b 34—359 b 26).

THE sea's saltness is our next subject ; this we must discuss, and also the question whether the sea remains the same for all time, or whether there was a time when it did not exist, or will be a time when it will cease to exist and disappear as some people think. ^(margin: Cosmos and sea coeval.)

It is, then, generally agreed that the sea had a beginning if the universe as a whole had ; for the two are supposed to have come into being at the same time. So, clearly, if the universe is eternal we must suppose that the sea is too. The belief held by Democritus [a] that the sea is decreasing in volume and that it will in the end disappear is like something out of Aesop's fables. For Aesop has a fable about ^(margin: Democritus.)

ὡς δὶς μὲν ἡ Χάρυβδις ἀναρροφήσασα τὸ μὲν πρῶτον τὰ ὄρη ἐποίησεν φανερά, τὸ δὲ δεύτερον

15 τὰς νήσους, τὸ δὲ τελευταῖον ῥοφήσασα ξηρὰν ποιήσει πάμπαν. ἐκείνῳ μὲν οὖν ἥρμοττεν ὀργιζομένῳ πρὸς τὸν πορθμέα τοιοῦτον εἰπεῖν μῦθον, τοῖς δὲ τὴν ἀλήθειαν ζητοῦσιν ἧττον· δι' ἣν γὰρ αἰτίαν ἔμεινε τὸ πρῶτον, εἴτε διὰ βάρος, ὥσπερ τινὲς καὶ τούτων φασίν (ἐν προχείρῳ γὰρ τούτου

20 τὴν αἰτίαν ἰδεῖν), εἴτε καὶ δι' ἄλλο τι, δῆλον ὅτι διὰ τοῦτο διαμένειν ἀναγκαῖον καὶ τὸν λοιπὸν χρόνον αὐτήν. ἢ γὰρ λεκτέον αὐτοῖς ὅτι οὐδὲ τὸ ἀναχθὲν ὕδωρ ὑπὸ τοῦ ἡλίου ἥξει πάλιν, ἢ εἴπερ τοῦτ' ἔσται, ἀναγκαῖον ἤτοι ἀεὶ ἢ μέχρι οὗπερ ἂν ᾖ τοῦτο ὑπολείπεσθαι τὴν θάλατταν, καὶ πάλιν ἀναχθῆναι ἐκεῖνο

25 πρότερον δεήσει τὸ πότιμον. ὥστε οὐδέποτε ξηρανεῖται· πάλιν γὰρ ἐκεῖνο φθήσεται καταβὰν εἰς τὴν αὐτὴν τὸ προανελθόν· διαφέρει γὰρ οὐδὲν ἅπαξ τοῦτ' εἰπεῖν ἢ πολλάκις. εἰ μὲν οὖν τὸν ἥλιον παύσει τις τῆς φορᾶς, τί ἔσται τὸ ξηραῖνον; εἰ δ' ἐάσει εἶναι τὴν περιφοράν, ἀεὶ πλησιάζων τὸ

30 πότιμον, καθάπερ εἴπομεν, ἀνάξει, ἀφήσει δὲ πάλιν ἀναχωρῶν. ἔλαβον δὲ ταύτην τὴν διάνοιαν κατὰ τῆς θαλάττης ἐκ τοῦ πολλοὺς τόπους φαίνεσθαι ξηροτέρους νῦν ἢ πρότερον· περὶ οὗ τὴν αἰτίαν εἴπομεν, ὅτι τῶν κατά τινα χρόνον ὑπερβολῶν γιγνομένων ὕδατος τοῦτ' ἐστὶν τὸ πάθος, ἀλλ' οὐ διὰ

35 τὴν τοῦ παντὸς γένεσιν καὶ τῶν μορίων· καὶ πάλιν

γ' ἔσται τοὐναντίον· καὶ ὅταν γένηται, ξηρανεῖται πάλιν· καὶ τοῦθ' οὕτως κατὰ κύκλον ἀναγκαῖον ἀεὶ

Charybdis in which he says that she took one gulp of the sea and brought the mountains to view, a second one and the islands appeared, and that her last gulp will dry the sea up altogether. A fable like this was a suitable retort for Aesop to make when the ferryman annoyed him, but is hardly suitable for those who are seeking the truth. For whatever cause originally made the sea come to rest where it does—whether it was its weight, as some even of these earlier thinkers say (for it is obvious that this is the reason), or whether some other cause—the same cause must clearly make it stay where it is for all time. For they must either say that the water drawn up by the sun does not fall again, or if it does, that the sea must remain, either for ever or at any rate as long as the process goes on, and that the fresh water must continue to be drawn up first. It follows that the sea will never dry up : for before it can do so the water that has left it will fall again into it, and to admit that this happens once is to admit it continues to happen. If, then, you arrest the sun's course, what is there to dry the water up ? But if you let it continue in its course it will, as we have explained, always draw up the fresh water when it approaches and let it fall again when it retires. This idea about the sea drying up arose because many places were observed to be drier than they were formerly ; and we have already explained [a] that the cause of this phenomenon is an excess of rain at certain periods, and that it is not due to the growth of the universe as a whole and its parts. Some day the opposite will happen, and after that the earth will again dry up. And so the process must go on in a cycle. For this is a more

Evaporation and rainfall balance.

[a] Book I. ch. 14, 352 a 25 ff.

357 a

βαδίζειν· μᾶλλον γὰρ οὕτως εὔλογον ὑπολαβεῖν ἢ
διὰ ταῦτα τὸν οὐρανὸν ὅλον μεταβάλλειν.

Ἀλλὰ περὶ μὲν τούτων πλείω τῆς ἀξίας ἐνδια-
5 τέτριφεν ὁ λόγος· περὶ δὲ τῆς ἁλμυρότητος, τοῖς
μὲν ἅπαξ γεννήσασι καὶ ὅλως αὐτὴν γεννῶσιν ἀδύνατόν ἐστιν ἁλμυρὰν ποιεῖν. εἰ γὰρ παντὸς τοῦ
ὑγροῦ τοῦ περὶ τὴν γῆν ὄντος καὶ ἀναχθέντος ὑπὸ
τοῦ ἡλίου τὸ ὑπολειφθὲν ἐγένετο θάλαττα, εἶτ᾽
ἐνυπῆρχε τοσοῦτος χυμὸς ἐν τῷ πολλῷ ὕδατι καὶ
10 γλυκεῖ διὰ τὸ συμμειχθῆναί τινα γῆν τοιαύτην,
οὐδὲν ἧττον ἐλθόντος πάλιν τοῦ διατμίσαντος
ὕδατος ἀνάγκη, ἴσου γ᾽ ὄντος τοῦ πλήθους, καὶ τὸ
πρῶτον· ἢ εἰ μηδὲ τὸ πρῶτον, μηδ᾽ ὕστερον ἁλμυρὰν αὐτὴν εἶναι. εἰ δὲ καὶ τὸ πρῶτον εὐθὺς ἦν,
λεκτέον τίς ἡ αἰτία, καὶ ἅμα διὰ τί οὐκ εἰ καὶ τότε
15 ἀνήχθη καὶ νῦν πάσχει ταὐτό. ἀλλὰ μὴν καὶ ὅσοι
τὴν γῆν αἰτιῶνται τῆς ἁλμυρότητος ἐμμειγνυμένην
(ἔχειν γάρ φασι πολλοὺς χυμοὺς αὐτήν, ὥσθ᾽ ὑπὸ
τῶν ποταμῶν συγκαταφερομένην διὰ τὴν μεῖξιν
ποιεῖν ἁλμυράν), ἄτοπον τὸ μὴ καὶ τοὺς ποταμοὺς
ἁλμυροὺς εἶναι· πῶς γὰρ δυνατὸν ἐν πολλῷ μὲν
20 πλήθει ὕδατος ἐπίδηλον οὕτως ποιεῖν τὴν μεῖξιν
τῆς τοιαύτης γῆς, ἐν ἑκάστῳ δὲ μή; δῆλον γὰρ
ὅτι ἡ θάλαττά ἐστιν ἅπαν τὸ ποτάμιον ὕδωρ· οὐδενὶ

ᵃ Anaxagoras (Diels 59 A 90 ; Aetius iii. 16. 2), Diogenes
(Diels 64 A 17).
ᵇ Anaxagoras (Diels 59 A 90 ; Alex. 67. 17), Xenophanes
(Diels 21 A 3 (4)), Metrodorus (Diels 70 A 19).

reasonable way of accounting for the facts than to suppose that the whole universe is in process of change.

But we have spent longer talking about these things than is really justified. To return to the sea's saltness. Those who make it come into existence all at once, or for a matter of that those who make it come into existence at all, cannot account for its saltness. For it is all the same whether they maintain (1) that sea is what is left of the moisture on the earth after evaporation by the sun,[a] or (2) that the taste inherent in the great mass of naturally sweet water is due to a suitable admixture of earth.[b] For (1) on the first view,[c] since the volume of water that falls as rain is equal to the volume evaporated, the sea must either have been salt in the first place, or if it was not it cannot have become salt subsequently. But if it was salt at first the reason for this should be given, and also the reason why if salt water was subject to evaporation then it is not now. While (2) as for those who attribute the sea's saltness to an admixture of earth, saying that the earth has many tastes and so when carried down by the rivers and mixed with the sea it makes it salt—if that is so it is odd that the rivers are not salt also. For how is it possible that the admixture of earth of this kind should have so obvious an effect in a large volume of water, but not in each individual river ? For it is clear that on this view the sea is composed of water from the rivers, as it does not differ from the rivers

---

[c] Thurot points out that the clause beginning οὐδὲν ἧττον deals only with the first of the two views put forward in the previous sentence, and that the passage makes better sense if it is supposed that some words have dropped out after τοιαύτην. But neither MSS. nor commentators give any indication of a lacuna.

357 a

γὰρ διέφερεν ἀλλ' ἢ τῷ ἁλμυρὰ εἶναι τῶν ποταμῶν·
τοῦτο δ' ἐν ἐκείνοις ἔρχεται εἰς τὸν τόπον εἰς ὃν
ἀθρόοι ῥέουσιν.

25 Ὁμοίως δὲ γελοῖον κἂν εἴ τις εἰπὼν ἱδρῶτα τῆς
γῆς εἶναι τὴν θάλατταν οἴεταί τι σαφὲς εἰρηκέναι,
καθάπερ Ἐμπεδοκλῆς· πρὸς ποίησιν μὲν γὰρ οὕτως
εἰπὼν ἴσως εἴρηκεν ἱκανῶς (ἡ γὰρ μεταφορὰ ποιητικόν), πρὸς δὲ τὸ γνῶναι τὴν φύσιν οὐχ ἱκανῶς·
οὐδὲ γὰρ ἐνταῦθα δῆλον πῶς ἐκ γλυκέος τοῦ
30 πόματος ἁλμυρὸς γίγνεται ὁ ἱδρώς, πότερον ἀπελθόντος τινὸς μόνον οἷον τοῦ γλυκυτάτου, ἢ συμ-
μειχθέντος τινός, καθάπερ ἐν τοῖς διὰ τῆς τέφρας
ἠθουμένοις ὕδασιν. φαίνεται δὲ τὸ αἴτιον ταὐτὸ
καὶ περὶ τὸ εἰς τὴν κύστιν περίττωμα συλλεγόμενον·
καὶ γὰρ ἐκεῖνο πικρὸν καὶ ἁλμυρὸν γίγνεται τοῦ
357 b πινομένου καὶ τοῦ ἐν τῇ τροφῇ ὑγροῦ γλυκέος
ὄντος. εἰ δὴ ὥσπερ τὸ διὰ τῆς κονίας ἠθούμενον
ὕδωρ γίγνεται πικρόν, καὶ ταῦτα, τῷ μὲν οὔρῳ
συγκαταφερομένης τοιαύτης τινὸς δυνάμεως οἵα
καὶ φαίνεται ὑφισταμένη ἐν τοῖς ἀγγείοις ἁλμυρίς,
5 τῷ δ' ἱδρῶτι συνεκκρινομένης ἐκ τῶν σαρκῶν, οἷον
καταπλύνοντος τὸ τοιοῦτον ἐκ τοῦ σώματος τοῦ
ἐξιόντος ὑγροῦ, δῆλον ὅτι κἂν τῇ θαλάττῃ τὸ ἐκ
τῆς γῆς συγκαταμισγόμενον τῷ ὑγρῷ αἴτιον τῆς
ἁλμυρότητος. ἐν μὲν οὖν τῷ σώματι γίγνεται τὸ
τοιοῦτον ἡ τῆς τροφῆς ὑπόστασις διὰ τὴν ἀπεψίαν·
10 ἐν δὲ τῇ γῇ τίνα τρόπον ὑπῆρχε, λεκτέον. ὅλως
δὲ πῶς οἷόν τε τοσοῦτον ὕδατος πλῆθος ξηραινομένης καὶ θερμαινομένης ἐκκριθῆναι; πολλοστὸν
γὰρ δεῖ μέρος αὐτὸ τοῦ λειφθέντος εἶναι ἐν τῇ γῇ.
ἔτι διὰ τί οὐ καὶ νῦν ὅταν ξηραινομένη τύχῃ γῆ,
εἴτε πλείων εἴτε ἐλάττων, ἰδίει; †ἡ γὰρ ὑγρότης

except in being salt and the salt is carried down in them to the place into which they all flow.

It is equally absurd (3) for anyone to think, like Empedocles,[a] that he has made an intelligible statement when he says that the sea is the sweat of the earth. Such a statement is perhaps satisfactory in poetry, for metaphor is a poetic device, but it does not advance our knowledge of nature. For it is by no means clear how salt sweat is produced in the body from sweet drink—whether, for example, it is simply by the loss of its sweetest constituent or whether it is due to the admixture of something else, as in the case of waters strained through ashes. The cause appears to be the same as that which makes the residue that collects in the bladder bitter and salty though our drink and the liquid in our food is sweet. If then the cause in both cases is the same as that which makes water filtered through ashes bitter, and if some substance like the salty deposit we see in chamber-pots is carried through the body with the urine, and secreted in sweat from the flesh, being washed out of the body as it were by the water on its way out, then the admixture of some substance from the earth must be responsible for the saltness of the water in the sea also. Now in the body the sediment of food caused by failure to digest is such a substance. But we still need to be told how anything of the kind is produced in the earth. Besides, more generally, how can the drying and heating of the earth cause the secretion of so large a volume of water? And this can only be a small proportion of what is still left in the earth. Again, why does not the earth still sweat to-day when dried in larger or smaller quantities? [For sweat and

---

[a] Diels 31 A 66.

357 b

15 καὶ ὁ ἱδρὼς γίγνεται πικρός.†[1] εἴπερ γὰρ καὶ τότε,
καὶ νῦν ἐχρῆν. οὐ φαίνεται δὲ τοῦτο συμβαῖνον,
ἀλλὰ ξηρὰ μὲν οὖσα ὑγραίνεται, ὑγρὰ δ' οὖσα οὐδὲν
πάσχει τοιοῦτον. πῶς οὖν οἷόν τε περὶ τὴν πρώτην
γένεσιν, ὑγρᾶς οὔσης τῆς γῆς, ἰδίειν ξηραινομένην; ἀλλὰ μᾶλλον εἰκός, ὥσπερ φασί τινες,
20 ἀπελθόντος τοῦ πλείστου καὶ μετεωρισθέντος τοῦ
ὑγροῦ διὰ τὸν ἥλιον, τὸ λειφθὲν εἶναι θάλατταν·
ὑγρὰν δ' οὖσαν ἰδίειν ἀδύνατον.

Τὰ μὲν οὖν λεγόμενα τῆς ἁλμυρότητος αἴτια δια-
φεύγειν φαίνεται τὸν λόγον· ἡμεῖς δὲ λέγωμεν
ἀρχὴν λαβόντες τὴν αὐτὴν ἣν καὶ πρότερον.

Ἐπειδὴ γὰρ κεῖται διπλῆν εἶναι τὴν ἀναθυμίασιν,
25 τὴν μὲν ὑγρὰν τὴν δὲ ξηράν, δῆλον ὅτι ταύτην
οἰητέον ἀρχὴν εἶναι τῶν τοιούτων.

Καὶ δὴ καὶ περὶ οὗ ἀπορῆσαι πρότερον ἀναγκαῖον, πότερον καὶ ἡ θάλαττα ἀεὶ διαμένει τῶν
αὐτῶν οὖσα μορίων ἀριθμῷ ἢ τῷ εἴδει καὶ τῷ
ποσῷ μεταβαλλόντων ἀεὶ τῶν μερῶν, καθάπερ ἀὴρ
30 καὶ τὸ πότιμον ὕδωρ καὶ πῦρ (ἀεὶ γὰρ ἄλλο καὶ
ἄλλο γίγνεται τούτων ἕκαστον, τὸ δ' εἶδος τοῦ
πλήθους ἑκάστου τούτων μένει, καθάπερ τὸ τῶν
ῥεόντων ὑδάτων καὶ τὸ τῆς φλογὸς ῥεῦμα)· φανερὸν
δὴ καὶ τοῦτο καὶ πιθανόν· ὡς ἀδύνατον μὴ τὸν
αὐτὸν εἶναι περὶ πάντων τούτων λόγον, καὶ δια-
358 a φέρειν ταχυτῆτι καὶ βραδυτῆτι τῆς μεταβολῆς, ἐπὶ

[1] ἡ γὰρ ὑγρότης om. 𝔄 H₁ N₁ Thurot : ἡ . . . πικρός om.
O.T.

---

[a] These words do not fit into the argument. " The point
is not that the earth secretes moisture but not salt moisture ;
but, as the following lines show, that it does not secrete any-
150

moisture are both bitter.] [a] For if it used to happen
once it should happen now. Yet in fact it does not
happen, but when earth is dry it absorbs moisture,
when it is moist it shows no sign of sweating. How
then can the earth when it first came into being and
was moist have sweated when dried ? The view that
most of the moisture left it and was drawn aloft by
the sun and that the sea is what was left is more
plausible. But it cannot possibly sweat when it is
moist.

Thus none of the current explanations of the sea's
saltness appear to stand examination, so let us offer
our own, starting from the principle already laid
down.

We have assumed that there are two kinds of exhalation, one moist and one dry ; and of these the latter must clearly be the origin of the phenomena in question. Saltness due to the dry exhalation.

But there is a difficulty which we must discuss first.
Does the sea always consist of identically the same
parts ; or does it remain the same in quality and
quantity though the parts are continually changing,
as in air, fresh water and fire ? For each of these is
in constant process of change, though the characteristic qualities of any aggregate of it remain the same,
as for instance with running water and a burning
flame. It is then obviously plausible to assume that
the same account must hold good of all of them, so
that they differ only in that their speed of change

thing at all under the conditions supposed " (O.T.). The
O.T. omits the words altogether : but if the passage is to be
emended it seems better to follow Thurot and to omit ἡ γὰρ
ὑγρότης and read ἰδίει, καὶ ὁ ἱδρὼς γίγνεται πικρός; " Why
does not the earth still sweat . . . and that sweat taste
salt ? "

πάντων τε φθορὰν εἶναι καὶ γένεσιν, ταύτην μέντοι
τεταγμένως συμβαίνειν πᾶσιν αὐτοῖς.

Τούτων δ' οὕτως ἐχόντων, πειρατέον ἀποδοῦναι
τὴν αἰτίαν καὶ περὶ τῆς ἁλμυρότητος. φανερὸν δὴ
5 διὰ πολλῶν σημείων ὅτι γίγνεται τοιοῦτος ὁ χυμὸς
διὰ σύμμειξίν τινος. ἔν τε γὰρ τοῖς σώμασι τὸ
ἀπεπτότατον ἁλμυρὸν καὶ πικρόν, ὥσπερ καὶ πρότερον εἴπομεν· ἀπεπτότατον γὰρ τὸ περίττωμα τῆς
ὑγρᾶς τροφῆς· τοιαύτη δὲ πᾶσα μὲν ἡ ὑπόστασις,
μάλιστα δὲ ἡ εἰς τὴν κύστιν (σημεῖον δ' ὅτι λεπτο-
10 τάτη ἐστίν· τὰ δὲ πεττόμενα πάντα συνίστασθαι
πέφυκεν)· ἔπειτα ἱδρὼς [ἀεί]¹· ἐν οἷς τὸ αὐτὸ σῶμα
συνεκκρίνεται, ὃ ποιεῖ τὸν χυμὸν τοῦτον. ὁμοίως
δὲ καὶ ἐν τοῖς καομένοις· οὗ γὰρ ἂν μὴ κρατήσῃ τὸ
θερμόν, ἐν μὲν τοῖς σώμασι γίγνεται περίττωσις,
ἐν δὲ τοῖς καομένοις τέφρα. διὸ καὶ τὴν θάλατταν
15 τινες ἐκ κατακεκαυμένης φασὶ γενέσθαι γῆς. ὃ
οὕτω μὲν εἰπεῖν ἄτοπον, τὸ μέντοι ἐκ τοιαύτης
ἀληθές· ὥσπερ γὰρ καὶ ἐν τοῖς εἰρημένοις, οὕτω
καὶ ἐν τῷ ὅλῳ ἔκ τε τῶν φυομένων καὶ γιγνομένων
κατὰ φύσιν ἀεὶ δεῖ νοεῖν, ὥσπερ ἐκ πεπυρωμένων
τὸ λειπόμενον τοιαύτην εἶναι γῆν, καὶ δὴ καὶ τὴν
20 ἐν τῇ ξηρᾷ ἀναθυμίασιν πᾶσαν· αὕτη γὰρ καὶ
παρέχεται τὸ πολὺ τοῦτο πλῆθος. μεμειγμένης
δ' οὔσης, ὥσπερ εἴπομεν, τῆς τε ἀτμιδώδους ἀναθυμιάσεως καὶ τῆς ξηρᾶς, ὅταν συνιστῆται εἰς
νέφη καὶ ὕδωρ, ἀναγκαῖον ἐμπεριλαμβάνεσθαί τι
πλῆθος ἀεὶ ταύτης τῆς δυνάμεως, καὶ συγκατα-
25 φέρεσθαι πάλιν ὕοντος, καὶ τοῦτ' ἀεὶ γίγνεσθαι

differs. In all the process of decay and generation is taking place, though in all it takes place in a fixed manner.

This being so, let us try and give the reason for the sea's saltness. There are many indications that this kind of salty taste is due to the admixture of something. For in living bodies it is the least digested matter that is salty and bitter, as we have remarked before. For the residue of liquid food is least digested ; this is true of all waste products, principally of that which collects in the bladder (whose extreme lightness proves it to be a waste product, as digestion naturally condenses), but also of sweat. In both of these the same substance is secreted and produces this taste. Something similar happens in combustion. What the heat fails to master becomes residue in living bodies, ash in combustion. So some have maintained that the sea is made of burnt earth. Thus expressed their opinion is absurd : but it is true that something of this sort makes it salt. For we must suppose that something happens in the world as a whole analogous to what happens in the phenomena just described : just as in combustion there is a residue of earth of this kind, so there is in all natural growth and generation, and all exhalation on dry land is such a residue. And it is dry land that provides the great bulk of the exhalation. Now since, as we have said, the moist and vaporous exhalation is mixed with the dry, when it condenses into clouds and rain it must necessarily include a certain amount of this property [a] which will subsequently be carried down in rain. The process follows a regular order,

---

[a] *i.e.* the dry exhalation which being a residue is salty.

---

[1] secl. Fobes.

358 a

κατά τινα τάξιν, ὡς ἐνδέχεται μετέχειν τὰ ἐνταῦθα
τάξεως. ὅθεν μὲν οὖν ἡ γένεσις ἔνεστιν τοῦ
ἁλμυροῦ ἐν τῷ ὕδατι, εἴρηται.

Καὶ διὰ τοῦτο τά τε νότια ὕδατα πλατύτερα καὶ
τὰ πρῶτα τῶν μετοπωρινῶν· ὅ τε γὰρ νότος καὶ

30 τῷ μεγέθει καὶ τῷ πνεύματι[1] ἀλεεινότατος ἄνεμός
ἐστιν, καὶ πνεῖ ἀπὸ τόπων ξηρῶν καὶ θερμῶν, ὥστε
μετ᾽ ὀλίγης ἀτμίδος. διὸ καὶ θερμός ἐστιν· εἰ γὰρ
καὶ μὴ τοιοῦτος, ἀλλ᾽ ὅθεν ἄρχεται πνεῖν ψυχρός,
οὐδὲν ἧττον προϊὼν διὰ τὸ συμπεριλαμβάνειν πολλὴν ἀναθυμίασιν ξηρὰν ἐκ τῶν σύνεγγυς τόπων

35 θερμός ἐστιν· ὁ δὲ βορέας ἅτε ἀφ᾽ ὑγρῶν τόπων

358 b ἀτμιδώδης· διὸ ψυχρός· τῷ δ᾽ ἀπωθεῖν αἴθριος
ἐνταῦθα, ἐν δὲ τοῖς ἐναντίοις ὑδατώδης. ὁμοίως
δὲ καὶ ὁ νότος αἴθριος τοῖς περὶ τὴν Λιβύην. πολὺ
οὖν ἐν τῷ καταφερομένῳ ὕδατι συμβάλλεται τοιοῦτον, καὶ τοῦ μετοπώρου πλατέα τὰ ὕδατα· ἀνάγκη

5 γὰρ τὰ βαρύτατα πρῶτα φέρεσθαι. ὥστ᾽ ἐν ὅσοις
ἔνεστι τῆς τοιαύτης γῆς πλῆθος, ῥέπει τάχιστα
κάτω ταῦτα. καὶ θερμή γε ἡ θάλαττα διὰ τοῦτό
ἐστιν· πάντα γὰρ ὅσα πεπύρωται, ἔχει δυνάμει
θερμότητα ἐν αὑτοῖς. ὁρᾶν δ᾽ ἔξεστι καὶ τὴν
κονίαν καὶ τὴν τέφραν καὶ τὴν ὑπόστασιν τῶν ζῴων

10 καὶ τὴν ξηρὰν καὶ τὴν ὑγράν· καὶ τῶν θερμοτάτων
γε κατὰ τὴν κοιλίαν ζῴων συμβαίνει θερμοτάτην
εἶναι τὴν ὑπόστασιν.

Γίγνεται μὲν οὖν ἀεί τε πλατυτέρα διὰ ταύτην
τὴν αἰτίαν, ἀνάγεται δ᾽ ἀεί τι μέρος αὐτῆς μετὰ
τοῦ γλυκέος (ἀλλ᾽ ἔλαττον τοσούτῳ ὅσῳ καὶ ἐν τῷ

[1] καὶ τῷ μεγέθει καὶ τῷ πνεύματι om. O.T.

154

so far as things in this world admit of regularity. This then accounts for the presence of salt in sea water.

This explains why the rains from the south and the first rains of autumn are brackish. For the south wind is the warmest of winds (both in size and strength [a]) and blows from regions that are dry and warm, and so contains little moist exhalation, which is the reason why it is hot. And even if it is not naturally hot but starts as a cold wind, it none the less becomes hot because it picks up large quantities of hot exhalation from the places that lie on its way. The north wind, on the other hand, carries moist vapour because it comes from damp places. So it is so cold. And it brings fine weather here because it drives the clouds away ; but in the south it brings rain. Similarly the south wind brings fine weather in Libya. There is then a great deal of this substance in the rain which falls ; and the rains of autumn are brackish because what is heaviest must fall first and so rain which contains any quantity of earth of this sort falls quickest. And this is the reason why the sea is warm. For everything which has been exposed to fire contains heat potentially. We can see this in ash, in cinders and in the excrement of animals, both solid and liquid. For the excrement of animals that have the hottest bellies is hottest.

This cause is always operating to make the sea more brackish. A certain amount of the salt water is always drawn up with the sweet, but this amount is always the less in the same proportion as the salt

Marginal notes: Southerly rains and autumn rains brackish.

Salt is left by evaporation.

---

[a] It is difficult to make sense of these words, which the O.T. omits. Alex. (84. 32) does not appear to have had them in his text.

358 b

15 ὑομένῳ τὸ ἁλμυρὸν καὶ πλατὺ τοῦ γλυκέος ἔλαττον·
διόπερ ἰσάζει ὡς ἐπίπαν εἰπεῖν). ὅτι δὲ γίγνεται
ἀτμίζουσα πότιμος καὶ οὐκ εἰς θάλατταν συγκρί-
νεται τὸ ἀτμίζον, ὅταν συνιστῆται πάλιν, πεπειρα-
μένοι λέγωμεν. πάσχει δὲ καὶ τἆλλα ταὐτό· καὶ
γὰρ οἶνος καὶ πάντες οἱ χυμοί, ὅσοι ἂν ἀτμίσαντες
20 πάλιν εἰς ὑγρὸν συστῶσιν, ὕδωρ γίγνονται· πάθη
γὰρ τἆλλα διά τινα σύμμειξιν τοῦ ὕδατός ἐστιν,
καὶ οἷον ἄν τι ᾖ τὸ συμμειχθέν, τοιοῦτον ποιεῖ τὸν
χυμόν. ἀλλὰ περὶ μὲν τούτων ἐν ἄλλοις καιροῖς
οἰκειοτέροις ποιητέον τὴν σκέψιν. νῦν δὲ τοσοῦτον
λέγωμεν, ὅτι τῆς θαλάττης ὑπαρχούσης αἰεί τι
25 ἀνάγεται καὶ γίγνεται πότιμον καὶ ἄνωθεν ἐν τῷ
ὑομένῳ κατέρχεται ἄλλο γεγενημένον, οὐ τὸ[ι]
χθέν· καὶ διὰ βάρος ὑφίσταται τῷ ποτίμῳ.[ ] καὶ
διὰ τοῦτο οὔτ᾿ ἐπιλείπει, ὥσπερ οἱ ποταμοί, ἀλλ᾿
ἢ τοῖς τόποις (τοῦτο δ᾿ ἐπ᾿ ἀμφοτέρων ἀνάγκη συμ-
30 βαίνειν ὁμοίως), οὔτε ἀεὶ τὰ αὐτὰ μέρη διαμένει,
οὔτε γῆς οὔτε θαλάττης, ἀλλ᾿ ἢ μόνον ὁ πᾶς ὄγκος
(καὶ[1] γὰρ καὶ περὶ γῆς ὁμοίως δεῖ ὑπολαβεῖν)[2]· τὸ
μὲν γὰρ ἀνέρχεται, τὸ δὲ πάλιν συγκαταβαίνει,
καὶ τοὺς τόπους μεταβάλλει τά τ᾿ ἐπιπολάζοντα
καὶ τὰ κατιόντα πάλιν.

Ὅτι δ᾿ ἐστὶν ἐν μείξει τινὸς τὸ ἁλμυρόν, δῆλον

---

[1] ὄγκος. καὶ Fobes.
[2] καὶ γὰρ . . . ὑπολαβεῖν interclusionem distinxi.

---

[a] i.e. as far as evaporation from the sea is concerned the
amount of salt lost is so small as to make no difference. The
following paragraph proceeds to confirm this by pointing out
that salt water when distilled loses its saltness ; so in the
process of evaporation from the sea little or no salt is lost.

[b] Aristotle had apparently only performed the experiment
with water : it is not true of wine.

and brackish element is less than the sweet in rain water, so that on the whole equality is preserved.[a] I have proved by experiment that salt water evaporated forms fresh and the vapour does not when it condenses condense into sea water again. The same is true in other cases. For wine [b] and all other tasting liquids which can be evaporated and subsequently condensed to liquid again become water on condensation. For the qualities they have other than those of water are due to admixture, and the taste varies according to what is mixed with the water. But we must investigate these subjects on another and more suitable opportunity. For the present let us confine ourselves to saying that a certain amount of the existing sea water is always being drawn up and becoming fresh; and that it subsequently falls down in rain in a different form [c] to that in which it was drawn up, and because of its weight sinks below the fresh water. So the sea like the rivers never dries up, except locally (as both sea and rivers alike must on occasion) ; nor do the same parts always remain sea, the same land, though the whole bulk of each remains constant (for we must suppose that the same thing is true of land as of the sea). For part of the sea rises up, part of it falls again, and both that which rises and that which falls change their positions.[d]

That saltness consists in an admixture is evident

Saltness an admixture: Examples.

[c] Because of the inclusion of dry exhalation, 358 a 33.

[d] Cf. 358 b 25-27 : it seems to make better sense to take τὸ μέν . . . τὸ δέ, ll. 31-32, as meaning the water of the sea and as referring to 358 b 25-27, with Saint-Hilaire, than to take them with the preceding sentence καὶ γάρ . . . ὑπολαβεῖν with the O.T. I have repunctuated Fobes' text accordingly. Ideler i. p. 83 punctuates as Fobes does, but translates in the same sense as Saint-Hilaire.

358 b

35 οὐ μόνον ἐκ τῶν εἰρημένων, ἀλλὰ καὶ ἐάν τις

359 a ἀγγεῖον πλάσας θῇ κήρινον εἰς τὴν θάλατταν, περι-
δήσας τὸ στόμα τοιούτοις ὥστε μὴ παρεγχεῖσθαι
τῆς θαλάττης· τὸ γὰρ εἰσιὸν διὰ τῶν τοίχων τῶν
κηρίνων γίγνεται πότιμον ὕδωρ· ὥσπερ γὰρ δι'
ἠθμοῦ τὸ γεῶδες ἀποκρίνεται καὶ τὸ ποιοῦν τὴν
5 ἁλμυρότητα διὰ τὴν σύμμειξιν. τοῦτο γὰρ αἴτιον
καὶ τοῦ βάρους (πλέον γὰρ ἕλκει τὸ ἁλμυρὸν ἢ τὸ
πότιμον) καὶ τοῦ πάχους· καὶ γὰρ τὸ πάχος διαφέρει τοσοῦτον ὥστε τὰ πλοῖα ἀπὸ τοῦ αὐτοῦ τῶν
ἀγωγίμων βάρους ἐν μὲν τοῖς ποταμοῖς ὀλίγου
10 καταδύνειν, ἐν δὲ τῇ θαλάττῃ μετρίως ἔχειν καὶ
πλευστικῶς· διόπερ ἔνιοι τῶν ἐν τοῖς ποταμοῖς
γεμιζόντων διὰ ταύτην τὴν ἄγνοιαν ἐζημιώθησαν.
τεκμήριον δὲ τοῦ μειγνυμένου τὸ παχύτερον εἶναι
τὸν ὄγκον· ἐὰν γάρ τις ὕδωρ ἁλμυρὸν ποιήσῃ
σφόδρα μείξας ἅλας, ἐπιπλέουσι τὰ ᾠά, κἂν ᾖ
15 πλήρη· σχεδὸν γὰρ ὥσπερ πηλὸς γίγνεται· τοσοῦτον
ἔχει σωματῶδες πλῆθος ἡ θάλαττα. ταὐτὸ δὲ τοῦτο
δρῶσι καὶ περὶ τὰς ταριχείας.

Εἰ δ' ἔστιν ὥσπερ μυθολογοῦσί τινες ἐν Παλαι-
στίνῃ τοιαύτη λίμνη, εἰς ἣν ἐάν τις ἐμβάλῃ συνδήσας
ἄνθρωπον ἢ ὑποζύγιον ἐπιπλεῖν καὶ οὐ καταδύεσθαι
20 κατὰ τοῦ ὕδατος, μαρτύριον ἂν εἴη τι τοῖς εἰρη-
μένοις· λέγουσι γὰρ πικρὰν οὕτως εἶναι τὴν λίμνην
καὶ ἁλμυρὰν ὥστε μηδένα ἰχθὺν ἐγγίγνεσθαι, τὰ

ᵃ Cf. *Hist. An.* viii. 2. 2, 590 a 24. As the O.T. notes, facts do not bear out Aristotle's statement, which makes it appear that he has not tried the experiment, but was taking it on hearsay. Pliny xxi. 37 and Aelian ix. 64 repeat Aris-

not only from what has now been said but also from the following experiment. Make a jar of wax and put it into the sea, having fastened its mouth in such a way as to prevent the sea getting in. It will be found that the water which gets through the wax walls is fresh, for the earthy substance whose admixture caused the saltness is separated off as though by a filter.[a] This substance is also the cause of its weight (for salt water weighs more than fresh) and of its density. For there is so great a difference in density between salt and fresh water that vessels laden with cargoes of the same weight almost sink in rivers, but ride quite easily at sea and are quite seaworthy. And an ignorance of this has sometimes cost people dear who load their ships in rivers. The following is a proof that the density of a fluid is greater when a substance is mixed with it. If you make water very salt by mixing salt in with it eggs will float on it, even when unblown, for the water becomes like mud. The sea contains a like quantity of earthy substance. The same thing is done in salting fish.[b]

If there were any truth in the stories they tell about the lake in Palestine [c] it would further bear out what I say. For they say if you bind a man or beast and throw him into it he floats and does not sink beneath the surface ; and that the lake is so bitter and salty that there are no fish in it, and that if you

totle's statement. κεράμινον (" earthenware ") has been conjectured for κήρινον (cf. O.T. note on *Hist. An. loc. cit.*) : but there is no ms. support for this and Pliny and Aelian have " wax."

[b] Alex. (88. 5) connects this with the statement about eggs, saying that the salt solution in which fish were salted was tested by floating an egg in it : when the egg floated the solution was strong enough.   [c] The Dead Sea.

359 a

δὲ ἱμάτια ῥύπτειν, ἐάν τις διασείσῃ βρέξας. ἔστι
δὲ καὶ τὰ τοιαῦτα σημεῖα πάντα τῶν εἰρημένων,
ὅτι τὸ ἁλμυρὸν ποιεῖ σῶμά τι, καὶ γεῶδές ἐστιν

25 τὸ ἐνυπάρχον· ἔν τε γὰρ τῇ Χαονίᾳ κρήνη τίς ἐστιν
ὕδατος πλατυτέρου, ἀπορρεῖ δ' αὕτη εἰς ποταμὸν
πλησίον γλυκὺν μέν, ἰχθῦς δ' οὐκ ἔχοντα· εἵλοντο
γὰρ δή, ὡς οἱ ἐκεῖ μυθολογοῦσιν, ἐξουσίας δοθείσης
ὑπὸ τοῦ Ἡρακλέους, ὅτ' ἦλθεν ἄγων ἐκ τῆς Ἐρυ-
θείας τὰς βοῦς, ἅλας ἀντὶ τῶν ἰχθύων, οἳ γίγνονται

30 αὐτοῖς ἐκ τῆς κρήνης· τούτου γὰρ τοῦ ὕδατος
ἀφέψοντές τι μέρος τιθέασι, καὶ γίγνεται ψυχθέν,
ὅταν ἀπατμίσῃ τὸ ὑγρὸν ἅμα τῷ θερμῷ, ἅλες, οὐ
χονδροὶ ἀλλὰ χαῦνοι καὶ λεπτοὶ ὥσπερ χιών.
εἰσίν τε τήν τε δύναμιν ἀσθενέστεροι τῶν ἄλλων
καὶ πλείους ἡδύνουσιν ἐμβληθέντες, καὶ τὴν χροιὰν

35 οὐχ ὁμοίως λευκοί. τοιοῦτον δ' ἕτερον γίγνεται
359 b καὶ ἐν Ὀμβρικοῖς· ἔστι γάρ τις τόπος ἐν ᾧ πε-
φύκασι κάλαμοι καὶ σχοῖνος· τούτων κατακάουσι,
καὶ τὴν τέφραν ἐμβάλλοντες εἰς ὕδωρ ἀφέψουσιν·
ὅταν δὲ λίπωσί τι μέρος τοῦ ὕδατος, τοῦτο ψυχθὲν
ἁλῶν γίγνεται πλῆθος.

5 Ὅσα δ' ἐστὶν ἁλμυρὰ ῥεύματα ποταμῶν ἢ κρηνῶν,
τὰ πλεῖστα θερμά ποτε εἶναι δεῖ νομίζειν, εἶτα τὴν
μὲν ἀρχὴν ἀπεσβέσθαι τοῦ πυρός, δι' ἧς δὲ δι-
ηθοῦνται γῆς, ἔτι μένειν οὖσαν οἷον κονίαν καὶ
τέφραν. εἰσὶ δὲ πολλαχοῦ καὶ κρῆναι καὶ ῥεύματα
ποταμῶν παντοδαποὺς ἔχοντα χυμούς, ὧν πάντων

10 αἰτιατέον τὴν ἐνοῦσαν ἢ ἐγγιγνομένην[1] δύναμιν
πυρός· καομένη γὰρ ἡ γῆ τῷ μᾶλλον καὶ ἧττον
παντοδαπὰς λαμβάνει μορφὰς καὶ χρόας χυμῶν·
στυπτηρίας γὰρ καὶ κονίας καὶ τῶν ἄλλων τῶν
τοιούτων γίγνεται πλήρης δυνάμεων, δι' ὧν τὰ

160

wet clothes in it and shake them out it cleans them.
The following facts also all support our contention
that it is the presence of a substance that makes
water salt, and that the substance present is earthy.
In Chaonia there is a spring of brackish water
which flows into a neighbouring river that is sweet
but contains no fish. For the inhabitants have a
story that when Heracles, on his way through with
the oxen from Erytheia, gave them the choice, they
chose to get salt instead of fish from the spring. For
they boil off some water from it and let the rest
stand ; and when it has cooled and the moisture has
evaporated with the heat salt is left, not in lumps
but in a loose powder like snow. It is also rather
weaker than other salt and more of it must be used
for seasoning, nor is it quite so white. Something of
a similar sort happens also in Umbria. There is a
place there where reeds and rushes grow : these they
burn and throw their ashes into water and boil it till
there is only a little left, and this when allowed to
cool produces quite a quantity of salt.

Most salt rivers and springs must be considered to
have once been hot ; subsequently the fiery principle in them was extinguished, but the earth through
which they filter retains qualities like those of ash
and cinders. And there are in various places many
springs and streams with many different tastes, the
cause of which is always a fiery element inherent or
produced in them. For the earth when subject to
combustion takes on to a greater or lesser degree all
kinds and shades of taste. For it becomes full of alum
and ash and substances of like qualities, and sweet

---

¹ ἐγγενομένην J O.T.

359 b

ἠθούμενα ὕδατα ὄντα γλυκέα μεταβάλλει, καὶ τὰ
15 μὲν ὀξέα γίγνεται, καθάπερ ἐν τῇ Σικάνῃ τῆς
Σικελίας· ἐκεῖ γὰρ ὀξάλμη γίγνεται, καὶ χρῶνται
καθάπερ ὄξει πρὸς ἔνια τῶν ἐδεσμάτων αὐτῷ.
ἔστι δὲ καὶ περὶ Λύγκον κρήνη τις ὕδατος ὀξέος,
περὶ δὲ τὴν Σκυθικὴν πικρά· τὸ δ' ἀπορρέον αὐτῆς
τὸν ποταμὸν εἰς ὃν εἰσβάλλει ποιεῖ πικρὸν ὅλον.
20 αἱ δὲ διαφοραὶ τούτων ἐκεῖθεν δῆλαι, ποῖοι χυμοὶ
ἐκ ποίων γίγνονται κράσεων· εἴρηται δὲ περὶ αὐτῶν
χωρὶς ἐν ἄλλοις.

Περὶ μὲν οὖν ὕδατος καὶ θαλάττης, δι' ἃς αἰτίας
αἰεί τε συνεχῶς εἰσι καὶ πῶς μεταβάλλουσι καὶ τίς
ἡ φύσις αὐτῶν, ἔτι δ' ὅσα πάθη κατὰ φύσιν αὐτοῖς
25 συμβαίνει ποιεῖν ἢ πάσχειν, εἴρηται σχεδὸν ἡμῖν
περὶ τῶν πλείστων.

---

[a] Cf. Eichholz in C.Q. xliii (July-Oct. 1949), p. 145 on
this passage.

CHAPTER IV

ARGUMENT

*The causes of winds. There are, as we have said, two kinds
of exhalation from the earth, dry and moist. These are
caused by the sun, whose movement in the ecliptic gives rise
to seasonal changes. The moist exhalation produces rain,
the dry exhalation wind (359 b 27—360 a 17). So rain and
wind differ in substance : and we cannot regard wind as air
in motion (360 a 17-21, 27-33). Air then is made up of two
exhalations, one moist and cold, one hot and dry, and is itself
in consequence moist and hot. The predominance of one or*

359 b 27 Περὶ δὲ πνευμάτων λέγωμεν, λαβόντες ἀρχὴν τὴν
εἰρημένην ἡμῖν ἤδη πρότερον. ἔστι γὰρ δύ' εἴδη

water changes when filtered through them.[a] Sometimes it becomes acid, as in Sicania in Sicily : for there it becomes both salt and acid and they use it as vinegar on some of their dishes. And there is an acid spring also at Lyncus, and a bitter one in Scythia the water from which makes the whole river into which it flows bitter.[b] These differences are clear from a knowledge of the different tastes produced by different mixtures, a subject which has been dealt with separately elsewhere.[c]

We have now dealt with the causes of the continued existence of water and the sea and of their changes, with their nature, and with most of their various natural characteristics active and passive.

[b] *Cf.* Herod. iv. 52, 81.
[c] *De Sensu*, ch. 4 ; or a lost work.

CHAPTER IV

ARGUMENT (*continued*)

other exhalation accounts for variations in rainfall from year to year (360 a 21-27, 33-b 26). Why wind occurs after rainfall, rainfall when wind drops (360 b 26—361 a 4). Why the prevailing winds are northerly or southerly (361 a 4-22). Winds originate from the earth (as exhalation), but their movement is determined by that of the celestial region. The exhalation of which they are composed collects gradually (361 a 22-b 8).

(With chs. 4-6 cf. Problems xxvi.)

LET us now give an account of winds, on the lines we have already laid down. For we have said [a] that there Two kinds of exhalation : wind

[a] *Cf.* Book I. ch. 4, 341 b 6 ff.

359 b

τῆς ἀναθυμιάσεως, ὥς φαμεν, ἡ μὲν ὑγρὰ ἡ δὲ
30 ξηρά· καλεῖται δ' ἡ μὲν ἀτμίς, ἡ δὲ τὸ μὲν ὅλον
ἀνώνυμος, τῷ δ' ἐπὶ μέρους ἀνάγκη χρωμένους
καθόλου προσαγορεύειν αὐτὴν οἷον καπνόν· ἔστι
δ' οὔτε τὸ ὑγρὸν ἄνευ τοῦ ξηροῦ οὔτε τὸ ξηρὸν
ἄνευ τοῦ ὑγροῦ, ἀλλὰ πάντα ταῦτα λέγεται κατὰ
τὴν ὑπεροχήν.

Φερομένου δὴ τοῦ ἡλίου κύκλῳ, καὶ ὅταν μὲν
35 πλησιάζῃ, τῇ θερμότητι ἀνάγοντος τὸ ὑγρόν, πορ-
360 a ρωτέρω δὲ γιγνομένου διὰ τὴν ψύξιν συνισταμένης
πάλιν τῆς ἀναχθείσης ἀτμίδος εἰς ὕδωρ (διὸ χει-
μῶνός τε μᾶλλον γίγνεται τὰ ὕδατα, καὶ νύκτωρ
ἢ μεθ' ἡμέραν· ἀλλ' οὐ δοκεῖ, διὰ τὸ λανθάνειν τὰ
5 νυκτερινὰ τῶν μεθ' ἡμέραν μᾶλλον), τὸ δὴ κατιὸν
ὕδωρ διαδίδοται πᾶν εἰς τὴν γῆν, ὑπάρχει δ' ἐν τῇ
γῇ πολὺ πῦρ καὶ πολλὴ θερμότης, καὶ ὁ ἥλιος οὐ
μόνον τὸ ἐπιπολάζον τῆς γῆς ὑγρὸν ἕλκει, ἀλλὰ
καὶ τὴν γῆν αὐτὴν ξηραίνει θερμαίνων· τῆς δ' ἀναθυμιάσεως, ὥσπερ εἴρηται, διπλῆς οὔσης, τῆς μὲν
10 ἀτμιδώδους τῆς δὲ καπνώδους, ἀμφοτέρας ἀναγκαῖον γίγνεσθαι. τούτων δ' ἡ μὲν ὑγροῦ πλέον
ἔχουσα πλῆθος ἀναθυμίασις ἀρχὴ τοῦ ὑομένου
ὕδατός ἐστιν, ὥσπερ εἴρηται πρότερον, ἡ δὲ ξηρὰ
τῶν πνευμάτων ἀρχὴ καὶ φύσις πάντων. ταῦτα
δὲ ὅτι τοῦτον τὸν τρόπον ἀναγκαῖον συμβαίνειν,
15 καὶ ἐξ αὐτῶν τῶν ἔργων δῆλον· καὶ γὰρ τὴν ἀναθυμίασιν διαφέρειν ἀναγκαῖον, καὶ τὸν ἥλιον καὶ
τὴν ἐν τῇ γῇ θερμότητα ταῦτα ποιεῖν οὐ μόνον
δυνατὸν ἀλλ' ἀναγκαῖόν ἐστιν.

Ἐπειδὴ δ' ἕτερον ἑκατέρας τὸ εἶδος, φανερὸν ὅτι
διαφέρει, καὶ οὐχ ἡ αὐτή ἐστιν ἥ τε ἀνέμου φύσις

are two kinds of exhalation—one moist and one dry : caused
of these the first is called vapour, the second has no by dry.
name that applies to it as a whole, and we are com-
pelled to apply to the whole a name which belongs
to a part only and call it a kind of smoke. The moist
exhalation does not exist without the dry nor the dry
without the moist, but we speak of them as dry or
moist according as either quality predominates.

When, therefore, the sun in its circular course
approaches the earth, its heat draws up the moist
exhalation ; when it recedes the vapour thus drawn
up is condensed again by the resulting cold into
water. (This is why there is more rain in the winter,
and more at night than by day—though this is not
commonly supposed to be so because rainfall at night
more often passes unnoticed than by day.) The water
thus formed falls and is all distributed over the earth.
Now there is in the earth a large amount of fire and
heat, and the sun not only draws up the moisture on
the earth's surface but also heats and so dries the
earth itself ; and this must produce exhalations
which are of the two kinds we have described, namely
vaporous and smoky. The exhalation containing the
greater amount of moisture is, as we have said before,[a]
the origin of rain water : the dry exhalation is the
origin and natural substance of winds. That this
must be the case is evident from the facts. For the
exhalations that produce rain and wind must differ
and it is not only possible but necessary that the sun
and the warmth in the earth should produce the
exhalations.

Since the two exhalations differ in kind, it is clear Rain and
that the substance of wind and of rain water also wind differ.

[a] Book I. ch. 9.

360 a

20 καὶ ἡ τοῦ ὑομένου ὕδατος, καθάπερ τινὲς λέγουσιν·
τὸν γὰρ αὐτὸν ἀέρα κινούμενον μὲν ἄνεμον εἶναι,
συνιστάμενον δὲ πάλιν ὕδωρ. καὶ γὰρ ἄτοπον εἰ
28 ὁ περὶ ἑκάστους περικεχυμένος ἀὴρ οὗτος γίγνεται
29 κινούμενος πνεῦμα, καὶ ὅθεν ἂν τύχῃ κινηθείς,
ἄνεμος ἔσται, ἀλλ' οὐ καθάπερ τοὺς ποταμοὺς ὑπο-
30 λαμβάνομεν οὐχ ὁπωσοῦν τοῦ ὕδατος εἶναι ῥέον-
31 τος, οὐδ' ἂν ἔχῃ πλῆθος, ἀλλὰ δεῖ πηγαῖον εἶναι
32 τὸ ῥέον· οὕτω γὰρ καὶ περὶ τῶν ἀνέμων ἔχει· κινη-
33 θείη γὰρ ἂν πολὺ πλῆθος ἀέρος ὑπό τινος μεγάλης
πτώσεως, οὐκ ἔχον ἀρχὴν οὐδὲ πηγήν.

21 Ὁ μὲν οὖν ἀήρ,[1] καθάπερ ἐν τοῖς πρὸ τούτων
22 λόγοις εἰρήκαμεν, γίγνεται ἐκ τούτων· ἡ μὲν γὰρ
23 ἀτμὶς ὑγρὸν καὶ ψυχρόν (εὐόριστον μὲν γὰρ ὡς
24 ὑγρόν, διὰ δὲ τὸ ὕδατος εἶναι ψυχρὸν τῇ οἰκείᾳ
25 φύσει, ὥσπερ ὕδωρ μὴ θερμανθέν), ὁ δὲ καπνὸς
26 θερμὸν καὶ ξηρόν· ὥστε καθάπερ ἐκ συμβόλων,
27 συνίσταιτο ἂν ὁ ἀὴρ ὑγρὸς καὶ θερμός. μαρτυρεῖ
34 δὲ τὰ γιγνόμενα τοῖς εἰρημένοις· διὰ γὰρ τὸ συν-
35 εχῶς μὲν μᾶλλον δὲ καὶ ἧττον καὶ πλείω καὶ
360 b ἐλάττω γίγνεσθαι τὴν ἀναθυμίασιν, ἀεὶ νέφη τε καὶ
πνεύματα γίγνεται κατὰ τὴν ὥραν ἑκάστην ὡς
πέφυκεν· διὰ δὲ τὸ ἐνίοτε μὲν τὴν ἀτμιδώδη γίγνεσθαι πολλαπλασίαν ὁτὲ δὲ τὴν ξηρὰν καὶ κα-
πνώδη, ὁτὲ μὲν ἔπομβρα τὰ ἔτη γίγνεται καὶ ὑγρά,
5 ὁτὲ δὲ ἀνεμώδη καὶ αὐχμοί. ὁτὲ μὲν οὖν συμβαίνει
καὶ τοὺς αὐχμοὺς καὶ τὰς ἐπομβρίας πολλοὺς ἅμα
καὶ κατὰ συνεχῆ γίγνεσθαι χώραν, ὁτὲ δὲ κατὰ
μέρη· πολλάκις γὰρ ἡ μὲν κύκλῳ χώρα λαμβάνει

---

[1] ὁ μὲν οὖν ἀήρ l. 21 . . . θερμός l. 27 post πηγήν l. 33 coll.
Thurot.

differ and are not the same, as some [a] maintain : for they say that the same substance, air, is wind when in motion, water when condensed again.[b] Yet it is absurd to suppose that the air which surrounds us becomes wind simply by being in motion, and will be wind whatever the source of its motion ; for we do not call a volume of water, however large, a river whatever its flow but only if it flows from a source, and the same thing is true of the winds, for a considerable volume of air might be set in motion by some large falling body, and have no origin or source.

Air then, as we have said before,[c] is made up of these two components, vapour which is moist and cold (it is unresistant because it is moist, and is naturally cold because derived from water, which is cold unless heated) and smoke which is hot and dry ; so that air, being composed, as it were, of complementary factors, is moist and hot. The facts confirm this view. For because the exhalation continually increases and decreases, expands and contracts, clouds and winds are always being produced in their natural season ; and because it is sometimes the vaporous exhalation that predominates, at other times the dry and smoky one, years are sometimes rainy and wet, at others windy and dry. And sometimes drought or rain is widespread and covers a large area of country, sometimes it is only local ; for often in the country at large the

Variations in rainfall.

---

[a] Metrodorus of Chios (Diels 70 A 19).

[b] The first sentence from the next paragraph follows here in the accepted Greek text : I have transposed it, following Thurot (see critical note), as the transposition seems to make better sense of the passage.

[c] *Cf.* Book I. ch. 3, 340 b 14-32 and note *a* on p. 20, ch. 4, 341 b 6 ff.; also *De Gen. et Corr.* ii. 4, and Joachim's note on 331 a 24.

360 b

τοὺς ὡραίους ὄμβρους ἢ καὶ πλείους, ἐν δέ τινι
10 μέρει ταύτης αὐχμός ἐστιν· ὁτὲ δὲ τοὐναντίον τῆς
κύκλῳ πάσης ἢ μετρίοις χρωμένης ὕδασιν ἢ καὶ
μᾶλλον αὐχμώσης, ἕν τι μόριον ὕδατος ἄφθονον
λαμβάνει πλῆθος. αἴτιον δ' ὅτι ὡς μὲν τὰ πολλὰ
τὸ αὐτὸ πάθος ἐπὶ πλείω διήκειν εἰκὸς χώραν,
διὰ τὸ παραπλησίως κεῖσθαι πρὸς τὸν ἥλιον τὰ
15 σύνεγγυς, ἐὰν μή τι διάφορον ἔχωσιν ἴδιον· οὐ μὴν
ἀλλ' ἐνίοτε κατὰ τοδὶ μὲν τὸ μέρος ἡ ξηρὰ ἀναθυμίασις ἐγένετο πλείων, κατὰ δὲ τὸ ἄλλο ἡ ἀτμιδώδης, ὁτὲ δὲ τοὐναντίον. καὶ αὐτοῦ δὲ τούτου
αἴτιον τὸ ἑκατέραν μεταπίπτειν εἰς τὴν τῆς ἐχομένης
χώρας ἀναθυμίασιν, οἷον ἡ μὲν ξηρὰ κατὰ τὴν
20 οἰκείαν ῥεῖ χώραν, ἡ δ' ὑγρὰ πρὸς τὴν γειτνιῶσαν,
ἢ καὶ εἰς τῶν πόρρω τινὰ τόπων ἀπεώσθη ὑπὸ
πνευμάτων· ὁτὲ δὲ αὕτη μὲν ἔμεινεν, ἡ δ' ἐναντία
ταὐτὸν ἐποίησεν. καὶ συμβαίνει τοῦτο πολλάκις,
ὥσπερ ἐπὶ τοῦ σώματος, ἐὰν ἡ ἄνω κοιλία ξηρὰ ᾖ,
τὴν κάτω ἐναντίως διακεῖσθαι, καὶ ταύτης ξηρᾶς
25 οὔσης ὑγρὰν εἶναι τὴν ἄνω καὶ ψυχράν, οὕτω καὶ
περὶ τοὺς τόπους ἀντιπεριίστασθαι καὶ μεταβάλλειν
τὰς ἀναθυμιάσεις.

Ἔτι δὲ μετά τε τοὺς ὄμβρους ἄνεμος ὡς τὰ πολλὰ
γίγνεται ἐν ἐκείνοις τοῖς τόποις καθ' οὓς ἂν συμ-
πέσῃ γενέσθαι τοὺς ὄμβρους, καὶ τὰ πνεύματα
30 παύεται ὕδατος γενομένου. ταῦτα γὰρ ἀνάγκη
συμβαίνειν διὰ τὰς εἰρημένας ἀρχάς· ὕσαντός τε
γὰρ ἡ γῆ ξηραινομένη ὑπό τε τοῦ ἐν αὐτῇ θερμοῦ
καὶ ὑπὸ τοῦ ἄνωθεν ἀναθυμιᾶται, τοῦτο δ' ἦν
ἀνέμου σῶμα· καὶ ὅταν ἡ τοιαύτη ἀπόκρισις ᾖ καὶ
ἄνεμοι κατέχωσι, παυομένων διὰ τὸ ἀποκρίνεσθαι

seasonal rainfall is normal or even above the normal, while in some districts of it there is a drought ; at other times, on the other hand, the rainfall in the country at large is meagre, or there is even a tendency to drought, while in a single district the rainfall is abundant in quantity. The reason is that as a rule a considerable area may be expected to be similarly affected, because neighbouring places lie in a similar relation to the sun, unless they have some local peculiarity : at the same time it may happen that at times the dry exhalation predominates in one district, the vaporous in another, while at times the opposite is the case. And the reason for this again is the movement of either of the two exhalations across to join that of the neighbouring district ; the dry, for instance, may circulate in its own, the moist flow to a neighbouring district or be driven by winds still farther afield, while on other occasions the moist exhalation may remain and the dry retire. Thus it often happens that just as in the human body if the upper belly is dry the lower is in the opposite condition, and if the lower is dry the upper is cold and wet, so the exhalations undergo reciprocal replacement [a] and change of place.

Moreover, wind as a rule occurs after rain in those places in which the rain has happened to fall, and when rain falls the wind drops. These are necessary consequences of the principles we have stated. For after rain the earth is dried by its own internal heat and the heat from above and gives off exhalations which are the substance of wind. And when this separation is in process winds prevail ; when they drop, because the hot element is constantly being

Wind follows rain.

[a] See Book I. ch. 12, note *b* on p. 82.

360 b

35 τὸ θερμὸν ἀεὶ καὶ ἀναφέρεσθαι εἰς τὸν ἄνω τόπον
συνίσταται ἡ ἀτμὶς ψυχομένη καὶ γίγνεται ὕδωρ·
καὶ ὅταν εἰς ταὐτὸν συνωσθῶσι τὰ νέφη καὶ ἀντι-
361 a περιστῇ εἰς αὐτὰ ἡ ψύξις, ὕδωρ γίγνεται καὶ καταψύχει τὴν ξηρὰν ἀναθυμίασιν. παύουσί τε οὖν τὰ
ὕδατα γιγνόμενα τοὺς ἀνέμους, καὶ παυομένων
αὐτὰ γίγνεται διὰ ταύτας τὰς αἰτίας.

5 Ἔτι δὲ τοῦ γίγνεσθαι μάλιστα πνεύματα ἀπό τε
τῆς ἄρκτου καὶ μεσημβρίας τὸ αὐτὸ αἴτιον· πλεῖστοι
γὰρ βορέαι καὶ νότοι γίγνονται τῶν ἀνέμων· ὁ γὰρ
ἥλιος τούτους μόνους οὐκ ἐπέρχεται τοὺς τόπους,
ἀλλὰ πρὸς τούτους καὶ ἀπὸ τούτων, ἐπὶ δυσμὰς
δὲ καὶ ἐπ' ἀνατολὰς ἀεὶ φέρεται· διὸ τὰ νέφη
10 συνίσταται ἐν τοῖς πλαγίοις, καὶ γίγνεται προσ-
ιόντος μὲν ἡ ἀναθυμίασις τοῦ ὑγροῦ, ἀπιόντος δὲ
πρὸς τὸν ἐναντίον τόπον ὕδατα καὶ χειμῶνες. διὰ
μὲν οὖν τὴν φορὰν τὴν ἐπὶ τροπὰς καὶ ἀπὸ τροπῶν
θέρος γίγνεται καὶ χειμών, καὶ ἀνάγεταί τε ἄνω
15 τὸ ὕδωρ καὶ γίγνεται πάλιν· ἐπεὶ δὲ πλεῖστον μὲν
καταβαίνει ὕδωρ ἐν τούτοις τοῖς τόποις ἐφ' οὓς
τρέπεται καὶ ἀφ' ὧν, οὗτοι δέ εἰσιν ὅ τε πρὸς
ἄρκτον καὶ μεσημβρίαν, ὅπου δὲ πλεῖστον ὕδωρ
ἡ γῆ δέχεται, ἐνταῦθα πλείστην ἀναγκαῖον γίγνεσθαι τὴν ἀναθυμίασιν παραπλησίως οἷον ἐκ
χλωρῶν ξύλων καπνόν, ἡ δ' ἀναθυμίασις αὕτη
20 ἄνεμός ἐστιν, εὐλόγως ἂν οὖν ἐντεῦθεν γίγνοιτο τὰ
πλεῖστα καὶ κυριώτατα τῶν πνευμάτων. καλοῦνται
δ' οἱ μὲν ἀπὸ τῆς ἄρκτου βορέαι, οἱ δὲ ἀπὸ τῆς
μεσημβρίας νότοι.

Ἡ δὲ φορὰ λοξὴ αὐτῶν ἐστιν· περὶ γὰρ τὴν γῆν
πνέουσιν εἰς ὀρθὸν γιγνομένης τῆς ἀναθυμιάσεως,
25 ὅτι πᾶς ὁ κύκλῳ ἀὴρ συνέπεται τῇ φορᾷ. διὸ καὶ

separated out and rising to the upper region,[a] the vaporous exhalation is cooled and condenses and becomes water. And when the clouds are driven together and the cold is compressed within them,[b] water is formed and cools the dry exhalation. For these reasons, therefore, when rain falls the wind drops, and when the wind drops the rain falls.

The same cause again accounts for the prevalence of winds from north and south [c]—for most winds are in fact either northerly or southerly. For over these regions alone the sun does not pass, but only approaches them or recedes from them ; but its course always passes over the east and west. So clouds form in these regions bordering on its course, and when it approaches it causes exhalation of moisture, when it recedes to the opposite side, rain and storms. The sun's movement in the ecliptic is thus the cause of summer and winter, and the water is drawn up and falls again. Now the largest amount of rain falls in the regions beyond the tropics, that is, the regions north and south of them ; and where the earth receives the most rainfall the exhalation must be correspondingly greatest, like the smoke from green sticks, and this exhalation is wind ; so it is only to be expected that the majority of winds and the most considerable should come from these quarters. Those that come from the north are called Boreae, those that come from the south Notoi. *Prevalence of northerly and southerly winds.*

Winds blow horizontally ; for though the exhalation rises vertically, the winds blow round the earth because the whole body of air surrounding the earth follows the motion of the heavens. So one might *Celestial sphere the moving cause of winds.*

[a] *Cf.* 341 a 4 and Book I. ch. 3, note a on p. 22.
[b] See Book I. ch. 12, note b on p. 82.
[c] *Cf.* ch. 5, 363 a 2-20.

361 a

ἀπορήσειεν ἄν τις ποτέρωθεν ἡ ἀρχὴ τῶν πνευμάτων ἐστί, πότερον ἄνωθεν ἢ κάτωθεν· ἡ μὲν γὰρ
κίνησις ἄνωθεν καὶ πρὶν πνεῖν ὁ [δ']¹ ἀὴρ ἐπίδηλος,
κἂν ᾖ νέφος ἢ ἀχλύς· σημαίνει γὰρ κινουμένην
πνεύματος ἀρχὴν πρὶν φανερῶς ἐληλυθέναι τὸν
30 ἄνεμον, ὡς ἄνωθεν αὐτῶν ἐχόντων τὴν ἀρχήν.
ἐπεὶ δ' ἐστὶν ἄνεμος πλῆθός τι τῆς ξηρᾶς ἐκ γῆς
ἀναθυμιάσεως κινούμενον περὶ τὴν γῆν, δῆλον ὅτι
τῆς μὲν κινήσεως ἡ ἀρχὴ ἄνωθεν, τῆς δὲ ὕλης καὶ
τῆς γενέσεως κάτωθεν· ᾗ μὲν γὰρ ῥευσεῖται τὸ
ἀνιόν, ἐκεῖθεν τὸ αἴτιον· ἡ γὰρ φορὰ τῶν πορρωτέρω
35 κυρία τῆς γῆς· καὶ ἅμα κάτωθεν μὲν εἰς ὀρθὸν
ἀναφέρεται, καὶ πᾶν ἰσχύει μᾶλλον ἐγγύς, ἡ δὲ τῆς
361 b γενέσεως ἀρχὴ δῆλον ὡς ἐκ τῆς γῆς ἐστιν.

Ὅτι δ' ἐκ πολλῶν ἀναθυμιάσεων συνιουσῶν κατὰ
μικρόν, ὥσπερ αἱ τῶν ποταμῶν ἀρχαὶ γίγνονται
νοτιζούσης τῆς γῆς, δῆλον καὶ ἐπὶ τῶν ἔργων· ὅθεν
γὰρ ἑκάστοτε πνέουσιν, ἐλάχιστοι πάντες εἰσί,
5 προϊόντες δὲ καὶ πόρρω λαμπροὶ πνέουσιν. ἔτι δὲ
καὶ τὰ περὶ τὴν ἄρκτον ἐν τῷ χειμῶνι νήνεμα καὶ
ἄπνοα, κατ' αὐτὸν ἐκεῖνον τὸν τόπον· ἀλλὰ τὸ
κατὰ μικρὸν ἀποπνέον καὶ λανθάνον ἔξω προϊὸν
ἤδη πνεῦμα γίγνεται λαμπρόν.

Τίς μὲν οὖν ἐστιν ἡ τοῦ ἀνέμου φύσις καὶ πῶς
10 γίγνεται, ἔτι δὲ αὐχμῶν τε πέρι καὶ ἐπομβρίας,
καὶ διὰ τίν' αἰτίαν καὶ παύονται καὶ γίγνονται μετὰ
τοὺς ὄμβρους, διὰ τί τε βορέαι καὶ νότοι πλεῖστοι
τῶν ἀνέμων εἰσίν, εἴρηται· πρὸς δὲ τούτοις καὶ
περὶ τῆς φορᾶς αὐτῶν.

¹ om. J_corr. O.T

raise the question whether winds originate from above or below, for their movement is derived from above, and even before they actually start to blow the air reveals their approach, even if there is cloud or mist ; for these show that a wind has started to blow even before its arrival is perceptible, which seems to indicate that winds originate from above. But since a wind is a body of dry exhalation moving about the earth, it is clear that though their motion takes its origin from above the material from which they are produced comes from below. Thus the direction of flow of the rising exhalation is determined from above, as the motion of the heavens controls things whose distance from the earth is considerable : at the same time the exhalation rises vertically from below, since any cause operates more strongly on its effect the nearer it is to it and the exhalation is clearly produced originally from the earth.

The facts also make it clear that winds are formed by the gradual collection of small quantities of exhalation, in the same way that rivers form when the earth is wet. For they are all least strong at their place of origin, but blow strongly as they travel farther from it. Besides, the north, that is the region immediately about the pole, is calm and windless in winter ; but the wind which blows so gently there that it passes unnoticed becomes strong as it moves farther afield.

We have thus given an account of the nature and origin of the wind, and of drought and rainfall. We have given the reason why winds fall and rise after rain and why the prevailing winds are northerly and southerly : finally we have dealt with the motion of the winds.

CHAPTER V

ARGUMENT

Extreme heat and cold prevent the rise of winds, which occur when the seasons are changing (361 b 14-35). This is shown by the Etesian winds and the fair weather winds which correspond to them (361 b 35—362 a 31). The south wind blows, not from the pole, but from the torrid zone. This is

361 b 14 Ὁ δ’ ἥλιος καὶ παύει καὶ συνεξορμᾷ τὰ πνεύ-
15 ματα· ἀσθενεῖς μὲν γὰρ καὶ ὀλίγας οὔσας τὰς ἀναθυμιάσεις μαραίνει τῷ πλείονι θερμῷ τὸ ἐν τῇ
ἀναθυμιάσει ἔλαττον ὄν, καὶ διακρίνει. ἔτι δὲ
αὐτὴν τὴν γῆν φθάνει ξηραίνων πρὶν γενέσθαι ἔκκρισιν ἀθρόαν, ὥσπερ εἰς πολὺ πῦρ ἐὰν ὀλίγον
ἐμπέσῃ ὑπέκκαυμα, φθάνει πολλάκις πρὶν καπνὸν
20 ποιῆσαι κατακαυθέν. διὰ μὲν οὖν ταύτας τὰς
αἰτίας καταπαύει τε τὰ πνεύματα καὶ ἐξ ἀρχῆς
γίγνεσθαι κωλύει, τῇ μὲν μαράνσει καταπαύων, τῷ
δὲ τάχει τῆς ξηρότητος γίγνεσθαι κωλύων· διὸ
περὶ Ὠρίωνος ἀνατολὴν μάλιστα γίγνεται νηνεμία,
καὶ μέχρι τῶν ἐτησίων καὶ προδρόμων. ὅλως δὲ
25 γίγνονται αἱ νηνεμίαι διὰ δύ’ αἰτίας· ἢ γὰρ διὰ
ψῦχος ἀποσβεννυμένης τῆς ἀναθυμιάσεως, οἷον ὅταν
γένηται πάγος ἰσχυρός, ἢ καταμαραινομένης ὑπὸ
τοῦ πνίγους. αἱ δὲ πλεῖσται καὶ ἐν ταῖς ἀνὰ μέσον
ὥραις, ἢ τῷ μήπω ἀναθυμιᾶσθαι, ἢ τῷ ἤδη ἐξ-
30 εληλυθέναι τὴν ἀναθυμίασιν καὶ ἄλλην μήπω
ἐπιρρεῖν.

Ἄκριτος δὲ καὶ χαλεπὸς ὁ Ὠρίων εἶναι δοκεῖ,
174

CHAPTER V

ARGUMENT (*continued*)

shown by a consideration of the two habitable zones of the earth ; one, in which we live, lies in the northern hemisphere, the other in the southern, and each has an analogous disposition of winds. The prevailing winds in our hemisphere are northerly or southerly (362 a 31—363 a 20).

THE sun both hinders and encourages the rise of winds. For when the exhalations are feeble and few its greater heat scorches up the lesser heat of the exhalation and disperses it. Also it dries up even the earth too quickly to allow the exhalation to gather in any quantity, just as a small amount of fuel thrown into a large fire is burnt up before it can produce any smoke. For these reasons, then, the sun hinders the rise of winds or prevents it altogether : it hinders it by scorching up the exhalation's heat ; it prevents it by the speed with which it dries the earth. Therefore the period from about the rise of Orion [a] to the coming of the Etesian winds [b] and their precursors is generally calm. There are two general causes of calm weather : either the exhalation is quenched by cold, as in a hard frost, or it is scorched up and stifled by the heat. Calm weather in the intervening periods [c] is mostly caused by lack of exhalation or by the exhalation having passed away and not yet being replaced.

The reason why Orion is commonly regarded as a constellation which brings uncertain and stormy

Extreme heat and cold prevent the rise of winds.

[a] Early July : the morning rising.
[b] *Cf.* 361 b 35 below.
[c] *i.e.* between the cold of winter and the heat of summer.

ARISTOTLE

καὶ δύνων καὶ ἐπιτέλλων, διὰ τὸ ἐν μεταβολῇ ὥρας
συμβαίνειν τὴν δύσιν καὶ τὴν ἀνατολήν, θέρους ἢ
χειμῶνος, καὶ διὰ τὸ μέγεθος[1] τοῦ ἄστρου ἡμερῶν
γίγνεται[1] πλῆθος· αἱ δὲ μεταβολαὶ πάντων ταρα-
35 χώδεις διὰ τὴν ἀοριστίαν εἰσίν.

Οἱ δ᾽ ἐτησίαι πνέουσι μετὰ τροπὰς καὶ κυνὸς
ἐπιτολήν, καὶ οὔτε τηνικαῦτα ὅτε μάλιστα πλησιάζει
362 a ὁ ἥλιος, οὔτε ὅτε πόρρω· καὶ τὰς μὲν ἡμέρας
πνέουσι, τὰς δὲ νύκτας παύονται. αἴτιον δ᾽ ὅτι
πλησίον μὲν ὢν φθάνει ξηραίνων πρὶν γενέσθαι
τὴν ἀναθυμίασιν· ὅταν δ᾽ ἀπέλθῃ μικρόν, σύμμετρος ἤδη γίγνεται ἡ ἀναθυμίασις καὶ ἡ[2] θερμότης,
5 ὥστε τὰ πεπηγότα ὕδατα τήκεσθαι, καὶ τῆς γῆς
ξηραινομένης ὑπό τε τῆς οἰκείας θερμότητος καὶ
ὑπὸ τῆς τοῦ ἡλίου οἷον τύφεσθαι καὶ θυμιᾶσθαι.
τῆς δὲ νυκτὸς λωφῶσι διὰ τὸ τὰ πεπηγότα τηκόμενα παύεσθαι διὰ τὴν ψυχρότητα τῶν νυκτῶν.
θυμιᾶται δ᾽ οὔτε τὸ πεπηγὸς οὔτε τὸ μηδὲν ἔχον
10 ξηρόν, ἀλλ᾽ ὅταν ἔχῃ τὸ ξηρὸν ὑγρότητα, τοῦτο
θερμαινόμενον θυμιᾶται.

Ἀποροῦσι δέ τινες διὰ τί βορέαι μὲν γίγνονται
συνεχεῖς, οὓς καλοῦμεν ἐτησίας, μετὰ τὰς θερινὰς
τροπάς, νότοι δὲ οὕτως οὐ γίγνονται μετὰ τὰς
χειμερινάς. ἔχει δὲ οὐκ ἀλόγως· γίγνονται μὲν
15 γὰρ οἱ καλούμενοι λευκόνοτοι τὴν ἀντικειμένην
ὥραν, οὐχ οὕτως δὲ γίγνονται συνεχεῖς· διὸ λαν-
θάνοντες ποιοῦσιν ἐπιζητεῖν. αἴτιον δ᾽ ὅτι ὁ μὲν
βορέας ἀπὸ τῶν ὑπὸ τὴν ἄρκτον πνεῖ τόπων, οἳ
πλήρεις ὕδατος καὶ χιόνος εἰσὶ πολλῆς, ὧν τηκομένων ὑπὸ τοῦ ἡλίου μετὰ τὰς θερινὰς τροπὰς

---

[1] " scribe διότι διὰ τὸ μέγεθος aut pro γίνεται corrige γίνε-
σθαι " (Ideler).   [2] ἀναθυμίασις καὶ ἡ om. E W Ap Ol Ideler.

weather when it rises and sets is that its rising and setting[a] occur at a change of season (summer or winter), and, owing to the size of the constellation, last many days : and all changes are uncertain and so unsettled.

The Etesian winds blow after the summer solstice and the rise of the Dog-star[b] ; they do not blow when the sun is at its nearest nor when it is far off. They blow in the day-time and drop at night. The reason for this is that when the sun is closer it dries the earth too quickly for the exhalation to form : when it withdraws a little, the balance between its heat and the exhalation is restored, with the result that frozen water melts and the earth, dried by its own internal heat and by that of the sun, gives off smoke and fumes.[c] These winds cease at night because the coldness of the nights stops frozen water melting. Moisture that is frozen or that contains no dry constituent does not give off fumes ; but a dry substance that contains moisture does so when heated.

The fair weather and Bird winds.

Some people find it difficult to see why the north winds which we call Etesian blow continuously after the summer solstice, but there are no corresponding south winds after the winter solstice. But this is not without reason. For the so-called fair weather winds do blow from the south at the corresponding time in winter, but as they do not blow so continuously, they escape notice ; and thus the difficulty arises. The reason for this is that the north wind blows from the polar regions, which are full of water and large quantities of snow ; so the Etesian winds blow when the sun melts these, which it does just

---

[a] Mid-November : the morning setting.
[b] Late July.   [c] Cf. 362 a 16-22 below.

177

362 a

20 μᾶλλον ἢ ἐν αὐταῖς πνέουσιν οἱ ἐτησίαι· οὕτω γὰρ
καὶ τὰ πνίγη γίγνεται, οὐχ ὅταν μάλιστα πλησιάζῃ
πρὸς ἄρκτον, ἀλλ᾽ ὅταν πλείων μὲν ᾖ χρόνος θερμαί-
νοντι, ἔτι δὲ ἐγγύς. ὁμοίως δὲ καὶ μετὰ χειμερινὰς
τροπὰς πνέουσιν οἱ ὀρνιθίαι· καὶ γὰρ οὗτοι ἐτησίαι
εἰσὶν ἀσθενεῖς· ἐλάττους δὲ καὶ ὀψιαίτεροι τῶν
25 ἐτησίων πνέουσιν· ἑβδομηκοστῇ γὰρ ἄρχονται πνεῖν
διὰ τὸ πόρρω ὄντα τὸν ἥλιον ἐνισχύειν ἧττον. οὐ
συνεχεῖς δ᾽ ὁμοίως πνέουσι, διότι τὰ μὲν ἐπιπολῆς
καὶ ἀσθενῆ τότε ἀποκρίνεται, τὰ δὲ μᾶλλον πεπηγότα πλείονος δεῖται θερμότητος. διὸ διαλεί-
ποντες οὗτοι πνέουσιν, ἕως ἂν ἐπὶ τροπαῖς πάλιν
30 ταῖς θεριναῖς πνεύσωσιν οἱ ἐτησίαι, ἐπεὶ θέλει γε
ὅτι μάλιστα συνεχῶς ἐντεῦθεν ἀεὶ πνεῖν ἄνεμος.

Ὁ δὲ νότος ἀπὸ τῆς θερινῆς τροπῆς πνεῖ, καὶ οὐκ
ἀπὸ τῆς ἑτέρας ἄρκτου. δύο γὰρ ὄντων τμημάτων
τῆς δυνατῆς οἰκεῖσθαι χώρας, τῆς μὲν πρὸς τὸν
ἄνω πόλον, καθ᾽ ἡμᾶς, τῆς δὲ πρὸς τὸν ἕτερον καὶ
35 πρὸς μεσημβρίαν, καὶ οὔσης οἷον τυμπάνου (τοιοῦ-
362 b τον γὰρ σχῆμα τῆς γῆς ἐκτέμνουσιν αἱ ἐκ τοῦ
κέντρου αὐτῆς ἀγόμεναι, καὶ ποιοῦσι δύο κώνους,
τὸν μὲν ἔχοντα βάσιν τὸν τροπικόν, τὸν δὲ τὸν διὰ
παντὸς φανερόν, τὴν δὲ κορυφὴν ἐπὶ τοῦ μέσου

---

[a] Alex. 99. 11 identifies these with the λευκόνοτοι " fair
weather winds " of a 14 above. Thus the whole passage
362 a 12-31 deals with the winds which blow after the winter
solstice and correspond to the Etesian winds. They must be
southerly winds, and are called " feeble Etesian " winds not
because they are northerly but because they correspond to
the Etesians. The name Bird wind seems to indicate a
southerly wind, with which the migrant birds return in early
spring. Yet De Mundo 395 a 4 refers to the Bird winds as
northerly.

after the solstice to a greater extent than at it. In the same way the most stifling heats occur not when the sun is at its most northerly point, but when it has had longer to make its heat felt and is still fairly close. Similarly after the winter solstice the Bird winds [a] blow. These are feeble Etesian winds, blowing later and with less force than the Etesian winds proper. They do not begin to blow till the seventieth day after the solstice, because the sun is then farther off and so has less power. They do not blow so continuously because at that time evaporation is confined to surface substances easily evaporated, and what is frozen to a greater degree requires a greater degree of heat. So they blow intermittently until the Etesian winds rise again at the summer solstice ; for from then onwards the wind tends to blow almost constantly.

But the south wind blows from the summer tropic and not from the south pole. For there are two habitable sectors of the earth's surface, one, in which we live, towards the upper pole,[b] the other towards the other, that is the south pole. These sectors are drum-shaped—for lines running from the centre of the earth cut out this shaped figure on its surface : they form two cones, one having the tropic as its base, the other the ever-visible circle,[c] while their vertex is the centre of the earth ; and two cones

The habitable zones of the earth.

[b] But *cf. De Caelo* ii. 2, 285 b 15.
[c] Strictly, this should mean the circumpolar stars, which, as the O.T. points out, and as Aristotle must surely have known (*cf. De Caelo* ii. 14, 297 b 30 ff.), vary with latitude, and therefore do not " serve the purpose of delineating zones at all well." Aristotle probably means the Arctic circle (Ideler ii. p. 562), though this way of referring to it is confusing.

179

τῆς γῆς· τὸν αὐτὸν δὲ τρόπον πρὸς τὸν κάτω πόλον

5 ἕτεροι δύο κῶνοι τῆς γῆς ἐκτμήματα ποιοῦσι.

Ταῦτα δ' οἰκεῖσθαι μόνα δυνατόν, καὶ οὔτ' ἐπέκεινα τῶν τροπῶν (σκιὰ γὰρ οὐκ ἂν ἦν πρὸς ἄρκτον,
νῦν δ' ἀοίκητοι πρότερον γίγνονται οἱ τόποι πρὶν
ἢ ὑπολείπειν ἢ μεταβάλλειν τὴν σκιὰν πρὸς μεσημβρίαν) τά θ' ὑπὸ τὴν ἄρκτον ὑπὸ ψύχους
ἀοίκητα.

10 [Φέρεται δὲ καὶ ὁ στέφανος κατὰ τοῦτον τὸν
τόπον· φαίνεται γὰρ ὑπὲρ κεφαλῆς γιγνόμενος ἡμῖν,
ὅταν ᾖ κατὰ τὸν μεσημβρινόν.][1]

Διὸ καὶ γελοίως γράφουσι νῦν τὰς περιόδους
τῆς γῆς· γράφουσι γὰρ κυκλοτερῆ τὴν οἰκουμένην,
τοῦτο δ' ἐστὶν ἀδύνατον κατά τε τὰ φαινόμενα καὶ
15 κατὰ τὸν λόγον. ὅ τε γὰρ λόγος δείκνυσιν ὅτι ἐπὶ

[1] seclusit O.T.

---

[a] It is difficult to give sense or point to this remark, which the O.T. brackets as a " learned interpolation " : cf. Heidel, op. cit. p. 96, note 204.

[b] Cf. Thomson, *Ancient Geography*, pp. 97-99.

constructed in the same way towards the lower pole cut out corresponding segments on the earth's surface.

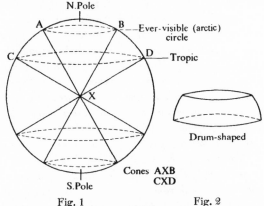

Fig. 1   Fig. 2

These are the only habitable regions ; for the lands beyond the tropics are uninhabitable, as there the shadow would not fall towards the north, and we know that the earth ceases to be habitable before the shadow disappears or falls towards the south, while the lands beneath the Bear are uninhabitable because of the cold.

[The Crown too passes over this region, for it appears to us to be directly overhead when it is on our meridian.] [a]

The way in which present maps of the world are drawn is therefore absurd. For they represent the inhabited earth as circular,[b] which is impossible both on factual and theoretical grounds. For theoretical

The dimensions of these zones.

181

362 b

πλάτος μὲν ὥρισται, τὸ δὲ κύκλῳ συνάπτειν ἐνδέχεται διὰ τὴν κρᾶσιν,—οὐ γὰρ ὑπερβάλλει τὰ καύ-
ματα καὶ τὸ ψῦχος κατὰ μῆκος, ἀλλ' ἐπὶ πλάτος,
ὥστ' εἰ μή που κωλύει θαλάττης πλῆθος, ἅπαν
εἶναι πορεύσιμον,—καὶ κατὰ τὰ φαινόμενα περί τε
20 τοὺς πλοῦς καὶ τὰς πορείας· πολὺ γὰρ τὸ μῆκος
διαφέρει τοῦ πλάτους. τὸ γὰρ ἀπὸ Ἡρακλείων
στηλῶν μέχρι τῆς Ἰνδικῆς τοῦ ἐξ Αἰθιοπίας πρὸς
τὴν Μαιῶτιν καὶ τοὺς ἐσχατεύοντας τῆς Σκυθίας
τόπους πλέον ἢ πέντε πρὸς τρία τὸ μέγεθός ἐστιν,
ἐάν τέ τις τοὺς πλοῦς λογίζηται καὶ τὰς ὁδούς, ὡς
25 ἐνδέχεται λαμβάνειν τῶν τοιούτων τὰς ἀκριβείας.
καίτοι ἐπὶ πλάτος μὲν μέχρι τῶν ἀοικήτων ἴσμεν
τὴν οἰκουμένην· ἔνθα μὲν γὰρ διὰ ψῦχος οὐκέτι
κατοικοῦσιν, ἔνθα δὲ διὰ τὴν ἀλέαν. τὰ δὲ τῆς
Ἰνδικῆς ἔξω καὶ τῶν στηλῶν τῶν Ἡρακλείων διὰ
τὴν θάλατταν οὐ φαίνεται συνείρειν τῷ[1] συνεχῶς
30 εἶναι πᾶσαν οἰκουμένην).

Ἐπεὶ δ' ὁμοίως ἔχειν ἀνάγκη τόπον τινὰ πρὸς
τὸν ἕτερον πόλον ὥσπερ ὃν ἡμεῖς οἰκοῦμεν πρὸς
τὸν ὑπὲρ ἡμῶν, δῆλον ὡς ἀνάλογον ἕξει τά τ' ἄλλα
καὶ τῶν πνευμάτων ἡ στάσις· ὥστε καθάπερ ἐνταῦθα βορέας ἐστίν, κἀκείνοις ἀπὸ τῆς ἐκεῖ ἄρκτου
35 τις ἄνεμος οὕτως ὤν, ὃν οὐδὲν δυνατὸν διέχειν
δεῦρο, ἐπεὶ οὐδ' ὁ βορέας οὗτος εἰς τὴν ἐνταῦθα
363 a οἰκουμένην πᾶσάν [ἐστιν][2]· ἔστιν γὰρ ὥσπερ ἀπό-
γειον τὸ πνεῦμα τὸ βόρειον [ἕως ὁ βορέας οὗτος εἰς

---

[1] συνείρειν, τῷ Fobes.   [2] ἔστιν om. E₁ O.T.

calculation shows that it is limited in breadth but
could, as far as climate is concerned, extend round the
earth in a continuous belt : for it is not difference of
longitude but of latitude that brings great variations
of temperature, and if it were not for the ocean which
prevents it, the complete circuit could be made. And
the facts known to us from journeys by sea and land
also confirm the conclusion that its length is much
greater than its breadth. For if one reckons up these
voyages and journeys, so far as they are capable of
yielding any accurate information, the distance from
the Pillars of Heracles to India exceeds that from
Aethiopia to Lake Maeotis and the farthest parts of
Scythia by a ratio greater than that of 5 to 3. Yet
we know the whole breadth of the habitable world up
to the unhabitable regions which bound it, where
habitation ceases on the one side because of the cold,
on the other because of the heat ; while beyond India
and the Pillars of Heracles it is the ocean which
severs the habitable land and prevents it forming a
continuous belt round the globe.[a]

Since, then, there must be a region which bears to
the other pole the same relation as that which we
inhabit bears to our pole, it is clear that this region
will be analogous to ours in the disposition of winds
as well as in other respects. Thus, just as we have a
north wind here, so they have a similar wind which
blows from their pole, and which cannot possibly
reach us ; for our own north wind does not blow
right across the region in which we live,[b] being in

Winds in the two zones correspond.

[a] So the disproportion of length and breadth may be still
greater : *cf. De Caelo* ii. 14, 298 a 9.

[b] Omit ἔστιν and understand διέχει from b 35 : it seems
unnecessary to alter διέχειν (b 35) to διήκειν with the O.T. as
διέχειν can bear the meaning required, to reach to.

363 a

τὴν ἐνταῦθα οἰκουμένην πνεῖ].[1] ἀλλὰ διὰ τὸ τὴν
οἴκησιν κεῖσθαι ταύτην πρὸς ἄρκτον, πλεῖστοι
βορέαι πνέουσιν. ὅμως δὲ καὶ ἐνταῦθα ἐλλείπει καὶ
5 οὐ δύναται πόρρω διήκειν, ἐπεὶ περὶ τὴν ἔξω
Λιβύης θάλατταν τὴν νοτίαν, ὥσπερ ἐνταῦθα οἱ
βορέαι καὶ οἱ νότοι πνέουσιν, οὕτως ἐκεῖ εὖροι καὶ
ζέφυροι διαδεχόμενοι συνεχεῖς ἀεὶ πνέουσιν.

Ὅτι μὲν οὖν ὁ νότος οὐκ ἔστιν ὁ ἀπὸ τοῦ ἑτέρου
πόλου πνέων ἄνεμος, δῆλον. ἐπεὶ δ' οὔτ' ἐκεῖνος,
10 οὔτε ὁ ἀπὸ χειμερινῆς τροπῆς (δέοι γὰρ ἂν ἄλλον
ἀπὸ θερινῆς εἶναι τροπῆς· οὕτως γὰρ τὸ ἀνάλογον
ἀποδώσει· νῦν δ' οὐκ ἔστιν· εἷς γὰρ μόνος φαίνεται
πνέων ἐκ τῶν ἐκεῖθεν τόπων)· ὥστ' ἀνάγκη τὸν
ἀπὸ τοῦ κατακεκαυμένου τόπου πνέοντα ἄνεμον
εἶναι νότον. ἐκεῖνος δ' ὁ τόπος διὰ τὴν τοῦ ἡλίου
15 γειτνίασιν οὐκ ἔχει ὕδατα καὶ νομάς,[2] αἳ διὰ τὴν
τῆξιν[3] ποιήσουσιν ἐτησίας· ἀλλὰ διὰ τὸ τὸν τόπον
εἶναι πολὺ πλείω ἐκεῖνον καὶ ἀναπεπταμένον, μείζων
καὶ πλείων καὶ μᾶλλον ἀλεεινὸς ἄνεμος ὁ νότος
ἐστὶ τοῦ βορέου, καὶ διήκει μᾶλλον δεῦρο ἢ οὗτος
ἐκεῖ.

Τίς μὲν οὖν αἰτία τούτων ἐστὶ τῶν ἀνέμων, καὶ
20 πῶς ἔχουσι πρὸς ἀλλήλους, εἴρηται.

[1] secl. Fobes.
[2] χίονας O.T. : cf. 362 a 18, 364 a 8-10.
[3] πῆξιν Ap Ol Fobes : τῆξιν codd.

this like a land wind. But because our region of habitation lies towards the north, most of our winds are north winds.[a] Yet even in our region they fail and are not strong enough to travel far ; for in the sea south of Libya east and west winds [b] alternate with each other continuously, just as here it is north and south winds that blow.

This proves that our south wind is not the wind that blows from the south pole. But it does not blow from the winter tropic any more than from the south pole. For there would have to be a wind from the summer tropic [c] if the correspondence is to be complete ; but in fact there is no such wind, but one wind only that blows from this region. The south wind must therefore be the wind that blows from the torrid zone. This region because of its proximity to the sun has no streams or pasture land to produce Etesian winds by thawing [d] ; but because the region is greater in extent and open, the south wind is greater, stronger and warmer than the north and reaches farther northwards than the north wind southwards.[e]

So much for the cause and mutual relations of these winds.

[a] Cf. 361 a 5.
[b] Perhaps the Trade Winds in the Indian Ocean.
[c] Blowing southwards.
[d] The O.T.'s τῆξιν is supported by 362 a 18 and 364 a 8-10, and has ms. authority : but though the parallel passages also suggest χίονας for νομάς, ms. authority for this change is lacking.
[e] Cf. 361 a 5 ff. ; and contrast 364 a 5-10.

ARISTOTLE

CHAPTER VI

ARGUMENT

The different winds and their directions are enumerated with the aid of a diagram (363 a 21—364 a 4). Why most winds are northerly (364 a 4-13). A more general classifica-

363 a 21 Περὶ δὲ θέσεως αὐτῶν, καὶ τίνες ἐναντίοι τίσι, καὶ ποίους ἅμα πνεῖν ἐνδέχεται καὶ ποίους οὔ, ἔτι δὲ καὶ τίνες καὶ πόσοι τυγχάνουσιν ὄντες, καὶ πρὸς τούτοις περὶ τῶν ἄλλων παθημάτων ὅσα μὴ συμ-
25 βέβηκεν ἐν τοῖς προβλήμασιν εἰρῆσθαι τοῖς κατὰ μέρος, νῦν λέγωμεν.

---

[a] With this chapter *cf. De Mundo*, ch. 4 and *Vent. Sit. et App.*; and see D'Arcy Thompson, " The Greek Winds," in *C.R.* xxxii (1918), pp. 49-56.

[b] *Cf. Problems* xxvi. *passim.*

CHAPTER VI

ARGUMENT *(continued)*

tion of the winds by the main points of the compass (364 a
13-27). *Miscellaneous characteristics of the winds described*
(364 a 27—365 a 13).

LET us go on to the positions of the winds [a] and their
mutual relations of opposition, and describe which Diagram-
kinds can blow simultaneously and which cannot and matic
what are their names and numbers, besides dealing exposition.
with any other of their characteristics that have not
already been treated as separate " problems." [b]

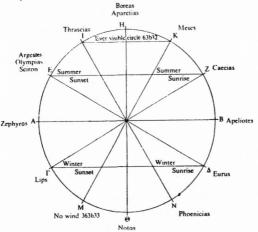

The *Vent. Sit.* supplies at M Leuconotos, the *De Mundo*
Libonotos : while for the doubtful (*cf.* 364 a 3) Phoenicias
De Mundo 393 b 33 has Euronotos, which should also
probably be read in *Vent. Sit.* 973 b 7 (O.T. note *ad loc.*).

363 a

Δεῖ δὲ περὶ τῆς θέσεως ἅμα τοὺς λόγους ἐκ τῆς ὑπογραφῆς θεωρεῖν. γέγραπται μὲν οὖν, τοῦ μᾶλλον εὐσήμως ἔχειν, ὁ τοῦ ὁρίζοντος κύκλος· διὸ καὶ στρογγύλος. δεῖ δὲ νοεῖν αὐτὸν[1] τὸ ἕτερον ἔκτμημα τὸ ὑφ' ἡμῶν οἰκούμενον· ἔσται γὰρ κἀ-
30 κεῖνο διελεῖν τὸν αὐτὸν τρόπον. ὑποκείσθω δὲ πρῶτον μὲν ἐναντία κατὰ τόπον εἶναι τὰ πλεῖστον ἀπέχοντα κατὰ τόπον, ὥσπερ κατ' εἶδος ἐναντία τὰ πλεῖστον ἀπέχοντα κατὰ τὸ εἶδος· πλεῖστον δ' ἀπέχει κατὰ τόπον τὰ κείμενα πρὸς ἄλληλα κατὰ διάμετρον.

Ἔστω οὖν τὸ μὲν ἐφ' ᾧ Α δυσμὴ ἰσημερινή,
363 b ἐναντίος δὲ τούτῳ τόπος, ἐφ' οὗ τὸ Β, ἀνατολὴ ἰσημερινή· ἄλλη δὲ διάμετρος ταύτην πρὸς ὀρθὴν τέμνουσα, ἧς τὸ ἐφ' οὗ Η ἔστω ἄρκτος· τούτῳ δ' ἐναντίον ἐξ ἐναντίας, τὸ ἐφ' οὗ Θ, μεσημβρία· τὸ
5 δ' ἐφ' οὗ Ζ ἀνατολὴ θερινή, τὸ δ' ἐφ' ᾧ Ε δυσμὴ θερινή, τὸ δ' ἐφ' οὗ Δ ἀνατολὴ χειμερινή, τὸ δ' ἐφ' οὗ Γ δυσμὴ χειμερινή. ἀπὸ δὲ τοῦ Ζ ἤχθω διάμετρος ἐπὶ τὸ Γ, καὶ ἀπὸ τοῦ Δ ἐπὶ τὸ Ε. ἐπεὶ οὖν τὰ μὲν πλεῖστον ἀπέχοντα κατὰ τόπον ἐναντία κατὰ τόπον, πλεῖστον δ' ἀπέχει τὰ κατὰ διάμετρον,
10 ἀναγκαῖον καὶ τῶν πνευμάτων ταῦτα ἀλλήλοις ἐναντία εἶναι, ὅσα κατὰ διάμετρόν ἐστιν.

Καλεῖται δὲ κατὰ τὴν θέσιν τῶν τόπων τὰ πνεύματα ὧδε· ζέφυρος μὲν τὸ ἀπὸ τοῦ Α· τοῦτο γὰρ δυσμὴ ἰσημερινή. ἐναντίος δὲ τούτῳ ἀπη-λιώτης ἀπὸ τοῦ Β· τοῦτο γὰρ ἀνατολὴ ἰσημερινή.
15 βορέας δὲ ⟨καὶ⟩[2] ἀπαρκτίας ἀπὸ τοῦ Η· ἐνταῦθα

---

[1] αὐτὸν F₁ H N O.T. : αὐτοῦ cett. Fobes.
[2] καὶ habent E_rec. 𝔚 : ὁ καὶ F_rec. : om. cett.

188

The treatment of their position must be followed with the help of the diagram. For the sake of clarity we have drawn the circle of the horizon ; that is why our figure is round. And it must be supposed to represent the section of the earth's surface in which we live ; for the other section could be divided in a similar way. Let us first define things as spatially opposite when they are farthest removed from each other in space (just as things formally opposite are things farthest removed from each other in form) ; and things are farthest removed from each other in space when they lie at opposite ends of the same diameter.

Let the point A be the equinoctial sunset, and the point B its opposite, the equinoctial sunrise. Let another diameter cut this at right angles, and let the point H on this be the north and its diametrical opposite Θ be the south. Let the point Z be the summer sunrise, the point E the summer sunset, the point Δ the winter sunrise, the point Γ the winter sunset. And from Z let the diameter be drawn to Γ, from Δ to E. Since, then, things spatially farthest removed from each other are spatially opposite, and things diametrically opposed are farthest removed, those winds must be mutually opposite which are opposed diametrically.

The names of the winds corresponding to these positions are as follows : Zephyros blows from A, for this is the equinoctial sunset. Its opposite is Apeliotes which blows from B, the equinoctial sunrise. Boreas or [a] Aparctias blows from H, the north. Its opposite

[a] Omitting καί the O.T. translates " the true north wind called Aparctias."

363 b

γὰρ ἡ ἄρκτος. ἐναντίος δὲ τούτῳ νότος ἀπὸ τοῦ
Θ· μεσημβρία τε γὰρ αὕτη ἀφ' ἧς πνεῖ, καὶ τὸ Θ
τῷ Η ἐναντίον· κατὰ διάμετρον γάρ. ἀπὸ δὲ τοῦ
Ζ καικίας· αὕτη γὰρ ἀνατολὴ θερινή. ἐναντίος δ'
οὐχ ὁ ἀπὸ τοῦ Ε πνέων, ἀλλ' ὁ ἀπὸ τοῦ Γ λίψ·
20 οὗτος γὰρ ἀπὸ δυσμῆς χειμερινῆς, ἐναντίος δὲ
τούτῳ (κατὰ διάμετρον γὰρ κεῖται). ἀπὸ δὲ τοῦ
Δ εὖρος· οὗτος γὰρ ἀπ' ἀνατολῆς χειμερινῆς πνεῖ,
γειτνιῶν τῷ νότῳ· διὸ καὶ πολλάκις εὐρόνοτοι
λέγονται πνεῖν. ἐναντίος δὲ τούτῳ οὐχ ὁ ἀπὸ τοῦ
Γ λίψ, ἀλλ' ὁ ἀπὸ τοῦ Ε, ὃν καλοῦσιν οἱ μὲν
25 ἀργέστην, οἱ δ' ὀλυμπίαν, οἱ δὲ σκίρωνα· οὗτος
γὰρ ἀπὸ δυσμῆς θερινῆς πνεῖ, καὶ κατὰ διάμετρον
αὐτῷ κεῖται μόνος.

Οὗτοι μὲν οὖν οἱ κατὰ διάμετρόν τε κείμενοι
ἄνεμοι καὶ οἷς εἰσιν ἐναντίοι· ἕτεροι δ' εἰσὶν καθ'
οὓς οὐκ ἔστιν ἐναντία πνεύματα. ἀπὸ μὲν γὰρ τοῦ
Ι ὃν καλοῦσι θρασκίαν· οὗτος γὰρ μέσος ἀργέστου
30 καὶ ἀπαρκτίου· ἀπὸ δὲ τοῦ Κ ὃν καλοῦσιν μέσην·
οὗτος γὰρ μέσος καικίου καὶ ἀπαρκτίου. ἡ δὲ τοῦ
ΙΚ διάμετρος βούλεται μὲν κατὰ τὸν διὰ παντὸς
εἶναι φαινόμενον, οὐκ ἀκριβοῖ δέ. ἐναντία δὲ τούτοις οὐκ ἔστι τοῖς πνεύμασιν, οὔτε τῷ μέση (ἔπνει
364 a γὰρ ἄν τις ἐφ' οὗ τὸ Μ· τοῦτο γὰρ κατὰ διάμετρον)
οὔτε τῷ Ι, τῷ θρασκίᾳ (ἔπνει γὰρ ἂν ἀπὸ τοῦ Ν·
τοῦτο γὰρ κατὰ διάμετρον τὸ σημεῖον, εἰ μὴ ἀπ'
αὐτοῦ καὶ ἐπ' ὀλίγον πνεῖ τις ἄνεμος, ὃν καλοῦσιν
οἱ περὶ τὸν τόπον ἐκεῖνον φοινικίαν).

5 Τὰ μὲν οὖν κυριώτατα καὶ διωρισμένα πνεύματα
ταῦτ' ἐστὶ καὶ τοῦτον τέτακται τὸν τρόπον· τοῦ δ'
εἶναι πλείους ἀνέμους ἀπὸ τῶν πρὸς ἄρκτον τόπων

is Notos which blows from Θ, the south, Θ and H being diametrically opposed. From Z blows Caecias, that is, from the summer sunrise. Its opposite is not the wind blowing from E, but the wind from Γ, Lips, which blows from the winter sunset, and so is opposite to Caecias, being diametrically opposed to it. From Δ blows Eurus, for it blows from the winter sunrise and is the neighbour of Notos ; so people often speak of the Euronotoi blowing. Its opposite is not Lips, the wind from Γ, but the wind from E called sometimes Argestes, sometimes Olympias, sometimes Sciron. For it blows from the summer sunset and is the only diametrical opposite to Eurus.

These, then, are the winds which have diametrical opposites ; but there are others which have no winds opposite them. From I blows the wind they call Thrascias, which lies between Argestes and Aparctias : from K the wind they call Meses, which lies between Caecias and Aparctias. The chord IK nearly corresponds to the ever-visible circle [a] but fails to do so exactly. There are no opposites to those winds : neither to Meses, otherwise there would be a wind from the point M diametrically opposite, nor to Thrascias at I, otherwise there would be a wind from N, the point diametrically opposite, which there is not, except perhaps a local wind called by the inhabitants Phoenicias.

These, then, are the most important different winds and their positions. There are two reasons for there being more winds from the northerly than from the

Most winds northerly.

---

[a] *Cf.* ch. 5, note *c* on p. 179.

ἢ τῶν πρὸς μεσημβρίαν αἴτιον τό τε τὴν οἰκουμένην ὑποκεῖσθαι πρὸς τοῦτον τὸν τόπον, καὶ ὅτι
πολλῷ πλέον ὕδωρ καὶ χιὼν ἀπωθεῖται εἰς τοῦτο
10 τὸ μέρος διὰ τὸ ἐκεῖνα ὑπὸ τὸν ἥλιον εἶναι καὶ τὴν
ἐκείνου φοράν, ὧν τηκομένων εἰς τὴν γῆν καὶ
θερμαινομένων ὑπὸ τοῦ ἡλίου καὶ τῆς γῆς ἀναγκαῖον πλείω καὶ ἐπὶ πλείω τόπον γίγνεσθαι τὴν
ἀναθυμίασιν διὰ ταύτην τὴν αἰτίαν.

Ἔστι δὲ τῶν εἰρημένων πνευμάτων βορέας μὲν
ὅ τ' ἀπαρκτίας κυριώτατα, καὶ θρασκίας καὶ
15 μέσης· ὁ δὲ καικίας κοινὸς ἀπηλιώτου καὶ βορέου·
νότος δὲ ὅ τε ἰθαγενὴς ὁ ἀπὸ μεσημβρίας καὶ λίψ·
ἀπηλιώτης δὲ ὅ τε ἀπ' ἀνατολῆς ἰσημερινῆς καὶ
ὁ εὖρος· ὁ δὲ φοινικίας κοινός· ζέφυρος δὲ ὅ τε
ἰθαγενὴς καὶ ὁ ἀργέστης καλούμενος. ὅλως δὲ τὰ
μὲν βόρεια τούτων καλεῖται, τὰ δὲ νότια· προσ-
20 τίθεται δὲ τὰ μὲν ζεφυρικὰ τῷ βορέᾳ (ψυχρότερα
γὰρ διὰ τὸ ἀπὸ δυσμῶν πνεῖν), νότῳ δὲ τὰ ἀπη-
λιωτικά (θερμότερα γὰρ διὰ τὸ ἀπ' ἀνατολῆς πνεῖν).
διωρισμένων οὖν τῷ ψυχρῷ καὶ τῷ θερμῷ καὶ
ἀλεεινῷ τῶν πνευμάτων οὕτως ἐκάλεσαν. θερμό-
25 τερα μὲν τὰ ἀπὸ τῆς ἔω τῶν ἀπὸ δυσμῆς, ὅτι
πλείω χρόνον ὑπὸ τὸν ἥλιόν ἐστι τὰ ἀπ' ἀνατολῆς·
τὰ δ' ἀπὸ δυσμῆς ἀπολείπει τε θᾶττον καὶ πλησιάζει τῷ τόπῳ ὀψιαίτερον.

Οὕτω δὲ τεταγμένων τῶν ἀνέμων, δῆλον ὅτι
ἅμα πνεῖν τοὺς μὲν ἐναντίους οὐχ οἷόν τε (κατὰ
διάμετρον γάρ· ἅτερος οὖν παύσεται ἀποβιασθείς),
30 τοὺς δὲ μὴ οὕτως κειμένους πρὸς ἀλλήλους οὐδὲν
κωλύει, οἷον τὸν Ζ καὶ Δ. διὰ τοῦτο ἅμα πνέουσιν

southerly regions.[a] First, our inhabited region lies towards the north ; second, far more rain and snow is pushed up into this region because the other lies beneath the sun and its course. These melt and are absorbed by the earth and when subsequently heated by the sun and the earth's own heat cause a greater and more extensive exhalation.[b]

Of the winds thus described the truest north winds are Aparctias, Thrascias and Meses. Caecias is part east and part north. South are the winds that come from due south and Lips. East are the winds that come from the equinoctial sunrise and Eurus. Phoenicias is part south, part east. West is the wind from due west and also the wind called Argestes. There is a general classification of these winds into northerly and southerly : westerly winds are counted as northerly, being colder because they blow from the sunset ; easterly winds are counted as southerly, being warmer because they blow from the sunrise. Winds are thus called northerly and southerly according to this division into cold and hot or warm. Winds from the sunrise are warmer than winds from the sunset, because those from the sunrise are exposed to the sun for longer ; while those from the sunset are reached by the sun later and it soon leaves them.[c] {Classification by points of compass.}

This being the arrangement of the winds, it is clear that opposite winds cannot blow at the same time, for one or other would be overpowered and stop blowing ; but there is nothing to prevent two winds not so related blowing at once, as, for instance, the winds from Z and Δ. So two winds may sometimes {Miscellaneous characteristics.}

[a] Cf. 361 a 4, 363 a 2.
[b] Cf. 361 a 6 ff., 362 a 3, a 17 : contrast 363 a 15.
[c] " A poor argument even for a flat-earth man ; and for Aristotle with his round earth lamentable. Perhaps the sentence should be condemned " (O.T.).

364 a

ἐνίοτε ἀμφότεροι οὔριοι, ἐπὶ τὸ αὐτὸ σημεῖον, οὐκ
ἐκ ταὐτοῦ οὐδὲ τῷ αὐτῷ πνεύματι.

Κατὰ δὲ τὰς ὥρας τὰς ἐναντίας οἱ ἐναντίοι
364 b μάλιστα πνέουσιν, οἷον περὶ ἰσημερίαν τὴν μὲν
ἐαρινὴν καικίας καὶ ὅλως τὰ ἐπέκεινα τροπῆς
θερινῆς, περὶ δὲ τὴν μετοπωρινὴν λίβες, περὶ δὲ
τροπὰς θερινὰς μὲν ζέφυρος, χειμερινὰς δὲ εὖρος.

Ἐπιπίπτουσι δὲ τοῖς ἄλλοις μάλιστα καὶ παύουσιν
5 ἀπαρκτίαι καὶ θρασκίαι καὶ ἀργέσται· διὰ τὸ ἐγγυτάτω γὰρ τὴν ὁρμὴν αὐτῶν εἶναι πολλοί τε καὶ
ἰσχυροὶ πνέουσι μάλιστα οὗτοι. διὸ καὶ αἰθριώ-
τατοί εἰσι τῶν ἀνέμων· πνέοντες γὰρ ἐγγύθεν μάλιστα ἀποβιαζόμενοί τε τἆλλα πνεύματα παύουσι,
καὶ ἀποφυσῶντες τὰ συνιστάμενα νέφη ποιοῦσιν
10 αἰθρίαν, ἂν μὴ ψυχροὶ σφόδρα τύχωσιν ἅμα ὄντες.
τότε δὲ οὐκ αἴθριοι· ἐὰν γὰρ ὦσι μᾶλλον ψυχροὶ ἢ
μεγάλοι, φθάνουσι πηγνύντες ἢ προωθοῦντες. ὁ
δὲ καικίας οὐκ αἴθριος, ὅτι ἀνακάμπτει εἰς αὑτόν·
ὅθεν καὶ λέγεται ἡ παροιμία " ἕλκων ἐφ' αὑτὸν
ὥστε καικίας νέφος."

Αἱ δὲ περιστάσεις γίγνονται αὐτῶν καταπαυο-
15 μένων εἰς τοὺς ἐχομένους κατὰ τὴν τοῦ ἡλίου
μετάστασιν, διὰ τὸ κινεῖσθαι μάλιστα τὸ ἐχόμενον
τῆς ἀρχῆς· ἡ δὲ ἀρχὴ οὕτω κινεῖται τῶν πνευμάτων
ὡς ὁ ἥλιος.

Οἱ ἐναντίοι δὲ ἢ ταὐτὸ ποιοῦσιν ἢ ἐναντίον, οἷον
ὑγροὶ λὶψ καὶ καικίας, ὃν ἑλλησποντίαν ἔνιοι
194

be favourable to ships making for the same point, though they are not blowing from the same quarter and are not the same wind.

As a rule, opposite winds blow in opposite seasons : for instance, at the time of the vernal equinox Caecias and winds from north of the summer sunrise prevail ; in the autumn Lips ; at the summer solstice Zephyros, at the winter Eurus.

Aparctias, Thrascias and Argestes are the winds that most often interrupt and stop others. For because their source is nearest to us they blow with the greatest frequency and strength of all winds. They therefore bring the fairest weather of all, for blowing from near at hand they force other winds away and stop them, and by blowing away any clouds that have formed make fair weather. If, however, they happen also to be very cold they do not bring fair weather ; for if they are cold rather than strong they freeze the clouds before they can drive them away. Caecias is not a fair-weather wind because it turns back on itself [a]—hence the proverb " Drawing it to himself as Caecias clouds."

When a wind drops it is succeeded by its neighbour in the direction of the sun's movement ; for what lies next to the source of a movement is set in motion first and the source of the winds moves round with the sun.[b]

Opposite winds produce either the same or opposite effects : for instance, Lips and Caecias (which some

[a] Cf. Problems xxvi. 1 and 29. Caecias, " descending from above, sweeps in a circular course up into the sky, and thence returns to the point from which it started " (O.T. note ad Problems xxvi. 1).

[b] Presumably because the sun is the controlling cause of the exhalation which produces wind.

364 b

20 καλοῦσιν [καὶ εὖρος, ὃν ἀπηλιώτην].¹ ξηροὶ δὲ
ἀργέστης καὶ εὖρος· ἀπ' ἀρχῆς δὲ οὗτος ξηρός,
τελευτῶν δὲ ὑδατώδης.

Νιφετώδης δὲ μέσης καὶ ἀπαρκτίας μάλιστα·
οὗτοι γὰρ ψυχρότατοι. χαλαζώδεις δὲ ἀπαρκτίας
καὶ θρασκίας καὶ ἀργέστης. καυματώδης δὲ νότος
καὶ ζέφυρος καὶ εὖρος. νέφεσι δὲ πυκνοῦσι τὸν
25 οὐρανὸν καικίας μὲν σφόδρα, λὶψ δὲ ἀραιοτέροις,
καικίας μὲν διά τε τὸ ἀνακάμπτειν πρὸς αὑτὸν καὶ
διὰ τὸ κοινὸς εἶναι βορέου καὶ εὔρου, ὥστε διὰ μὲν
τὸ ψυχρὸς εἶναι πηγνὺς τὸν ἀτμίζοντα ἀέρα συν-
ίστησι, διὰ δὲ τὸ τῷ τόπῳ ἀπηλιωτικὸς εἶναι ἔχει
πολλὴν ὕλην καὶ ἀτμίδα ἣν προωθεῖ. αἴθριοι δὲ
30 ἀπαρκτίας, θρασκίας, ἀργέστης· ἡ δ' αἰτία εἴρηται
πρότερον. ἀστραπὰς δὲ ποιοῦσιν μάλιστα οὗτοί
τε καὶ ὁ μέσης· διὰ μὲν γὰρ τὸ ἐγγύθεν πνεῖν
ψυχροί εἰσιν, διὰ δὲ τὸ ψυχρὸν ἀστραπὴ γίγνεται·
ἐκκρίνεται γὰρ συνιόντων τῶν νεφῶν. διὸ καὶ
365 a ἔνιοι τῶν αὐτῶν τούτων χαλαζώδεις εἰσίν· ταχὺ
γὰρ πηγνύουσιν.

Ἐκνεφίαι δὲ γίγνονται μετοπώρου μὲν μάλιστα,
εἶτα ἔαρος, καὶ μάλιστα ἀπαρκτίας καὶ θρασκίας
καὶ ἀργέστης. αἴτιον δ' ὅτι οἱ ἐκνεφίαι γίγνονται
μάλιστα ὅταν τῶν ἄλλων πνεόντων ἐμπίπτωσιν
5 ἕτεροι, οὗτοι δὲ μάλιστα ἐμπίπτουσιν τοῖς ἄλλοις
πνέουσιν· ἡ δ' αἰτία εἴρηται καὶ τούτου πρότερον.

Οἱ δ' ἐτησίαι περιίστανται τοῖς μὲν περὶ δυσμὰς
οἰκοῦσιν ἐκ τῶν ἀπαρκτίων εἰς θρασκίας καὶ

¹ seclusit O.T.

METEOROLOGICA, II. vi

call Hellespontias) are both wet winds.[a] Dry are Argestes and Eurus—the latter, however, though it starts by being dry, ends up by being rainy.

Meses and Aparctias are the most snowy, because they are the coldest. Aparctias, Thrascias and Argestes bring hail. Notos, Zephyros and Eurus bring heat. Caecias fills the sky with thick clouds, Lips with thinner. Caecias does this because it turns back on itself, and because it is part north and part east and so, being cold, collects and freezes the vaporized air, and being easterly in position has a great deal of vapour as material which it drives before it. Aparctias, Thrascias and Argestes are fair-weather winds for the reason we have given before.[b] They and Meses most often produce lightning. For they are cold because their origin is near, and lightning is produced by cold, being driven out by the condensation of the clouds.[c] For this reason some of these same winds sometimes bring hail, for they freeze quickly.

Hurricanes occur most often in autumn, and next in spring : and Aparctias, Thrascias and Argestes most often cause them. The reason for this is that hurricanes are usually the result of one wind falling on another while it is still blowing, and these are the winds that do this most often. Why they do it we have already explained.[d]

The Etesian winds veer round, for people living in the west, from Aparctias to Thrascias, Argestes

---

[a] I omit the words καὶ εὗρος, ὃν ἀπηλιώτην with the O.T., since the argument requires that *pairs* of contrary winds should be named and the introduction of a *third* wind makes nonsense.

[b] 364 b 7.

[c] *Cf.* below, ch. 9.   [d] 364 b 3.

365 a

ἀργέστας καὶ ζεφύρους [(ὁ γὰρ ἀπαρκτίας . . .
ζέφυρός ἐστιν),]¹ ἀρχόμενοι μὲν ἀπὸ τῆς ἄρκτου,
10 τελευτῶντες δ' εἰς τοὺς πόρρω· τοῖς δὲ πρὸς ἔω
περιίστανται μέχρι τοῦ ἀπηλιώτου.

Περὶ μὲν οὖν ἀνέμων, τῆς τε ἐξ ἀρχῆς αὐτῶν
γενέσεως καὶ οὐσίας καὶ τῶν συμβαινόντων κοινῇ
τε παθημάτων καὶ περὶ ἕκαστον, τοσαῦθ' ἡμῖν
εἰρήσθω.

CHAPTER VII

ARGUMENT

Earthquakes. The views of Anaxagoras (365 a 18-35),

365 a 14   Περὶ δὲ σεισμοῦ καὶ κινήσεως γῆς μετὰ ταῦτα
15 λεκτέον· ἡ γὰρ αἰτία τοῦ πάθους ἐχομένη τούτου
τοῦ γένους ἐστίν.

Ἔστι δὲ τὰ παρειλημμένα μέχρι γε τοῦ νῦν
χρόνου τρία καὶ παρὰ τριῶν. Ἀναξαγόρας τε γὰρ
ὁ Κλαζομένιος καὶ πρότερον Ἀναξιμένης ὁ Μιλήσιος ἀπεφήναντο, καὶ τούτων ὕστερον Δημόκριτος
ὁ Ἀβδηρίτης.

20   Ἀναξαγόρας μὲν οὖν φησι τὸν αἰθέρα πεφυκότα
φέρεσθαι ἄνω, ἐμπίπτοντα δ' εἰς τὰ κάτω τῆς γῆς
καὶ κοῖλα κινεῖν αὐτήν· τὰ μὲν γὰρ ἄνω συναλη-
λεῖφθαι διὰ τοὺς ὄμβρους (ἐπεὶ φύσει γε ἅπασαν
ὁμοίως εἶναι σομφήν), ὡς ὄντος τοῦ μὲν ἄνω τοῦ
δὲ κάτω τῆς ὅλης σφαίρας, καὶ ἄνω μὲν τούτου

─────────────────────
ᵃ Diels 56 A 1 (9), 42 (12), 89.

and Zephyros, beginning from north and ending farther south ; for people living in the east, they veer from the north to Apeliotes.

This completes our account of winds, their original genesis, their substance, and the attributes common to all and peculiar to each.

---

[1] seclusit O.T.

CHAPTER VII

ARGUMENT (continued)

Democritus (365 b 1-6), and Anaximenes (365 b 6-20) are stated and criticized.

We must next deal with earthquakes and earth tremors, a subject which follows naturally on our last, as the cause of these phenomena is akin to that of wind.

Up to the present three theories have been put forward by three separate men. For Anaxagoras of Clazomenae and before him Anaximenes of Miletus both published views on the subject, and after them Democritus of Abdera. Three views :

Anaxagoras [a] says that the air, whose natural motion is upwards, causes earthquakes when it is trapped in hollows beneath the earth, which happens when the upper parts of the earth get clogged by rain, all earth being naturally porous. For he regards the globe [b] as having an upper and a lower part, the Anaxagoras ;

---

[b] σφαῖρα presumably means the earth : but Anaxagoras thought the earth was flat : Diels 59 A 42 (3).

365 a

25 ὄντος τοῦ μορίου ἐφ᾽ οὗ τυγχάνομεν οἰκοῦντες,
κάτω δὲ θατέρου.

Πρὸς μὲν οὖν ταύτην τὴν αἰτίαν οὐδὲν ἴσως δεῖ
λέγειν ὡς λίαν ἁπλῶς εἰρημένην· τό τε γὰρ ἄνω
καὶ τὸ κάτω νομίζειν οὕτως ἔχειν ὥστε μὴ πρὸς
μὲν τὴν γῆν πάντῃ φέρεσθαι τὰ βάρος ἔχοντα τῶν
σωμάτων, ἄνω δὲ τὰ κοῦφα καὶ τὸ πῦρ, εὔηθες,
30 καὶ ταῦθ᾽ ὁρῶντας τὸν ὁρίζοντα τὴν οἰκουμένην
ὅσην ἡμεῖς ἴσμεν, ἕτερον ἀεὶ γιγνόμενον μεθισταμένων, ὡς οὔσης κυρτῆς καὶ σφαιροειδοῦς· καὶ τὸ
λέγειν μὲν ὡς διὰ τὸ μέγεθος ἐπὶ τοῦ ἀέρος μένειν,
σείεσθαι δὲ φάσκειν τυπτομένην κάτωθεν ἄνω δι᾽
ὅλης. πρὸς δὲ τούτοις οὐδὲν ἀποδίδωσι τῶν συμ-
35 βαινόντων περὶ τοὺς σεισμούς· οὔτε γὰρ χῶραι
οὔτε ὧραι αἱ τυχοῦσαι μετέχουσι τούτου τοῦ πάθους.

365 b

Δημόκριτος δέ φησι πλήρη τὴν γῆν ὕδατος οὖσαν,
καὶ πολὺ δεχομένην ἕτερον ὄμβριον ὕδωρ, ὑπὸ τούτου κινεῖσθαι· πλείονός τε γὰρ γιγνομένου διὰ τὸ
μὴ δύνασθαι δέχεσθαι τὰς κοιλίας ἀποβιαζόμενον
5 ποιεῖν τὸν σεισμόν, καὶ ξηραινομένην ἕλκουσαν εἰς
τοὺς κενοὺς τόπους ἐκ τῶν πληρεστέρων τὸ μετα-
βάλλον ἐμπῖπτον κινεῖν.

Ἀναξιμένης δέ φησιν βρεχομένην τὴν γῆν καὶ
ξηραινομένην ῥήγνυσθαι, καὶ ὑπὸ τούτων τῶν ἀπορ-
ρηγνυμένων κολωνῶν ἐμπιπτόντων σείεσθαι· διὸ
καὶ γίγνεσθαι τοὺς σεισμοὺς ἔν τε τοῖς αὐχμοῖς καὶ
10 πάλιν ἐν ταῖς ἐπομβρίαις· ἔν τε γὰρ τοῖς αὐχμοῖς,

---

[a] Aristotle is here criticizing Anaxagoras for a mistake of
which he himself has often in turn been accused, that of

part on which we live being the upper part, the other the lower.

It is perhaps hardly necessary to say anything to refute this very elementary account. For it is very silly to think of up and down as if heavy bodies did not fall down to the earth from all directions and light ones (*e.g.* fire) rise up from it, especially when we see that throughout the known world the horizon always changes as we move, which indicates that we live on the convex surface of a sphere.[a] It is silly, too, to think that the earth rests on the air because of its size, and that it is jarred right through by a shock from below. Besides, he fails to account for any of the peculiar features of earthquakes, which do not occur in any district or at any time indiscriminately.

Democritus [b] says the earth is full of water and that earthquakes are caused when a large amount of rain water falls besides this ; for when there is too much for the existing cavities in the earth to contain, it causes an earthquake by forcing its way out. Similarly, when the earth gets dried up water is drawn to the empty places from the fuller and causes earthquakes by the impact of its passage.

Anaximenes [c] says that when the earth is in process of becoming wet or dry it breaks, and is shaken by the high ground breaking and falling. Which is why earthquakes occur in droughts and again in heavy rains : for in droughts the earth is dried and so, as

Demo-
critus ;

Anaxi-
menes.

supposing that up and down are absolute and not relative terms. The absoluteness in Aristotle's own use of the terms is due to his belief that the centre of the earth is the absolute centre of the universe.

[b] Diels 68 A 97, 98.

[c] Diels 13 A 7 (8), 21.

ὥσπερ εἴρηται, ξηραινομένην ῥήγνυσθαι, καὶ ὑπὸ
τῶν ὑδάτων ὑπερυγραινομένην διαπίπτειν.

Ἔδει δὲ τούτου συμβαίνοντος ὑπονοστοῦσαν πολλαχῇ φαίνεσθαι τὴν γῆν. ἔτι δὲ διὰ τίν᾿ αἰτίαν
15 περὶ τόπους τινὰς πολλάκις γίγνεται τοῦτο τὸ
πάθος οὐδεμιᾷ διαφέροντας ὑπερβολῇ τοιαύτῃ παρὰ
τοὺς ἄλλους; καίτοι ἐχρῆν. ὅλως δὲ τοῖς οὕτως
ὑπολαμβάνουσιν ἀναγκαῖον ἧττον ἀεὶ τοὺς σεισμοὺς
φάναι γίγνεσθαι, καὶ τέλος παύσασθαί ποτε σειο-
μένην· τὸ γὰρ σαττόμενον τοιαύτην ἔχει φύσιν.
ὥστ᾿ εἰ τοῦτ᾿ ἀδύνατον, δῆλον ὅτι ἀδύνατον καὶ
20 ταύτην εἶναι τὴν αἰτίαν.

CHAPTER VIII

ARGUMENT

*Earthquakes (continued). The cause of earthquakes is wind
(i.e. dry exhalation) when it gets trapped in the earth (365
b 21—366 a 5). So most earthquakes occur in calm weather,
having exhausted all the available wind : if an earthquake is
accompanied by a wind it is likely to be less violent as the
motive cause is divided (366 a 5-23). Earthquakes are severest
in places where the earth is hollow (366 a 23–b 1) ; and most
frequent in spring and autumn and during rains and
droughts, since exhalation is produced in the greatest quantities at these times (366 b 1-14). Analogies from the human
body and confirmatory examples (366 b 14—367 a 20).
Various concomitants and signs of earthquakes all confirm
our theory (367 a 20–b 19). Earthquakes and eclipses (367
b 19-33). After a severe earthquake the shocks may last for
some time (367 b 33—368 a 14). Wind the cause of subterranean noises (368 a 14-25). Earthquakes are sometimes
accompanied by an outbreak of water : but their cause is*

just explained, breaks, and when the rains make it excessively wet it falls apart.

But (i) if this is so the earth ought to be sinking obviously in many places, (ii) and why do earthquakes occur often in some places which, compared with others, are by no means conspicuous for any such excess of drought or rain, as on this theory they should be? (iii) Besides, on this theory it must be maintained that earthquakes are getting progressively fewer, and will some day cease altogether. For this would be the natural result of the packing down process it describes. But if this is impossible, then this account of their cause must be impossible too.

CHAPTER VIII

ARGUMENT (*continued*)

nevertheless air (368 a 26-33). Why tidal waves accompany earthquakes (368 a 33–b 12). Why earthquakes are confined to one locality, while winds are more general (368 b 12-22). Two types of earthquake shock (368 b 22-32). Earthquakes rare in islands at a distance from the mainland (368 b 32— 369 a 7). Conclusion (369 a 7-9).

Note.—*In this chapter the word normally translated " wind " is πνεῦμα : but on occasion ἄνεμος is used as an alternative, and twice, apparently, ἀήρ (367 a 11, 20). More strictly, ἀήρ is atmospheric air, a combination of the dry and moist exhalations. πνεῦμα and ἄνεμος, both translated " wind," and both composed of dry exhalation, are closely similar : but ἄνεμος is the narrower term, meaning wind in the strict sense, whereas πνεῦμα, both in this and the following chapters (ii. 8, 9, iii. 1), is used in a wider sense to mean the dry exhalation in so far as it is the material which manifests itself not only in wind in the strict sense, but in earthquakes,*

*thunder, lightning, etc. With the parallel with the human
body drawn in 366 b 14 ff. compare Shakespeare*, Henry IV,
Pt. I. *iii. i :*

> Diseased nature oftentimes breaks forth
> In strange eruptions ; oft the teeming earth

365 b 21 Ἀλλ' ἐπειδὴ φανερὸν ὅτι ἀναγκαῖον καὶ ἀπὸ
ὑγροῦ καὶ ἀπὸ ξηροῦ γίγνεσθαι ἀναθυμίασιν, ὥσπερ
εἴπομεν ἐν τοῖς πρότερον, ἀνάγκη τούτων ὑπαρχόντων γίγνεσθαι τοὺς σεισμούς. ὑπάρχει γὰρ ἡ
25 γῆ καθ' αὑτὴν μὲν ξηρά, διὰ δὲ τοὺς ὄμβρους
ἔχουσα ἐν αὑτῇ νοτίδα πολλήν, ὥσθ' ὑπό τε τοῦ
ἡλίου καὶ τοῦ ἐν αὑτῇ πυρὸς θερμαινομένης πολὺ
μὲν ἔξω πολὺ δ' ἐντὸς γίγνεσθαι τὸ πνεῦμα· καὶ
τοῦτο ὁτὲ μὲν συνεχὲς ἔξω ῥεῖ πᾶν, ὁτὲ δ' εἴσω πᾶν,
ἐνίοτε δὲ καὶ μερίζεται.

Εἰ δὴ τοῦτ' ἀδύνατον ἄλλως ἔχειν, τὸ μετὰ τοῦτο
30 σκεπτέον ἂν εἴη ποῖον κινητικώτατον εἴη τῶν σω-
μάτων· ἀνάγκη γὰρ τὸ ἐπὶ πλεῖστόν τε πεφυκὸς
ἰέναι καὶ σφοδρότατον μάλιστα τοιοῦτον εἶναι.
σφοδρότατον μὲν οὖν ἐξ ἀνάγκης τὸ τάχιστα φερό-
μενον· πλήσσει γὰρ μάλιστα διὰ τὸ τάχος· ἐπὶ
πλεῖστον δὲ πέφυκε διιέναι τὸ διὰ παντὸς ἰέναι
35 μάλιστα δυνάμενον, τοιοῦτον δὲ τὸ λεπτότατον.
366 a ὥστ' εἴπερ ἡ τοῦ πνεύματος φύσις τοιαύτη, μάλιστα
τῶν σωμάτων τὸ πνεῦμα κινητικόν· καὶ γὰρ τὸ
πῦρ ὅταν μετὰ πνεύματος ᾖ, γίγνεται φλὸξ καὶ
φέρεται ταχέως. οὐκ ἂν οὖν ὕδωρ οὐδὲ γῆ αἴτιον
εἴη, ἀλλὰ πνεῦμα τῆς κινήσεως, ὅταν εἴσω τύχῃ
5 ῥυὲν τὸ ἔξω ἀναθυμιώμενον.

Διὸ γίγνονται νηνεμίας οἱ πλεῖστοι καὶ μέγιστοι
τῶν σεισμῶν· συνεχὴς γὰρ οὖσα ἡ ἀναθυμίασις

Is with a kind of colic pinch'd and vex'd
By the imprisoning of unruly wind
Within her womb ; which, for enlargement striving,
Shakes the old beldam earth, and topples down
Steeples and moss-grown towers.

Now it is clear, as we have already said,[a] that there must be exhalation both from moist and dry, and earthquakes are a necessary result of the existence of these exhalations. For the earth is in itself dry but contains much moisture because of the rain that falls on it ; with the result that when it is heated by the sun and its own internal fire, a considerable amount of wind is generated both outside it and inside, and this sometimes all flows out, sometimes all flows in, while sometimes it is split up. *The cause of earthquakes is wind, produced by exhalation.*

This process is inevitable. Our next step should therefore be to consider what substance has the greatest motive power. This must necessarily be the substance whose natural motion is most prolonged and whose action is most violent. The substance most violent in action must be that which has the greatest velocity, as its velocity makes its impact most forcible. The farthest mover must be the most penetrating, that is, the finest. If, therefore, the natural constitution of wind is of this kind, it must be the substance whose motive power is the greatest. For even fire when conjoined with wind is blown to flame and moves quickly. So the cause of earth tremors is neither water nor earth but wind, which causes them when the external exhalation flows inwards.

This is why the majority of earthquakes and the greatest occur in calm weather. For the exhalation *Earthquakes commonest in calm weather.*

<hr>

[a] Book I. ch. 4, 341 b 6.

366 a

ἀκολουθεῖ ὡς ἐπὶ τὸ πολὺ τῇ ὁρμῇ τῆς ἀρχῆς,
ὥστε ἢ ἔσω ἅμα ἢ ἔξω ὁρμᾷ πᾶσα. τὸ δ᾽ ἐνίους
γίγνεσθαι καὶ πνεύματος ὄντος οὐδὲν ἄλογον· ὁρῶ-
10 μεν γὰρ ἐνίοτε ἅμα πλείους πνέοντας ἀνέμους, ὧν
ὅταν εἰς τὴν γῆν ὁρμήσῃ θάτερον, ἔσται πνεύματος
ὄντος ὁ σεισμός. ἐλάττους δ᾽ οὗτοι τὸ μέγεθος
γίγνονται διὰ τὸ διῃρῆσθαι τὴν ἀρχὴν καὶ τὴν
αἰτίαν αὐτῶν. νυκτὸς δ᾽ οἱ πλείους καὶ μείζους
15 γίγνονται τῶν σεισμῶν, οἱ δὲ τῆς ἡμέρας περὶ
μεσημβρίαν· νηνεμώτατον γάρ ἐστιν ὡς ἐπὶ τὸ πολὺ
τῆς ἡμέρας ἡ μεσημβρία (ὁ γὰρ ἥλιος ὅταν μάλιστα
κρατῇ, κατακλείει τὴν ἀναθυμίασιν εἰς τὴν γῆν·
κρατεῖ δὲ μάλιστα περὶ τὴν μεσημβρίαν), καὶ αἱ
νύκτες δὲ τῶν ἡμερῶν νηνεμώτεραι διὰ τὴν ἀπου-
σίαν τὴν τοῦ ἡλίου· ὥστ᾽ ἔσω γίγνεται πάλιν ἡ
20 ῥύσις, ὥσπερ ἄμπωτις, εἰς τοὐναντίον τῆς ἔξω
πλημμυρίδος, καὶ πρὸς ὄρθρον μάλιστα· τηνικαῦτα
γὰρ καὶ τὰ πνεύματα πέφυκεν ἄρχεσθαι πνεῖν.
ἐὰν οὖν εἴσω τύχῃ μεταβάλλουσα ἡ ἀρχὴ αὐτῶν
ὥσπερ Εὔριπος, διὰ τὸ πλῆθος ἰσχυρότερον ποιεῖ
τὸν σεισμόν.

Ἔτι δὲ περὶ τόπους τοιούτους οἱ ἰσχυρότατοι
25 γίγνονται τῶν σεισμῶν, ὅπου θάλαττα ῥοώδης ἢ
ἡ χώρα σομφὴ καὶ ὕπαντρος· διὸ καὶ περὶ Ἑλλής-
ποντον καὶ περὶ Ἀχαΐαν καὶ Σικελίαν, καὶ τῆς
Εὐβοίας περὶ τούτους τοὺς τόπους· δοκεῖ γὰρ
διαυλωνίζειν ὑπὸ τὴν γῆν ἡ θάλαττα· διὸ καὶ τὰ
θερμὰ τὰ περὶ Αἰδηψὸν ἀπὸ τοιαύτης αἰτίας γέγονε.
30 περὶ δὲ τοὺς εἰρημένους τόπους οἱ σεισμοὶ γίγνονται
μάλιστα διὰ τὴν στενότητα· τὸ γὰρ πνεῦμα γιγνόμενον σφοδρὸν καὶ διὰ τὸ πλῆθος τῆς θαλάττης
πολλῆς προσφερομένης ἀπωθεῖται πάλιν εἰς τὴν

being continuous in general follows its initial impulse and tends either all to flow inwards at once or all outwards. There is, however, nothing inexplicable in the fact that some earthquakes occur when a wind is blowing; for we sometimes see several winds blowing at the same time, and when one of these plunges into the earth the resultant earthquake is accompanied by wind. But these earthquakes are less violent, because the energy of their original cause is divided. Most major earthquakes occur at night, and those that occur in daytime at midday, this being as a rule the calmest time of day, because when the sun is at its strongest it confines the exhalation within the earth, and it is at its strongest about midday; and the night again is calmer than the day because of the sun's absence. So at these times the flow turns inwards again, like an ebb as opposed to the outward flood. This happens especially towards dawn, for it is then that winds normally begin to blow. If, then, the original impulse of the exhalation changes direction, like the Euripus, and turns inwards, it causes a more violent earthquake because of its quantity.

Again, the severest earthquakes occur in places where the sea is full of currents or the earth is porous and hollow. So they occur in the Hellespont and Achaea and Sicily, and in the districts in Euboea where the sea is supposed to run in channels beneath the earth. The hot springs at Aedepsus [a] are due to a similar cause. In the places mentioned earthquakes occur mostly because of the constricted space. For when a violent wind arises the volume of the inflowing sea drives it back into the earth, when it would

Where earthquakes are severest.

---

[a] In Euboea.

γῆν, τὸ πεφυκὸς ἀποπνεῖν ἐκ τῆς γῆς. αἵ τε χῶραι
366 b ὅσαι σομφοὺς ἔχουσι τοὺς κάτω τόπους, πολὺ δεχό-
μεναι πνεῦμα σείονται μᾶλλον.

Καὶ ἔαρος δὲ καὶ μετοπώρου μάλιστα καὶ ἐν
ἐπομβρίαις καὶ ἐν αὐχμοῖς γίγνονται διὰ τὴν αὐτὴν
αἰτίαν· αἵ τε γὰρ ὧραι αὗται πνευματωδέσταται·
5 τὸ γὰρ θέρος καὶ ὁ χειμών, τὸ μὲν διὰ τὸν πάγον,
τὸ δὲ διὰ τὴν ἀλέαν ποιεῖ τὴν ἀκινησίαν· τὸ μὲν γὰρ
ἄγαν ψυχρόν, τὸ δ' ἄγαν ξηρόν ἐστι· καὶ ἐν μὲν
τοῖς αὐχμοῖς πνευματώδης ὁ ἀήρ· τοῦτο γὰρ αὐτό
ἐστιν ὁ αὐχμός, ὅταν πλείων ἡ ἀναθυμίασις ἡ ξηρὰ
γίγνηται τῆς ὑγρᾶς· ἐν δὲ ταῖς ὑπερομβρίαις πλείω
10 τε ποιεῖ τὴν ἐντὸς ἀναθυμίασιν, καὶ τῷ ἐναπολαμ-
βάνεσθαι ἐν στενοτέροις τόποις καὶ ἀποβιάζεσθαι
εἰς ἐλάττω τόπον τὴν τοιαύτην ἀπόκρισιν, πληρου-
μένων τῶν κοιλιῶν ὕδατος, ὅταν ἄρξηται κρατεῖν
διὰ τὸ πολὺ εἰς ὀλίγον πιληθῆναι τόπον, ἰσχυρῶς
15 κινεῖ ῥέων ὁ ἄνεμος καὶ προσπίπτων· δεῖ γὰρ νοεῖν
ὅτι ὥσπερ ἐν τῷ σώματι ἡμῶν καὶ τρόμων καὶ
σφυγμῶν αἴτιόν ἐστιν ἡ τοῦ πνεύματος ἐναπολαμ-
βανομένη δύναμις, οὕτω καὶ ἐν τῇ γῇ τὸ πνεῦμα
παραπλήσιον ποιεῖν, καὶ τὸν μὲν τῶν σεισμῶν οἷον
τρόμον εἶναι τὸν δ' οἷον σφυγμόν, καὶ καθάπερ
20 συμβαίνει πολλάκις μετὰ τὴν οὔρησιν (διὰ τοῦ
σώματος γὰρ γίγνεται ὥσπερ τρόμος τις ἀντιμεθ-
ισταμένου τοῦ πνεύματος ἔξωθεν εἴσω ἀθρόου),
τοιαῦτα [γὰρ]¹ γίγνεσθαι καὶ περὶ τὴν γῆν. ὅσην
δ' ἔχει τὸ πνεῦμα δύναμιν, οὐ μόνον ἐκ τῶν ἐν τῷ
ἀέρι δεῖ θεωρεῖν γιγνομένων (ἐνταῦθα μὲν γὰρ διὰ
τὸ μέγεθος ὑπολάβοι τις ἂν τοιαῦτα δύνασθαι
25 ποιεῖν) ἀλλὰ καὶ ἐν τοῖς σώμασι τοῖς τῶν ζῴων·
οἵ τε γὰρ τέτανοι καὶ οἱ σπασμοὶ πνεύματος μέν

naturally be exhaled from it. And places whose sub-
soil is porous are shaken more because of the large
amount of wind they absorb.

For the same reason earthquakes occur most often _{When}
in spring and autumn and during rains and droughts, _{earthquakes are most}
since these periods produce most wind. For summer _{frequent.}
and winter both bring calm weather, the one because
of its frosts, the other because of its warmth, the one
thus being too cold, the other being too dry to produce winds. But in times of drought the air is full
of wind, drought simply being an excess of dry over
moist exhalation. In times of rain the exhalation is
produced within the earth in greater quantity,[a] and
when what has been so produced is caught in a constricted space and forcibly compressed as the hollows
within the earth fill with water, the impact of the
stream of the wind on the earth causes a severe shock,
once the compression of a large quantity of it into a
small space begins to have its effect. For we must _{Analogies}
suppose that the wind in the earth has effects similar _{from the human}
to those of the wind in our bodies whose force when _{body.}
it is pent up inside us can cause tremors and throbbings, some earthquakes being like a tremor, some
like a throbbing. We must suppose, again, that the
earth is affected as we often are after making water,
when a sort of tremor runs through the body as a body
of wind turns inwards again from without.[b] For the
force that wind has can be seen not only by studying
its effects in the air, when one would expect it to be
able to produce them because of its volume, but also
in the bodies of living things. Tetanus and spasms

---

[a] Cf. 361 a 17.
[b] Cf. Problems viii. 8, 13, xxxiii. 16.

[1] γὰρ seclusit Fobes.

366 b

εἰσιν κινήσεις, τοσαύτην δὲ ἔχουσιν ἰσχὺν ὥστε
πολλοὺς ἅμα πειρωμένους ἀποβιάζεσθαι μὴ δύνασθαι κρατεῖν τῆς κινήσεως τῶν ἀρρωστούντων.
τοιοῦτον δὴ δεῖ νοεῖν τὸ γιγνόμενον καὶ ἐν τῇ γῇ,
30 ὡς εἰκάσαι πρὸς μικρὸν μεῖζον.

Σημεῖα δὲ τούτων καὶ πρὸς τὴν ἡμετέραν αἴσθησιν πολλαχῇ γέγονεν· ἤδη γὰρ σεισμὸς ἐν τόποις
τισὶν γιγνόμενος οὐ πρότερον ἔληξε πρὶν ἐκρήξας
εἰς τὸν ὑπὲρ τῆς γῆς τόπον φανερῶς ὥσπερ ἐκ-
367 a νεφίας ἐξῆλθεν ὁ κινήσας ἄνεμος, οἷον καὶ περὶ
Ἡράκλειαν ἐγένετο τὴν ἐν τῷ Πόντῳ νεωστί,
καὶ πρότερον περὶ τὴν Ἱερὰν νῆσον (αὕτη δ᾽ ἐστὶν
μία τῶν Αἰόλου καλουμένων νήσων)· ἐν ταύτῃ γὰρ
5 ἀνῴδει τι τῆς γῆς, καὶ ἀνῄει οἷον λοφώδης ὄγκος
μετὰ ψόφου· τέλος δὲ ῥαγέντος ἐξῆλθεν πνεῦμα
πολὺ καὶ τὸν φέψαλον καὶ τὴν τέφραν ἀνῆκεν καὶ
τήν τε Λιπαραίων πόλιν οὖσαν οὐ πόρρω πᾶσαν
κατετέφρωσε καὶ εἰς ἐνίας τῶν ἐν Ἰταλίᾳ πόλεων
ἦλθεν· καὶ νῦν ὅπου τὸ ἀναφύσημα τοῦτο ἐγένετο,
10 δῆλόν ἐστιν. καὶ γὰρ δὴ τοῦ γιγνομένου πυρὸς
ἐν τῇ γῇ ταύτην οἰητέον εἶναι τὴν αἰτίαν, ὅταν
κοπτόμενον ἐκπρησθῇ πρῶτον εἰς μικρὰ κερμα-
τισθέντος τοῦ ἀέρος.

Τεκμήριον δ᾽ ἐστὶ τοῦ ῥεῖν ὑπὸ γῆν τὰ πνεύματα
καὶ τὸ γιγνόμενον περὶ ταύτας τὰς νήσους· ὅταν
γὰρ ἄνεμος μέλλῃ πνευσεῖσθαι νότος, προσημαίνει
πρότερον· ἠχοῦσι γὰρ οἱ τόποι ἐξ ὧν γίγνεται τὰ
15 ἀναφυσήματα, διὰ τὸ τὴν θάλατταν μὲν προωθεῖσθαι
ἤδη πόρρωθεν, ὑπὸ δὲ ταύτης τὸ ἐκ τῆς γῆς ἀνα-
φυσώμενον ἀπωθεῖσθαι πάλιν εἴσω, ᾗπερ ἐπέρχεται
ἡ θάλαττα ταύτη. ποιεῖ δὲ ψόφον ἄνευ σεισμοῦ

are movements caused by wind, and are so strong that the combined strength and efforts of a number of men is unable to master the movements of their victims. And if we may compare great things with small, we must suppose that the same sort of thing happens to the earth.

As evidence we may cite occurrences which have been observed in many places. For in some places there has been an earthquake which has not ceased until the wind which was its motive force has broken out like a hurricane and risen into the upper region. This happened recently, for instance, in Heracleia in Pontus, and before that in Hiera, one of the so-called Aeolian islands. For in this island part of the earth swelled up and rose with a noise in a crest-shaped lump ; this finally exploded and a large quantity of wind broke out, blowing up cinders and ash which smothered the neighbouring city of Lipara, and even reached as far as some of the cities in Italy. The place where this eruption took place can still be seen. (This too must be regarded as the cause of the fire that there is in the earth ; for when the air is broken up into small particles, percussion then causes it to catch fire.) [a]

And there is a proof that winds circulate beneath the earth in something else that happens in these islands. For when a south wind is going to blow it is heralded by noises from the places from which eruptions occur. This is because the sea, which is being driven forward from far off, thrusts the wind that is erupting out of the earth back again when it meets it. This causes a noise but no earthquake

Con-
firmatory
examples.

_____

[a] The warm and dry (and so inflammable) exhalation is one of the constituents of air.

211

367 a

διά τε τὴν εὐρυχωρίαν τῶν τόπων (ὑπερχεῖται γὰρ
20 εἰς τὸ ἀχανὲς ἔξω) καὶ δι' ὀλιγότητα τοῦ ἀπωθου-
μένου ἀέρος.

Ἔτι τὸ γίγνεσθαι τὸν ἥλιον ἀχλυώδη καὶ ἀμαυρό-
τερον ἄνευ νέφους, καὶ πρὸ τῶν ὀρθρίων σεισμῶν
ἐνίοτε νηνεμίαν τε καὶ κρύος ἰσχυρόν, σημεῖον τῆς
εἰρημένης αἰτίας ἐστίν. τόν τε γὰρ ἥλιον ἀχλυώδη
καὶ ἀμαυρὸν ἀναγκαῖον εἶναι ὑπονοστεῖν ἀρχομένου
25 τοῦ πνεύματος εἰς τὴν γῆν τοῦ διαλύοντος τὸν ἀέρα
καὶ διακρίνοντος, καὶ πρὸς τὴν ἔω καὶ περὶ τοὺς
ὄρθρους νηνεμίαν τε καὶ ψῦχος. τὴν μὲν γὰρ νηνεμίαν ἀναγκαῖον ὡς ἐπὶ τὸ πολὺ συμβαίνειν, καθάπερ
εἴρηται καὶ πρότερον, οἷον μεταρροίας εἴσω γιγνομένης τοῦ πνεύματος, καὶ μᾶλλον πρὸ τῶν
30 μειζόνων σεισμῶν· μὴ διασπώμενον γὰρ τὸ μὲν
ἔξω τὸ δ' ἐντός, ἀλλ' ἀθρόως φερόμενον ἀναγκαῖον
ἰσχύειν μᾶλλον. τὸ δὲ ψῦχος συμβαίνει διὰ τὸ
τὴν ἀναθυμίασιν εἴσω τρέπεσθαι, φύσει θερμὴν
οὖσαν καθ' αὑτήν. οὐ δοκοῦσι δ' οἱ ἄνεμοι εἶναι
θερμοὶ διὰ τὸ κινεῖν τὸν ἀέρα πλήρη πολλῆς ὄντα
367 b καὶ ψυχρᾶς ἀτμίδος, ὥσπερ τὸ πνεῦμα ⟨τὸ⟩ διὰ
τοῦ στόματος φυσώμενον· καὶ γὰρ τοῦτο ἐγγύθεν
μέν ἐστι θερμόν, ὥσπερ καὶ ὅταν ἀάζωμεν, ἀλλὰ
δι' ὀλιγότητα οὐχ ὁμοίως ἐπίδηλον, πόρρωθεν δὲ
ψυχρὸν διὰ τὴν αὐτὴν αἰτίαν τοῖς ἀνέμοις. ἐκ-
5 λειπούσης οὖν εἰς τὴν γῆν τῆς τοιαύτης δυνάμεως,
συνιοῦσα δι' ὑγρότητα¹ ἡ ἀτμιδώδης ἀπόρροια ποιεῖ
τὸ ψῦχος, ἐν οἷς συμβαίνει τόποις γίγνεσθαι τοῦτο
τὸ πάθος. τὸ δ' αὐτὸ αἴτιον καὶ τοῦ εἰωθότος
ἐνίοτε γίγνεσθαι σημείου πρὸ τῶν σεισμῶν. ἢ γὰρ

because there is plenty of room for the wind, of which there is only a small quantity and which can overflow into the void outside.

Further evidence that our account of the cause of earthquakes is correct is afforded by the facts that before them the sun becomes misty and dimmer though there is no cloud, and that before earthquakes that occur at dawn there is often a calm and a hard frost. The sun is necessarily misty and dim when the wind which dissolves and breaks up the air begins to retreat into the earth. Calm and cold towards sunrise and dawn are also necessary concomitants. Calm must usually fall, as we have explained,[a] because the wind drains back as it were into the earth, and the greater the earthquake the more this happens ; for the earthquake is bound to be more severe if the wind is not dispersed, some outside and some in, but moves in a mass. The reason for the cold is that the exhalation, which is by nature essentially warm, is directed inwards. (Winds are not usually supposed to be warm because they set the air in motion and the air contains large quantities of cold vapour. This can be seen when wind is blown out of the mouth : close by it is warm, as when we breathe with open mouth, though there is too little of it to be very noticeable, while farther off it is cool for the same reason as the winds.) So the warm element disappears into the earth, and wherever this happens, the vaporous exhalation being moist condenses and causes cold. The cause of a sign which often heralds earthquakes is the same. In clear weather, either

[a] 366 a 5 ff.

[1] δι' ὑγρότητα om. O.T.

μεθ' ἡμέραν ἢ μικρὸν μετὰ δυσμάς, αἰθρίας οὔσης,
10 νεφέλιον λεπτὸν φαίνεται διατεῖνον καὶ μακρόν,
οἷον γραμμῆς μῆκος εὐθύτητι διηκριβωμένον, τοῦ
πνεύματος ἀπομαραινομένου διὰ τὴν μετάστασιν.
τὸ δ' ὅμοιον συμβαίνει καὶ ἐν τῇ θαλάττῃ περὶ τοὺς
αἰγιαλούς· ὅταν μὲν γὰρ κυμαίνουσα ἐκβάλλῃ, σφόδρα παχεῖαι καὶ σκολιαὶ γίγνονται αἱ ῥηγμῖνες,
15 ὅταν δὲ γαλήνη ᾖ, [διὰ τὸ μικρὰν ποιεῖσθαι τὴν
ἔκκρισιν][1] λεπταί εἰσι καὶ εὐθεῖαι. ὅπερ οὖν ἡ
θάλαττα ποιεῖ περὶ τὴν γῆν, τοῦτο τὸ πνεῦμα περὶ
τὴν ἐν τῷ ἀέρι ἀχλύν, ὥσθ' ὅταν γένηται νηνεμία,
πάμπαν εὐθεῖαν καὶ λεπτὴν καταλείπεσθαι ὥσπερ
ῥηγμῖνα οὖσαν ἀέρος τὴν νεφέλην.
20   Διὰ ταῦτα δὲ καὶ περὶ τὰς ἐκλείψεις ἐνίοτε τῆς
σελήνης συμβαίνει γίγνεσθαι σεισμόν· ὅταν γὰρ
ἤδη πλησίον ᾖ ἡ ἀντίφραξις, καὶ μήπω μὲν ᾖ
πάμπαν ἀπολελοιπὸς τὸ φῶς καὶ τὸ ἀπὸ τοῦ ἡλίου
θερμὸν ἐκ τοῦ ἀέρος, ἤδη δ' ἀπομαραινόμενον,
25 εἰς τὴν γῆν, ὃ ποιεῖ τὸν σεισμὸν πρὸ τῶν ἐκλείψεων. γίγνονται γὰρ καὶ ἄνεμοι πρὸ τῶν ἐκλείψεων
πολλάκις, ἀκρόνυχον μὲν πρὸ τῶν μεσονυκτίων
ἐκλείψεων, μεσονύκτιον δὲ πρὸ τῶν ἑῴων. συμβαίνει δὲ τοῦτο διὰ τὸ ἀμαυροῦσθαι τὸ θερμὸν τὸ
ἀπὸ τῆς σελήνης, ὅταν πλησίον ἤδη γίγνηται ἡ
30 φορὰ ἐν ᾧ γενομένων ἔσται ἡ ἔκλειψις. ἀνιεμένου
οὖν ᾧ κατείχετο ὁ ἀὴρ καὶ ἠρέμει, πάλιν κινεῖται
καὶ γίγνεται πνεῦμα τῆς ὀψιαίτερον ἐκλείψεως
ὀψιαίτερον.
   Ὅταν δ' ἰσχυρὸς γένηται σεισμός, οὐκ εὐθὺς οὐδ'

---

[1] διὰ . . . ἔκκρισιν seclusit O.T.

^a Into the earth, cf. 367 a 26.

by day or a little after sunset, a fine long streak of cloud appears, like a long straight line carefully drawn, the reason being that the wind is dying down and running away.[a] Something like it happens on the seashore too. For when the sea runs high the breakers are large and uneven, but when there is a calm they are fine and straight [because the amount of exhalation is small].[b] The wind produces the same effects on the cloud in the sky as the sea on the shore, so that when there is a calm the clouds that are left are all straight and fine like breakers in the air.

For the same reason an earthquake sometimes occurs at an eclipse of the moon. For when the interposition is approaching but the light and warmth from the sun,[c] though already fading, have not entirely disappeared from the air, a calm falls when the wind runs back into the earth. And this causes the earthquake before the eclipse. For there are often winds also before eclipses, at nightfall before a midnight eclipse, at midnight before an eclipse at dawn. The reason for this is the failure of the heat from the moon when its course approaches the point at which [d] the eclipse will take place. Thus when the cause which held it quiet ceases to operate the air is set in motion again and a wind rises, and the later the eclipse, the later this happens.[e]

When an earthquake is severe the shocks do not

Earth-quakes and eclipses.

Shocks con-tinue after a severe earthquake.

[b] The O.T. omits these words as " a misguided gloss on γαλήνη." Alex. shows no sign of having had them in his text.

[c] Reflected from the moon (Alex.).

[d] " Lit. ' at which, when the moon and its sphere (φορά) have got there ' " (O.T.).

[e] With this somewhat obscure paragraph cf. Problems xxvi. 18, 942 a 22.

εἰσάπαξ παύεται σείσας, ἀλλὰ τὸ πρῶτον μὲν μέχρι
περὶ τετταράκοντα πρόεισι πολλάκις ἡμέρας, ὥστε-
368 a ρον δὲ καὶ ἐφ' ἓν καὶ ἐπὶ δύο ἔτη ἐπισημαίνει κατὰ
τοὺς αὐτοὺς τόπους. αἴτιον δὲ τοῦ μὲν μεγέθους
τὸ πλῆθος τοῦ πνεύματος καὶ τῶν τόπων τὰ σχήματα δι' οἵων ἂν ῥυῇ· ᾗ γὰρ ἂν ἀντιτυπήσῃ καὶ μὴ
ῥᾳδίως διέλθῃ, μάλιστά τε σείει καὶ ἐγκαταλεί-
5 πεσθαι ἀναγκαῖον ἐν ταῖς δυσχωρίαις, οἷον ὕδωρ
ἐν σκεύει οὐ δυνάμενον διεξελθεῖν.   διὸ καθάπερ
ἐν σώματι οἱ σφυγμοὶ οὐκ ἐξαίφνης παύονται οὐδὲ
ταχέως, ἀλλ' ἐκ προσαγωγῆς ἅμα καταμαραινο-
μένου τοῦ πάθους, καὶ ἡ ἀρχὴ ἀφ' ἧς ἡ ἀναθυμίασις
ἐγένετο καὶ ἡ ὁρμὴ τοῦ πνεύματος δῆλον ὅτι οὐκ
10 εὐθὺς ἅπασαν ἀνήλωσεν τὴν ὕλην, ἐξ ἧς ἐποίησε
τὸν ἄνεμον, ὃν καλοῦμεν σεισμόν.   ἕως ἂν οὖν
ἀναλωθῇ τὰ ὑπόλοιπα τούτων, ἀνάγκη σείειν, ἠρε-
μαιότερον δὲ καὶ μέχρι τούτου ἕως ἂν ἔλαττον ᾖ
τὸ ἀναθυμίωμενον ἢ ὥστε δύνασθαι κινεῖν ἐπιδήλως.

Ποιεῖ δὲ καὶ τοὺς ψόφους τοὺς ὑπὸ τὴν γῆν
15 γιγνομένους τὸ πνεῦμα, καὶ τοὺς πρὸ τῶν σεισμῶν·
καὶ ἄνευ δὲ σεισμῶν ἤδη που γεγόνασιν ὑπὸ γῆν·
ὥσπερ γὰρ καὶ ῥαπιζόμενος ὁ ἀὴρ παντοδαποὺς
ἀφίησι ψόφους, οὕτως καὶ τύπτων αὐτός· οὐδὲν
γὰρ διαφέρει· τὸ γὰρ τύπτον ἅμα καὶ αὐτὸ τύπτεται
πᾶν.   προέρχεται δὲ ὁ ψόφος τῆς κινήσεως διὰ τὸ
20 λεπτομερέστερον εἶναι καὶ μᾶλλον διὰ παντὸς ἰέναι
τοῦ πνεύματος τὸν ψόφον.   ὅταν δ' ἔλαττον ᾖ ἢ
ὥστε κινῆσαι τὴν γῆν διὰ λεπτότητα, διὰ μὲν τὸ
ῥᾳδίως διηθεῖσθαι οὐ δύναται κινεῖν, διὰ δὲ τὸ
προσπίπτειν στερεοῖς ὄγκοις καὶ κοίλοις καὶ παντο-
δαποῖς σχήμασι παντοδαπὴν ἀφίησι φωνήν, ὥστ'

cease immediately or at once, but frequently go on
for forty days or so in the first instance, and symptoms
appear subsequently for one or two years in the same
district. The cause of the severity is the amount of
the wind and the shape of the passages through
which it has to flow. When it meets with resistance
and cannot easily get through, the shocks are severest
and air is bound to be left in the narrow places, like
water that cannot get out of a vessel. Therefore,
just as throbbings in the body do not stop at once or
quickly, but gradually as the affliction which is their
cause dies away, so the originating cause of the exhalation and the source of the wind clearly do not
expend all at once the material which produces the
wind which we call an earthquake. Until, therefore,
the rest of it is expended shocks must continue, their
force decreasing until there is too little exhalation
to cause a shock that is noticeable.

Wind is also the cause of noises beneath the earth, Wind the
among them the noises that precede earthquakes, cause of
though they have also been known to occur without ranean
an earthquake following. For as the air when struck noises.
gives out all sorts of noises, so also it does when it
is itself the striker ; the effect is the same in either
case, since every striker is itself also struck. The
sound precedes the shock because the sound is of
finer texture and so more penetrating than the wind
itself. When the wind is too fine to communicate any
impulse to the earth, being unable to do so because
of the ease with which it filters through it, nevertheless when it strikes hard or hollow masses of all shapes
it gives out all sorts of noises, so that sometimes the

368 a

25 ἐνίοτε δοκεῖν ὅπερ λέγουσιν οἱ τερατολογοῦντες,
μυκᾶσθαι τὴν γῆν.

Ἤδη δὲ καὶ ὕδατα ἀνερράγη γιγνομένων σεισμῶν·
ἀλλ' οὐ διὰ τοῦτο αἴτιον τὸ ὕδωρ τῆς κινήσεως,
ἀλλ' ἂν ᾖ ἐξ ἐπιπολῆς ἢ κάτωθεν βιάζηται τὸ
πνεῦμα, ἐκεῖνο τὸ κινοῦν ἐστιν, ὥσπερ τῶν κυμά-
30 των οἱ ἄνεμοι ἀλλ' οὐ τὰ κύματα τῶν ἀνέμων εἰσὶν
αἴτια, ἐπεὶ καὶ τὴν γῆν οὕτως ἄν τις αἰτιῷτο τοῦ
πάθους· ἀνατρέπεται γὰρ σειομένη, καθάπερ ὕδωρ
(ἡ γὰρ ἔκχυσις ἀνάτρεψίς τίς ἐστιν). ἀλλ' αἴτια
ταῦτα μὲν ἄμφω ὡς ὕλη (πάσχει γάρ, ἀλλ' οὐ
ποιεῖ), τὸ δὲ πνεῦμα ὡς ἀρχή.

Ὅπου δ' ἄμα κῦμα σεισμῷ γέγονεν, αἴτιον, ὅταν
35 ἐναντία γίγνηται τὰ πνεύματα. τοῦτο δὲ γίγνεται
368 b ὅταν τὸ σεῖον τὴν γῆν πνεῦμα φερομένην ὑπ' ἄλλου
πνεύματος τὴν θάλατταν ἀπῶσαι μὲν ὅλως μὴ
δύνηται, προωθοῦν δὲ καὶ συστέλλον εἰς ταὐτὸν
συναθροίσῃ πολλήν· τότε γὰρ ἀναγκαῖον ἡττηθέντος
5 τούτου τοῦ πνεύματος ἀθρόαν ὠθουμένην ὑπὸ τοῦ
ἐναντίου πνεύματος ἐκρήγνυσθαι καὶ ποιεῖν τὸν
κατακλυσμόν. ἐγένετο δὲ τοῦτο καὶ περὶ Ἀχαΐαν·
ἐκεῖ[1] μὲν γὰρ ἦν νότος, ἔξω[1] δὲ βορέας, νηνεμίας
δὲ γενομένης καὶ ῥυέντος εἴσω τοῦ ἀνέμου ἐγένετο
τό τε κῦμα καὶ ὁ σεισμὸς ἄμα, καὶ μᾶλλον διὰ τὸ
10 τὴν θάλατταν μὴ διδόναι διαπνοὴν τῷ ὑπὸ τὴν γῆν
ὡρμημένῳ πνεύματι, ἀλλ' ἀντιφράττειν· ἀποβια-
ζόμενα γὰρ ἄλληλα τὸ μὲν πνεῦμα τὸν σεισμὸν
ἐποίησεν, ἡ δ' ὑπόστασις τοῦ κύματος τὸν κατακλυσμόν.

[1] ἐκεῖ—ἔξω O.T. : ἔξω—ἐκεῖ Fobes.

---

[a] Cf. l. 34 below.   [b] Cf. 343 b 2 and note.

earth seems to bellow as they say it does in fairy stories.

Water has sometimes burst out of the earth when there has been an earthquake. But this does not mean that the water was the cause of the shock. It is the wind which is the cause, whether it exerts its force on the surface [a] or from beneath—just as the winds are the cause of waves and not the waves of winds. Indeed one might as well suppose that the earth is the cause of the shock as that the water is ; for in an earthquake it is overturned like water, and upsetting water is a form of overturning. But in fact both earth and water are material causes, being passive not active, but wind the motive cause. *Water produced by earthquakes.*

When a tidal wave coincides with an earthquake the cause is an opposition of winds. This happens when the wind which is causing the earthquake is unable quite to drive out the sea which is being driven in by another wind, but pushes it back and piles it together till a large mass has collected. Then if the first wind gives way the whole mass is driven in by the opposing wind and breaks on the land and causes a flood. This is what happened in Achaea.[b] For in Achaea there was a south wind, outside a north wind [c]; this was followed by a calm when the wind plunged into the earth, and so there was a tidal wave at the same time as the earthquake—an earthquake which was all the more violent because the sea gave no vent to the wind that had run into the earth, but blocked its passage. So in their mutual struggle the wind caused the earthquake, the wave by its subsidence the flood. *Earthquakes and tidal waves.*

[c] " Transpose ἔξω and ἐκεῖ ll. 6, 7. The map makes it clear that the received text is impossible " (O.T.).

Κατὰ μέρος δὲ γίγνονται οἱ σεισμοὶ τῆς γῆς, καὶ
πολλάκις ἐπὶ μικρὸν τόπον, οἱ δ' ἄνεμοι οὔ· κατὰ
15 μέρος μέν, ὅταν αἱ ἀναθυμιάσεις αἱ κατὰ τὸν τόπον
αὐτὸν καὶ τὸν γειτνιῶντα συνέλθωσιν εἰς ἕν, ὥσπερ
καὶ τοὺς αὐχμοὺς ἔφαμεν γίγνεσθαι καὶ τὰς ὑπερομ-
βρίας τὰς κατὰ μέρος. καὶ οἱ μὲν σεισμοὶ γίγνονται
διὰ¹ τοῦτον τὸν τρόπον, οἱ δ' ἄνεμοι οὔ· τὰ μὲν
γὰρ ἐν τῇ γῇ τὴν ἀρχὴν ἔχει, ὥστ' ἐφ' ἓν ἁπάσας
20 ὁρμᾶν· ὁ δ' ἥλιος² οὐχ ὁμοίως δύναται, τὰς δὲ
μετεώρους μᾶλλον, ὥστε ῥεῖν, ὅταν ἀρχὴν λάβωσιν
ἀπὸ τῆς τοῦ ἡλίου φορᾶς ἤδη κατὰ τὰς διαφορὰς
τῶν τόπων, ἐφ' ἕν.

Ὅταν μὲν οὖν ᾖ πολὺ τὸ πνεῦμα, κινεῖ τὴν γῆν,
ὥσπερ δὲ ὁ τρόμος, ἐπὶ πλάτος· γίγνεται δ' ὀλιγάκις
25 καὶ κατά τινας τόπους, οἷον σφυγμός, ἄνω κάτωθεν·
διὸ καὶ ἐλαττονάκις σείει τοῦτον τὸν τρόπον· οὐ
γὰρ [δίδωσιν]³ ῥᾴδιον οὕτω πολλὴν συνελθεῖν ἀρχήν·
ἐπὶ μῆκος γὰρ πολλαπλασία τῆς ἀπὸ τοῦ βάθους
ἡ διάκρισις. ὅπου δ' ἂν γένηται τοιοῦτος σεισμός,
ἐπιπολάζει πλῆθος λίθων, ὥσπερ τῶν ἐν τοῖς
30 λίκνοις ἀναβραττομένων· τοῦτον γὰρ τὸν τρόπον
γενομένου σεισμοῦ τά τε περὶ Σίπυλον ἀνετράπη
καὶ τὸ Φλεγραῖον καλούμενον πεδίον καὶ τὰ περὶ
τὴν Λιγυστικὴν χώραν.

Ἐν δὲ ταῖς νήσοις ταῖς ποντίαις ἧττον γίγνονται
σεισμοὶ τῶν προσγείων· τὸ γὰρ πλῆθος τῆς θαλάτ-
35 της καταψύχει τὰς ἀναθυμιάσεις καὶ κωλύει τῷ

¹ κατὰ W.
² ὁρμᾶν ὁ ἥλιος O.T.
³ seclusit Fobes.

ᵃ Cf. 360 b 17.
ᵇ The O.T., following Thurot, regards the text of ll. 17-22

Earthquakes are confined to one locality, often quite a small one, but winds are not. They are localized when the exhalations of a particular locality and its neighbour combine, which was what we said [a] happens in local droughts and rainy seasons. Earthquakes are produced in this way, but not winds. For rains, droughts and earthquakes originate in the earth, and so their constituent exhalations tend to move all in one direction ; the sun has less power over them than it has with the exhalations in the air which therefore flow on in one direction when the sun's movement gives them an impulse, differing according to the difference of its position.[b]

Why earthquakes are local.

So then, when the quantity of wind is large it causes an earthquake shock which runs horizontally, like a shudder: occasionally in some places the shock runs up from below, like a throb. The latter type of shock is therefore the rarer, for sufficient force to cause it does not easily collect since there is many times as much of the exhalation that causes shocks horizontally as of that which causes them from below. But whenever this type of earthquake does occur, large quantities of stones come to the surface, like the chaff in a winnowing sieve. This kind of earthquake it was that devastated the country round Sipylos, the so-called Phlegraean plain and the districts of Liguria.

Horizontal and vertical shocks.

Earthquakes are rarer in islands that are far out at sea than in those close to the mainland. For the quantity of the sea cools the exhalations and its

Earthquakes and islands.

as corrupt. In my attempt to make sense of it I follow Alex.'s explanation (124. 28 ff.), taking τὰ μέν l. 18 to mean rains, etc., and understanding τὰς ἀναθυμιάσεις with ἁπάσας l. 19. The general point of the paragraph, as the O.T. remarks, is to contrast the local nature of earthquakes with the wide range of winds.

368 b

βάρει καὶ ἀποβιάζεται· ἔτι δὲ ῥεῖ καὶ οὐ σείεται
369 a κρατουμένη ὑπὸ τῶν πνευμάτων· καὶ διὰ τὸ πολὺν
ἐπέχειν τόπον οὐκ εἰς ταύτην ἀλλ' ἐκ ταύτης αἱ
ἀναθυμιάσεις γίγνονται, καὶ ταύταις ἀκολουθοῦσιν
αἱ ἐκ τῆς γῆς. αἱ δ' ἐγγὺς τῆς ἠπείρου μόριόν
5 εἰσιν τῆς ἠπείρου· τὸ γὰρ μεταξὺ διὰ μικρότητα
οὐδεμίαν ἔχει δύναμιν· τὰς δὲ ποντίας οὐκ ἔστιν
κινῆσαι ἄνευ τῆς θαλάττης ὅλης, ὑφ' ἧς περιεχό-
μεναι τυγχάνουσιν.

Περὶ μὲν οὖν σεισμῶν, καὶ τίς ἡ φύσις, καὶ διὰ
τίνα αἰτίαν γίγνονται, καὶ περὶ τῶν ἄλλων τῶν
συμβαινόντων περὶ αὐτούς, εἴρηται σχεδὸν περὶ
τῶν μεγίστων.

CHAPTER IX

ARGUMENT

*Thunder is due to the forcible ejection of the dry exhalation
trapped in the clouds in the process of condensation (369 a 10–
b 3). The ejected exhalation usually catches fire, and this
produces lightning (which thus occurs, in spite of appearances,*

369 a 10 Περὶ δὲ ἀστραπῆς καὶ βροντῆς, ἔτι δὲ περὶ
τυφῶνος καὶ πρηστῆρος καὶ κεραυνῶν λέγωμεν·
καὶ γὰρ τούτων τὴν αὐτὴν ἀρχὴν ὑπολαβεῖν δεῖ
πάντων.

Τῆς γὰρ ἀναθυμιάσεως, ὥσπερ εἴπομεν, οὔσης
διττῆς, τῆς μὲν ὑγρᾶς τῆς δὲ ξηρᾶς, καὶ τῆς συγ-
15 κρίσεως ἐχούσης ἄμφω ταῦτα δυνάμει καὶ συνισταμένης εἰς νέφος, ὥσπερ εἴρηται πρότερον, ἔτι
δὲ πυκνοτέρας τῆς συστάσεως τῶν νεφῶν γιγνο-

weight crushes them and prevents their forming; and the force of the winds causes waves and not shocks in the sea. Again, its extent is so great that the exhalations do not run into it but are produced from it and joined by those from the land. On the other hand, islands close to the mainland are for all practical purposes part of it, the interval between them being too small to be effective. And islands out at sea can feel no shock that is not felt by the whole of the sea by which they are surrounded.

This completes our explanation of the nature and cause of earthquakes, and of their most important attendant circumstances.

CHAPTER IX

ARGUMENT (continued)

after thunder) (369 b 3-11). *Theories of Empedocles and Anaxagoras stated and criticized* (369 b 11—370 a 10). *Theory of Cleidemus and others* (370 a 10-21). *Summary and conclusion* (370 a 21-34).

LET us now explain lightning and thunder, and then whirlwinds, firewinds and thunderbolts : for the cause of all of them must be assumed to be the same. As we have said,[a] there are two kinds of exhalation, moist and dry ; and their combination (air) contains both potentially. It condenses into cloud, as we have explained before,[b] and the condensation of clouds

Thunder caused by the forcible ejection of dry exhalation from cloud.

---

[a] Cf. 341 b 6 ff.
[b] Cf. 346 b 23 ff., 359 b 34 ff.

μένης πρὸς τὸ ἔσχατον πέρας (ᾗ γὰρ ἐκλείπει τὸ
θερμὸν διακρινόμενον εἰς τὸν ἄνω τόπον, ταύτῃ
πυκνοτέραν καὶ ψυχροτέραν ἀναγκαῖον εἶναι τὴν
20 σύστασιν· διὸ καὶ οἱ κεραυνοὶ καὶ οἱ ἐκνεφίαι καὶ
πάντα τὰ τοιαῦτα φέρεται κάτω, καίτοι πεφυκότος
ἄνω τοῦ θερμοῦ φέρεσθαι παντός· ἀλλ' εἰς τοὐναντίον τῆς πυκνότητος ἀναγκαῖον γίγνεσθαι τὴν
ἔκθλιψιν, οἷον οἱ πυρῆνες οἱ ἐκ τῶν δακτύλων
ἐκπηδῶντες· καὶ γὰρ ταῦτα βάρος ἔχοντα φέρεται
25 πολλάκις ἄνω)· ἡ μὲν οὖν ἐκκρινομένη θερμότης
εἰς τὸν ἄνω διασπείρεται τόπον· ὅση δ' ἐμπερι-
λαμβάνεται τῆς ξηρᾶς ἀναθυμιάσεως ἐν τῇ μεταβολῇ ψυχομένου τοῦ ἀέρος, αὕτη συνιόντων τῶν
νεφῶν ἐκκρίνεται, βίᾳ δὲ φερομένη καὶ προσπίπτουσα τοῖς περιεχομένοις νέφεσι ποιεῖ πληγήν, ἧς
30 ὁ ψόφος καλεῖται βροντή. γίγνεται δ' ἡ πληγὴ
τὸν αὐτὸν τρόπον, ὡς παρεικάσαι μείζονι μικρὸν
πάθος, τῷ ἐν τῇ φλογὶ γιγνομένῳ ψόφῳ, ὃν καλοῦσιν οἱ μὲν τὸν Ἥφαιστον γελᾶν, οἱ δὲ τὴν
Ἑστίαν, οἱ δ' ἀπειλὴν τούτων. γίγνεται δ' ὅταν
ἡ ἀναθυμίασις εἰς τὴν φλόγα συνεστραμμένη φέ-
35 ρηται, ῥηγνυμένων καὶ ξηραινομένων τῶν ξύλων·
οὕτως γὰρ καὶ ἐν τοῖς νέφεσι ἡ γιγνομένη τοῦ
πνεύματος ἔκκρισις πρὸς τὴν πυκνότητα τῶν νεφῶν
369 b ἐμπίπτουσα ποιεῖ τὴν βροντήν. παντοδαποὶ δὲ
ψόφοι διὰ τὴν ἀνωμαλίαν τε γίγνονται τῶν νεφῶν
καὶ διὰ τὰς μεταξὺ κοιλίας, ᾗ τὸ συνεχὲς ἐκλείπει
τῆς πυκνότητος.

Ἡ μὲν οὖν βροντὴ τοῦτ' ἔστι, καὶ γίγνεται διὰ
5 ταύτην τὴν αἰτίαν· τὸ δὲ πνεῦμα τὸ ἐκθλιβόμενον
τὰ πολλὰ μὲν ἐκπυροῦται λεπτῇ καὶ ἀσθενεῖ πυρώσει, καὶ τοῦτ' ἔστιν ἣν καλοῦμεν ἀστραπήν, ᾗ ἂν

is thicker towards their farther limit. (Condensation must be denser and colder where the heat gives out as it radiates into the upper region. This is the reason why thunderbolts and hurricanes and all such phenomena move downwards ; for although all heat naturally rises, they must be projected away from the dense formation. Analogously, when we make fruit stones jump from between our fingers, they often move upwards in spite of their weight.) Heat[a] when radiated disperses into the upper region. But any of the dry exhalation that gets trapped when the air is in process of cooling is forcibly ejected as the clouds condense and in its course strikes the surrounding clouds, and the noise caused by the impact is what we call thunder. The impact is produced in the same way (to compare small things with great) as the noise you get in a flame, which some people call Hephaestus's or Hestia's laugh, some their threat. This noise occurs when the exhalation is hurled bodily against the flame as the logs crack and dry ; similarly the windy exhalation in the clouds produces thunder when it strikes a dense cloud formation. Different kinds of sound are produced because of the lack of uniformity in the clouds and because hollows occur where their density is not continuous.

This, then, is what thunder is and this is its cause. As a rule, the ejected wind burns with a fine and gentle fire, and it is then what we call lightning,

Lightning due to the same cause.

---

[a] *i.e.* the dry, warm exhalation.

ὥσπερ ἐκπῖπτον τὸ πνεῦμα χρωματισθὲν ὀφθῇ.
γίγνεται δὲ μετὰ τὴν πληγὴν καὶ ὕστερον τῆς
βροντῆς· ἀλλὰ φαίνεται πρότερον διὰ τὸ τὴν ὄψιν
10 προτερεῖν τῆς ἀκοῆς. δηλοῖ. δ' ἐπὶ τῆς εἰρεσίας
τῶν τριήρων· ἤδη γὰρ ἀναφερόντων πάλιν τὰς κώ-
πας ὁ πρῶτος ἀφικνεῖται ψόφος τῆς κωπηλασίας.

Καίτοι τινὲς λέγουσιν ὡς ἐν τοῖς νέφεσιν ἐγγίγνεται πῦρ· τοῦτο δ' Ἐμπεδοκλῆς μέν φησιν εἶναι
τὸ ἐμπεριλαμβανόμενον τῶν τοῦ ἡλίου ἀκτίνων,
15 Ἀναξαγόρας δὲ τοῦ ἄνωθεν αἰθέρος, ὃ δὴ ἐκεῖνος
καλεῖ πῦρ κατενεχθὲν ἄνωθεν κάτω. τὴν μὲν οὖν
διάλαμψιν ἀστραπὴν εἶναι τὴν τούτου τοῦ πυρός,
τὸν δὲ ψόφον ἐναποσβεννυμένου καὶ τὴν σίξιν βροντήν, ὡς καθάπερ φαίνεται καὶ γιγνόμενον οὕτως
καὶ πρότερον τὴν ἀστραπὴν οὖσαν τῆς βροντῆς.

Ἄλογος δὲ καὶ ἡ τοῦ πυρὸς ἐμπερίληψις, ἀμφο-
20 τέρως μέν, μᾶλλον δ' ἡ κατάσπασις τοῦ ἄνωθεν
αἰθέρος. τοῦ τε γὰρ κάτω φέρεσθαι τὸ πεφυκὸς
ἄνω δεῖ λέγεσθαι τὴν αἰτίαν, καὶ διὰ τί ποτε τοῦτο
γίγνεται κατὰ τὸν οὐρανὸν ὅταν ἐπινέφελον ᾖ μόνον,
ἀλλ' οὐ συνεχῶς οὕτως· αἰθρίας δὲ οὔσης οὐ γίγνεται. τοῦτο γὰρ παντάπασιν ἔοικεν εἰρῆσθαι
25 προχείρως. ὁμοίως δὲ καὶ τὸ τὴν ἀπὸ τῶν ἀκτίνων
θερμότητα φάναι τὴν ἀπολαμβανομένην ἐν τοῖς
νέφεσιν εἶναι τούτων αἰτίαν οὐ πιθανόν· καὶ γὰρ
οὗτος ὁ λόγος ἀπραγμόνως εἴρηται λίαν· ἀποκεκριμένον τε γὰρ ἀναγκαῖον εἶναι τὸ αἴτιον ἀεὶ καὶ
ὡρισμένον, τό τε τῆς βροντῆς καὶ τῆς ἀστραπῆς

which occurs when the falling wind appears to us as it were coloured. Lightning is produced after the impact and so later than thunder, but appears to us to precede it because we see the flash before we hear the noise. You can see this by watching the rowing of a trireme ; for the oars are already drawing back again when the sound of the stroke which they have made first reaches us.

Some, however, say that there is fire in the clouds. Views of This Empedocles [a] supposes to be some of the sun's Empedocle and Anaxa rays trapped in the clouds, Anaxagoras [b] to be a part goras of the upper aether which he calls fire and which has stated, descended into the lower atmosphere. Lightning they then suppose to be this fire flashing through the clouds, thunder the noise of it hissing when quenched ; so the apparent order of the two is the real order and lightning precedes thunder.

The enclosure of the fire is difficult to account for and criti- on both views. The difficulty is greater on the view cized. that it is drawn down from the upper aether. For we should be told the reason for the downward move- ment of something whose natural movement is up- wards, and further why this happens only when the sky is cloudy and not all the time, since it does not happen in clear weather. The theory seems alto- gether too hasty. It is, however, equally unconvincing to say that the cause is the heat of the sun's rays cut off in the clouds, and this theory too must be pro- nounced to be ill-considered. For there must be a separate and distinct cause of the occurrence of each phenomenon, whether thunder or lightning or any-

[a] Diels 31 A 62.
[b] Diels 59 A 1 (9), 42 (11), 84 : *cf.* 339 b 21 (Book I. ch. 3) for Anaxagoras on the aether.

369 b

30 καὶ τῶν ἄλλων τῶν τοιούτων, καὶ οὕτω γίγνεσθαι.
τοῦτο δὲ διαφέρει πλεῖστον· ὅμοιον γὰρ κἂν εἴ τις
οἴοιτο τὸ ὕδωρ καὶ τὴν χιόνα καὶ τὴν χάλαζαν
ἐνυπάρχοντα πρότερον ὕστερον ἐκκρίνεσθαι καὶ
μὴ γίγνεσθαι, οἷον ὑπὸ χεῖρα ποιούσης ἀεὶ τῆς
συγκρίσεως ἕκαστον αὐτῶν· ὡσαύτως γὰρ ἐκεῖνά
35 τε συγκρίσεις καὶ ταῦτα διακρίσεις ὑποληπτέον
εἶναι, ὥστ' εἰ θάτερα τούτων μὴ γίγνεται ἀλλ' ἔστι,
370 a περὶ ἀμφοτέρων ὁ αὐτὸς ἁρμόσει λόγος. τὴν τ'
ἐναπόληψιν τί ἂν ἀλλοιότερον λέγοι τις ἢ καθάπερ
ἐν τοῖς πυκνοτέροις; καὶ γὰρ τὸ ὕδωρ ὑπὸ τοῦ
ἡλίου καὶ τοῦ πυρὸς γίγνεται θερμόν· ἀλλ' ὅμως
ὅταν πάλιν συνίῃ καὶ ψύχηται τὸ ὕδωρ πηγνύμενον,
5 οὐδεμίαν συμβαίνει γίγνεσθαι τοιαύτην ἔκπτωσιν
οἵαν ἐκεῖνοι λέγουσιν· καίτοι[1] γ' ἐχρῆν κατὰ λόγον
τοῦ μεγέθους. τὴν[2] δὲ ζέσιν ποιεῖν τὸ ἐγγιγνό-
μενον πνεῦμα ὑπὸ τοῦ πυρός, ἣν οὔτε δυνατὸν
ἐνυπάρχειν πρότερον, οὔτ' ἐκεῖνοι τὸν ψόφον ζέσιν
ποιοῦσιν ἀλλὰ σίξιν· ἔστι δὲ καὶ ἡ σίξις μικρὰ
10 ζέσις· ᾗ γὰρ τὸ προσπῖπτον κρατεῖ σβεννύμενον,
ταύτῃ ζέον ποιεῖ τὸν ψόφον.

Εἰσὶ δέ τινες οἳ τὴν ἀστραπήν, ὥσπερ καὶ
Κλείδημος, οὐκ εἶναί φασιν ἀλλὰ φαίνεσθαι, παρει-
κάζοντες ὡς τὸ πάθος ὅμοιον ὂν καὶ ὅταν τὴν
θάλατταν τις ῥάβδῳ τύπτῃ· φαίνεται γὰρ τὸ ὕδωρ
ἀποστίλβον τῆς νυκτός· οὕτως ἐν τῇ νεφέλῃ ῥαπι-

---

[1] λέγουσι. καίτοι Fobes.

[2] μεγέθους. τὴν interpunxit O.T.: δὲ E $\mathfrak{W}_1$ F$_1$ O.T., om.
Fobes.

---

[a] I have followed the O.T. readings in ll. 5, 6, though
Fobes's text is that which Alex. had. On the readings I have
adopted Aristotle seems to be making two points in 370 a 1-10:

228

thing else. But the cause proposed is far from ful-
filling this requirement. It is rather as if one supposed that water and snow and hail emerged ready-
made, and did not have to be formed because the
atmosphere has a stock ready to hand for each occasion. For we must suppose that the same is true of
products of condensation, like water, snow and hail,
and of products of ejection like thunder and lightning;
so that if it is true of either that they are not formed
but exist ready made, the same argument will apply
to both. Again, how are we to say that interception
by cloud differs from interception by denser bodies ?
For water too is warmed by the sun and by fire. Yet
when it contracts again and is cooled still further and
freezes there is no ejection such as they describe,
though on their theory there should be to a duly pro-
portionate extent. And boiling is caused by the wind
produced in water by fire and cannot exist in the
water beforehand ; and though they do not call the
noise boiling but hissing, yet hissing is boiling in
miniature (for when the fire on impact is quenched
yet masters the moisture, it boils and causes the
noise).[a]

There are some, for instance Cleidemus,[b] who say
that lightning has no objective existence but is an
appearance only. They compare it to the visual
experience one has when the sea is struck with a
stick at night and the water seems to flash, and say

View of
Cleidemus
and others
stated and
criticized.

(1) Fire ought also to be intercepted by water when heated and
a noise analogous to lightning therefore be produced when it
is cooled. (2) We know that boiling is not produced by fire
already in water ; yet hissing, to which thunder is compared,
is merely boiling in miniature (and so hissing cannot be
produced by fire already in water either).

  [b] Diels 62. 1.

370 a

15 ζομένου τοῦ ὑγροῦ τὴν φάντασιν τῆς λαμπρότητος
εἶναι τὴν ἀστραπήν. οὗτοι μὲν οὖν οὔπω συνήθεις
ἦσαν ταῖς περὶ τῆς ἀνακλάσεως δόξαις, ὅπερ αἴτιον
δοκεῖ τοῦ τοιούτου πάθους εἶναι· φαίνεται γὰρ τὸ
ὕδωρ στίλβειν τυπτόμενον ἀνακλωμένης ἀπ' αὐτοῦ
τῆς ὄψεως πρός τι τῶν λαμπρῶν. διὸ καὶ γί-
20 γνεται μᾶλλον τοῦτο νύκτωρ· τῆς γὰρ ἡμέρας οὐ
φαίνεται διὰ τὸ πλέον ὂν τὸ φέγγος τὸ τῆς ἡμέρας
ἀφανίζειν.

Τὰ μὲν οὖν λεγόμενα περὶ βροντῆς τε καὶ ἀστραπῆς παρὰ τῶν ἄλλων ταῦτ' ἐστί, τῶν μὲν ὅτι
ἀνάκλασις ἡ ἀστραπή, τῶν δ' ὅτι πυρὸς μὲν ἡ
ἀστραπὴ διάλαμψις, ἡ δὲ βροντὴ σβέσις, οὐκ ἐγγι-
25 γνομένου παρ' ἕκαστον πάθος τοῦ πυρὸς ἀλλ' ἐνυπάρχοντος. ἡμεῖς δέ φαμεν τὴν αὐτὴν εἶναι φύσιν
ἐπὶ μὲν τῆς γῆς ἄνεμον, ἐν δὲ τῇ γῇ σεισμόν, ἐν
δὲ τοῖς νέφεσι βροντήν· πάντα γὰρ εἶναι ταῦτα τὴν
οὐσίαν ταὐτόν, ἀναθυμίασιν ξηράν, ἣ ῥέουσα μέν
πως ἄνεμός ἐστιν, ὡδὶ δὲ ποιεῖ τοὺς σεισμούς, ἐν
30 δὲ τοῖς νέφεσι μεταβάλλουσι[1] ἐκκρινομένη,[2] συνιόντων καὶ συγκρινομένων αὐτῶν εἰς ὕδωρ, βροντάς
τε καὶ ἀστραπὰς καὶ πρὸς τούτοις τἆλλα τὰ τῆς
αὐτῆς φύσεως τούτοις ὄντα. καὶ περὶ μὲν βροντῆς
εἴρηται καὶ ἀστραπῆς.

---

[1] μεταβάλλουσι ci. Thurot : μεταβάλλουσα Fobes codd. :
om. J F 𝔐.
[2] ἐκκρινομένη E 𝔚 (Ap) : διακρινομένη Fobes.

that lightning is a similar appearance of brightness produced when the moisture in the cloud is struck. These people had no acquaintance with theories of reflection, which is now generally recognized as the cause of this kind of phenomenon. The water seems to flash when struck because our line of vision is reflected from it to some bright object. This happens more often at night, for the greater brightness of the daylight prevents it being observed.

These are the views held by others about thunder Conclusion. and lightning : some think lightning is a reflection, others that lightning is fire flashing through the clouds, thunder the noise of its quenching, and that the fire does not come into being on each occasion but exists already. Our own view is that the same natural substance causes wind on the earth's surface, earthquakes beneath it, and thunder in the clouds ; for all these have the same substance, the dry exhalation. If it flows in one way it is wind, in another it causes earthquakes ; and when the clouds change in the process of contracting and condensing into water, it is ejected and causes thunder and lightning, and all other phenomena of the same nature. So much for thunder and lightning.

Γ

CHAPTER I

ARGUMENT

Hurricanes, typhoons, firewinds and thunderbolts. These are all products of the dry exhalation (just as the rain is the moist exhalation) ; thunder and lightning of small quantities, hurricanes of large (370 b 3-17). When the exhalation or wind meets resistance an eddy is formed, and the result is a

370 b 3 Περὶ δὲ τῶν ὑπολοίπων εἴπωμεν ἔργων τῆς ἐκκρίσεως ταύτης, τὸν ὑφηγημένον ἤδη τρόπον λέγοντες.

5 Τὸ γὰρ πνεῦμα τοῦτο ἐκκρινόμενον κατὰ μικρὰ μὲν καὶ σποράδην διαχεόμενον καὶ πολλάκις γιγνόμενον καὶ διαπνέον καὶ λεπτομερέστερον ὂν βροντὰς ποιεῖ καὶ ἀστραπάς· ἂν δ᾽ ἀθρόον καὶ πυκνότερον, ἧττον δ᾽ ἐκκριθῇ λεπτόν, ἐκνεφίας ἄνεμος γίγνεται· διὸ καὶ βίαιος (τὸ γὰρ τάχος τῆς ἐκκρίσεως ποιεῖ 10 τὴν ἰσχύν).

Ὅταν μὲν οὖν σ·νακολουθήσῃ πολλὴ καὶ συνεχὴς ἔκκρισις, τὸν αὐτὸν γίγνεται τρόπον ὥσπερ ὅταν πάλιν εἰς τοὐναντίον ὁρμήσῃ· τότε γὰρ ὑετὸς καὶ ὕδατος γίγνεται πλῆθος. ὑπάρχει μὲν οὖν ἄμφω

BOOK III

CHAPTER I

LET us deal now with the remaining effects of this process of exhalation, proceeding on the method we have before adopted.

Thunder, lightning and hurricanes the products of exhalation.

The windy exhalation causes thunder and lightning when it is produced in small quantities, widely dispersed, and at frequent intervals, and when it spreads quickly and is of extreme rarity. But when it is produced in a compact mass and is denser, the result is a hurricane, which owes its violence to the force which the speed of its separation gives it.

When there is an abundant and constant flow of exhalation the process is similar to the opposite process which produces rain and large quantities of water. Both possibilities are latent in the material,[a]

[a] Alex. (134. 15) thinks the " material " is cloud, which contains exhalations of both kinds, *cf.* 358 a 21 : but so also does air, *cf.* 340 b 14-32, 341 b 6.

370 b

δυνάμει ταῦτα κατὰ τὴν ὕλην· ὅταν δὲ ἀρχὴ γένηται
15 τῆς δυνάμεως ὁποτερασοῦν, ἀκολουθεῖ συγκρινό-
μενον ἐκ τῆς ὕλης ὁποτέρου ἂν ᾖ πλῆθος ἐνυπάρχον
πλέον, καὶ γίγνεται τὸ μὲν ὄμβρος, τὸ δὲ τῆς
ἑτέρας ἀναθυμιάσεως ἐκνεφίας.

Ὅταν δὲ τὸ ἐκκρινόμενον πνεῦμα τὸ ἐν τῷ νέφει
ἑτέρῳ ἀντιτυπήσῃ οὕτως ὥσπερ ὅταν ἐξ εὐρέος εἰς
στενὸν βιάζηται ὁ ἄνεμος ἐν πύλαις ἢ ὁδοῖς (συμ-
20 βαίνει γὰρ πολλάκις ἐν τοῖς τοιούτοις ἀπωσθέντος
τοῦ πρώτου μορίου τοῦ ῥέοντος σώματος διὰ τὸ
μὴ ὑπείκειν, ἢ διὰ στενότητα ἢ διὰ τὸ ἀντιπνεῖν,
κύκλον καὶ δίνην γίγνεσθαι τοῦ πνεύματος· τὸ μὲν
γὰρ εἰς τὸ πρόσθεν κωλύει προϊέναι, τὸ δ' ὄπισθεν
ἐπωθεῖ, ὥστε ἀναγκάζεται εἰς τὸ πλάγιον, ᾗ οὐ
25 κωλύεται, φέρεσθαι, καὶ οὕτως ἀεὶ τὸ ἐχόμενον,
ἕως ἂν ἓν γένηται, τοῦτο δ' ἐστὶ κύκλος· οὗ γὰρ
μία φορὰ σχήματος, τοῦτο καὶ αὐτὸ ἀνάγκη ἓν
εἶναι)· ἐπί τε τῆς γῆς οὖν διὰ ταῦτα γίγνονται οἱ
δῖνοι, καὶ ἐν τοῖς νέφεσιν ὁμοίως κατὰ τὴν ἀρχήν,
πλὴν ὅτι, ὥσπερ, ὅταν ἐκνεφίας γίγνηται, ἀεὶ τοῦ
30 νέφους[1] ἐκκρίνεται καὶ γίγνεται συνεχὴς ἄνεμος,
οὕτως ἐνταῦθα ἀεὶ τὸ ⟨νέφος⟩[2] συνεχὲς ἀκολουθεῖ
[τοῦ νέφους][3]· διὰ δὲ πυκνότητα οὐ δυνάμενον ἐκκριθῆναι τὸ πνεῦμα ἐκ τοῦ νέφους στρέφεται μὲν
κύκλῳ τὸ πρῶτον διὰ τὴν εἰρημένην αἰτίαν, κάτω
371 a δὲ φέρεται διὰ τὸ ἀεὶ τὰ νέφη πυκνοῦσθαι, ᾗ
ἐκπίπτει τὸ θερμόν. καλεῖται δ', ἂν ἀχρωμάτιστον

---

[1] τοῦ νέφους 𝔅 var. H.corr. m. 1 𝔚 Ap (ut videtur) O.T. : τὸ
νέφος Fobes cett.
[2] νέφος ci. Thurot.
[3] τοῦ νέφους del. Thurot.

---

[a] The text of ll. 28-31 (πλὴν ὅτι . . . νέφους) and the mean-

and when an impulse is given which may lead to the development of either, the one of which there is the greater quantity latent in the material is forthwith formed from it, and either rain, or, if it is the other exhalation that predominates, a hurricane is produced.

When the wind produced in the cloud runs against Whirlwinds. another the result is similar to that produced when the wind is forced from a wide into a narrow place in a gateway or road. In such circumstances the first part of the stream is thrust aside by the resistance either of the narrow entrance or of the contrary wind and as a result forms a circular eddy of wind. For its forward part prevents it from going forward, while its hinder part pushes it from behind, and so it is forced to flow sideways where there is no resistance. This happens to each succeeding part of the stream, till finally it forms a single body whose shape is circular ; for any figure that is formed by a single motion must itself be single. This, then, is the cause of wind eddies on the earth, and they start in a similar way in the clouds. There, however, just as when a hurricane is produced, the wind is in continuous process of separation from the cloud, so in a whirlwind the cloud follows the windstream continuously[a] ; and because of the cloud's density the wind is unable to separate itself from it and so is forced round in a circle at first (for the reason given above), and then descends because the clouds always condense where the heat leaves them.[b] The

ing of the passage are uncertain. With the text as printed the point appears to be a comparison of hurricane and whirlwind ; in both these is a constant production of wind from cloud, but in the whirlwind the cloud *follows* the wind. This comparison is incidental to the main comparison in 370 b 17— 371 a 2 of the wind eddy on land and the wind eddy in the air.

[b] *Cf.* 369 a 16.

371 a

ἦ, τοῦτο τὸ πάθος τυφῶν ἄνεμος, ὧν οἷον[1] ἐκνεφίας
ἄπεπτος. βορείοις δ' οὐ γίγνεται τυφῶν, οὐδὲ
νιφετῶν[2] ὄντων ἐκνεφίας, διὰ τὸ πάντα ταῦτ' εἶναι
5 πνεῦμα, τὸ δὲ πνεῦμα ξηρὰν εἶναι καὶ θερμὴν
ἀναθυμίασιν. ὁ οὖν πάγος καὶ τὸ ψῦχος διὰ τὸ
κρατεῖν σβέννυσιν εὐθὺς γιγνομένην ἔτι τὴν ἀρχήν.
ὅτι δὲ κρατεῖ, δῆλον· οὐδὲ γὰρ ἂν ἦν νιφετός, οὐδὲ
βόρεια τὰ ὑγρά· ταῦτα γὰρ συμβαίνει κρατούσης
εἶναι τῆς ψυχρότητος. γίγνεται μὲν οὖν τυφῶν,
10 ὅταν ἐκνεφίας γιγνόμενος μὴ δύνηται ἐκκριθῆναι
τοῦ νέφους· ἔστι δὲ διὰ τὴν ἀντίκρουσιν τῆς δίνης,
ὅταν ἐπὶ γῆν φέρηται ἡ ἕλιξ συγκατάγουσα τὸ
νέφος, οὐ δυναμένη ἀπολυθῆναι. ᾗ δὲ κατ' εὐθυωρίαν ἐκπνεῖ, ταύτῃ τῷ πνεύματι κινεῖ, καὶ τῇ
κύκλῳ κινήσει στρέφει καὶ ἀναφέρει ᾧ ἂν προσπέσῃ
15 βιαζόμενον.

Ὅταν δὲ κατασπώμενον ἐκπυρωθῇ (τοῦτο δ'
ἐστὶν ἐὰν λεπτότερον τὸ πνεῦμα γένηται), καλεῖται
πρηστήρ· συνεκπίμπρησι γὰρ τὸν ἀέρα τῇ πυρώσει
χρωματίζων.

Ἐὰν δ' ἐν αὐτῷ τῷ νέφει πολὺ καὶ λεπτὸν ἐκ-
θλιφθῇ πνεῦμα, τοῦτο γίγνεται κεραυνός, ἐὰν μὲν
20 πάνυ λεπτόν, οὐκ ἐπικάων διὰ λεπτότητα, ὃν οἱ
ποιηταὶ ἀργῆτα καλοῦσιν, ἐὰν δ' ἧττον, ἐπικάων,
ὃν ψολόεντα καλοῦσιν· ὁ μὲν γὰρ διὰ τὴν λεπτότητα
φέρεται, διὰ δὲ τὸ τάχος φθάνει διιὼν πρὶν ἢ ἐκ-
πυρῶσαι καὶ ἐπιδιατρίψας μελᾶναι· ὁ δὲ βραδύτερος
ἔχρωσε μέν, ἔκαυσε δ' οὔ, ἀλλ' ἔφθασε. διὸ καὶ

---

[1] τυφῶν, ἄνεμος ὤν, οἷον Fobes.
[2] νιφετῶν ὄντων E$_{corr.}$ 𝔐 𝔅 F H N Ol : νιπτικῶς ἐχόντων 𝔚 :
aut νιπτικῶς ἐχόντων aut νιπτικῶν ἐχόντων E$_1$: νιπτικῶς ἐχόντων
Fobes.

resulting phenomenon, when colourless, is called a whirlwind, being a kind of unripe hurricane. Whirlwinds do not occur when the wind is in the north, nor hurricanes when there is snow. For all these phenomena are wind, and wind is dry and warm exhalation ; frost and cold therefore master and smother this at the outset. It is clear that they do master it, otherwise there would be no snow nor would rains come from the north, which can only happen when the cold has the mastery. A whirlwind thus arises when a hurricane that has been produced is unable to free itself from the cloud : it is caused by the resistance of the eddy, and occurs when the spiral sinks to the earth and carries with it the cloud from which it is unable to free itself. Its blast overturns anything that lies in its path, and its circular motion whirls away and carries off by force anything it meets.

When the wind that is drawn down catches fire— Firewinds. which happens when it is finer in texture—it is called a firewind ; for its conflagration sets on fire and so colours the neighbouring air.

If a large quantity of wind of fine texture is squeezed Thunder-out in the cloud itself, the result is a thunderbolt ; bolts. if the wind is very fine in texture and in consequence does not scorch, the bolt is of the kind called by the poets gleaming ; if the wind is less fine textured and so scorches, the bolt is of the kind they call smoky. For the one kind moves rapidly [a] because of its fineness, and because of its rapidity passes through the object before it can burn it or remain long enough to blacken it ; while the other kind, moving more slowly, blackens the object but still moves too fast to burn

[a] The sense demands a complement to φέρεται : Thurot suggests διὰ τάχους.

371 a

25 τὰ μὲν ἀντιτυπήσαντα πάσχει τι, τὰ δὲ μὴ οὐδέν,
οἷον ἀσπίδος ἤδη τὸ μὲν χάλκωμα ἐτάκη, τὸ δὲ
ξύλον οὐδὲν ἔπαθεν· διὰ γὰρ μανότητα ἔφθασε τὸ
πνεῦμα διηθηθέν· καὶ διελθὸν[1] καὶ δι᾽ ἱματίων
ὁμοίως οὐ κατέκαυσεν, ἀλλ᾽ οἷον τρῦχος ἐποίησεν.
30 Ὥστε ὅτι γε πνεῦμα ταῦτα πάντα, δῆλον καὶ ἐκ
τῶν τοιούτων. ἔστι δ᾽ ἐνίοτε καὶ τοῖς ὄμμασιν
θεωρεῖν, οἷον καὶ νῦν ἐθεωροῦμεν περὶ τὸν ἐν
Ἐφέσῳ ναὸν καόμενον· πολλαχῇ γὰρ ἡ φλὸξ ἐφέρετο συνεχής, ἀποσπωμένη χωρίς. ὅτι μὲν γὰρ
371 b ὅ τε καπνὸς πνεῦμα καὶ κάεται ὁ καπνός, φανερόν,
καὶ εἴρηται ἐν ἑτέροις πρότερον· ὅταν δ᾽ ἀθρόον
χωρῇ, τότε φανερῶς δοκεῖ πνεῦμα εἶναι. ὅπερ
οὖν ἐν ταῖς μικραῖς πυρκαϊαῖς φαίνεται, τοῦτο καὶ
τότε πολλῆς ὕλης καομένης ἐγίγνετο πολλῷ ἰσχυ-
5 ρότερον. ῥηγνυμένων οὖν τῶν ξύλων, ὅθεν ἡ ἀρχὴ
τοῦ πνεύματος ἦν, πολὺ ἐχώρει ἀθρόον, ᾗ ἐξέπνει,
καὶ ἐφέρετο ἄνω πεπυρωμένον. ὥστ᾽ ἐφαίνετο ἡ
φλὸξ φέρεσθαι καὶ εἰσπίπτειν εἰς τὰς οἰκίας. ἀεὶ
γὰρ οἴεσθαι δεῖ ἐπακολουθεῖν τοῖς κεραυνοῖς πνεῦμα
καὶ προϊέναι· ἀλλ᾽ οὐχ ὁρᾶται, διὰ τὸ ἀχρωμά-
10 τιστον εἶναι. διὸ καὶ ᾗ μέλλει πατάξειν, κινεῖται
πρὶν πληγῆναι, ἅτε πρότερον προσπιπτούσης τῆς
ἀρχῆς τοῦ πνεύματος. καὶ αἱ βρονταὶ δὲ διιστᾶσιν
οὐ τῷ ψόφῳ, ἀλλ᾽ ὅτι ἅμα συνεκκρίνεται τὸ τὴν
πληγὴν ποιῆσαν καὶ τὸν ψόφον πνεῦμα· ὃ ἐὰν
πατάξῃ, διέστησεν, ἐπέκαυσε δ᾽ οὔ.

---

[1] διηθηθὲν καὶ διελθόν· Fobes : διηθηθέν· καὶ διελθὸν Thurot
O.T.

---

[a] So Alex. 138. 3.
[b] 356 B.C.
[c] 341 b 21, cf. 388 a 2 ; De Gen. et Corr. 331 b 25.

it. So objects which offer resistance suffer, those which offer none do not—for instance, the bronze head of a spear has been known to melt while the wooden handle was unaffected, the reason being that the wind percolated through the wood without affecting it because of the rareness of its texture. Similarly it has passed through garments without burning them, but leaving them threadbare.[a]

Such instances are in themselves conclusive evidence that all these phenomena are due to wind. But sometimes we get ocular evidence too, the burning of the temple of Ephesus [b] being a recent example; for it was observed then that sheets of flame were torn off from the main conflagration and carried in all directions. It is evident, and we have already demonstrated elsewhere,[c] that smoke is wind and that smoke burns; and when the flame moves in a body, then it can be seen clearly that it is wind. Thus what is obvious in small conflagrations took place on that occasion with considerably more violence owing to the quantity of material that was being burned. For when the beams in which the wind originated cracked, it issued in a body at the place where it burst out and went up in flames. So the flame was seen moving through the air and falling on the neighbouring houses. We must, indeed, suppose that wind always follows and precedes thunderbolts, but remains invisible because colourless. So a place that is going to be struck moves before the blow falls, because the wind in which the bolt originates strikes the object first. Thunder also splits things, not by its noise, but because a single wind is produced which deals the blow and causes the noise; this if it strikes an object splits it but does not burn it.

371 b

15 Περὶ μὲν οὖν βροντῆς καὶ ἀστραπῆς καὶ ἐκνεφίου,
ἔτι δὲ πρηστήρων τε καὶ τυφώνων καὶ κεραυνῶν,
εἴρηται, καὶ ὅτι ταὐτὸ πάντα, καὶ τίς ἡ διαφορὰ
πάντων αὐτῶν.

CHAPTER II

ARGUMENT

*Haloes, rainbows, mock suns and rods are our next sub-
ject : and the characteristics of each must first be described
(371 b 18-22). Haloes (371 b 22-26). Rainbows (371 b
26—372 a 10). Mock suns and rods (372 a 10-16). All are*

371 b 18 Περὶ δὲ ἅλω καὶ ἴριδος, τί τε ἑκάτερον καὶ διὰ
τίν᾽ αἰτίαν γίγνεται, λέγωμεν, καὶ περὶ παρηλίων
20 καὶ ῥάβδων· καὶ γὰρ ταῦτα γίγνεται πάντα διὰ τὰς
αὐτὰς αἰτίας ἀλλήλοις.

Πρῶτον δὲ δεῖ λαβεῖν τὰ πάθη καὶ τὰ συμβαίνοντα περὶ ἕκαστον αὐτῶν.

Τῆς μὲν οὖν ἅλω φαίνεται πολλάκις κύκλος ὅλος,
καὶ γίγνεται περὶ ἥλιον καὶ σελήνην καὶ περὶ τὰ
25 λαμπρὰ τῶν ἄστρων, ἔτι δ᾽ οὐδὲν ἧττον νυκτὸς ἢ
ἡμέρας καὶ περὶ μεσημβρίαν ἢ δείλην· ἕωθεν δ᾽
ἐλαττονάκις καὶ περὶ δύσιν.

Τῆς δ᾽ ἴριδος οὐδέποτε γίγνεται κύκλος οὐδὲ
μεῖζον ἡμικυκλίου τμῆμα· καὶ δύνοντος μὲν καὶ
ἀνατέλλοντος ἐλαχίστου μὲν κύκλου, μεγίστη δ᾽ ἡ
ἁψίς, αἰρομένου δὲ μᾶλλον κύκλου μὲν μείζονος,
30 ἐλάττων δ᾽ ἡ ἁψίς· καὶ μετὰ μὲν τὴν μετοπωρινὴν
ἰσημερίαν, ἐν ταῖς βραχυτέραις ἡμέραις, πᾶσαν
ὥραν γίγνεται τῆς ἡμέρας, ἐν δὲ ταῖς θεριναῖς οὐ
γίγνεται περὶ μεσημβρίαν. οὐδὲ δὴ δυοῖν πλείους

240

This concludes our treatment of thunder, lightning Conclusion. and hurricanes, of firewinds, whirlwinds and thunderbolts ; we have shown that they are all materially the same and described the differences between them.

CHAPTER II

ARGUMENT (*continued*)

caused by reflection (372 a 16-21). *Rainbows occur both by day and night* (372 a 21-29). *We must refer to the science of optics for the explanation of reflections. Reflecting surfaces sometimes reflect shape, sometimes colour only* (372 a 29–b 11).

WE must now deal with haloes, rainbows, mock suns and rods, explaining what they are and what are their causes ; for the same causes account for all of them.

First we must describe what the actual characteristics of each of these phenomena are.

The complete circle of a halo is often visible, round Halo. the sun and moon and round bright stars, and as frequently by night as by day, that is, at midday or in the afternoon ; for they occur more rarely at dawn and sunset.

The rainbow never forms a complete circle, nor a Rainbow. segment of a circle larger than a semicircle. At sunrise and sunset the circle is smallest and the segment largest ; when the sun is higher the circle is larger, the segment smaller.[a] After the autumn equinox, during the shorter days, it occurs at all hours of the day ; but in summer it does not occur round about midday. Nor do more than two rainbows occur

---

[a] The size of the circle does not in fact vary.

ARISTOTLE

ἴριδες οὐ γίγνονται ἅμα. τούτων δὲ τρίχρως μὲν
ἑκατέρα, καὶ τὰ χρώματα ταὐτὰ καὶ ἴσα τὸν
ἀριθμὸν ἔχουσιν ἀλλήλαις, ἀμυδρότερα δ' ἐν τῇ
ἐκτὸς καὶ ἐξ ἐναντίας κείμενα κατὰ τὴν θέσιν· ἡ
μὲν γὰρ ἐντὸς τὴν πρώτην ἔχει περιφέρειαν τὴν
μεγίστην φοινικίαν, ἡ δ' ἔξωθεν τὴν ἐλαχίστην μὲν
5 ἐγγύτατα δὲ πρὸς ταύτην, καὶ τὰς ἄλλας ἀνάλογον.
ἔστι δὲ τὰ χρώματα ταῦτα ἅπερ μόνα σχεδὸν οὐ
δύνανται ποιεῖν οἱ γραφεῖς· ἔνια γὰρ αὐτοὶ κεραν-
νύουσι, τὸ δὲ φοινικοῦν καὶ πράσινον καὶ ἁλουργὸν
οὐ γίγνεται κεραννύμενον· ἡ δὲ ἶρις ταῦτ' ἔχει τὰ
10 χρώματα. τὸ δὲ μεταξὺ τοῦ φοινικοῦ καὶ πρασίνου φαίνεται πολλάκις ξανθόν.

Παρήλιοι δὲ καὶ ῥάβδοι γίγνονται ἐκ πλαγίας
αἰεὶ καὶ οὔτ' ἄνωθεν οὔτε πρὸς τῆς γῆς οὔτ' ἐξ
ἐναντίας, οὐδὲ δὴ νύκτωρ, ἀλλ' ἀεὶ περὶ τὸν ἥλιον,
ἔτι δὲ ἢ αἰρομένου ἢ καταφερομένου· τὰ πλεῖστα
δὲ πρὸς δυσμάς· μεσουρανοῦντος δὲ σπάνιον εἴ τι
15 γέγονεν, οἷον ἐν Βοσπόρῳ ποτὲ συνέπεσε· δι' ὅλης
γὰρ τῆς ἡμέρας συνανασχόντες δύο παρήλιοι διε-
τέλεσαν μέχρι δυσμῶν.

Τὰ μὲν οὖν περὶ ἕκαστον αὐτῶν συμβαίνοντα
ταῦτ' ἐστίν· τὸ δ' αἴτιον οὕτων ἁπάντων ταὐτό·
πάντα γὰρ ἀνάκλασις ταῦτ' ἐστί. διαφέρουσι δὲ
τοῖς τρόποις καὶ ἀφ' ὧν, καὶ ὡς συμβαίνει γί-

ᵃ The colours of the rainbow are six : red, orange, yellow,
green, blue, violet. Aristotle reduces them to three by grouping red-orange-yellow, and blue-violet. But he notes that
a yellow band (grouping orange-yellow) is often seen between
the red and the green. The painters' primary colours are red,
yellow, and blue ; not red, *green*, and blue as Aristotle says.
Green can be produced by mixing yellow and blue, but yellow
cannot be produced by any mixture of red, green and blue.

at the same time. Of two such simultaneous rainbows each is three-coloured, the colours being the same in each and equal in number, but dimmer in the outer bow and placed in the reverse order. For in the inner bow it is the first and largest band that is red, in the outer it is the smallest and closest to the red band of the inner. And the other bands correspond similarly. These colours are almost the only ones that painters cannot manufacture ; for they produce some colours by a mixture of others, but red, green and blue cannot be produced in this way, and these are the colours of the rainbow—though between the red and green band there often appears a yellow one.[a]

Mock suns and rods always appear beside the sun, and not either above or below it or opposite it [b] ; nor of course do they appear at night, but always in the neighbourhood of the sun and either when it is rising or setting, and mostly towards sunset. They rarely if ever occur when the sun is high, though this did happen once in the Bosporus, where two mock suns rose with the sun and continued all day till sunset.

Mock sun, rod.

These, then, are the characteristics of these phenomena. The cause of all is the same, for they are all phenomena of reflection.[c] They differ in the manner of the reflection and in the reflecting surface, and

All due to reflection.

---

[b] *Cf.* 377 b 27 ff.

[c] Here as elsewhere in the *Meteorologica* (*e.g.* Book I. ch. 6, 343 a 2 and note) Aristotle speaks as if our sight were reflected *to* the object and not the object (or rays therefrom) reflected *to* our sight. Alex. (141) connects this with the view that in sight rays are projected from the eye to the object, for which *cf.* Plato, *Timaeus* 45 ʙ ff., a view which Aristotle himself rejects (*De Anima* ii. 7). But so far as the mathematics of the matter are concerned, which is all that is at issue here, it makes (as Alex. also remarks 141. 20) little difference which view is taken of reflection. *Cf.* Ideler ii. pp. 273-274.

372 a

20 γνεσθαι τὴν ἀνάκλασιν πρὸς τὸν ἥλιον ἢ πρὸς ἄλλο
τι τῶν λαμπρῶν.

Καὶ μεθ᾽ ἡμέραν μὲν ἶρις γίγνεται, νύκτωρ δ᾽
ἀπὸ σελήνης, ὡς μὲν οἱ ἀρχαῖοι ᾤοντο, οὐκ ἐγί-
γνετο· τοῦτο δ᾽ ἔπαθον διὰ τὸ σπάνιον· ἐλάνθανε
γὰρ αὐτούς· γίγνεται μὲν γάρ, ὀλιγάκις δὲ γίγνεται.
25 τὸ δ᾽ αἴτιον ὅτι τ᾽ ἐν τῷ σκότει λανθάνει τὰ χρώματα, καὶ ἄλλα πολλὰ δεῖ συμπεσεῖν, καὶ ταῦτα
πάντα ἐν ἡμέρᾳ μιᾷ τοῦ μηνός· ἐν τῇ πανσελήνῳ
γὰρ γενέσθαι ἀνάγκη τὸ μέλλον ἔσεσθαι, καὶ τότε
ἀνατελλούσης ἢ δυνούσης· διόπερ ἐν ἔτεσιν ὑπὲρ
τὰ πεντήκοντα δὶς ἐνετύχομεν μόνον.

30 Ὅτι μὲν οὖν ἡ ὄψις ἀνακλᾶται, ὥσπερ καὶ ἀφ᾽
ὕδατος, οὕτω καὶ ἀπὸ ἀέρος καὶ πάντων τῶν ἐχόντων τὴν ἐπιφάνειαν λείαν, ἐκ τῶν περὶ τὴν ὄψιν
δεικνυμένων δεῖ λαμβάνειν τὴν πίστιν, καὶ διότι
τῶν ἐνόπτρων ἐν ἐνίοις μὲν καὶ τὰ σχήματα ἐμφαίνεται, ἐν ἐνίοις δὲ τὰ χρώματα μόνον· τοιαῦτα δ᾽
372 b ἐστὶν ὅσα μικρὰ τῶν ἐνόπτρων, καὶ μηδεμίαν αἰσθητὴν ἔχει διαίρεσιν· ἐν γὰρ τούτοις τὸ μὲν σχῆμα
ἀδύνατον ἐμφαίνεσθαι (δόξει γὰρ εἶναι διαιρετόν·
πᾶν γὰρ σχῆμα ἅμα δοκεῖ σχῆμά τ᾽ εἶναι καὶ δι-
5 αίρεσιν ἔχειν), ἐπεὶ δ᾽ ἐμφαίνεσθαί τι ἀναγκαῖον,
τοῦτο δὲ ἀδύνατον, λείπεται τὸ χρῶμα μόνον ἐμφαίνεσθαι. τὸ δὲ χρῶμα ὀτὲ μὲν λαμπρὸν φαίνεται
τῶν λαμπρῶν, ὀτὲ δέ, ἢ τῷ μείγνυσθαι τῷ τοῦ
ἐνόπτρου ἢ διὰ τὴν ἀσθένειαν τῆς ὄψεως, ἄλλου
χρώματος ἐμποιεῖ φαντασίαν.

---

[a] " Since divisibility is involved in the notion of figure"
(O.T.).

according as the reflection is to the sun or some other bright object.

The rainbow occurs by day, and also at night, when it is due to the moon, though early thinkers did not think this ever happened. Their opinion was due to the rarity of the phenomenon, which thus escaped their observation : for though it does occur, it only does so rarely. And the reason for this is that the darkness hides the colours, and a conjunction of many other circumstances is necessary, all of which must coincide upon a single day of the month, the day of the full moon. For it is on that day that the phenomenon must occur if it is to occur at all, and occur then only at the moon's rising or setting. So we have only met with two instances of it over a period of more than fifty years. *Rainbows by day and night.*

We must refer to what has been demonstrated by the science of optics as our ground for believing that our vision is reflected from the air and other substances which have a smooth surface, just as it is from water, and to the fact that in some mirrors shapes are reflected, in others colours only. Colours only are reflected in mirrors that are small and incapable of subdivision by our sense of sight. In these shape cannot be reflected. If it could be, it would be capable of subdivision, as all shape has the characteristics both of shape and of divisibility.[a] Since, then, something must necessarily be reflected, but shape cannot be, the only remaining possibility is that colour should be. The colour of bright objects sometimes appears bright in the reflection, but sometimes, either owing to contamination by the colour of the mirror or owing to the feebleness of our sight, produces an appearance of another colour. *Optics provides the explanation.*

245

372 b

Ἔστω δὲ περὶ τούτων ἡμῖν τεθεωρημένον ἐν τοῖς
10 περὶ τὰς αἰσθήσεις δεικνυμένοις· διὸ τὰ μὲν λέγωμεν, τοῖς δ᾽ ὡς ὑπάρχουσι χρησώμεθα αὐτῶν.

CHAPTER III

ARGUMENT

*The shape of the halo. Reflection takes place in certain
conditions of cloud formation, and is a sign of various
weather conditions (372 b 12-34). The circularity of the halo*

372 b 12   Πρῶτον δὲ περὶ τῆς ἅλω τοῦ σχήματος εἴπωμεν,
διότι τε κύκλος γίγνεται, καὶ διότι περὶ τὸν ἥλιον
ἢ τὴν σελήνην, ὁμοίως δὲ καὶ περί τι τῶν ἄλλων
15 ἄστρων· ὁ γὰρ αὐτὸς ἐπὶ πάντων ἁρμόσει λόγος.

Γίγνεται μὲν οὖν ἡ ἀνάκλασις τῆς ὄψεως συνισταμένου τοῦ ἀέρος καὶ τῆς ἀτμίδος εἰς νέφος,
ἐὰν ὁμαλὴς καὶ μικρομερὴς συνισταμένη τύχῃ. διὸ
καὶ σημεῖον ἡ μὲν σύστασις ὕδατός ἐστιν, αἱ μέντοι
διασπάσεις ἢ μαράνσεις, αὗται μὲν εὐδιῶν, αἱ δὲ
20 διασπάσεις πνεύματος. ἐὰν μὲν γὰρ μήτε καταμα-
ρανθῇ μήτε διασπασθῇ, ἀλλ᾽ ἐαθῇ τὴν φύσιν ἀπο-
λαμβάνειν τὴν αὐτῆς, ὕδατος εἰκότως σημεῖόν ἐστι·
δηλοῖ γὰρ ἤδη γίγνεσθαι τοιαύτην τὴν σύστασιν,
ἐξ ἧς τὸ συνεχὲς λαμβανούσης τῆς πυκνώσεως
25 ἀναγκαῖον εἰς ὕδωρ ἐλθεῖν· διὸ καὶ μέλαιναι γί-

---

[a] The rest of this paragraph deals mainly with the halo
as a weather-sign. But Aristotle's wording at the outset is
confusing because σύστασις l. 18, after συνισταμένη in l. 17, at

But let us in these matters accept the results of our investigation of sensation, and mention some points only while taking the rest for granted.

CHAPTER III

ARGUMENT (*continued*)

geometrically explained (372 b 34—373 a 19). Further characteristics of the reflecting cloud (373 a 19-27). Haloes more frequent round the moon than the sun. They also form round the stars (373 a 27-31).

Let us first deal with the shape of the halo and explain why it is round and why it appears round the sun or moon or similarly round one of the other stars. For the same explanation will fit all these cases. The shape of the halo.

The reflection of our vision takes place when the air and vapour are condensed into cloud, if the condensation is uniform and its constituent particles small. This formation [a] is therefore a sign of rain, while if it is broken it is a sign of wind, if it fades, of fine weather. For if it neither fades nor breaks, but is allowed to reach its full development, it is reasonable to regard it as a sign of rain, since it shows that a condensation is taking place of the kind, which, if the condensing process continues, will necessarily lead to rain. And for this reason these haloes are Conditions of reflection : the halo as a weather sign.

first sight seems to refer to the cloud formation and not to the halo. But it seems clear from what he says later (*e.g.* l. 25) that it is of the halo he is thinking : and the parallels quoted by Ideler (ii. p. 277) confirm this. A full halo is a sign of rain, a broken halo of wind, a fading, dim halo of fine weather.

372 b

γνονται τὴν χρόαν αὗται μάλιστα τῶν ἄλλων.
ὅταν δὲ διασπασθῇ, πνεύματος σημεῖον· ἡ γὰρ
διαίρεσις ὑπὸ πνεύματος γέγονεν ἤδη μὲν ὄντος,
οὔπω δὲ παρόντος. σημεῖον δὲ τούτου διότι ἐντεῦθεν γίγνεται ὁ ἄνεμος, ὅθεν ἂν ἡ κυρία γίγνηται
30 διάσπασις. ἀπομαραινομένη δὲ εὐδίας· εἰ γὰρ μὴ
ἔχει πως οὕτως ὁ ἀὴρ ὥστε κρατεῖν τοῦ ἐναπο-
λαμβανομένου θερμοῦ μηδ' ἔρχεσθαι εἰς πύκνωσιν
ὑδατώδη, δῆλον ὡς οὔπω ἡ ἀτμὶς ἀποκέκριται τῆς
ἀναθυμιάσεως [ἀπὸ][1] τῆς ξηρᾶς καὶ πυρώδους·
τοῦτο δὲ εὐδίας αἴτιον.

Πῶς μὲν οὖν ἔχοντος τοῦ ἀέρος γίγνεται ἡ ἀνά-
373 a κλασις, εἴρηται. ἀνακλᾶται δ' ἀπὸ τῆς συνισταμένης ἀχλύος περὶ τὸν ἥλιον ἢ τὴν σελήνην ἡ ὄψις·
διὸ οὐκ ἐξ ἐναντίας ὥσπερ ἶρις φαίνεται. πάντοθεν
δὲ ὁμοίως ἀνακλωμένης ἀναγκαῖον κύκλον εἶναι ἢ
κύκλου μέρος· ἀπὸ γὰρ τοῦ αὐτοῦ σημείου πρὸς
5 τὸ αὐτὸ σημεῖον αἱ ἴσαι κλασθήσονται ἐπὶ κύκλου
γραμμῆς ἀεί. ἔστω γὰρ ἀπὸ τοῦ σημείου ἐφ' ᾧ
τὸ Α πρὸς τὸ Β κεκλασμένη ἥ τε τὸ ΑΓΒ καὶ ἡ τὸ
ΑΖΒ καὶ ἡ τὸ ΑΔΒ· ἴσαι δὲ αὗταί τε αἱ ΑΓ ΑΖ
ΑΔ ἀλλήλαις, καὶ αἱ πρὸς τὸ Β ἀλλήλαις, οἷον αἱ
10 ΓΒ ΖΒ ΔΒ· καὶ ἐπεζεύχθω ἡ ΑΕΒ, ὥστε τὰ τρίγωνα ἴσα· καὶ γὰρ ἐπ' ἴσης τῆς ΑΕΒ. ἤχθωσαν
δὴ κάθετοι ἐπὶ τὴν ΑΕΒ ἐκ τῶν γωνιῶν, ἀπὸ μὲν
τῆς Γ ἡ τὸ ΓΕ, ἀπὸ δὲ τῆς Ζ ἡ τὸ ΖΕ, ἀπὸ δὲ τῆς
Δ ἡ τὸ ΔΕ. ἴσαι δὴ αὗται· ἐν ἴσοις γὰρ τριγώνοις
15 καὶ ἐν ἑνὶ ἐπιπέδῳ πᾶσαι· πρὸς ὀρθὰς γὰρ πᾶσαι
τῇ ΑΕΒ, καὶ ἐφ' ἓν σημεῖον τὸ Ε συνάπτουσι.
κύκλος ἄρα ἔσται ἡ γραφομένη, κέντρον δὲ τὸ Ε.
ἔστι δὴ τὸ μὲν Β ὁ ἥλιος, τὸ δὲ Α ἡ ὄψις, ἡ δὲ περὶ

[1] seclusit Fobes.

248

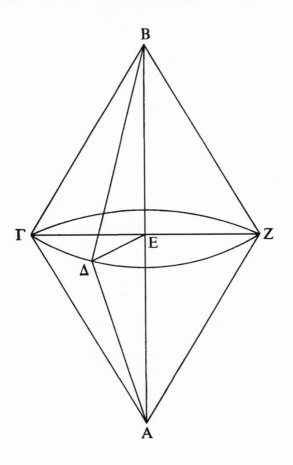

the darkest of all in colour. But when it is broken
it is a sign of wind; for its break up is due to a wind
that is already in being but has not yet arrived. An
indication that this is so is that the wind springs from
the quarter in which the main break occurs. When
it fades it is a sign of fine weather. For if the air is
not yet in a state to overcome the heat contained in
it and to develop into a watery condensation, it is clear
that the vapour has not yet separated from the dry
and fiery exhalation which causes fine weather.

These, then, are the atmospheric conditions in which
reflection takes place. Our vision is reflected from
the mist which condenses round the sun and moon;
which is why a halo does not appear opposite the sun
like a rainbow. And as the reflection is symmetrical
on all sides, the result is bound to be a circle or a
segment of a circle. For when lines drawn from the
same point and to the same point are equal, the points
at which they form an angle will always lie on a
circle.[a] For let the lines AΓB, AZB and AΔB be
drawn from the point A to the point B, each forming
an angle : let the lines AΓ, AZ, AΔ be equal to each
other, and the lines drawn to B, that is ΓB, ZB, ΔB,
also equal to each other. Let the line AEB be drawn
and the triangles so formed will be equal as they
stand on the equal base AEB. Let perpendiculars
be dropped from the angles to AEB, ΓE from Γ, ZE
from Z, ΔE from Δ. These perpendiculars are then
equal, being in equal triangles and in one plane.
For all meet AEB at right angles and at the single
point E. The figure thus drawn will be a circle with
centre E. B is of course the sun, A the eye, and the

Why the halo is circular.

---

[a] Here Aristotle in effect assumes what he is setting out
to prove.

τὸ ΓΖΔ περιφέρεια τὸ νέφος ἀφ' οὗ ἀνακλᾶται ἡ
ὄψις πρὸς τὸν ἥλιον.

Δεῖ δὲ νοεῖν συνεχῆ τὰ ἔνοπτρα· ἀλλὰ διὰ μικρό-
20 τητα ἕκαστον μὲν ἀόρατον, τὸ δ' ἐξ ἁπάντων ἓν
εἶναι δοκεῖ διὰ τὸ ἐφεξῆς. φαίνεται δὲ τὸ μὲν
λευκόν, ὁ ἥλιος, κύκλῳ συνεχῶς ἐν ἑκάστῳ φαινό-
μενος τῶν ἐνόπτρων, καὶ μηδεμίαν ἔχων αἰσθητὴν
διαίρεσιν, πρὸς δὲ τῇ γῇ μᾶλλον διὰ τὸ νηνεμώτερον
25 εἶναι· πνεύματος γὰρ ὄντος οὐκ εἶναι στάσιν φανερόν. παρὰ δὲ τοῦτο μέλαινα ἡ ἐχομένη περιφέρεια, διὰ τὴν ἐκείνης λευκότητα δοκοῦσα εἶναι
μελαντέρα.

Πλεονάκις δὲ γίγνονται αἱ ἅλῳ περὶ τὴν σελήνην
διὰ τὸ τὸν ἥλιον θερμότερον ὄντα θᾶττον διαλύειν
τὰς συστάσεις τοῦ ἀέρος. περὶ δὲ τοὺς ἀστέρας
30 γίγνονται μὲν διὰ τὰς αὐτὰς αἰτίας, οὐ σημειώδεις
δ' ὁμοίως, ὅτι μικρὰς πάμπαν ἐπιδηλοῦσι τὰς
συστάσεις καὶ οὔπω γονίμους.

ᵃ Each particle thus reflecting colour only and not shape :
372 a 32.
ᵇ The O.T. would transpose these words, inserting them
after the next sentence. It is not clear exactly where Aristotle

CHAPTER IV

ARGUMENT

*The physical basis of reflection. Our vision is reflected
from all smooth surfaces. Air reflects when condensed (sometimes even when not condensed) : water reflects still better,
and especially water in process of formation by condensation
from air. Each particle of it forms a mirror, which reflects*

circumference drawn through ΓΖΔ the cloud from which the vision is reflected to the sun.

The reflecting particles must be thought of as being continuous. Each individually is so small as to be invisible, but because they are continuous they appear in aggregate as a single surface. The bright light, that is, the sun, thus appears as a continuous ring, being mirrored in each of the reflecting particles as a point of light indivisible by sense.[a] It appears in closer proximity to the earth because it is calmer there, and if there is a wind the halo cannot maintain its position.[b] Next to the bright ring of the halo is a dark ring, which appears still darker beside the brightness of the halo. *(Character-istics of the reflecting cloud.)*

Haloes round the moon are more frequent than those round the sun because the sun being hotter more quickly dissolves the condensations of the air. They are formed round the stars from the same causes, but are not weather signs in the same way, because they indicate condensations that are insignificant and so not productive of weather changes. *(Haloes round the moon and stars.)*

does suppose that haloes form: *cf.* note on Aristotle's views of the stratification of the atmosphere at end of Book I. ch. 3.

CHAPTER IV

ARGUMENT *(continued)*

colour only, not shape : an agglomeration of particles forms a continuous mirror in which the colours mirrored by the constituent particles appear. So when sun and cloud are suitably related a rainbow is formed (373 a 32–b 32). The rainbow is coloured, the halo not coloured because the rainbow is a reflection from water, the halo from air, and air (being light) cannot reflect colours, water (being dark) can. Examples (373 b 32—374 b 7). The colours of the rainbow are due to the weakening of our sight by reflection. This takes place in three stages : at the first the bright light of the sun, reflected in the dark medium of water, turns red : further weakening of the sight produces green and then blue. These are the

373 a 32 Ἡ δ' ἶρις ὅτι μὲν ἐστιν ἀνάκλασις, εἴρηται πρό-
τερον· ποία δέ τις ἀνάκλασις, καὶ πῶς καὶ διὰ τίν'
αἰτίαν ἕκαστα γίγνεται τῶν συμβαινόντων περὶ
ταύτην, λέγωμεν νῦν.

35 Ἀνακλωμένη μὲν οὖν ἡ ὄψις ἀπὸ πάντων φαί-
373 b νεται τῶν λείων, τούτων δ' ἐστὶν καὶ ἀὴρ καὶ ὕδωρ.
γίγνεται δὲ ἀπὸ μὲν ἀέρος, ὅταν τύχῃ συνιστάμενος·
διὰ δὲ τὴν τῆς ὄψεως ἀσθένειαν πολλάκις καὶ ἄνευ
συστάσεως ποιεῖ ἀνάκλασιν, οἷόν ποτε συνέβαινέ
5 τινι πάθος ἠρέμα καὶ οὐκ ὀξὺ βλέποντι· ἀεὶ γὰρ
εἴδωλον ἐδόκει προηγεῖσθαι βαδίζοντι αὐτῷ, ἐξ
ἐναντίας βλέπον πρὸς αὐτόν. τοῦτο δ' ἔπασχε διὰ
τὸ τὴν ὄψιν ἀνακλᾶσθαι πρὸς αὐτόν· οὕτω γὰρ
ἀσθενὴς ἦν καὶ λεπτὴ πάμπαν ὑπὸ τῆς ἀρρωστίας,
ὥστ' ἔνοπτρον ἐγίγνετο καὶ ὁ πλησίον ἀήρ, καὶ οὐκ
10 ἐδύνατο ἀπωθεῖν—ὡς ὁ πόρρω καὶ πυκνός· διόπερ
αἵ τ' ἄκραι ἀνεσπασμέναι φαίνονται ἐν τῇ θαλάττῃ,
καὶ μείζω τὰ μεγέθη πάντων, ὅταν εὖροι πνέωσι,
καὶ τὰ ἐν ταῖς ἀχλύσιν, οἷον καὶ ἥλιος καὶ ἄστρα
ἀνίσχοντα καὶ δύνοντα μᾶλλον ἢ μεσουρανοῦντα.

Ἀπὸ δὲ ὕδατος μάλιστα ἀνακλᾶται, καὶ ἀπὸ
15 ἀρχομένου γίγνεσθαι μᾶλλον ἔτι ἢ ἀπ' ἀέρος· ἕκαστον γὰρ τῶν μορίων ἐξ ὧν γίγνεται συνισταμένων

three colours of the rainbow (374 b 7—375 a 7). The yellow in the rainbow due to contrast of colours and not to reflection (375 a 7-28). The same causes account for the double rainbow ; in the outer of the two the order of colours is reversed. More than two rainbows are not seen at a time (375 a 28- b 15).

It has already been stated that the rainbow is a reflection. We must now proceed to explain what kind of a reflection it is, how its various character- istics arise, and to what cause they are due.

Our vision, then, is reflected from all smooth sur- faces, among them air and water. Air reflects when it is condensed ; but even when not condensed it can produce a reflection when the sight is weak. An example of this is what used to happen to a man whose sight was weak and unclear : he always used to see an image going before him as he walked, and facing towards him. And the reason why this used to happen to him was that his vision was re- flected back to him ; for its enfeebled state made it so weak and faint that even the neighbouring air be- came a mirror and it was unable to thrust it aside. Distant and dense air does of course normally act as a mirror in this way, which is why when there is an east wind promontories on the sea appear to be elevated above it and everything appears abnormally large [a] ; the same is true of objects seen in a mist, or twilight—for instance the sun and stars which at their rising and setting appear larger than at their meridian.

But reflection takes place chiefly from water, and still better from water in process of formation than from air : for each of the particles which when con-

How the rainbow is formed by reflection.

---

[a] It is not clear exactly how Aristotle supposed this effect to be produced : cf. *Problems* xxvi. 53.

ἡ ψακὰς ἔνοπτρον ἀναγκαῖον εἶναι μᾶλλον τῆς
ἀχλύος. ἐπεὶ δὲ καὶ δῆλον καὶ εἴρηται πρότερον
ὅτι ἐν τοῖς τοιούτοις ἐνόπτροις τὸ χρῶμα μόνον
ἐμφαίνεται, τὸ δὲ σχῆμα ἄδηλον, ἀναγκαῖον, ὅταν
20 ἄρχηται ὕειν καὶ ἤδη μὲν συνιστῆται εἰς ψακάδας
ὁ ἐν τοῖς νέφεσιν ἀήρ, μήπω δὲ ὕῃ, ἐὰν ἐξ ἐναντίας
ᾖ ὁ ἥλιος ἢ ἄλλο τι οὕτω λαμπρὸν ὥστε γίγνεσθαι
ἔνοπτρον τὸ νέφος, καὶ τὴν ἀνάκλασιν γίγνεσθαι
πρὸς τὸ λαμπρὸν ἐξ ἐναντίας, γίγνεσθαι ἔμφασιν
25 χρώματος, οὐ σχήματος. ἑκάστου δ᾽ ὄντος τῶν
ἐνόπτρων μικροῦ καὶ ἀοράτου, τῆς δ᾽ ἐξ ἁπάντων
αὐτῶν συνεχείας τοῦ μεγέθους ὁρωμένης, ἀνάγκη
συνεχὲς μέγεθος τοῦ αὐτοῦ φαίνεσθαι χρώματος·
ἕκαστον γὰρ τῶν ἐνόπτρων τὸ αὐτὸ ἀποδίδωσι
χρῶμα τῷ συνεχεῖ. ὥστ᾽ ἐπεὶ ταῦτ᾽ ἐνδέχεται
30 συμβαίνειν, ὅταν τοῦτον ἔχῃ τὸν τρόπον ὅ τε ἥλιος
καὶ τὸ νέφος καὶ ἡμεῖς ὦμεν μεταξὺ αὐτῶν, ἔσται
διὰ τὴν ἀνάκλασιν ἔμφασίς τις. ἀλλὰ μὴν καὶ
φαίνεται τότε καὶ οὐκ ἄλλως ἐχόντων γιγνομένη
ἡ ἶρις.

Ὅτι μὲν οὖν ἀνάκλασις ἡ ἶρις τῆς ὄψεως πρὸς
τὸν ἥλιόν ἐστι, φανερόν· διὸ καὶ ἐξ ἐναντίας ἀεὶ
35 γίγνεται, ἡ δ᾽ ἅλως περὶ αὐτόν· καίτοι ἄμφω ἀνά-
374 a κλασις· ἀλλ᾽ ἥ γε τῶν χρωμάτων ποικιλία διαφέρει·
ἡ μὲν γὰρ ἀφ᾽ ὕδατος καὶ μέλανος γίγνεται ἀνάκλασις καὶ πόρρωθεν, ἡ δ᾽ ἐγγύθεν καὶ ἀπὸ ἀέρος
λευκοτέρου τὴν φύσιν.

Φαίνεται δὲ τὸ λαμπρὸν διὰ τοῦ μέλανος ἢ ἐν
5 τῷ μέλανι (διαφέρει γὰρ οὐδέν) φοινικοῦν (ὁρᾶν δ᾽

---

densed forms a raindrop will necessarily be a better mirror than mist. Now it is clear, and has already [a] been stated, that in mirrors of this kind colour only is reflected and shape does not appear. When, therefore, it is about to rain and the air in the clouds is already condensing into raindrops but the rain is not yet falling, if there is, opposite the cloud, the sun or any other object so bright that the cloud mirrors it and reflection takes place from the cloud to the bright object opposite, an image of colour but not of shape must be produced. Each of the reflecting particles is invisibly small, and the continuous magnitude formed by them all is what we see ; what appears to us is therefore necessarily a continuous magnitude of a single colour, since each of the reflecting particles gives off a colour the same as that of the continuous whole. Since, therefore, these conditions are theoretically possible, we may suppose that when the sun and the cloud stand in this relation and we are situated between them, the process of reflection will give rise to an image. And it is under these conditions and no others that the rainbow in fact appears.

It is clear, then, that the rainbow is a reflection of our sight to the sun. And so the rainbow is always opposite the sun, the halo round it. Both are reflections, but the variety of its colours distinguishes the rainbow, which is a reflection from a distance and from water that is dark, while the halo is a reflection from near by and from air which is naturally lighter.

Bright light shining through a dark medium or reflected in a dark surface (it makes no difference which) looks red.[b] Thus one can see how the flames

Difference in colour between rainbow and halo.

[b] *De Sensu* 440 a 10, *De Col.* ch. 2, 792 a 8 ff.

ἔξεστι τό γε τῶν χλωρῶν ξύλων πῦρ, ὡς ἐρυθρὰν
ἔχει τὴν φλόγα διὰ τὸ τῷ καπνῷ πολλῷ μεμεῖχθαι
τὸ πῦρ λαμπρὸν ὂν καὶ λευκόν)· καὶ δι᾽ ἀχλύος
καὶ καπνοῦ ὁ ἥλιος φαίνεται φοινικοῦς. διὸ ἡ μὲν
τῆς ἴριδος ἀνάκλασις ἡ μὲν πρώτη τοιαύτην ἔχειν
10 φαίνεται τὴν χρόαν (ἀπὸ ῥανίδων γὰρ μικρῶν γίγνεται ἡ ἀνάκλασις), ἡ δὲ τῆς ἅλω οὔ. περὶ δὲ τῶν
ἄλλων χρωμάτων ὕστερον ἐροῦμεν. ἔτι δὲ περὶ
αὐτὸν μὲν τὸν ἥλιον οὐ γίγνεται διατριβὴ τοιαύτης
συστάσεως, ἀλλ᾽ ἢ ὕει ἢ διαλύεται. ἐκ δὲ τῶν
ἐναντίων ἐν τῷ μεταξὺ τῆς τοῦ ὕδατος γενέσεως
15 γίγνεταί τις χρόνος· τούτου γὰρ μὴ συμβαίνοντος
ἦσαν ἂν κεχρωματισμέναι αἱ ἅλως ὥσπερ ἡ ἶρις.
νῦν δ᾽ ὅλα μὲν οὐ γίγνεται τοιαύτην ἔχοντα τὴν
ἔμφασιν, οὐδὲ κύκλῳ, μικρὰ δὲ καὶ κατὰ μόριον,
αἱ καλοῦνται ῥάβδοι, ἐπεὶ εἰ συνίστατο τοιαύτη
ἀχλὺς οἷα γένοιτ᾽ ἂν ὕδατος ἤ τινος ἄλλου μέλανος,
20 καθάπερ λέγομεν, ἐφαίνετο ἂν ἡ ἶρις ὅλη, ὥσπερ
ἡ περὶ τοὺς λύχνους. περὶ γὰρ τούτους τὰ πλεῖστα
νοτίων ὄντων ἶρις γίγνεται τοῦ χειμῶνος, μάλιστα
δὲ δήλη γίγνεται τοῖς ὑγροὺς ἔχουσι τοὺς ὀφθαλ-
μούς. τούτων γὰρ ἡ ὄψις ταχὺ δι᾽ ἀσθένειαν ἀνακλᾶται. γίγνεται δ᾽ ἀπό τε τῆς τοῦ ἀέρος ὑγρότητος
25 καὶ ἀπὸ λιγνύος τῆς ἀπὸ τῆς φλογὸς ἀπορρεούσης
καὶ μειγνυμένης· τότε γὰρ γίγνεται ἔνοπτρον,[1] καὶ
διὰ τὴν μελανίαν· καπνώδης γὰρ ἡ λιγνύς· τὸ δὲ
τοῦ λύχνου φῶς οὐ λευκὸν ἀλλὰ πορφυροῦν φαίνεται κύκλῳ καὶ ἰριῶδες, φοινικοῦν δ᾽ οὔ· ἔστι

---

[1] τότε . . . ἔνοπτρον interclusionem distinguit Thurot.

---

[a] And water is dark.

of a fire made of green wood are red, because the fire-light which is bright and clear is mixed with a great deal of smoke ; and the sun looks red when seen through mist or smoke. The reflection which is the rainbow therefore has its outermost circumference of this colour, since the reflection is from minute water-drops [a] ; but in the halo this colour does not appear. With the other colours we will deal later. Further, a condensation of this kind does not linger long round the sun itself, but either turns to rain or disperses : but during the formation of water opposite the sun some time elapses. If this were not so haloes would be coloured like the rainbow. As it is, no complete or circular halo presents this appearance, but only the small, partial formations called " rods " ; for if a formation of the kind of mist which arises from water or any other dark substance in the way we maintain [b] were present, we should see a complete rainbow, like the one we see round lamps. For a rainbow does form round lamps in the winter, especially when there is a south wind, and is most clearly visible to those whose eyes are watery, for their sight is weak and so easily reflected. The rainbow is due to the moisture of the air and to the soot which is given off by and mixed with the flame, and so forms a mirror owing to the dark colour derived from the smokiness of the soot [c] : and the light of the lamp appears not white but purple, and forms a ring like a rainbow, except that the colour red is

[b] a 1 above : the rainbow is a reflection in a dark medium.

[c] Or take τότε γὰρ γίνεται ἔνοπτρον (l. 25) as a parenthesis, and the meaning is that the rainbow is due to moisture, to soot and the dark colour derived from the soot, which between them constitute the mirror. But Alex. seems to have had a text punctuated as that printed here.

374 a

γὰρ ἥ τε ὄψις ὀλίγη ἡ ἀνακλωμένη, καὶ μέλαν τὸ
30 ἔνοπτρον. ἡ δ' ἀπὸ τῶν κωπῶν τῶν ἀναφερομένων
ἐκ τῆς θαλάττης ἶρις τῇ μὲν θέσει τὸν αὐτὸν γίγνεται τρόπον τῇ ἐν τῷ οὐρανῷ, τὸ δὲ χρῶμα
ὁμοιοτέρα τῇ περὶ τοὺς λύχνους· οὐ γὰρ φοινικῆν
ἀλλὰ πορφυρᾶν ἔχουσα φαίνεται τὴν χρόαν. ἡ δ'
ἀνάκλασις ἀπὸ τῶν μικροτάτων μὲν συνεχῶν δὲ
35 γίγνεται ῥανίδων· αὗται δ' ὕδωρ ἀποκεκριμένον
374 b εἰσὶν ἤδη παντελῶς. γίγνεται δὲ κἄν τις λεπταῖς
ῥαίνῃ ῥανίσιν εἴς τι τοιοῦτον χωρίον ὃ τὴν θέσιν
πρὸς τὸν ἥλιον ἐστραμμένον ἐστὶ καὶ τῇ μὲν ὁ ἥλιος
ἀνέχῃ τῇ δὲ σκιάζῃ· ἐν τῷ τοιούτῳ γάρ, ἐὰν εἴσω
5 τις ῥαίνῃ, τῷ ἑστῶτι ἐκτός, ᾗ ἐπαλλάττουσιν αἱ
ἀκτῖνες καὶ ποιοῦσι τὴν σκιάν, φαίνεται ἶρις. ὁ
δὲ τρόπος καὶ ἡ χρόα ὁμοία καὶ τὸ αἴτιον τὸ αὐτὸ
τῇ ἀπὸ τῶν κωπῶν· τῇ γὰρ χειρὶ κώπῃ χρῆται
ὁ ῥαίνων.

Ὅτι δὲ τὸ χρῶμα τοιοῦτον, ἅμα δῆλον ἔσται καὶ
περὶ τῶν ἄλλων χρωμάτων τῆς φαντασίας, ἐκ
τῶνδε. δεῖ γὰρ νοήσαντας, ὥσπερ εἴρηται, καὶ
10 ὑποθεμένους πρῶτον μὲν ὅτι τὸ λαμπρὸν ἐν τῷ
μέλανι ἢ διὰ τοῦ μέλανος χρῶμα ποιεῖ φοινικοῦν,
δεύτερον δ' ὅτι ἡ ὄψις ἐκτεινομένη ἀσθενεστέρα
γίγνεται καὶ ἐλάττων, τρίτον δ' ὅτι τὸ μέλαν οἷον
ἀπόφασίς ἐστιν· τῷ γὰρ ἐκλείπειν τὴν ὄψιν φαίνεται
15 μέλαν· διὸ τὰ πόρρω πάντα μελάντερα φαίνεται,
διὰ τὸ μὴ δικνεῖσθαι τὴν ὄψιν. θεωρείσθω μὲν
οὖν ταῦτ' ἐκ τῶν περὶ τὰς αἰσθήσεις συμβαινόντων·
ἐκείνων γὰρ ἴδιοι οἱ περὶ τούτων λόγοι· νῦν δ' ὅσον

---

[a] " It is bound to be weak by lamplight " (O.T.).
[b] 372 a 1, ch. 2 above.

missing, as the reflected vision is weak [a] and the mirror dark. The rainbow produced by oars breaking water is the outcome of the same relative positions as a rainbow in the sky but is more like the rainbow round a lamp in colour, since it appears purple and not red. The reflection takes place from a number of minute water-drops which form between them a continuous surface, and which are of course water already fully formed. A rainbow is also produced when someone sprinkles a fine spray into a room so placed that it faces the sun and is partly illuminated by it, partly in shadow. When anyone sprinkles water inside a room so placed a rainbow appears, to anyone standing outside, at the point where the sun's rays stop and the shadow begins. It arises in the same way as the rainbow produced by the oars, is similar to it in colour and due to the same cause, for the sprinkler uses his hand like an oar.

The following considerations will make clear both that the colours of the rainbow are such as we have described [b] and how the other colours appear in it. We must, as has been said, [c] bear in mind and assume the following principles. (1) White light reflected on a dark surface or passing through a dark coloured medium produces red ; (2) our vision becomes weaker and less effective with distance ; (3) dark colour is a kind of negation of vision, the appearance of darkness being due to the failure of our sight ; hence objects seen at a distance appear darker because our sight fails to reach them. These principles should be examined in the light of the processes of sensation, and the discussion of them properly belongs to the theory of sensation ; here let us say no more about

The colours of the rainbow explained.

[c] Cf. 373 b 9, 374 a 3.

374 b

ἀνάγκη, τοσοῦτον περὶ αὐτῶν λέγωμεν. φαίνεται
δ' οὖν διὰ ταύτην τὴν αἰτίαν τά τε πόρρω μελάντερα
20 καὶ ἐλάττω καὶ λειότερα, καὶ τὰ ἐν τοῖς ἐνόπτροις,
καὶ τὰ νέφη μελάντερα βλέπουσιν εἰς τὸ ὕδωρ ἢ
εἰς αὐτὰ τὰ νέφη. καὶ τοῦτο πάνυ ἐπιδήλως· διὰ
γὰρ τὴν ἀνάκλασιν ὀλίγη τῇ ὄψει θεωροῦνται. διαφέρει δ' οὐδὲν τὸ ὁρώμενον μεταβάλλειν ἢ τὴν
ὄψιν· ἀμφοτέρως γὰρ ἔσται ταὐτόν. πρὸς δὲ τού-
25 τοις δεῖ μὴ λεληθέναι καὶ τόδε· συμβαίνει γὰρ ὅταν
ᾖ τοῦ ἡλίου νέφος πλησίον, εἰς μὲν αὐτὸ βλέποντι
μηδὲν φαίνεσθαι κεχρωματισμένον ἀλλ' εἶναι λευκόν,
ἐν δὲ τῷ ὕδατι αὐτὸ τοῦτο θεωροῦντι χρῶμά τι
ἔχειν τῆς ἴριδος. δῆλον τοίνυν ὅτι ἡ ὄψις ὥσπερ
καὶ τὸ μέλαν κλωμένη δι' ἀσθένειαν μελάντερον
30 ποιεῖ φαίνεσθαι, καὶ τὸ λευκὸν ἧττον λευκόν, καὶ
προσάγει πρὸς τὸ μέλαν. ἡ μὲν οὖν ἰσχυροτέρα
ὄψις εἰς φοινικοῦν χρῶμα μετέβαλεν, ἡ δ' ἐχομένη
εἰς τὸ πράσινον, ἡ δὲ ἔτι ἀσθενεστέρα εἰς τὸ
ἁλουργόν. ἐπὶ δὲ τὸ πλέον οὐκέτι φαίνεται, ἀλλ'
ἐν τοῖς τρισίν, ὥσπερ καὶ τῶν ἄλλων τὰ πλεῖστα,
35 καὶ τούτων ἔσχεν τέλος· τῶν δ' ἄλλων ἀναίσθητος
375 a ἡ μεταβολή. διὸ καὶ ἡ ἶρις τρίχρως φαίνεται,
ἑκατέρα μέν, ἐναντίως δέ. ἡ μὲν οὖν πρώτη τὴν
ἔξω φοινικῆν ἔχει· ἀπὸ μεγίστης γὰρ περιφερείας
πλείστη προσπίπτει ὄψις πρὸς τὸν ἥλιον, μεγίστη
δ' ἡ ἔξω· ἡ δ' ἐχομένη καὶ ἡ τρίτη ἀνάλογον. ὥστ'
5 εἰ τὰ περὶ τῶν χρωμάτων τῆς φαντασίας εἴρηται
καλῶς, ἀνάγκη τρίχρων τε εἶναι αὐτὴν καὶ τούτοις

---

[a] " i.e. whether the object is actually further from the eye
in space or whether (owing to reflection) the sight travels to
it by a longer route " (O.T.).   [b] Cf. De Caelo 268 a 9 ff.
  [c] i.e. inner, cf. 375 b 6.   [d] 374 b 9.

them than is necessary for our present purpose. At any rate, they give the reason why distant objects appear darker and smaller and less irregular, as do also objects seen in mirrors, and why too the clouds appear darker when one looks at their reflection in water than directly at them. This last example is a particularly clear one: for we view them with a vision diminished by the reflection. And it makes no difference whether the change is in the object or in our vision [a]; the result is the same in either case. The following fact also must not be overlooked; when a cloud is close to the sun, when we look directly at it, it appears to have no colour but to be white, but when we look at its reflection in water it seems to be partially rainbow-coloured. The reason is clearly that, just as our vision when reflected through an angle and so weakened makes a dark colour appear still darker, so also it makes white appear less white and approach nearer to black. When the sight is fairly strong the colour changes to red, when it is less strong to green, and when it is weaker still to blue. There is no further change of colour, the complete process consisting, like most others,[b] of three stages; any further change is imperceptible. This is why the rainbow is three-coloured, and why, when there are two of them, each is three-coloured, but the colours are in the reverse order in each. In the primary [c] rainbow the outermost band is red. For the vision is reflected most strongly on to the sun from the largest circumference, and the outermost band is the largest: and corresponding remarks apply to the second and third bands. So if our assumptions [d] about the appearance of colours are correct, the rainbow must be three-coloured and its only colours must be these three.

ARISTOTLE

τοῖς χρώμασι κεχρῶσθαι μόνοις. τὸ δὲ ξανθὸν
φαίνεται διὰ τὸ παρ' ἄλληλα φαίνεσθαι. τὸ γὰρ
φοινικοῦν παρὰ τὸ πράσινον λευκὸν φαίνεται. σημεῖον δὲ τούτου· ἐν γὰρ τῷ μελαντάτῳ νέφει
10 μάλιστα ἄκρατος γίγνεται ἶρις· συμβαίνει δὲ τότε
ξανθότερον εἶναι δοκεῖν τὸ φοινικοῦν. ἔστι δὲ τὸ
ξανθὸν ἐν τῇ ἴριδι χρῶμα μεταξὺ τοῦ τε φοινικοῦ
καὶ πρασίνου χρώματος.[1] διὰ τὴν μελανίαν οὖν
τοῦ κύκλῳ νέφους ὅλον αὐτοῦ φαίνεται τὸ φοινικοῦν
λευκόν· ἔστι γὰρ πρὸς ἐκεῖνα[2] λευκόν. καὶ πάλιν
15 ἀπομαραινομένης τῆς ἴριδος [ἐγγύτατα],[3] ὅταν λύη-
ται τὸ φοινικοῦν· ἡ γὰρ νεφέλη λευκὴ οὖσα, προσπίπτουσα παρὰ τὸ πράσινον, μεταβάλλει εἰς τὸ
ξανθόν. μέγιστον δὲ σημεῖον τούτων ἡ ἀπὸ τῆς
σελήνης ἶρις· φαίνεται γὰρ λευκὴ πάμπαν. γίγνεται
δὲ τοῦτο ὅτι ἔν τε τῷ νέφει ζοφερῷ φαίνεται καὶ
20 ἐν νυκτί. ὥσπερ οὖν πῦρ ἐπὶ πῦρ, μέλαν παρὰ
μέλαν ποιεῖ τὸ ἠρέμα λευκὸν παντελῶς φαίνεσθαι
λευκόν· τοῦτο δ' ἐστὶν τὸ φοινικοῦν. γίγνεται δὲ
τοῦτο τὸ πάθος καταφανὲς καὶ ἐπὶ τῶν ἀνθῶν· ἐν
γὰρ τοῖς ὑφάσμασιν καὶ ποικίλμασιν ἀμύθητον δια-
25 φέρει τῇ φαντασίᾳ ἄλλα παρ' ἄλλα τιθέμενα τῶν

---

[1] ἔστι . . . χρώματος post φαίνεται l. 8 fortasse traiiciendum:
post μόνοις l. 7 coll. Thurot, et pro τὸ δὲ ξανθὸν φαίνεται ci.
φαίνεται δέ.   [2] ἐκεῖνο E_corr. N_rec.
[3] ἐγγύτατα seclusi : om. E₁ Ap Ol O.T.

---

[a] In what follows (ll. 7-17), Aristotle is trying to account
for the orange colour in the rainbow. This he regards as due
not to reflection, like its other three colours, but to the contrast of two colours in juxtaposition. The argument of the
passage is not easy to follow in detail. What seems certain
is that Aristotle is trying to explain two things: (i) the occurrence of a yellow band *between* the red and the green; this
he has already noticed (372 a 9) and refers to here (ll. 11-12);

The yellow colour [a] that appears in the rainbow is due to the contrast of two others; for red in contrast to green appears light. (And the yellow colour in the rainbow lies between the red and green.)[a] An example of such contrast is the fact that the rainbow is purest when the cloud is blackest, and that in these circumstances the red appears more yellow. So the whole of the red appears light because of the contrast with the blackness of the surrounding cloud; for compared with the cloud it is light-coloured. The same thing happens when the rainbow is fading and the red dissolving: for the cloud, which is white, changes to yellow when brought next to the green.[b] But the best illustration of colour contrast is afforded by the moon rainbow. This appears entirely white, simply because it appears in dark cloud and at night. For as fire increases fire,[c] so dark placed by dark makes a dim light (like red) appear clear and bright. The same effect can also be seen in dyes: for there is an indescribable difference in the appearance of the colours in woven or embroidered materials when

(ii) the replacement of the red band by a yellow, which is apparently what he has in mind in ll. 10-14 and certainly what he has in mind in ll. 14-16 (see note b). As Thurot pointed out, the sentence ἔστι δέ . . . χρώματος (ll. 11-12) in its present position breaks the sequence of thought. I have suggested that it would come more naturally after φαίνεται (l. 8) and translated accordingly. Aristotle thus starts by accounting for the yellow *between* green and red by colour contrast, and then goes on (l. 9 σημεῖον δὲ τούτου, sc. τοῦ παρ' ἄλληλα φαίνεσθαι) to give further examples of such contrast in which the whole of the red is *replaced* by yellow. ἐκεῖνο should then be read for ἐκεῖνα in l. 14.

[b] When the rainbow fades the red disappears first. It is to this that Aristotle refers here when he speaks of a yellow band replacing the red as a result of colour contrast.

[c] Proverbial.

χρωμάτων, οἷον καὶ τὰ πορφυρᾶ ἐν λευκοῖς ἢ
μέλασιν ἐρίοις, ἔτι δ' ἐν αὐγῇ τοιαδὶ ἢ τοιαδί· διὸ
καὶ οἱ ποικιλταί φασι διαμαρτάνειν ἐργαζόμενοι
πρὸς τὸν λύχνον πολλάκις τῶν ἀνθῶν, λαμβάνοντες
ἕτερα ἀνθ' ἑτέρων.

Διότι μὲν οὖν τρίχρως τε, καὶ ὅτι ἐκ τούτων
30 φαίνεται τῶν χρωμάτων μόνων ἡ ἶρις, εἴρηται.
διπλῆ¹ δὲ καὶ ἀμαυροτέρα τοῖς χρώμασιν ἡ περι-
έχουσα, καὶ τῇ θέσει τὰς χρόας ἐξ ἐναντίας ἔχει
κειμένας διὰ τὴν αὐτὴν αἰτίαν· μακροτέρα γὰρ
ἀποτεινομένη ἡ ὄψις ὥσπερ τὸ πορρώτερον ὁρᾷ, καὶ
τὸ ἐνταῦθα τὸν αὐτὸν τρόπον. ἀσθενεστέρα οὖν
375 b ἀπὸ τῆς ἔξωθεν ἡ ἀνάκλασις γίγνεται διὰ τὸ πορρώτερον ποιεῖσθαι τὴν ἀνάκλασιν, ὥστ' ἐλάττων
προσπίπτουσα τὰ χρώματα ποιεῖ ἀμαυρότερα φαίνεσθαι. καὶ ἀντεστραμμένως δὴ διὰ τὸ πλείω ἀπὸ
τῆς ἐλάττονος καὶ τῆς ἐντὸς περιφερείας προσ-
5 πίπτειν πρὸς τὸν ἥλιον· ἐγγυτέρω γὰρ τῆς ὄψεως
οὖσα ἀνακλᾶται ἀπὸ τῆς ἐγγυτάτω περιφερείας τῆς
πρώτης ἴριδος. ἐγγυτάτω δὲ ἐν τῇ ἔξωθεν ἴριδι ἡ
ἐλαχίστη περιφέρεια, ὥστε αὕτη ἕξει τὸ χρῶμα
φοινικοῦν· ἡ δ' ἐχομένη καὶ ἡ τρίτη κατὰ λόγον.

---

¹ διπλῆς ci. Thurot.

they are differently arranged ; for instance, purple is quite different on a white or a black background, and variations of light can make a similar difference. So embroiderers say they often make mistakes in their colours when they work by lamplight, picking out one colour in mistake for another.

This, then, is why the rainbow is three-coloured and why the rainbow is made up of these three colours only. The same cause accounts for the double rainbow and for the colours in the outer bow being dimmer and in the reverse order. For the effects here are the same as those produced by an increase in the distance of vision on our perception of distant objects.[a] The reflection from the outer rainbow is weaker because it has farther to travel ; its impulse is therefore feebler, which makes the colours seem dimmer. The colours are in the reverse order because the impulse reaching the sun is greater from the smaller and inner band ; for the reflection that is closer to our sight is the one reflected from the band that is closest to the primary rainbow, that is, the smallest band in the outer rainbow, which will consequently be coloured red. And the second and third bands are to be explained analogously.

[a] *Cf.* 374 b 9 ff.

Ἡ ἔξω ἶρις ἐφ' ᾧ τὸ Β· ἡ ἔσω, ἡ πρώτη, ἐφ' ᾧ
10 τὸ Α· τὰ χρώματα δ', ἐφ' ᾧ τὸ Γ, φοινικοῦν, ἐφ'
ᾧ τὸ Δ, πράσινον, ἐφ' ᾧ Ε, ἁλουργόν· τὸ ξανθὸν
δὲ φαίνεται ἐφ' οὗ τὸ Ζ.

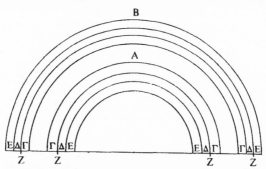

Τρεῖς δ' οὐκέτι γίγνονται, οὐδὲ πλείους ἴριδες,
διὰ τὸ καὶ τὴν δευτέραν γίγνεσθαι ἀμαυροτέραν,
ὥστε καὶ τὴν τρίτην ἀνάκλασιν πάμπαν ἀσθενῆ γίγ-
15 νεσθαι καὶ ἀδυνατεῖν ἀφικνεῖσθαι πρὸς τὸν ἥλιον.

CHAPTER V

ARGUMENT

(I) Demonstration that when the sun is on the horizon the
rainbow cannot be greater than a semicircle (375 b 16—376
b 22). (II) Demonstration that when the sun is above the
horizon the rainbow must be less than a semicircle (376 b
28—377 a 11). (III) The differences in the size of the sun's
arc above the horizon account for the fact that rainbows do not
occur at midday in the summer months (377 a 11-28).

Let B be the outer and A the inner, primary rainbow : and to symbolize the colours, let us use Γ for red, Δ for green, E for purple. Yellow will appear at Z.

Three or more rainbows are never seen, because even the second is dimmer than the first, and so the third reflection is altogether too feeble to reach the sun.

CHAPTER V

ARGUMENT (continued)

Note.—*The general intention of these geometrical demonstrations is clear. In the first the eye is imagined to be at the centre K of the horizon (Fig. 1) : the lines of vision form a cone with apex K and base the circle MMM. The sun or other heavenly body is imagined to be rising on the horizon at H. Then MMM is the rainbow. It is evident at once that in the limiting case represented by the figure the rainbow will be a*

*semicircle, and that in all other possible cases it will be an arc
of a circle less than a semicircle. So much is already made
clear in para. 1, and is the substance of what the first figure
is designed to prove. But Aristotle proceeds in paragraphs
2-4 to elaborate the figure (Fig. 2) and to prove at greater
length that in whatever plane the triangle HKM is drawn the
point M will be on the circle MN, and that the segment of the
circle MN cut off by the horizon will be a semicircle. The
first demonstration has thus shown that a rainbow formed
when the sun is on the horizon will be a semicircle. The
second (Fig. 4) proceeds to show that if the sun is at any point
above the horizon the rainbow will be less than a semicircle.
For the segment of the circle ΨΥΩ cut off by the horizon is
necessarily less than a semicircle.*

*Finally, the last paragraph points out that the figures given
assume that the arc of the sun's course above the horizon is a
semicircle. This will only be true at the equinoxes ; but the*

375 b 16 Ὅτι δ' οὔτε κύκλον οἷόν τε γενέσθαι τῆς ἴριδος
οὔτε μεῖζον ἡμικυκλίου τμῆμα, καὶ περὶ τῶν ἄλλων
τῶν συμβαινόντων περὶ αὐτήν, ἐκ τοῦ διαγράμ-
ματος ἔσται θεωροῦσι δῆλον.

Ἡμισφαιρίου γὰρ ὄντος ἐπὶ τοῦ ὁρίζοντος κύ-
20 κλου τοῦ ἐφ' ᾧ τὸ Α, κέντρου δὲ τοῦ Κ, ἄλλου δέ
τινος ἀνατέλλοντος σημείου ἐφ' ᾧ τὸ Η, ἐὰν ἀπὸ
τοῦ Κ γραμμαὶ κατὰ κῶνον ἐκπίπτουσαι ποιῶσιν
ὡσπερεὶ ἄξονα τὴν ἐφ' ᾗ ΗΚ, καὶ ἀπὸ τοῦ Κ ἐπὶ

268

*figure can be drawn for other seasons with the sun's course
shown as a segment greater or less than a semicircle. And
this variation of the arc accounts for the fact that whereas
in the shorter days rainbows occur at any time of day, during
the longer days they cannot occur at midday.*

IT will be clear from a study of the diagram that the
rainbow can never be a complete circle or a segment
of a circle greater than a semicircle ; the diagram
will also make clear its other properties.

(I) (1) Let A be a hemisphere resting on the circle Demon-
of the horizon whose centre is K : let H be another stration (I).
point rising on the horizon. If the lines that fall in
a cone from K rotate about HK as an axis, and if lines

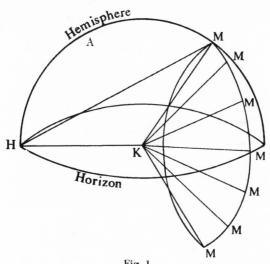

Fig. 1

375 b

τὸ Μ ἐπιζευχθεῖσαι ἀνακλασθῶσιν ἀπὸ τοῦ ἡμισφαιρίου ἐπὶ τὸ Η ἐπὶ τὴν μείζω γωνίαν, πρὸς
25 κύκλου περιφέρειαν προσπεσοῦνται αἱ ἀπὸ τοῦ Κ·
καὶ ἐὰν μὲν ἐπ' ἀνατολῆς ἢ ἐπὶ δύσεως τοῦ ἄστρου
ἡ ἀνάκλασις γένηται, ἡμικύκλιον ἀποληφθήσεται
τοῦ κύκλου ὑπὸ τοῦ ὁρίζοντος τὸ ὑπὲρ γῆν γιγνόμενον, ἐὰν δ' ἐπάνω, ἀεὶ ἔλαττον ἡμικυκλίου· ἐλάχιστον δέ, ὅταν ἐπὶ τοῦ μεσημβρινοῦ γένηται τὸ
ἄστρον.
30 Ἔστω γὰρ ἐπ' ἀνατολῆς πρῶτον, οὗ τὸ Η, καὶ
ἀνακεκλάσθω ἡ ΚΜ ἐπὶ τὸ Η, καὶ τὸ ἐπίπεδον

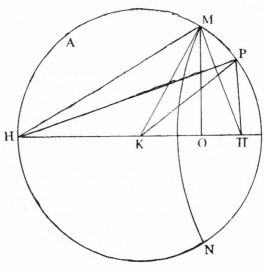

Fig. 2

drawn joining K and M are reflected (at M) from the surface of the hemisphere back to H over the obtuse angle (HKM), the lines from K fall on the circumference of a circle. If the reflection takes place at the rising or setting of a heavenly body, the segment of the circle cut off above the earth by the horizon will be a semicircle ; if the body has risen higher, the segment will be less than a semicircle, and it will be smallest when the body reaches its meridian.

(2) For let the heavenly body be just rising at the point H, and let the line KM be reflected to H, and

375 b

ἐκβεβλήσθω [ἐν ᾧ ἡ Α,][1] τὸ ἀπὸ τοῦ τριγώνου ἐν
ᾧ[2] τὸ ΗΚΜ. κύκλος οὖν ἡ τομὴ ἔσται τῆς
σφαίρας ὁ μέγιστος. ἔστω ὁ ἐφ᾽ ᾧ Α· διοίσει γὰρ
οὐδὲν ἂν ὁποιονοῦν τῶν ἐπὶ τῆς ΗΚ κατὰ τὸ

376 a τρίγωνον τὸ ΚΜΗ ἐκβληθῇ τὸ ἐπίπεδον. αἱ οὖν
ἀπὸ τῶν Η Κ ἀναγόμεναι γραμμαὶ ἐν τούτῳ τῷ
λόγῳ οὐ συσταθήσονται τοῦ ἐφ᾽ ᾧ Α ἡμικυκλίου
πρὸς ἄλλο καὶ ἄλλο σημεῖον· ἐπεὶ γὰρ τά τε Κ Η

5 σημεῖα δέδοται καὶ ἡ ΗΚ, δεδομένη ἂν εἴη καὶ ἡ
ΜΗ, ὥστε καὶ λόγος τῆς ΜΗ πρὸς ΜΚ. δεδο-
μένης οὖν περιφερείας ἐφάψεται τὸ Μ. ἔστω δὴ
αὕτη ἐφ᾽ ἧς τὰ Ν Μ· ὥστε ἡ τομὴ τῶν περιφερειῶν
δέδοται. πρὸς ἄλλῃ δέ γε ἢ τῇ ΜΝ περιφερείᾳ
ἀπὸ τῶν αὐτῶν σημείων ὁ αὐτὸς λόγος ἐν τῷ αὐτῷ
ἐπιπέδῳ οὐ συνίσταται.

10 Ἐκκείσθω οὖν τις γραμμὴ ἡ ΔΒ, καὶ τετμήσθω
ὡς ἡ ΜΗ πρὸς ΜΚ ἡ Δ πρὸς Β. μείζων δὲ ἡ ΜΗ
τῆς ΚΜ, ἐπείπερ ἐπὶ τὴν μείζω γωνίαν ἡ ἀνάκλασις
τοῦ κώνου· ὑπὸ γὰρ τὴν μείζω γωνίαν ὑποτείνει
τοῦ ΚΜΗ τριγώνου. [μείζων ἄρα καὶ ἡ Δ τῆς Β.][3]

15 προσπεπορίσθω οὖν πρὸς τὴν Β, ἐφ᾽ ἧς τὸ Ζ· ὥστ᾽
εἶναι ὅπερ τὴν Δ πρὸς τὴν Β, τὴν ΒΖ πρὸς τὴν Δ.
εἶτα ὅπερ ἡ Ζ πρὸς τὴν ΚΗ, ἡ τὸ Β πρὸς ἄλλην
πεποιήσθω τὴν ΚΠ, καὶ ἀπὸ τοῦ Π ἐπὶ τὸ Μ ἐπεζεύχθω ἡ τὸ ΜΠ. ἔσται οὖν τὸ Π πόλος τοῦ κύ-

---

[1] seclusi : scilicet A posuit hemisphaerium supra ll. 19, 20.
[2] ἐφ᾽ ᾧ ci. O.T.
[3] μείζων . . . τῆς Β secl. Fobes : habent E_corr. F_corr. H N.

---

[a] I have omitted the words ἐν ᾧ ἡ Α since A has so far only
occurred as a hemisphere (ll. 19-20), and so to speak of it lying
on a plane is nonsense. Sense can only be made of the words
by supposing that A refers here to something else (*e.g.* "a

272

let the plane of the triangle HKM be produced.[a] It will cut the sphere in a great circle : let this be called A. (It makes no difference which of the planes passing through HK and determined by the triangle KMH is produced.) Then lines drawn from the points H and K to any point on the semicircle A other than M will not bear the same relation to each other (as HM and KM). For if the points K and H and the line HK are given, the line MH will be given too, and so the ratio of MH to MK. The point on M thus touches a given circumference, which we will call NM, and so the intersection of the two circumferences [b] is given. But the same ratio will not hold between lines drawn from the same points H and K and in the same plane to any circumference other than MN.

(3) Draw a line ΔB outside the figure, and divide

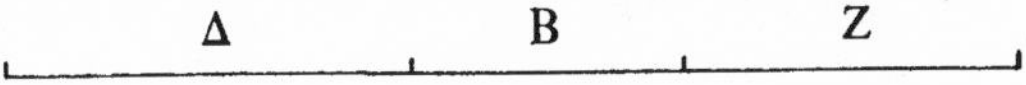

Fig. 3

it into two parts Δ and B in the ratio MH : MK. MH is greater than MK since the reflection of the cone is over the greater angle, subtending the greater angle of the triangle KMH. [Δ is therefore greater than B.] Produce the line B to form a line Z, so that B + Z has the same ratio to Δ as Δ has to B. Produce HK to Π so that B has the same ratio to KΠ as Z to KH. Join Π and M to form the line MΠ. Π will

great circle of the whole sphere " (O.T.)). But Alex. does not seem to have had the words, and the passage makes better sense without them.

[b] *i.e.* of the great circle formed by producing the plane of the triangle HKM and called A (l. 375 b 33) and the circle forming the base of the cone (MMM Fig. 1).

κλου, πρὸς ὃν αἱ ἀπὸ τοῦ Κ γραμμαὶ προσπίπτουσιν·
20 ἔσται γὰρ ὅπερ ἡ Ζ πρὸς ΚΗ, καὶ ἡ Β πρὸς ΚΠ,
καὶ ἡ Δ πρὸς ΠΜ. μὴ γὰρ ἔστω, ἀλλ' ἢ πρὸς
ἐλάττω ἢ πρὸς μείζω τῆς ΠΜ· οὐδὲν γὰρ διοίσει.
ἔστω πρὸς ΠΡ. τὸν αὐτὸν ἄρα λόγον αἱ ΗΚ καὶ
ΚΠ καὶ ἡ ΠΡ πρὸς ἀλλήλας ἕξουσιν ὅνπερ αἱ
25 Ζ Β Δ.[1] αἱ δὲ Ζ Β Δ[1] ἀνὰ λόγον ἦσαν, ὅπερ ἡ Δ
πρὸς Β, ἡ ΖΒ πρὸς Δ· ὥστε ὅπερ ἡ ΠΗ πρὸς τὴν
ΠΡ, ἡ τὸ ΠΡ πρὸς τὴν ΠΚ. ἂν οὖν ἀπὸ τῶν
Κ Η αἱ ΗΡ καὶ ΚΡ ἐπὶ τὸ Ρ ἐπιζευχθῶσιν, αἱ
ἐπιζευχθεῖσαι αὗται τὸν αὐτὸν ἕξουσι λόγον ὅνπερ
ἡ ΗΠ πρὸς τὴν ΠΡ· περὶ γὰρ τὴν αὐτὴν γωνίαν
30 τὴν Π ἀνάλογον αἵ τε τοῦ ΗΠΡ τριγώνου καὶ τοῦ
ΚΡΠ. ὥστε καὶ ἡ ΠΡ πρὸς τὴν ΚΡ τὸν αὐτὸν
ἕξει λόγον, καὶ ἡ τὸ ΗΠ πρὸς τὴν ΠΡ. ἔχει δὲ
καὶ ἡ ΜΗ πρὸς ΚΜ τοῦτον τὸν λόγον· ὅνπερ γὰρ
376 b ἡ τὸ Δ πρὸς τὴν Β ἀμφότεραι. ὥστε ἀπὸ τῶν
Η Κ σημείων οὐ μόνον πρὸς τὴν Μ Ν περιφέρειαν
συσταθήσονται τὸν αὐτὸν ἔχουσαι λόγον, ἀλλὰ καὶ
ἄλλοθι· ὅπερ ἀδύνατον. ἐπεὶ οὖν ἡ Δ οὔτε πρὸς
5 ἔλαττον τοῦ ΜΠ οὔτε πρὸς μείζω (ὁμοίως γὰρ
δειχθήσεται), δῆλον ὅτι πρὸς αὐτὴν ἂν εἴη τὴν ἐφ'
ᾗ Μ Π. ὥστ' ἔσται ὅπερ ἡ ΜΠ πρὸς ΠΚ, ἡ ΠΗ
πρὸς τὴν ΜΠ [καὶ λοιπὴ ἡ τὸ ΜΗ πρὸς ΜΚ].[2]
    Ἐὰν οὖν τῷ ἐφ' ᾧ τὸ Π πόλῳ χρώμενος, δια-
στήματι δὲ τῷ ἐφ' ᾧ Μ Π, κύκλος γραφῇ, ἁπασῶν
10 ἐφάψεται τῶν γωνιῶν ἃς ἀνακλώμεναι ποιοῦσιν αἱ
ἀπὸ τοῦ Η καὶ Κ[3]· εἰ δὲ μή, ὁμοίως δειχθήσονται
τὸν αὐτὸν ἔχουσαι λόγον αἱ ἄλλοθι καὶ ἄλλοθι τοῦ
ἡμικυκλίου συνιστάμεναι, ὅπερ ἦν ἀδύνατον. ἐὰν
οὖν περιαγάγῃς τὸ ἡμικύκλιον τὸ ἐφ' ᾧ τὸ Α περὶ
τὴν ἐφ' ᾗ Η Κ Π διάμετρον, αἱ ἀπὸ τοῦ ΗΚ ἀνα-

then be the pole of the circle on which the lines from K fall : for the ratio of Z to KH and B to KII is the same as that of Δ to ΠΜ. For suppose it is not so, and Δ bears this ratio to a line greater or less than ΠΜ (it does not matter which). Let this line be ΠΡ. Then HK and KII and ΠΡ will stand in the same ratio to each other as Z, B and Δ. But Z, B and Δ stood in ratios such that Δ was to B as Z + B to Δ : so that ΠΗ is to ΠΡ as ΠΡ to ΠΚ. If, therefore, from the points K and H the lines HP and KP are drawn to P, the lines so drawn will bear the same ratio to each other as HΠ to ΠΡ, for the triangles HΠΡ and KΡΠ are homologous about the angle Π. So ΠΡ will bear the same ratio to KP as HΠ to ΠΡ. But MH and KM also stand in this ratio, as the ratio of both HΠ to ΠΡ and MK to MH is the same as that of Δ to B. Therefore, from the points H and K lines standing in the same ratio to each other will have been drawn both to the circumference MN and to another point. Which is impossible. Since, therefore, Δ cannot bear the ratio in question to a line either less or greater than ΜΠ (the proof in either case is the same), it follows that it must bear that ratio to ΜΠ itself. So the ratio of ΜΠ to ΠΚ is the same as that of ΠΗ to ΜΠ [and finally MH to MK].

(4) If, then, a circle is drawn with Π as pole and distance ΜΠ, it will touch all the angles made by the reflection of the lines from H and K. If not, it can be shown as before that lines drawn to different points on the semicircle A bear the same relation to each other, which is an impossibility. If, then, you revolve the semicircle A about HKΠ as diameter, the

---

[1] Z B Δ E₁ 𝔚 Ap O.T. : Δ B Z Fobes. [2] secl. Fobes.
[3] H καὶ K ci. O.T., cf. Ap : MA κύκλου Fobes.

376 b

15 κλώμεναι πρὸς τὸ ἐφ' ᾧ τὸ Μ ἐν πᾶσι τοῖς ἐπι-
πέδοις ὁμοίως ἕξουσι, καὶ ἴσην ποιήσουσι γωνίαν
τὴν ΚΜΗ· καὶ ἣν ποιήσουσι δὲ γωνίαν αἱ ΗΠ
καὶ ΜΠ ἐπὶ τῆς ΗΠ, ἀεὶ ἴση ἔσται. τρίγωνα οὖν
ἐπὶ τῆς ΗΠ καὶ ΚΠ ἴσα τῷ ΗΜΠ ΚΜΠ συν-
εστήκασι. τούτων δὲ αἱ κάθετοι ἐπὶ τὸ αὐτὸ
20 σημεῖον πεσοῦνται τῆς ΗΠ καὶ ἴσαι ἔσονται. πι-
πτέτωσαν ἐπὶ τὸ Ο. κέντρον ἄρα τοῦ κύκλου τὸ
Ο, ἡμικύκλιον δὲ τὸ περὶ τὴν ΜΝ¹ ἀφῄρηται ὑπὸ²
τοῦ ὁρίζοντος.

[Τῶν μὲν γὰρ ἄνω τὸν ἥλιον οὐ κρατεῖν, τῶν δὲ
†προσπτεριζομένων† κρατεῖν, καὶ διαχεῖν τὸν ἀέρα·
καὶ διὰ τοῦτο τὴν ἶριν οὐ συμβάλλειν τὸν κύκλον.
25 γίγνεσθαι δὲ καὶ νύκτωρ ἀπὸ τῆς σελήνης ὀλιγάκις·
οὔτε γὰρ ἀεὶ πλήρης, ἀσθενεστέρα τε τὴν φύσιν
⟨ἢ⟩³ ὥστε κρατεῖν τοῦ ἀέρος· μάλιστα δ' ἵστασθαι
τὴν ἶριν, ὅπου μάλιστα κρατεῖται ὁ ἥλιος· πλείστη
γὰρ ἐν αὐτῇ ἰκμὰς ἐνέμεινεν.]⁴

Πάλιν ἔστω ὁρίζων μὲν ἐφ' οὗ τὸ ΑΚΓ, ἐπανα-
30 τεταλκέτω δὲ τὸ Η, ὁ δ' ἄξων ἔστω νῦν ἐφ' οὗ τὸ
ΗΠ. τὰ μὲν οὖν ἄλλα πάντα ὁμοίως δειχθήσεται
ὡς καὶ πρότερον, ὁ δὲ πόλος τοῦ κύκλου ὁ ἐφ' ᾧ
Π κάτω ἔσται τοῦ· ὁρίζοντος τοῦ ἐφ' ᾧ τὸ ΑΓ,

377 a ἀρθέντος τοῦ ἐφ' ᾧ τὸ Η σημείου. ἐπὶ δὲ τῆς
αὐτῆς ὅ τε πόλος καὶ τὸ κέντρον τοῦ κύκλου καὶ
τὸ τοῦ ὁρίζοντος νῦν τὴν ἀνατολήν· ἔστι γὰρ οὗτος

¹ τοῦ περὶ τὴν ΜΝ (sc. κύκλου) ci. O.T.
² ὑπὸ 𝔐 𝔅ʳᵉᶜ· Fcorr. m. 1 H N O.T. : ἀπὸ Fobes.
³ ἢ ci. O.T.
⁴ τῶν μὲν l. 22 . . . ἐνέμεινεν l. 28 damnaverunt O.T.
Ideler : om. Ap.

lines reflected from H and K to the point M will bear
the same ratio to each other in all planes, and the angle
KMH will remain constant, as will also the angle made
by HΠ and MΠ upon HΠ. So the triangles on HΠ
and KΠ are equal to the triangles HMΠ and KMΠ.
Their perpendiculars will fall on the same point in
HΠ and all be equal. Let the point on which they
fall be O. Then O is the centre of the circle, of which
a semicircle MN is cut off by the horizon.[a]

[For the sun does not master the parts above, but
does master those near the earth and dissolve the
air. And that is why the circle of the rainbow is not
complete. A rainbow at night, due to the moon, is
rare. For the moon is not always full, and is naturally
too feeble to master the air. The rainbow stands
most firmly when the sun is most mastered : for then
most moisture remains in it.][b]

(II) Again, let the horizon be AKΓ, and let H be
raised some way above the horizon. And let the axis
now be HΠ. The proof will be the same in most
respects as the one above, but the pole of the circle
Π will be below the horizon AΓ, since the point H
has risen above it. The pole, and the centre of the
circle (O),[c] and the centre (K) of the circle on whose
arc the sun rises (that is, the circle HΠ) are all in

Demonstration (II).

[a] This seems to assume that the great circle A (*cf.* 375
b 33 : MPNH of Fig. 2) is the circle of the horizon, which
is not what the earlier parts of the demonstration would lead
one to suppose, *cf.* 375 b 30 ff. But Aristotle may be speaking
carelessly, or the words may be a gloss (O.T. : there is no trace
of them in Alex.). The O.T.'s conjecture, " a semicircle of
the circle about MN," would avoid the difficulty.

[b] As Ideler and O.T. remark, this passage is certainly out
of place here : and I agree with the O.T. that " it is incoherent in itself and certainly an interpolation."

[c] *i.e.* the circle which is the base of the cone.

ἐφ' ᾧ τὸ ΗΠ. ἐπεὶ δὲ τῆς διαμέτρου τῆς ΑΓ τὸ
5 ΚΗ ἐπάνω, τὸ κέντρον εἴη ἂν ὑποκάτω τοῦ ὁρίζοντος πρότερον τοῦ ἐφ' ᾧ τὸ ΑΓ, ἐπὶ τῆς ΚΠ
γραμμῆς, ἐφ' οὗ τὸ Ο.[1] ὥστ' ἔλαττον ἔσται τὸ
ἐπάνω τμῆμα ἡμικυκλίου τὸ ἐφ' ᾧ Ψ Υ· τὸ γὰρ
ΨΥΩ[2] ἡμικύκλιον ἦν, νῦν δὲ ἀποτέτμηται ὑπὸ[3]
τοῦ ΑΓ ὁρίζοντος. τὸ δὴ ΥΩ[2] ἀφανὲς ἔσται αὐτοῦ,
10 ἐπαρθέντος τοῦ ἡλίου· ἐλάχιστον δ', ὅταν ἐπὶ μεσ-
ημβρίας· ὅσον γὰρ ἀνώτερον τὸ Η, κατώτερον ὅ
τε πόλος καὶ τὸ κέντρον τοῦ κύκλου ἔσται.

"Οτι δ' ἐν μὲν ταῖς ἐλάττοσιν ἡμέραις ταῖς μετ'
ἰσημερίαν τὴν μετοπωρινὴν ἐνδέχεται ἀεὶ γίγνεσθαι

---

[1] B Op Fobes : Ο E_rec. B_rec. F_corr. m. 1 Bekker O.T.
[2] ΨΥΟ, ΟΥ Fobes.
[3] ἀπὸ Fobes : ὑπὸ B_corr. F_corr. Η Ν O.T.

---

[a] Though Fobes' readings, ΨΥΟ and ΟΥ, have good
authority, it is clear from Fig. 4 that the sense of the passage
demands the readings given here, which are those adopted by
Bekker and the O.T.

the same straight line. But since KH is above the diameter AΓ, the centre will be below the former horizon AΓ on the line KΠ at the point O. The seg-

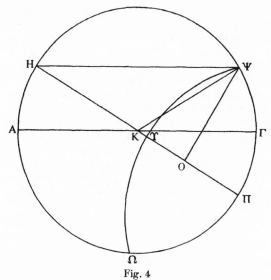

Fig. 4

ment ΨΥ above the horizon will thus be less than a hemisphere: for ΨΥΩ *a* is a semicircle and is now cut off by the horizon AΓ. So part of it, ΥΩ,*a* will be invisible when the sun has risen above the horizon, and the visible segment will be the smallest when the sun is on its meridian. For the higher H is, the lower will be the pole and the centre of the circle.

(III) The reason why, during the shorter days after the autumn equinox, it is possible for a rainbow to (III) The effect of the differences

279

377 a

ἴριν, ἐν δὲ ταῖς μακροτέραις ἡμέραις ταῖς ἀπὸ ἰσημε-
ρίας τῆς ἑτέρας ἐπὶ τὴν ἰσημερίαν τὴν ἑτέραν περὶ
15 μεσημβρίαν οὐ γίγνεται ἶρις, αἴτιον ὅτι τὰ μὲν πρὸς
ἄρκτον τμήματα πάντα μείζω ἡμικυκλίου καὶ ἀεὶ
ἐπὶ μείζω ἡμικυκλίου, τὸ δ' ἀφανὲς μικρόν, τὰ δὲ
πρὸς μεσημβρίαν τμήματα τοῦ ἰσημερινοῦ, τὸ μὲν
ἄνω τμῆμα μικρόν, τὸ δ' ὑπὸ γῆν μέγα, καὶ ἀεὶ
20 δὴ μείζω τὰ πορρώτερα· ὥστ' ἐν μὲν ταῖς πρὸς
θερινὰς τροπὰς ἡμέραις διὰ τὸ μέγεθος τοῦ τμήματος, πρὶν ἐπὶ τὸ μέσον ἐλθεῖν τοῦ τμήματος καὶ
ἐπὶ τὸν μεσημβρινὸν τὴν τὸ Η, κάτω ἤδη τελέως
γίγνεται ἡ τὸ Π, διὰ τὸ πόρρω ἀφεστάναι τῆς γῆς
τὴν μεσημβρίαν διὰ τὸ μέγεθος τοῦ τμήματος. ἐν
25 δὲ ταῖς πρὸς τὰς χειμερινὰς τροπὰς ἡμέραις, διὰ
τὸ μὴ πολὺ ὑπὲρ γῆς εἶναι τὰ τμήματα τῶν κύκλων, τοὐναντίον ἀναγκαῖον γίγνεσθαι· βραχὺ γὰρ
ἀρθείσης τῆς ἐφ' ᾧ τὸ Η, ἐπὶ τῆς μεσημβρίας
γίγνεται ὁ ἥλιος.

CHAPTER VI

ARGUMENT

(1) *Mock suns and rods. Rods are due to the reflection
of our sight to the sun from clouds of uneven consistency
(377 a 29-b 15). Mock suns are due to reflection from even
and dense cloud. Mock suns as signs of rain (377 b 15-27).
Why mock suns and rods appear only at the side of the sun,
and not above or beneath it (377 b 27—378 a 14).* (2) *We*

377 a 29   Τὰς δ' αὐτὰς αἰτίας ὑποληπτέον καὶ περὶ παρ-
30 ηλίων καὶ ῥάβδων ταῖς εἰρημέναις.

occur at any time of day, but during the longer days between the spring and autumn equinoxes no rainbow occurs about midday, is as follows : When the sun's orbit is north of the equator the visible segment of it is greater than a semicircle and continues to increase, while the segment that is invisible is small ; when it is south of the equator the upper, visible segment is small, while the segment below the earth is large, and increases as the sun recedes. In the days of the summer solstice, therefore, the size of the segment is so large that before the point H reaches the middle of the segment, that is, the meridian, the point H is already well below the horizon, because the segment is large and therefore the distance of the meridian from the earth great. But in the days of the winter solstice the opposite result must follow, because the segments of the sun's orbit above the earth are not large : for the sun reaches its meridian when the point H has risen only a small distance.

in the sun's arc.

CHAPTER VI

ARGUMENT (continued)

have still to study the effects produced by the two forms of exhalation within the earth. They give rise to two types of substance, minerals and metals (378 a 15–b 6).

With 378 a 15 ff. cf. Eichholz, " Aristotle's Theory of the Formation of Metals and Minerals," C.Q. xliii (July-Oct. 1949).

(1) Mock suns and rods must again be supposed to be produced by the same causes.

(1) Mock suns and rods also

377 a

Γίγνεται γὰρ παρήλιος μὲν ἀνακλωμένης τῆς ὄψεως πρὸς τὸν ἥλιον, ῥάβδοι δὲ διὰ τὸ προσπίπτειν τοιαύτην οὖσαν τὴν ὄψιν, οἵαν εἴπομεν ἀεὶ γίγνεσθαι ὅταν πλησίον ὄντων τοῦ ἡλίου νεφῶν ἀπό τινος ἀνακλασθῇ τῶν ὑγρῶν πρὸς τὸ νέφος· φαί-

377 b νεται γὰρ αὐτὰ μὲν ἀχρωμάτιστα τὰ νέφη κατ' εὐθυωρίαν εἰσβλέπουσιν, ἐν δὲ τῷ ὕδατι ῥάβδων μεστὸν τὸ νέφος· πλὴν τότε μὲν ἐν τῷ ὕδατι δοκεῖ τὸ χρῶμα τοῦ νέφους εἶναι, ἐν δὲ ταῖς ῥάβδοις ἐπ' αὐτοῦ τοῦ νέφους. γίγνεται δὲ τοῦτο ὅταν ἀνώ-
5 μαλος ἡ τοῦ νέφους ᾖ σύστασις, καὶ τῇ μὲν πυκνό-τερον τῇ δὲ μανόν, καὶ τῇ μὲν ὑδατωδέστερον τῇ δ' ἧττον· ἀνακλασθείσης γὰρ τῆς ὄψεως πρὸς τὸν ἥλιον, τὸ σχῆμα μὲν [τοῦ ἡλίου][1] οὐχ ὁρᾶται [διὰ μικρότητα τῶν ἐνόπτρων],[1] τὸ δὲ χρῶμα· διὰ δὲ τὸ ἐν ἀνωμάλῳ φαίνεσθαι λαμπρὸν καὶ λευκὸν τὸν
10 ἥλιον, πρὸς ὃν ἀνεκλάσθη ἡ ὄψις, τὸ μὲν φοινικοῦν φαίνεται, τὸ δὲ πράσινον ἢ ξανθόν. διαφέρει γὰρ οὐδὲν διὰ τοιούτων ὁρᾶν ἢ ἀπὸ τοιούτων ἀνακλω-μένην· ἀμφοτέρως γὰρ φαίνεται τὴν χρόαν ὅμοιον, ὥστ' εἰ κἀκείνως φοινικοῦν, καὶ οὕτως.

Αἱ μὲν οὖν ῥάβδοι γίγνονται δι' ἀνωμαλίαν τοῦ
15 ἐνόπτρου οὐ τῷ σχήματι ἀλλὰ τῷ χρώματι· ὁ δὲ παρήλιος, ὅταν ὅτι μάλιστα ὁμαλὸς ᾖ ὁ ἀὴρ καὶ πυκνὸς ὁμοίως· διὸ φαίνεται λευκός. ἡ μὲν γὰρ ὁμαλότης τοῦ ἐνόπτρου ποιεῖ χρόαν μίαν τῆς ἐμ-φάσεως· ἡ δ' ἀνάκλασις ἀθρόας τῆς ὄψεως, διὰ τὸ ἅμα προσπίπτειν πρὸς τὸν ἥλιον ἀπὸ πυκνῆς οὔσης
20 τῆς ἀχλύος, καὶ οὔπω μὲν οὔσης ὕδωρ[2] ἐγγὺς δ'

---

[1] secl. Fobes.
[2] ὕδωρ Fobes codd. : ὕδατος ci. Thurot qui ὕδωρ non con-strui posse censet : cf. Ἀρ ὑδατώδους.

A mock sun is caused by the reflection of our sight due to reflection. Rods. to the sun. Rods are caused when our sight reaches the sun in the condition in which we have said [a] it does when it is reflected from some liquid surface to a cloud, when there are clouds near the sun : for the clouds when we look directly at them appear colourless, but their reflection in water is full of rods. The only difference is that it is the reflection of the cloud in water that appears coloured, while the colours of the rod appear on the cloud itself. This takes place when the consistency of the cloud is uneven, and part of it is dense and part rare, part more and part less, watery. For when the sight is reflected to the sun its shape is not seen owing to the smallness of the reflecting particles,[b] but its colour is : and the clear, bright light of the sun to which our sight is reflected, seen on an uneven reflecting surface, appears partly red, partly green or yellow.[c] It makes no difference whether sight passes through a medium or is reflected from a surface of this kind : in either case a similar colour appears, and if it is red in the one case it will be in the other.

The colour, therefore, of rods, though not their Mock suns. shape, is caused by the unevenness of the reflecting surface. A mock sun appears when the air is very even and at the same time dense. Hence its bright colour. For the evenness of the reflecting surface produces an image of a single colour ; and our sight is reflected as a whole and projected all at once to the sun from the mist, which is dense and very nearly water though not yet quite, and this reflection causes

[a] 374 b 9 ff.   *Cf.* esp. 374 b 20.
[b] 372 a 32, 373 b 17.
[c] *Cf.* 374 b 30.

377 b

ὕδατος, [διὰ]¹ τὸ ὑπάρχον τῷ ἡλίῳ ἐμφαίνεσθαι χρῶμα ποιεῖ, ὥσπερ ἀπὸ χαλκοῦ λείου κλωμένην διὰ τὴν πυκνότητα. ὥστ᾽ ἐπεὶ τὸ χρῶμα τοῦ ἡλίου λευκόν, καὶ ὁ παρήλιος φαίνεται λευκός. διὰ δὲ τὸ αὐτὸ τοῦτο μᾶλλον ὕδατος σημεῖον ὁ παρήλιος
25 τῶν ῥάβδων· μᾶλλον γὰρ συμβαίνει τὸν ἀέρα εὐεργῶς ἔχειν πρὸς γένεσιν ὕδατος. ὁ δὲ νότιος τοῦ βορείου μᾶλλον, ὅτι μᾶλλον ὁ νότιος ἀὴρ εἰς ὕδωρ μεταβάλλει τοῦ πρὸς ἄρκτον.

Γίγνονται δ᾽, ὥσπερ εἴπομεν, περί τε δυσμὰς καὶ περὶ τὰς ἀνατολάς, καὶ οὔτε ἄνωθεν οὔτε κάτω-
30 θεν, ἀλλ᾽ ἐκ τῶν πλαγίων καὶ ῥάβδοι καὶ παρήλιοι· καὶ οὔτ᾽ ἐγγὺς τοῦ ἡλίου λίαν οὔτε πόρρω παντελῶς· ἐγγὺς μὲν γὰρ οὖσαν ὁ ἥλιος διαλύει τὴν σύστασιν, πόρρω δ᾽ οὔσης ἡ ὄψις οὐκ ἀνακλασθήσεται· ἀπὸ γὰρ μικροῦ ἐνόπτρου πόρρω ἀποτεινομένη ἀσθενὴς γίγνεται· διὸ καὶ αἱ ἅλως οὐ γίγνονται ἐξ ἐναντίας
378 a τοῦ ἡλίου. ἄνω μὲν οὖν ἐὰν γίγνηται καὶ ἐγγύς, διαλύσει ὁ ἥλιος· ἐὰν δὲ πόρρω, ἐλάττων ἡ ὄψις οὖσα ἢ ὥστε ποιεῖν ἀνάκλασιν οὐ προσπεσεῖται. ἐν δὲ τῷ πλαγίῳ [ὑπὸ τὸν ἥλιον]² ἐστὶ τοσοῦτον ἀποστῆναι τὸ ἔνοπτρον, ὥστε μήτε τὸν ἥλιον δια-
5 λῦσαι, τήν τε ὄψιν ἀθρόαν ἐλθεῖν, διὰ τὸ πρὸς τῇ γῇ³ φερομένην μὴ διασπᾶσθαι ὥσπερ δι᾽ ἀχανοῦς φερομένην. ὑπὸ δὲ τὸν ἥλιον οὐ γίγνεται διὰ τὸ πλησίον μὲν τῆς γῆς διαλύεσθαι ἂν ὑπὸ τοῦ ἡλίου, ἄνω δὲ μεσουρανίου ⟨γιγνομένης συστάσεως⟩⁴ τὴν ὄψιν διασπᾶσθαι. καὶ ὅλως οὐδ᾽ ἐκ πλαγίου μεσ-

---

¹ secl. Fobes.　　　　² secl. Fobes.
³ τῇ γῇ O.T.　τὴν γῆν Fobes.

the sun's real colour to appear, as it does when our sight is reflected by the density of a polished copper surface. As the colour of the sun is bright, so, therefore, is the colour of the mock sun. For this same reason the mock sun is more a sign of rain than of rods, the air being in a more favourable condition for the production of water. And a mock sun in the south is more of a sign of rain than one in the north, because the air in the south is more liable to change to water than the air towards the north.

Both rods and mock suns occur, as we said,[a] at sunset and sunrise, and neither above nor below the sun, but beside it. Nor do they occur very close to the sun, nor very far off. For if the condensation is close the sun dissolves it, and if it is far off the sight is not reflected. For when the reflecting surface is small the sight grows progressively weaker as the distance increases, which is why haloes do not occur opposite the sun. If, then, the condensation is close to the sun and above it, the sun will dissolve it : if it is far at a distance from it, the sight is too weak to produce a reflection and does not reach it. But at the side of the sun the reflecting material can be far enough away for the sun not to dissolve it, yet near enough for sight to reach it as a whole, because its course is near the earth and it is not, as it were, dissipated on its journey through space. Reflection does not take place below the sun because close to the earth the sun would dissolve the reflecting material, whereas when it forms high in the heavens the sight is dissipated. Indeed it does not take place even at the

[a] 372 a 10.

_____

[4] γιγνομένης συστάσεως ci. Fobes, cf. Ap : ὄντος E 𝔚.

10 οὐρανίου γίγνεται· ἡ γὰρ ὄψις οὐ πρὸς τῇ γῇ[1]
φέρεται, ὥστε ὀλίγη ἀφικνεῖται πρὸς τὸ ἔνοπτρον,
καὶ ἡ ἀνακλωμένη γίγνεται πάμπαν ἀσθενής.

Ὅσα μὲν οὖν ἔργα συμβαίνει παρέχεσθαι τὴν
ἔκκρισιν ἐν τοῖς τόποις τοῖς ὑπὲρ τῆς γῆς, σχεδόν
15 ἐστι τοσαῦτα καὶ τοιαῦτα. ὅσα δ' ἐν αὐτῇ τῇ γῇ,
ἐγκατακλειομένη τοῖς τῆς γῆς μέρεσιν, ἀπεργάζε-
ται, λεκτέον.

Ποιεῖ γὰρ δύο διαφορὰς σωμάτων διὰ τὸ διπλῆ
πεφυκέναι καὶ αὐτή, καθάπερ καὶ ἐν τῷ μετεώρῳ·
δύο μὲν γὰρ αἱ ἀναθυμιάσεις, ἡ μὲν ἀτμιδώδης ἡ δὲ
20 καπνώδης, ὥς φαμεν, εἰσίν· δύο δὲ καὶ τὰ εἴδη τῶν
ἐν τῇ γῇ γιγνομένων, τὰ μὲν ὀρυκτὰ τὰ δὲ μεταλ-
λευτά. ἡ μὲν οὖν ξηρὰ ἀναθυμίασίς ἐστιν ἥ τις
ἐκπυροῦσα ποιεῖ τὰ ὀρυκτὰ πάντα, οἷον λίθων τε
γένη τὰ ἄτηκτα καὶ σανδαράκην καὶ ὦχραν καὶ μίλ-
τον καὶ θεῖον καὶ τἆλλα τὰ τοιαῦτα. τὰ δὲ πλεῖστα
25 τῶν ὀρυκτῶν ἐστιν τὰ μὲν κονία κεχρωματισμένη,
τὰ δὲ λίθος ἐκ τοιαύτης γεγονὼς συστάσεως, οἷον τὸ
κιννάβαρι. τῆς δ' ἀναθυμιάσεως τῆς ἀτμιδώδους,
ὅσα μεταλλεύεται, καὶ ἔστιν ἢ χυτὰ ἢ ἐλατά, οἷον
σίδηρος, χρυσός, χαλκός. ποιεῖ δὲ ταῦτα πάντα
ἡ ἀναθυμίασις ἡ ἀτμιδώδης ἐγκατακλειομένη, καὶ
30 μάλιστα ἐν τοῖς λίθοις, διὰ ξηρότητα εἰς ἓν συνθλι-
βομένη καὶ πηγνυμένη, οἷον ἢ δρόσος ἢ πάχνη,
ὅταν ἀποκριθῇ. ἐνταῦθα δὲ πρὶν ἀποκριθῆναι
γεννᾶται ταῦτα. διὸ ἔστι μὲν ὡς ὕδωρ ταῦτα,
ἔστιν δ' ὡς οὔ· δυνάμει μὲν γὰρ ἡ ὕλη ὕδατος ἦν,
ἔστι δ' οὐκέτι, οὐδ' ἐξ ὕδατος γενομένου διά τι

---

[1] πρὸς τῇ γῇ Ap : ὑπὸ τὴν γῆν Fobes codd.

---

[a] Lit. substances dug or quarried and substances mined.
" The ' fossils ' include not only certain minerals such as

side of the sun when it is high : for our sight is not then travelling close to the earth, and so when it reaches the reflecting surface it is already weak and its reflection lacks force entirely.

(2) This, then, completes our enumeration of the kind of effects produced by exhalation in the regions above the earth's surface : we have still to describe those which it produces when enclosed in the parts of the earth.

It produces two different kinds of body, being itself twofold just as it is in the upper regions. For there are, we maintain, two exhalations, one vaporous and one smoky ; and there are two corresponding kinds of body produced within the earth, " fossiles " and metals.[a] The dry exhalation by the action of its heat produces all the " fossiles," for example, all kinds of stones that are infusible—realgar, ochre, ruddle, sulphur and all other substances of this kind. Most " fossiles " are coloured dust or stone formed of a similar composition, for instance cinnabar. Metals are the product of the vaporous exhalation, and are all fusible or ductile, for example, iron, gold, copper. These are all produced by the enclosure of the vaporous exhalation, particularly within stones, whose dryness compresses it together and solidifies it, just as dew and frost [b] solidify when they have been separated—only metals are produced before separation has taken place. So they are in a sense water and in another sense not : it was possible for their material to turn into water, but it can no longer do so, nor are they, like tastes, the result of some change of

realgar, ochre, ruddle, sulphur and cinnabar, but also those stones which cannot be melted " (Eichholz, *loc. cit.*).

   [b] Book I. ch. 10.

373 b πάθος, ὥσπερ οἱ χυμοί· οὐδὲ γὰρ οὕτω γίγνεται
τὸ μὲν χαλκὸς τὸ δὲ χρυσός, ἀλλὰ πρὶν γενέσθαι
παγείσης τῆς ἀναθυμιάσεως ἕκαστα τούτων ἐστίν.
διὸ καὶ πυροῦται πάντα καὶ γῆν ἔχει· ξηρὰν γὰρ
ἔχει ἀναθυμίασιν· ὁ δὲ χρυσὸς μόνος οὐ πυροῦται.
5 Κοινῇ μὲν οὖν εἴρηται περὶ αὐτῶν ἁπάντων, ἰδίᾳ
δὲ σκεπτέον προχειριζομένοις περὶ ἕκαστον γένος.

quality in water that has already formed. For this is not the way in which copper or gold is produced, but each is the result of the solidification of the exhalation before it turns to water. So all metals are affected by fire and contain earth, for they contain dry exhalation. The only exception is gold, which is not affected by fire.

So much for a general account of these bodies; we must now take each kind separately and examine it in detail.

Δ

CHAPTER I

ARGUMENT

*Of the four constituent qualities of the four elements, two,
heat and cold, are active, two, moist and dry, are passive
(378 b 10-26). These factors, active and passive, give rise to
generation, change and destruction (378 b 26—379 a 11). Destruction is due to the failure of the active factors in a thing
to master the passive. Decay is due to the destruction of a
moist body's natural heat by external heat, and so may be
said to be due to internal cold or external heat. Confirmatory
examples (379 a 11–b 9).*

378 b 10 Ἐπεὶ δὲ τέτταρα αἴτια διώρισται τῶν στοιχείων,
τούτων δὲ κατὰ συζυγίας καὶ τὰ στοιχεῖα τέτταρα
συμβέβηκεν εἶναι, ὧν τὰ μὲν δύο ποιητικά, τὸ
θερμὸν καὶ τὸ ψυχρόν, τὰ δὲ δύο παθητικά, τὸ ξηρὸν
καὶ τὸ ὑγρόν· ἡ δὲ πίστις τούτων ἐκ τῆς ἐπαγωγῆς·
15 φαίνεται γὰρ ἐν πᾶσιν ἡ μὲν θερμότης καὶ ψυχρότης
ὁρίζουσαι καὶ συμφύουσαι καὶ μεταβάλλουσαι τά
θ' ὁμογενῆ καὶ τὰ μὴ ὁμογενῆ, καὶ ὑγραίνουσαι
καὶ ξηραίνουσαι καὶ σκληρύνουσαι καὶ μαλάττουσαι,
τὰ δὲ ξηρὰ καὶ ὑγρὰ ὁριζόμενα καὶ τἆλλα τὰ εἰρη-

---

[a] *Cf.* Book I. ch. 2. For the general doctrine of the four
elements, each of which is composed of prime matter and a

290

BOOK IV

CHAPTER I

ARGUMENT (*continued*)

Note.—*The word translated " generation " in this chapter (γένεσις) covers all processes of coming into existence of whatever kind ; " destruction " (φθορά), correspondingly, covers all kinds of passing out of existence ; " decay " (σῆψις) is a particular, but very common, type of " destruction " (φθορά), covering generally cases in which a thing decays, disintegrates or perishes in the ordinary course of nature (cf. 379 a 3), its literal meaning being " putrefaction."*

WE have distinguished in the elements four causal factors whose combinations yield four elements [a] : two of the factors are active, the hot and the cold, two are passive, the moist and the dry. This can be confirmed by considering some examples. (1) It is always heat and cold that are observed to determine, combine and change things both of the same and of different kinds, as well as moistening, drying, hardening and softening : things dry and moist, on the other hand, are the subjects of determination and the other changes just

The active and passive qualities,

---

[a] pair of the prime contrarieties (fire = hot-dry, air = moist-hot, water = moist-cold, earth = dry-cold), see *De Caelo* iii-iv, *De Gen. et Corr.* ii. 1-6. For the view that hot and cold are active, moist and dry passive, *cf.* in particular *De Gen. et Corr.* ii. 2, 329 b 20-33, and Joachim's note *ad* 329 b 24-26.

378 b

μένα πάθη πάσχοντα αὐτά τε καθ᾽ αὑτὰ καὶ ὅσα
20 κοινὰ ἐξ ἀμφοῖν σώματα συνέστηκεν· ἔτι δ᾽ ἐκ τῶν
λόγων δῆλον, οἷς ὁριζόμεθα τὰς φύσεις αὐτῶν· τὸ
μὲν γὰρ θερμὸν καὶ ψυχρὸν ὡς ποιητικὰ λέγομεν
(τὸ γὰρ συγκριτικὸν ὥσπερ ποιητικόν τί ἐστι), τὸ
δὲ ὑγρὸν καὶ ξηρὸν παθητικόν (τὸ γὰρ εὐόριστον
25 καὶ δυσόριστον τῷ πάσχειν τι λέγεται τὴν φύσιν
αὐτῶν).

Ὅτι μὲν οὖν τὰ μὲν ποιητικὰ τὰ δὲ παθητικά, φανερόν. διωρισμένων δὲ τούτων ληπτέον ἂν εἴη τὰς
ἐργασίας αὐτῶν, αἷς ἐργάζονται τὰ ποιητικά, καὶ
τῶν παθητικῶν τὰ εἴδη. πρῶτον μὲν οὖν καθόλου
ἡ ἁπλῆ γένεσις καὶ ἡ φυσικὴ μεταβολὴ τούτων τῶν
30 δυνάμεών ἐστιν ἔργον, καὶ ἡ ἀντικειμένη φθορὰ
κατὰ φύσιν. αὗται μὲν οὖν τοῖς τε φυτοῖς ὑπάρχουσι καὶ ζῴοις καὶ τοῖς μέρεσιν αὐτῶν. ἔστι δ᾽
ἡ ἁπλῆ καὶ ἡ φυσικὴ γένεσις μεταβολὴ ὑπὸ τούτων
τῶν δυνάμεων, ὅταν ἔχωσι λόγον, ἐκ τῆς ὑποκει-
μένης ὕλης ἑκάστη φύσει· αὗται δ᾽ εἰσὶν αἱ εἰρη-
379 a μέναι δυνάμεις παθητικαί. γεννῶσι δὲ τὸ θερμὸν
καὶ ψυχρὸν κρατοῦντα τῆς ὕλης· ὅταν δὲ μὴ κρατῇ,
κατὰ μέρος μὲν μόλυνσις καὶ ἀπεψία γίγνεται. τῇ
δ᾽ ἁπλῇ γενέσει ἐναντίον μάλιστα κοινὸν σῆψις·
πᾶσα γὰρ ἡ κατὰ φύσιν φθορὰ εἰς τοῦθ᾽ ὁδός ἐστιν,
5 οἷον γῆρας καὶ αὔανσις. τέλος δὲ πάντων [τῶν
ἄλλων τούτων][1] σαπρότης, ἐὰν μή τι βίᾳ φθαρῇ,[2]
τῶν φύσει συνεστώτων· ἔστι γὰρ καὶ σάρκα καὶ
ὀστοῦν καὶ ὁτιοῦν κατακαῦσαι, ὧν τὸ τέλος τῆς

---

[1] seclusi. τούτων ἁπάντων O.T. γὰρ τῶν ἄλλων ἁπάντων E₁:
γὰρ τούτων ἁπάντων E_corr. ꟽ: *enim horum cunctorum* Hen-
ricus : δὲ τῶν ἄλλων ἁπάντων Bekker.
[2] post φθαρῇ virgulam ponunt Thurot O.T.

enumerated, both in isolation and in combination with each other. (2) We can see the same thing by examining the terms of the definitions we give of the natures of these factors. For we speak of the hot and the cold as active (for what causes combination is in a sense active) and the moist and the dry as passive (for what is unresistant or resistant is so described in virtue of being affected in a certain way).

It is clear, therefore, that of the four factors two are active, two passive. Having established this, we must describe the operations of the active factors and the forms taken by the passive. First, then, simple generation and natural change are the result of these properties, as well as the corresponding natural destruction : and these processes occur both in plants and in animals and their constituent parts. Simple, natural generation is a change effected by these properties, when present in the right proportions, in the matter underlying a particular natural thing, this matter being the passive properties of which we have spoken. The hot and the cold produce change by mastering the matter : when they fail to master it the result is half-cooked [a] and undigested. But the most general contrary to simple generation is decay. For all natural destruction leads to decay, for instance old age and withering, and all compound natural bodies rot in the end,[b] unless they are destroyed by violence : for it is of course quite possible to destroy by burning either flesh, bone or anything else which in the ordinary course of nature is finally destroyed by

their mutual relations cause generation, change and destruction.

[a] Cf. 381 a 12 and ch. 3, note b on p. 306.
[b] The omission of τῶν ἄλλων τούτων gives the sense that seems to be required, though there is no MS. justification for the omission ; the passage is clearly corrupt and the words may be a gloss on πάντων.

κατὰ φύσιν φθορᾶς σῆψίς ἐστιν. διὸ ὑγρὰ πρῶτον,
εἶτα ξηρὰ τέλος γίγνεται τὰ σηπόμενα· ἐκ τούτων
10 γὰρ ἐγένετο, καὶ ὡρίσθη τῷ ὑγρῷ τὸ ξηρὸν ἐργα-
ζομένων τῶν ποιητικῶν.

Γίγνεται δ' ἡ φθορὰ ὅταν κρατῇ τοῦ ὁρίζοντος
τὸ ὁριζόμενον διὰ τὸ περιέχον. (οὐ μὴν ἀλλ' ἰδίως
γε λέγεται σῆψις ἐπὶ τῶν κατὰ μέρος φθειρομένων,
ὅταν χωρισθῇ τῆς φύσεως.) διὸ καὶ σήπεται πάντα
15 τἆλλα πλὴν πυρός· καὶ γὰρ γῆ καὶ ὕδωρ καὶ ἀὴρ
σήπεται· πάντα γὰρ ὕλη τῷ πυρί ἐστι ταῦτα.
σῆψις δ' ἐστὶν φθορὰ τῆς ἐν ἑκάστῳ ὑγρῷ οἰκείας
καὶ κατὰ φύσιν θερμότητος ὑπ' ἀλλοτρίας θερμό-
τητος· αὕτη δ' ἐστὶν ἡ τοῦ περιέχοντος. ὥστε
ἐπεὶ κατ' ἔνδειαν πάσχει θερμοῦ, ἐνδεὲς δὲ ὂν
20 τοιαύτης δυνάμεως ψυχρὸν πᾶν, ἄμφω ἂν αἴτια
εἴη, καὶ κοινὸν τὸ πάθος ἡ σῆψις, ψυχρότητός τε
οἰκείας καὶ θερμότητος ἀλλοτρίας. διὰ τοῦτο γὰρ
καὶ ξηρότερα γίγνεται τὰ σηπόμενα πάντα, καὶ
τέλος γῆ καὶ κόπρος· ἐξιόντος γὰρ τοῦ οἰκείου
θερμοῦ συνεξατμίζεται τὸ κατὰ φύσιν ὑγρόν, καὶ
25 τὸ σπῶν τὴν ὑγρότητα οὐκ ἔστιν· ἐπάγει γὰρ
ἕλκουσα ἡ οἰκεία θερμότης. καὶ ἐν τοῖς ψύχεσι δ'
ἧττον σήπεται ἢ ἐν ταῖς ἀλέαις (ἐν μὲν γὰρ τῷ
χειμῶνι ὀλίγον ἐν τῷ περιέχοντι ἀέρι καὶ ὕδατι
τὸ θερμόν, ὥστ' οὐδὲν ἰσχύει, ἐν δὲ τῷ θέρει πλέον)·
30 καὶ οὔτε τὸ πεπηγός (μᾶλλον γὰρ ψυχρὸν ἢ ὁ ἀὴρ
θερμόν· οὔκουν κρατεῖται, τὸ δὲ κινοῦν κρατεῖ) οὔτε

---

a Cf. Joachim, loc. cit. ; for the importance of σύμφυτον
θερμόν cf. Jaeger, Hermes xlviii. pp. 43-55, and Joachim,
Journal of Philology, xxix (1903), pp. 72-86, and De Part. An.

decay. Things, therefore, that are decaying become first moist and then in the end dry : for it was from these properties that they originated, the moist being determined by the dry through the operation of the active properties.

Destruction takes place when what is being determined gets the better of what is determining it with the help of its environment (though there is a special sense in which decay is used of things which are partially destroyed, when they have departed from their true nature). So everything else decays except fire : for earth, water and air all decay, since all are matter in relation to fire. Decay is the destruction of a moist body's own natural heat by heat external to it, that is, the heat of its environment.[a] Since, therefore, a thing is so affected because of lack of heat, and as everything that lacks this property is cold, decay is caused by and is the common result alike of internal coldness and external heat. That is why everything that decays gets drier, until it ends as earth or dung : for as its own heat leaves it its natural moisture evaporates, and there is nothing to suck moisture into it (this being the function of its own heat, which attracts and draws moisture in). And there is less decay in cold than in warm weather : for in winter the amount of heat in the surrounding air and water is so small as to be ineffective, while in summer it is greater. Again, what is frozen does not decay, as its cold is greater than the air's heat, and therefore is not mastered by it : but what causes change in a thing does master it. Nor does any-

ii. 3, 650 a 2 ff., *De Gen. An.* 736 b 33 ff., 742 a 14, 784 a 34 ff., *De Vit. et Mort.* 469 b 7-20, with Book II. ch. 2, 355 b 9 above.

379 a

τὸ ζέον ἢ θερμόν (ἐλάττων γὰρ ἡ ἐν τῷ ἀέρι θερμότης τῆς ἐν τῷ πράγματι, ὥστ᾽ οὐ κρατεῖ οὐδὲ ποιεῖ
μεταβολὴν οὐδεμίαν). ὁμοίως δὲ καὶ τὸ κινούμενον
καὶ ῥέον ἧττον σήπεται τοῦ ἀκινητίζοντος· ἀσθενε-
35 στέρα γὰρ γίγνεται ἡ ὑπὸ τῆς ἐν τῷ ἀέρι θερμό-
379 b τητος κίνησις τῆς ἐν τῷ πράγματι προϋπαρχούσης,
ὥστε οὐδὲν ποιεῖ μεταβάλλειν. ἡ δ᾽ αὐτὴ αἰτία καὶ
τοῦ τὸ πολὺ ἧττον τοῦ ὀλίγου σήπεσθαι· ἐν γὰρ
τῷ πλέονι πλέον ἐστὶν πῦρ οἰκεῖον καὶ ψυχρὸν ἢ
ὥστε κρατεῖν τὰς ἐν τῷ περιεστῶτι δυνάμεις. διὸ
5 ἡ θάλαττα κατὰ μέρος μὲν διαιρουμένη ταχὺ σήπεται, ἅπασα δ᾽ οὔ, καὶ τἆλλα ὕδατα ὡσαύτως.
καὶ ζῷα ἐγγίγνεται τοῖς σηπομένοις διὰ τὸ τὴν
ἀποκεκριμένην θερμότητα φυσικὴν οὖσαν συνι-
στάναι τὰ ἐκκριθέντα.

Τί μὲν οὖν ἐστι γένεσις καὶ τί φθορά, εἴρηται.

---

[a] *Cf.* 389 b 5: Aristotle believed that living things
(*e.g.* maggots) are produced spontaneously from decaying

CHAPTER II

ARGUMENT

*Chapter I has dealt with heat and cold as causes of growth
and decay in general, the processes which produce or destroy
natural bodies : Chapter II goes on to deal with their effects
on bodies so produced. The effect of heat on bodies is con-*

379 b 10 Λοιπὸν δ᾽ εἰπεῖν τὰ ἐχόμενα εἴδη, ὅσα αἱ εἰρη-
μέναι δυνάμεις ἐργάζονται ἐξ ὑποκειμένων τῶν
φύσει συνεστώτων ἤδη.

thing boiling or hot decay, because the heat in the surrounding air is less than that in the object, and so does not master it or cause any change. Similarly, what is in motion or flowing decays less easily than what is static. For the motive force of the heat in the air is less than that of the heat residing in the object, and so causes no change. For the same reason large quantities decay less than small ones : for the larger quantity has too much native heat and cold in it for the properties of its environment to master. Therefore sea water in small quantities decays rapidly, but in bulk it does not : and the same is true of other kinds of water. Living things are generated in decaying matter because the natural heat which is expelled compounds them out of the material thrown off with it.[a]

This completes our description of generation and destruction.

matter : *cf. Hist. An.* v. 2 and Bonitz, *Index,* 124 b 3-22, for further references.

CHAPTER II

ARGUMENT (continued)

coction, of which there are three species, ripening, boiling and roasting : the effect of cold is inconcoction, whose species are rawness, scalding and scorching (379 b 10-18). Concoction and inconcoction. Concoction is maturity, produced by heat : inconcoction its opposite (379 b 18—380 a 10).

WE must next describe the kind of effect which the properties in question produce when operating on already constituted natural bodies as their material.

Ἔστι δὴ θερμοῦ μὲν πέψις, πέψεως δὲ πέπανσις,
ἕψησις, ἔτι ὄπτησις· ψυχρότητος δὲ ἀπεψία, ταύτης
δὲ ὠμότης, μόλυνσις, στάτευσις. δεῖ δὲ ὑπολαμ-
15 βάνειν μὴ κυρίως ταῦτα λέγεσθαι τὰ ὀνόματα τοῖς
πράγμασιν, ἀλλ᾽ οὐ κεῖται καθόλου τοῖς ὁμοίοις,
ὥστε οὐ ταῦτα ἀλλὰ τοιαῦτα δεῖ νομίζειν εἶναι τὰ
εἰρημένα εἴδη.

Εἴπωμεν δ᾽ αὐτῶν ἕκαστον τί ἐστιν.

Πέψις μὲν οὖν ἐστιν τελείωσις ὑπὸ τοῦ φυσικοῦ
καὶ οἰκείου θερμοῦ ἐκ τῶν ἀντικειμένων παθη-
20 τικῶν· ταῦτα δ᾽ ἐστὶν ἡ οἰκεία ἑκάστῳ ὕλη. ὅταν
γὰρ πεφθῇ, τετελείωταί τε καὶ γέγονεν. καὶ ἡ
ἀρχὴ τῆς τελειώσεως ὑπὸ θερμότητος τῆς οἰκείας
συμβαίνει, κἂν διά τινος τῶν ἐκτὸς βοηθείας συν-
επιτελεσθῇ, οἷον ἡ τροφὴ συμπέττεται καὶ διὰ λου-
τρῶν καὶ δι᾽ ἄλλων τοιούτων· ἀλλ᾽ ἥ γε ἀρχὴ ἡ ἐν
25 αὐτῷ θερμότης ἐστίν. τὸ δὲ τέλος τοῖς μὲν ἡ
φύσις ἐστίν, φύσις δὲ ἣν λέγομεν ὡς εἶδος καὶ
οὐσίαν· τοῖς δὲ εἰς ὑποκειμένην τινὰ μορφὴν τὸ
τέλος ἐστὶ τῆς πέψεως, ὅταν τοιονδὶ γένηται καὶ
τοσονδὶ τὸ ὑγρὸν ἢ ὀπτώμενον ἢ ἑψόμενον ἢ ση-
πόμενον[1] ἢ ἄλλως πως θερμαινόμενον· τότε γὰρ
30 χρήσιμόν ἐστι καὶ πεπέφθαι φαμέν, ὥσπερ τὸ
γλεῦκος καὶ τὰ ἐν τοῖς φύμασιν συνιστάμενα, ὅταν
γένηται πύον, καὶ τὸ δάκρυον, ὅταν γένηται λήμη·
ὁμοίως δὲ καὶ τἆλλα.

---

[1] πεπαινόμενον (in O glossam) ci. Thurot.

---

a Notice that Aristotle assimilates chemical change of all

The effect of heat is concoction, and there are three species of concoction, ripening, boiling and roasting : the effect of cold is inconcoction, whose species are their rawness, scalding and scorching. It must, however, be understood that these terms do not properly describe the subject-matter under discussion, nor cover all the phenomena which should be classed together as similar : the terms just mentioned must therefore be interpreted to cover all phenomena which should be classed with them and not only those covered by their normal meaning.[a]

Concoction, inconcoction and their species.

Let us deal with them in order.

Concoction is maturity, produced from the opposite, passive characteristics by a thing's own natural heat, these passive characteristics being the matter proper to the particular thing. For when a thing has been concocted it has become fully mature. And the maturing process is initiated by the thing's own heat, even though external aids may contribute to it : as, for instance, baths and the like may aid digestion, but it is initiated by the body's own heat. In some cases the end of the process is a thing's nature, in the sense of its form and essence. In others the end of concoction is the realization of some latent form, as when moisture takes on a certain quality and quantity when cooked or boiled or rotted [b] or otherwise heated ; for then it is useful for something and we say it has been concocted. Examples are must, the pus that gathers in boils, and tears when they become rheum ; and so on.

Concoction.

kinds (for this is, in our terms, what he is trying to explain) to the two easily observable processes of cooking food and ripening fruit : *cf.* 380 a 16, 381 a 10, b 3 below.

[b] The sense given by Thurot's alternative reading, " ripened," is better.

Συμβαίνει δὲ τοῦτο πάσχειν ἅπασιν, ὅταν κρα-
τηθῇ ἡ ὕλη καὶ ἡ ὑγρότης· αὕτη γάρ ἐστιν ἡ ὁρι-
35 ζομένη ὑπὸ τῆς ἐν τῇ φύσει θερμότητος. ἕως γὰρ
380 a ἂν ἐνῇ ἐν αὐτῇ ὁ λόγος, φύσις τοῦτ᾽ ἐστίν. διὸ
καὶ ὑγιείας σημεῖα τὰ τοιαῦτα, καὶ οὖρα καὶ ὑποχωρήσεις καὶ ὅλως τὰ περιττώματα. καὶ λέγεται
πεπέφθαι, ὅτι δηλοῖ κρατεῖν τὴν θερμότητα τὴν
οἰκείαν τοῦ ἀορίστου. ἀνάγκη δὲ τὰ πεττόμενα
5 παχύτερα καὶ θερμότερα εἶναι· τοιοῦτον γὰρ ἀπο-
τελεῖ τὸ θερμόν, εὐογκότερον καὶ παχύτερον καὶ
ξηρότερον.

Πέψις μὲν οὖν τοῦτό ἐστιν· ἀπεψία δὲ ἀτέλεια
δι᾽ ἔνδειαν τῆς οἰκείας θερμότητος (ἡ δὲ ἔνδεια
τῆς θερμότητος ψυχρότης ἐστίν)· ἡ δ᾽ ἀτέλειά
ἐστιν τῶν ἀντικειμένων παθητικῶν, ἥπερ ἐστὶν
ἑκάστῳ φύσει ὕλη.

10 Πέψις μὲν οὖν καὶ ἀπεψία διωρίσθω τοῦτον τὸν
τρόπον.

CHAPTER III

ARGUMENT

*The species of concoction and inconcoction. Ripening
(380 a 11-27), rawness (380 a 27-b 11), boiling (380 b 12—*

380 a 11 Πέπανσις δ᾽ ἐστὶν πέψις τις· ἡ γὰρ τῆς ἐν τοῖς
περικαρπίοις τροφῆς πέψις πέπανσις λέγεται. ἐπεὶ
δ᾽ ἡ πέψις τελέωσις, τότε ἡ πέπανσις τελέα ἐστὶν
ὅταν τὰ ἐν τῷ περικαρπίῳ σπέρματα δύνηται ἀπο-
15 τελεῖν τοιοῦτον ἕτερον οἷον αὐτό· καὶ γὰρ ἐπὶ τῶν
ἄλλων τὸ τέλεον οὕτω λέγομεν. περικαρπίου μὲν

Concoction, in fact, is what happens to everything when its constituent moisture is mastered ; for this is the material that is determined by a thing's natural heat, and as long as the determining proportion holds a thing's nature is maintained. So urine and excreta and the waste products of the body in general are a sign of health, and we say they have been concocted because they show that its own inherent heat has mastered the indeterminate matter. Things concocted are necessarily denser and hotter, for the effect of heat is to make things compacter, denser and drier.

So much for concoction. Inconcoction is a failure to reach maturity owing to a deficiency in natural heat, and lack of heat is of course cold. This immaturity is one of the opposite passive qualities which are the natural matter of all things. *Inconcoction.*

This completes our description of concoction and inconcoction.

CHAPTER III

ARGUMENT (*continued*)

381 a 12), *scalding* (381 a 12-23), *roasting* (381 a 23–b 13) *and its opposite* (381 b 13-20).

RIPENING is a sort of concoction. For the concoction of the nourishing element in fruit is called ripening, and since concoction is maturity, the process of ripening is complete when the seeds in the fruit are capable of producing another fruit of the same kind : for this is what we mean by mature in other cases also. This, *Ripening.*

380 a

οὖν αὕτη πέπανσις, λέγεται δὲ καὶ ἄλλα πολλὰ
πέπονα τῶν πεπεμμένων, κατὰ μὲν τὴν αὐτὴν
ἰδέαν, μεταφοραῖς δέ, διὰ τὸ μὴ κεῖσθαι, καθάπερ
εἴρηται καὶ πρότερον, ὀνόματα καθ' ἑκάστην τε-
20 λείωσιν περὶ τὰ ὁριζόμενα ὑπὸ τῆς φυσικῆς θερμότητος καὶ ψυχρότητος. ἔστιν δὲ ἡ φυμάτων καὶ
φλέγματος καὶ τῶν τοιούτων πέπανσις ἡ ὑπὸ τοῦ
φυσικοῦ θερμοῦ τοῦ ἐνόντος ὑγροῦ πέψις· ἀδύνατον
γὰρ ὁρίζειν μὴ κρατοῦν. ἐκ μὲν οὖν τῶν πνευμα-
τικῶν ὑδατώδη, ἐκ δὲ τῶν τοιούτων τὰ γεηρὰ
25 συνίσταται, καὶ ἐκ λεπτῶν αἰεὶ παχύτερα γίγνεται
πεπαινόμενα πάντα. καὶ τὰ μὲν εἰς αὑτὴν[1] ἡ φύσις
ἄγει κατὰ τοῦτο, τὰ δὲ ἐκβάλλει.

Πέπανσις μὲν οὖν εἴρηται τί ἐστιν. ὠμότης δ'
ἐστὶν τὸ ἐναντίον· ἐναντίον δὲ πεπάνσει ἀπεψία τῆς ἐν τῷ περικαρπίῳ τροφῆς· αὕτη δ' ἐστὶν
ἡ ἀόριστος ὑγρότης. διὸ ἢ πνευματικὴ ἢ ὑδα-
30 τώδης ἢ τῶν ἐξ ἀμφοῖν ἐστιν ἡ ὠμότης. ἐπεὶ δ'
ἡ πέπανσις τελέωσίς τίς ἐστιν ἡ ὠμότης ἀτέλεια
ἔσται. γίγνεται δ' ἡ ἀτέλεια δι' ἔνδειαν τοῦ φυσικοῦ θερμοῦ καὶ ἀσυμμετρίαν πρὸς τὸ ὑγρὸν τὸ
πεπαινόμενον. οὐδὲν δὲ ὑγρὸν αὐτὸ καθ' αὑτὸ
πεπαίνεται ἄνευ ξηροῦ· ὕδωρ γὰρ οὐ παχύνεται
380 b μόνον τῶν ὑγρῶν. συμβαίνει δὲ τοῦτο ἢ τῷ τὸ
θερμὸν ὀλίγον εἶναι ἢ τῷ τὸ ὁριζόμενον πολύ· διὸ
καὶ λεπτοὶ οἱ χυμοὶ τῶν ὠμῶν, καὶ ψυχροὶ μᾶλλον
ἢ θερμοί, καὶ ἄβρωτοι καὶ ἄποτοι. λέγεται δὲ καὶ
ἡ ὠμότης ὥσπερ καὶ ἡ πέπανσις, πολλαχῶς. ὅθεν
5 καὶ οὖρα καὶ ὑποχωρήσεις καὶ κατάρροι ὠμοὶ λέ-

---

[1] ἑαυτὴν 𝔚 O.T. : αὐτὴν cett. Fobes.

[a] This sentence breaks the sequence of thought and seems

then, is what ripening is in the case of fruit, but many other things that have been concocted are said to be ripe ; the process is specifically the same but the term used metaphorically, since, as we remarked earlier, there are no specific names for each type of maturity that occurs when matter is determined by natural heat and cold. In the case of boils and phlegm and the like ripening is the concoction of the moisture in them by their natural heat, for that which does not master material cannot determine it. So when things are ripened, if the material is of an airy nature, the product is watery ; if the material is watery, the product is earthy, and generally what is rare becomes denser. In this process nature assimilates some of the material to itself, and some it rejects.

So much for ripening. Rawness is its opposite, Rawness. which means that it is an inconcoction of the nourishing element in fruit, that is to say, of the undetermined moisture. So rawness is either of an airy or watery nature or a mixture of both : and as ripening is maturity, rawness will be immaturity. Immaturity results from a deficiency of natural heat and its lack of proportion to the moisture that is being ripened. (Nothing moist ripens of itself without the admixture of something dry : for water is the only liquid that does not thicken.[a]) This disproportion occurs either because the amount of heat is small or else because the amount of material being determined is large : hence the juice of raw things is thin, cold rather than hot, and unfit for food or drink. Rawness too, like ripeness, has many senses. Thus urine and excreta and catarrhs are all called raw, the reason for the

out of place here. For what Aristotle says about water cf. 383 a 12 and note.

γονται διὰ τὸ αὐτὸ αἴτιον· τῷ γὰρ μὴ κεκρατῆσθαι
ὑπὸ τῆς θερμότητος μηδὲ συνεστάναι ὠμὰ πάντα
προσαγορεύεται. πόρρω δὲ προϊόντων καὶ κέραμος
ὠμὸς καὶ γάλα ὠμὸν καὶ ἄλλα πολλὰ λέγεται, ἐὰν
10 δυνάμενα μεταβάλλειν καὶ συνίστασθαι ὑπὸ θερμότητος ἀπαθῆ ᾖ. διὸ τὸ ὕδωρ ἑφθὸν μὲν λέγεται,
ὠμὸν δ' οὔ, ὅτι οὐ παχύνεται.

Πέπανσις μὲν οὖν καὶ ὠμότης εἴρηται τί ἐστιν,
καὶ διὰ τί ἐστιν ἑκάτερον αὐτῶν.

Ἕψησις δ' ἐστὶν τὸ μὲν ὅλον πέψις ὑπὸ θερμότητος ὑγρᾶς τοῦ ἐνυπάρχοντος ἀορίστου ἐν τῷ
15 ὑγρῷ, λέγεται δὲ τοὔνομα κυρίως μόνον ἐπὶ τῶν
ἑψομένων. τοῦτο δ' ἂν εἴη, ὥσπερ εἴρηται, πνευ-
ματῶδες ἢ ὑδατῶδες. ἡ δὲ πέψις γίγνεται ἀπὸ
τοῦ ἐν τῷ ὑγρῷ πυρός· τὸ γὰρ ἐπὶ τῶν τηγάνων
ὀπτᾶται (ὑπὸ γὰρ τοῦ ἔξωθεν θερμοῦ πάσχει, ἐν
ᾧ δ' ἐστὶν ὑγρῷ, ποιεῖ ἐκεῖνο μᾶλλον ξηρόν, εἰς
20 αὐτὸ ἀναλαμβάνον), τὸ δ' ἑψόμενον τοὐναντίον ποιεῖ
(ἐκκρίνεται γὰρ ἐξ αὐτοῦ τὸ ὑγρὸν ὑπὸ τῆς ἐν τῷ
ἔξω ὑγρῷ θερμασίας)· διὸ ξηρότερα τὰ ἑφθὰ τῶν
ὀπτῶν· οὐ γὰρ ἀνασπᾷ εἰς ἑαυτὰ τὸ ὑγρὸν τὰ
ἑψόμενα· κρατεῖ γὰρ ἡ ἔξωθεν θερμότης τῆς ἐντός·
εἰ δ' ἐκράτει ἡ ἐντός, εἷλκεν ἂν εἰς ἑαυτήν.

25 Ἔστιν δ' οὐ πᾶν σῶμα ἑψητόν· οὔτε γὰρ ἐν ᾧ
μηδέν ἐστιν ὑγρόν, οἷον ἐν λίθοις, οὔτ' ἐν οἷς ἔνεστι
μέν, ἀλλ' ἀδύνατον κρατηθῆναι διὰ πυκνότητα,
οἷον ἐν τοῖς ξύλοις· ἀλλ' ὅσα τῶν σωμάτων ἔχει
ὑγρότητα παθητικὴν ὑπὸ τῆς ἐν τῷ ὑγρῷ πυρώσεως.
λέγεται δὲ καὶ χρυσὸς ἕψεσθαι καὶ ξύλον καὶ ἄλλα

---

^a 380 a 29.
^b *i.e.* the water in which the thing is boiled.

term being applied to them being the same in each case, namely, that the material has not been mastered by the heat or acquired consistency. And if we go farther, brick and milk and many other things also are called raw if they have remained unaffected by heat, though they normally change and acquire consistency when subjected to it. That is why we speak of water being boiled, but not raw, because it does not thicken.

This completes our description of ripening and rawness and of their several causes.

Boiling, as a general term, is concoction by moist heat of the undetermined material present in the moisture of a thing, but the term is properly applicable only to things cooked by boiling. This material, as we have said,[a] is either of an airy or watery nature. The concoction arises from the fire in the moisture.[b] For what is cooked in a pan is roasted, being acted upon by the external heat, and in turn acting upon the moisture which contains it, by drying it up and absorbing it into itself : what is boiled, on the other hand, produces the opposite effect, its moisture being drawn out of it by the heat of the moisture surrounding it. This is why boiled food is drier than roast : for things boiled do not draw moisture into themselves, because the external heat is stronger than their own internal heat—if their internal heat were the stronger they would draw it in.

Not every body can be boiled. Bodies which contain no moisture, like stones, cannot, nor can bodies which contain moisture but which are too solid for it to be mastered, like wood. Bodies which can are those which contain moisture which is subject to action by the heat in moisture outside them. Of course, gold and wood and many other things are

380 b

30 πολλά, κατὰ μὲν τὴν ἰδέαν οὐ¹ τὴν αὐτήν, μεταφορᾷ
δέ· οὐ γὰρ κεῖται ὀνόματα ταῖς διαφοραῖς. καὶ τὰ
ὑγρὰ δὲ ἕψεσθαι λέγομεν, οἷον γάλα καὶ γλεῦκος,
ὅταν ἐν τῷ ὑγρῷ ὁ χυμὸς εἰς εἶδός τι μεταβάλλῃ ὑπὸ
τοῦ κύκλῳ καὶ ἔξωθεν πυρὸς θερμαίνοντος, ὥστε
381 a τρόπον τινὰ παραπλήσιον τῇ εἰρημένῃ ἑψήσει ποιεῖ.
(τέλος δὲ οὐ ταὐτὸ πᾶσιν, οὔτε ἑψομένοις οὔτε πετ-
τομένοις, ἀλλὰ τοῖς μὲν πρὸς ἐδωδήν, τοῖς δὲ πρὸς
ῥόφησιν, τοῖς δὲ πρὸς ἄλλην χρείαν, ἐπεὶ καὶ τὰ
φάρμακα ἕψειν λέγομεν.) ὥστε ὅσα παχύτερα δύ-
5 ναται γίγνεσθαι ἢ ἐλάττω ἢ βαρύτερα, ἢ τὰ μὲν
αὐτῶν τοιαῦτα τὰ δ' ἐναντία, διὰ τὸ διακρινόμενα
τὰ μὲν παχύνεσθαι τὰ δὲ λεπτύνεσθαι, ὥσπερ τὸ
γάλα εἴς τε ὀρὸν καὶ πυετίαν, πάντα ἑψητά ἐστιν.
τὸ δὲ ἔλαιον οὐχ ἕψεται αὐτὸ καθ' ἑαυτό, ὅτι τούτων
οὐδὲν πάσχει. ἡ μὲν οὖν κατὰ τὴν ἕψησιν λεγομένη
10 πέψις τοῦτ' ἐστίν· καὶ οὐδὲν διαφέρει ἐν ὀργάνοις
τεχνικοῖς καὶ φυσικοῖς ἐάν τι γίγνηται· διὰ τὴν
αὐτὴν γὰρ αἰτίαν πάντα ἔσται.

Μόλυνσις δὲ ἀπεψία μὲν ἡ ἐναντία ἑψήσει· εἴη δ'
ἂν ἐναντία ἥ τε πρώτη λεχθεῖσα² ἀπεψία τοῦ ἐν τῷ
σώματι ἀορίστου δι' ἔνδειαν τῆς ἐν τῷ ὑγρῷ τῷ
15 πέριξ θερμότητος (ἡ δ' ἔνδεια μετὰ ψυχρότητος
ὅτι ἐστίν, εἴρηται)· γίγνεται δὲ διὰ κίνησιν ἄλλην·
ἐκκρούεται γὰρ ἡ πέττουσα, καὶ ἡ ἔνδεια δὲ ἢ διὰ
τὸ πλῆθος τῆς ἐν τῷ ὑγρῷ ψυχρότητος ἢ διὰ τὸ ἐν
τῷ ἑψομένῳ [πλῆθος]³· τότε γὰρ συμβαίνει τὴν ἐν

---

¹ οὐ om. Thurot O.T.
² τῇ πρώτῃ λεχθείσῃ Thurot O.T.
³ seclusi : del. Thurot.

ᵃ Thurot and O.T. consider this sentence out of place here.
ᵇ μόλυνσις = half-cooking, " imperfect boiling " (O.T.).

commonly said to be boiled, but it is not the same kind of process, and is only so called metaphorically as there are no separate words to mark the difference. We also speak of liquids like milk and must being boiled, when the flavour of the liquid undergoes some form of change when heated by the fire surrounding it externally, which thus has an effect on it somewhat similar to boiling as we have defined it. (The end for which things are boiled or concocted is not the same in all cases ; in some it is for eating, in others for drinking, in others, again, for some other purpose, as, for instance, we speak of drugs being boiled.) [a] Everything, then, can be boiled which can become denser and smaller and heavier, or of which part can so behave while the remainder behaves in the opposite way, in which case the parts divide, and part thickens, part grows thinner, as milk divides into whey and curds. Olive oil, because it cannot be affected in any of these ways, will not boil by itself. This, then, is what is called concoction by boiling : and it makes no difference whether it takes place in an artificial or a natural vessel, for the cause is the same in all cases.

Scalding [b] is the species of inconcoction opposite to boiling : and the opposite to boiling, and so the primary sense of scalding, will be an inconcoction of the undetermined matter due to a lack of heat in the surrounding liquid. (It has already been stated [c] that lack of heat means presence of cold.) This is caused by another kind of motion, which takes place when the concocting heat is driven out, the lack of heat being due to the amount of cold either in the surrounding liquid or in the thing to be boiled : for

Scalding.

[c] 379 a 19.

381 a

τῷ ὑγρῷ θερμότητα πλείω μὲν εἶναι ἢ ὥστε μὴ
20 κινῆσαι, ἐλάττω δὲ ἢ ὥστε ὁμαλῦναι καὶ συμπέψαι.
διὸ σκληρότερα μὲν τὰ μεμωλυσμένα γίγνεται τῶν
ἐφθῶν, τὰ δ᾽ ὑγρὰ διωρισμένα μᾶλλον.

Ἕψησις μὲν οὖν καὶ μόλυνσις εἴρηται, καὶ τί
ἐστιν καὶ διὰ τί ἐστιν.

Ὄπτησις δ᾽ ἐστὶν πέψις ὑπὸ θερμότητος ξηρᾶς
καὶ ἀλλοτρίας. διὰ τοῦτο κἂν ἕψων τις ποιῇ μετα-
25 βάλλειν καὶ πέττεσθαι, μὴ ὑπὸ τῆς τοῦ ὑγροῦ θερμότητος ἀλλ᾽ ὑπὸ τῆς τοῦ πυρός, ὅταν τελεσθῇ, ὀπτὸν
γίγνεται καὶ οὐχ ἐφθόν, καὶ τῇ ὑπερβολῇ προσκε-
καῦσθαι λέγεται· ὑπὸ ξηρᾶς δὲ θερμότητος γίγνεται
ὅταν ξηρότερον γίγνηται ἐπιτελεσθέν. διὸ καὶ τὰ
30 ἐκτὸς ξηρότερα τῶν ἐντός· τὰ δ᾽ ἐφθὰ τοὐναντίον.
καὶ ἔργον ἐπὶ τῶν χειροκμήτων τὸ ὀπτῆσαι μεῖζον
ἢ ἑψῆσαι· χαλεπὸν γὰρ τὰ ἐκτὸς καὶ τὰ ἐντὸς ὁμα-
λῶς θερμαίνειν. ἀεὶ γὰρ τὰ ἐγγύτερον τοῦ πυρὸς
381 b ξηραίνεται θᾶττον, ὥστε καὶ μᾶλλον. συνιόντων
οὖν τῶν ἔξω πόρων οὐ δύναται ἐκκρίνεσθαι τὸ
ἐνυπάρχον ὑγρόν, ἀλλ᾽ ἐγκατακλείεται, ὅταν οἱ
πόροι μύσωσιν. ὄπτησις μὲν οὖν καὶ ἕψησις γί-
5 γνονται μὲν τέχνῃ, ἔστιν δ᾽, ὥσπερ λέγομεν, τὰ
εἴδη καθόλου ταὐτὰ καὶ φύσει· ὅμοια γὰρ τὰ γιγνόμενα πάθη, ἀλλ᾽ ἀνώνυμα· μιμεῖται γὰρ ἡ τέχνη
τὴν φύσιν, ἐπεὶ καὶ ἡ τῆς τροφῆς ἐν τῷ σώματι
πέψις ὁμοία ἑψήσει ἐστίν· καὶ γὰρ ἐν ὑγρῷ καὶ

ᵃ So we speak of *burning* porridge, which we *boil*.
ᵇ Aristotle's habit of explaining natural processes in terms
of artificial comes out very clearly in this passage : *cf.* ch. 2,
note *a* on p. 298, and 379 b 14, 380 a 16, 381 a 10.

in these circumstances the heat in the liquid is too great to cause no change at all but too small to produce uniform concoction. So things scalded are harder than things boiled and the moisture in them more discrete.

This completes our account of boiling and scalding, their nature and causes.

Roasting is concoction by extrinsic dry heat. So, even if you cause a thing to change and be concocted by boiling it, yet if the change is due to the heat of the fire and not to the heat in the liquid, when the process is complete the thing is roasted and not boiled, while if it is overdone we say it is burnt [a] : but the cause is dry heat if at the end the thing is drier. This is why the outside is drier than the inside of things that have been roasted, while the opposite is true of things that have been boiled. And when done artificially, roasting is more difficult than boiling, as it is difficult to heat both outside and inside evenly ; for the parts nearer the fire dry faster and so more thoroughly. When, therefore, the outer pores contract, the moisture contained in the thing cannot escape, but is trapped inside when the pores shut. Roasting and boiling are of course artificial processes, but, as we have said, in nature too there are processes specifically the same ; for the phenomena are similar though we have no terms for them. For human operations imitate natural.[b] So the digestion [c] of food in the body is similar to boiling, for it takes

[c] I have translated πέψις by the narrower term " digestion " here, rather than the wider term " concoction " used to translate it elsewhere, as Aristotle is in fact talking of digestion. But the fact that he uses the same word for both shows that he thinks that digestion is to be explained as a form of *cooking*.

381 b

θερμῷ ὑπὸ τῆς τοῦ σώματος θερμότητος γίγνεται.
καὶ ἀπεψίαι ἔνιαι ὅμοιαι τῇ μολύνσει. καὶ ζῷον
10 οὐκ ἐγγίγνεται ἐν τῇ πέψει, ὥσπερ τινές φασιν,
ἀλλ' ἐν τῇ ἀποκρίσει σηπομένη ἐν τῇ κάτω κοιλίᾳ,
εἶτ' ἐπανέρχεται ἄνω· πέττεται μὲν γὰρ ἐν τῇ ἄνω
κοιλίᾳ, σήπεται δ' ἐν τῇ κάτω τὸ ἀποκριθέν· δι'
ἣν δ' αἰτίαν, εἴρηται ἐν ἑτέροις.

Ἡ μὲν οὖν μόλυνσις τῇ ἑψήσει ἐναντίον· τῇ δὲ
15 ὡς ὀπτήσει λεγομένῃ πέψει ἔστι μέν τι ἀντικείμενον
ὁμοίως, ἀνωνυμώτερον δέ. εἴη δ' ἂν οἷον εἰ γένοιτο
στάτευσις ἀλλὰ μὴ ὄπτησις δι' ἔνδειαν θερμότητος,
ἣ συμβαίη ἂν ἢ δι' ὀλιγότητα τοῦ ἔξω πυρὸς ἢ διὰ
πλῆθος τοῦ ἐν τῷ ὀπτωμένῳ ὕδατος· τότε γὰρ
πλείων μέν ἐστιν ἢ ὥστε μὴ κινῆσαι, ἐλάττων δὲ
20 ἢ ὥστε πέψαι.

Τί μὲν οὖν ἐστι πέψις καὶ ἀπεψία, καὶ πέπανσις
καὶ ὠμότης, καὶ ἕψησις καὶ ὄπτησις καὶ τἀναντία
τούτοις, εἴρηται.

---

^a The reference is uncertain.

CHAPTER IV

ARGUMENT

*The passive factors, moist and dry (i.e. in practice water
and earth as the elements in which these qualities predominate),
are necessary constituents of all physical bodies, whose characteristics vary according to the predominance of one or the*

381 b 23 Τῶν δὲ παθητικῶν, τοῦ ὑγροῦ καὶ τοῦ ξηροῦ,
λεκτέον τὰ εἴδη.

310

place under the influence of the heat of the body in a hot and moist medium. And some forms of indigestion are like scalding. And it is not true that worms are generated in the process of digestion as some say ; they are generated in the excrement which decays in the lower belly, and subsequently make their way upwards. For digestion takes place in the upper belly and the excrement decays in the lower. The reason for this we have explained elsewhere.[a]

Now scalding is the opposite to boiling, and there is a process similarly opposed to the form of concoction we have called roasting, but it is less easy to find a term for it. It is the sort of thing you will find happening when a thing gets scorched and not properly roasted, as a result of lack of heat caused either through a deficiency of the external fire or an undue amount of water in the thing to be roasted : for then the amount of heat is too great to give rise to no change but too small to concoct properly.

So much for concoction and inconcoction, for ripeness and rawness, and for boiling and roasting and their opposites.

The opposite to roasting.

CHAPTER IV

ARGUMENT (continued)

other (381 b 23—382 a 8). So hardness and softness are the primary qualities, anything whose surface does not yield being hard, anything whose surface does yield being soft (382 a 8-21).

WE must now describe the forms taken by the passive factors, moist and dry.

381 b

Εἰσὶν δ' αἱ μὲν ἀρχαὶ τῶν σωμάτων αἱ παθητικαὶ
25 ὑγρὸν καὶ ξηρόν, τὰ δ' ἄλλα μεικτὰ μὲν ἐκ τούτων,
ὁποτέρου δὲ μᾶλλον, τούτου μᾶλλον τὴν φύσιν
ἐστίν, οἷον τὰ μὲν ξηροῦ μᾶλλον τὰ δ' ὑγροῦ.
πάντα δὲ τὰ μὲν ἐντελεχείᾳ ἔσται, τὰ δ' ἐν τῷ
ἀντικειμένῳ· ἔχει δ' οὕτως τῆξις πρὸς τὸ τηκτόν.
ἐπεὶ δ' ἐστὶν τὸ μὲν ὑγρὸν εὐόριστον, τὸ δὲ ξηρὸν
30 δυσόριστον, ὅμοιόν τι τῷ ὄψῳ καὶ τοῖς ἡδύσμασι
πρὸς ἄλληλα πάσχουσι· τὸ γὰρ ὑγρὸν τῷ ξηρῷ
αἴτιον τοῦ ὁρίζεσθαι, καὶ ἑκάτερον ἑκατέρῳ οἷον
382 a κόλλα γίγνεται, ὥσπερ καὶ Ἐμπεδοκλῆς ἐποίησεν
ἐν τοῖς φυσικοῖς "ἄλφιτον ὕδατι κολλήσας." καὶ
διὰ τοῦτο ἐξ ἀμφοῖν ἐστιν τὸ ὡρισμένον σῶμα.
λέγεται δὲ τῶν στοιχείων ἰδιαίτατα ξηροῦ μὲν γῆ,
ὑγροῦ δὲ ὕδωρ. διὰ τοῦτο ἅπαντά τε τὰ ὡρισμένα
5 σώματα ἐνταῦθα οὐκ ἄνευ γῆς καὶ ὕδατος (ὁποτέρου δὲ πλέον, κατὰ τὴν δύναμιν τούτου ἕκαστον
φαίνεται)· καὶ ἐν γῇ καὶ ἐν ὕδατι ζῷα μόνον ἐστίν,
ἐν ἀέρι δὲ καὶ πυρὶ οὐκ ἔστιν, ὅτι τῶν σωμάτων
ὕλη ταῦτα. τῶν δὲ σωματικῶν παθημάτων ταῦτα
πρῶτα ἀνάγκη ὑπάρχειν τῷ ὡρισμένῳ, σκληρότητα
10 ἢ μαλακότητα· ἀνάγκη γὰρ τὸ ἐξ ὑγροῦ καὶ ξηροῦ
ἢ σκληρὸν εἶναι ἢ μαλακόν. ἔστι δὲ σκληρὸν μὲν
τὸ μὴ ὑπεῖκον εἰς αὑτὸ κατὰ τὸ ἐπίπεδον, μαλακὸν
δὲ τὸ ὑπεῖκον τῷ μὴ ἀντιπεριίστασθαι· τὸ γὰρ ὕδωρ
οὐ μαλακόν· οὐ γὰρ ὑπείκει τῇ θλίψει τὸ ἐπίπεδον

---

[a] Cf. *De Gen. et Corr.* ii. 2, 329 b 30-32 and Joachim, *ad loc.* [b] Diels 31 B 34.

[c] *De Gen. et Corr.* ii. 3, 331 a 3-6, says that air is character-istically moist (ὑγρόν), water characteristically cold : yet *De Gen. et Corr.* ii. 8, 334 b 34, implies that water is character-

The passive elements of physical bodies are moist and dry and all bodies are compounds of them, the nature of the body varying according as to which predominates, dry doing so in some cases, moist in others. And all will exist either actually or in the opposite sense, potentially : this, for example, is the relationship borne by the process of melting to the capacity for being melted. The moist is unresistant, the dry resistant,[a] and their mutual relationship is therefore something like that of a dish and its seasoning : for the moist causes the dry to take shape, and each serves as a kind of glue to the other, as Empedocles says, in his poem *On Nature*, "gluing meal together with water."[b] So the body formed is a compound of both. And of the four elements earth is regarded as having the most specific characteristics of dry, water of moist.[c] It is for this reason that all definite physical bodies in our world require earth and water for their composition (and each body manifests the properties of the one which predominates in it), and that animals exist only on land and in water, which are the matter from which their bodies are compounded, but not in air or fire. Of the qualities of body hardness or softness are those which must primarily belong to a determinate thing, for anything compounded of moist and dry must be either hard or soft. Hard is anything whose surface does not yield inwards, soft is anything whose surface yields but not by displacement ; for water is not soft, and its surface does not yield downwards to pressure, but

istically moist, and this is certainly the doctrine of the *Meteorologica* as a whole. Perhaps too much stress should not be laid on what Aristotle says in *De Gen. et Corr.* 331 a 3-6 when he is speaking from a particular point of view: *cf.* Joachim, *ad loc.*, and above, Introduction, pp. xix-xx.

313

382 a

εἰς βάθος, ἀλλ᾽ ἀντιπεριίσταται. ἁπλῶς μὲν οὖν
15 σκληρὸν ἢ μαλακὸν τὸ ἁπλῶς τοιοῦτον, πρὸς
ἕτερον δὲ τὸ πρὸς ἐκεῖνο τοιοῦτον. πρὸς μὲν οὖν
ἄλληλα ἀόριστά ἐστιν τῷ μᾶλλον καὶ ἧττον· ἐπεὶ
δὲ πρὸς τὴν αἴσθησιν πάντα κρίνομεν τὰ αἰσθητά,
δῆλον ὅτι καὶ τὸ σκληρὸν καὶ τὸ μαλακὸν ἁπλῶς
πρὸς τὴν ἀφὴν ὡρίκαμεν, ὡς μεσότητι χρώμενοι
20 τῇ ἀφῇ· διὸ τὸ μὲν ὑπερβάλλον αὐτὴν σκληρόν, τὸ
δ᾽ ἐλλεῖπον μαλακὸν εἶναί φαμεν.

---

^a Cf. Book I. ch. 12, note b on p. 82.
^b Cf. De Anima ii. 11, 423 b 27 ff.

CHAPTER V

ARGUMENT

*Any self-contained body must be hard or soft : whatever
is hard or soft is a solid, so we must discuss solidification.
This also we shall find to be due to the two active properties,*

382 a 22 Ἀνάγκη δὲ σκληρὸν ἢ μαλακὸν εἶναι τὸ ὡρισμένον σῶμα οἰκείῳ ὅρῳ (ἢ γὰρ ὑπείκει ἢ μή)· ἔτι
πεπηγὸς εἶναι (τούτῳ γὰρ ὁρίζεται)· ὥστ᾽ ἐπεὶ πᾶν
25 μὲν τὸ ὡρισμένον καὶ συνεστὸς ἢ μαλακὸν ἢ
σκληρόν, ταῦτα δὲ πήξει ἐστίν, ἅπαντ᾽ ἂν εἴη τὰ
σώματα τὰ σύνθετα καὶ ὡρισμένα οὐκ ἄνευ πήξεως.
πήξεως οὖν πέρι ῥητέον.

Ἔστιν δὴ τὰ αἴτια τὰ παρὰ τὴν ὕλην δύο, τό τε
ποιοῦν καὶ τὸ πάθος (τὸ μὲν οὖν ποιοῦν ὡς ὅθεν ἡ
30 κίνησις, τὸ δὲ πάθος ὡς εἶδος)· ὥστε καὶ πήξεως
καὶ διαχύσεως, καὶ τοῦ ξηραίνεσθαι καὶ τοῦ
ὑγραίνεσθαι. ποιεῖ δὲ τὸ ποιοῦν δυσὶ δυνάμεσι,

314

is merely displaced.[a]   Things which possess these characteristics without qualification are hard and soft absolutely ; things which possess them in relation to something else are hard and soft relatively.   Degrees of hardness and softness are indefinable with relation to each other ; but since we judge all sensible qualities by sensation, it is clear that both hard and soft are defined absolutely with reference to touch, which we use as a mean saying that what exceeds it is hard and what falls short of it is soft.[b]

CHAPTER V

ARGUMENT (continued)

heat and cold (382 a 22–b 1).   Drying is a form of solidification, and is due to heat or cold (382 b 1-27).

A BODY defined by its own limit must be either hard or soft, for it either yields or does not.   Further, it must be solid ; for this gives it its definite limits.   So, since every definite and formed body is either soft or hard, and softness and hardness are the result of solidification, no composite and definite thing can exist without solidification.   We must therefore discuss solidification.

   Now there are two causes besides matter, the efficient and the qualitative, the efficient being the source of movement or change, the qualitative being the formal element.   This will apply to solidification and dispersal and to drying and moistening.   The efficient cause acts through two properties and the

Solidification.

315

382 a

καὶ πάσχει παθήμασιν δυσίν, ὥσπερ εἴρηται· ποιεῖ
μὲν θερμῷ καὶ ψυχρῷ, τὸ δὲ πάθος ἢ ἀπουσίᾳ ἢ
382 b παρουσίᾳ θερμοῦ ἢ ψυχροῦ.

Ἐπεὶ δὲ τὸ πήγνυσθαι ξηραίνεσθαί πώς ἐστιν,
περὶ τούτου εἴπωμεν πρῶτον.[1] τὸ δὴ[2] πάσχον ἢ
ὑγρὸν ἢ ξηρὸν ἢ ἐκ τούτων. τιθέμεθα δὲ ὑγροῦ
σῶμα ὕδωρ, ξηροῦ δὲ γῆν· ταῦτα γὰρ τῶν ὑγρῶν
5 καὶ τῶν ξηρῶν παθητικά. διὸ καὶ τὸ ψυχρὸν τῶν
παθητικῶν μᾶλλον· ἐν τούτοις γάρ ἐστιν· καὶ γὰρ
ἡ γῆ καὶ τὸ ὕδωρ ψυχρὰ ὑπόκειται. ποιητικὸν δὲ
τὸ ψυχρὸν ὡς φθαρτικὸν ἢ ὡς κατὰ συμβεβηκός,
καθάπερ εἴρηται πρότερον· ἐνίοτε γὰρ καὶ κάειν
λέγεται καὶ θερμαίνειν τὸ ψυχρόν, οὐχ ὡς τὸ θερμόν,
10 ἀλλὰ τῷ συνάγειν ἢ ἀντιπεριστάναι τὸ θερμόν.
ξηραίνεται δὲ ὅσα ἐστὶν ὕδωρ καὶ ὕδατος εἴδη, ἢ
ἔχει ὕδωρ εἴτ' ἐπακτὸν εἴτε συμφυές (λέγω δὲ
ἐπακτὸν μὲν οἷον ἐν ἐρίῳ, σύμφυτον δ' οἷον ἐν
γάλακτι). ὕδατος δ' εἴδη τὰ τοιάδε, οἶνος, οὖρον,
ὀρός, καὶ ὅλως ὅσα μηδεμίαν ἢ βραχεῖαν ἔχει
15 ὑπόστασιν, μὴ διὰ γλισχρότητα· ἐνίοις γὰρ αἴτιον
τοῦ μὴ ὑφίστασθαι μηδὲν ἡ γλισχρότης, ὥσπερ
ἐλαίῳ ἢ πίττῃ. ξηραίνεται δὲ πάντα ἢ θερμαινόμενα ἢ ψυχόμενα, ἀμφότερα δὲ θερμῷ, καὶ ὑπὸ
τῆς ἐντὸς θερμότητος ἢ τῆς ἔξω· καὶ γὰρ τὰ τῇ
ψύξει ξηραινόμενα, ὥσπερ ἱμάτιον, ἐὰν ᾖ κεχωρι-
20 σμένον αὐτὸ καθ' αὑτὸ τὸ ὑγρόν, ὑπὸ τοῦ ἐντὸς
θερμοῦ συνεξατμίζοντος τὸ ὑγρὸν ξηραίνεται, ἂν
ὀλίγον ᾖ τὸ ὑγρόν, ἐξιούσης τῆς θερμότητος ὑπὸ
τοῦ περιεστῶτος ψυχροῦ.

[1] ἐπεὶ ... πρῶτον post ὑγραίνεσθαι a 30 transponit O.T.
[2] δὲ O.T.

---

[a] Ch. 1, 378 b 21.   [b] e.g. 347 b 2-7, 348 b 2-8.

thing acted on is affected in virtue of two properties as has been explained [a] : the two properties by which action takes place are heat and cold. and the qualitative effect is produced either by the absence or presence of heat and cold.

Since solidification is a form of drying, let us deal Drying. with drying first. The thing acted on is either moist or dry or a mixture of both. Water we regard as a largely moist substance, earth as largely dry : for among substances that can be moist or dry these are passive. And so cold is more on the side of the passive qualities, since it is contained in water and earth, both of which we assume to be cold. But cold is an active property either because it disrupts or incidentally, as explained before [b] ; for sometimes cold is said both to burn and heat, not in the way that heat does, but by concentrating and compressing heat.[c] Water and all kinds of watery liquids are affected by drying, as well as all things containing water either extraneous or natural (by extraneous I mean like the water in wool, by natural like the water in milk). The watery liquids are, for example, wine, urine, whey, and generally those which have either no sediment or very little, and yet are not viscous ; for some liquids have little sediment because they are viscous, like olive oil and pitch. Things are dried either by being heated or by being cooled, heat internal or external being the active cause in either case. For even things which are dried by cooling, like wet clothes, and in which the water has a separate existence, are dried by their internal heat which, when driven out by the surrounding cold, evaporates the moisture if the amount of it is small.

[c] *Cf.* Book I. ch. 12, note *b* on p. 82.

382 b

Ξηραίνεται μὲν οὖν, ὥσπερ εἴρηται, ἅπαντα ἢ
θερμαινόμενα ἢ ψυχόμενα, καὶ πάντα θερμῷ, ἢ τῷ
25 ἐντὸς ἢ τῷ ἐκτὸς συνεξατμίζοντι τὸ ὑγρόν (λέγω
δ' ἐκτὸς μὲν ὥσπερ τὰ ἑψόμενα, ἐντὸς δὲ ὅταν
ἀφαιρεθέντος ὑφ' ἧς ἔχει θερμότητος ἀναλωθῇ ἀπο-
πνεούσης).

Περὶ μὲν οὖν τοῦ ξηραίνεσθαι εἴρηται.

CHAPTER VI

ARGUMENT

*Liquefaction and solidification. Liquefaction is the result
either of condensation or of melting : solids are formed either
(1) from watery liquids or (2) from water and earth by the
action of heat or of cold ; they are liquefied again by the action*

382 b 28 Τὸ δ' ὑγραίνεσθαί ἐστιν ἓν μὲν τὸ ὕδωρ γίγνεσθαι
συνιστάμενον, ἓν δὲ τὸ τήκεσθαι τὸ πεπηγός. τού-
30 των δὲ συνίσταται μὲν ψυχόμενον τὸ πνεῦμα· περὶ
δὲ τήξεως ἅμα καὶ περὶ πήξεως ἔσται δῆλον.
πήγνυται δὲ ὅσα πήγνυνται ἢ ὕδατος ὄντα ἢ γῆς
καὶ ὕδατος, καὶ ταῦτα ἢ θερμῷ ξηρῷ ἢ ψυχρῷ.
383 a διὸ καὶ λύεται τοῖς ἐναντίοις, ὅσα λύεται τῶν ὑπὸ
θερμοῦ παγέντων ἢ ὑπὸ ψυχροῦ· τὰ μὲν γὰρ ὑπὸ
ξηροῦ θερμοῦ παγέντα ὑπὸ ὕδατος λύεται, ὅ ἐστιν
ὑγρὸν ψυχρόν, τὰ δὲ ὑπὸ ψυχροῦ παγέντα ὑπὸ πυρὸς
λύεται, ὅ ἐστιν θερμόν. πήγνυσθαι δ' ἔνια δόξειεν

---

[a] " Aristotle does not distinguish in this or the next chapter
between solution (λύεσθαι) and melting (τῆξις) : they are
treated indifferently as the correlate of πῆξις " (O.T.). An
exception is 383 b 7, 12, when a distinction is assumed (see

Drying, then, as we have said, is always due to heat or cold, heat internal or external always being the active cause and evaporating the moisture. By external heat I mean, for example, what happens in boiling, by internal what happens when the moisture is removed and consumed by the action of the thing's own heat as it leaves it.

So much for drying.

CHAPTER VI

ARGUMENT (continued)

of the opposite of these two properties to that which caused solidification (382 b 28—383 a 6). (1) Watery liquids (383 a 6-13). (2) Compounds of earth and water, (a) in which earth predominates (383 a 13-b 17).

LIQUEFACTION takes two forms : the one is condensation into water, the other the melting of a solid. Of these, condensation takes place when air is cooled, while melting will be explained at the same time as solidification. Everything that solidifies is (1) a watery liquid or (2) a compound of water and earth, and the cause is either dry heat or cold. So of things which solidify owing to hot or cold, those that dissolve [a] are dissolved by the opposite property : for those that solidify owing to dry heat are dissolved by water, that is, by moist cold, while those that solidify owing to cold are dissolved by fire, that is, by heat. (Some things would appear indeed to be

Liquefaction and solidification : due to heat or cold.

note *c* on p. 323). In chs. 8 and 9, again, solution and melting are not clearly distinguished : *cf.* ch. 8, note *a* on p. 343.

ARISTOTLE

5 ἂν ὑπὸ ὕδατος, ὡς τὸ μέλι τὸ ἐφθόν· πήγνυται δὲ
οὐχ ὑπὸ τοῦ ὕδατος, ἀλλ’ ὑπὸ τοῦ ἐν αὐτῷ ψυχροῦ.

Ὅσα μὲν οὖν ἐστιν ὕδατος, οὐ πήγνυται ὑπὸ
πυρός· λύεται γὰρ ὑπὸ πυρός, τὸ δὲ αὐτὸ τῷ αὐτῷ
κατὰ ταὐτὸ οὐκ ἔσται αἴτιον τοῦ ἐναντίου. ἔτι τῷ
ἀπιέναι τὸ θερμὸν πήγνυται, ὥστε δῆλον ὅτι τῷ
10 εἰσιέναι λυθήσεται· ὥστε ποιοῦντος τοῦ ψυχροῦ
πήγνυται. διὸ καὶ οὐ παχύνεται τὰ τοιαῦτα πηγνύ-
μενα· ἡ γὰρ πάχυνσις ὑγροῦ μὲν ἀπιόντος γίγνεται,
τοῦ ξηροῦ δὲ συνισταμένου· ὕδωρ δὲ τῶν ὑγρῶν οὐ
παχύνεται μόνον.[1]

Ὅσα δὲ κοινὰ γῆς καὶ ὕδατος, καὶ ὑπὸ πυρὸς
15 πήγνυται καὶ ὑπὸ ψυχροῦ, παχύνεται δὲ ὑπ’ ἀμφοῖν
ἔστι μὲν ὡς τὸν αὐτὸν τρόπον, ἔστι δ’ ὡς ἄλλως,
ὑπὸ μὲν θερμοῦ τὸ ὑγρὸν ἐξάγοντος (ἐξατμίζοντος
γὰρ τοῦ ὑγροῦ παχύνεται τὸ ξηρὸν καὶ συνίσταται),
ὑπὸ δὲ ψυχροῦ τὸ θερμὸν ἐκθλίβοντος, μεθ’ οὗ τὸ
ὑγρὸν συναπέρχεται συνεξατμίζον. ὅσα μὲν οὖν
20 μαλακὰ ἀλλὰ μὴ ὑγρά, οὐ παχύνεται ἀλλὰ πήγνυται
ἐξιόντος τοῦ ὑγροῦ, οἷον ὁ ὀπτώμενος κέραμος·
ὅσα δὲ ὑγρὰ τῶν μεικτῶν, καὶ παχύνεται, οἷον γάλα.
πολλὰ δὲ καὶ ὑγραίνεται πρῶτον, ὅσα ἢ παχέα ἢ
σκληρὰ ὑπὸ ψυχροῦ προϋπῆρχεν ὄντα, ὥσπερ καὶ
25 ὁ κέραμος τὸ πρῶτον ὀπτώμενος ἀτμίζει καὶ μα-
λακώτερος γίγνεται· διὸ καὶ διαστρέφεται ἐν ταῖς
καμίνοις.

[1] ὕδωρ . . . μόνον alio quo traiciendum censet Thurot.

[a] These words seem to be a parenthesis. Contrast ch. 8,
385 b 1 ff. and cf. Hist. An. v. 22, 354 a 6.
[b] If any sense is to be made of this sentence, ὕδωρ must be
taken (as by the O.T.) as =τὰ ὕδατος. Aristotle is distinguish-
320

solidified by water, for instance, boiled honey : but in fact it is not the water but the cold in the water which causes it to solidify.) [a]

(1) Watery liquids, then, are not solidified by fire, for they are dissolved by fire, and the same cause operating on the same substance in the same way cannot produce opposite effects. Besides, it is decrease of heat that solidifies them, and so, clearly, increase of heat will liquefy them ; it follows, therefore, that cold is what causes solidification. This is why watery liquids when they solidify do not increase in density, for increase in density takes place when the moisture in a thing evaporates and its dry constituents are packed closer, and only watery fluids do not increase in density.[b]

(1) Watery liquids.

(2) Compounds of earth and water are solidified both by fire and by cold, and are also increased in density by both, their mode of operation being in some respects the same, in others different. Heat draws out the moisture, and when the moisture evaporates the dry constituents increase in density and pack closer ; cold expels the heat and the moisture evaporates and passes off with it. So things that are soft but not moist do not increase in density when moisture leaves them but solidify, like clay when baked : but compounds that are moist, like milk, do increase in density. And bodies which have been made dense or hard by cold often become moist at first when heated, like clay again, which when baked steams at first and becomes softer (which is why it sometimes becomes distorted in the kiln).

(2) Compounds of earth and water :

ing between solidification and thickening or increase in density, and says that watery liquids are liable to the first but not to the second.

321

383 a

Ὅσα μὲν οὖν ὑπὸ ψυχροῦ πήγνυται τῶν κοινῶν
γῆς καὶ ὕδατος, πλέον δὲ ἐχόντων γῆς, τὰ μὲν τῷ
τὸ θερμὸν ἐξεληλυθέναι πηγνύμενα, ταῦτα τήκεται
θερμῷ εἰσιόντος πάλιν τοῦ θερμοῦ, οἷον ὁ πηλὸς
30 ὅταν παγῇ· ὅσα δὲ διὰ ψύξιν, καὶ τοῦ θερμοῦ συν-
εξατμίσαντος ἅπαντος, ταῦτα δὲ ἄλυτα μὴ ὑπερ-
βαλλούσῃ θερμότητι, ἀλλὰ μαλάττεται, οἷον σίδηρος
καὶ κέρας. τήκεται δὲ καὶ ὁ εἰργασμένος σίδηρος,
ὥστε ὑγρὸς γίγνεσθαι καὶ πάλιν πήγνυσθαι. καὶ
τὰ στομώματα ποιοῦσιν οὕτως· ὑφίσταται γὰρ καὶ
383 b ἀποκαθαίρεται κάτω ἡ σκωρία· ὅταν δὲ πολλάκις
πάθῃ καὶ καθαρὸς γένηται, τοῦτο στόμωμα γίγνεται. οὐ ποιοῦσι δὲ πολλάκις αὐτὸ διὰ τὸ ἀπου-
σίαν γίγνεσθαι πολλὴν καὶ τὸν σταθμὸν ἐλάττω
5 ἀποκαθαιρομένου. ἔστιν δ᾽ ἀμείνων σίδηρος ὁ
ἐλάττω ἔχων ἀποκάθαρσιν. τήκεται δὲ καὶ ὁ λίθος
ὁ πυρίμαχος ὥστε στάζειν καὶ ῥεῖν· τὸ δὲ πηγνύμενον ὅταν ῥυῇ, πάλιν γίγνεται σκληρόν. καὶ αἱ
μύλαι τήκονται ὥστε ῥεῖν· τὸ δὲ ῥέον πηγνύμενον
τὸ μὲν χρῶμα μέλαν, ὅμοιον δὲ γίγνεται τῇ τιτάνῳ.
τήκεται δὲ καὶ ὁ πηλὸς καὶ ἡ γῆ.[1]
10 Ὅσα δ᾽ ὑπὸ ξηροῦ θερμοῦ πήγνυται, τὰ μὲν
ἄλυτα, τὰ δὲ λυτὰ ὑγρῷ. κέραμος μὲν οὖν καὶ
λίθων ἐνίων γένη, ὅσοι ὑπὸ πυρὸς τῆς γῆς συγκαυ-
θείσης γίγνονται, οἷον οἱ μυλίαι, ἄλυτα, νίτρον δὲ
καὶ ἅλες λυτὰ ὑγρῷ, οὐ παντὶ δὲ ἀλλὰ ψυχρῷ· διὸ

---

[1] τήκεται . . . γῆ del. Thurot O.T.

[a] See Note on Ancient Iron Making at the end of this
chapter.

Now, of the compounds of earth and water in which *(a)* in which earth predominates and which are solidified by cold, earth predominates; those that solidify because the heat has left them melt when the heat returns to them again, like frozen mud ; but those that solidify because of cold and the evaporation of all their heat are indissoluble save by excessive heat, but can be softened, like iron and horn. Wrought iron indeed will melt and grow soft, and then solidify again. And this is the way in which steel is made.[a] For the dross sinks to the bottom and is removed from below, and by repeated subjection to this treatment the metal is purified and steel produced. They do not repeat the process often, however, because of the great wastage and loss of weight in the iron that is purified. But the better the quality of the iron the smaller the amount of impurity. Pyrimachus stone will also melt and form drops and become fluid : when it solidifies after having been fluid it regains its former hardness. Millstones [b] too melt and become fluid : and when they solidify again afterwards they are black in colour but like lime in texture. [Mud and earth also melt.]

Things solidified by dry heat are some of them altogether insoluble, some of them soluble by liquid. Earthenware and some kinds of stone which are made of earth calcined by fire, like millstones, are insoluble [c] : but soda [d] and salt are soluble in liquid, not in all liquid but only in cold. So they melt in water

---

[b] Millstones were often made of various kinds of lava.

[c] There is no *prima facie* contradiction between this and l. 7 above. Millstones can be melted by fire but are insoluble in water. Yet the μυλίαι of 383 b 12, having been solidified by heat (383 b 10), can hardly be the same as the μύλαι of 383 b 7 which have solidified by cold (383 a 26).

[d] νίτρον = sodium carbonate.

383 b

ὕδατι καὶ ὅσα ὕδατος εἴδη τήκεται, ἐλαίῳ δ' οὐ
15 τήκεται· τῷ γὰρ ξηρῷ θερμῷ ἐναντίον ψυχρὸν
ὑγρόν. εἰ οὖν ἔπηξεν θάτερον, θάτερον λύσει· οὕτω
γὰρ τἀναντία ἔσται αἴτια τῶν ἐναντίων.

NOTE ON ANCIENT IRON MAKING [a]
383 A 32–B 5

In order to understand this passage, an interesting and apparently neglected one in the history of ancient metallurgy, it is necessary to know something of the method by which iron was produced in the ancient world.

In what follows, I have been guided especially by the following articles : H. C. Richardson, " Iron, Prehistoric and Ancient," *American Journal of Archaeology*, xxxviii (1934) ; R. J. Forbes, " The Coming of Iron," *Jaarbericht No. 9 van het voraziatischegyptisch gezelschap* " *ex Oriente Lux* " ; Campbell and Thum, " Ancient Iron," *Metal Progress*, vol. 20 (1931) ; Rudolf Schaur, " Entwicklungsgeschichte der Hochofen in Steiermark," *Stahl und Eisen*, xlix (April 1929) ; article *s.v.* " ferrum " in Daremberg-Saglio, *Dictionnaire des antiquités grecques et romaines*. An exhaustive bibliography can be found in R. J. Forbes, *Bibliographia Antiqua, Philosophia Naturalis ii*, part J (Leiden, 1942).[b]

To-day *iron* is produced in the blast furnace, in which the fuel is coke and the ore is completely liquefied. The product of the blast furnace is pig-iron, which has a high carbon content and is therefore very brittle. *Steel* is produced by a further process in which the pig-iron is again made molten and its carbon content reduced, steel being, in fact, iron with a particular range of carbon content (approximately 0·25% to 1·5%). The two steel-making processes now in common use are the Bessemer process and the Siemens open-hearth process ; it is unnecessary to enter here into details of either process, the purpose of both being to reduce the carbon

[a] I am very grateful to Mr. Herbert Maryon of the British Museum for advice and help in writing this note.
[b] To this should now be added his *Metallurgy in Antiquity* (Leiden, Brill, 1950).

and the watery liquids but not in olive oil. For moist cold is opposite to dry heat, and what one solidifies the other will dissolve ; for opposite causes will thus produce opposite effects.

content of the raw material (pig-iron or pig-iron and scrap iron) sufficiently to make steel. In the blast furnace (and in the Siemens furnace) certain impurities in the charge also liquefy to form a molten " slag " or " gangue " which floats on top of the metal and can be run off separately from it.

The method of making iron in the ancient world was entirely different. The fuel used was charcoal ; and in the charcoal furnaces of the ancient world it was impossible to reach the temperature at which iron melts (1600° C.). The blast furnace, which can reach this temperature, was not developed until the end of the Middle Ages, and even after its invention the possibilities of the new method were limited so long as charcoal remained the fuel ; it was not until 1735 that Abraham Darby of Colebrooke in Shropshire perfected the coke blast furnace which made iron production on a large scale possible. The ancient charcoal furnace was, by comparison, a very simple affair. It consisted of a shallow excavation, perhaps two feet deep, whose sides were built up with turf and stone to a height of two or three feet above ground level and lined with some sort of refractory clay. There was a channel which ran into the bottom of the excavation and through which air could reach the furnace, which to facilitate the construction was commonly built on the side of a hill facing the prevailing wind. The ore was broken up small and charged into the furnace with the charcoal. Bellows were sometimes used to raise the heat, but the furnace was often allowed to burn with a natural draught only. The ore did not become molten but did become pasty and gradually coagulate. This process took some 8-12 hours. At the end of it the furnace was broken open, and the iron " bloom " which had formed as a result of the smelting process was removed. This bloom still contained many impurities, the dross, gangue or slag. The melting-point of the slag is lower than that of the ore, and can be still further reduced by the addition of suitable fluxes, which the ancients may have used.

It would therefore liquefy first, and find its way to the lower part of the furnace. Next the heavier iron would trickle down, sink through the slag and gradually form a bloom at the bottom of the furnace, with the slag next above it and the infusible remainder of the ore on top. When the furnace was opened, the bloom would be raked from its position at the bottom and the slag would run or fall or be knocked off it. But much of the slag would, nevertheless, remain adhering to or included in the bloom, and this would be, so far as possible, forced out or knocked off by hammering or forging. In order to remove it more completely the bloom would be reheated and reforged a number of times ; but complete removal would hardly be possible, and specimens of ancient iron that have been analysed still contain much slag.

The iron bloom that was finally produced after hammering would, if the iron remained pure, be *wrought iron*. But wrought iron has a very low carbon content and is therefore soft and unsuitable for tools. The problem of the ancient iron-worker was thus the opposite of that of the modern steel-maker : the modern steel-maker has to take the carbon *out* of his raw material (pig-iron) in order to toughen it; the ancient iron-worker had to get carbon *into* his iron so that it could be hardened for tools and weapons. This carburization was effected in the process of repeated reheating ; for the iron bloom would pick up carbon from the charcoal fuel, and specimens of ancient iron in fact show a carbon content equivalent to that of mild steel. But the process of carburization was a tricky one, and its results uncertain : and it seems unlikely that the ancient iron-workers really understood it, though they knew quite empirically that repeated reheating did produce an iron or mild steel that could be used for tools and weapons. Hence the quality of the ore was an important factor as some ores, especially those containing manganese, more easily produced iron of the requisite quality when treated by this method than others. The ores of Noricum were especially suited to produce a good quality metal by ancient methods, and that area (the seat of the Halstatt civilization) remained celebrated for its iron throughout the Greco-Roman period.

To render the iron or mild steel so produced hard enough for tool purposes, it was necessary to quench it in water from a white heat. This process was certainly known to the Greeks, and passing reference to it is not uncommon. It is

NOTE ON ANCIENT IRON MAKING

effective only when the iron has a certain minimum carbon content : hence the importance of the carburization process without which iron will not harden enough to use for tools and weapons. There are, therefore, two main stages in ancient iron-working : (a) the smelting of the ore and the production of a bloom of forgeable iron ; (b) the forging of the iron bloom so produced into a tool or weapon with the quenching as its final stage. (Tempering may have been known to the Romans, but can be ignored for our present purpose.)

It remains to interpret the present passage (383 a 32–b 5) in terms of ancient methods. By εἰργασμένος σίδηρος (" wrought iron "), Aristotle presumably refers to the produce of the iron furnace, the bloom that has been forged or " wrought." It is doubtful if any ancient furnace could have melted this (even though its melting-point would be less than that of pure iron), and no ancient smith would have wished to do so, for the casting of iron was unknown in the ancient world. Though, therefore, Aristotle speaks of the iron " melting "(τήκεται l. 32), he probably does not mean complete liquefaction. In the previous line he speaks of iron as softening (μαλάττεται l. 31), and ὑγρός (l. 33) can be used of substances that are soft and pliant as well as of those that are liquid. Aristotle should therefore be understood to mean that " wrought iron " when heated will become soft and pliable rather than that it will become liquid.

It is not immediately obvious to which of the two main stages of the iron-making process defined above the remainder of the passage refers. The critical word is στόμωμα (" steel "). The word is not common in classical authors, as reference to L & S⁹ and Stephanus will show.[a] Basically it seems to mean the capacity of steel to take an edge (cf. Latin acies) : so στόμα is used (e.g. by Homer, Il. xv. 389) of the edge or point of a weapon. But ancient iron would only take an edge when it had been hardened by quenching : so L & S⁹ give " hardened iron," " steel," as the meaning, L & S⁸ " iron hardened to take a sharp edge," and we find the connexion of στόμωμα with quenching explicitly made by Plutarch, Moralia 73 c : ὥσπερ ὁ σίδηρος πυκνοῦται τῇ περιψύξει καὶ δέχεται τὴν στόμωσιν ἀνεθεὶς πρῶτον ὑπὸ θερμότητος καὶ· μαλακὸς γενόμενος, οὕτω τοῖς φίλοις διακεχυμένοις καὶ

[a] The only occurrence before the 4th century is in a fragment of Cratinus : fr. 247 Kock, Pollux 10. 186. Aristophanes has στομόω (Nub. 1108, 1110).

ARISTOTLE

θερμοῖς οὖσι ὑπὸ τῶν ἐπαίνων ὥσπερ βαφὴν ἀτρέμα τὴν παρ-
ρησίαν ἐπάγειν. Other passages in Plutarch bear this out
(*ibid.* 156 B, 943 E, *Lyc.* 9), and so also does a passage from
Aetius quoted by Stephanus. Metaphorically στόμωμα is
used either with reference to its hardness or to its cutting
power (Plutarch, *Mor.* 625 B, 693 A ; Arrian, *Tact.* 12. 2, *cf.*
Ael. *Tact.* 13. 2 : compare Aristophanes' use of στομόω " to
harden" in the sense of "to train" *Nub.* 1108, 1110). στόμωμα
then means the iron-steel product of the ancient furnace after
it has been hardened by quenching and made capable of
taking a cutting edge.

At first sight, therefore, one would expect our passage to
refer to the second main stage of ancient iron making. The
smith when making a tool would start with the εἰργασμένος
σίδηρος, the iron bloom, and would heat it in his charcoal
furnace. He would have to reheat it a number of times, since
it would not remain long at a workable heat when taken out
of the furnace. But his bloom would, as we have seen, still
contain many impurities, and these would melt (as in the
iron-furnace, stage (*a*)) and drop off the bloom and be raked
away with the ash of the furnace (ὑφίσταται . . . καὶ ἀποκαθαίρεται κάτω 383 a 34). Too frequent reheating would lead
to loss of weight, and would be avoided : and the better the
iron the less the impurity and the less the loss. Also, though
Aristotle could not know this, the bloom would pick up
carbon from the charcoal furnace, and so become more suitable for quenching.

But Aristotle makes no mention of quenching, and he
may be thinking of the former of the two stages, and using
στόμωμα as a general term for iron, which becomes hard after
quenching. We must then suppose that he is reminded by
his reference to wrought iron of the smelting process which
also (καί 383 a 33) depends on the reaction of iron ore to heat.
The words ὑφίσταται . . . καὶ ἀποκαθαίρεται κάτω ἡ σκωρία
383 a 34 refer to the slag sinking to the bottom of the furnace
and being raked away. Ideler and the O.T. find the words

NOTE ON ANCIENT IRON MAKING

puzzling because both think in terms of the blast furnace in which the metal *liquefies* and the melted slag floats on top of it. But in the ancient furnace the slag would " sink to the bottom " with the iron. Several reheatings and reforgings are necessary before the impurities are sufficiently removed (πολλάκις παθῇ 383 b 1), and the purer the ore (σίδηρος covering the ore as well as the product) the smaller the amount of impurity to be removed. Too frequent reheating was avoided because of the loss of weight consequent upon it (383 b 2).

The translation of οὐ ποιοῦσι δὲ πολλάκις αὐτό (383 b 2) as " they do not repeat the process often " follows Ideler, St.-Hilaire and O.T. (and is supported by Alex. 207. 23). There is at first sight a contradiction with πολλάκις παθῇ " frequent subjection to this treatment " (383 b 1), since both contexts refer to the process of reheating. The contradiction can be resolved by supposing that what Aristotle means is that while reheating was necessary (πολλάκις 383 b 1), it inevitably entailed some loss of metal and so was not repeated unduly often (πολλάκις 383 b 2), not more often, we may suppose, than was absolutely necessary. St.-Hilaire makes the point by translating πολλάκις " plusieurs fois " and " souvent " in the two contexts.

Either interpretation of the passage is consistent with ancient practice : but Aristotle's characteristic brevity makes a decision between them difficult. Nor is there much evidence elsewhere in ancient literature to throw light on the subject. [Arist.] *De Mirab. Ausc.* 48 tells us very little, though it perhaps suggests that the pyrimachus stone (mentioned also here 383 b 5) was used as a flux. I doubt whether, as Richardson suggests, it is evidence for the use of a crucible process. Hippocrates, περὶ Διαίτης i. 13, refers briefly to the process of forging and quenching (possibly to smelting also). And Pliny, *Nat. Hist.* xxxiv, has a number of miscellaneous and not very illuminating remarks. But in the main we must rely on non-literary evidence.

CHAPTER VII

ARGUMENT

Liquefaction and solidification (continued.). Compounds of earth and water, (b) in which water predominates: the

383 b 18 Παχύνεται μὲν οὖν ὑπὸ πυρὸς μόνον, ὅσα ὕδατος πλέον ἔχει ἢ γῆς, πήγνυται δέ, ὅσα γῆς. διὸ καὶ τὸ 20 νίτρον καὶ οἱ ἅλες γῆς εἰσιν μᾶλλον, καὶ λίθος καὶ κέραμος.

Ἀπορώτατα δὲ ἔχει ἡ τοῦ ἐλαίου φύσις. εἰ μὲν γὰρ ὕδατος, ἔδει πήγνυσθαι ὑπὸ ψυχροῦ, εἰ δὲ γῆς πλέον, ὑπὸ πυρός· νῦν δὲ πήγνυται μὲν ὑπ' οὐδε-τέρου, παχύνεται δὲ ὑπ' ἀμφοῖν. αἴτιον δ' ἐστὶν 25 ὅτι ἀέρος ἐστὶν πλῆρες. διὸ καὶ ἐν τῷ ὕδατι ἐπι-πολάζει· καὶ γὰρ ὁ ἀὴρ φέρεται ἄνω. τὸ μὲν οὖν ψυχρὸν ἐκ τοῦ ἐνόντος πνεύματος ὕδωρ ποιοῦν παχύνει· ἀεὶ γάρ, ὅταν μειχθῇ ὕδωρ καὶ ἔλαιον, ἀμφοῖν γίγνεται παχύτερον. ὑπὸ δὲ πυρὸς καὶ χρόνου παχύνεται καὶ λευκαίνεται, λευκαίνεται μὲν 30 ἐξατμίζοντος εἴ τι ἐνῆν ὕδατος, παχύνεται δὲ διὰ τὸ μαραινομένου τοῦ θερμοῦ ἐκ τοῦ ἀέρος γίγνεσθαι ὕδωρ. ἀμφοτέρως μὲν οὖν τὸ αὐτὸ γίγνεται πάθος, καὶ διὰ τὸ αὐτό, ἀλλ' οὐχ ὡσαύτως. παχύνεται μὲν οὖν ὑπ' ἀμφοτέρων, οὐ ξηραίνεται δ' ὑπ' οὐδετέρου· οὔτε γὰρ ὁ ἥλιος οὔτε τὸ ψῦχος ξηραίνει· οὐ μόνον 384 a διότι γλίσχρον, ἀλλὰ καὶ διότι ἀέρος ἐστίν. οὐ

CHAPTER VII

ARGUMENT (*continued*)

special case of olive oil (383 b 18—384 a 1). *Liquefaction and solidification of various particular compounds of earth and water discussed* (384 a 2–b 23).

COMPOUNDS which contain more water than earth are only increased in density by fire, but those that contain more earth than water are solidified. Soda and salt, therefore, contain more earth, and also stone and clay.

(b) in which water predominates.

The nature of olive oil is the most difficult to determine.[a] For if it contained more water, cold should solidify it, if more earth, fire should do so. In fact, however, its density is increased by both, while it is solidified by neither. The reason is that it is full of air, which is why it floats on water, since air naturally moves upwards. Cold therefore increases its density by turning the air in it to water, for when oil and water are mixed the density of the compound is greater than that of either constituent. Oil is also increased in density and turned white by fire and by age : it is turned white because of the evaporation of any water it contained ; its density is increased because as its heat fades the air in it is turned to water. The effect, therefore, is the same in either case, and so also is the cause, but it operates in a different way. But while its density is increased both by heat and cold, it is not dried by either (for neither sun nor frost dries it), not only because it is viscous but because it contains air ; for it is not dried

[a] *Cf. De Gen. An.* ii. 2, 735 b 13 ff.

384 a

ξηραίνεται δὲ [τὸ ὕδωρ]¹ οὐδ' ἕψεται ὑπὸ πυρός,
ὅτι οὐκ ἀτμίζει διὰ γλισχρότητα.

Ὅσα δὲ μεικτὰ ὕδατος καὶ γῆς, κατὰ τὸ πλῆθος
ἑκατέρου ἄξιον λέγεσθαι· οἶνος γάρ τις καὶ πήγνυται
5 καὶ ἕψεται, οἷον τὸ γλεῦκος. ἀπέρχεται δὲ ἀπὸ
πάντων τῶν τοιούτων ξηραινομένων τὸ ὕδωρ.
σημεῖον δ' ὅτι τὸ ὕδωρ· ἡ γὰρ ἀτμὶς συνίσταται εἰς
ὕδωρ, ἐάν τις βούληται συλλέγειν· ὥστε ὅσοις
λείπεταί τι, τοῦτο γῆς. ἔνια δὲ τούτων καὶ ὑπὸ
ψυχροῦ, ὥσπερ εἴρηται, παχύνεται καὶ ξηραίνεται·
10 τὸ γὰρ ψυχρὸν οὐ μόνον πήγνυσιν, ἀλλὰ ξηραίνει
μὲν ὕδωρ, παχύνει δὲ τὸν ἀέρα ὕδωρ ποιοῦν· ἡ δὲ
πῆξις εἴρηται ξηρασία τις οὖσα. ὅσα μὲν οὖν μὴ
παχύνεται ὑπὸ τοῦ ψυχροῦ ἀλλὰ πήγνυται, ὕδατός
ἐστι μᾶλλον, οἷον οἶνος καὶ οὖρον καὶ ὄξος καὶ
κονία καὶ ὀρός· ὅσα δὲ παχύνεται μὴ ἐξατμίζοντα
15 ὑπὸ πυρός, τὰ μὲν γῆς, τὰ δὲ κοινὰ ὕδατος καὶ
ἀέρος, μέλι μὲν γῆς, ἔλαιον δ' ἀέρος. ἔστιν δὲ καὶ
τὸ γάλα καὶ τὸ αἷμα ἀμφοῖν μὲν κοινὰ καὶ ὕδατος
καὶ γῆς, μᾶλλον δὲ τὰ πολλὰ γῆς, ὥσπερ καὶ ἐξ
ὅσων ὑγρῶν νίτρον γίγνεται καὶ ἅλες (καὶ λίθοι δ'
ἔκ τινων συνίστανται τοιούτων). διὸ ἐὰν μὴ χω-
20 ρισθῇ ὁ ὀρός, ἐκκάεται ὑπὸ τοῦ πυρὸς ἑψόμενος.
τὸ δὲ γεῶδες συνίσταται καὶ ὑπὸ τοῦ ὀποῦ, ἐάν
πως ἕψῃ τις, οἷον οἱ ἰατροὶ ὀπίζοντες. οὕτω δὲ
χωρίζεται ὁ ὀρὸς καὶ ὁ τυρός. ὁ δὲ χωρισθεὶς ὀρὸς

¹ del. O.T.   τὸ ἔλαιον F H N.

ᵃ And so are a compound of earth and water, and not
" watery liquids," the heading under which wine in general
is classified at 382 b 13.

up or boiled off by fire because its viscous character prevents evaporation.

Compounds of water and earth should be classified according to which predominates. For some kinds of wine, for example must, solidify when boiled.[a] In all such cases it is the water that is driven off in the process of drying. This is shown by the fact that if you collect the vapour it condenses into water[b] : and so where there is any sediment left it must be earthy. But some of these compounds, as we have said,[c] are also increased in density and dried by cold. For cold not only solidifies, but also dries water and increases density by turning air to water ; and solidification we have already[d] described as a kind of drying. Things, therefore, which cold solidifies but does not increase in density, contain more water, like wine, urine, vinegar, lye and whey[e] : and of things which it increases in density (but which are not evaporated by fire), some contain more earth while others are a compound of water and air—honey, for example, contains more earth, oil contains air. Milk and blood are both compounds of earth and water, containing for the most part more earth, as also are the liquids from which soda and salt are formed. Stones are also formed from some liquids of the same kind. So whey, if it has not been separated, will boil away on a fire. The earthy constituent in milk can also be coagulated by rennet, if you boil it in the way doctors do when they curdle it : and this is the way in which the whey and the cheese are commonly separated.

Various examples discussed.

[b] *Cf.* Book II. ch. 3, note *b* on p. 156.
[c] 383 a 13.   [d] 382 b 1.
[e] Yet at 382 b 13 wine, urine and whey were classified as " watery liquids " ($\H{\upsilon}\delta\alpha\tau\sigma\varsigma$ $\epsilon\H{\iota}\delta\eta$), which should imply that they have no admixture of earth : *cf.* also 384 a 4, 385 b 1.

384 a

οὐκέτι παχύνεται, ἀλλ' ἐκκάεται ὥσπερ ὕδωρ. εἰ
δέ τι μὴ ἔχει τυρὸν γάλα ἢ ὀλίγον, τοῦτο μᾶλλον
25 ὕδατος καὶ ἄτροφον. καὶ τὸ αἷμα δὲ ὁμοίως·
πήγνυται γὰρ τῷ ξηραίνεσθαι ψυχόμενον. ὅσα δὲ
μὴ πήγνυται, οἷον τὸ τῆς ἐλάφου, τὰ τοιαῦτα
ὕδατος μᾶλλον, καὶ ψυχρὰ ταῦτα. διὸ καὶ οὐκ
ἔχει ἶνας· αἱ γὰρ ἶνές εἰσιν γῆς καὶ στερεόν· ὥστε
καὶ ἐξαιρεθεισῶν οὐ πήγνυται· τοῦτο δ' ἐστὶν ὅτι
30 οὐ ξηραίνεται· ὕδωρ γὰρ τὸ λοιπόν, ὡς τὸ γάλα τοῦ
τυροῦ ἐξαιρεθέντος. σημεῖον δέ· τὰ νοσώδη γὰρ
αἵματα οὐ θέλει πήγνυσθαι· ἰχωροειδῆ γάρ, τοῦτο
δὲ φλέγμα καὶ ὕδωρ,[1] διὰ τὸ ἄπεπτον εἶναι καὶ
ἀκράτητον ὑπὸ τῆς φύσεως. ἔτι δὲ τὰ μὲν λυτά
384 b ἐστιν, οἷον νίτρον, τὰ δὲ ἄλυτα, οἷον κέραμος, καὶ
τούτων τὰ μὲν μαλακτά, οἷον κέρας, τὰ δὲ ἀμάλακτα, οἷον κέραμος καὶ λίθος. αἴτιον δ' ὅτι
τἀναντία τῶν ἐναντίων αἴτια, ὥστ' εἰ πήγνυται
δυοῖν, ψυχρῷ καὶ ξηρῷ, λύεσθαι ἀνάγκη θερμῷ καὶ
5 ὑγρῷ· διὸ πυρὶ καὶ ὕδατι (ταῦτα γὰρ ἐναντία), ὕδατι
μὲν ὅσα πυρὶ μόνῳ, πυρὶ δὲ ὅσα ψυχρῷ μόνῳ· ὥστ'
εἴ τι ὑπ' ἀμφοῖν συμβαίνει πήγνυσθαι, ταῦτα ἄλυτα
μάλιστα. γίγνεται δὲ τοιαῦτα ὅσα θερμανθέντα
ἔπειτα τῷ ψυχρῷ πήγνυται· συμβαίνει γάρ, ὅταν
τὸ θερμὸν ἐξικμάσῃ ἐξιὸν τὸ πλεῖστον ὑγρόν,[2] συν-
10 θλίβεσθαι πάλιν ὑπὸ τοῦ ψυχροῦ, ὥστε μηδὲ ὑγρῷ
διδόναι δίοδον. καὶ διὰ ταῦτα οὔτε τὸ θερμὸν λύει·

---

[1] interpunxi.
[2] interpunxit O.T. : ἐξιόν, τὸ πλεῖστον Fobes.

---

[a] Cf. De Part. An. ii. 4 : and for the deer in particular
De Part. An. ii. 4, 650 b 15, Hist. An. iii. 6, 515 b 34.

[b] Adopting the O.T.'s punctuation, and taking ἐξικμάσῃ
b 9 as transitive : there is indeed no real authority for its use
as intransitive, for the only instance, apart from this passage,

Whey when separated will no longer increase in density but boil away like water : and if milk contains little or no cheese, then water predominates in its composition and it is not nutritious. Blood [a] behaves similarly, for it solidifies when dried by cooling. But in kinds of blood that do not solidify, like that of the deer, water predominates and the temperature is cold. Hence they do not contain fibres, fibres being composed of earth and solid. So blood from which fibres have been removed does not solidify, because it will not dry, the residuum being watery, which is what happens to milk when the cheese is removed. A proof of this is that diseased blood will not solidify, being serous, that is, made up of phlegm and water, nature having failed to control and concoct it. Again, some compounds are soluble, like soda, others are insoluble, like earthenware, and of these some can be softened, like horn, others cannot, like earthenware and stone. The reason is that opposite causes produce opposite effects, so if the two properties cold and dry cause solidification, it follows that hot and moist cause dissolution. So fire and water are dissolving agents (being opposites), water dissolving what fire alone solidifies, fire what cold alone solidifies, while anything that is solidified by both is least liable to dissolution. For when the heat as it leaves them vaporizes most of their moisture, they become compressed again by the cold and so afford no entrance even to moisture. [b] And for this reason even heat will not dissolve them, for it dis-

given by L & S⁹ (*Problems* 930 b 34) may be corrupt (Stephanus suggests that ἐξήτμικε is the correct reading). Fobes' punctuation (following Ideler and Bekker) does not yield the sense clearly required : for, as 383 a 12 shows, it is not τὸ ὑγρόν that is compressed, but τὸ ξηρόν.

384 b

ὅσα γὰρ ὑπὸ ψυχροῦ πήγνυται μόνον, ταῦτα λύει·
οὔθ' ὑπὸ ὕδατος· ὅσα γὰρ ὑπὸ ψυχροῦ πήγνυται,
οὐ λύει, ἀλλ' ὅσα ὑπὸ θερμοῦ ξηροῦ μόνον. ὁ δὲ
15 σίδηρος τακεὶς ὑπὸ θερμοῦ ψυχθεὶς πήγνυται. τὰ
δὲ ξύλα ἐστὶν γῆς καὶ ἀέρος· διὸ καυστὰ καὶ οὐ
τηκτὰ οὐδὲ μαλακτά, καὶ ἐπὶ τῷ ὕδατι ἐπιπλεῖ,
πλὴν ἐβένου· αὕτη δ' οὔ· τὰ μὲν γὰρ ἄλλα ἀέρος
ἔχει πλέον, ἐκ δὲ τῆς ἐβένου τῆς μελαίνης δια-
πέπνευκεν ὁ ἀήρ, καὶ ἔστι πλέον ἐν αὐτῇ γῆς.
20 κέραμος δὲ γῆς μόνον διὰ τὸ ξηραινόμενος παγῆναι
κατὰ μικρόν· οὔτε γὰρ τὸ ὕδωρ εἰσόδους ἔχει, δι'
ὧν μόνον πνεῦμα ἐξῆλθεν, οὔτε πῦρ· ἔπηξε γὰρ
αὐτό.

Τί μὲν οὖν ἐστι πῆξις καὶ τῆξις, καὶ διὰ πόσα
καὶ ἐν πόσοις ἐστίν, εἴρηται.

CHAPTER VIII

ARGUMENT

*Differentiating qualities of bodies. All bodies thus contain
the four primary qualities of heat, cold, wet and dry. They
are also differentiated by the ways in which they affect our
senses and by certain intrinsic properties (384 b 24—385 a
10). Eighteen such properties, each grouped with its contrary, are enumerated (385 a 10-20). The first two pairs
dealt with (385 a 20–b 5).*

Note.—*The compounds with which Aristotle is primarily
concerned in the remaining chapters (even when he does not
mention them specifically, as in ch. 11) are the " homoeomerous " bodies. A substance is homoeomerous if it is
homogeneous in the sense of being a chemical compound*

336

solves only such things as are solidified by cold : nor will water, which will not dissolve things solidified by cold but only those solidified by dry heat. But iron is melted by heat and solidifies when cooled. Wood is composed of earth and air and so is combustible, but not meltable or softenable, and (except for ebony) floats. Ebony does not, for while in other woods there is a greater proportion of air, in black ebony it has been exhaled and the proportion of earth is greater. Earthenware is composed of earth only because when dried it solidifies gradually ; neither can water gain entry through pores from which only vapour could escape, nor can fire, which was the solidifying agent.

This completes our account of solidification and melting, their causes and the substances in which they occur.

CHAPTER VIII

ARGUMENT (continued)

(μίξις), as opposed to a mechanical mixture (σύνθεσις) : cf. De Gen. et Corr. i. 10, esp. 328 a 10 φαμὲν δὲ δεῖν, εἴπερ μέμικται, τὸ μιχθὲν ὁμοιομερὲς εἶναι. The homoeomerous substances thus play an important part in Aristotle's theory of the physical world. The simplest physical substances are the four elements, analysable in theory but not in fact into combinations of the four prime contraries and prime matter (De Caelo iii-iv, De Gen. et Corr. ii. 1-6). From the four elements the homoeomerous substances are made, comprising all simple homogeneous substances, animal and mineral : from the homoeomerous substances in turn are composed more complex

337

(*anhomoeomerous*) *organic and inorganic bodies :* cf. 388 a
13 *ff.*, 389 b 27 *ff.*, and De Part. An. *ii.* 1, 646 a 8-21, De
Gen. An. 715 a 8-11. *The distinction between homoeomerous*

334 b 24 Ἐκ δὲ τούτων φανερὸν ὅτι ὑπὸ θερμοῦ καὶ
25 ψυχροῦ συνίσταται τὰ σώματα, ταῦτα δὲ παχύνοντα
καὶ πηγνύντα ποιεῖται τὴν ἐργασίαν αὐτῶν. διὰ
δὲ τὸ ὑπὸ τούτων δημιουργεῖσθαι ἐν ἅπασιν ἔνεστι
θερμότης, τισὶ δὲ καὶ ψυχρότης ᾗ ἐκλείπει. ὥστ'
ἐπεὶ ταῦτα μὲν ὑπάρχει διὰ τὸ ποιεῖν, ὑγρὸν δὲ καὶ
30 ξηρὸν διὰ τὸ πάσχειν, μετέχει αὐτῶν τὰ κοινὰ πάντων. ἐκ μὲν οὖν ὕδατος καὶ γῆς τὰ ὁμοιομερῆ
σώματα συνίσταται, καὶ ἐν φυτοῖς καὶ ἐν ζῴοις,
καὶ τὰ μεταλλευόμενα, οἷον χρυσὸς καὶ ἄργυρος
καὶ ὅσα ἄλλα τοιαῦτα, ἐξ αὐτῶν τε καὶ ἐκ τῆς
ἀναθυμιάσεως τῆς ἑκατέρου ἐγκατακλειομένης,
385 a ὥσπερ εἴρηται ἐν ἄλλοις. ταῦτα δὲ διαφέρει ἀλλήλων τοῖς τε πρὸς τὰς αἰσθήσεις ἰδίοις ἅπαντα, τῷ
ποιεῖν τι δύνασθαι (λευκὸν γὰρ καὶ εὐῶδες καὶ
ψοφητικὸν καὶ γλυκὺ καὶ θερμὸν καὶ ψυχρὸν τῷ
ποιεῖν τι δύνασθαι τὴν αἴσθησίν ἐστι), καὶ ἄλλοις
5 οἰκειοτέροις πάθεσιν, ὅσα τῷ πάσχειν λέγονται,
λέγω δ' οἷον τὸ τηκτὸν καὶ πηκτὸν καὶ καμπτὸν
καὶ ὅσα ἄλλα τοιαῦτα· πάντα γὰρ τὰ τοιαῦτα παθητικά, ὥσπερ τὸ ὑγρὸν καὶ τὸ ξηρόν. τούτοις δ'
ἤδη διαφέρει ὀστοῦν καὶ σὰρξ καὶ νεῦρον καὶ ξύλον
10 καὶ φλοιὸς καὶ λίθος καὶ τῶν ἄλλων ἕκαστον τῶν
ὁμοιομερῶν μὲν φυσικῶν δὲ σωμάτων.

Εἴπωμεν δὲ πρῶτον τὸν ἀριθμὸν αὐτῶν, ὅσα κατὰ
δύναμιν καὶ ἀδυναμίαν λέγεται. ἔστιν δὲ τάδε·

Πηκτὸν ἄπηκτον.
Τηκτὸν ἄτηκτον.

338

and anhomoeomerous is particularly important in biology,
where you have the homoeomerous parts (blood, bone, sinew,
flesh), the anhomoeomerous parts composed of them (hands,
feet, eyes) and finally the complete creature (man, horse).

FROM this it is clear that bodies are formed by heat The
and cold, which operate by increasing density and qualities
solidifying. And because they are manufactured by classified
them, all bodies contain heat and some contain cold
in so far as they lack heat. So, since heat and cold
are present as active constituents, moist and dry as
passive, compound bodies contain them all. The
homoeomerous bodies, therefore, vegetable and animal, and also the metals,[a] such as gold, silver and the
like, are composed of water and earth and of their
exhalations when, as has been explained elsewhere,[b]
they are enclosed underground. All these bodies
differ from each other, firstly, in the particular ways in
which they can act on the senses (for a thing is white,
fragrant, resonant, sweet, hot or cold in virtue of the
way it acts on sensation), and, secondly, in other more
intrinsic qualities commonly classed as passive—I
mean solubility, solidification, flexibility and the like,
all of which, like moist and dry, are passive qualities.
It is by these passive qualities that bone, flesh,
sinew, wood, bark, stone and all the other natural
homoeomerous bodies are differentiated.

Let us begin by enumerating them, grouping each and
property with its converse. They are as follows : enumerated
in pairs.

1. Capable or incapable of solidification.
2. Meltable or unmeltable.

---

[a] τὰ μεταλλευόμενα are said to be a species of ὁμοιομερῆ at
388 a 13.
[b] Book III. ch. 6, 378 a 15 ff.

Μαλακτὸν ἀμάλακτον.

Τεγκτὸν ἄτεγκτον.

Καμπτὸν ἄκαμπτον.

Κατακτὸν ἀκάτακτον.

Θραυστὸν ἄθραυστον.

15 Θλαστὸν ἄθλαστον.

Πλαστὸν ἄπλαστον.

Πιεστὸν ἀπίεστον.

Ἑλκτὸν ἄνελκτον.

Ἐλατὸν ἀνήλατον.

Σχιστὸν ἄσχιστον.

Τμητὸν ἄτμητον.

Γλίσχρον ψαθυρόν.

Πιλητὸν ἀπίλητον.

Καυστὸν ἄκαυστον.

Θυμιατὸν ἀθυμίατον.

Τὰ μὲν οὖν πλεῖστα σχεδὸν τῶν σωμάτων τού-
20 τοις διαφέρει τοῖς πάθεσιν· τίνα δ᾽ ἕκαστον τούτων
ἔχει δύναμιν, εἴπωμεν.

Περὶ μὲν οὖν πηκτοῦ καὶ ἀπήκτου καὶ τηκτοῦ καὶ
ἀτήκτου εἴρηται μὲν καθόλου πρότερον, ὅμως δ᾽
ἐπανέλθωμεν καὶ νῦν. τῶν γὰρ σωμάτων ὅσα
πήγνυται καὶ σκληρύνεται, τὰ μὲν ὑπὸ θερμοῦ
πάσχει τοῦτο τὰ δ᾽ ὑπὸ ψυχροῦ, ὑπὸ μὲν τοῦ
25 θερμοῦ ξηραίνοντος τὸ ὑγρόν, ὑπὸ δὲ τοῦ ψυχροῦ
ἐκθλίβοντος τὸ θερμόν. ὥστε τὰ μὲν ἀϋγροῦπουσίᾳ
τὰ δὲ θερμοῦ τοῦτο πάσχει, ὅσα μὲν ὕδατος, θερμοῦ,
ὅσα δὲ γῆς, ὑγροῦ. τὰ μὲν οὖν ὑγροῦ ἀπουσίᾳ ὑπὸ
ὑγροῦ διατήκεται, ἂν μὴ οὕτως συνέλθῃ ὥστε ἐλάτ-
30 τους τοὺς πόρους λειφθῆναι τῶν τοῦ ὕδατος ὄγκων,

3. Softenable or unsoftenable by heat.
4. Softenable or unsoftenable by water.
5. Flexible or inflexible.
6. Breakable or unbreakable.
7. Capable or incapable of fragmentation.
8. Capable or incapable of taking an impression.
9. Plastic or non-plastic.
10. Capable or incapable of being squeezed.
11. Ductile or non-ductile.
12. Malleable or non-malleable.
13. Fissile or non-fissile.
14. Cuttable or uncuttable.
15. Viscous or friable.
16. Compressible or incompressible.
17. Combustible or incombustible.
18. Capable or incapable of giving off fumes.

The great majority of bodies are differentiated by these qualities, whose nature we will therefore go on to describe.

We have already [a] given a general description of the first two pairs of qualities, but let us return to them again now. Bodies which solidify and harden do so under the influence of cold or heat, heat drying their moisture and cold expelling their heat : they are so affected, in fact, either by lack of moisture or of heat, those in which water predominates by lack of heat, those in which earth predominates by lack of moisture. Bodies so affected by lack of moisture are melted by moisture, unless their composition is such that their pores [b] are too small for the particles of water to enter, as, for instance, earthenware ; but

(marginal note: (1 and 2) Solidification, melting and their contraries.)

---

[a] Chs. 6 and 7.
[b] On Aristotle's use of " pores " in this and the following passages see Introd. p. xvii.

385 a

οἷον ὁ κέραμος· ὅσα δὲ μὴ οὕτω, πάντα ὑγρῷ τήκεται, οἷον νίτρον, ἅλες, γῆ ἡ ἐκ πηλοῦ· τὰ δὲ
θερμοῦ στερήσει ὑπὸ θερμοῦ τήκεται, οἷον κρύσταλλος, μόλυβδος, χαλκός. ποῖα μὲν οὖν πηκτὰ

385 b καὶ τηκτά, εἴρηται, καὶ ποῖα ἄτηκτα. ἄπηκτα δὲ
ὅσα μὴ ἔχει ὑγρότητα ὑδατώδη, μηδὲ ὕδατός ἐστιν,
ἀλλὰ πλέον θερμοῦ καὶ γῆς, οἷον μέλι καὶ γλεῦκος
(ὥσπερ ζέοντα γάρ ἐστιν), καὶ ὅσα ὕδατος μὲν ἔχει,
ἔστιν δὲ πλέον ἀέρος, ὥσπερ τὸ ἔλαιον καὶ ὁ ἄρ-
5 γυρος ὁ χυτός, καὶ εἴ τι γλίσχρον, οἷον ⟨πίττα
καὶ⟩[1] ἰξός.

---

[1] πίττα καὶ om. codd. : habent Al Ol.

CHAPTER IX

ARGUMENT

*The remaining sixteen properties and their contraries are
dealt with in order.*

385 b 6 Μαλακτὰ δ' ἐστὶ τῶν πεπηγότων ὅσα μὴ ἐξ
ὕδατος, οἷον κρύσταλλος ὕδατος, ἀλλ' ὅσα γῆς
μᾶλλον, καὶ μήτ' ἐξίκμασται πᾶν τὸ ὑγρὸν ὥσπερ
ἐν νίτρῳ ἢ ἁλσί, μήτ' ἔχει ἀνωμάλως ὥσπερ ὁ κέ-
10 ραμος, ἀλλ' ἢ ἑλκτὰ μὴ ὄντα διαντά, ἢ ἐλατὰ μὴ
ὄντα ὕδατος, καὶ μαλακτὰ πυρί, οἷον σίδηρος καὶ
κέρας [καὶ ξύλα.][1]

Ἔστι δὲ καὶ τῶν τηκτῶν καὶ τῶν ἀτήκτων τὰ
μὲν τεγκτὰ τὰ δὲ ἄτεγκτα, οἷον χαλκὸς ἄτεγκτον,
τηκτὸν ὄν, ἔριον δὲ καὶ γῆ τεγκτόν· βρέχεται γάρ.
15 καὶ χαλκὸς μὲν δὴ τηκτόν, οὐχ ὑπὸ ὕδατος δὲ

unless this is so they are all melted by moisture, like
soda, salt and dried mud. Bodies solidified by deficiency of heat are melted by heat, for instance ice,
lead or bronze.[a] This deals with bodies capable of
solidification and with bodies that will and will not
melt. Incapable of solidification are bodies which
contain no watery moisture and are not watery, and
in which heat and earth predominate rather than
water, like honey and must (for they are in a kind of
ferment), and also bodies in which, though they
contain water, air predominates, like oil, quicksilver
and viscous liquids such as pitch and birdlime.

[a] Aristotle uses the same word ($\tau\eta\kappa\tau\acute{o}\nu$), both of substances
that can be *dissolved* in water (*e.g.* salt) and *melted* by fire.

CHAPTER IX

SOLID bodies can be softened by heat if they are not (3) Soften-
composed of water (as ice is) but are predominantly able by
earthy : their moisture must not have been all
evaporated (as in soda or salt) nor be disproportion-
ately small in quantity (as in potter's clay), and if they
are either tensile but not absorbent or ductile without
a preponderance of moisture, fire will soften them.
Examples are iron and horn.

Of bodies that can and cannot be melted some can (4) Soften-
be softened in water, some cannot ; thus bronze, able by
water.
which will melt, cannot, but wool and earth can, for
they can be soaked. Bronze, of course, though it can
be melted, cannot be melted in water : but some

[1] secl. O.T., cf. 384 b 15-16.

385 b

τηκτόν. ἀλλὰ καὶ τῶν ὑπὸ ὕδατος τηκτῶν ἔνια
ἄτεγκτα, οἷον νίτρον καὶ ἅλες· οὐδὲ γὰρ ἄλλο
τεγκτὸν οὐδὲν ὃ μὴ μαλακώτερον γίγνεται βρεχό-
μενον. ἔνια δὲ τεγκτὰ ὄντα οὐ τηκτά ἐστιν, οἷον
ἔριον καὶ οἱ καρποί. ἔστι δὲ τεγκτὰ μὲν ὅσα γῆς
20 ὄντα ἔχει τοὺς πόρους μείζους τῶν τοῦ ὕδατος
ὄγκων, ὄντας δὲ σκληροτέρους[1] τοῦ ὕδατος. τηκτὰ
δὲ ὕδατι ὅσα δι' ὅλου. διὰ τί δ' ἡ μὲν γῆ καὶ
τήκεται καὶ τέγγεται ὑπὸ τοῦ ὑγροῦ, τὸ δὲ νίτρον
τήκεται μέν, τέγγεται δ' οὔ; ὅτι ἐν μὲν τῷ νίτρῳ
δι' ὅλου οἱ πόροι, ὥστε διαιρεῖται εὐθὺς ὑπὸ τοῦ
25 ὕδατος τὰ μόρια, ἐν δὲ τῇ γῇ καὶ παραλλάξ εἰσι
πόροι, ὥστε ὁποτέρως ἂν δέξηται, διαφέρει τὸ
πάθος.[2]

Ἔστι δὲ καὶ τὰ μὲν τῶν σωμάτων καμπτὰ καὶ
εὐθυντά, οἷον κάλαμος καὶ λύγος, τὰ δ' ἄκαμπτα
τῶν σωμάτων, οἷον κέραμος καὶ λίθος. ἔστιν δὲ
30 ἄκαμπτα μὲν καὶ ἀνεύθυντα ὅσων σωμάτων οὐ
δύναται τὸ μῆκος εἰς εὐθύτητα ἐκ περιφερείας καὶ
ἐξ εὐθύτητος εἰς περιφέρειαν μεταβάλλειν, καὶ τὸ
κάμπτεσθαι καὶ τὸ εὐθύνεσθαί ἐστιν τὸ εἰς εὐθύτητα
ἢ περιφέρειαν μεθίστασθαι ἢ κινεῖσθαι· καὶ γὰρ τὸ
386 a ἀνακαμπτόμενον καὶ τὸ κατακαμπτόμενον κάμπτεται. ἡ μὲν οὖν εἰς κυρτότητα ἢ κοιλότητα κίνησις
τοῦ μήκους σῳζομένου κάμψις ἐστίν· εἰ γὰρ καὶ εἰς
τὸ εὐθύ, εἴη ἂν ἅμα κεκαμμένον καὶ εὐθύ· ὅπερ
ἀδύνατον, τὸ εὐθὺ κεκάμφθαι. καὶ εἰ κάμπτεται
5 πᾶν ἢ ἀνακάμψει ἢ κατακάμψει, τούτων δὲ τὸ μὲν

---

[1] ὄντας δὲ σκληροτέρους 𝔐 : ὄντας σκληροτέρους Eᵣₑ𝒸. Nᵣₑ𝒸. :
ὄντων σκληροτέρων Fobes.

things also which can be melted in water cannot be softened, like soda and salt, for nothing is softened in water which does not become softer when soaked. On the other hand, some things which water softens do not melt, like wool and grain. Anything which is earthy and has pores larger than the particles of water and harder than water can be softened by water. But bodies that can be melted by water are porous throughout.[a] But why is earth melted and softened by moisture while soda is melted but is not softened ? Because soda is porous throughout and so its parts are dispersed at once by water ; but in earth the pores alternate and the effect differs according to which set the water enters.

Some bodies can be bent and straightened, like reeds and withies; some cannot be bent, like earthenware and stone. Things which cannot be bent and straightened are those which when curved cannot be bent straight and when straight cannot be bent into a curve, bending and straightening being the motion of bending straight or into a curve, for a thing is bent whether it is bent in or out. Bending, therefore, is alteration of shape to convex or concave, length remaining unchanged. If we were to add " or to straight," it would imply that a thing could be simultaneously bent and straight, and it is of course impossible for what is bent to be straight. And if everything that is bent is bent either in or out, and

(5) Flexible and inflexible.

---

[a] If the pores remain intact the body is softenable : if they yield the body melts. The latter alternative is expressed rather obscurely in the words τηκτὰ . . . δι' ὅλου (l. 21), with which we must presumably supply ἔχει πόρους from ll. 19-20.

---

2 διὰ τί l. 21 . . . τὸ πάθος secludendum censent O.T. Ideler.

εἰς τὸ κυρτὸν τὸ δ' εἰς τὸ κοῖλον μετάβασις, οὐκ
ἂν εἴη καὶ εἰς τὸ εὐθὺ κάμψις, ἀλλ' ἔστι κάμψις
καὶ εὔθυνσις ἄλλο καὶ ἄλλο. καὶ ταῦτά ἐστιν
καμπτὰ καὶ εὐθυντά, καὶ ἄκαμπτα καὶ ἀνεύθυντα.

Καὶ τὰ μὲν κατακτὰ καὶ θραυστὰ ἅμα ἢ χωρίς,
10 οἷον ξύλον μὲν κατακτόν, θραυστὸν δ' οὔ, κρύσταλλος δὲ καὶ λίθος θραυστόν, κατακτὸν δ' οὔ, κέραμος
δὲ καὶ θραυστὸν καὶ κατακτόν. διαφέρει δ', ὅτι
κάταξις μέν ἐστιν εἰς μεγάλα μέρη διαίρεσις καὶ
χώρισις, θραῦσις δὲ εἰς τὰ τυχόντα καὶ πλείω δυοῖν.
15 ὅσα μὲν οὖν οὕτω πέπηγεν ὥστε πολλοὺς ἔχειν
παραλλάττοντας πόρους, θραυστά (μέχρι γὰρ τούτου
διίσταται), ὅσα δ' εἰς πολύ, κατακτά, ὅσα δ' ἄμφω,
ἀμφότερα.

Καὶ τὰ μὲν θλαστά, οἷον χαλκὸς καὶ κηρός,
τὰ δ' ἄθλαστα, οἷον κέραμος καὶ ὕδωρ. ἔστιν δὲ
θλάσις ἐπιπέδου κατὰ μέρος εἰς βάθος μετάστασις
20 ὥσει ἢ πληγῇ, τὸ δ' ὅλον ἀφῇ. ἔστιν δὲ τὰ τοιαῦτα
καὶ μαλακά,[1] οἷον κηρὸς μένοντος τοῦ ἄλλου ἐπιπέδου κατὰ μέρος μεθίσταται, καὶ σκληρά, οἷον
χαλκός. καὶ τὰ[2] ἄθλαστα καὶ σκληρά, οἷον κέραμος
(οὐ γὰρ ὑπείκει εἰς βάθος τὸ ἐπίπεδον), καὶ ὑγρά,
25 οἷον ὕδωρ (τὸ γὰρ ὕδωρ ὑπείκει μέν, ἀλλ' οὐ κατὰ
μέρος, ἀλλ' ἀντιμεθίσταται). τῶν δὲ θλαστῶν ὅσα
μὲν μένει θλασθέντα καὶ εὔθλαστα χειρί, ταῦτα μὲν
πλαστά, τὰ δὲ ἢ μὴ εὔθλαστα, ὥσπερ λίθος ἢ ξύλον,
ἢ εὔθλαστα μέν, μὴ μένει δὲ ἡ θλάσις, ὥσπερ ἐρίου

---

[1] μαλακά E O.T. Thurot : μαλακτά Fobes cett.
[2] χαλκός. καὶ τὰ ἄθλαστα O.T. Thurot : χαλκός, καὶ ἄθλαστα
Fobes : θλαστὰ alii.

if this means an alteration of shape either to convex or to concave, there is no such process as bending straight, but two different processes, bending and straightening. These, then, are the things that can and cannot be bent and can and cannot be straightened.

Some things can be both broken and fragmented, others only one or the other. Thus wood can be broken but not fragmented, ice and stone can be fragmented but not broken, while earthenware can be both fragmented and broken. The difference is that breaking is division and separation into large parts, fragmentation into any number of parts greater than two. Things, therefore, that solidify in such a way as to have many alternating pores fragment (the pores allowing this degree of dispersion), and things that have long continuous pores break, while things that have pores of both kinds do both. (6, 7) Breaking and fragmentation.

Some things will take an impression, like bronze and wax, some things cannot, like earthenware and water. *An impression is an indentation of part of a thing's surface by pressure or impact*, or, generally speaking, by contact ; and such things are either soft,[a] like wax, part of whose surface only is indented, or hard, like bronze. Things that cannot take an impression are either hard, like earthenware (for its surface will not yield inwards), or moist, like water (for water yields not by any part of it being indented, but by displacement). Of things that take an impression, those that retain it and are easily moulded by hand are plastic ; while those not easily moulded, like stone or wood, or easily moulded but incapable (8) Capable of taking an impression. (9) Plasticity.

---

[a] μαλακά must be the right reading, for the contrast is with σκληρά : *cf.* 382 a 10.

386 a

ἢ σπόγγου, οὐ πλαστά, ἀλλὰ πιεστὰ ταῦτ᾽ ἐστίν.
30 ἔστι δὲ πιεστὰ ὅσα ὠθούμενα εἰς αὑτὰ συνιέναι
δύναται, εἰς βάθος τοῦ ἐπιπέδου παραλλάττοντος,
οὐ διαιρουμένου, καὶ ⟨μὴ⟩ μεθισταμένου ἄλλου
ἄλλῳ μορίου, οἷον τὸ ὕδωρ ποιεῖ· τοῦτο γὰρ ἀντιμεθίσταται. ἔστι δὲ ὦσις ἡ κίνησις ὑπὸ τοῦ κι-
386 b νοῦντος, ἢ γίγνεται ἀπὸ τῆς ἅψεως· πληγὴ δέ, ὅταν
ἀπὸ τῆς φορᾶς. πιέζεται δὲ ὅσα πόρους ἔχει κενοὺς
συγγενοῦς σώματος· καὶ πιεστὰ ταῦτα ὅσα δύναται
εἰς τὰ ἑαυτῶν κενὰ συνιέναι ἢ εἰς τοὺς ἑαυτῶν
πόρους· ἐνίοτε γὰρ οὐ κενοί εἰσιν εἰς οὓς συνέρχεται,[1]
5 οἷον ὁ βεβρεγμένος σπόγγος (πλήρεις γὰρ αὐτοῦ
οἱ πόροι), ἀλλ᾽ ὧν ἂν οἱ πόροι πλήρεις ὦσι μαλακω-
τέρων ἢ αὐτὸ τὸ πεφυκὸς συνιέναι εἰς αὑτό.[2]
πιεστὰ μὲν οὖν ἐστιν οἷον σπόγγος, κηρός, σάρξ.
ἀπίεστα δὲ τὰ μὴ πεφυκότα συνιέναι ὦσει εἰς
τοὺς ἑαυτῶν πόρους διὰ τὸ ἢ μὴ ἔχειν ἢ σκληρο-
10 τέρων ἔχειν πλήρεις· ὁ γὰρ σίδηρος ἀπίεστος καὶ
λίθος καὶ ὕδωρ καὶ πᾶν ὑγρόν.

Ἑλκτὰ δ᾽ ἐστὶν ὅσων δυνατὸν εἰς τὸ πλάγιον
μεθίστασθαι τὸ ἐπίπεδον· τὸ γὰρ ἕλκεσθαί ἐστι τὸ
ἐπὶ τὸ κινοῦν μεθίστασθαι τὸ ἐπίπεδον συνεχὲς ὄν.
ἔστιν δὲ τὰ μὲν ἑλκτά, οἷον θρίξ, ἱμάς, νεῦρον,
15 σταίς, ἰξός, τὰ δ᾽ ἄνελκτα, οἷον ὕδωρ καὶ λίθος. τὰ
μὲν οὖν ταῦτά ἐστιν ἑλκτὰ καὶ πιεστά, οἷον ἔριον,
τὰ δ᾽ οὐ ταῦτά, οἷον φλέγμα πιεστὸν μὲν οὐκ
ἔστιν, ἑλκτὸν δέ, καὶ ὁ σπόγγος πιεστὸν μέν, οὐχ
ἑλκτὸν δέ.

348

of retaining an impression, like wool or sponge, are non-plastic but can be squeezed. Now things that (10) Squeez-can be squeezed are those that can contract into ability. themselves on pressure, their surface sinking in without being broken and without displacement of one part by another such as occurs in water. Pressure is action by a moving force which remains in contact with its object : impact is action by impulse. And things can be squeezed which have pores empty of their own material and which can therefore contract under pressure into the empty space within them, that is, into their own pores ; for sometimes the pores into which they contract are not empty, as, for instance, in a wet sponge, whose pores are full, but in that case the material filling the pores must be softer than the body which is to contract on itself. Sponges, wax and flesh can therefore all be squeezed : things that cannot be squeezed are those which are not constituted to contract on pressure into their own pores either because they have none or because they are full of a material harder than themselves. So iron cannot be squeezed, or stone, or water, or any liquid.

Ductile are things whose surface will extend in the (11) Duc-same plane, for to be drawn out is to have the surface tility. extended in the direction of the motive force without breaking. And some things are ductile, like hair, leather, sinew, dough and birdlime, some are not, like water and stone. And some things are both ductile and squeezable, like wool, some are not, like phlegm, which is not squeezable but is ductile, or sponge, which is squeezable but is not ductile.

---

[1] ἐνίοτε . . . συνέρχεται secl. Fobes : om. J 𝔐 𝔅₁ H.
[2] αὐτό O.T. : αὐτό E_corr. 𝔚 N : αὐτό 𝔅_rec. : ἑαυτά J₁ 𝔅₁ H : ἑαυτό J_rec. : αὐτά Fobes.

386 b

Ἔστιν δὲ καὶ τὰ μὲν ἐλατά, οἷον χαλκός, τὰ δ'
ἀνήλατα, οἷον λίθος καὶ ξύλον. ἔστιν δ' ἐλατὰ μὲν
20 ὅσα τῇ αὐτῇ πληγῇ δύναται ἅμα καὶ εἰς πλάτος
καὶ εἰς βάθος τὸ ἐπίπεδον μεθίστασθαι κατὰ μέρος,
ἀνήλατα δὲ ὅσα ἀδύνατα. ἔστιν δὲ τὰ μὲν ἐλατὰ
ἅπαντα καὶ θλαστά, τὰ δὲ θλαστὰ οὐ πάντα ἐλατά,
οἷον ξύλον· ὡς μέντοι ἐπίπαν εἰπεῖν, ἀντιστρέφει.
25 τῶν δὲ πιεστῶν τὰ μὲν ἐλατὰ τὰ δ' οὔ, κηρὸς μὲν
καὶ πηλὸς ἐλατά, ἔριον δ' οὔ [οὐδ' ὕδωρ].[1]

Ἔστιν δὲ καὶ τὰ μὲν σχιστά, οἷον ξύλον, τὰ δὲ
ἄσχιστα, οἷον κέραμος. ἔστιν δὲ σχιστὸν τὸ δυνάμενον διαιρεῖσθαι ἐπὶ πλέον ἢ τὸ διαιροῦν διαιρεῖ·
σχίζεται γάρ, ὅταν ἐπὶ πλέον διαιρῆται ἢ τὸ δι-
30 αιροῦν διαιρεῖ, καὶ προηγεῖται ἡ διαίρεσις· ἐν δὲ
τῇ τμήσει οὐκ ἔστιν τοῦτο. ἄσχιστα δὲ ὅσα μὴ
δύνανται τοῦτο πάσχειν. ἔστιν δὲ οὔτε μαλακὸν
οὐδὲν σχιστόν (λέγω δὲ τῶν ἁπλῶς μαλακῶν καὶ
μὴ πρὸς ἄλληλα· οὕτω μὲν γὰρ καὶ σίδηρος ἔσται
387 a μαλακός) οὔτε τὰ σκληρὰ πάντα, ἀλλ' ὅσα μήτε
ὑγρά ἐστιν μήτε θλαστὰ μήτε θραυστά· τοιαῦτα δ'
ἐστὶν ὅσα κατὰ μῆκος ἔχει τοὺς πόρους, καθ' οὓς
προσφύεται ἀλλήλοις, ἀλλὰ μὴ κατὰ πλάτος.

Τμητὰ δ' ἐστὶν τῶν συνεστώτων σκληρῶν ἢ
5 μαλακῶν ὅσα δύναται μήτ' ἐξ ἀνάγκης προηγεῖσθαι
τῆς διαιρέσεως μήτε θραύεσθαι διαιρούμενα· ὅσα
δὲ μὴ ὑγρὰ ᾖ,[2] τὰ τοιαῦτα ἄτμητα. ἔνια δ' ἐστὶν
ταὐτὰ καὶ τμητὰ καὶ σχιστά, οἷον ξύλον· ἀλλ' ὡς
ἐπὶ τὸ πολὺ σχιστὸν μὲν κατὰ τὸ μῆκος, τμητὸν δὲ
κατὰ τὸ πλάτος· ἐπεὶ γὰρ διαιρεῖται ἕκαστον εἰς
10 πολλά, ᾗ μὲν μήκη πολλὰ τὸ ἕν, σχιστὸν ταύτῃ, ᾗ
δὲ πλάτη πολλὰ τὸ ἕν, τμητὸν ταύτῃ.

[1] del. Thurot Fobes.

Similarly some things are malleable, like bronze, some are not, like stone and wood. And things are malleable part of whose surface will yield and extend simultaneously under the same blow, while things with which this is impossible are non-malleable. All malleable things will take an impression, but not all things that will take an impression are malleable, wood for example : but, generally speaking, the two terms are convertible. Of things that can be squeezed some are malleable, some are not, wax and mud being malleable, wool not. (12) Malleability.

Some things are fissile, like wood, some non-fissile, like earthenware. Fissile are things in which division can continue beyond the dividing agent : for a thing is split when it is divided to a point beyond that reached by the dividing agent and the division runs in advance of it, whereas in cutting this is not so. Non-fissile are things which have not this property. Nothing soft is fissile (I mean absolutely and not relatively soft, for iron can be relatively soft), nor are all hard things, but only things which are not liquid or impressible or fragmentable, that is to say, in which the pores along which they cohere run lengthwise and not crosswise. (13) Fissility.

Cuttable are hard or soft solid bodies which when divided do not necessarily split in advance of the tool or break into fragments ; and everything that is not moist is uncuttable. Some things, like wood, can both be cut and split, but, generally speaking, things split lengthwise and cut crosswise ; for things are divisible into many parts, and if the parts making up the unit run lengthwise it is fissile, if they run crosswise it is cuttable. (14) Cuttable and uncuttable.

---

[2] ἢ ὑγρὰ ἢ Bekker O.T.

Γλίσχρον δ' ἐστὶν ὅταν ἑλκτὸν ᾖ ὑγρὸν ὂν ἢ μαλακόν. τοιοῦτον δὲ γίγνεται τῇ ἐπαλλάξει ὅσα
ὥσπερ αἱ ἁλύσεις σύγκεινται τῶν σωμάτων· ταῦτα
γὰρ ἐπὶ πολὺ δύναται ἐκτείνεσθαι καὶ συνιέναι.
15 ὅσα δὲ μὴ τοιαῦτα, ψαθυρά.

Πιλητὰ δ' ὅσα τῶν πιεστῶν μόνιμον ἔχει τὴν
πίεσιν, ἀπίλητα δὲ ὅσα ἢ ὅλως ἀπίεστα ἢ μὴ μόνιμον ἔχει τὴν πίεσιν.

Καὶ τὰ μὲν καυστά ἐστιν τὰ δὲ ἄκαυστα, οἷον
ξύλον μὲν καυστὸν καὶ ἔριον καὶ ὀστοῦν, λίθος δὲ
καὶ κρύσταλλος ἄκαυστον. ἔστιν δὲ καυστὰ ὅσα
20 ἔχει πόρους δεκτικοὺς πυρὸς καὶ ὑγρότητα ἐν τοῖς
κατ' εὐθυωρίαν πόροις ἀσθενεστέραν πυρός. ὅσα
δὲ μὴ ἔχει ἢ ἰσχυροτέραν, οἷον κρύσταλλος καὶ τὰ
σφόδρα χλωρά, ἄκαυστα.

Θυμιατὰ δ' ἐστὶ τῶν σωμάτων ὅσα ὑγρότητα ἔχει
μέν, οὕτω δ' ἔχει ὥστε μὴ ἐξατμίζειν πυρουμένων
25 χωρίς· ἔστιν γὰρ ἀτμὶς ἡ ὑπὸ θερμοῦ καυστικοῦ
εἰς ἀέρα καὶ πνεῦμα ἔκκρισις ἐξ ὑγροῦ διαντική.
τὰ δὲ θυμιάματα[1] χρόνῳ εἰς ἀέρα ἐκκρίνεται, καὶ
τὰ μὲν ἀφανιζόμενα ξηρά, τὰ δὲ γῇ γίγνεται.
διαφέρει δ' αὕτη ἡ ἔκκρισις, ὅτι οὔτε διαίνει οὔτε
πνεῦμα γίγνεται. ἔστιν δὲ πνεῦμα ῥύσις συνεχὴς
30 ἀέρος ἐπὶ μῆκος· θυμίασις δ' ἐστὶν ἡ ὑπὸ θερμοῦ
καυστικοῦ κοινὴ ἔκκρισις ξηροῦ καὶ ὑγροῦ ἀθρόως·

A thing is viscous when it is ductile as well as being (15) Vis-liquid or soft. And this characteristic belongs to all cous or friable. bodies with interlocking parts, whose composition is like that of chains ; for they admit of considerable extension and contraction. Bodies which have not this characteristic are friable.

Compressible bodies are those which can be (16) Com-squeezed and retain the shape into which they have pressibility. been squeezed : incompressible are either those which cannot be squeezed at all or those which when squeezed do not retain the shape into which they have been squeezed.

Some things are combustible, some incombustible ; (17) Com-for example, wood is combustible and wool and bone, bustibility. while stone and ice are incombustible. All things are combustible which have pores which fire can penetrate and which contain in their longitudinal pores too little moisture to overcome the fire. But things which have no pores or contain enough moisture to master the fire are incombustible, as, for example, ice and very green matter.

Fumes are given off by bodies which contain (18) Giving moisture, but in such a way that it does not evaporate off fumes. separately when they are exposed to fire. For vapour is a moist exhalation into air and wind, given off by moisture in a body when exposed to burning heat ; but fumes can be exhaled into the air in course of time, and either dry up and vanish or turn into earth, being a different form of exhalation which is not moist and does not become wind. (Wind is a continuous current of air in a given direction.) But fuming is the exhalation of dry and moist together due to burning heat : hence it does not wet, but

---

[1] θυμιάματα E$_1$: θυμιατὰ Fobes.

387 a

διόπερ οὐ διαίνει, ἀλλὰ χρωματίζει μᾶλλον. ἔστι

387 b δ' ἡ μὲν ξυλώδους σώματος θυμίασις καπνός. λέγω
γὰρ καὶ ὀστᾶ καὶ τρίχας καὶ πᾶν τὸ τοιοῦτον ἐν
ταὐτῷ· οὐ γὰρ κεῖται ὄνομα κοινόν, ἀλλὰ κατ'
ἀναλογίαν ὅμως ἐν ταὐτῷ πάντ' ἐστίν, ὥσπερ καὶ
Ἐμπεδοκλῆς φησιν

5 ταὐτὰ τρίχες καὶ φύλλα καὶ οἰωνῶν πτερὰ πυκνὰ
καὶ λοπίδες γίγνονται ἐπὶ στιβαροῖσι μέλεσσιν.

ἡ δὲ πίονος θυμίασις λιγνύς, ἡ δὲ λιπαροῦ κνῖσα.
διὰ τοῦτο τὸ ἔλαιον οὐχ ἕψεται οὐδὲ παχύνεται, ὅτι
θυμιατόν ἐστιν ἀλλ' οὐκ ἀτμιστόν· ὕδωρ δ' οὐ θυμιατὸν ἀλλ' ἀτμιστόν. οἶνος δ' ὁ μὲν γλυκὺς θυμιᾶ-
10 ται. πίων γάρ, καὶ ταὐτὰ ποιεῖ τῷ ἐλαίῳ· οὔτε
γὰρ ὑπὸ ψύχους πήγνυται, καίεταί τε. ἔστιν δὲ
ὀνόματι οἶνος, ἔργῳ δ' οὐκ ἔστιν· οὐ γὰρ οἰνώδης ὁ
χυμός· διὸ οὐ μεθύσκει, ὁ τυχὼν δ' οἶνος (μικρὰν
δ' ἔχει θυμίασιν· διὸ ἀνίησιν φλόγα).

Καυστὰ δὲ δοκεῖ εἶναι ὅσα εἰς τέφραν διαλύεται
15 τῶν σωμάτων. πάσχει δὲ τοῦτο πάντα ὅσα πέπηγεν ἢ ὑπὸ θερμοῦ ἢ ὑπ' ἀμφοῖν, ψυχροῦ καὶ
θερμοῦ· ταῦτα γὰρ φαίνεται κρατούμενα ὑπὸ τοῦ
πυρός· ἥκιστα δὲ τῶν λίθων ἡ σφραγίς, ὁ καλούμενος ἄνθραξ. τῶν δὲ καυστῶν τὰ μὲν φλογιστά
ἐστιν τὰ δ' ἀφλόγιστα· τούτων δ' ἔνια ἀνθρακευτά.
20 φλογιστὰ μὲν οὖν ὅσα φλόγα δύναται παρέχεσθαι·
ὅσα δὲ ἀδύνατα, ἀφλόγιστα. ἔστι δὲ φλογιστὰ ὅσα

---

[a] The text and meaning of 387 a 24 ἔστιν γάρ . . . 31-32
χρωματίζει μᾶλλον is uncertain. I follow Fobes's text, with
the substitution of θυμιάματα for θυμιατά in l. 26, and take
the argument to be as follows : Fumes are given off by bodies
containing moisture when the moisture does not evaporate
separately (θυμιατά, θυμιάματα, θυμίασις contrasted with

rather discolours things.[a] The fumes of woody material are smoke. And I include in this designation bones and hair and all such things : for there is no common term for them but they are analogous and so classified together. So Empedocles says : " The same are hair and leaves and birds' thick feathers and scales upon strong limbs." [b] The fumes of fat are sooty, of oily substances steamy. The reason why oil does not boil or thicken is that it gives off fumes but does not evaporate : water, on the other hand, evaporates but does not fume. Sweet wine fumes, being fat and behaving in the same way as oil, for cold does not solidify it and it will burn. And though called wine, it has not the effect of wine, for it does not taste like wine and does not intoxicate like ordinary wine. It gives off few fumes and so is inflammable.

Combustible bodies are those which dissolve into ash. And all bodies do this which have been solidified by heat or by both heat and cold, for we find them mastered by fire. Least affected by fire is the gem commonly called carbuncle. Of combustible [c] bodies some are inflammable, some are not, and some of the former can be carbonized. Inflammable bodies are those which can produce flame ; those which cannot are uninflammable. Bodies which are not moist but

Combustibility, inflammability and fumes.

ἀτμίς, ἀτμίζειν : cf. the contrast between θυμιατόν and ἀτμιστόν in b 7-8). Evaporation (ἀτμίς) is also a moist exhalation, but fuming differs from it in that evaporation takes moisture off and is moist, fuming takes moist and dry off together and does not moisten but discolours. Cf. also the moist and dry exhalations of Book II. ch. 4.   [b] Diels 31 B 82.

[c] Aristotle returns to combustibility ((17) above) and considers certain forms it takes (e.g. inflammability) and its relation to fuming.

387 b

μὴ ὑγρὰ ὄντα θυμιατά ἐστιν· πίττα δὲ ἢ ἔλαιον ἢ
κηρὸς μᾶλλον μετ' ἄλλων ἢ καθ' αὑτὰ φλογιστά·
μάλιστα δ' ὅσα καπνὸν ἀνίησιν. ἀνθρακευτὰ δ'
ὅσα τῶν τοιούτων γῆς πλέον ἔχει ἢ καπνοῦ. ἔτι

25 δ' ἔνια τηκτὰ ὄντα οὐ φλογιστά ἐστιν, οἷον χαλκός,
καὶ φλογιστὰ οὐ τηκτά, οἷον ξύλον, τὰ δ' ἄμφω,
οἷον λιβανωτός. αἴτιον δ' ὅτι τὰ μὲν ξύλα ἀθρόον
ἔχει τὸ ὑγρόν, καὶ δι' ὅλου συνεχές ἐστιν, ὥστε
διακάεσθαι, ὁ δὲ χαλκὸς παρ' ἕκαστον μὲν μέρος,

30 οὐ συνεχὲς δέ, καὶ ἔλαττον ἢ ὥστε φλόγα ποιῆσαι·
ὁ δὲ λιβανωτὸς τῇ μὲν οὕτως τῇ δ' ἐκείνως ἔχει.
φλογιστὰ δ' ἐστὶν τῶν θυμιατῶν ὅσα μὴ τηκτά
ἐστιν διὰ τὸ μᾶλλον εἶναι γῆς. τὸ ξηρὸν γὰρ ἔχει

388 a κοινὸν τῷ πυρί· τοῦτ' οὖν θερμὸν ἂν γένηται τὸ
ξηρόν, πῦρ γίγνεται. διὰ τοῦτο ἡ φλὸξ πνεῦμα
ἢ καπνὸς καόμενός ἐστιν.[1] ξύλων μὲν οὖν ἡ θυ-
μίασίς καπνός, κηροῦ δὲ καὶ λιβανωτοῦ καὶ τῶν
τοιούτων καὶ πίττης, καὶ ὅσα ἔχει πίτταν ἢ τοιαῦτα,

5 λιγνύς, ἐλαίου δὲ καὶ ὅσα ἐλαιώδη, κνῖσα, καὶ ὅσα
ἥκιστα καίεται μόνα, ὅτι ὀλίγον ξηροῦ ἔχει, ἡ δὲ
μετάβασις διὰ τούτου, μετὰ δ' ἑτέρου τάχιστα·
τοῦτο γάρ ἐστιν τὸ πῖον, ξηρὸν λιπαρόν. τὰ μὲν
οὖν ἐκθυμιώμενα [τῶν ὑγρῶν][2] ὑγροῦ μᾶλλον, ὡς
ἔλαιον καὶ πίττα, τὰ δὲ καόμενα ξηροῦ.

---

[1] τὸ ξηρὸν l. 32 . . . ἐστιν interclusionem distinxit Thurot,
habet Fobes.
[2] seclusi : del. O.T.

---

[a] Cf. 387 b 22.

356

contain fumes are inflammable. Pitch, oil and wax are more inflammable when mixed with other things than by themselves. Most inflammable of all are things which produce smoke. All materials of this sort which contain more earth than smoke can be carbonized. Some bodies that can be melted are not inflammable, like bronze, and some inflammable bodies will not melt, like wood, while some bodies melt and burn like frankincense. The reason is that the moisture in wood is concentrated and distributed evenly so that it can be burnt out, while in bronze it is dispersed into each part and not continuous and is not sufficient in quantity to give rise to flame, whereas in frankincense both conditions obtain. Bodies which fume and do not melt because earth preponderates in them are inflammable. For in their dryness they have a factor in common with fire, and when this dryness becomes hot, fire is produced : flame, therefore, is burning wind or smoke. The fumes, then, of wood are smoke, the fumes of wax and frankincense and the like, of pitch and materials containing pitch or similar constituents, are sooty, and the fumes of oil and oily substances are steamy, as are also those of substances which do not burn readily by themselves, having little dryness (by which the transition to fire is effected) but do burn readily with other things [a] ; for fat is a combination of dry and oily. And bodies which give off fumes are predominantly moist (*e.g.* oil and pitch), bodies which burn are predominantly dry.

CHAPTER X

ARGUMENT

Dry and moist in homoeomerous bodies. Having thus described the properties which distinguish homoeomerous bodies, we must determine in what proportion dry and moist, i.e. earth and water, their material cause, are present in them (388 a 10-25). All bodies are either liquid or solid, and there

388 a 10 Τούτοις δὲ τοῖς παθήμασιν καὶ ταύταις ταῖς διαφοραῖς τὰ ὁμοιομερῆ τῶν σωμάτων, ὥσπερ εἴρηται,
διαφέρει ἀλλήλων κατὰ τὴν ἀφήν, καὶ ἔτι χυμοῖς
καὶ ὀσμαῖς καὶ χρώμασιν· λέγω δ᾽ ὁμοιομερῆ οἷον
τά τε μεταλλευόμενα—χαλκόν, χρυσόν, ἄργυρον,
15 καττίτερον, σίδηρον, λίθον, καὶ τἆλλα τὰ τοιαῦτα,
καὶ ὅσα ἐκ τούτων γίγνεται ἐκκρινόμενα—καὶ τὰ
ἐν τοῖς ζῴοις καὶ φυτοῖς, οἷον σάρκες, ὀστᾶ, νεῦρον,
δέρμα, σπλάγχνον, τρίχες, ἶνες, φλέβες, ἐξ ὧν ἤδη
συνέστηκε τὰ ἀνομοιομερῆ, οἷον πρόσωπον, χείρ,
πούς, καὶ τἆλλα τὰ τοιαῦτα, καὶ ἐν φυτοῖς ξύλον,
20 φλοιός, φύλλον, ῥίζα, καὶ ὅσα τοιαῦτα. ἐπεὶ δὲ
ταῦτα μὲν ὑπ᾽ ἄλλης αἰτίας συνέστηκεν, ἐξ ὧν δὲ
ταῦτα ὕλη μὲν τὸ ξηρὸν καὶ ὑγρόν, ὥστε ὕδωρ καὶ
γῆ (ταῦτα γὰρ προφανεστάτην ἔχει τὴν δύναμιν
ἑκάτερον ἑκατέρου), τὰ δὲ ποιοῦντα τὸ θερμὸν καὶ
25 ψυχρόν (ταῦτα γὰρ συνίστησιν καὶ πήγνυσιν ἐξ

---

[a] 385 a 8.

[b] If we take ἐν φυτοῖς . . . τοιαῦτα (ll. 19-20) as parallel
to the whole clause καὶ τὰ ἐν τοῖς ζῴοις καὶ φυτοῖς . . . τἆλλα τὰ
τοιαῦτα (ll. 16-19) with the O.T., wood, bark, etc., are given
as examples of homoeomerous bodies : if we take them as
part of the clause beginning ἐξ ὧν (l. 18) they are examples
of anhomoeomerous bodies. In fact, wood and bark are

CHAPTER X

ARGUMENT (*continued*)

are various principles by which the proportion can be deter-
mined for liquids and solids (388 a 25—389 a 7). *The*
proportions for homoeomerous bodies are determined and these
bodies classified accordingly (389 a 7-23).

THESE are the different characteristics which, as we
have said,[a] distinguish homoeomerous bodies from
each other to touch ; and they are further distinguished by taste, smell and colour. By homoeomerous
bodies I mean, for example, metallic substances (*e.g.*
bronze, gold, silver, tin, iron, stone and similar materials and their by-products) and animal and vegetable tissues (*e.g.* flesh, bone, sinew, skin, intestine,
hair, fibre, veins) from which in turn the anhomoeomerous bodies, face, hand, foot and the like, are composed ;
in plants, examples are wood, bark, leaf, root and the
like.[b] The non-homoeomerous [c] bodies owe their
constitution to another cause ; the *material* cause of
the homoeomerous bodies which make them up is
dry and moist, that is, water and earth, which display
most clearly these two characteristics ; their *efficient*
cause is heat and cold, which produce concrete

The homoe-
omerous
bodies :
what pro-
portions of
earth and
water do
they con-
tain ?

clearly homoeomerous, leaf and root pretty clearly not
homoeomerous (*De An.* 412 b 2-3 : though at 389 a 13 below
φύλλα are listed among homoeomerous substances). I suggest
that Aristotle is writing loosely and that the phrase is added
on to the end of the sentence to give examples from plants
parallel to those given for animals, and that examples of both
kinds of substance are therefore included.

[c] ταῦτα (l. 20) must refer to the *last-named*, *i.e.* anhomoeomerous bodies (Alex. 219. 20), and not to the homoeomerous
(O.T., Ideler) ; ἐξ ὧν . . . ὕλη (l. 21), if expanded, would be
ἐκείνων δέ, ἐξ ὧν ταῦτα συνέστηκεν, ὕλη (Alex. 219. 21-22).

388 a

ἐκείνων), λάβωμεν τῶν ὁμοιομερῶν ποῖα γῆς εἴδη
καὶ ποῖα ὕδατος καὶ ποῖα κοινά.

Ἔστι δὴ τῶν σωμάτων τῶν δεδημιουργημένων
τὰ μὲν ὑγρά, τὰ δὲ μαλακά, τὰ δὲ σκληρά· τούτων
δὲ ὁπόσα σκληρὰ ἢ μαλακὰ ⟨ὅτι⟩[1] πήξει ἐστίν,
εἴρηται πρότερον.

30 Τῶν μὲν οὖν ὑγρῶν ὅσα μὲν ἐξατμίζεται, ὕδατος,
ὅσα δὲ μή, ἢ γῆς ἢ κοινὰ γῆς καὶ ὕδατος, οἷον γάλα,
ἢ γῆς καὶ ἀέρος, οἷον ξύλον,[2] ἢ ὕδατος καὶ ἀέρος,
οἷον ἔλαιον. καὶ ὅσα μὲν ὑπὸ θερμοῦ παχύνεται,
κοινά (ἀπορήσειε δ᾽ ἄν τις περὶ οἴνου τῶν ὑγρῶν·

388 b τοῦτο γὰρ καὶ ἐξατμισθείη ἄν, καὶ παχύνεται ὥσπερ
ὁ νέος· αἴτιον δ᾽ ὅτι οὔτε ἐν ἑνὶ εἴδει λέγεται ὁ οἶνος,
καὶ ὅτι ἄλλος ἄλλως· ὁ γὰρ νέος μᾶλλον γῆς ἢ ὁ
παλαιός· διὸ καὶ παχύνεται τῷ θερμῷ μάλιστα καὶ
5 πήγνυται ἧττον ὑπὸ τοῦ ψυχροῦ· ἔχει γὰρ καὶ
θερμὸν πολὺ καὶ γῆς, ὥσπερ ὁ ἐν Ἀρκαδίᾳ οὕτως
ἀποξηραίνεται ὑπὲρ τοῦ καπνοῦ ἐν τοῖς ἀσκοῖς ὥστε
ξυόμενος πίνεσθαι· εἰ δὴ ἅπας ἰλὺν ἔχει, οὕτως
ἑκατέρου ἐστίν, ἢ γῆς ἢ ὕδατος, ὡς ταύτης ἔχει
πλῆθος)· ὅσα δὲ ὑπὸ ψυχροῦ παχύνεται, γῆς· ὅσα
10 δ᾽ ὑπ᾽ ἀμφοῖν, κοινὰ πλειόνων, οἷον ἔλαιον καὶ μέλι
καὶ ὁ γλυκὺς οἶνος.

Τῶν δὲ συνεστώτων ὅσα μὲν πέπηγεν ὑπὸ ψυχροῦ,
ὕδατος, οἷον κρύσταλλος, χιών, χάλαζα, πάχνη·
ὅσα δ᾽ ὑπὸ θερμοῦ, γῆς, οἷον κέραμος, τυρός,

---

[1] ὅτι ci. O.T.   [2] μέλι ci. Vicomercatus.

[a] 382 a 25.
[b] Ideler accepts Vicomercato's conjecture " honey."
[c] Cf. 380 b 32, 384 a 5, 387 b 9.

homoeomerous bodies out of water and earth. Let us therefore consider which of the homoeomerous bodies are composed of earth, which of water, and which of both.

Bodies which are finished products are either liquid or soft or hard: and those which are soft or hard are, as has been explained, the result of solidification.[a] Bodies classified as

Liquids which evaporate are made of water; those which do not are made of earth or are a mixture of earth and water, like milk, or of earth and air, like wood,[b] or of water and air, like oil. Liquids whose density heat increases are a mixture. (Among the liquids, wine[c] presents a difficulty, for it evaporates and also thickens, as new wine does. The reason is that there is more than one kind of liquid called wine and that different kinds behave differently. For new wine contains more earth than old, and so thickens most under the influence of heat, but solidifies less under the influence of cold; for it contains considerable quantities of heat and earth, as in Arcadia where the smoke dries it up in the skins to such an extent that it must be scraped off before it is drunk. If, then, all wine has some sediment, whether earth or water predominates in it will depend on the amount of sediment present.) Liquids whose density cold increases are earthy: bodies whose density is increased both by heat and cold are compounded of more than one element, like oil and honey and sweet wine. (1) Liquid.

(a) Solids which solidify as a result of cold are composed of water, for example, ice, snow, hail and frost; (b) those which solidify as a result of heat are composed of earth, for example, earthenware, cheese, (2) Solid.

νίτρον, ἅλες· ὅσα δ᾽ ὑπ᾽ ἀμφοῖν (τοιαῦτα δ᾽ ἐστὶν
ὅσα ψύξει· ταῦτα δ᾽ ἐστὶν ὅσα ἀμφοῖν στερήσει,
15 καὶ θερμοῦ καὶ ὑγροῦ συνεξιόντος τῷ θερμῷ· οἱ
μὲν γὰρ ἅλες ὑγροῦ μόνου στερήσει πήγνυνται, καὶ
ὅσα εἰλικρινῆ γῆς, ὁ δὲ κρύσταλλος θερμοῦ μόνου),
ταῦτα δ᾽ ἀμφοῖν. διὸ καὶ ὑπ᾽ ἀμφοῖν καὶ εἶχεν
ἄμφω. ὅσων μὲν οὖν ἅπαν ἐξικμάσθη, οἷον κέ-
20 ραμος ἢ ἤλεκτρον (καὶ γὰρ τὸ ἤλεκτρον, καὶ ὅσα
λέγεται ὡς δάκρυα, ψύξει ἐστίν, οἷον σμύρνα,
λιβανωτός, κόμμι· καὶ τὸ ἤλεκτρον δὲ τούτου τοῦ
γένους ἔοικεν, καὶ πήγνυται· ἐμπεριειλημμένα γοῦν
ζῷα ἐν αὐτῷ φαίνεται· ὑπὸ δὲ τοῦ ποταμοῦ τὸ
θερμὸν ἐξιὸν ὥσπερ τοῦ ἑψομένου μέλιτος, ὅταν
εἰς ὕδωρ ἀφεθῇ, ἐξατμίζει τὸ ὑγρόν), ταῦτα πάντα
25 γῆς. καὶ τὰ μὲν ἄτηκτα καὶ ἀμάλακτα, οἷον τὸ
ἤλεκτρον καὶ λίθοι ἔνιοι, ὥσπερ οἱ πῶροι οἱ ἐν τοῖς
σπηλαίοις· καὶ γὰρ οὗτοι ὁμοίως γίγνονται τούτοις,
καὶ οὐχ ὡς ὑπὸ πυρὸς ἀλλ᾽ ὡς ὑπὸ τοῦ ψυχροῦ
διεξιόντος τοῦ θερμοῦ συνεξέρχεται τὸ ὑγρὸν ὑπὸ
τοῦ ἐξ αὐτοῦ ἐξιόντος θερμοῦ· ἐν δὲ τοῖς ἑτέροις
30 ὑπὸ τοῦ ἔξωθεν πυρός. ὅσα δὲ μὴ ὅλα, γῆς μέν
ἐστι μᾶλλον, μαλακτὰ δέ, οἷον σίδηρος καὶ κέρας.
(λιβανωτοὶ δὲ καὶ τὰ τοιαῦτα παραπλησίως τοῖς
ξύλοις ἀτμίζει.)[1] ἐπεὶ οὖν τηκτά γε θετέον καὶ ὅσα
τήκεται ὑπὸ πυρός, ταῦτ᾽ ἐστὶν ὑδατωδέστερα, ἔνια
389 a δὲ καὶ κοινά, οἷον κηρός· ὅσα δὲ ὑπὸ ὕδατος, ταῦτα

---

[1] λιβανωτοὶ . . . ἀτμίζει fortasse post κόμμι l. 20 supra
traiciendum.

soda, salt ; (c) those which solidify as a result of both [a] are composed of both and so are solidified by both causes and contain both constituents. (Into this last category fall things solidified by cooling, that is by deprivation both of heat and moisture, the moisture escaping with the heat : for salt and things composed purely of earth solidify when deprived of moisture only, while ice, on the other hand, does so when deprived of heat only.) (d) Solids from which all moisture has been evaporated, as e.g. earthenware or amber, are composed of earth. (For both amber and substances called tears are formed by cooling, for example myrrh, frankincense and gum : and amber appears to belong to this class, as the insects trapped in it show that it has formed by solidification. The heat expelled by the cold of the river evaporates the moisture in it, as it does in boiled honey when it is dropped into water.) And some of these solids cannot be melted or softened, like amber and some kinds of stone, for example stalactites in caves ; for these too are formed in the same way, being solidified not by fire but because their heat is driven out by cold and their moisture accompanies the heat when it retires. In the others [b] the cause is external fire. (e) Solids from which the moisture has not wholly evaporated contain a preponderance of earth but can be softened by heat like iron and horn. (Frankincense and similar bodies give off vapour rather as wood does.) (f) Finally, since things that are melted by fire must be included in the class of things that melt, they will in general be composed largely of water, though some, like wax, will be composed of both water and earth : on the other hand, things that

---

[a] Cf. 383 a 13.   [b] i.e. that can be melted, e.g. salt.

δὲ γῆς· ὅσα δὲ μηδ᾽ ὑφ᾽ ἑτέρου, ταῦτα ἢ γῆς ἢ
ἀμφοῖν.

Εἰ οὖν ἅπαντα μὲν ἢ ὑγρὰ ἢ πεπηγότα, τούτων
δὲ τὰ ἐν τοῖς εἰρημένοις πάθεσιν, καὶ οὐκ ἔστιν
5 μεταξύ, ἅπαντ᾽ ἂν εἴη εἰρημένα οἷς διαγνωσόμεθα
πότερον γῆς ἢ ὕδατος ἢ πλειόνων κοινόν, καὶ
πότερον ὑπὸ πυρὸς συνέστηκεν ἢ ψυχροῦ ἢ ἀμφοῖν.

Χρυσὸς μὲν δὴ καὶ ἄργυρος καὶ χαλκὸς καὶ
καττίτερος καὶ μόλυβδος καὶ ὕαλος καὶ λίθοι πολλοὶ
ἀνώνυμοι ὕδατος· πάντα γὰρ τήκεται ταῦτα θερμῷ.
10 ἔτι οἶνοι ἔνιοι καὶ οὖρον καὶ ὄξος καὶ κονία καὶ ὀρὸς
καὶ ἰχὼρ ὕδατος· πάντα γὰρ πήγνυται ψυχρῷ.
σίδηρος δὲ καὶ κέρας καὶ ὄνυξ καὶ ὀστοῦν καὶ
νεῦρον καὶ ξύλον καὶ τρίχες καὶ φύλλα καὶ φλοιὸς
γῆς μᾶλλον· ἔτι ἤλεκτρον, σμύρνα, λίβανος, καὶ
15 πάντα τὰ δάκρυα λεγόμενα, καὶ πῶρος, καὶ οἱ
καρποί, οἷον τὰ χεδροπά, καὶ σῖτος (τὰ τοιαῦτα γὰρ
τὰ μὲν σφόδρα, τὰ δὲ ἧττον μὲν τούτων, ὅμως δὲ
γῆς· τὰ μὲν γὰρ μαλακτά, τὰ δὲ θυμιατὰ καὶ ψύξει
γεγενημένα)· ἔτι νίτρον, ἅλες, λίθων γένη, ὅσα μήτε
ψύξει μήτε τηκτά. αἷμα δὲ καὶ γονὴ κοινὰ γῆς καὶ
20 ὕδατος καὶ ἀέρος, τὸ μὲν ἔχον αἷμα ἶνας μᾶλλον
γῆς (διὸ ψύχει πήγνυται καὶ ὑγρῷ τήκεται), τὰ δὲ
μὴ ἔχοντα ἶνας ὕδατος (διὸ καὶ οὐ πήγνυται). γονὴ
δὲ πήγνυται ψύξει ἐξιόντος τοῦ ὑγροῦ μετὰ τοῦ
θερμοῦ.

are melted by water will be composed of earth, and things melted by neither of earth or both.

If, then, all things are either liquid or solid, and if the things qualified by the characteristics we have described are covered by this alternative, and there is no intermediate possibility, it follows that we have enumerated all the criteria whereby we can distinguish whether a thing is composed of earth or of water or of more than one element, and whether it is formed by fire, by cold or by both.

The following are therefore composed of water : gold, silver, bronze, tin, lead, glass and many kinds of stone which have no name, for all of these are melted by heat ; in addition, some wines, urine, vinegar, lye, whey and serum, for all of these are solidified by cold. Earth preponderates in the following : iron, horn, nail, bone, sinew, wood, hair, leaves and bark, besides amber, myrrh, frankincense, the drop-like substances, stalactites, and produce such as vegetables and corn (in these the proportion of earth varies but all are earthy, for some can be softened by fire, others give off fumes and are produced by cooling) ; in addition there are soda, salt, and those kinds of stone that are neither formed by cooling nor able to be melted. Blood and semen, on the other hand, are composed of earth, water and air, blood which contains fibres having a preponderance of earth (and so being solidified by cooling and melted by liquid), blood which contains no fibres having a preponderance of water (and so not solidifying) ; semen is solidified by cooling when its moisture leaves it at the same time as its heat.

The proportions for the homoeomerous bodies determined.

CHAPTER XI

ARGUMENT

Hot and cold in solids and liquids. (1) *Bodies composed of water are, generally speaking, cold,* (2) *bodies composed of earth hot, though bodies composed of either alone tend to be cold.* (3) *Bodies composed of more than one element tend to*

389 a 24 Ποῖα δὲ θερμὰ ἢ ψυχρὰ τῶν πεπηγότων ἢ τῶν
25 ὑγρῶν, ἐκ τῶν εἰρημένων δεῖ μεταδιώκειν. ὅσα
μὲν οὖν ὕδατος, ὡς ἐπὶ τὸ πολὺ ψυχρά, ἐὰν μὴ
ἀλλοτρίαν ἔχῃ θερμότητα, οἷον κονία, οὖρον, οἶνος·
ὅσα δὲ γῆς, ὡς ἐπὶ τὸ πολὺ θερμὰ διὰ τὴν τοῦ
θερμοῦ δημιουργίαν, οἷον τίτανος καὶ τέφρα.

Δεῖ δὲ λαβεῖν τὴν ὕλην ψυχρότητά τινα εἶναι·
30 ἐπεὶ γὰρ τὸ ξηρὸν καὶ τὸ ὑγρὸν ὕλη (ταῦτα γὰρ
παθητικά), τούτων δὲ σώματα μάλιστα γῆ καὶ
ὕδωρ ἐστίν (ταῦτα γὰρ ψυχρότητι ὥρισται), δῆλον
389 b ὅτι πάντα τὰ σώματα ὅσα ἑκατέρου ἁπλῶς τοῦ
στοιχείου, ψυχρὰ μᾶλλόν ἐστιν, ἐὰν μὴ ἔχῃ ἀλλοτρίαν θερμότητα, οἷον τὸ ζέον ὕδωρ ἢ τὸ διὰ τέφρας
ἠθημένον· καὶ γὰρ τοῦτο ἔχει τὴν ἐκ τῆς τέφρας
θερμότητα· ἐν ἅπασι γάρ ἐστι θερμότης, ἢ πλείων
5 ἢ ἐλάττων, τοῖς πεπυρωμένοις· διὸ καὶ ἐν τοῖς
σαπροῖς ζῷα ἐγγίγνεται· ἔνεστι γὰρ θερμότης ἡ
φθείρασα τὴν ἑκάστου οἰκείαν θερμότητα.

Ὅσα δὲ κοινά, ἔχει θερμότητα· συνέστηκε γὰρ
τὰ πλεῖστα ὑπὸ θερμότητος πεψάσης. ἔνια δὲ

CHAPTER XI

ARGUMENT (*continued*)

be hot, though those that contain a predominance of water
tend to be cold.

 Note.—Ch. 11 is complementary to ch. 10 ; ch. 10 deals
with the proportions of dry and moist in homoeomerous
bodies, ch. 11 with the proportions of hot and cold.

WE must proceed to examine on the basis of what
has been said which solids and which liquids are hot
or cold. (1) Those composed of water are, generally
speaking, cold, unless they have some external source
of heat (as have lye, urine and wine) ; (2) those composed of earth are generally hot, having been manufactured by heat, like lime and ash.

 It must be understood that cold is in a sense the
material factor. For as dry and moist are matter
(being passive), and find their principal embodiments
in earth and water which have cold as a defining
characteristic, it is clear that all bodies that are made
of either element alone tend to be cold unless they
have an external source of heat like boiling water or
water strained through ash, which contains the heat
from the ash ; for everything that has been burned
contains heat to a greater or lesser degree. The
presence of heat is the reason why worms are gener-
ated in rotten material, the presence, that is, of the
heat which has destroyed the material's own natural
heat.[a]

 (3) Things composed of more than one element
contain heat, having most of them been formed by
concoction by heat, though some are the products

  [a] *Cf.* 379 b 6, ch. 1, note *a* on p. 296.

389 b

σήψεις εἰσίν, οἷον τὰ συντήγματα[1]· ὥστε ἔχοντα
10 μὲν τὴν φύσιν θερμὰ καὶ αἷμα καὶ γονὴ καὶ μυελὸς
καὶ ὀπὸς καὶ πάντα τὰ τοιαῦτα, φθειρόμενα δὲ καὶ
ἐξιστάμενα τῆς φύσεως οὐκέτι· λείπεται γὰρ ἡ
ὕλη, γῆ οὖσα ἢ ὕδωρ· διὸ ἀμφότερα δοκεῖ τισιν,
καὶ οἱ μὲν ψυχρὰ οἱ δὲ θερμὰ ταὐτά φασιν εἶναι,
ὁρῶντες, ὅταν μὲν ἐν τῇ φύσει ὦσιν, θερμά, ὅταν
15 δὲ χωρισθῶσιν, πηγνύμενα. ἔχει μὲν οὖν οὕτως,
ὅμως δέ, ὥσπερ διώρισται, ἐν οἷς μὲν ἡ ὕλη ὕδατος
τὸ πλεῖστον, ψυχρά (ἀντίκειται γὰρ μάλιστα τοῦτο
τῷ πυρί), ἐν οἷς δὲ γῆς ἢ ἀέρος, θερμότερα.

Συμβαίνει δέ ποτε ταὐτὰ γίγνεσθαι ψυχρότατα
καὶ θερμότατα ἀλλοτρίᾳ θερμότητι· ὅσα γὰρ μά-
20 λιστα πέπηγε καὶ στερεώτερά ἐστιν, ταῦτα ψυχρά
τε μάλιστα, ἐὰν στερηθῇ θερμότητος, καὶ κάει
μάλιστα, ἐὰν πυρωθῇ, οἷον ὕδωρ καπνοῦ καὶ ὁ λίθος
ὕδατος καίει μᾶλλον.

---

[1] συντήγματα 𝔚 𝔐 𝔅ᵣₑ꜀ Ap : συντηκτά Fobes : cf. L&S⁹, s.v.

[a] Cf. De Gen. An. i. 18, 724 b 21 ff.

CHAPTER XII

ARGUMENT

The next step is to deal in detail with the homoeomerous bodies, which we are now in a position to classify according to their material constituents, and which are in their turn the material of anhomoeomerous bodies (389 b 23-28). In all cases the formal element is even more important than the material, though the more elementary the body the less obvious this is. Even the elements have their final cause, which is still more obvious in the parts of the body, each of which has

of decay like the waste products [a] of the body. So as long as blood, semen, marrow, rennet and the like keep their proper nature they are warm, but once they perish and lose their proper nature they lose their warmth, for all that is left is their material factors, earth and water. So there are two views about them, and some regard them as cold, some as hot, seeing that as long as they retain their nature they are hot, but when they depart from it they solidify.[b] This is true. Nevertheless, as we have laid down, things in which the material factor is mainly water are cold (for water is the extreme opposite of fire), things in which it is mainly earth or air contain more heat.

It sometimes happens that bodies which are excessively cold become excessively hot under the influence of external heat—for the most solid and rigid bodies are also the coldest if deprived of heat, but they give the most heat after exposure to fire : thus water gives more heat than smoke and stone than water.

[b] *Cf.* 389 a 20-21.

CHAPTER XII

ARGUMENT (*continued*)

its specific function. So we may lay it down in general that things are what they are because of their ability to perform some function. And though heat and cold and their effects may be sufficient to account for the production of homoeomerous substances, it is clear that they are not sufficient to account for bodies made from those substances ; for in their production human craftsmanship or nature is also a factor (389 b 28—390 b 14). In dealing with the homoeomerous

bodies we should therefore, if possible, look for formal,
material and efficient causes. We can then proceed to an-

389 b 23 Ἐπεὶ δὲ περὶ τούτων διώρισται, καθ' ἕκαστον
λέγωμεν τί σὰρξ ἢ ὀστοῦν ἢ τῶν ἄλλων τῶν ὁμοιο-
25 μερῶν· ἔχομεν γὰρ ἐξ ὧν ἡ τῶν ὁμοιομερῶν φύσις
συνέστηκεν, τὰ γένη αὐτῶν, τίνος ἕκαστον γένους,
διὰ τῆς γενέσεως· ἐκ μὲν γὰρ τῶν στοιχείων τὰ
ὁμοιομερῆ, ἐκ δὲ τούτων ὡς ὕλης τὰ ὅλα ἔργα
τῆς φύσεως.

Ἔστιν δ' ἅπαντα ὡς μὲν ἐξ ὕλης ἐκ τῶν εἰρημένων, ὡς δὲ κατ' οὐσίαν τῷ λόγῳ. ἀεὶ δὲ μᾶλλον
30 δῆλον ἐπὶ τῶν ὑστέρων καὶ ὅλως ὅσα οἷον ὄργανα
καὶ ἕνεκά του. μᾶλλον γὰρ δῆλον ὅτι ὁ νεκρὸς
ἄνθρωπος ὁμωνύμως. οὕτω τοίνυν καὶ χεὶρ τελευ-
390 a τήσαντος ὁμωνύμως, καθάπερ καὶ αὐλοὶ λίθινοι
λεχθείησαν ⟨ἂν⟩[1]· οἷον γὰρ καὶ ταῦτα ὄργανα ἄττα
ἔοικεν εἶναι. ἧττον δ' ἐπὶ σαρκὸς καὶ ὀστοῦ τὰ
τοιαῦτα δῆλα. ἔτι δ' ἐπὶ πυρὸς καὶ ὕδατος ἧττον·
τὸ γὰρ οὗ ἕνεκα ἥκιστα ἐνταῦθα δῆλον, ὅπου δὴ
5 πλεῖστον τῆς ὕλης· ὥσπερ γὰρ εἰ καὶ τὰ ἔσχατα
ληφθείη, ἡ μὲν ὕλη οὐδὲν ἄλλο παρ' αὐτήν, ἡ δ'
οὐσία οὐδὲν ἄλλο ἢ λόγος, τὰ δὲ μεταξὺ ἀνάλογον
τῷ ἐγγὺς εἶναι ἕκαστον, ἐπεὶ καὶ τούτων ὁτιοῦν
ἐστιν ἕνεκά του, καὶ οὐ πάντως ἔχον ὕδωρ ἢ πῦρ,
ὥσπερ οὐδὲ σὰρξ οὐδὲ σπλάγχνον. τούτων δ' ἔτι
10 μᾶλλον πρόσωπον καὶ χείρ. ἅπαντα δ' ἐστὶν ὡρισμένα τῷ ἔργῳ· τὰ μὲν γὰρ δυνάμενα ποιεῖν τὸ αὐτῶν ἔργον ἀληθῶς ἐστιν ἕκαστον, οἷον ὀφθαλμὸς

[1] ἂν suppl. Thurot O.T.

homoeomerous bodies and, finally, to things made up of them (390 b 14-22).

HAVING dealt with these matters, let us proceed to give separate accounts of flesh and bone and the other homoeomerous bodies. We can tell from their generation what is the constitution of the homoeomerous bodies, what are the classes into which they fall and to which class each belongs ; for the homoeomerous bodies are composed of the elements, and serve in turn as material for all the works of nature.

But while the material of all the homoeomerous bodies is the elements we have mentioned, their essential reality is comprised in their formal definition. This is always clearer in the higher products of nature and, generally speaking, in things which are instrumental and serve a particular end. Thus it is only too clear that a corpse is a man in name only. So also the hand of a dead man is a hand in name only, just as a sculptured flute might still be called a flute, for it also is an instrument of a kind. The distinction is less clear in the case of flesh and bone, and less clear again in the case of fire and water. For the final cause is least obvious where matter predominates. For just as, to take the two extremes, matter is simply matter, essential reality is simply formal definition, so things intermediate are related to these two extremes according to their proximity to each ; for each of them has some final cause, and is not just water or fire, nor just flesh and intestines. And the same is even truer of face and hand. All these things, in fact, are determined by their function, and the true being of each consists in its ability to perform its particular function, of the eye, for instance, in its ability

390 a

εἰ ὁρᾷ, τὸ δὲ μὴ δυνάμενον ὁμωνύμως, οἷον ὁ
τεθνεὼς ἢ ὁ λίθινος· οὐδὲ γὰρ πρίων ὁ ξύλινος,
ἀλλ' ἢ ὡς εἰκών. οὕτω τοίνυν καὶ σάρξ· ἀλλὰ
15 τὸ ἔργον αὐτῆς ἧττον δῆλον ἢ τὸ τῆς γλώττης.
ὁμοίως δὲ καὶ πῦρ· ἀλλ' ἔτι ἧττον ἴσως δῆλον φυσικῶς ἢ τὸ τῆς σαρκὸς ἔργον. ὁμοίως δὲ καὶ τὰ
ἐν τοῖς φυτοῖς καὶ τὰ ἄψυχα, οἷον χαλκὸς καὶ
ἄργυρος· πάντα γὰρ δυνάμει τινί ἐστιν ἢ τοῦ ποιεῖν
ἢ τοῦ πάσχειν, ὥσπερ σὰρξ καὶ νεῦρον· ἀλλ' οἱ
20 λόγοι αὐτῶν οὐκ ἀκριβεῖς. ὥστε πότε ὑπάρχει καὶ
πότε οὔ, οὐ ῥᾴδιον διιδεῖν, ἂν μὴ σφόδρα ἐξίτηλον
ᾖ καὶ τὰ σχήματα μόνα ᾖ λοιπά, οἷον καὶ τὰ τῶν
παλαιουμένων νεκρῶν σώματα ἐξαίφνης τέφρα γίγνεται ἐν ταῖς θήκαις· καὶ καρποὶ μόνον τῷ σχή-
390 b ματι, τῇ δ' αἰσθήσει[1] οὐ φαίνονται, παλαιούμενοι
σφόδρα· καὶ τὰ ἐκ τοῦ γάλακτος πηγνύμενα.

Τὰ μὲν οὖν τοιαῦτα μόρια θερμότητι καὶ ψυχρότητι καὶ ταῖς ὑπὸ τούτων κινήσεσιν ἐνδέχεται γίγνεσθαι, πηγνύμενα τῷ θερμῷ καὶ τῷ ψυχρῷ·
5 λέγω δ' ὅσα ὁμοιομερῆ, οἷον σάρκα, ὀστοῦν, τρίχας,
νεῦρον, καὶ ὅσα τοιαῦτα· πάντα γὰρ διαφέρει ταῖς
πρότερον εἰρημέναις διαφοραῖς, τάσει, ἕλξει, θραύ-
σει, σκληρότητι, μαλακότητι καὶ τοῖς ἄλλοις τοῖς
τοιούτοις· ταῦτα δὲ ὑπὸ θερμοῦ καὶ ψυχροῦ καὶ τῶν
10 κινήσεων γίγνεται μειγνυμένων. τὰ δ' ἐκ τούτων
συνεστῶτα οὐδενὶ ἂν ἔτι δόξειεν τὰ ἀνομοιομερῆ,
οἷον κεφαλὴ ἢ χεὶρ ἢ πούς, ἀλλ' ὥσπερ καὶ τοῦ
χαλκὸν μὲν ἢ ἄργυρον γενέσθαι αἰτία ψυχρότης καὶ

---

[1] τῇ δ' αἰσθήσει 𝔐 𝔚 : κατὰ τὴν δ' αἴσθησιν ci. Thurot : τὴν δ'
αἴσθησιν Fobes.

372

to see ; while if it cannot perform its function it is that thing in name only, like a dead man or a stone figure of a man. Nor is a wooden saw, properly speaking, a saw but merely a representation of one. This is all equally true of flesh, but its function is less obvious than that of, *e.g.*, the tongue ; it is true of fire, but its natural function is even less obvious than that of flesh. It is equally true of plants and inorganic bodies like bronze and silver, for they are all what they are because of their ability to perform some active or passive function, like flesh and sinew, but their precise formal definitions are not apparent, and so it is difficult to perceive when they are operative and when they are not, unless the particular body is very decayed and retains few of its properties but its outward appearance. For example, ancient corpses sometimes suddenly turn to dust in their tombs, and some fruits when they get very old retain only their appearance and not their other sensible qualities, as do also solids formed from milk.

Heat and cold and the motions set up by them are therefore, since solidification is due to heat and cold, sufficient to produce all parts of this sort,[a] that is to say, all homoeomerous parts like flesh, bone, hair, sinew and the like : for these are all distinguished by the differentia we have already described (tension, ductility, fragmentability, hardness, softness and the rest) which are produced by heat and cold and the combination of their motions. But no one would suppose that this was the case with the anhomoeo-merous bodies which they in turn compose (for example, head, hand or foot), for though cold and heat and their motion will account for the production

---

[a] *Cf.* Introduction, pp. xv-xvi.

390 b

θερμότης καὶ κίνησις, τοῦ δὲ πρίονα ἢ φιάλην ἢ κιβωτὸν οὐκέτι, ἀλλ᾽ ἐνταῦθα μὲν τέχνη, ἐκεῖ δὲ φύσις ἢ ἄλλη τις αἰτία.

15 Εἰ οὖν ἔχομεν τίνος γένους ἕκαστον τῶν ὁμοιομερῶν, ληπτέον καθ᾽ ἕκαστον τί ἐστιν, οἷον τί αἷμα ἢ σὰρξ ἢ σπέρμα καὶ τῶν ἄλλων ἕκαστον· οὕτω γὰρ ἴσμεν ἕκαστον διὰ τί καὶ τί ἐστιν, ἐὰν ἢ τὴν ὕλην ἢ τὸν λόγον ἔχωμεν, μάλιστα δ᾽ ὅταν ἄμφω τῆς τε γενέσεως καὶ φθορᾶς, καὶ πόθεν ἡ ἀρχὴ τῆς

20 κινήσεως. δηλωθέντων δὲ τούτων ὁμοίως τὰ ἀνομοιομερῆ θεωρητέον, καὶ τέλος τὰ ἐκ τούτων συνεστῶτα, οἷον ἄνθρωπον, φυτόν, καὶ τἆλλα τὰ τοιαῦτα.

---

a Cf. De Gen. et Corr. ii. 9, De Part. An. ii. 1.

of bronze or silver, they will not account for the production of a saw or a cup or a box. Here human craftsmanship is the cause, while in other cases it is nature or some other cause.

Knowing, therefore, into which class each of the homoeomerous bodies fall, we should proceed to describe each of them, giving the definition of blood, flesh, semen and all the rest. For we know the cause and nature of a thing when we understand either the material or formal factor in its generation and destruction, or best of all if we know both, and also its efficient cause. When we have thus explained the homoeomerous bodies we must similarly examine the anhomoeomerous, and finally the bodies composed from them, such as men, plants and the like.[a]

INDEX OF NAMES AND TOPICS [1]

INDEX OF NAMES AND TOPICS

INDEX OF NAMES AND TOPICS

INDEX OF NAMES AND TOPICS

INDEX OF NAMES AND TOPICS

GREEK INDEX[1]

ἀάζω, 367 b 2
Ἀβδηρίτης, 365 a 19
ἄβρωτος, 380 b 3
ἀγγεῖον, 349 a 34, 35, b 15, 353 b 21, 357 b 4, 358 b 35
ἄγνοια, 359 a 11
ἄγονος, 346 b 35
ἄγω, 359 a 28, 362 b 1, 363 b 6, 373 a 11, 380 a 26
ἀγώγιμος, 359 a 8
ἄδηλος, 339 b 7, 13, 354 a 9, 356 a 35, 373 b 19
ἀδήλως, 355 b 32
ἀδιαίρετος, 343 b 34, 35, 344 a 1
ἀδυναμία, 385 a 11
ἀδυνατέω, 375 b 14
ἀδύνατος, 340 b 1, 343 a 21, b 7, 345 a 32, b 12, 18, 353 b 17, 31, 355 a 11, b 33, 356 a 19, 32, 357 a 6, b 21, 33, 362 b 14, 365 b 19 (bis), 29, 372 b 2, 5, 376 b 3, 12, 380 a 22, b 26, 386 a 4, b 22, 387 b 20
ἀέναος, 349 b 9 (bis), 12, 352 b 5, 12, 353 a 27
ἀήρ, 338 b 24, 339 a 16, 18, 36, b 3, 32, 340 a 3, 10 (bis),

12, 17, 20, 22, 24 (bis), 32, 34, 35, 36, b 2, 7, 10, 21, 24, 31, 34, 341 a 3, 8, 17, 27, 30, b 18, 342 a 1, 29, b 1, 5, 7, 344 a 11, b 5, 22, 32, 345 b 33, 34, 346 a 6, 9, b 18, 29, 31, 32, 347 a 3, 34, 348 a 8, 10, b 13, 28, 349 a 17, 20, 22, b 22, 24, 354 b 8, 24, 355 a 24, 30, 357 b 29, 360 a 20, 21, 26, 28, 32, 361 a 24, 27, 364 b 27, 365 a 32, 366 b 7, 23, 367 a 11, 20, 25, 34, b 17, 19, 23, 30, 368 a 16, 369 a 27, 371 a 17, 372 a 30, b 16, 30, 34, 373 a 29, b 1, 2, 9, 15, 21, 374 a 2, 24, 376 b 23, 26, 377 b 16, 25, 27, 379 a 15, 28, 30, 31, 35, 382 a 7, 383 b 24, 26, 31, 384 a 1, 11, 15, 16, b 16, 18, 19, 385 b 4, 387 a 25, 26, 29, 388 a 31, 32, 389 a 20, b 17
Ἀθήνησιν, 343 b 4
ἄθλαστος, 385 a 15, 386 a 18, 22
ἄθραυστος, 385 a 14

[1] The Greek Index is that of Professor Fobes' edition with prepositions, conjunctions and certain minor or common words omitted. I am grateful to Professor Fobes for permission to use his Index in this way. The references are to pages and lines of the Bekker edition.

GREEK INDEX

b 33, 374 b 6, 377 a 15,
378 b 10, 379 a 20, 380 b 6,
381 b 31, 382 a 27, b 15,
383 a 8, b 16, 24, 384 b 2,
3, 387 b 27, 388 b 1

ἄκαμπτος, 385 a 14, b 28, 29,
386 a 8

ἀκαριαῖος, 352 a 26

ἀκάτακτος, 385 a 14

ἄκαυστος, 385 a 18, 387 a 18,
19, 22

ἀκινησία, 340 b 18, 366 b 6

ἀκινητίζω, 379 a 34

ἀκμάζω, 351 a 29

ἀκμή, 351 a 28

ἀκοή, 369 b 9

ἀκολουθέω, 340 b 17, 366 a 7,
369 a 3, 370 b 14, 31

ἀκούω, 348 a 25

ἄκρα, 373 b 10

ἀκράτητος, 384 a 33

ἄκρατος, 375 a 10

ἀκρίβεια, 362 b 25

ἀκριβής, 390 a 19

ἀκριβόω, 363 b 32

ἀκριβῶς, 341 a 14

ἄκριτος, 361 b 30

ἀκρόνυχον, 367 b 26

ἄκρος, 350 a 32

ἀκτίς, 340 a 29, 32, 345 a 29,
b 6, 346 b 24, 348 a 17,
369 b 14, 25, 374 b 4

ἀλέα, 341 a 19, 347 a 20, 348
b 4, 362 b 27, 366 b 5, 379
a 27

ἀλεεινός, 348 a 19, b 4, 9, 349
a 4, 8, 363 a 17, 364 a 23

ἀλεεινότατος, 358 a 30

ἀλεεινότερος, 347 a 21, 348 b 6

ἀλήθεια, 356 b 17

ἀληθής, 343 a 35, 352 a 21, 22,
358 a 16

ἀληθῶς, 390 a 11

ἅλμα, 343 b 23

ἁλμυρίς, 357 b 4

ἁλμυρός, 353 a 33, b 13 (bis),
15, 16, 354 b 18, 21, 355
a 33, b 4, 9, 357 a 6, 12, 18,
19, 22, 29, 34, 358 a 6, 27,
b 14, 34, 359 a 6, 13, 21,
23, b 4

ἁλμυρότης, 353 b 13, 354 b 2,
356 b 4, 357 a 5, 16, b 7,
22, 358 a 4, 359 a 5

ἄλογος, 355 a 21, 35, 366 a 9,
369 b 19

ἀλόγως, 362 a 14

ἁλουργός, 372 a 8, 374 b 33,
375 b 11

ἅλς, 359 a 13, 29, 32, b 4, 383
b 13, 20, 384 a 18, 385 a 31,
b 9, 16, 388 b 13, 15, 389
a 18

ἅλυσις, 387 a 13

ἄλυτος, 383 a 30, b 10, 12,
384 a 34, b 7

ἄλφιτον, 382 a 1

ἅλως, 344 b 2, 6, 13, 18, 346
a 5, 371 b 18, 22, 372 b 12,
373 a 27, b 34, 374 a 10, 15,
377 b 34

ἀμάλακτος, 384 b 1, 385 a 13,
388 b 25

ἀμαυρός, 343 b 12, 367 a 23

ἀμαυρότερος, 344 b 29, 367
a 21, 375 a 30, b 3, 13

ἀμαυρόω, 367 b 28

Ἀμμώνιος, 352 b 32

ἄμπωτις, 366 a 19

ἀμυδρός, 343 b 13

ἀμυδρότερος, 372 a 2

ἀμύθητον, 375 a 23

ἀναβαίνω, 344 a 20

ἀναβλέπω, 346 a 34

GREEK INDEX

ἀντιφράττω, 345 a 29, b 9, 368 b 10
ἀνωθέω, 348 a 20
ἀνωμαλία, 369 b 1, 377 b 14
ἀνώμαλος, 377 b 4, 8
ἀνωμάλως, 385 b 9
ἀνώνυμος, 341 b 15, 359 b 30, 381 b 6, 389 a 8
ἀνωνυμώτερος, 381 b 15
ἀξία, 357 a 4
ἄξιος, 384 a 4
ἄξων, 375 b 22, 376 b 30
ἀοίκητος, 362 b 7, 9, 26
ἀόρατος, 373 a 20, b 25
ἀοριστία, 361 b 34
ἀόριστος, 380 a 3, 29, b 14, 381 a 14, 382 a 16
ἀπαθής, 380 b 10
ἀπαντάω, 353 b 22
ἀπαρκτίας, 363 b 14, 29, 31, 364 a 14, b 4, 21, 22, 29, 365 a 2, 7, 8
ἀπαρτίζω, 340 b 35
ἀπατμίζω, 359 a 31
ἀπειλή, 369 a 32
ἄπειμι (εἶμι), 350 b 26, 351 b 6, 361 a 11, 383 a 9, 12
ἀπειράκις, 339 b 29
ἄπειρος, 351 a 12
ἄπεπτος, 371 a 3, 384 a 33
ἀπεπτότατος, 358 a 6, 7
ἀπεργάζομαι, 378 a 16
ἀπέρχομαι, 357 a 30, b 19, 362 a 3, 384 a 5
ἀπέχω, 345 b 21, 363 a 31, 32, 33, b 8, 9
ἀπεψία, 357 b 9, 379 a 2, b 13, 380 a 6, 9, 28, 381 a 12, 13, b 9, 20
ἄπηκτος, 385 a 12, 21, b 1
ἀπηλιώτης, 363 b 13, 364 a 15, 16, b 19, 365 a 10

ἀπηλιωτικός, 364 a 21, b 28
ἀπίεστος, 385 a 15, 386 b 8, 10, 387 a 16
ἀπίλητος, 385 a 17, 387 a 16
ἄπιστος, 348 a 27
ἀπλανής, 343 b 9, 29, 344 a 36
ἄπλαστος, 385 a 15
ἄπλετος, 355 b 23
ἁπλοῦς, 339 b 34, 341 b 7, 378 b 28, 32, 379 a 3
ἁπλῶς, 365 a 26, 382 a 14, 15, 19, 386 b 32, 389 a 32
ἄπνους, 354 a 22, 361 b 6
ἀποβιάζομαι, 351 a 6, 364 a 29, b 8, 365 b 4, 366 b 11, 27, 368 b 10, 35
ἀπόγειος, 363 a 1
ἀποδείκνυμι, 344 a 6
ἀποδέχομαι, 346 b 1
ἀποδίδωμι, 339 a 7, 355 a 27, 28, 358 a 3, 363 a 11, 365 a 34, 373 b 28
ἀποκαθαίρω, 383 a 34, b 3
ἀποκάθαρσις, 383 b 4
ἀποκρίνω, 340 b 20, 345 b 34, 346 b 8 (bis), 349 b 26, 29, 359 a 4, 360 b 34, 362 a 27, 369 b 28, 372 b 32, 374 a 35, 378 a 31, 32, 379 b 7, 381 b 13
ἀπόκρισις, 360 b 33, 366 b 12, 381 b 11
ἀπολαμβάνω, 369 b 26, 372 b 21, 375 b 27
ἀπολείπω, 346 b 26, 353 a 22, 364 a 26, 367 b 22
ἀπόλειψις, 346 b 30, 351 a 21, b 19
ἀπολύω, 371 a 12
ἀπομαραίνομαι, 343 b 16, 367 b 11, 23, 372 b 29, 375 a 14
ἀποξηραίνω, 388 b 6

GREEK INDEX

αὐγή, 375 a 26
αὐλός, 389 b 32
αὔξω, 351 a 31, 355 a 24
αὐτόματος, 353 b 28, 34
αὐτόπτης, 350 a 17
αὐχμάω, 360 b 11
αὐχμός, 344 b 20, 360 b 5
    (bis), 9, 361 b 9, 365 b 9,
    10, 366 b 3, 7, 8, 368 b 16
ἀφαιρέω, 351 b 32, 376 b 21,
    382 b 26
ἀφανής, 344 a 5, 377 a 8, 17
ἀφανίζω, 343 b 15, 31, 351 b 1,
    4, 354 a 31, 355 b 13, 29,
    356 a 24, 370 a 21, 387 a 27
ἀφέψω, 359 a 30, b 3
ἀφή, 382 a 19, 20, 386 a 20,
    388 a 12
ἄφθονος, 360 b 11
ἀφίημι, 347 a 33, 349 a 35, b 2,
    356 b 30, 368 a 17, 24, 388
    b 23
ἀφικνέομαι, 341 a 29, 343 a 20,
    355 a 5, b 31, 369 b 11, 375
    b 14, 378 a 10
ἀφίστημι, 347 a 4, 377 a 23,
    378 a 4
ἀφλόγιστος, 387 b 18, 20
ἀφορία, 351 b 14
ἀφορίζω, 339 b 10, 350 b 23
Ἀχαΐα, 343 b 2, 366 a 26,
    368 b 6
ἀχανής, 340 a 32, 355 b 31,
    367 a 19, 378 a 6
Ἀχελῷος, 350 b 15, 352 a 35
ἀχλύς, 361 a 28, 367 b 17, 373
    a 1, b 12, 17, 374 a 7, 18,
    377 b 19
ἀχλυώδης, 367 a 20, 23
ἀχρωμάτιστος, 371 a 2, b 9,
    377 b 1
ἄχυρον, 344 a 26

ἄψις, 386 b 1
ἀψίς, 371 b 28, 29
ἄψυχος, 390 a 17

βαδίζω, 357 a 2, 373 b 5
βάθος, 339 b 12, 341 b 34, 342
    a 23, b 15, 350 a 31, 351
    a 6, 13, 354 a 18, 368 b 28,
    382 a 14, 386 a 19, 23, 30,
    b 20
βαθύς, 351 a 12, 354 a 27 (bis)
βαθύτατος, 354 a 21
βαθύτερος, 354 a 19
Βάκτρος, 350 a 23
βάρος, 341 b 12, 355 a 34, b 5,
    356 b 18, 358 b 26, 359 a 6,
    8, 365 a 28, 368 b 35, 369
    a 23
βαρύνω, 341 a 5
βαρύτατος, 340 b 20, 358 b 5
βαρύτερος, 381 a 5
βασιλεύς, 352 b 24
βάσις, 362 b 2
βέλτιον, 349 a 26
βία, 341 a 26, 31, 342 a 25,
    369 a 28, 379 a 6
βιάζω, 368 a 28, 370 b 19, 371
    a 15
βίαιος, 370 b 9
βιώσκομαι, 351 a 35
βλέπω, 352 a 17, 373 b 4, 6,
    374 b 20, 26
βοήθεια, 379 b 23
βόθυνος, 342 a 36
βορέας, 343 a 17, 345 a 1, 347
    b 2, 6, 358 a 35, 361 a 6, 22,
    b 11, 362 a 11, 16, b 33, 35,
    363 a [2], 4, 6, 17, b 14,
    364 a 13, 15, 20, b 26, 368
    b 7
βόρειος, 344 b 35, 347 a 36,
    37, b 9 (bis), 363 a 2, 364

391

GREEK INDEX

a 19, 371 a 3, 8, 377 b 26

Βόσπορος, 353 a 7, 372 a 15

βούλομαι, 348 b 33, 349 a 20, b 15, 354 b 32, 363 b 31, 384 a 7

βοῦς, 359 a 29

βραδύς, 341 a 23

βραδύτατα, 343 a 5

βραδύτερος, 371 a 23

βραδυτής, 357 b 34

βραχύ, 377 a 26

βραχύς, 347 b 22, 348 b 24, 354 a 22, 382 b 14

βραχύτερος, 371 b 30

βραχύτης, 354 a 18

βρέχω, 359 a 22, 365 b 6, 385 b 14, 18, 386 b 5

βροντή, 369 a 10, 29, b 1, 3, 8, 17, 19, 29, 370 a 22, 24, 27, 31, 33, b 7, 371 b 11, 14

γάλα, 338 b 22, 339 a 34, 342 b 25, 345 a 9, 12, 20, 25, 26, 31, 32, 36, b 11, 19, 23, 26, 346 a 17, b 2, 5, 13, 380 b 8, 32, 381 a 7, 382 b 12, 383 a 22, 384 a 16, 24, 30, 388 a 31, 390 b 2

γαλήνη, 367 b 15

Γαμηλιών, 343 b 5

γεηρός, 380 a 24

γειτνίασις, 363 a 14

γειτνιάω, 338 b 21, 350 a 5, 360 b 20, 363 b 22, 368 b 15

γελάω, 369 a 32

γελοῖος, 352 a 26, 354 b 33, 357 a 24

γελοίως, 362 b 12

γεμίζω, 359 a 11

γένεσις, 338 a 24, 340 b 37, 342 a 14, 346 b 19, 23, 347 b

22, 34, 348 a 15, 349 b 2, 351 a 20, b 9, 352 a 25, b 17, 353 a 34, b 6, 354 b 1, 28, 355 a 30, 356 b 8, 35, 357 b 17, 358 a 2, 27, 361 a 32, 36, 365 a 11, 374 a 14, 377 b 25, 378 b 28, 32, 379 a 3, b 8, 389 b 26, 390 b 19

γεννάω, 341 b 36, 357 a 5, 6, 378 a 32, 379 a 1

γένος, 353 b 32, 365 a 15, 378 a 22, b 6, 383 b 11, 388 b 21, 389 a 18, b 25, 26, 390 b 15

γεώδης, 359 a 4, 24, 384 a 20

γῆ, 338 b 25, 339 a 16, 17, 19 (bis), 28, 37, b 4, 6, 11, 13, 31, 340 a 6, 7, 22, 27, 28, 29, 34, b 3, 10, 21, 25, 26, 35, 37, 341 a 11, b 6, 9 (bis), 10, 20, 342 a 10, 343 a 12, 344 a 9, 12, b 12, 345 a 27, 30, b 3, 4, 5, 6, 7, 9, 346 b 11, 17, 24, 29, 31, 347 a 8, 10, b 27, 29, 348 a 9, 17, 20, 24, 29, 34, b 4, 349 b 4, 18, 20, 22, 23, 24, 29, 31, 33, 34, 350 a 2, 16, b 24, 36, 351 a 2, 11, 14, 19, 22, 25, 27, 30, 33, b 9, 352 a 27, b 6, 28, 353 a 21, 23, 25, b 1, 7, 12, 14, 16, 18, 354 a 7, 10, 12, 25, 28, 30 (bis), 32, b 9, 23, 31, 355 a 22, 23, b 18, 35, 356 a 14, 24, 357 a 7, 10, 15, 20, 25, b 6, 9, 12, 13, 18, 358 a 15, 19, b 6, 30, 31, 359 b 7, 10, 360 a 5, 6, 7, 8, 16, b 31, 361 a 17, 23, 31 (bis), 34, b 1, 3, 17, 362 a 5, 35, b 4, 5, 13, 364 a 10, 11,

392

GREEK INDEX

393

GREEK INDEX

διάσπασις, 372 b 19, 20, 29

διασπάω, 367 a 29, 372 b 21, 26, 378 a 6, 8

διασπείρω, 341 b 33, 369 a 25

διάστασις, 350 b 36

διάστημα, 340 a 1, 37, 345 b 3, 17, 376 b 8

διαστρέφω, 383 a 25

διατείνω, 355 b 26, 367 b 10

διατελέω, 341 a 8, 351 a 23, 372 a 16

διατήκω, 385 a 28

διατμίζω, 344 b 23, 353 b 8, 357 a 11

διατριβή, 374 a 12

διατρίβω, 353 a 35

διάττω, 341 b 35

διαυλωνίζω, 366 a 27

διαφαίνω, 342 b 6

διαφέρω, 340 a 13, 341 b 5, 24, 347 b 15, 349 a 23 (bis), 350 a 10, 351 a 33, 353 b 25, 355 b 27, 356 b 12, 26, 357 a 22, b 34, 359 a 7, 360 a 15, 18, 362 b 20, 365 b 15, 368 a 18, 369 b 30, 372 a 19, 374 a 1, 4, b 22, 375 a 24, b 33, 376 a 22, 377 b 11, 381 a 10, 385 a 1, 8, 19, b 26, 386 a 12, 387 a 28, 388 a 11, 390 b 6

διαφεύγω, 357 b 22

διαφθείρω, 352 b 29

διαφορά, 340 b 9, 347 a 10, 353 b 29, 359 b 20, 368 b 22, 371 b 16, 378 a 16, 380 b 31, 388 a 10, 390 b 7

διάφορος, 360 b 14

διαχέω, 370 b 5, 376 b 23

διάχυσις, 382 a 30

δίδυμος, 343 b 31

δίδωμι, 359 a 27, 368 b 9,

[26], 376 a 4 (bis), 5, 7, 384 b 10

δίειμι (εἶμι), 365 b 34, 371 a 22

διέξειμι, 388 b 28

διεξέρχομαι, 368 a 6

διέρχομαι, 339 a 5, 344 a 30, 368 a 4, 371 a 27

διέχω, 362 b 35

διηθέω, 354 b 17, 359 b 7, 368 a 22, 371 a 27

διήκω, 360 b 13, 363 a 5, 18

δικνέομαι, 374 b 15

διΐστημι, 339 a 27, 371 b 12, 14, 386 a 16

δίνη, 370 b 22, 371 a 11

δῖνος, 370 b 28

δίοδος, 351 a 6, 384 b 10

διονομάζω, 350 b 12

διοράω, 390 a 20

διορίζω, 339 a 11, b 15, 26, 340 b 5, 341 b 1, 353 b 30, 364 a 4, 22, 378 b 10, 26, 380 a 10, 381 a 21, 389 b 15, 23

διορισμός, 339 a 34

διορύττω, 352 b 25, 29

διπλοῦς, 339 a 14, 341 b 8, 357 b 24, 360 a 9, 375 a 30, 378 a 17

δίπλωμα, 346 a 24

δίς, 339 b 28, 356 b 13, 372 a 29

διττός, 369 a 13

διῶρυξ, 350 a 1

δοκέω, 339 b 23, 340 a 36, 341 a 35, b 34, 342 a 32, b 3, 16, 18, 29, 343 b 34, 344 a 24, 25, 347 b 35, 348 a 14, 349 a 23, b 3, 354 b 4, 15, 360 a 3, 361 b 30, 366 a 27, 367 a 33, 368 a 24, 370

395

GREEK INDEX

a 17, 371 b 2, 372 b 2, 3,
373 a 20, 26, b 5, 375 a 11,
377 b 3, 383 a 4, 387 b 13,
389 b 12, 390 b 10
δόξα, 339 b 19, 29, 34, 343
b 25, 354 b 19, 370 a 17
δράω, 359 a 16
δρόσος, 347 a 16, 18, 22, 36,
b 17, 20, 31, 349 a 9, 378
a 31
δύναμαι, 339 a 6, 341 a 17, 343
a 13, 347 a 27, 32, 351 a 13,
34, b 18, 352 a 11, 355 a 2,
363 a 5, 365 b 3, 34, 366
b 24, 28, 368 a 5, 13, 22,
b 2, 20, 370 b 31, 371 a 10,
12, 372 a 6, 373 b 9, 380
a 14, b 9, 381 a 4, b 2, 385
a 2, 4, b 30, 386 a 30, b 3,
20, 27, 30, 387 a 4, 14,
b 20, 390 a 10, 12
δυνάμει, 339 b 1, 340 b 15, 28,
29, 358 b 8, 369 a 14, 370
b 13, 378 a 33, 390 a 18
δύναμις, 339 a 23, 32, b 17,
24, 340 a 14, 16, 345 b 33,
347 a 8, 351 a 33, 357 b 3,
358 a 24, 359 a 33, b 10, 13,
366 b 16, 22, 367 b 5, 369
a 5, 370 b 14, 378 b 29, 33,
34, 379 a 20, b 4, 11, 382 a
5, 31, 385 a 11, 20, 388 a 23
δυνατός, 344 a 6, 345 b 28, 348
a 5, 357 a 19, 360 a 17, 362
a 33, b 6, 34, 370 a 7, 386
b 11
δύνω, 361 b 31, 371 b 27, 372
a 28, 373 b 13
δύσις, 343 b 15, 361 b 32, 371
b 26, 375 b 26
δυσμή, 343 b 3, 350 b 1, 361
a 9, 363 a 34, b 5, 6, 12, 19,

25, 364 a 21, 24, 26, 365
a 7, 367 b 9, 372 a 14, 16,
377 b 28
δυσόριστος, 378 b 24, 381 b 29
δυσχωρία, 368 a 5
δύω (verbum), 342 b 10, 343
b 22

Δωδώνη, 352 a 35

ἔαρ, 347 b 37, 348 b 26, 28,
365 a 2, 366 b 2
ἐαρινός, 364 b 1
ἐάω, 347 b 10, 356 b 28, 372
b 21
ἑβδομηκοστός, 362 a 24
ἔβενος, 384 b 17, 18
Ἕβρος, 350 b 17
ἐγγίγνομαι, 359 a 21, b 10,
369 b 12, 370 a 6, 24, 379
b 6, 381 b 10, 389 b 5
ἐγκατακλείω, 378 a 15, 29,
381 b 2, 384 b 34
ἐγκαταλείπω, 368 a 4
ἐγκύκλιος, 339 a 4, 341 b 14,
344 a 9
ἐγκυκλίως, 339 a 12
ἐγχειρέω, 352 b 27
ἔγχωσις, 352 b 34
ἔδεσμα, 359 b 16
ἕδρα, 350 a 34, 35, 356 a 4
ἐδωδή, 381 a 2
ἐθέλω, 347 a 5
ἔθνος, 350 a 34, 351 b 11, 16,
23
ἔθω, 367 b 7
εἶδος, 338 b 25, 339 a 29, 357
b 28, 31, 359 b 28, 360
a 18, 363 a 32 (bis), 378
a 20, b 28, 379 b 10, 17, 26,
380 b 32, 381 b 4, 24, 382
a 29, b 11, 13, 383 b 14,
388 a 26, b 2

396

GREEK INDEX

εἴδωλον, 373 b 5
εἰκάζω, 366 b 29
εἰκότως, 372 b 22
εἰκών, 390 a 13
εἰλέω, 356 a 5
εἰλικρινής, 340 b 8, 388 b 16
εἰμι, 365 b 31, 34, 368 a 20
εἰρεσία, 369 b 10
εἰσβάλλω, 351 a 10, 356 a 11,
    359 b 19
εἰσβλέπω, 377 b 1
εἴσειμι, 359 a 2, 383 a 9, 28
εἰσέρχομαι, 355 b 7
εἴσοδος, 384 b 21
εἰσοικίζω, 351 b 31
εἰσπίπτω, 371 b 7
εἰσπλέω, 350 a 31, 353 a 3
εἰσρέω, 356 a 16
ἐκβάλλω, 367 b 13, 375 b 31,
    376 a 1, 380 a 26
ἐκδίδωμι, 351 a 11
ἐκθλίβω, 341 a 5, 342 a 1, 9,
    369 b 5, 371 a 18, 383 a 18,
    385 a 25
ἔκθλιψις, 342 a 15, 369 a 22
ἐκθυμιάω, 388 a 8
ἐκκαίω, 341 b 16, 20, 36, 342
    a 17, 344 a 18
ἔκκαυσις, 342 a 2, 15
ἐκκάω, 341 b 23, 384 a 20, 23
ἔκκειμαι, 376 a 10
ἐκκρίνω, 342 a 1, 18, 345 a 7,
    357 b 11, 364 b 32, 369
    a 24, 27, b 32, 370 b 5, 8,
    17, 29, 32, 371 a 10, 379
    b 8, 380 b 20, 381 b 2, 387
    a 26, 388 a 15
ἔκκρισις, 342 a 15, 344 b 21,
    346 a 1, b 6, 361 b 18, 367
    b 15, 369 a 36, 370 b 3, 9,
    11, 378 a 12, 387 a 25, 28,
    30

ἐκκρούω, 381 a 16
ἐκλείπω, 342 b 34, 347 b 29,
    367 b 4, 369 a 17, b 3, 374
    b 13, 384 b 28
ἔκλειψις, 367 b 20, 25, 26, 27,
    30, 31
ἐκνεφίας, 365 a 1, 3, 366 b 33,
    369 a 19, 370 b 8, 17, 29,
    371 a 3, 4, 10, b 15
ἐκπηδάω, 369 a 23
ἐκπίμπρημι, 346 b 12, 367
    a 10
ἐκπίπτω, 342 a 17, 344 b 33,
    345 a 14, 369 b 7, 371 a 1,
    375 b 22
ἐκπνέω, 371 a 13, b 5
ἔκπτωσις, 370 a 5
ἐκπυρόω, 338 b 23, 340 b 13,
    341 a 18, 32, 34, 342 b 2,
    22, 344 a 14, 369 b 5, 371
    a 15, 23, 378 a 21
ἐκπύρωσις, 342 b 2
ἐκρέω, 356 a 16
ἐκρήγνυμι, 366 b 32, 368 b 5
ἐκριπίζω, 346 a 9
ἐκροή, 351 a 4, 356 a 10
ἔκρους, 351 a 10
ἔκρυσις, 351 a 5
ἐκτείνω, 374 b 11, 387 a 14
ἐκτέμνω, 362 a 35
ἔκτμημα, 362 b 5, 363 a 29
ἔκχυσις, 354 a 26, 368 a 32
ἔλαιον, 381 a 8, 382 b 16, 383
    b 14, 21, 28, 384 a 16, 385
    b 4, 387 b 7, 10, 22, 388 a 5
    9, 32, b 10
ἐλαιώδης, 388 a 5
ἐλατός, 378 a 27, 385 a 16,
    b 10, 386 b 18, 19, 22, 23,
    24, 25
ἔλαφος, 384 a 27
ἕλιξ, 371 a 12

397

GREEK INDEX

GREEK INDEX

399

GREEK INDEX

400

GREEK INDEX

Ζεύς, 343 b 30
ζεφυρικός, 364 a 20
ζέφυρος, 363 a 7, b 12, 364
  a 18, b 3, 23, 365 a 8 (bis)
ζέω, 370 a 10, 379 a 31, 385
  b 3, 389 b 2
ζημιόω, 359 a 11
ζητέω, 354 b 11, 355 b 20, 356
  b 17
ζήτησις, 349 a 27 (bis)
ζοφερός, 375 a 19
ζῴδιον, 343 a 24, 345 a 20,
  346 a 12
ζωή, 351 b 10
ζώνη, 343 b 24
ζῷον, 339 a 7, 351 a 28, 355
  b 6, 358 b 9, 11, 366 b 25,
  378 b 31, 379 b 6, 381 b 9,
  382 a 6, 384 b 31, 388 a 16,
  b 22, 389 b 5

ἡγέομαι, 339 b 22
ἡδύνω, 359 a 34
ἥδυσμα, 381 b 30
ἡθέω, 353 b 15, 357 a 31, b 1,
  359 b 13, 389 b 2
ἠθμός, 359 a 4
ἥκω, 356 b 22
ἤλεκτρον, 388 b 18, 19, 20, 25,
  389 a 13
ἡλιόομαι, 350 a 31
ἥλιος, 341 a 13, 20, 23, 24, 35,
  b 7, 342 a 33, b 19, 343 a 4,
  10, 14, 15, 20, 34, 36, b 6,
  21, 344 b 3, 5, 15, 345 a 7,
  16, 22, 27, 29, 30, 34, 35,
  b 2, 4, 5, 6, 8, 11, 20, 27,
  346 a 4, 12, 14, b 21, 36,
  347 a 4, 348 b 33, 349 b 3,
  351 a 32, 353 b 7, 8, 12,
  354 a 29, b 27, 34, 355 a 6,
  8, 11, 13, 15, 17, 19, 23,

b 19, 356 b 22, 28, 357 a 8,
  b 20, 359 b 34, 360 a 7, 16,
  b 14, 361 a 7, b 14, 36, 362
  a 6, 18, 25, 363 a 14, 364
  a 9, 11, 25, b 15, 17, 365
  b 25, 366 a 15, 18, 367 a 20,
  23, b 22, 368 b 20, 21, 369
  b 14, 370 a 3, 371 b 23, 372
  a 13, 20, b 13, 373 a 1, 17,
  19, 21, 28, b 12, 21, 30, 33,
  374 a 7, 12, b 2 (bis), 25,
  375 a 3, b 5, 15, 376 b 22,
  28, 377 a 9, 28, 31, 33, b 7,
  [7], 9, 19, 21, 22, 30, 31, 34,
  378 a 1, [3], 4, 6, 7, 383
  b 34
ἡμέρα, 342 a 12, b 19, 344
  b 33, 345 a 2, 347 a 13, 348
  b 9, 349 a 7, b 16, 28, 354
  b 14, 29, 355 b 22, 28, 360
  a 3, 4, 361 b 33, 362 a 1,
  366 a 14, 15, 18, 367 b 9,
  34, 370 a 20, 21, 371 b 25,
  31 (bis), 372 a 15, 21, 26,
  377 a 12, 13, 20, 25
ἡμέρη, 355 a 14
ἡμέτερος, 343 a 3, 345 b 11,
  351 b 10, 366 b 30
ἡμικύκλιον, 345 a 23, 346 a 24,
  371 b 27, 375 b 17, 27, 28,
  376 a 3, b 12, 13, 21, 377
  a 6, 7, 16 (bis)
ἡμισφαίριον, 375 b 19, 24
ἤπειρος, 351 a 21, 353 a 24,
  369 a 4 (bis)
Ἡράκλεια, 367 a 1
Ἡράκλειος, 354 a 12, 362
  b 21, 28
Ἡράκλειτος, 355 a 14
Ἡρακλῆς, 359 a 28
ἠρέμα, 343 b 14, 373 b 4, 375
  a 21

401

GREEK INDEX

19, 23, 25, 28, b 8, 17, 382
b 18, 21, 26, 383 a 31, 384
b 27, 389 a 26, b 2, 3, 4, 6
(bis), 7, 8, 19, 21, 390 b 3, 12
θέρος, 348 a 18, b 26, 28, 349
a 5, b 8, 361 a 13, b 32, 366
b 4, 379 a 29
θέσις, 339 a 33, 340 a 20, 341
b 24, 342 a 22, 346 a 18,
34, b 16, 356 a 10, 363 a 21,
25, b 11, 372 a 3, 374 a 30,
b 1, 375 a 31
θετέον, 388 b 32
θέω, 339 b 25
θεωρέω, 338 a 25, b 26, 339
a 6, b 32, 35, 345 b 27, 346
a 31, 353 b 18, 363 a 26,
366 b 23, 371 a 30, 31, 372
b 9, 374 b 15, 22, 27, 375
b 18
θεώρημα, 339 b 8, 37, 345 b 2
θεωρητέον, 390 b 20
Θῆβαι, 351 b 34
θήκη, 390 a 23
θημών, 344 a 26
θήρα, 348 b 35
θηρεύω, 348 b 35
θιγγάνω, 342 b 29
θλάσις, 386 a 18, 28
θλαστός, 385 a 15, 386 a 17,
25, b 22, 23, 387 a 1
θλάω, 386 a 26
θλῖψις, 382 a 13
θνήσκω, 390 a 12
θρασκίας, 363 b 29, 364 a 1,
14, b 4, 22, 29, 365 a 3, 7
θραῦσις, 386 a 13, 390 b 7
θραυστός, 385 a 14, 386 a 9,
10, 11 (bis), 15, 387 a 1
θραύω, 387 a 5
θρίξ, 386 b 14, 387 b 1, 4, 388
a 17, 389 a 12, 390 b 5

θυμίασις, 387 a 30, 32, b 6, 13,
388 a 3
θυμιατός, 385 a 18, 387 a 23,
26, b 7, 8, 21, 31, 389 a 17
θυμιάω, 362 a 7, 9, 11, 387 b 9

ἰατρός, 384 a 21
ἰδέα, 380 a 17, b 30
ἰδίᾳ, 378 b 5
ἰδιαίτατος, 382 a 3
ἴδιος, 360 b 15, 374 b 16, 385
a 1
ἰδίω, 350 a 1, 357 b 14, 18, 21
ἰδίως, 379 a 12
ἰδρύω, 339 b 11
ἱδρώς, 353 b 12, 13, 357 a 25,
29, b 4, 14, 358 a 10
Ἱερὰ (νῆσος), 367 a 2
ἰθαγενής, 364 a 16, 18
ἰκμάς, 376 b 28
ἰλύς, 388 b 7
ἱμάς, 386 b 14
ἱμάτιον, 359 a 22, 371 a 28,
382 b 19
Ἴναχος, 350 b 16
Ἰνδική, 362 b 21, 28
Ἰνδός, 350 a 25
ἰξός, 385 b 5, 386 b 14
Ἱπποκράτης, 342 b 36, 343
a 28, 344 b 15
ἶρις, 371 b 18, 26, 32, 372 a 9,
21, 373 a 2, 32, b 32, 33,
374 a 8, 15, 20, 21, 30, b 5,
28, 375 a 1, 10, 11, 15, 18,
30, b 6, 7, 9, 12, 16, 376
b 24, 27, 377 a 13, 15
ἰριώδης, 374 a 28
ἴς, 384 a 28 (bis), 388 a 17,
389 a 20, 21
ἰσάζω, 358 b 15
ἰσημερία, 364 b 1, 371 b 30,
377 a 12, 14 (bis)

GREEK INDEX

ἰσημερινός (adiectivum), 343
b 3, 345 a 3, 350 b 1, 363
a 34, b 1, 12, 14 364 a 17
ἰσημερινός(substantivum),377
a 18
ἰσοταχῶς, 345 b 17
ἰσότης, 340 a 4, 15
ἵστημι, 374 b 4, 376 b 27
Ἴστρος, 350 b 2, 3, 9, 356 a 28
ἰσχίον, 343 b 11
ἰσχυρός, 361 b 27, 364 b 6,
367 a 22, b 32
ἰσχυρότατος, 366 a 24
ἰσχυρότερος, 366 a 23, 371
b 4, 374 b 31, 387 a 21
ἰσχυρῶς, 349 a 9, 366 b 14
ἰσχύς, 366 b 27, 370 b 10
ἰσχύω, 361 a 35, 367 a 31, 379
a 28
ἴσχω, 343 a 27, 30, 356 a 13
Ἰταλία, 367 a 7
Ἰταλικός, 342 b 30
ἰχθύς, 348 b 35, 359 a 21, 26,
29
ἰχώρ, 389 a 10
ἰχωροειδής, 384 a 32

καθαρός, 339 b 30, 344 b 14,
383 b 1
καθαρώτερος, 340 b 8
κάθεσις, 356 a 11
κάθετος, 373 a 11, 376 b 19
καθίημι, 351 a 13
καθόλου, 339 a 7, 359 b 31,
378 b 28, 379 b 16, 381 b 4,
385 a 21
καικίας, 363 b 17, 30, 364
a 15, b 1, 12, 14, 18, 24, 25
καιρός, 344 b 26, 358 b 23
καίω, 341 b 2, 26, 27, 30, 342
b 3, 343 a 9, 371 a 24, 387
b 10, 388 a 6, 389 b 22

καλάμη, 341 b 27
κάλαμος, 349 a 1, 3, 359 b 1,
385 b 27
κάμινος, 383 a 25
καμπτός, 385 a 6, 13, b 27,
386 a 8
κάμπτω, 385 b 31, 386 a 1, 3,
4 (bis)
κάμψις, 386 a 2, 7 (bis)
Κανωβικός, 351 b 33
καπνός, 341 b 21, 342 b 11,
19, 359 b 32, 360 a 25, 361
a 19, b 19, 371 a 33 (bis),
374 a 6, 7, 387 b 1, 23, 24,
388 a 2, 3, b 6, 389 b 22
καπνώδης, 341 b 10, 15, 360
a 10, b 3, 374 a 26, 378 a 19
καρπός, 385 b 19, 389 a 15,
390 a 23
Κάσπιος, 354 a 3
καταβαίνω, 349 b 32, 355 a 26,
356 b 26, 361 a 15
καταβολή, 352 b 15
καταδύνω, 359 a 9
καταδύω, 359 a 19
κατακαίω, 358 a 14, 361 b 20,
363 a 13, 371 a 28, 379 a
7
κατακάμπτω, 386 a 1
κατάκαμψις, 386 a 5
κατακάω, 359 b 2
κατακλείω, 366 a 16
κατακλυσμός, 352 a 33,368 b 5,
12
κατακτός, 385 a 14, 386 a 9,
10, 11 (bis), 16
καταλείπω, 367 b 18
καταλήγω, 340 b 9
καταμαραίνω, 344 a 30, 361
b 27, 368 a 7, 372 b 20
καταξηραίνω, 340 b 1
κάταξις, 386 a 12

404

GREEK INDEX

GREEK INDEX

GREEK INDEX

κύαθος, 355 b 29
κυανοῦς, 342 b 15
κυβερνάω, 339 a 23
κύκλος, 343 a 7, 12, 19, 24, 25,
  345 a 3, 16, 20, 22, 25, 33, b
  19, 346 a 16, 23, 27, 28, 31,
  35, b 4, 6, 21, 36 (bis), 357
  a 1, 363 a 28, 370 b 22, 26,
  371 b 23, 26, 28, 29, 372 b
  13, 373 a 3, 4, 5, 16, 375 b
  16, 19, 24, 27, 32, 376 a 18,
  b 8, 10, 21, 24, 31, 377 a 2,
  11, 26
κυκλοτερής, 362 b 13
κύκλῳ, 340 b 11, 32, 34, 341
  a 2, 344 a 13, 347 a 2, 7,
  348 b 7, 354 a 4, 356 a 8,
  359 b 34, 360 b 8, 10, 361
  a 24, 362 b 15, 370 b 32,
  371 a 14, 373 a 22, 374
  a 17, 27, 375 a 13, 380 b
  33
κῦμα, 343 b 2, 344 b 35, 368
  a 29 (bis), 34, b 8, 12
κυμαίνω, 356 a 17, 367 b 13
κύριος (adiectivum), 346 b 20,
  361 a 34, 372 b 29
κυρίως, 379 b 14, 380 b 14
κυριώτατος, 361 a 20, 364 a 4,
  14
κυρτός, 350 a 11, 365 a 31,
  386 a 5
κυρτότης, 386 a 1
κύστις, 357 a 33, 358 a 9
κύων, 343 b 12, 361 b 35
κωλύω, 340 a 29, b 32, 33, 341
  a 4, 342 b 20, 345 a 29, 348
  b 20, 361 b 21, 23, 362 b 18,
  364 a 30, 368 b 34, 370
  b 23, 24
κῶνος, 345 b 6, 362 b 2, 5,
  375 b 22, 376 a 12

κώπη, 369 b 10, 374 a 29, b 6
  (bis)
κωπηλασία, 369 b 11

λαβρότερος, 348 b 10 (bis), 23
λαμβάνω, 339 b 4, 21, 340
  b 35, 341 a 10, 25, 343 a 2,
  17, b 9, 346 a 7, 347 b 34,
  349 a 34, 351 a 33, 354
  b 22, 355 a 8, 29, 356 b 30,
  357 b 23, 359 b 11, 27,
  360 b 8, 11, 362 b 24, 368
  b 21, 371 b 21, 372 a 32,
  b 23, 375 a 28, 388 a 25,
  389 a 29, 390 a 5
λαμπρός, 361 b 5, 8, 370 a 19,
  371 b 24, 372 a 21, b 6, 7,
  373 b 22, 23, 374 a 3, 7,
  b 10, 377 b 9
λαμπρότατος, 346 a 20
λαμπρότης, 370 a 15
λανθάνω, 351 b 10, 15, 23, 354
  a 4, 360 a 4, 361 b 7, 362
  a 15, 372 a 23, 25, 374 b 24
λεῖος, 372 a 31, 373 a 35, 377
  b 21
λειότερος, 374 b 19
λείπω, 340 b 2, 351 b 17, 353
  b 9, 357 b 12, 20, 358 a 19,
  359 b 3, 372 b 5, 384 a 8,
  385 a 29, 389 b 11
λεπτομερέστερος, 368 a 19,
  370 b 6
λεπτός, 359 a 32, 367 b 9, 15,
  18, 369 b 5, 370 b 8, 371
  a 18, 19, 373 b 8, 374 b 1,
  380 a 24, b 2
λεπτότατος, 354 b 28, 358 a 9,
  365 b 35
λεπτότερος, 371 a 16
λεπτότης, 368 a 21, 371 a 20,
  22

GREEK INDEX

GREEK INDEX

μέσος, 339 a 15 (bis), 340
b 19, 20, 345 b 22, 356 a 1,
5, 11, 15, 361 b 28, 362 b 3,
363 b 29, 30, 377 a 21
μεσότης, 382 a 19
μεσουρανέω, 372 a 14, 373
b 13
μεσουράνιος, 378 a 8, 9
μεστός, 377 b 2
μεταβάλλω, 347 a 1, 351 a 20,
21, b 4, 24, 352 a 5, b 1,
353 a 21, 24, 354 b 6, 355
a 9, 357 a 3, b 28, 358 b 33,
359 b 14, 23, 360 b 26, 362
b 8, 365 b 5, 366 a 22, 370
a 30, 374 b 23, 31, 375 a 17,
377 b 27, 378 b 16, 379 b 1,
380 b 9, 33, 381 a 24, 385
b 31
μετάβασις, 386 a 6, 388 a 6
μεταβολή, 338 a 23, 351 b 12,
36, 352 a 18, 26, b 16, 354
b 27, 358 a 1, 361 b 31, 34,
369 a 26, 374 b 35, 378
b 29, 32, 379 a 33
μεταδιώκω, 389 a 25
μεταλλευτός, 378 a 21
μεταλλεύω, 378 a 27, 384 b 32,
388 a 13
μετανάστασις, 351 b 16
μεταπίπτω, 360 b 18
μετάρροια, 367 a 28
μετάστασις, 364 b 15, 367
b 12, 386 a 19
μεταφορά, 357 a 27, 380 a 18,
b 30
μετέχω, 358 a 26, 365 a 35,
384 b 29
μετεωρίζω, 346 b 28, 347
a 13, 29, 32, 357 b 20
μετεωρολογία, 338 a 26
μετεωρολόγος, 354 a 29

μετέωρος, 343 a 31, 348 a 6,
b 20, 368 b 20, 378 a 18
μετοπωρινός, 358 a 29, 364
b 2, 371 b 30, 377 a 12
μετόπωρον, 348 a 1, b 27, 28,
358 b 4, 365 a 2, 366 b 2
μέτριος, 360 b 10
μετρίως, 346 b 2, 359 a 9
μῆκος, 341 b 25, 27, 29, 32,
344 a 23, 29, 351 b 32, 356
a 27, 362 b 17, 20, 367 b 10,
368 b 27, 385 b 30, 386 a 2,
387 a 2, 8, 10, 30
μηνύω, 344 b 13
μικρομέρεια, 348 a 9
μικρομερής, 372 b 17
μικρότης, 348 a 8, 369 a 5, 373
a 19, [377 b 8]
Μιλήσιος, 365 a 18
μίλτος, 378 a 23
μιμέομαι, 346 b 36, 381 b 6
μιμνήσκομαι, 343 b 18
μνεία, 352 a 1
μνημονεύω, 351 b 12, 20, 26
μόλυβδος, 349 a 2, 385 a 32,
389 a 8
μόλυνσις, 379 a 2, b 14, 381
a 12, 22, b 9, 14
Μόλων, 343 b 5
μονή, 344 a 24, 25
μόνιμος, 387 a 15, 17
μόριον, 340 a 6, 341 a 5, 345
a 24, b 23, 347 a 12, 353
b 3, 356 b 35, 357 b 28,
360 b 11, 365 a 24, 369 a 4,
370 b 20, 373 b 15, 374
a 17, 385 b 25, 386 a 32,
390 b 3
μορφή, 359 b 11, 379 b 27
μυελός, 389 b 10
μυθολογέω, 356 b 12, 359
a 17, 27

410

GREEK INDEX

μῦθος, 356 b 11, 17
μυθώδης, 350 b 8
μυκάομαι, 368 a 25
Μυκηναῖος, 352 a 9, 11
μύλη, 383 b 7
μυλίας, 383 b 12
μύω, 381 b 3
μωλύνω, 381 a 21

ναός, 371 a 31
ναυσιπέρατος, 351 a 18
Νεῖλος, 350 b 14, 351 b 30,
    353 a 16, 356 a 28
νεκρός, 389 b 31, 390 a 22
νέος, 355 a 14 (bis), 388 b 1, 3
Νέσσος, 350 b 16
νεῦρον, 385 a 8, 386 b 14, 388
    a 17, 389 a 12, 390 a 19, b 5
νεφέλη, 346 b 33, 35, 348 a 20,
    367 b 19, 370 a 14, 375 a 16
νεφέλιον, 367 b 9
νέφος, 340 a 25, 31, b 30, 33,
    341 a 10, 346 b 33, 347
    b 12, 23, 26, 348 a 16, 23,
    26, b 8, 349 a 18, 350 b 25,
    358 a 23, 360 b 1, 361 a 1,
    9, 27, 364 b 9, 14, 24, 33,
    367 a 21, 369 a 15, 16, 27,
    28, 35, 36, b 2, 12, 26, 370
    a 27, 29, b 18, 28, 29, 31,
    32, 371 a 1, 10, 12, 18, 372
    b 17, 373 a 18, b 20, 22, 30,
    374 b 20, 21, 25, 375 a 9,
    13, 19, 377 a 33, 34, b 1, 2,
    3, 4, 5
νηνεμία, 347 a 26, 361 b 23,
    25, 366 a 5, 367 a 22, 26
    (bis), b 18, 23, 368 b 7
νήνεμος, 361 b 6
νηνεμώτατος, 366 a 14
νηνεμώτερος, 366 a 18, 373
    a 24

νῆσος, 356 b 14, 367 a 2, 3, 13,
    368 b 32
Νικόμαχος, 345 a 2
νιπτικῶς, 371 a 4
νίτρον, 383 b 12, 19, 384 a 18,
    34, 385 a 31, b 9, 16, 23
    (bis), 388 b 13, 389 a 18
νιφετός, 349 a 9, 371 a 8
νιφετώδης, 364 b 21
νοέω, 340 b 14, 24, 341 b 18,
    345 b 36, 347 a 2, 349 b 17,
    353 b 21, 358 a 18, 363
    a 28, 366 b 15, 29, 373 a 19,
    374 b 9
νομή, 363 a 14
νομίζω, 339 a 29, b 24, 25, 34,
    344 a 5, b 19, 348 b 5, 349
    b 21, 25, 350 b 22, 35, 351
    a 25, b 22, 352 a 16, b 4,
    355 b 12, 356 b 9, 359 b 5,
    365 a 27, 379 b 17
νομιστέον, 339 a 24, b 14
νόσος, 351 b 14
νοσώδης, 384 a 31
νοτίζω, 361 b 2
νότιος, 347 a 36, 37, b 9, 10,
    358 a 28, 363 a 6, 364 a 19,
    374 a 21, 377 b 26, 27
νοτίς, 343 a 11, 350 b 29, 365
    b 25
νότος, 343 a 8, 10, b 3, 345 a 1,
    347 b 2, 5, 358 a 29, b 2,
    361 a 6, 22, b 11, 362 a 12,
    31, 363 a 6, 8, 13, 17, b 15,
    22, 364 a 15, 21, b 23, 367
    a 13, 368 b 7
νυκτερινός, 360 a 4
νύκτωρ, 342 a 11, 34, 345
    b 25, 347 a 15, 360 a 3, 370
    a 20, 372 a 12, 21, 376 b 25
νύξ, 342 b 20, 345 a 23, b 8,
    22, 350 a 32, 354 a 31, 362

411

GREEK INDEX

GREEK INDEX

GREEK INDEX

GREEK INDEX

368 a 8, 31, 369 a 31, 370
a 12, 17, 25, 371 a 2, b 21,
373 b 4, 375 a 22, 378 a 34,
b 19, 379 a 21, 381 b 5, 382
a 28, 29, 33, 383 b 32, 385
a 5, 19, b 26, 389 a 4
παιδικός, 339 b 33
παλαιός, 339 b 21, 352 b 27,
388 b 3
παλαιόω, 390 a 22, b 1
Παλαιστίνη, 359 a 17
παμμήκης, 351 b 10
πανσέληνος, 372 a 27
παντάπασιν, 369 b 24
παραβλέπω, 343 b 13
παραδίδωμι, 345 b 30
παρακολουθέω, 344 b 3, 346 a 3
παραλαμβάνω, 349 a 15, 365
a 16
παραλλάξ, 385 b 25
παραλλάττω, 342 a 33, 386
a 15, 31
παράλογος, 347 b 35
παραπλήσιος, 344 a 25, 366
b 17, 380 b 34
παραπλησίως, 342 b 35, 349
a 25, 360 b 13, 361 a 18,
388 b 31
παρασκευάζω, 341 a 20, 355
a 2
παρεγχέω, 359 a 2
παρεικάζω, 369 a 30, 370 a 12
παρεκπυρόω, 341 b 30
παρέχω, 341 a 13, 355 a 25,
358 a 20, 378 a 12, 387 b 20
παρήλιος, 371 b 19, 372 a 10,
16, 377 a 29, 30, b 15, 23,
24, 30
Παρνασσός, 350 a 19
παροιμία, 364 b 13
παροράω, 355 a 20
παρουσία, 382 a 33

πάσχω, 339 a 30, 345 a 18, 23,
348 b 14, 351 a 29, 352 a 21,
353 b 34, 357 a 15, b 17,
358 b 18, 359 b 25, 368
a 33, 371 a 25, 26, 372 a 23,
373 b 6, 378 b 19, 24, 379
a 19, b 33, 380 b 18, 381
a 9, b 30, 382 a 31, b 2, 383
b 1, 384 b 29, 385 a 5, 24,
26, 386 b 31, 387 b 14, 390
a 18
πατάσσω, 371 b 9, 13
παύω, 339 b 33, 352 b 29, 356
b 28, 360 b 29, 33, 361 a 3,
4, b 10, 14, 362 a 2, 8, 364
a 29, b 4, 8, 365 b 17, 367
b 33, 368 a 7
πάχνη, 347 a 16 (bis), 23, 30,
b 16, 23, 24, 30, 349 a 10,
378 a 31, 388 b 12
πάχος, 359 a 7 (bis)
πάχυνσις, 383 a 11
παχύνω, 380 a 34, b 11, 381
a 6, 383 a 11, 13, 14, 17,
20, 22, b 18, 24, 27, 29, 30,
32, 384 a 9, 10, 12, 14, 23,
b 25, 387 b 7, 388 a 32,
b 1, 4, 9
παχύς, 367 b 14, 383 a 23
παχύτερος, 359 a 12, 380 a 4,
5, 25, 381 a 4, 383 b 28
πεδίον, 350 a 6, 368 b 31
πείθω, 354 a 29, 356 b 12
πειρατέον, 358 a 3
πειράω 352 b 24, 358 b 18,
366 b 27
πέλαγος, 354 a 7, 10, 15, 27
Πελοπόννησος, 351 a 2
πεπαίνω, 380 a 25, 33 (bis)
πέπανσις, 379 b 12, 380 a 11,
12, 13, 16, 21, 26, 28, 30,
b 4, 11, 381 b 20

GREEK INDEX

GREEK INDEX

(bis), 4, 5, 10, 11, 23, 369 a 1, 35, b 4, 7, 370 a 7, b 4, 17, 22, 32, 371 a 4, 5, 13, 16, 18, 27, 29, 33, b 2, 5, 8, 11, 13, 372 b 20, 26, 27, 373 a 24, 382 b 30, 383 b 26, 384 b 21, 387 a 25, 29 (bis), 388 a 2

πνευματικός, 380 a 23, 29

πνευματωδέστατος, 366 b 4

πνευματωδέστερος, 341 b 9

πνευματώδης, 341 b 11, 344 b 27, 366 b 7, 380 b 16

πνέω, 345 a 1, 347 a 28, 358 a 30, 32, 361 a 23, 27, b 4, 5, 35, 362 a 1, 17, 19, 23, 24, 25, 26, 29 (bis), 31 (bis), 363 a [3], 4, 6, 8 (bis), 12, 13, 22, b 16, 18, 21, 23, 25, 34, 364 a 1, 3, 21, 22, 28, 31, 33, b 6, 7, 31, 365 a 4, 5, 366 a 10, 21, 367 a 13, 373 b 12

πνῖγος, 361 b 27, 362 a 20

ποιέω, 340 b 13, 342 a 21, b 7, 11, 15, 18, 23, 343 b 35, 345 a 3, 346 a 9, 347 b 2, 5, 348 b 8, 17, 349 b 16, 35, 351 b 6, 352 a 1, b 9, 12, 353 a 10, 35, b 6, 9, 354 a 15, 31, b 3, 32, 355 a 1, 25, 356 a 3, 6, b 8, 14, 15, 357 a 6, 18, 20, 358 a 11, b 22, 359 a 4, 13, 24, b 19, 25, 360 a 17, b 22, 361 b 19, 362 a 16, b 2, 5, 363 a 15, 364 b 9, 18, 30, 365 b 4, 366 a 23, b 5, 10, 17, 25, 367 a 17, b 6, 15, 16, 24, 368 a 10, 14, 33, b 5, 11, 369 a 29, b 1, 33, 370 a 6, 8, 10, 29, b 7, 9, 371

a 29, b 13, 372 a 6, 373 b 3, 374 b 4, 11, 29, 375 a 20, b 1, 2, 22, 376 a 17, b 10, 15, 16, 377 b 17, 21, 378 a 2, 16, 22, 28, 379 a 32, b 1, 380 b 18, 20, 381 a 1, 24, 382 a 1, 28 (bis), 31 (bis), 32, 383 a 10, 34, b 2, 27, 384 a 11, b 26, 28, 385 a 2, 4, 386 a 32, 387 b 10, 30, 388 a 23, 390 a 11, 18

ποίησις, 357 a 26

ποιητέον, 358 b 23

ποιητής, 371 a 20

ποιητικός, 357 a 27, 378 b 12, 22, 23, 25, 27, 379 a 11, 382 b 6

ποικιλία, 342 b 18, 373 b 35

ποίκιλμα, 375 a 23

ποικιλτής, 375 a 27

πόλεμος, 351 b 14

πόλις, 367 a 6, 7

πόλος, 362 a 33, b 4, 31, 363 a 8, 376 a 18, b 8, 31, 377 a 1, 10

πόμα, 357 a 29

πόντιος, 368 b 33, 369 a 5

πόντος, 350 b 4

Πόντος, 347 a 36, b 4, 348 b 34, 351 a 12, 354 a 14, 20, 367 a 1

πορεία, 344 b 5, 362 b 20

πορεύσιμος, 362 b 19

πορθμεύς, 356 b 16

πόρος, 381 b 1, 3, 385 a 29, b 20, 24, 25, 386 a 15, b 2, 4, 5, 6, 9, 387 a 2, 19, 21

πορφυροῦς, 342 b 8, 374 a 27, 32, 375 a 25

ποτάμιος, 353 b 28, 357 a 22

ποταμός (vide etiam Αἰγὸς ποταμοί), 339 b 12, 347 a 2,

418

GREEK INDEX

419

GREEK INDEX

GREEK INDEX

366 a 4, b 14, 367 a 11, 368
  a 3, b 7, 21, 35, 370 a 28,
  b 21, 379 a 33, 383 b 6
  (bis), 7 (bis)
ῥηγμίν, 367 b 14, 19
ῥήγνυμι, 365 b 7, 11, 367 a 4,
  369 a 34, 371 b 4
ῥητέον, 382 a 27
ῥίζα, 353 b 1, 388 a 20
Ῥῖπαι, 350 b 7
ῥιπτέω, 342 a 9, 12, 32
ῥῖψις, 342 a 2, 6, 7, 21
Ῥοδανός, 351 a 16, 18
Ῥοδόπη, 350 b 18
ῥοῦς, 353 a 10
ῥοφέω, 356 b 15
ῥόφησις, 381 a 2
ῥοώδης, 366 a 25
ῥύπτω, 359 a 22
ῥύσις, 353 b 27, 355 b 17, 366
  a 19, 387 a 29
ῥυτός, 353 b 19 (bis)

σαλεύω, 356 a 3
σανδαράκη, 378 a 23
σαπρός, 389 b 5
σαπρότης, 379 a 6
Σαρδονικός, 354 a 21
σάρξ, 355 b 10, 357 b 5, 379
  a 7, 385 a 8, 386 b 8, 388
  a 16, 389 b 24, 390 a 2, 8,
  14, 16, 19, b 5, 16
σάττω, 365 b 18
σαφέστερον, 344 b 25
σαφής, 357 a 25
σβέννυμι, 346 b 28, 347 b 4,
  10, 370 a 10, 371 a 6
σβέσις, 370 a 24
σεισμός, 338 b 26, 343 b 2,
  365 a 14, 34, b 4, 9, 17, 23,
  366 a 6, 11, 13, 23, 24, 30,
  b 18, 31, 367 a 18, 21, 29,

b 8, 20, 25, 32, 368 a 11,
  15 (bis), 26, 34, b 8, 11, 13,
  18, 28, 30, 33, 369 a 7, 370
  a 27, 29
σείω, 365 a 32, b 8, 18, 366 b 1,
  367 b 33, 368 a 4, 12, 31,
  b 1, 26, 35
σελήνη, 340 b 6, 341 a 22, 342
  a 30, 33, 344 b 3, 345 b 5,
  346 a 15, 353 b 9, 367 b 20,
  28, 371 b 23, 372 a 22, b 13,
  373 a 2, 27, 375 a 18, 376
  b 25
Σελλός, 352 b 2
σεμνότερος, 353 b 2
Σέσωστρις, 352 b 26
σημαίνω, 339 b 23, 344 b 19,
  361 a 28
σημεῖον, 341 a 31, 342 a 30,
  345 b 14, 346 a 23, b 34,
  347 a 28, b 24, 348 a 33,
  350 a 30, 354 a 28, 358 a 4,
  9, 359 a 23, 364 a 2, 31, 366
  b 30, 367 a 22, b 8, 372
  b 18, 22, 26, 28, 373 a 4, 5,
  6, 15, 375 a 9, 17, b 21, 376
  a 3, 4, 8, b 1, 19, 377 a 1,
  b 24, 380 a 1, 384 a 6, 31
σημειώδης, 373 a 30
σήπω, 379 a 9, 14, 15, 22, 26,
  34, b 2, 5, 7, 28, 381 b 11,
  12
σῆψις, 379 a 3, 8, 13, 16, 21,
  389 b 8
σίδηρος, 378 a 28, 383 a 31.
  32, b 4, 384 b 14, 385 b 11.
  386 b 10, 33, 388 a 14, b 31.
  389 a 11
Σικάνη, 359 b 15
Σικελία, 359 b 15, 366 a 26
Σικελικός, 354 a 21
σίξις, 369 b 17, 370 a 8, 9

421

GREEK INDEX

GREEK INDEX

συγκατάγω, 371 a 12
συγκαταμίσγω, 357 b 7
συγκαταφέρω, 357 a 17, b 2, 358 a 24
σύγκειμαι, 387 a 13
συγκρίνω, 341 a 4, 342 a 29, b 17, 346 b 22, 347 a 17, 19, 350 a 13, 358 b 17, 370 a 30, b 15
σύγκρισις, 341 a 10, 344 b 9, 346 a 4, 16, 23, b 34, 369 a 14, b 33, 34
συγκριτικός, 378 b 22
συζυγία, 378 b 11
συλλαμβάνω, 340 a 7
συλλέγω, 347 b 20, 349 b 6, 10, 357 a 33, 384 a 7
συλλείβω, 349 b 33, 350 a 9
συλλογιμαῖος, 353 b 23
συμβαίνω, 338 b 20, 339 a 5, 21, 27, 341 a 27, 342 b 33, 344 a 8, 346 a 6, b 4, 18, 347 b 34, 348 a 20, b 2, 17, 349 b 20, 25, 350 a 17, b 21, 32, 351 a 1, 29, b 1, 27, 352 a 2, 8, 15, 16, 353 a 9, 12, 26, 354 a 16, 355 a 3, 12, 21, b 30, 356 a 14, 18, 32, 357 b 16, 358 a 2, b 11, 29, 359 b 24, 360 a 14, b 5, 22, 30, 361 b 32, 363 a 24, 365 a 12, 34, b 12, 366 b 19, 367 a 27, 31, b 6, 12, 20, 27, 369 a 8, 370 a 4, b 19, 371 a 8, b 21, 372 a 17, 19, 373 a 34, b 4, 29, 374 a 14, b 16, 24, 375 a 10, b 17, 377 b 25, 378 a 12, b 11, 379 b 22, 32, 380 a 34, 381 a 18, b 17, 382 b 7, 384 b 6, 8, 389 b 18

συμβάλλω, 345 b 6, 348 b 30, 358 b 3, 376 b 24
σύμβολον, 360 a 26
συμμειγνύω, 352 b 30, 354 a 1, 357 a 10, 30, 358 b 22
σύμμειξις, 358 a 5, b 21, 359 a 5
σύμμετρος, 362 a 4
συμπεριάγω, 344 a 12
συμπεριλαμβάνω, 358 a 33
συμπέττω, 379 b 23, 381 a 20
συμπίπτω, 343 a 21, 344 a 20, 345 a 5, 349 a 22, 360 b 28, 372 a 15, 25
συμπληρόω, 340 a 18
σύμφασις, 342 b 28
συμφυής, 382 b 11
σύμφυτος, 382 b 12
συμφύω, 348 a 12, 378 b 15
συνάγω, 350 a 1, 354 a 7, 382 b 9
συναθροίζω, 368 b 3
συνακολουθέω, 370 b 10
συναλείφω, 365 a 21
συναναφέρω, 341 a 7
συνανέχω, 372 a 15
συναπέρχομαι, 383 a 19
συνάπτω, 345 a 24, 362 b 16, 373 a 15
σύναψις, 343 b 8
συνδέω, 359 a 18
σύνειμι (εἰμί), 342 a 19, 20, b 17, 361 b 1, 364 b 33, 367 b 5, 369 a 27, 370 a 4, 30, 381 b 1, 386 a 30, b 3, 7, 8, 387 a 14
συνείρω, 362 b 29
συνεκκρίνω, 357 b 4, 358 a 11, 371 b 12
συνεκπίμπρημι, 371 a 17
συνεξατμίζω, 379 a 24, 382 b 20, 24, 383 a 19, 30

GREEK INDEX

συνέξειμι, 388 b 14
συνεξέρχομαι, 388 b 28
συνεξορμάω, 361 b 14
συνεπιτελέω, 379 b 23
συνέπομαι, 361 a 24
συνέρχομαι, 343 b 31, 344 a 1,
  348 a 10, 368 b 16, 27, 385
  a 28, 386 b 4
συνεφέλκω, 341 a 2
συνέχεια, 373 b 26
συνεχής, 339 a 22, 341 a 3,
  344 a 11, 346 b 11, 351
  a 15, 352 b 31, 355 a 9,
  360 b 6, 362 a 11, 15, 26,
  363 a 7, 365 b 27, 366 a 6,
  369 b 3, 370 b 10, 30 (bis),
  371 a 32, 372 b 23, 373 a 19,
  b 26, 28, 374 a 34, 386 b 13,
  387 a 29, b 28, 29
συνεχῶς, 341 a 7, 346 a 22,
  b 8, 349 b 17, 27, 355 a 15,
  b 30, 359 b 23, 360 a 34,
  362 a 30, b 29, 369 b 23,
  373 a 22
συνήθεια, 340 b 22
συνήθης, 370 a 16
σύνθετος, 382 a 26
συνθλίβω, 378 a 30, 384 b 9
συνίστημι, 339 a 12, 20, b 9,
  340 a 2, 25, 29, 34, b 30,
  33, 342 a 1, 17, 34, b 1, 5,
  344 a 36, b 11, 24, 345 a 8,
  346 a 16, b 29, 347 a 27,
  b 10, 13, 349 a 3, 18, b 23,
  31, 353 b 4, 354 b 20, 31,
  355 a 32, 358 a 10, 22, b 17,
  20, 360 a 1, 21, 26, b 35,
  361 a 10, 364 b 9, 27, 369
  a 15, 372 b 16, 17, 373 a 1,
  b 2, 16, 20, 374 a 18, 376
  a 2, 9, b 2, 12, 18, 378 b 20,
  379 a 6, b 8, 11, 31, 380

  a 24, b 7, 9, 382 a 25, b 28,
  29, 383 a 12, 17, 384 a 7,
  19, 20, b 25, 31, 387 a 4,
  388 a 18, 21, 24, b 10, 389
  a 6, b 7, 25, 390 b 10, 21
συννοέω, 345 a 19
σύνοδος, 343 b 30
σύνταξις, 355 b 10
συντηκτός, 389 b 8
συντιτράω, 355 b 34
συνωθέω, 361 a 1
συρρέω, 350 b 28, 353 b 22
σύστασις, 340 a 30, 341 b 23,
  342 b 14, 344 a 34, b 18,
  345 b 34, 346 a 13, b 10,
  347 a 35, b 21, 352 b 10,
  369 a 16, 19, 372 b 18, 23,
  373 a 28, 31, b 3, 374 a 12,
  377 b 5, 32, 378 a 8, 26
συστέλλω, 368 b 3
σύστοιχος, 340 a 5
συστρέφω, 369 a 34
σφαῖρα, 341 b 20, 346 a 33,
  354 b 24, 365 a 23, 375 b 33
σφαιροειδής, 340 b 36, 365
  a 31
σφραγίς, 387 b 17
σφιγμός, 366 b 15, 18, 368
  a 6, b 25
σχῆμα, 342 b 12, 348 a 28, 33,
  36, 362 a 35, 368 a 3, 24,
  370 b 26, 372 a 33, b 2, 3
  (bis), 12, 373 b 19, 24, 377
  b 7, 14, 390 a 21, 23
σχηματίζω, 344 a 21
σχίζω, 340 a 31, 386 b 28
σχιστός, 385 a 16, 386 b 26,
  27, 31, 387 a 7, 8, 10
σχοῖνος, 359 b 1
σώζω, 351 b 21, 356 a 21, 386
  a 2
σῶμα, 338 b 21, 339 a 5, 12

GREEK INDEX

429

GREEK INDEX

φέγγος, 343 b 13, 22, 346 a 26,
370 a 21
φέρω, 339 a 12, b 31, 35, 340
b 10, 341 a 6, 18, 26, 31,
342 a 16, 23, 25, 26, b 3,
343 a 10, 13, 344 a 13, b 10,
345 a 16, 21, 27, b 19, 346
b 25, 31, 347 a 9, 11, 31,
348 a 24, 34, 35, b 19, 24,
354 a 29, b 26, 29, 358 b
5, 359 b 34, 361 a 9, 362
b 9, 365 a 20, 28, b 33, 366
a 3, 367 a 30, 368 b 1, 369
a 20, 21, 24, 28, 34, b 21,
370 b 24, 33, 371 a 11, 22,
32, b 6 (bis), 378 a 5, 6, 10,
383 b 26
φέψαλος, 367 a 5
φθάνω, 349 b 14, 356 b 26,
361 b 17, 19, 362 a 2, 364
b 11, 371 a 22, 24, 27
φθαρτικός, 382 b 7
φθείρω, 353 a 20, 355 a 3, 31,
379 a 6, 13, 389 b 6, 10
φθίνω, 351 a 30, 31
φθορά, 338 a 24, 345 a 16, 346
b 23, 351 b 12, 13, 352 b 17,
354 b 28, 358 a 1, 378 b 30,
379 a 4, 8, 11, 16, b 9, 390
b 19
φιάλη, 390 b 13
φλέγμα, 380 a 21, 384 a 32,
386 b 16
Φλεγραῖος, 368 b 31
φλέψ, 388 a 17
φλογιστός, 387 b 18, 19, 21,
23, 25, 26, 31
φλοιός, 385 a 9, 388 a 19, 389
a 13
φλόξ, 341 b 2, 21, 26, 342 a 4,
b 3, 19, 346 b 12, 355 a 7,
9, 357 b 32, 366 a 3, 369

a 31, 33, 371 a 32, b 6, 374
a 6, 24, 387 b 13, 20, 29,
388 a 2
φοβερός, 348 a 24
φοινικίας, 364 a 4, 17
φοινίκιος, 372 a 4
φοινικοῦς, 342 b 7, 11, 20, 372
a 7, 9, 374 a 4, 8, 28, 32,
b 11, 31, 375 a 2, 8, 11, 12,
13, 15, 22, b 8, 10, 377 b 10,
13
φοιτάω, 347 b 12
φορά, 338 a 21, b 22, 339 a 22,
b 18, 340 b 32, 341 a 20,
b 14, 342 a 2, 25, 27, 29,
343 a 10, 344 a 9, 12, 23,
24, 31, b 10, 12, 345 a 18,
346 a 4, 8, 12, 27, b 11,
22, 348 a 29, b 18, 22,
352 b 12, 356 a 12, b 28,
361 a 12, 22, 25, 34, b 12,
364 a 10, 367 b 29, 368
b 21, 370 b 26, 386 b 1
φορτίον, 347 a 31
φρέαρ, 347 b 9
φρεατιαῖος, 353 b 26
φροντίζω, 355 a 19
φροῦδος, 340 a 2, 353 a 1
φύλλον, 387 b 4, 388 a 20, 389
a 13
φῦμα, 379 b 31, 380 a 21
φυσάω, 367 b 1
φύσει, 342 a 25, 365 a 22, 367
a 32, 379 a 6, b 11, 380 a 9,
381 b 5
φυσικός, 338 a 21, 351 b 8,
378 b 29, 32, 379 b 7, 18,
380 a 20, 22, 32, 381 a 11,
382 a 1, 385 a 10
φυσικῶς, 390 a 16
φύσις, 338 a 20, b 20, 339
a 13, b 4, 9, 15, 26, 340

430

GREEK INDEX

GREEK INDEX